Teachers Discovering Computers

Integrating Technology in the Classroom

Third Edition

Gary B. Shelly
Thomas J. Cashman
Randolph E. Gunter
Glenda A. Gunter

THOMSON
COURSE TECHNOLOGY

COURSE TECHNOLOGY
25 THOMSON PLACE
BOSTON MA 02210

SHELLY
CASHMAN
SERIES®

Australia • Canada • Denmark • Japan • Mexico • New Zealand • Philippines • Puerto Rico • Singapore
South Africa • Spain • United Kingdom • United States

THOMSON

COURSE TECHNOLOGY

Teachers Discovering Computers
Integrating Technology in the Classroom
Third Edition

Gary B. Shelly
Thomas J. Cashman
Randolph E. Gunter
Glenda A. Gunter

Executive Editor:
Cheryl Costantini

Developmental Editor:
Marjorie Hunt

Senior Product Manager:
Alexandra Arnold

Product Manager:
Erin Runyon

Associate Product Manager:
Reed Cotter

Editorial Assistant:
Emilie Perreault

Print Buyer:
Laura Burns

Director of Production:
Becky Herrington

Production Editor:
Kristen Guevara

Production Assistant:
Jennifer Quiambao

Copy Editor:
Ginny Harvey

Proofreader:
Cherilyn King

Illustrators:
Kenny Tran
Rich Herrera

Cover Design:
Kenny Tran

Signing Representative:
Cheryl Costantini

Compositors:
Betty Hopkins
Kenny Tran
Andrew Bartel

Printer:
Banta Menasha

CONTENTS

Teachers Discovering Computers
Integrating Technology in the Classroom
Third Edition

Preface   vii

Introduction to Using Computers in Education — Chapter 1

Objectives	1.01
Curriculum-Specific Learning	1.02
Computer, Information, and Integration Literacy	1.03
What Is a Computer and What Does It Do?	1.04
The Components of a Computer	1.05
Input Devices	1.05
Output Devices	1.06
System Unit	1.06
Storage Devices	1.07
Communications Devices	1.08
Categories of Computers Typically Used in Education	1.09
Personal Computers	1.09
Mobile Computers and Mobile Devices	1.10
Notebook Computers	1.10
Tablet PC	1.10
Mobile Devices	1.11
Why Is a Computer So Powerful?	1.11
Speed	1.11
Reliability	1.11
Accuracy	1.11
Storage	1.11
Communications	1.12
Computer Software	1.12
System Software	1.13
Application Software	1.14
Software Development	1.16
Networks and the Internet	1.16
Why Use Computer Technology in Education?	1.18
An Example of How One School Uses Computers	1.21
Superintendent	1.21
Principal	1.22
School Secretary	1.22
Technology Coordinator	1.22
Cafeteria Manager	1.23
Media Specialist	1.23
Teachers	1.23
Parent	1.24
Community	1.25
Using the Textbook Web Site	1.25
Interacting with End-of-Chapter Materials	1.26
Timeline — Milestones in Computer History	1.27
Summary of Introduction to Integrating Technology in Education	1.27
In Brief	1.28
Key Terms	1.30
Checkpoint	1.31
Teaching Today	1.32
Education Issues	1.34
Integration Corner	1.35
Software Corner	1.36
In the Lab	1.37
Learn It Online	1.40
Special Feature	1.42

Timeline — Milestones in Computer History

Communications Networks, the Internet, and the World Wide Web — Chapter 2

Objectives	2.01
What Is Communications?	2.03
Communications Networks	2.03
Local Area Networks	2.06
Wide Area Networks	2.06
Home Networks	2.06
Networking the Classroom, School, and District	2.07
Wireless Schools and Classrooms	2.10
High Speed or Broadband Access	2.10
The Benefits of Computer Networks in Education	2.11
What Is the Internet?	2.11
History of the Internet	2.13
How the Internet Works	2.15
Internet Service Providers versus Online Service Providers	2.16
Connecting to the Internet	2.17
The Internet Backbone	2.18
Internet Addresses	2.19
The World Wide Web	2.21
How a Web Page Works	2.22
Web Browser Software	2.23
Searching for Information on the Web	2.25
Multimedia on the Web	2.25
Other Internet Services	2.31
E-Mail	2.31
FTP	2.32
Newsgroups and Message Boards	2.33
Mailing Lists	2.34
Chat Rooms	2.34
Instant Messaging	2.35
Short Message Service	2.35
Netiquette	2.35
Internet Security	2.35
The Impact of the Internet and the World Wide Web on Education	2.36
The Future of the Internet and the World Wide Web	2.38
Guide to World Wide Web Sites and Searching Techniques	2.38
Summary of Communications, Networks, the Internet, and the World Wide Web	2.39
In Brief	2.40
Key Terms	2.42

Checkpoint	2.43
Teaching Today	2.44
Education Issues	2.45
Integration Corner	2.46
Software Corner	2.47
In the Lab	2.48
Learn It Online	2.51

Special Feature — 2.52
GUIDE TO WORLD WIDE WEB SITES AND SEARCHING TECHNIQUES

Application Software Productivity Tools for Educators — Chapter 3

Objectives	**3.01**
The Operating System	**3.02**
The Role of the Operating System	3.02
Using Different Operating Systems	3.03
The Role of the User Interface	3.04
Application Software	**3.04**
Starting a Software Application	3.05
Working with Software Applications	3.06
Productivity Software	**3.10**
Word Processing Software	3.10
Spreadsheet Software	3.13
Database Software	3.15
Presentation Graphics Software	3.17
Personal Information Managers	3.22
PDA Software	3.23
Software Suites and Integrated Software	3.24
Graphics and Multimedia Software	**3.25**
Desktop Publishing Software	3.25
Paint/Image Editing Software	3.26
Video and Audio Editing Software	3.27
Clip Art/Image Gallery	3.27
Multimedia Authoring Software	3.27
Web Page Authoring Software	3.28
Software for School Use	**3.28**
School and Student Management Software	3.29
Grade Book Software	3.30
Educational AND Reference SOFTWARE	3.30
Special Needs Software	3.32
Software for Homeand Personal Use	**3.32**
Personal Finance Software	3.32
Tax Preparation Software	3.33
Legal Software	3.34
Entertainment Software	3.34
Learning Aids and Support Tools	**3.34**
Using Help	3.34
Other Learning Resources	3.35
Software Versions and Upgrades	**3.35**
Using Different Software Versions	3.36
Working with Macintosh Computers and PCs	3.36
Creating a Teacher's Web Page	**3.37**
Summary of Application Software Productivity Tools for Educators	**3.37**
In Brief	**3.38**
Key Terms	**3.40**
Checkpoint	**3.41**
Teaching Today	**3.42**
Education Issues	**3.43**
Integration Corner	**3.44**

Software Corner	3.45
In the Lab	3.46
Learn It Online	3.49

Special Feature — 3.50
Creating a Teacher's Web Page Using Microsoft Word

Hardware for Educators — Chapter 4

Objectives	**4.01**
The System Unit	**4.02**
Data Representation	**4.03**
The Components of the System Unit	**4.04**
The Motherboard	4.04
THE CPU and Microprocessor	4.05
Memory	4.07
Expansion Slots and Expansion Cards	4.09
Ports and Connectors	4.10
What Is Input?	**4.12**
What Are Input Devices?	**4.13**
The Keyboard	4.13
Pointing Devices	4.15
Optical Readers	4.18
Optical Scanners	4.18
Digital Cameras	4.19
Audio and Video Input	4.19
Input Devices for Handheld Computers	4.19
Input Devices for Students with Special Needs	4.20
What Is Output?	**4.21**
What Are Output Devices?	**4.22**
Monitors and Display Devices	4.22
Printers	4.25
Data Projectors	4.26
Facsimile (Fax) Machine	4.27
Multifunction Devices	4.28
Audio Output	4.28
Output Devices for Students with Special Needs	4.28
What Is Storage?	**4.29**
Storage Media and Devices	**4.29**
Floppy Disks	4.30
High-Capacity Removable Disks	4.31
Hard Disks	4.32
CDs and DVDs	4.33
Miniature Mobile Storage Media	4.38
Buyer's Guide	**4.38**
A World Without Wires	**4.38**
Summary of Hardware for Educators	**4.39**
In Brief	**4.40**
Key Terms	**4.42**
Checkpoint	**4.43**
Teaching Today	**4.44**
Education Issues	**4.45**
Integration Corner	**4.46**
Software Corner	**4.47**
In the Lab	**4.48**
Learn It Online	**4.51**

Special Feature — 4.52
Buyer's Guide 2004

Integrating Multimedia and Educational Software Applications — Chapter 5

Objectives	**5.01**
What Is Multimedia?	**5.02**
Text	5.04
Graphics	5.04
Animation	5.06
Audio	5.06
Video	5.07
Multimedia Applications	**5.08**
Computer-Based Training (CBT)	5.09
Electronic Books and References	5.09
How-To Guides	5.12
Multimedia Newspapers and Magazines (E-Zines)	5.12
Entertainment and Edutainment	5.14
Virtual Reality	5.15
Information Kiosks	5.16
Multimedia and the World Wide Web	5.16
Web-Based Training (WBT) and Distance Learning	5.17
K-12 Educational Software Applications	**5.20**
Computer-Assisted Instruction (CAI)	5.21
Drill-and-Practice Software	5.21
Educational Games	5.22
Tutorials	5.22
Educational Simulations	5.23
Integrated Learning Systems	5.23
Applications for Students with Disabilities	5.24
Curriculum-Specific Educational Software	5.25
Creating and Presenting Multimedia Applications	**5.28**
Obtaining Graphics for a Multimedia Application	5.28
Multimedia and Web Authoring Software	5.29
Presenting Multimedia	5.30
Why Are Multimedia and Educational Software Applications Important for Education?	**5.32**
Digital Imaging and Video Technology	**5.33**
Summary of Integrating Multimedia and Educational Software Applications	**5.33**
In Brief	**5.34**
Key Terms	**5.36**
Checkpoint	**5.37**
Teaching Today	**5.38**
Education Issues	**5.39**
Integration Corner	**5.40**
Software Corner	**5.41**
In the Lab	**5.42**
Learn It Online	**5.45**
Special Feature — Digital Imaging and Video Technology	**5.46**

Technology and Curriculum Integration — Chapter 6

Objectives	**6.01**
What Is Curriculum?	**6.02**
Curriculum Standards and Benchmarks	6.03
What Is Technology Integration?	**6.05**
Classroom Integration versus Traditional Computer Labs	6.06
The Classroom in Action	**6.07**
Integrating Technology into the Curriculum	**6.08**
Changing Instructional Strategies	**6.09**
Barriers to Technology Integration	**6.10**
Technology Integration and the Learning Process	**6.11**
The Learning Process	6.12
Technology and the Learning Process	6.13
Strategies for Integrating Technology into Teaching	**6.16**
The Role of the School District	**6.16**
Planning for Technology Integration in the Classroom	**6.17**
One-Computer Classroom	6.17
Two-Computer Classroom	6.18
More Than Two Computers	6.18
Using a Computer Lab	6.19
Using a Wireless Mobile Lab	6.19
Planning Lessons with Technology	**6.20**
KWL Charts	6.20
Instructional Models	**6.22**
The ASSURE Model	6.22
Getting Started at a New School	**6.25**
Information About Technology	6.25
Technology Training	6.26
Hardware	6.26
Software	6.26
Other Technologies	6.27
Technology Supplies	6.28
Putting It All Together	**6.28**
Creating an Integrated Learning Environment	6.28
The Classroom Centers	6.29
The Results of Technology Integration	6.30
Learning Theories and Educational Research	**6.31**
Summary of Technology and Curriculum Integration	**6.31**
In Brief	**6.32**
Key Terms	**6.34**
Checkpoint	**6.35**
Teaching Today	**6.36**
Education Issues	**6.37**
Integration Corner	**6.38**
Software Corner	**6.39**
In the Lab	**6.40**
Learn It Online	**6.44**
Special Feature — Learning Theories and Educational Research	**6.45**

Evaluating Educational Technology and Integration Strategies — Chapter 7

Objectives	**7.01**
Evaluating Educational Technology	**7.02**
Sources of Information	7.02
Evaluating Software Applications	7.06
Evaluating Web Resources	7.09
Evaluating the Effectiveness of Technology Integration	**7.12**
Assessment Tools for Evaluating the Effectiveness of Technology Integration	7.12
Evaluating Technology-Based Student Projects	7.17
Putting it All Together — Evaluating Technology Integration	7.20
Integration Strategies	**7.21**
One-Computer Classroom	7.22
Multicomputer Classroom	7.24
Computer Labs	7.26
Curriculum Integration Activities	**7.26**
Curriculum Pages	7.26
Creating Lesson Plans	7.28
Finding Funds to Support Classroom Technology Integration	**7.42**
Fund-Raising Drives and Academic Contests	7.43
Grants	7.44
Creating a Curriculum Page	**7.45**
Summary of Evaluating Educational Technology and Integration Strategies	**7.45**
In Brief	**7.46**
Key Terms	**7.48**
Checkpoint	**7.49**
Teaching Today	**7.50**
Education Issues	**7.51**
Integration Corner	**7.53**
Software Corner	**7.54**
In the Lab	**7.55**
Learn It Online	**7.59**
Special Feature	**7.60**

Creating a Curriculum Page Using Microsoft Word

Security Issues, Ethics, and Emerging Technologies in Education — Chapter 8

Objectives	**8.01**
Computer Security: Risks and Safeguards	**8.02**
Computer Viruses	8.02
Virus Detection and Removal	8.05
Unauthorized Access and Use	8.07
Firewalls	8.08
Hardware Theft and Vandalism	8.09
Software Theft	8.10
Information Theft	8.12
System Failure	8.13
Backup Procedures	8.15
Ethics and the Information Age	**8.16**
Information Privacy	8.16
Copyright Laws	8.18
Internet Ethics and Objectionable Materials	**8.22**
Recent Government Actions	8.24
Parental Controls	8.24
Educational Controls	8.26
Health Issues	**8.28**
Computers and Health Issues	8.28
Ergonomics	8.29
Emerging Technologies	**8.31**
The World Wide Web	8.32
Educational Software on DVD	8.32
Assistive Technologies	8.32
Web-Enhanced Textbooks	8.33
Web-Based Distance Learning	8.34
A World Without Wires	8.34
Summary of Security Issues, Ethics, and Emerging Technologies in Education	**8.35**
Summary of Teachers Discovering Computers	**8.35**
In Brief	**8.36**
Key Terms	**8.38**
Checkpoint	**8.39**
Teaching Today	**8.40**
Education Issues	**8.41**
Integration Corner	**8.42**
Software Corner	**8.43**
In the Lab	**8.44**
Learn It Online	**8.48**
Special Feature	**8.49**

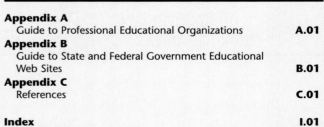

A World Without Wires

Appendix A	
Guide to Professional Educational Organizations	**A.01**
Appendix B	
Guide to State and Federal Government Educational Web Sites	**B.01**
Appendix C	
References	**C.01**
Index	**I.01**
Photo Credits	**I.15**

Preface

The Shelly Cashman Series® offers the finest textbooks in computer education. We are proud of the fact that our previous *Teachers Discovering Computers* books have been so well received by instructors and students. This latest edition continues with the innovation, quality, and reliability you have come to expect from this series. The previous edition's popularity was due to (1) the integration of the World Wide Web; (2) the currency of the materials; (3) readability; (4) extensive exercises; (5) supplements; and (6) the ancillaries that allow an instructor to teach the way he or she wants to teach.

We are pleased to announce the publication of *Teachers Discovering Computers: Integrating Technology in the Classroom, Third Edition*. In addition to the standard technological updates and appropriate content changes, the third edition of *Teachers Discovering Computers* includes these enhancements:

- Increased emphasis on technology integration
- A new companion Web site
- New Frequently Asked Questions (FAQ) boxes offer common questions and answers about subjects related to the topic at hand
- Two new features: Digital Imaging and Video Technology and A World Without Wires
- Three appendices added: Guide to Professional Educational Organizations, Guide to State and Federal Government Educational Web Sites, and a new list of References
- Two new corners added to Integration Corner: Reading/Language Arts Corner and Social Studies/History Corner

The content of the textbook and the companion Web site also have been enhanced to allow for curriculum-specific learning by all K-12 educators. That is, students using the *Teachers Discovering Computers* textbook will be able to learn both how to use, and more importantly, how to integrate technology into their current or future classroom curriculum. In addition, this third edition of *Teachers Discovering Computers* has been updated to address the National Educational Technology Standards for Teachers (NETS-T), the Technology Standards for School Administrators (TSSA), and applicable Internet and Computing Core Certification (IC³) program standards.

Objectives of This Textbook

Teachers Discovering Computers: Integrating Technology in the Classroom, Third Edition is intended for use in a one-quarter or one-semester undergraduate or graduate-level introductory computer course for educators. Students will finish the course with a solid understanding of educational technology, including how to use computers, how to access and evaluate information on the World Wide Web, and how to integrate computers and educational technology into classroom curriculum. This book also can be used for in-service training workshops that train teachers, administrators, and counselors how to use and effectively integrate educational technology.

The objectives of this textbook are to:

- Present practical, efficient ways to integrate technology resources and technology-based methods into everyday curriculum-specific practices

- Provide students with an understanding of the concepts and skills outlined in the National Educational Technology Standards for Teachers (NETS-T) and the Technology Standards for School Administrators (TSSA)
- Present the fundamentals of computers and educational technology in an easy-to-understand format
- Make use of the World Wide Web as a repository of the latest information and as an educational resource and learning tool for K-12 education
- Provide information about both Macintosh computers and PCs
- Give students an in-depth understanding of why computers are essential components in society, the business world, and K-12 education
- Provide students with the knowledge of how to use educational technology with diverse student populations
- Offer numerous examples of how to use educational technology in various subject areas and with students who have special needs
- Provide students with the knowledge of how to use educational technology with diverse student populations
- Offer numerous examples of how to use educational technology in various subject areas and with students who have special needs
- Provide students with knowledge of responsible, ethical, and legal uses of technology, information, and software resources
- Provide students with knowledge of technology to enhance their personal and professional productivity

Distinguishing Features

Teachers Discovering Computers: Integrating Technology in the Classroom, Third Edition includes the following distinguishing features.

The Proven Shelly and Cashman Pedagogy

More than five million students have learned about computers using Shelly and Cashman computer fundamental textbooks. With World Wide Web integration and interactivity, streaming audio and animations, extraordinary visual drawings and photographs, unprecedented currency, and the Shelly and Cashman touch, this book will make your introductory educational technology course for educators exciting and dynamic — an experience your students will remember as a highlight of their educational careers. Students, teachers, and course instructors will find this to be the finest textbook they have ever used.

World Wide Web

Teachers Discovering Computers continues the Shelly and Cashman tradition of innovation with its extensive integration of the World Wide Web. The purpose of integrating the World Wide Web into the book is to (1) offer students additional information and currency on topics of importance; (2) make available alternative learning techniques with Web-based curriculum-specific content, learning games, practice tests, and Interactive Labs; (3) underscore the relevance of the World Wide Web as a basic information tool that can be used in all facets of K-12 education and society; and (4) offer instructors the opportunity to organize and administer their campus-based or distance education-based courses on the Web. The World Wide Web is integrated into the book in three central ways:

- End-of-chapter pages, many of the features, and two of the appendices in the book are stored as Web pages on the World Wide Web. While working on an end-of-chapter page, students can display the corresponding Web page to obtain additional information on a term or exercise, explore the vast resources the Web has for education, or get an alternative point of view. The end-of-chapter Web pages provide students with thousands of links to additional sources of information. These sources that have been evaluated for appropriateness and are maintained by a team of educators. See page xv for more information.

- *Teachers Discovering Computers* uses streaming audio on the Web in the end-of-chapter In Brief sections and the 18 Interactive Labs in the end-of-chapter Learn It Online sections.

- Throughout the text, marginal annotations titled Web Info provide suggestions on how to obtain additional information via the World Wide Web about an important topic covered on the page. The textbook Web site provides links to these additional sources of information.

This textbook, however, does not depend on Web access to be used successfully. The Web access adds to the already complete treatment of topics within the book.

A Visually Appealing Book that Maintains Student Interest

The latest technology, pictures, drawings, and text have been artfully combined to produce a visually appealing and easy-to-understand book. Many of the figures show a step-by-step pedagogy, which simplifies the more complex computer and educational technology concepts. Pictures and drawings reflect the latest trends in computer and educational technology. Finally, the text was set in two columns, which research shows is easier for students to read. This combination of pictures, step-by-step drawings, and tested text layout sets a new standard for education textbook design.

Latest Educational Technology and Computer Trends

The terms and examples of educational technology described in this book are the same ones your students will encounter when using computers in the school setting and at home. The latest educational software packages and programs are shown throughout this book.

Macintosh Computers and PCs

Unlike many businesses, both Macintosh computers and PCs are used in the K-12 school environment. This textbook addresses both computer platforms and describes the appropriateness and use of educational software for both Macintosh computers and PCs.

Shelly Cashman Series Interactive Labs

Eighteen unique, hands-on exercises allow students to use the computer to learn about computer technology. Students can step through each Lab exercise in about 15 minutes. Assessment also is available. The Interactive Labs are described in detail on page xvi.

End-of-Chapter Activities

Unlike other books on educational technology fundamentals, a major effort was undertaken in *Teachers Discovering Computers* to offer exciting, rich, and thorough end-of-chapter materials to reinforce the chapter objectives and assist you in making your course the finest ever offered. As indicated earlier, each and every one of the

end-of-chapter pages is stored as a Web page on the World Wide Web to provide your students in-depth information and alternative methods of preparing for examinations. Each chapter ends with the following activities:

- **In Brief** This section summarizes the chapter material for the purpose of reviewing and preparing for examinations. Links on the Web pages provide additional current information. With a single click on the Web page, the review section is read to the student using streaming audio.

- **Key Terms** This list of the key terms with page references will aid students in mastering the chapter material. A complete summary of all key terms in the book, together with their definitions, appears in the index at the end of the book. On the Web page, students can click terms to view a definition and a picture, and then click a link to visit a Web page that provides supplemental information.

- **Checkpoint** Matching and short-answer questions, together with a figure from the chapter that can be labeled, are used to reinforce the material presented within the chapter. Students accessing the Web page answer the questions in an interactive forum.

- **Teaching Today** This section is designed to help students gain an appreciation of the value that technology and the World Wide Web have for K-12 education by visiting exciting educational Web pages and completing suggested curriculum integration tasks. The Web pages provide links to challenge students further on a vast array of interesting teacher-related topics.

- **Education Issues** The use of computers and other technologies in education are not without controversy. At the end of each chapter, several scenarios are presented that challenge students to examine critically their perspective of the use of technology in K-12 education and society in general. Other nontechnology related scenarios allow students to explore many current controversial issues in education, such as school violence. The Web pages provide links to challenge students further.

- **Integration Corner** This innovative section provides students with extensive ideas and resources for integrating technology into their classroom-specific curriculum. Each chapter provides information on and links to approximately 90 outstanding educational Web sites organized in 12 Corners: Early Childhood, Elementary, Middle School, Secondary, Reading/Language Arts, Social Studies/History, Math, Science, Special Education, Post Secondary, Administrator, and Research.

- **Software Corner** Today's educators can choose from a variety of high-quality and often inexpensive educational software. Students learn about popular software programs by researching them on the Web and, in many cases, even download or order a free evaluation copy so they can evaluate a program before buying it.

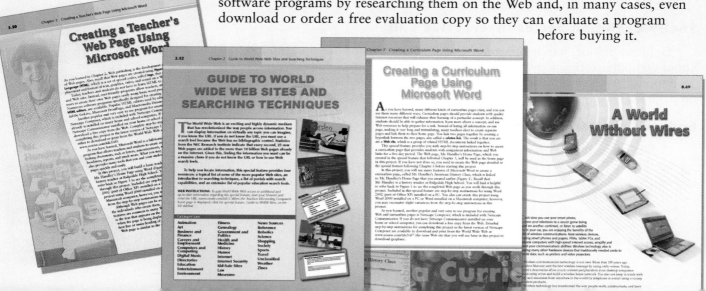

- **In the Lab** These exercises are divided into two areas: productivity and integration. Students can use the productivity exercises to improve their software-specific skills in using word processing, spreadsheets, database, desktop publishing, curriculum and Web page development, and other productivity software programs. They can use the integration ideas for incorporating these programs into their classroom-specific curriculum. The Web pages provide links to tutorials, productivity ideas, integration examples and ideas, and more.

- **Learn It Online** These exercises allow students to improve their computer and integration skills by learning exciting new skills online. This section includes Interactive Lab exercises, software tutorials, Windows and Macintosh exercises, scavenger hunts, practice tests, learning games, and much more.

Timeline: Milestones in Computer History

A colorful, highly informative, 15-page timeline following Chapter 1 steps students through the major computer technology developments of the past 50 years, including the most recent advances.

Guide to World Wide Web Sites and Searching Techniques

More than 150 popular Web sites are listed and described in a general guide to Web sites that follows Chapter 2. These Web sites are organized into general categories, such as Entertainment, Health and Medicine, Government and Politics, Shopping, and more. This guide also introduces students to searching techniques and provides links to numerous popular education search tools.

Creating a Teacher's Web Page Using Microsoft Word

Following Chapter 3, a 17-page project provides students with instructions on how to create a basic teacher's Web page using Microsoft Word. By completing this step-by-step project, students will acquire many of the basic skills needed to create educational Web pages. Step-by-step instructions for creating this project using the latest version of Netscape Composer are available for download at the textbook Web site.

Buyer's Guide 2004: How to Purchase, Install, and Maintain a Personal Computer

A 21-page guide following Chapter 4 introduces students to purchasing, installing, and maintaining a desktop computer, notebook computer, Tablet PC, and PDA.

Digital Imaging and Video Technology

This special feature following Chapter 5 introduces students to using a personal computer, digital camera, and video camera to manipulate photographs and video.

Learning Theories and Educational Research

At the end of Chapter 6, a 22-page special feature provides information about educational learning theories and research. This feature introduces students to educational terms, learning theories and theorists, educational research, and learning strategies.

Creating a Curriculum Page Using Microsoft Word

Following Chapter 7, a 23-page project presents instructions on how to create a curriculum page using Microsoft Word. By completing this step-by-step project, students will acquire many of the skills needed to create educational Web sites and curriculum pages. Step-by-step instructions for creating this project using the latest version of Netscape Composer are available for download at the textbook Web site.

A World Without Wires

This special feature following Chapter 8 presents an overview of the Wi-Fi revolution. It describes the growth of wireless technology and presents the latest in hardware and applications.

Guide to Professional Educational Organizations

More than 30 popular, professional educational organizations are listed and described in Appendix A. Updated links to the most current URLs for these professional organizations are located at the textbook Web site.

Guide to State and Federal Government Educational Web Sites

The federal government, state governments, and state institutions and organizations are providing a multitude of Web resources for K-12 teachers and students. Educational resources provided by 30 federal government agencies and all 50 states and the District of Columbia are listed and described in Appendix B. Updated links to the most current URLs for these state and government organizations are located at the textbook Web site.

References

Appendix C lists the various books, articles, and other sources of information used in developing *Teachers Discovering Computers*.

Shelly Cashman Series Instructor Resources

The two categories of ancillary materials that accompany this textbook are Instructor Resources (ISBN 0-619-20179-7) and Online Content. These ancillaries are available to adopters through your Course Technology representative or by calling one of the following telephone numbers: Colleges and Universities, 1-800-648-7450; High Schools, 1-800-824-5179; Private Career Colleges, 1-800-347-7707; Canada, 1-800-268-2222; Corporations with IT Training Centers, 1-800-648-7450; and Government Agencies, Health-Care Organizations, and Correctional Facilities, 1-800-477-3692.

Instructor Resources CD-ROM

The Instructor Resources for this textbook include both teaching and testing aids. The contents of the Instructor Resources CD-ROM are listed below.

- **Instructor's Manual** The Instructor's Manual is made up of Microsoft Word files. The Instructor's Manual includes detailed lesson plans with page number references, lecture notes, teaching tips, classroom activities, discussion topics, projects to assign, and transparency references. The transparencies are available through the Figure Files described below.

- **Syllabus** Any instructor who has been assigned a course at the last minute knows how difficult it is to come up with a course syllabus. For this reason, sample syllabi are included that can be customized easily to a course.

- **Figure Files** Illustrations for every figure in the textbook are available in electronic form. Use this ancillary to present a slide show in lecture or to print transparencies for use in lecture with an overhead projector.

- **Solutions to Exercises** Solutions and required files for all the chapter projects, Checkpoint exercises, Teaching Today, Education Issues, Integration Corner, Software Corner, and In the Lab at the end of each chapter are available.

- **Test Bank & Test Engine** The test bank includes 110 questions for every chapter (25 multiple-choice, 50 true/false, and 35 fill-in-the-blank) with page number references, and when appropriate, figure references. A version of the test bank you can print also is included. The test bank comes with a copy of the test engine, ExamView. ExamView is a state-of-the-art test builder that is easy to use. ExamView enables you quickly to create printed tests, Internet tests, and computer (LAN-based) tests. You can enter your own test questions or use the test bank that accompanies ExamView.

- **Data Files for Students** The author-supplied files for the two projects created in this book are included.

- **PowerPoint Presentation** PowerPoint Presentation is a multimedia lecture presentation system that provides PowerPoint slides for each chapter. Presentations are based on the chapters' objectives. Use this presentation system to present well-organized lectures that are both interesting and knowledge based. PowerPoint Presentation provides consistent coverage at schools that use multiple lecturers in their courses.

Course Technology provides the following Online Content options so you can customize your classes using the latest course management tools.

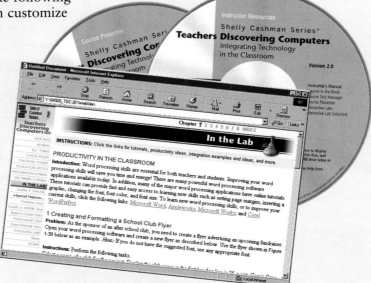

MyCourse 2.0 - Course Management Made Easy

MyCourse 2.0 is a flexible, easy-to-use course management tool that gives you true customization over the online components of your course. MyCourse 2.0 allows you to personalize your course home page, schedule your course activities and assignments, post messages, administer tests, and file the results in a grade book. You also can use text-specific preloaded content for this book, add your own content, select from a pool of test bank questions, or create questions yourself. MyCourse 2.0 is hosted by Thomson Learning, allowing you hassle-free maintenance and student access at all times. For more information, visit course.com/onlinecontent.

Blackboard and WebCT Online Content

Course Technology offers you options for online content. For those who want online testing, we provide a Blackboard test bank and a WebCT test bank, available for download in the Instructor Resources section on course.com. For those who desire more content, we offer course management and access to a Web site that is fully populated with content for this book. Also see Blackboard and WebCT Online Content in the Supplements section. For more information, visit course.com/onlinecontent.

Shelly Cashman Series Interactive Labs with Audio on CD-ROM

The Shelly Cashman Series Interactive Labs with Audio on CD-ROM (ISBN 0-7895-6111-5) may be used in combination with this textbook to augment your students' learning process and reinforce computer and technology-related concepts. See page xvi for a description of each Lab. These Interactive Labs also are available at no cost on the Web by clicking the appropriate button on the Learn It Online exercise pages (see page 1.40).

Acknowledgements

The Shelly Cashman Series would not be the leading computer education series without the contributions of outstanding publishing professionals. First, and foremost, among them is Becky Herrington, director of production and designer. She is the heart and soul of the Shelly Cashman Series, and it is only through her leadership, dedication, and tireless efforts that superior products are made possible.

Under Becky's direction, the following individuals made significant contributions to these books: Kristen Guevara, production editor; Jennifer Quiambao, production assistant; Ken Russo, senior Web and graphic designer; Betty Hopkins, interior designer; Kenny Tran, cover designer; Kenny Tran and Rich Herrera, interior illustrators; Betty Hopkins, Andrew Bartel and Kenny Tran, QuarkXPress compositors; Marjorie Hunt, developmental editor; Ginny Harvey, copy editor; Cherilyn King, proofreader; and Cristina Haley, indexer.

Special thanks go to Vicki Rath, Cindy Brown, Brandi Evans, Shannon Hamilton, Denise Palmieri, Jane Ingoglia, Maria Garlick, Sonya Otero, Kristina Harvey, Amy Scheick, Nirsa Gautier, Mary Edmonds, Michael Brown, and Joel Hartman for assisting in the development of the end-of-chapter materials and features. We also want to thank Julie Kittrell for assisting in the development of the instructor's materials.

We also would like to thank Kristen Duerr, senior vice president and publisher; Cheryl Costantini, executive editor; Jim Quasney, series consulting editor; Alexandra Arnold, senior product manager; Erin Runyon, product manager; Reed Cotter, associate product manager; and Emilie Perreault, editorial assistant.

Finally, we were fortunate to have a truly dedicated group of reviewers whose critical evaluations of the initial manuscript were of great value during the preparation of this book. Special thanks go to the following:

David J. Bullock, Ed.D., Portland State University – Graduate School of Education
Sarah Huyvaert, Eastern Michigan University
Thomas E. Love, Malone College
Cordelia R. Twomey, Ph.D., New Jersey City University
Professor Beverly Woolery, Polk Community College

Gary B. Shelly
Thomas J. Cashman
Randolph E. Gunter
Glenda A. Gunter

Shelly Cashman Series Interactive Labs with Audio

Each of the eight chapters in this book includes the Learn It Online exercises that utilize the World Wide Web. The 17 Shelly Cashman Series Interactive Labs described below are included as exercises in the Learn It Online section. These Interactive Labs are available on the Web (see page 1.40) or on CD-ROM. The CD-ROM version (ISBN 0-7895-6111-5) is available for a small additional cost. A nonaudio version also is available at no extra cost on the Shelly Cashman Series Teaching Tools CD-ROM that is available free to adopters. Each Lab takes students approximately 15 minutes to complete using a personal computer and helps them gain a better understanding of a specific subject covered in the chapter.

Shelly Cashman Series Interactive Labs with Audio		
Lab	*Function*	*Page*
Using the Mouse	**Master how to use a mouse. The Lab includes exercises on pointing, clicking, double-clicking, and dragging.**	**1.40**
Using the Keyboard	**Learn how to use the keyboard. The Lab discusses different categories of keys, including the edit keys, function keys, ESC, CTRL, and ALT keys and how to press keys simultaneously.**	**1.40**
Connecting to the Internet	**Learn how a computer is connected to the Internet. The Lab presents using the Internet to access information.**	**2.51**
The World Wide Web	**Understand the significance of the World Wide Web and how to use Web browser software and search tools.**	**2.51**
Word Processing	**Gain a basic understanding of word processing concepts, from creating a document to printing and saving the final result.**	**3.49**
Working with Spreadsheets	**Learn how to create and utilize spreadsheets, including entering formulas, creating charts, and performing what-if analysis.**	**3.49**
Designing a Database	**Create a database structure and optimize a database to support searching.**	**3.49**
Evaluating Operating Systems	**Evaluate the advantages and disadvantages of different categories of operating systems.**	**3.49**
Understanding the Motherboard	**Step through the components of a motherboard. The Lab shows how different motherboard configurations affect the overall speed of a computer.**	**4.51**
Configuring Your Display	**Recognize the different monitor configurations available, including screen size, display cards, and number of colors.**	**4.51**
Maintaining Your Hard Drive	**Understand how files are stored on disk, what causes fragmentation, and how to maintain an efficient hard drive.**	**4.51**
Understanding Multimedia	**Gain an understanding of the types of media used in multimedia applications, the components of a multimedia PC, and the newest applications of multimedia.**	**5.45**
Scanning Documents	**Understand how document scanners work.**	**5.45**
Setting Up to Print	**See how information flows from the system unit to the printer and how drivers, fonts, and physical connections play a role in generating a printout.**	**6.44**
Working at Your Computer	**Learn the basic ergonomic principles that prevent back and neck pain, eye strain, and other computer-related physical ailments.**	**6.44**
Keeping Your Computer Virus Free	**Learn what a virus is and about the different kinds of viruses. The Lab discusses how to prevent your computer from being infected with a virus.**	**8.48**
Exploring the Computers of the Future	**Learn about computers of the future and how they will work.**	**8.48**

Introduction to Integrating Technology in Education

Objectives

After completing this chapter, you will be able to:

- Explain the difference between computer, information, and integration literacy

- Define and describe computers and their functions

- Identify the major components of a computer

- Explain the four operations of the information processing cycle: input, process, output, and storage

- Explain how speed, reliability, accuracy, storage, and communications enable computers to be powerful tools

- Differentiate among the various categories of software

- Explain the purpose of a network

- Discuss the uses of the Internet and the World Wide Web

- Explain why computer technology is important for education

- Describe the National Educational Technology Standards (NETS-T) for Teachers

- Provide examples of how computers are changing the way people teach and learn

Computers play an essential role in how individuals work, live, and learn. Organizations of all sizes — even the smallest schools and businesses — rely on computers to help them operate more efficiently and effectively. At home, work, and school, computers help people do work faster, more accurately, and in some cases, in ways that previously were not possible. People use computers at home for education, entertainment, information management, and business purposes. They also use computers as tools to access information and to communicate with others around the world. In the classroom, computers and computer-related technologies are having a profound influence on the way teachers instruct and students learn. Even the activities that are part of your daily routine — typing a report, driving a car, paying for goods and services with a credit card, or using an ATM — involve the use of computers.

WEB INFO

For more information and ideas about classroom teachers integrating technology, visit the Teachers Discovering Computers Web site, click Chapter 1, click Web Info, and then click Integration Ideas.

As they have for a number of years, computers continue to influence the lives of most individuals. Today, teachers in K-12 schools are educating students who will spend all of their adult lives in a technology-rich society. To help schools better educate students, the federal government, state governments, and school districts are spearheading massive funding efforts to equip classrooms with computers, with connectivity to networks and access to the Internet and the World Wide Web. Teachers in these classrooms must be prepared to utilize both current and emerging computer technologies.

The purpose of this book is to provide you with the knowledge to begin to use and integrate technology into your specific classroom curriculum. Chapter 1 introduces you to basic computer concepts, such as what a computer is, how it works, and how teachers and administrators integrate computers into K-12 education. As you read, you also will begin to understand the vocabulary used to describe computers and educational technology. While you are reading, remember that this chapter is an overview and that many of the terms and concepts that are introduced are presented in detail in later chapters.

Curriculum-Specific Learning

As you review the materials and concepts presented in this textbook and the accompanying Web site, continuously ask yourself how you can use and integrate the knowledge you are gaining into your specific curricular interests. Reflect how you can use your newly acquired knowledge in three ways: (1) for your own professional development; (2) using technology as a productivity tool in your classroom; and most importantly (3) extensively integrating technology in your teaching, lessons, student-based projects, and student assessments to improve student learning; in other words, throughout your curriculum. By doing this, you will be involved in **curriculum-specific learning** or **discipline-specific learning**, which is when you are learning how to apply teaching principles, knowledge, and ideas to authentic and practical classroom lessons and projects that can benefit your students.

Traditional twentieth century educational practices will no longer provide you with the necessary skills you need to teach your students effectively how to become productive citizens in today's high-tech, global workplace. Figure 1-1 lists characteristics representing traditional approaches to learning and corresponding strategies associated with new learning environments for K-12 students. As you continue to use and integrate educational technology, you will find yourself transitioning from using traditional teaching and learning strategies to using many new and exciting technology-enriched teaching and learning strategies. Refer back to this chart often as you learn how to integrate

Establishing New Learning Environments
Incorporating New Strategies

Traditional Learning Environments	→	New Learning Environments
Teacher-centered instruction	→	Student-centered learning
Single-sense stimulation	→	Multisensory stimulation
Single-path progression	→	Multipath progression
Single media	→	Multimedia
Isolated work	→	Collaborative work
Information delivery	→	Information exchange
Passive learning	→	Active/exploratory/inquiry-based learning
Factual, knowledge-based learning	→	Critical thinking and informed decision making
Reactive response	→	Proactive/planned action
Isolated, artificial context	→	Authentic, real-world context

Source: International Society for Technology in Education (ISTE)

Figure 1-1 This chart shows the characteristics that represent traditional approaches to learning and corresponding strategies often associated with new learning environments for K-12 students.

technology into your classroom curriculum and practice using these new teaching strategies.

Another important issue is that teachers no longer have the time to create their various lesson plans and other documents from scratch, or in other words, constantly to reinvent the wheel. The primary reason for extensively Web-enhancing this textbook is to provide you with hundreds of outstanding curriculum-specific sources of information and integration ideas that you can modify for use in your classroom curriculum. These resources are organized so you can choose the best curriculum-specific content to improve your students' learning. We encourage you to interact with the curriculum-specific content that works for you and then adopt and modify the content and other information, integrating it into your classroom curriculum.

Computer, Information, and Integration Literacy

Today, the vocabulary of computing is all around you. Before the advent of computers, memory was an individual's mental ability to recall previous experiences; storage was a place for out-of-season clothing; and communication was the act of exchanging opinions and information through writing, speaking, or sign language. In today's world, these words and countless others have taken on new meanings as part of the vocabulary used to describe computers and their uses.

When you hear the word, computer, initially you may think of computers used in schools to perform activities such as creating flyers, memos, and letters; managing student rosters and calculating grades; or tracking library books. In the course of a day or week, however, you encounter many other computers. Your home, for instance, can contain a myriad of electronic devices, such as cordless telephones, VCRs, DVD players, handheld video games, digital cameras, and stereo systems including small computers.

Computers help you with your banking when you use automatic teller machines (ATMs) to deposit or withdraw funds. When you buy groceries, a computer tracks your purchases and calculates the amount of money you owe; it may even generate custom coupons based on your buying patterns. Even your car is equipped with computers that run the electrical system, control the temperature, and run sophisticated antitheft devices.

Experts anticipate that by the year 2010, all occupations will involve the use of computers on a daily basis [Figure 1-2]. As the world of computers advances, it is

Figure 1-2
Computers are present in every aspect of daily living — in the workplace, at home, in the classroom, and for entertainment.

FAQ

What is media literacy?

Media literacy, similar to information literacy, is when a person understands, analyzes, evaluates, and can communicate in a variety of forms.

FAQ

Is data singular or plural?

With respect to computers, it is accepted and common practice to use the word data in both singular and plural context.

essential that you gain some level of **computer literacy**; that is, you must have a knowledge and understanding of computers and their uses.

Information literacy means knowing how to find, analyze, and use information. Information literacy is the ability to gather information from multiple sources, select relevant material, and organize it into a form that will allow the user to make decisions or take specific actions.

Students must learn to make informed decisions based on information obtained in all areas of their lives. For example, suppose you decide to move to a new city and need a place to live. You could find a home by driving around the city looking for a house or apartment within your price range that is close to school or work. As an information literate person, however, you may search for a home using the Internet, which is a global network of computers that contains information on a multitude of subjects. Using these resources to locate potential homes before you leave will make your drive through the city more efficient and focused.

How do computers relate to information literacy? They relate because, increasingly, information on housing, cars, and other products, as well as information on finances, school systems, travel, and weather, is accessible by computers. For example, with communications equipment, you can use a computer to connect to the Internet to access information on countless topics. After you have accessed the desired information, computers can help you analyze and use that information.

While computer and information literacy are very important for educators, today's teachers also must use computers as a tool to facilitate learning. Teachers must be able to assess technology resources and plan classroom activities using available technologies. These skills are part of **integration literacy**, which is the ability to use computers and other technologies combined with a variety of teaching and learning strategies to enhance students' learning. Integration literacy means that teachers can understand how to match appropriate technology to learning objectives, goals, and outcomes. A solid foundation of computer and information

literacy is essential to understanding how to integrate technology into classroom curriculum successfully.

As an educator, computers will affect your work and your life every day — and will continue to do so in the future. Today, school administrators use computers to access and manage information, and teachers use computers to enhance teaching and learning. The computer industry continually is developing new and different uses for computers and making improvements to existing technologies. Learning about computers and other technologies will help you function effectively in society and become a better facilitator of learning.

What Is a Computer and What Does It Do?

A **computer** is an electronic machine, operating under the control of instructions stored in its own memory, that can accept data (input), manipulate the data according to specified rules (process), produce results (output), and store the results for future use.

Data is a collection of unorganized facts, which can include words, numbers, images, and sounds. Computers manipulate and process data to create information. **Information** is data that is organized, has meaning, and is useful. Examples are reports, newsletters, a receipt, a picture, an invoice, or a check. In Figure 1-3, data is processed and manipulated to create a check.

Data entered into a computer is called **input**. The processed results are called **output**. Thus, a computer processes input to create output. A computer also can hold data and information for future use in an area called **storage**. This cycle of input, process, output, and storage is called the **information processing cycle**.

A person who communicates with a computer or uses the information it generates is called a **user**.

The electric, electronic, and mechanical equipment that makes up a computer is called **hardware**. **Software** is the series of instructions that tells the hardware how to perform tasks. Without software, hardware is useless; hardware needs the

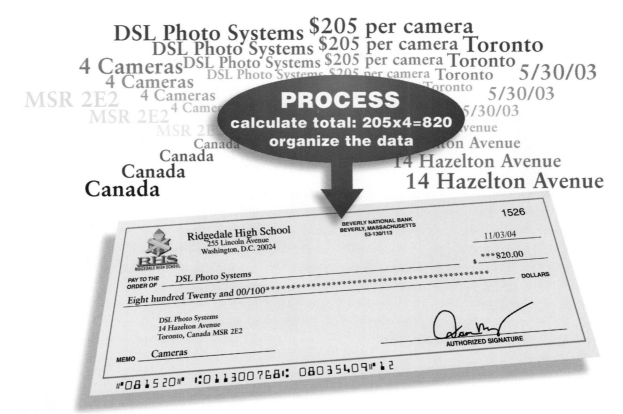

Figure 1-3 Data is processed into information. In this example, the company name, the date, the number of cameras, and cost per camera each represent data. These items are processed into information, which in this case is a check.

instructions provided by software to process data into information.

The next section discusses various hardware components. Later in the chapter, categories of software are discussed.

The Components of a Computer

A computer consists of a variety of hardware components that work together with software to perform calculations, organize data, and communicate with other computers.

These hardware components include input devices, output devices, a system unit, storage devices, scanners, digital cameras, PC cameras, and communications devices. Figure 1-4 on the next page shows some common computer hardware components.

INPUT DEVICES

An **input device** allows a user to enter data and commands into the memory of a computer. Three commonly used input devices are a keyboard, a mouse, and a microphone. Other input devices include scanners and digital cameras.

A computer keyboard contains keys that allow you to type letters of the alphabet, numbers, spaces, punctuation marks, and other symbols. A computer keyboard also contains special keys that allow you to perform specific functions on the computer.

A mouse is a small handheld device that contains at least one button. The mouse controls the movement of a symbol on the screen called a pointer. For example, moving the mouse across a flat surface allows you to move the pointer on the screen. You also can make choices and initiate processing on the computer by using a mouse.

A microphone allows you to speak to the computer in order to enter data and control the actions of the computer. Using a scanner you can capture an entire page of text or images. A digital camera allows you to take pictures and store them digitally instead of on traditional film.

WEB INFO

For more information about input devices, visit the Teachers Discovering Computers Web site, click Chapter 1, click Web Info, and then click Input Devices.

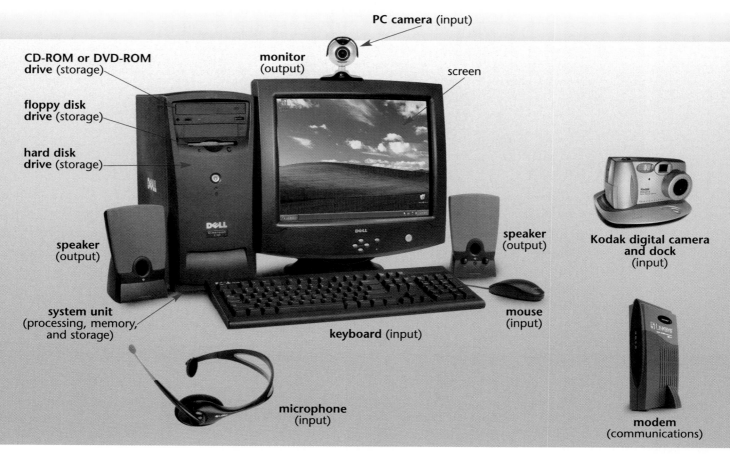

Figure 1-4 Common computer hardware components include a keyboard, mouse, microphone, system unit, disk drives, PC camera, scanner, digital camera, monitor, and speakers.

OUTPUT DEVICES

An **output device** is any hardware component used to convey the information generated by a computer to a user. Three commonly used output devices are a printer, a monitor, and speakers.

A printer produces text and graphics, such as photographs, on paper or another hard-copy medium. A monitor, which looks like a television screen, is used to display text and graphics. Speakers allow you to hear music, voice, and other sounds generated by the computer.

SYSTEM UNIT

The **system unit** is a box-like case made from metal or plastic that houses the computer electronic circuitry. The circuitry in the system unit usually is part of or is connected to a circuit board called the motherboard.

Two main components on the motherboard are the central processing unit (CPU) and memory. The **central processing unit (CPU)**, also called a **processor**, is the electronic device that interprets and carries out the instructions that operate the computer.

Memory is a series of electronic elements that temporarily holds data and instructions while they are being processed by the CPU.

Both the processor and memory are chips. A chip is an electronic device that contains many microscopic pathways designed to carry electrical current. Chips, which usually are no bigger than a one-half-inch square, are packaged so they can be connected to a motherboard or other circuit boards [Figure 1-5].

Some computer components, such as the processor and memory, reside inside the system unit; that is, they are internal. Other components, such as the keyboard, mouse, microphone, monitor, and printer, are located outside the system unit. These

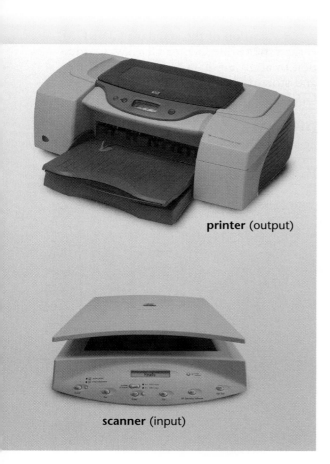

printer (output)

scanner (input)

devices are considered external. Any external device that attaches to the system unit is called a **peripheral device**.

STORAGE DEVICES

Storage holds data, information, and instructions for future use. Storage differs from memory, in that it can hold these items permanently, whereas memory holds these items only temporarily during processing operations. A **storage medium** (media is the plural) is the physical material used to store data, instructions, and information. One commonly used storage medium is a disk, which is a round, flat piece of plastic or metal on which data is encoded, or written.

A **storage device** is the mechanism used to record and retrieve data, information, and instructions to and from a storage medium. Storage devices often function as a source of input because they transfer items from storage into memory. Common storage devices are a floppy disk drive, a Zip drive, a hard disk drive, a CD-ROM drive, a CD-RW drive, and a DVD-ROM drive. A disk drive is a device that reads from and may write onto a disk.

For an overview of hardware, including discussions of the CPU and memory, visit the Teachers Discovering Computers Web site, click Chapter 1, click Web Info, and then click Hardware.

memory chip

processor chip packaging

Figure 1-5 Computer chips are packaged so they may be connected to a circuit board.

FAQ

Which spelling is correct, disk or disc?

Both are correct, depending on usage. When referring to CD, DVD, and other optical (laser) storage media, the term, disc, commonly is used. Floppy disks, Zip disks, hard disks, and other nonoptical storage media use the term, disk.

A floppy disk consists of a thin, circular flexible disk enclosed in a plastic shell. A floppy disk stores data and information using magnetic patterns and can be inserted into and removed from a floppy disk drive [Figure 1-6]. A floppy disk drive reads from and writes on a floppy disk. A Zip disk is a higher-capacity floppy disk that can store the equivalent of 170 to 500 floppy disks.

Figure 1-6 A floppy disk is inserted and removed from a floppy disk drive.

A hard disk provides much greater storage capacity than a floppy disk. A hard disk usually consists of several circular disks on which data, information, and instructions are stored magnetically. Sealed in an airtight case, hard disks often are housed inside the system unit.

A compact disc is a flat, round, portable medium that stores data using microscopic pits, which are created by a laser light. One type of compact disc is a CD-ROM, which you access using a CD-ROM drive. A Picture CD is a special type of CD-ROM that stores digital versions of photographs for consumers.

A variation of the standard CD-ROM is the rewriteable CD, or CD-RW. In addition to accessing data, you also can erase and store data on a CD-RW. To use a CD-RW, you need a CD-RW drive.

Another type of compact disc is a DVD-ROM, which has tremendous storage capacities — enough for a full-length movie. To use a DVD-ROM, you need a DVD-ROM drive [Figure 1-7].

Figure 1-7 A compact disc stores data in microscopic pits, which are created by a laser light. Two types of compact discs are CD-ROMs and DVD-ROMs.

COMMUNICATIONS DEVICES

A **communications device** enables a computer to exchange data, information, and instructions with another computer. Communications devices transmit data and information over transmission media, such as cables, telephone lines, or other means used to establish a connection between two computers. A modem is a communications device that enables computers to communicate via telephone lines.

WEB INFO

For details about disk drives, visit the Teachers Discovering Computers Web site, click Chapter 1, click Web Info, and then click Disk Drive.

Categories of Computers Typically Used in Education

Computers found in K-12 schools can be organized in three general categories: personal computers or desktop computers, mobile computers and devices, and servers. All of these types of computers are discussed in detail in later chapters and special features.

Personal Computers

A **personal computer**, or **PC**, is a computer designed for use by one person at a time. A personal computer can perform all of its input, processing, output, and storage activities by itself.

Many people associate the term, personal computer, or PC, with computers that use Microsoft Windows, which is a popular operating system used on many of today's computers. All personal computers, however, do not use Windows. For example, Apple Macintosh computers use a different operating system, **Mac OS**, but still are a type of personal computer. Why the confusion?

In 1981, IBM Corporation released its first personal computer, the IBM Personal Computer [Figure 1-8]. The IBM

Personal Computer was an instant business success and quickly became known by its nickname — the PC. For marketing reasons, IBM allowed other companies to copy its computer design; therefore, many companies started making IBM-compatible computers. These computers were called IBM-compatible because they used software that was the same as or similar to the IBM PC software. All subsequent IBM computers and IBM-compatibles were called PCs.

Three years after the introduction of the first IBM PC, the Apple Computer Company introduced the **Macintosh computer** [Figure 1-9]. Macintosh computers could accomplish many of the same tasks as IBM PCs, but were very different. The Macintosh computer used a pointing device called a mouse. Macintosh computers were incompatible with the IBM PC because they used different software than the IBM and IBM-compatible computers. As a result, a distinction developed between the terms Macintosh and PC, even though Macintosh computers are personal computers. This distinction and confusion between the two types of computers continues today. To avoid confusion, users often refer to these two types of personal computers as Windows environment or Mac environment.

For more information about Macintosh computers, visit the Teachers Discovering Computers Web site, click Chapter 1, click Web Info, and then click Macintosh.

Figure 1-9 Apple Computer Company produced the Macintosh computer in 1984.

Figure 1-8 The original IBM Personal Computer was introduced in 1981.

Today, businesses, homes, and K-12 schools use dozens of different models of Apple and IBM-compatible personal computers. To avoid confusion in this textbook, personal computers that use Microsoft Windows will be referred to as PCs and all Macintosh personal computers will be referred to as Macintosh computers [Figure 1-10]. When this textbook refers to the terms personal computer, desktop computer, or computer, the subject matter being discussed is applicable to Apple, IBM, and IBM-compatible computers. Most of the concepts and terms covered in this textbook are applicable to all types of personal computers.

Personal computers shown in Figure 1-10a and Figure 1-10b also are called **desktop computers** because they are designed so the system unit, input devices, output devices, and any other devices fit entirely on a desk.

How long have schools used Tablet PCs?

In December 2002, Ocoee Middle School in Orlando, Florida, was the first public school to provide students with this new technology.

[a] IBM computer (PC)

[b] Apple Macintosh (Mac)

Figure 1-10 Figure 1-10a shows a typical PC and Figure 1-10b shows a typical Macintosh computer.

Mobile Computers and Mobile Devices

A mobile computer is a personal computer that you can carry from place to place. The most popular type of mobile computer is the notebook computer. A mobile device is a computing device small enough to hold in your hand. Popular mobile devices include handheld computers, PDAs, and smart phones.

NOTEBOOK COMPUTERS

A **notebook computer**, also called a laptop computer, is a portable, personal computer small enough to fit on you lap. Today's notebook computers are thin and lightweight, yet they can be as powerful as the average desktop computer [Figure 1-11]. Notebook computers normally are more expensive than desktop computers with equal capabilities.

Figure 1-11 Notebook computers are available in Windows and Mac environments. Shown is an Apple iBook.

TABLET PC

Resembling a letter-sized slate, the **Tablet PC** is a special type of notebook computer that allows you to write on the screen using a digital pen [Figure 1-12].

Figure 1-12 The Tablet PC combines the features of a traditional notebook computer with the simplicity of pencil and paper.

Users also can use the attached keyboard. Tablet PCs will be covered in later chapters and the special feature that follows Chapter 8.

MOBILE DEVICES

Some mobile devices are **Web-enabled**, meaning they can connect to the Internet wirelessly. Mobile devices usually do not have disk drives. Instead, these devices store programs and data permanently on memory inside the system unit or on small storage media such as memory cards. Three popular mobile devices are handheld computers, PDAs, and smart phones. Some combination mobile devices also are available, for example, a PDA/smart phone.

HANDHELD COMPUTER
A **handheld computer** is a computer small enough to fit in one hand while you operate it with the other hand. Because of their reduced size, the screens on handheld computers are quite small. The primary input device on a handheld computer is a small keyboard.

PDA
A **personal digital assistant**, or **PDA**, provides personal organizer functions such as a calendar, appointment book, address book, calculator, and notepad [Figure 1-13]. The PDA is one of the more popular light-weight mobile devices in use today. Most PDAs also offer a variety of other application software, such as word processing, spreadsheets, and games. In addition, a large array of educational software is available for use on PDAs, including concept mapping tools, periodic tables, graphic calculators, and much more. Many PDAs are Web-enabled so users can check e-mail and access the Internet.

Figure 1-13 PDAs are widely used in both business and education.

SMART PHONES
Offering the convenience of one-handed operation, a **smart phone** is a Web-enabled telephone. In addition to basic telephone capabilities, smart phones allow you to send and receive e-mail and access the Internet. Some models have color screens, play music, and allow you to take and send digital photos.

Why Is a Computer So Powerful?

A computer's power derives from its capability of performing the **information processing cycle** (input, process, output, and storage) with speed, reliability, and accuracy; its capacity to store large amounts of data and information; and its capability of communicating with other computers.

SPEED

Inside the system unit, operations occur through electronic circuits. When data and information flow along these circuits, they travel at close to the speed of light. As a result, computers process billions of operations in a single second.

RELIABILITY

The electronic components in modern computers are dependable because they have a low failure rate. The high reliability of their components enables computers to produce consistent results.

ACCURACY

Computers can process large amounts of data and generate error-free results, provided the user enters the data correctly. If a user enters inaccurate data, the resulting output will be incorrect. This computing principle, called garbage in, garbage out (GIGO), points out that the accuracy of a computer's output depends on the accuracy of the input. In fact, human mistakes cause most instances of computer errors.

STORAGE

Many computers can store enormous amounts of data and make this data available for processing when needed. Using current storage methods, a computer can

transfer data from storage to memory quickly, process the data, and then store the processed data for future use.

COMMUNICATIONS

Most computers today can communicate with other computers. Computers with this capability can share any of the four information processing cycle operations, input, process, output, and storage, with another computer. For example, two computers connected by a communications device such as a modem can share stored data, instructions, and information. A **network** consists of two or more computers connected together via communications media and devices. The most widely known network is the Internet, linking together millions of businesses, government installations, educational institutions, and individuals.

Today, hundreds of millions of people routinely send and receive messages using **electronic mail** (**e-mail**), which is the electronic exchange of messages to and from other computer users. The Internet also allows individuals to access a global network of computers to gather information on practically any subject, send e-mail and other types of messages, and obtain products and services [Figure 1-14].

Figure 1-14 The Internet is a worldwide collection of networks that links together millions of businesses, the government, educational institutions, and individuals.

Computer Software

Software, also called a **computer program** or simply a **program**, is a series of instructions that tells the hardware of a computer what to do and how to do it. For example, some instructions direct the computer to allow you to input data from the keyboard and store it in memory. Other instructions cause data stored in memory to be used in calculations, such as adding a series of numbers to obtain a total. Some instructions compare two values stored in memory and direct the computer to perform alternative operations based on the results of the comparison; and some instructions direct the computer to print a report, display information on the monitor, draw a color graph on the monitor, or store information on a disk.

Before a computer can perform, or **execute**, a program, the instructions in the program must be placed, or loaded, into the memory of the computer. Usually, they are loaded into memory from storage. For example, a program might be loaded from the hard disk of a computer into memory for execution.

When you purchase a program, you will receive one or more floppy disks, one or more CD-ROMs, or a single DVD-ROM on which the software is stored [Figure 1-15]. To use this software, you often must **install** the software on the computer's hard disk. Many programs also may be purchased and downloaded from the Internet.

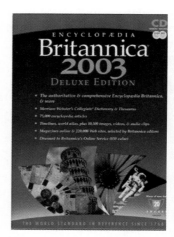

Figure 1-15 When you buy software, you receive media, such as a CD-ROM or a DVD-ROM, which contains the software program.

Sometimes, a program can be loaded in memory directly from a floppy disk, CD-ROM, or DVD-ROM so you do not have to install it on a hard disk first.

When you buy a computer, it usually has some software already installed on its hard disk. Thus, you can use the computer as soon as you receive it.

Figure 1-16 illustrates the steps required when a user installs and runs an encyclopedia program.

Software is the key to productive use of computers. With the correct software, a computer is an invaluable tool.

Software can be categorized into two types: system software and application software. The following sections describe these categories of software.

SYSTEM SOFTWARE

System software consists of programs that control the operations of a computer and its devices. System software also serves as the liaison between a user and the computer's hardware. Two types of system software are the operating system and utility programs.

OPERATING SYSTEM   One of the more important programs on a computer, the **operating system** contains instructions that coordinate all of the activities of hardware devices. The operating system also contains instructions that allow you to run application software.

When you start a computer, the computer loads, or copies, the operating system into memory from the hard disk. The operating system remains in memory while the computer runs and allows you to communicate with the computer and other software. Many Macintosh computers use a unique operating system called the Macintosh operating system, or **Mac OS**; many of today's PCs use a popular operating system called **Microsoft Windows**.

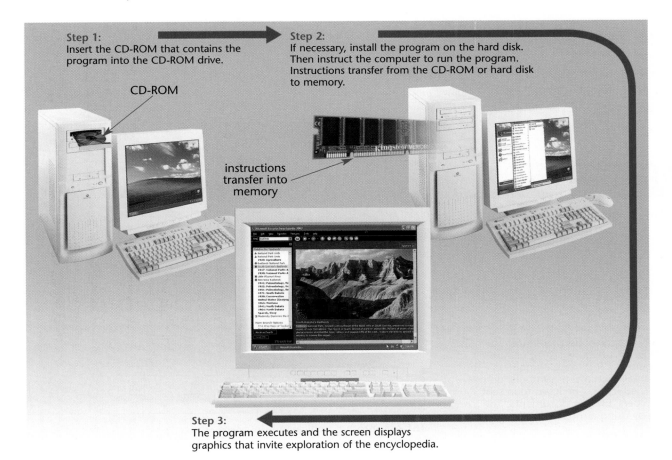

Step 1:
Insert the CD-ROM that contains the program into the CD-ROM drive.

CD-ROM

instructions transfer into memory

Step 2:
If necessary, install the program on the hard disk. Then instruct the computer to run the program. Instructions transfer from the CD-ROM or hard disk to memory.

Step 3:
The program executes and the screen displays graphics that invite exploration of the encyclopedia.

Figure 1-16 This figure shows the steps involved in installing and running a computer program.

WEB INFO

For more information about Windows graphical user interface, visit the Teachers Discovering Computers Web site, click Chapter 1, click Web Info, and then click GUI.

USER INTERFACE   All software has a **user interface**, which is the part of the software with which the user interacts. The user interface controls how you enter data and instructions. The user interface also controls how the computer presents information on the screen. Many of today's software programs use a **graphical user interface**, or **GUI** (pronounced *gooey*), which allows you to interact with the software using visual items such as icons. An **icon** is a small image that represents a program, an instruction, or some other object. Figure 1-17a shows the Windows graphical user interface and Figure 1-17b shows the Mac OS graphical user interface.

UTILITY PROGRAMS   A **utility program** is a type of system software that performs a specific task, usually related to managing a computer, its devices, or its programs. An example of a utility program is an uninstaller, which removes a program previously installed on a computer. Most operating systems include several utility programs for managing disk drives, printers, and other devices. You also can buy stand-alone utility programs to perform additional computer management functions.

APPLICATION SOFTWARE

    Application software consists of programs designed to perform specific tasks for users. When you think of the different ways people use computers in their careers or personal lives, you are thinking of examples of application software. Educational, business, and scientific computer programs are all examples of application software.

icons

[a] Windows graphical user interface.

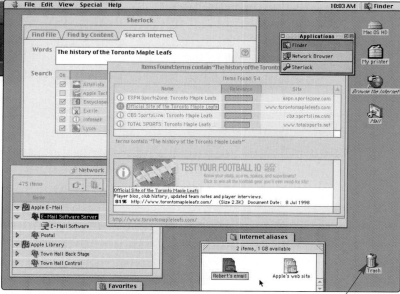

[b] Macintosh graphical user interface.

icons

Trash icon

Figure 1-17 Graphical user interfaces, such as Microsoft Windows [Figure 1-17a] or Apple's Mac OS [Figure 1-17b], make computers easier to use. The small pictures, or symbols, on the screen are called icons. The icons represent programs, folders, files, or documents. The icons are selected by using a mouse or other pointing device.

Popular application software includes word processing, spreadsheet, database, and presentation graphics. Word processing software allows you to create documents such as letters and reports. Spreadsheet software allows you to calculate numbers arranged in rows and columns and create charts and graphs. Teachers and schools use spreadsheet software for gradebooks, lesson plans, and other school-related tasks. Database software allows you to store data in an organized fashion, as well as to retrieve, manipulate, and display that data in a meaningful form. With presentation graphics software, you can create electronic slides for use when giving classroom presentations. Computer software manufacturers frequently package these four applications together as a single unit, called a software suite. A software suite contains individual software applications sold in the same box for a price that is significantly less than buying the applications separately [Figure 1-18].

Many other types of application software exist that enable users to perform a variety of tasks. Some widely used software applications include: reference, education, and entertainment; desktop publishing; photo and video editing; multimedia authoring; network, communications, electronic mail, and Web browsers; accounting; school and student record keeping; and personal information management. Each of these applications is discussed in future chapters.

The number and quality of software applications designed specifically for the K-12 learning environment have increased dramatically in the past few years. Education software and the use of productivity software in education are discussed extensively in Chapters 3 and 5. In addition, you can learn about dozens of education software programs by reviewing Software Corner at the end of each chapter.

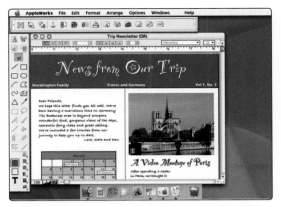

Figure 1-18 AppleWorks is a popular suite used by teachers and students primarily on Macintosh computers and includes word processing, spreadsheet, database, presentation graphics, and communications software.

WEB INFO

For more information about application software packages, visit the Teachers Discovering Computers Web site, click Chapter 1, click Web Info, and then click Application Software.

PACKAGED SOFTWARE   Packaged software is designed to meet the needs of a variety of users, not just a single user, school, or business. Programs required for common educational, business, and personal applications are available for purchase off the shelf from software vendors or stores that sell computer products [Figure 1-19]. You also can purchase packaged software on the Internet.

Figure 1-19 You can buy packaged software programs from computer stores, office equipment suppliers, retailers, and the Internet.

CUSTOM SOFTWARE   Sometimes a user or organization with unique software requirements cannot find packaged software that meets all of its needs. In this case, the user or organization can use **custom software**, which is a program developed at a user's request to perform specific functions. For example, a state Department of Education may design a custom gradebook and attendance program for use by its school districts.

SHAREWARE, FREEWARE, AND PUBLIC-DOMAIN SOFTWARE   Shareware is software distributed to a user free for a trial period. If you want to use a shareware program beyond the trial period, the person or company that developed the program expects you to send a small fee. When you send this small fee, the developer registers you to receive service assistance and updates. **Freeware** is software provided at no cost to a user by an individual or company. Thousands of inexpensive shareware and freeware programs are available for download from the Internet. **Public-domain software** also is free software, but has been donated for public use and has no copyright restrictions.

SOFTWARE DEVELOPMENT

People who write software programs are called **computer programmers** or **programmers**. Programmers write the instructions necessary to direct the computer to process data into information. Programmers must place the correct instructions in the right sequence so the program performs the desired actions. Complex programs can require hundreds of thousands of program instructions. Many programmers use a programming language to write computer programs.

When writing complex programs for large businesses, programmers often follow a plan developed by a systems analyst. A **systems analyst** manages the development of a program, working with both the user and the programmer to design the program.

WEB INFO

For more information about shareware, freeware, and evaluation software, visit the Teachers Discovering Computers Web site, click Chapter 1, click Web Info, and then click Shareware.

Networks and the Internet

A **network** is a collection of computers and devices connected together via communications media and devices such as cables, telephone lines, modems, or other means. When you connect your computer to a network, you are online with the network.

Businesses and schools continue to network their computers so users can share **resources**, such as hardware devices, software programs, data, and information. Sharing resources saves time and money. For example, instead of purchasing one printer for every Macintosh and PC in a computer lab, schools can connect a single printer and all the computers using a local area network, or LAN. The network enables all of the computers within a lab to access the same printer.

These networks can be relatively small or quite extensive. A local area network (LAN) is a network that connects computers in a limited geographic area, such as a school computer laboratory, business office, or group of adjacent buildings [Figure 1-20]. A wide area network (WAN) is a network that covers a large geographical area, such as one that connects the district offices of a statewide school system or the offices of a national corporation [Figure 1-21].

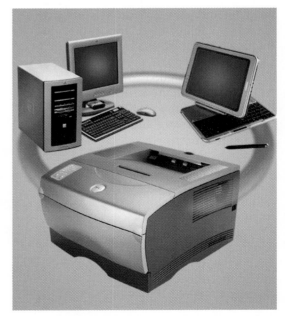

Figure 1-20 A local area network (LAN) enables two separate computers to share the same printer.

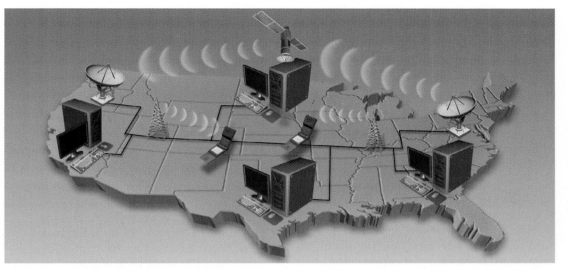

Figure 1-21 A wide area network (WAN) can be quite large and complex, connecting users in offices around the country.

WEB INFO

For more information about aspects of the Internet, visit the Teachers Discovering Computers Web site, click Chapter 1, click Web Info, and then click Internet.

The world's largest network is the **Internet**, which is a worldwide collection of networks that links together millions of businesses, governments, educational institutions, and individuals using modems, telephone lines, and other communications devices and media. More than 400 million users around the world access the Internet for a variety of reasons [Figure 1-22]. For teachers, the Internet opens doors to a myriad of educational activities including the following:

- Sending messages to other connected users, including teachers and students

- Accessing a wealth of information, including curriculum and lesson plans, activities, and teacher's guides

Figure 1-22 Users access the Internet for a variety of reasons: to send messages to other connected users, to access a wealth of information, to shop for goods and services, to meet and converse with people around the world, and for entertainment.

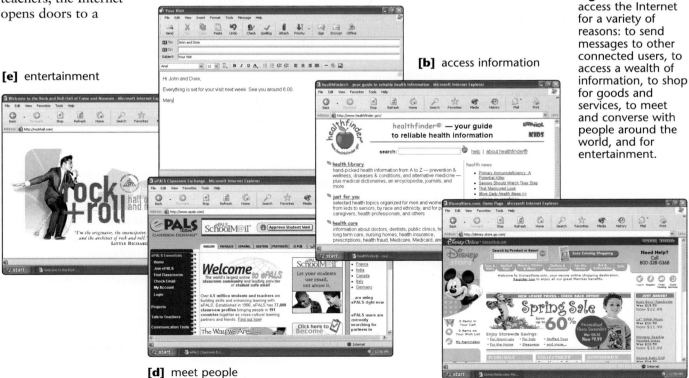

[a] send a message

[b] access information

[e] entertainment

[d] meet people

[c] shop

FAQ

How do I find the right access provider for me?

The Web has many comprehensive lists of access providers. One of the more popular lists on the Web is called The List of ISPs (www.thelist.com).

WEB INFO

For more information about the World Wide Web, visit the Teachers Discovering Computers Web site, click Chapter 1, click Web Info, and then click Web.

- Joining an educational community to collaborate with teachers and students around the world

- Accessing sources of educational content such as encyclopedias, online museums, magazines, and other project collections

- Taking an online class or even enrolling in an online Master's Degree program

Most users connect to the Internet in one of two ways: through an Internet service provider or using an online service. An Internet service provider (ISP) is an organization that supplies connections to the Internet for a monthly fee. Like an ISP, an online service provides access to the Internet, but it also provides a variety of other specialized content and services such as financial data, hardware and software guides, news, weather, legal information, and numerous similar commodities. For this reason, the fees for using an online service usually are slightly higher than fees for using an ISP. Two popular online services are America Online and The Microsoft Network (MSN).

One of the more popular parts of the Internet is the **World Wide Web**, also called the **Web**. The Web portion of the Internet consists of computer sites that contain billions of electronic documents called Web pages. A Web page is an electronic document that contains text, graphics, sound, animation, or video, and has built-in connections, or links, to other documents. Web pages are stored on computers throughout the world. A Web site is a collection of related Web pages that you can access electronically for information on thousands of topics. You access and view Web pages using a software program called a Web browser. The most popular Web browsers are Microsoft Internet Explorer, Netscape, and Mozilla. Figure 1-23 illustrates one method of connecting to the Web and displaying a Web page.

Why Use Computer Technology in Education?

In any society, educators have the ability to make an enormous positive contribution. Making such a contribution is a challenge and teachers must willingly embrace new teaching and learning opportunities. Educators are beginning to recognize that they must teach future leaders and citizens of society the technologies that will be a major part of their future.

Technology is everywhere and integrated into every aspect of individuals' lives. Today's educators must provide students with the skills they will need to excel in a technology-rich society. Parents no longer are urging schools to incorporate technology into the classroom; they are insisting on it. When used appropriately, technology has the potential to enhance students' achievement and assist them in meeting learning objectives.

An extensive body of education research is showing that technology can support learning in many ways. Using technology in the classroom, for example, can be motivational. Teachers have found that using modern computers or computer-related technologies can capture and hold students' attention. Computers also can provide many unique, effective, and powerful opportunities for teaching and learning. These opportunities include skill-building practice, real-world problem solving, interactive learning, discovery learning, and linking learners to instructional resources.

Computers also support communications beyond classroom walls, thus enabling schools and communities to provide an environment for cooperative learning, for development of high-order thinking skills, and for solving complex problems. As demonstrated by these examples, computers, when placed in the hands of teachers and students, can provide unique, effective, and powerful opportunities for many different types of instruction and learning.

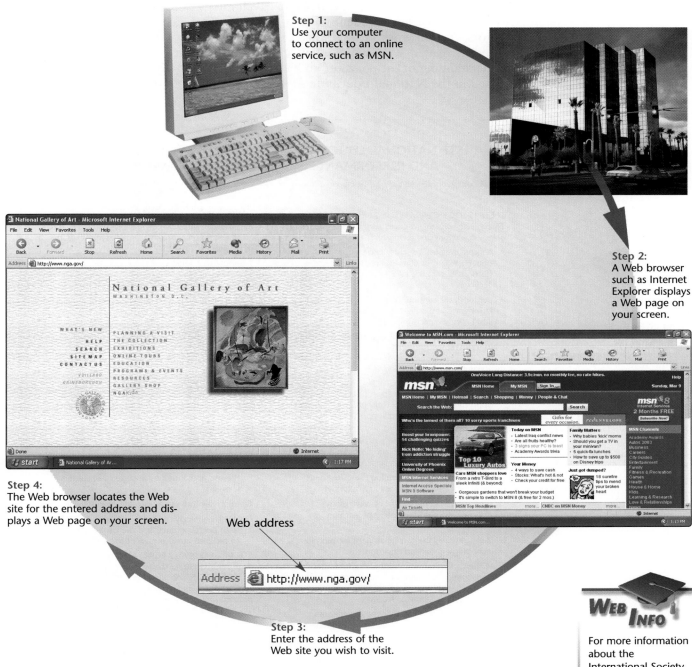

Step 1:
Use your computer to connect to an online service, such as MSN.

Step 2:
A Web browser such as Internet Explorer displays a Web page on your screen.

Step 4:
The Web browser locates the Web site for the entered address and displays a Web page on your screen.

Web address

Step 3:
Enter the address of the Web site you wish to visit.

Figure 1-23 One method of connecting to the Web and displaying a Web page.

Several national and international organizations support education and educators in the use of technology. The leading organization is the **International Society for Technology in Education** (**ISTE**), which is a nonprofit group that promotes the use of technology to support and improve teaching and learning. ISTE supports all areas of K-12 education, community colleges and universities, administration of K-12 education, and teacher education organizations.

ISTE has been instrumental in developing the National Educational Technology Standards (NETS) for the **National Council for Accreditation for Teacher Education** (**NCATE**). NCATE is the official body for accrediting teacher education programs. To date, ISTE has developed standards for K-12 teachers, students, and administrators. As you work through this textbook and its related Web site, you will gain an understanding of the concepts and skills outlined in the **National Educational**

Technology Standards for Teachers (**NETS-T**), which define the fundamental concepts, knowledge, skills, and attitudes for applying technology in K-12 educational settings [Figure 1-24].

WEB INFO

For more information about ISTE's standards for students, teachers, and administrators, visit the Teachers Discovering Computers Web site, click Chapter 1, click Web Info, and then click Students, Teachers, or Administrators.

ISTE NATIONAL EDUCATIONAL TECHNOLOGY STANDARDS AND PERFORMANCE INDICATORS FOR TEACHERS

All classroom teachers should be prepared to meet the following standards and performance indicators.

I. TECHNOLOGY OPERATIONS AND CONCEPTS
Teachers demonstrate a sound understanding of technology operations and concepts. Teachers:

A. demonstrate introductory knowledge, skills, and understanding of concepts related to technology (as described in the ISTE *National Educational Technology Standards for Students*).

B. demonstrate continual growth in technology knowledge and skills to stay abreast of current and emerging technologies.

II. PLANNING AND DESIGNING LEARNING ENVIRONMENTS AND EXPERIENCES
Teachers plan and design effective learning environments and experiences supported by technology. Teachers:

A. design developmentally appropriate learning opportunities that apply technology-enhanced instructional strategies to support the diverse needs of learners.

B. apply current research on teaching and learning with technology when planning learning environments and experiences.

C. identify and locate technology resources and evaluate them for accuracy and suitability.

D. plan for the management of technology resources within the context of learning activities.

E. plan strategies to manage student learning in a technology-enhanced environment.

III. TEACHING, LEARNING, AND THE CURRICULUM
Teachers implement curriculum plans that include methods and strategies for applying technology to maximize student learning. Teachers:

A. facilitate technology-enhanced experiences that address content standards and student technology standards.

B. use technology to support learner-centered strategies that address the diverse needs of students.

C. apply technology to develop students' higher-order skills and creativity.

D. manage student learning activities in a technology-enhanced environment.

IV. ASSESSMENT AND EVALUATION
Teachers apply technology to facilitate a variety of effective assessment and evaluation strategies. Teachers:

A. apply technology in assessing student learning of subject matter using a variety of assessment techniques.

B. use technology resources to collect and analyze data, interpret results, and communicate findings to improve instructional practice and maximize student learning.

C. apply multiple methods of evaluation to determine students' appropriate use of technology resources for learning, communication, and productivity.

V. PRODUCTIVITY AND PROFESSIONAL PRACTICE
Teachers use technology to enhance their productivity and professional practice. Teachers:

A. use technology resources to engage in ongoing professional development and lifelong learning.

B. continually evaluate and reflect on professional practice to make informed decisions regarding the use of technology in support of student learning.

C. apply technology to increase productivity.

D. use technology to communicate and collaborate with peers, parents, and the larger community in order to nurture student learning.

VI. SOCIAL, ETHICAL, LEGAL, AND HUMAN ISSUES
Teachers understand the social, ethical, legal, and human issues surrounding the use of technology in PK–12 schools and apply that understanding in practice. Teachers:

A. model and teach legal and ethical practice related to technology use.

B. apply technology resources to enable and empower learners with diverse backgrounds, characteristics, and abilities.

C. identify and use technology resources that affirm diversity.

D. promote safe and healthy use of technology resources.

E. facilitate equitable access to technology resources for all students.

Source: International Society for Technology in Education (ISTE)

Figure 1-24 The ISTE technology standards and performance indicators provide a framework for implementing technology in teaching and learning.

An Example of How One School Uses Computers

To illustrate how a typical school might use computers and other computer-based technologies, this section takes you on a visual and narrative tour of a typical day at Ridgedale High School, home of the Fighting Tigers. Ridgedale High School is taking advantage of the Federal Communications Commission's **Education Rate**, or **E-Rate**, program, which is a government initiative designed to provide discounts to schools and libraries on all communications services, including network installation and Internet access.

All of the computers at Ridgedale High School are part of a local area network that allows teachers and students to share information with one another and with others around the world. First, Ridgedale networked the computers in all three of its computer labs. Two of these labs contain 30 PCs and the third lab contains 30 Macintosh computers. The school then installed at least three computers connected to the Internet in each classroom. Ridgedale High School also maintains a Web site to provide up-to-date information for students, teachers, and parents [Figure 1-25].

As the day starts, students are hurrying down the halls toward their classrooms, trying to reach them before the first period bell rings. For these students, the day is just beginning. For the administrators, teachers, and staff of Ridgedale High School, their day started much earlier.

SUPERINTENDENT

Early this morning, Dr. Helen Hartley, superintendent of Washington County Public School District, put the final touches on the district's Three-Year Technology Plan [Figure 1-26]. Dr. Hartley is very interested in the progress of the district's Technology Committee, whose members include administrators, teachers, parents, media specialists, technology coordinators, and business partners from the community.

While pleased with the work the committee has accomplished thus far, the superintendent has found that, as more technology initiatives are launched, the committee's planning meetings are becoming too long (and are hard to fit into the extremely busy schedules of the members). To help with this problem, Dr. Hartley asked the district Webmaster and network specialist, Bob Still, to develop an interactive template for the committee's Web page. Now, all the committee members can access the page with their password and work on their sections of the report.

WEB INFO

For more information about the FCC's E-Rate Universal Service Program for Schools & Libraries, visit the Teachers Discovering Computers Web site, click Chapter 1, click Web Info, and then click E-Rate.

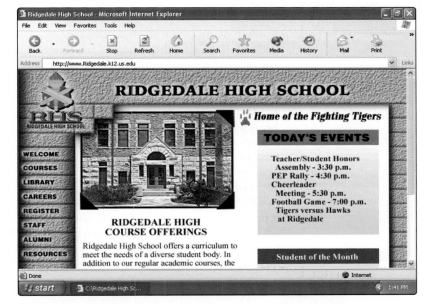

Figure 1-25 Ridgedale High School's Web site allows teachers, students, and parents to have direct access to extensive and up-to-date school-related information.

Figure 1-26 The superintendent shows her staff the final touches of the school district's Three-Year Technology Plan. She will use charts and graphs to present the plan at the next school board meeting.

For more information about national Technology Standards for School Administrators (TSSA), visit the Teachers Discovering Computers Web site, click Chapter 1, click Web Info, and then click TSSA.

Dr. Hartley has several other items to attend to and people to visit before heading to Ridgedale High School for the 3:30 P.M. Teacher/Student Honors Assembly. Ridgedale's new multimedia presentation system, which was purchased with money donated by a local store, would be up and running for the assembly and Dr. Hartley was looking forward to seeing the presentation. She also wanted to review the national Technology Standards for School Administrators (TSSA) with the principal of Ridgedale High School.

PRINCIPAL

Mr. Tony Hidalgo, the principal at Ridgedale High School, starts his day by completing several administrative tasks, which he accomplishes by sending several e-mail messages to teachers and staff. He sends an e-mail message to Ms. Jenny Marcus, Ridgedale's technology coordinator, to remind her to install and test the new presentation system before the Teacher/Student Honors Assembly. Mr. Hidalgo also sends an e-mail message to Dr. Hartley requesting an update on his latest budgeting request — $8,300 for new educational software for the math and science teachers and $3,150 for new computer software to run the school's security system [Figure 1-27].

Figure 1-27 Mr. Hidalgo is pondering the wording of his important e-mail message to the superintendent.

Finally, before the students arrive, Mr. Hidalgo sends an e-mail message to all teachers and staff reminding them that the Teacher/Student Honors Assembly begins promptly at 3:30 P.M. Mr. Hidalgo finishes his early morning administrative tasks in time to walk the halls and greet students arriving for school.

SCHOOL SECRETARY

When she first started at Ridgedale High School, Ms. Clara Rich, the school secretary, spent much of her day answering and routing incoming telephone calls. Last year, however, the school board approved the installation of a computerized telephone system that routes calls directly to the appropriate person. Ms. Rich's day now starts in a different manner, as she checks her e-mail and voice mail messages to determine if any teachers are going to be late or absent. If necessary, Ms. Rich accesses the school's teacher database to identify potential substitute teachers.

Next, Ms. Rich uses the school's inventory database to check the quantities of certain supplies and confirm delivery of recent purchases [Figure 1-28]. Ms. Rich reviews the customized certificates she has created for the Honors Assembly. She is sure the certificates, which she created using her desktop publishing program and the school's color printer, will impress students, teachers, and parents.

Figure 1-28 By using various databases, the school secretary easily can locate potential substitute teachers and manage equipment purchases, inventory, and supplies.

TECHNOLOGY COORDINATOR

Ms. Jenny Marcus, technology coordinator, arrives early to attend to several items and browse the Web to locate information on installing and testing the new presentation system. Ms. Marcus has several questions that she is unable to find answers for on the company's Web site. By accessing its technical assistance chat room, she is able to talk directly with a technician. The technician promptly answers most of her questions, but several deal with individual decisions that the principal needs to approve before the installation can be completed. Ms. Marcus calls and leaves a message on Mr. Hidalgo's voice mail asking if they can meet in her office at 10:00 A.M. to resolve these details [Figure 1-29].

Figure 1-29 The technology coordinator leaves a voice message for the principal after she has gathered technical information on the new presentation system from the World Wide Web.

CAFETERIA MANAGER

Ms. Kim Johnson, the cafeteria manager, starts working at 6:00 A.M. making sure the computerized purchasing and inventory system is ready to use for her morning training session. Ms. Johnson knows her staff is excited about the new system, which includes a database to track purchases, inventory, and student favorites, and keeps accurate records of students enrolled in the school lunch program [Figure 1-30].

Figure 1-30 The cafeteria manager is enthusiastic about her new purchasing and inventory system. Here, she shows her staff how the new computer program will save time and money.

MEDIA SPECIALIST

Mr. Chris Finley, the media specialist, arrives at school very early because many students need access to media center resources before first period classes begin. While the students are searching the online catalog for materials, both in their own media center and other centers in the district, Mr. Finley completes his final preparations for Mrs. Acosta's tenth grade class [Figure 1-31]. Mr. Finley and Mrs. Acosta work together to create activities that help students learn history while sharpening their research skills.

Figure 1-31 After locating electronic resources, textbooks, and other materials in the school media center, the media specialist works with students on their research projects.

After confirming that all of the center's computers are up and running, Mr. Finley starts gathering resources for Mrs. Acosta's students; including books, CD-ROMs, DVD-ROMs, and videotapes. The biggest excitement every morning is the live broadcast of the *Ridgedale News Show* in the TV Production Lab. Students gain experiences in TV production and communications and learn what it is like to work in front of and behind the camera. Students form the complete production team, from the camera operator to reporters. Crew members rotate on a weekly basis through each of the broadcast production jobs.

TEACHERS

Early the same day, Mrs. Ana Acosta uses presentation graphics software to put the finishing touches on the PowerPoint presentation she created to introduce her class to their research assignments [Figure 1-32].

Figure 1-32 Using presentation graphics software, a teacher instructs her students on how to do their research assignment.

Mrs. Acosta plans to start class by showing a video that Mr. Finley obtained through the state's interlibrary loan program. The video shows how history students across the country are using technology to create their own projects.

Mr. Victor Reamy is in his classroom preparing for his advanced placement biology class. He is having his students work on their class projects in groups of three. The class is using 10 wireless notebook computers that are part of a 10-station wireless mobile lab that the students call the 10 pack. Each wireless notebook computer is connected without wires to the school's network, providing students with instant and wireless access to the Internet and dozens of educational and productivity software programs. Mr. Reamy shares this new wireless mobile lab with four other science teachers and has found using the new wireless mobile lab to be easy and extremely beneficial both for his instruction and student learning. Before, he had to take his students to a traditional computer lab that was located in a different building on the other side of campus. Now, he simply rolls the lab to his students for use in his classroom, saving valuable instructional and on-task time.

The students' first assignment is to visit numerous biology Web sites that Mr. Reamy has evaluated for appropriateness and instructional value. Then, each group uses the wireless notebook computers to run experiments, log their research findings, type their findings into a report, and create presentations for the class [Figure 1-33].

At the other end of school, two of the physical education instructors, Mrs. Rita Simpson and Mr. Gary Roberts, are

installing and testing video equipment so they can tape gymnastics routines for personal and class evaluation of techniques. Mr. Roberts, who also is the girls' soccer coach, taped last week's soccer game and wants to show the soccer team how they can improve for the state finals competition next week.

The school recently received 30 Palm handheld computers and software from a physical education improvement grant [Figure 1-34]. They also purchased a new software program so students can evaluate their running techniques, cardiovascular activities, and nutritional needs. The software interfaces with their Palm so they can enter data in the Palm handheld computers wherever they are. When they are back at their classroom computer, they connect the Palm and download all the pertinent data onto the school's network. This way, they can keep track of and analyze the data.

Figure 1-34 Physical education students are downloading personal information into a software program that will monitor and chart their personal fitness.

PARENT

Using her home computer, Catherine Rosa accesses Ridgedale's Web site to check the time of the Teacher/Student Honors Assembly [Figure 1-35]. While she was looking up the time, Catherine notices a new graphic that reads, We Need Your Support! Curious, she clicks the graphic and links to a Web page requesting parent volunteers to chaperone the girls' soccer team on its trip to the state finals. Catherine sends an e-mail message to Mr. Roberts, stating that she gladly will chaperone the trip. Catherine then quickly browses

WEB INFO

For more information and ideas on integrating technology into your lessons and to learn more about Integration Literacy, visit the Teachers Discovering Computer Web site, click Chapter 1, click Web Info, and then click Integration Literacy.

Figure 1-33 Students create projects, experiments, research reports, and papers using a wireless notebook computer.

through the state Department of Education Web site to read the latest information released on Ridgedale High School before heading to the school for the assembly.

Figure 1-35 A parent of a Ridgedale High School student logs onto the school's Web site to find out the start time for a special event.

COMMUNITY

Kevin Lee, a 72-year-old, retired construction worker, starts his day by reading e-mail messages from 16-year-old Brian Johnson, a student at Ridgedale High School [Figure 1-36]. Kevin and Brian communicate online regularly as part of a program called Seniors Online. Seniors Online is a school program designed to match students with special needs with senior citizens, who serve as mentors. Each week Kevin, along with 13 other senior citizens, visits the school to work with a student, one on one.

The students teach the senior citizens how to use a computer, send and receive e-mail messages, and browse the Web. Their mentors, in turn, help the students understand the challenges and opportunities they likely are going to experience after they graduate from high school. The interaction between the seniors and students with special needs is a remarkable success story.

The students send e-mail messages to their mentors to seek advice or just to share everyday news. For seniors such as Kevin, learning to use a computer is a great experience, but working directly with the students is the most rewarding experience of all.

Figure 1-36 A successful program at Ridgedale High School matches senior citizens with students with special needs. In this photo, a retired construction worker is checking his e-mail for a message from his new friend.

Using the Textbook Web Site

Each chapter in this textbook contains nine end-of-chapter sections, all of which are stored as Web pages on the World Wide Web. In addition, the textbook includes eight special features (one follows each chapter) and three appendices; many of these also are located at the textbook Web site. To enhance your learning experience, be sure to view the end-of-chapter materials, special features, and Appendices A and B on the Web, where you will find curriculum-specific information, integration ideas, interactive exercises, and links to thousands of popular educational sites.

In all eight chapters, annotations in the margins, called Web Info [Figure 1-37], send students to the textbook Web site, where they will find links to current and additional information about Web Info topics. Also located in the margins are FAQ boxes that consist of frequently asked questions and their answers.

For more information about Macintosh computers, visit the Teachers Discovering Computers Web site, click Chapter 1, click Web Info, and then click Macintosh.

Figure 1-37 An example of the Web Info features that are located in the margins throughout this textbook.

To access the textbook Web site, start your browser and enter the following Web address, www.course.com/tdc3 [Figure 1-38]. To display an end-of-chapter section, click the desired chapter number at the top and then click any of the end-of-chapter sections displayed on the left sidebar; for example, click Chapter 1 and then click Teaching Today [Figure 1-39]. The special features located below the end-of-chapter sections may be accessed at anytime. Use the scroll bar to view the links to all of the special features [Figure 1-38].

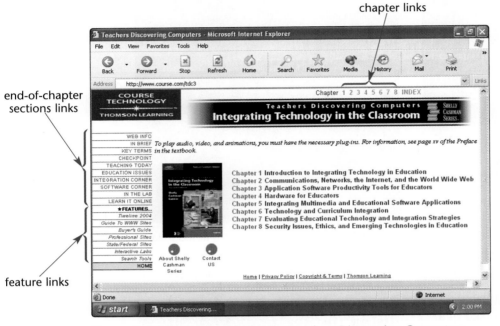

Figure 1-38 The home page of the Teachers Discovering Computers Web site.

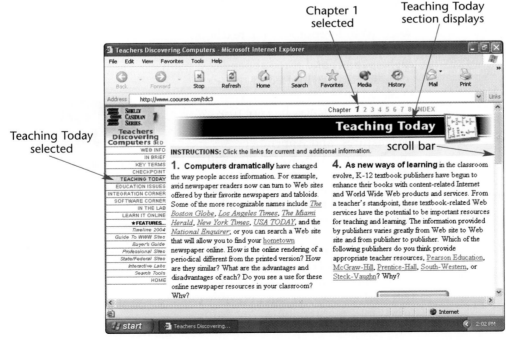

Figure 1-39 Teaching Today end-of-chapter section for Chapter 1 displayed at the textbook Web site. Use the scroll bar to see the additional Teaching Today segments.

INTERACTING WITH END-OF-CHAPTER MATERIALS

The following sections explain how you can interact in a curriculum-specific way with the resources available at the various end-of-chapter materials. This will help you transition to using the new learning environments described in Figure 1-1 on page 1.02.

IN BRIEF This section summarizes the chapter materials; you can use these short summaries to prepare for examinations. Click the Audio button at the top and the summaries will be read to you in streaming audio; click the links in the summaries for additional current information.

KEY TERMS Click any term to see and hear a term definition. A picture and animation of the term will appear with a Web Link. Click the Web Link to visit a Web page for supplemental information on the term.

CHECKPOINT Use these interactive questions and answers to prepare for quizzes and examinations. Click the various links for more in-depth information on the topic.

TEACHING TODAY This section contains five segments that will provide you with an appreciation of the value that technology and the Web have for K-12 education. Each segment contains one or more links that reinforce the information presented in the segment.

EDUCATION ISSUES Education Issues contains several scenarios that will allow you to explore controversial and current issues in education; for example, school violence. Click the links for additional information on the issue.

INTEGRATION CORNER This innovative section provides you with extensive ideas and resources for integrating technology into your classroom-specific curriculum. Each chapter provides information on and links to approximately 100 outstanding educational Web sites organized in the following 12 corners: Early Childhood, Elementary, Middle School, Secondary, Reading/Language Arts; Social Studies/ History, Math, Science, Special Education, Post Secondary, Administrator, and Research. Choose your area and explore the resources to learn how to integrate technology into your specific classroom curriculum and how other educators are integrating technology.

SOFTWARE CORNER Today's educators can choose from a variety of high quality and often inexpensive educational software programs. You can learn about popular software programs by researching them on the Web and in many cases even download or order a free evaluation copy so you can evaluate a program prior to you or your school buying it. Software Corner provides you with information on and links to additional information and download instructions for dozens of educational software programs used by teachers from all disciplines.

IN THE LAB These exercises are divided into two areas: productivity and integration. Use the productivity exercises to improve your software-specific skills in using word processing, spreadsheet, database, desktop publishing, curriculum and Web page development, and other productivity software programs. Use the integration ideas for incorporating these programs into your specific classroom curriculum. Click the links for tutorials, productivity ideas, integration examples and ideas, and more.

LEARN IT ONLINE These exercises allow you to improve your computer and integration skills by learning exciting new skills online. This section includes interactive lab exercises, software tutorials, scavenger hunts, practice tests, learning games, and much more.

Timeline — Milestones in Computer History

At the end of Chapter 1 is an interactive, colorful, and highly informative multipage timeline of the history of computers from 1937 to the present. This entire special feature also is stored as Web pages at the textbook Web site. The Timeline contains dozens of links to extensive supplemental information, including historical audio segments from National Public Radio, animations, videos, and much more.

To display this interactive special feature, click Timeline on the left sidebar at the textbook Web site [Figure 1-38]. All of the graphics and pictures contain links to the Web. Explore the special feature with your mouse; to access the interactive links, click when your mouse pointer changes to a hand.

Summary of Introduction to Integrating Technology in Education

This chapter presented a broad introduction to concepts and terminology related to computers and computers in education. You now have a basic understanding of what a computer is and how it processes data into information. You also have seen some examples of how computers are being used in K-12 schools and integrated into classroom settings. Reading and learning the concepts in this chapter will help you understand these topics as they are presented in more detail in future chapters.

In Brief

WEB INFO

IN BRIEF

KEY TERMS

CHECKPOINT

TEACHING TODAY

EDUCATION ISSUES

INTEGRATION CORNER

SOFTWARE CORNER

IN THE LAB

LEARN IT ONLINE

✶ FEATURES...

Timeline 2004

Guide to WWW Sites

Buyer's Guide 2004

Professional Sites

State/Federal Sites

Interactive Labs

Search Tools

HOME

Web Instructions: To display this page from the Web, start your browser and enter the URL, www.course.com/tdc3. Click Chapter 1 at the top of the Web page and then click In Brief on the left sidebar. Click the links for current and additional information. To listen to an audio version of this In Brief, click the Audio button to the top left of these instructions.

1. Personal Computers

A **personal computer**, or **PC**, is a computer designed for use by one person at a time. Macintosh computers and PCs are the two primary types of personal computers used in schools, businesses, and homes. Apple Computer Company manufactures Macintosh computers; several companies manufacture PCs.

2. Computer, Information, and Integration Literacy

As the world of computers advances, it is essential that you gain some level of **computer literacy**; that is, you should have a knowledge and understanding of computers and their uses. Information literacy means knowing how to find, analyze, and use information. In addition, teachers must know how to integrate technology into K-12 curriculum, or integration literacy. **Integration literacy** is the ability to use computers and other technologies combined with a variety of teaching and learning strategies to enhance students' learning of required basic skills.

3. Computers, Data, Information, and Processing

A **computer** is an electronic machine, operating under the control of instructions stored in its own memory, that can accept data (input), manipulate the data according to specified rules (process), produce results (output), and store the results for future use. **Data** is a collection of unorganized facts, which can include words, numbers, pictures, and sounds. **Information** is data that is organized, has meaning, and is useful, such as a report, graphic, newsletter, invoice, check, video, or photograph. **Processing** is the activity of organizing data into information. Computers perform four basic operations: input, process, output, and storage. Computer professionals often refer to these four operations as the **information processing cycle** because a computer performs these actions repeatedly while the computer is running.

4. Computer Components

A computer consists of a variety of hardware components that work together with software to carry out various computer activities. These hardware components include input devices, output devices, a system unit, storage devices, and communications devices. An **input device** allows a user to enter data and commands into the memory of a computer. An **output device** is used to convey the information generated by a computer to the user. The **system unit** is a box-like case made from metal or plastic that houses the computer circuitry. A **storage device** is the mechanism used to record and retrieve data, information, and instructions to and from a storage medium. A **communications device** enables a computer to exchange data and information with another computer.

5. Computer Power

A computer's power derives from its capability of performing the **information processing cycle** (input, process, output, storage) with speed, reliability, and accuracy; its capacity to store large amounts of data and information; and its capability of communicating with other computers.

6. Computer Software

Software, also called a **computer program** or simply a **program**, is a series of instructions that tells the hardware of a computer what to do. System software and application software are the two main categories of software. **System software** consists of programs that control the operations of a computer and its devices. **Application software** consists of programs designed to perform a specific task for a user.

In Brief

WEB INFO

IN BRIEF

KEY TERMS

CHECKPOINT

TEACHING TODAY

EDUCATION ISSUES

INTEGRATION CORNER

SOFTWARE CORNER

IN THE LAB

LEARN IT ONLINE

✱ FEATURES...

Timeline 2004

Guide to WWW Sites

Buyer's Guide 2004

Professional Sites

State/Federal Sites

Interactive Labs

Search Tools

HOME

7. Networks

A **network** is a collection of computers and devices connected together via communications media and devices such as cables, telephone lines, modems, or other means. Businesses and schools <u>network</u> their computers so users can share **resources**, such as hardware devices, software programs, data, and information. Sharing resources saves time and money.

8. The Internet

The world's largest network is the **Internet**, which is a worldwide collection of networks that links together millions of businesses, the government, educational institutions, and individuals. Millions of people use the <u>Internet</u> to gain information, send messages, and obtain products or services. The **World Wide Web**, or **Web**, portion of the Internet consists of computer sites, called Web sites that can be accessed electronically for information on thousands of topics.

9. Computer Technology and Education

When used appropriately, technology has the potential to enhance students' achievement and assist them in meeting learning objectives. Networked computers allow communications <u>beyond classroom walls</u>, thus enabling schools and communities to provide an environment for cooperative learning, development of high-order thinking skills, and solving of complex problems. Computers can provide unique, effective, and powerful opportunities for many different types of instruction and learning. Several leading national and international organizations, including the **International Society for Technology in Education** (ISTE) support education and educators in the use of technology.

Key Terms

Web Instructions: To display this page from the Web, start your browser and enter the URL, www.course.com/tdc3. Click Chapter 1 at the top of the Web page and then click Key Terms on the left sidebar. Scroll through the list of terms. Click a term to display its definition and a picture. Click Key Terms on the left to redisplay the Key Terms page. Click the TO WEB button for current and additional information about the term from the Web.

WEB INFO

IN BRIEF

KEY TERMS

CHECKPOINT

TEACHING TODAY

EDUCATION ISSUES

INTEGRATION CORNER

SOFTWARE CORNER

IN THE LAB

LEARN IT ONLINE

✱ FEATURES...

Timeline 2004

Guide to WWW Sites

Buyer's Guide 2004

Professional Sites

State/Federal Sites

Interactive Labs

Search Tools

HOME

application software [1.14]

central processing unit (CPU) [1.06]
communications device [1.08]
computer [1.04]
computer literacy [1.04]
computer program [1.12]
computer programmers [1.16]
curriculum-specific learning [1.02]
custom software [1.16]

data [1.04]
desktop computer [1.10]
discipline-specific learning [1.02]

Education Rate (E-Rate) [1.21]
electronic mail (e-mail) [1.12]
execute [1.12]

freeware [1.16]

graphical user interface (GUI) [1.14]

handheld computer [1.11]
hardware [1.04]

icon [1.14]
information [1.04]
information literacy [1.04]

information processing cycle [1.04, 1.11]
input [1.04]
input device [1.05]
install [1.12]
integration literacy [1.04]
International Society for Technology in Education (ISTE) [1.19]
Internet [1.17]

Macintosh computer [1.09]
Mac OS [1.09, 1.13]
memory [1.06]
Microsoft Windows [1.13]
mobile computer [1.10]
mobile device [1.10]

National Council for Accreditation for Teacher Education (NCATE) [1.19]
National Educational Technology Standards for Teachers (NETS-T) [1.20]
network [1.12, 1.16]
notebook computer [1.10]

operating system [1.13]
output [1.04]
output device [1.06]

packaged software [1.15]
PDA [1.11]
peripheral device [1.07]
personal computer (PC) [1.09]
personal digital assistant [1.11]
processor [1.06]
program [1.12]
programmers [1.16]
public-domain software [1.16]

resources [1.16]

shareware [1.16]
smart phone [1.11]
software [1.04, 1.10]
storage [1.04]
storage device [1.07]
storage medium [1.07]
system software [1.13]
system unit [1.06]
systems analyst [1.16]

Tablet PC [1.10]

user [1.04]
user interface [1.14]
utility program [1.14]

Web [1.18]
Web-enabled [1.11]
World Wide Web [1.18]

Checkpoint

WEB INFO

IN BRIEF

KEY TERMS

CHECKPOINT

TEACHING TODAY

EDUCATION ISSUES

INTEGRATION CORNER

SOFTWARE CORNER

IN THE LAB

LEARN IT ONLINE

★ FEATURES...

Timeline 2004

Guide to WWW Sites

Buyer's Guide 2004

Professional Sites

State/Federal Sites

Interactive Labs

Search Tools

HOME

1. Label the Figure

Instructions: Identify each element of an information system by placing the correct label on the numbered lines.

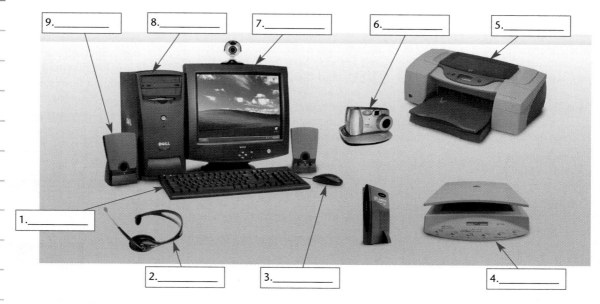

9._____   8._____   7._____   6._____   5._____

1._____

2._____   3._____   4._____

2. Matching

Instructions: Match each term from the column on the left with the best description from the column on the right.

____ 1. software
____ 2. input devices
____ 3. output devices
____ 4. storage device
____ 5. information

a. data that is organized has meaning and is useful, such as a report, newsletters, a receipt, a picture, an invoice, or a check

b. allows a user to enter data and commands into the memory of a computer

c. examples include CD-ROM drives, floppy disk drives, and hard disk drives

d. conveys information generated by a computer to a user; examples include printers, monitors, and speakers

e. a series of instructions that tells the hardware how to perform tasks

3. Short Answer

Instructions: Write a brief answer to each of the following questions.

1. What is the difference between computer literacy, information literacy, and integration literacy? _____

2. What are the components of a Macintosh computer or PC? How does each component contribute to information processing? _____

3. What capabilities make a computer a powerful tool? Describe each. How does a computer's ability to communicate enhance a computer's power? _____

4. What is computer software? How is system software different from application software? _____

5. Briefly summarize why computers should be used in K-12 schools. _____

Teaching Today

Web Instructions: To display this page from the Web, start your browser and enter the URL www.course.com/tdc3. Click Chapter 1 at the top of the Web page and then click Teaching Today on the left sidebar. Click the links for current and additional information.

WEB INFO

IN BRIEF

KEY TERMS

CHECKPOINT

TEACHING TODAY

EDUCATION ISSUES

INTEGRATION CORNER

SOFTWARE CORNER

IN THE LAB

LEARN IT ONLINE

✱ FEATURES...

Timeline 2004

Guide to WWW Sites

Buyer's Guide 2004

Professional Sites

State/Federal Sites

Interactive Labs

Search Tools

HOME

1. **Computers have changed** the way people access information dramatically. For example, avid newspaper readers now can turn to Web sites offered by their favorite newspapers and tabloids. Some of the more recognizable names include *The Boston Globe*, *Los Angeles Times*, *The Miami Herald*, *New York Times*, *USA TODAY*, and the *National Enquirer*; or you can search a Web site that will allow you to find your hometown newspaper online. How is the online rendering of a periodical different from the printed version? How are they similar? What are the advantages and disadvantages of each? Do you see a use for these online newspaper resources in your classroom? Why?

2. **As the automobile** led to the end of the horse and buggy, will the growth of the Internet lead to the demise of printed media? Probably not; in fact, booksellers are turning to the Internet to promote their products. Many online bookstores sell books, videos, and games. Some of these are Amazon.com, Barnes & Noble College Bookstores, and Books-A-Million, or you can visit a bookstore directory that links and describes dozens of top book-

store sites and book publishers. Visit a bookstore Web site and compare searching for a book online with finding a book in a traditional bookstore. Try looking for a particular title, a book by a certain author, and books on a specific subject. What are the advantages and disadvantages of shopping for a book online? How likely would you be to buy a book through a bookstore Web site? Why?

3. **The health-care industry** has made significant breakthroughs during the past few years, and continued advances are expected in many health-related areas. For example, major prescription drug companies currently are developing/testing more than 1,000 new medicines. The Web offers an up-to-date source for information on virtually every area of health care. You can locate current information on diseases and other health aliments such as migraines. People can obtain an abundance of important information in a very short time, such as the latest treatment options. Visit the following medical site and research one specific area of health care that is of personal importance to you.

Teaching Today

WEB INFO

IN BRIEF

KEY TERMS

CHECKPOINT

TEACHING TODAY

EDUCATION ISSUES

INTEGRATION CORNER

SOFTWARE CORNER

IN THE LAB

LEARN IT ONLINE

✳ FEATURES...

Timeline 2004

Guide to WWW Sites

Buyer's Guide 2004

Professional Sites

State/Federal Sites

Interactive Labs

Search Tools

HOME

4. **As new ways of learning** in the classroom evolve, K-12 textbook publishers have begun to enhance their books with content-related Internet and World Wide Web products and services. From a teacher's standpoint, these textbook-related Web services have the potential to be important resources for teaching and learning. The information provided by publishers varies greatly from Web site to Web site and from publisher to publisher. Which of the following publishers do you think provide appropriate teacher resources: Pearson Education, McGraw-Hill, Prentice-Hall, South-Western, or Steck-Vaughn? Why?

5. **You are a middle school teacher** with numerous computers in your classroom. You keep catching your students spending class time receiving and answering instant messages (IM) instead of working on class assignments. Your students say that the IMs are a great way to keep in touch with friends and ask questions about class work. To them, instant messaging is totally cool! Should you allow your students to use instant messaging during class time? Is this a misuse of class time? If you think that it is a misuse of class time, what can you do to manage the sending and receiving of IMs in your class?

Education Issues

Web Instructions: To display this page from the Web, start your browser and enter the URL, www.course.com/tdc3. Click Chapter 1 at the top of the Web page and then click Education Issues on the left sidebar. Click the links for current and additional information.

WEB INFO

IN BRIEF

KEY TERMS

CHECKPOINT

TEACHING TODAY

EDUCATION ISSUES

INTEGRATION CORNER

SOFTWARE CORNER

IN THE LAB

LEARN IT ONLINE

✱ FEATURES...

Timeline 2004

Guide to WWW Sites

Buyer's Guide 2004

Professional Sites

State/Federal Sites

Interactive Labs

Search Tools

HOME

1. School Violence

Numerous polls have shown that school safety is now the number-one concern of both parents and teachers. National leaders are calling the increase in school violence a national crisis. Do you agree that school violence should be the main concern of parents? One popular answer to the dramatic increase in the incidences of school violence is to build protective nets around the nation's schools; including fences, metal detectors, high-tech video surveillance, body searches, and armed guards. Do you agree with this solution? Other political and educational leaders stress that turning schools into armed camps is not the solution. Instead, schools and communities must address and attempt to find solutions for the causes of school violence. Do you agree with this solution? If so, what are some of the causes of school violence? What would you suggest to reduce the incidences of school violence?

2. Possible Child Abuse

During your student internship, you notice that 9-year-old Juan Gonzales has bruises all over his arms and legs. He has been one of your more inquisitive students, but lately you have noticed that he has become moody, seems uninterested in class, and his grades are falling. The school nurse casually informs you that she has noticed that Juan has been losing weight the past couple of months. You suspect that Juan may be a victim of child abuse. You ask your supervising teacher what you should do and she says, "Oh! He is the son of a member of the school board; I am sure he is just growing and is at a clumsy age." You really like the school and would like to work there after graduation. Do you tell someone or do you ignore it? If so, who do you tell? What else could you do?

3. Reality or Fantasy

The space shuttle was first flown in July 1969 and landed on the moon that same year. An ingredient in many popular shampoos has been proven to cause cancer. It is illegal to contact space aliens. None of these statements is true, but each appeared on the Web. In today's society, some people, especially young students, think that anything in print is true, and the Web adds to that because anyone can publish anything on a Web page. Authors with a wide range of expertise, authority, and biases create Web pages. Web pages can be as accurate as the most scholarly journal or no truer than some articles in supermarket tabloids. Ultimately, who is responsible for the accuracy of information on the Web? Why? How can you verify information on the Web? How would you teach your students to make sure information is accurate?

4. Possible Cheating

Today, students come to class with cellular telephones, graphing calculators, pagers, personal digital assistants (PDAs), notebook computers, and other devices. During a geometry test, you notice that a student is using a cell phone. As you approach the student, you realize that the student is looking at a smart phone with a picture on the screen. The student puts away the phone and apologizes, indicating that he had forgotten to turn off the phone when a call came in. After class, another student informs you that the other student was making calls to another student in the classroom, and they were taking pictures of the equations. This student was almost positive the two students were cheating by sending each other pictures of the answers over their smart phones. What should you do? How are you going to handle this situation? Does a way to gather proof exist? What next? Should telephones of any kind be banned in classrooms? If so, how? Explain.

Integration Corner

Web Instructions: To display this page from the Web, start your browser and enter the URL, www.course.com/tdc3. Click Chapter 1 at the top of the Web page and then click Integration Corner on the left sidebar. Click any Corner and then click the various links for extensive and curriculum-specific information.

WEB INFO

IN BRIEF

KEY TERMS

CHECKPOINT

TEACHING TODAY

EDUCATION ISSUES

INTEGRATION CORNER

SOFTWARE CORNER

IN THE LAB

LEARN IT ONLINE

✳ FEATURES...

Timeline 2004

Guide to WWW Sites

Buyer's Guide 2004

Professional Sites

State/Federal Sites

Interactive Labs

Search Tools

HOME

Integration Corner is designed for teachers and other educators who are looking for innovative ways to integrate technology into their content-specific curriculum. Integration Corner not only provides great Web sites with current information but also shows what other educators are doing in the field of educational technology. These Corners are designed for all educators regardless of their interest. Review information and sites outside of your teaching area because many great integration ideas in one area easily can be modified for use in other curricular areas.

Teachers and administrators will find other colleagues in their areas with whom to connect and share the successes and hurdles of integrating technology in a classroom or an entire school system. Consider this your one stop for integration ideas and resources. Links to educational Web sites are organized in the following 12 Corners, and different Web resources are available for each chapter. Figure 1-40 shows examples of the Web resources provided in the Chapter 1 Early Childhood Corner.

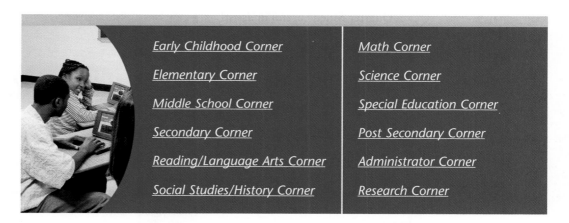

Early Childhood Corner

Elementary Corner

Middle School Corner

Secondary Corner

Reading/Language Arts Corner

Social Studies/History Corner

Math Corner

Science Corner

Special Education Corner

Post Secondary Corner

Administrator Corner

Research Corner

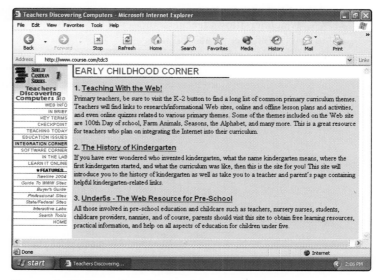

Figure 1-40 Examples of the Web resources provided in the Chapter 1 Early Childhood Corner.

Software Corner

WEB INFO

IN BRIEF

KEY TERMS

CHECKPOINT

TEACHING TODAY

EDUCATION ISSUES

INTEGRATION CORNER

SOFTWARE CORNER

IN THE LAB

LEARN IT ONLINE

✱ FEATURES...

Timeline 2004

Guide to WWW Sites

Buyer's Guide 2004

Professional Sites

State/Federal Sites

Interactive Labs

Search Tools

HOME

Web Instructions: To display this page from the Web, start your browser and enter the URL, www.course.com/tdc3. Click Chapter 1 at the top of the Web page and then click Software Corner on the left sidebar. Click the links for additional information and instructions on how to download or receive an evaluation copy.

1. Kid Pix is a suite of creativity programs for students from kindergarten through eighth grade. This program allows students to express themselves using electronic drawing and art tools to create pictures, illustrate their own stories, and unleash their natural creative desires. All sound effects are realistic, making this program exciting for students to use. Storybooks, projects, and movies are included with the package for use when creating multimedia projects. Two interesting features of this software are voice painting and photo editing. Kid Pix is a valuable resource for student expression through art.

2. BodyWorks, from Borderbund, is a visual and textual classroom reference software of the human body. Included with BodyWorks are video lectures, high-resolution images, and thousands of audio pronunciations of medical terms, and a searchable database of more than 400,000 words with useful information for classroom lectures, presentations, and reports. A teacher's guide also is available for this intermediate and secondary science program.

3. Quarter Mile is useful in assisting students to learn math skills from basic math facts to difficult skills such as integers, converting percents and fractions, and advanced equations. Quarter Mile is a super remediation program for the exceptional student classroom as well as a great skills practice program for the regular classroom at all educational levels. What makes this program interesting for students is that they race against their own time, allowing them to see their own progress.

4. Timeliner allows teachers and students to create, print, and illustrate timelines using pictures or text with ease for any time period. Timeliner can be used at the elementary level by having students create timelines of their life using personal events in order to help them gain an understanding of the concept of time and sequence of important events. Elementary teachers can use this program to teach the concept of decade, century, millennium, and more. At the middle and high school levels, Timeliner can be used to show historical progress of specific time periods, chart world changing occurrences and causes of important events, or even illustrate the different stages of a novel, like *The Red Badge of Courage*.

5. If you need assistance with classroom record keeping and planning, then Making the Grade is for you. Making the Grade allows teachers to manage and track student grades and academic performance as well as keeping attendance and planning seating charts. Teachers can drop grades, apply grading curves, customize a grading scale, and make necessary changes to student records with ease. Making the Grade provides teachers the ability to create charts, export data to word processing, database, or spreadsheet programs and print detailed reports for student and parent conferences.

In the Lab

Web Instructions: To display this page from the Web, start your browser and enter the URL, www.course.com/tdc3. Click Chapter 1 at the top of the Web page and then click In The Lab on the left sidebar. Click the links for tutorials, productivity ideas, integration examples and ideas, and more.

WEB INFO

IN BRIEF

KEY TERMS

CHECKPOINT

TEACHING TODAY

EDUCATION ISSUES

INTEGRATION CORNER

SOFTWARE CORNER

IN THE LAB

LEARN IT ONLINE

✷ FEATURES...

Timeline 2004

Guide to WWW Sites

Buyer's Guide 2004

Professional Sites

State/Federal Sites

Interactive Labs

Search Tools

HOME

PRODUCTIVITY IN THE CLASSROOM

Introduction: Word processing skills are essential for both teachers and students. Improving your word processing skills will save you time and energy! Many powerful word processing software applications are available today. In addition, many of the major word processing applications have online tutorials. These tutorials can provide fast and easy access to learning new skills such as setting page margins, inserting a graphic, and changing the font, font color, and font size. To learn new word processing skills or improve your current skills, click the following links: Microsoft Word; Appleworks; Microsoft Works; and Corel WordPerfect.

1 Creating and Formatting a School Activity Flyer

Problem: As the 7th grade class trip sponsor, you need to create a flyer to notify parents and students of an upcoming informational meeting. Open your word processing software and create a new flyer as described below. Use the flyer shown in Figure 1-41 on the next page as an example. (*Hint:* If you do not have the suggested font, use any appropriate font.)

Instructions: Perform the following tasks.

1. Select a class trip destination/title for the project. Display the title in the first heading line centered in 36-point Comic Sans MS font.
2. Select a school name and display the second heading line centered in 22-point Arial Narrow bold font.
3. Choose an appropriate picture, image, or clip art graphic and insert it centered on the page.
4. Describe the field trip in three lines of text. Display the text in 14-point Times or Times New Roman font.
5. Create a bulleted list that provides specific information about the meeting. Display the bulleted list with a one-half-inch margin in 12-point Arial bold font. Display a portion of each bulleted phrase in orange.
6. Provide contact information at the bottom of the flyer (your name, e-mail address, and current date). Display the information in 14-point Times or Times New Roman blue font.
7. Save the document on a floppy disk with a name of your choice. Print the document and then follow your instructor's directions for submitting the assignment.

2 Creating and Formatting a Band Fund-Raiser Flyer

Problem: As the band teacher, you need to create a flyer advertising the fall fund-raiser. Open your word processing software and create a new flyer as described below. (*Hint:* If you do not have the suggested font, use any appropriate font.)

Instructions: Display the first heading line in 30-point Lucinda Sans font. Insert an appropriate picture, image, or clip art graphic centered on the page. Enter a second heading line below the image in 22-point Verdana red font. Next, enter four lines of text describing the purpose of the fall fund-raiser in 16-point Times or Times New Roman font. Create a bulleted list with a one and a half-inch margin in 14-point Times or Times New Roman font listing the dates, items to be sold, and place of the fund-raising event. Enter a closing phrase following the bulleted list in 18-point Verdana blue font. Finally, enter two lines of contact information in 12-point Times or Times New Roman font that includes the current date, your name, and e-mail address. Display the entire document in bold.

In the Lab

WEB INFO

IN BRIEF

KEY TERMS

CHECKPOINT

TEACHING TODAY

EDUCATION ISSUES

INTEGRATION CORNER

SOFTWARE CORNER

IN THE LAB

LEARN IT ONLINE

✱ FEATURES...

Timeline 2004

Guide to WWW Sites

Buyer's Guide 2004

Professional Sites

State/Federal Sites

Interactive Labs

Search Tools

HOME

7th Grade Sea Camp Trip
Indian Trails Middle School

The 7th grade class at Indian Trails Middle School has the opportunity to attend Sea Camp April 21 through April 23. This is an exciting educational opportunity! Please join us at the informational meeting to learn more.

❖ November 19 **- Join us at 7:00 p.m. in the Media Center**
❖ Slide Show **- Watch an informational slide show about Sea Camp**
❖ Application Packet **- Packets will be available for distribution**

For more information, please contact:
Mr. Mark Allman
m_allman@ssms.k12.ca.us
November 5, 2005

Figure 1-41

In the Lab

WEB INFO

IN BRIEF

KEY TERMS

CHECKPOINT

TEACHING TODAY

EDUCATION ISSUES

INTEGRATION CORNER

SOFTWARE CORNER

IN THE LAB

LEARN IT ONLINE

✱ FEATURES...

Timeline 2004

Guide to WWW Sites

Buyer's Guide 2004

Professional Sites

State/Federal Sites

Interactive Labs

Search Tools

HOME

After you have typed and formatted the document, save the document on a floppy disk with a file name of your choice. Print the document and then follow your instructor's directions for submitting the assignment.

3 Creating and Formatting an Announcement Flyer

Problem: You have been asked to create a flyer announcing the upcoming school play.

Instructions: Create a document similar to the flyer illustrated in Figure 1-41. Use appropriate fonts styles, font sizes, font colors, and images. Include the current date, your name, and e-mail address on the bottom of the flyer. After you have typed and formatted the document, save the document on a floppy disk using an appropriate file name. Print the document and then follow your instructor's directions for submitting the assignment.

INTEGRATION IN THE CLASSROOM

1 Your class is studying geometric shapes in architecture. Students will locate pictures of buildings and identify at least three geometric shapes. They will create a flyer that contains the following information: a heading line, an image of the building, a few lines explaining what they found, and a bulleted list with the three different geometric shapes. Create a flyer to use as an example for your students. Include two final lines listing the current date, your name, and school name.

2 Your students are studying various careers. They conduct research on the Internet and gather information about pay scales, educational requirements, and other benefits of their chosen profession. The students then prepare a flyer to share their information with the class. Create a flyer to present as an example for your students. Use appropriate font styles, font sizes, font colors, and images. Include the current date, your name, and e-mail address on the bottom of the flyer.

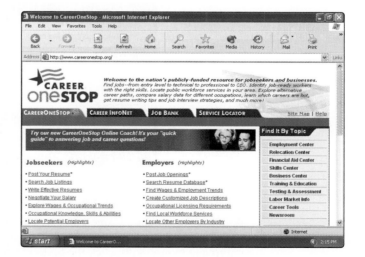

3 You are teaching your elementary students about famous painters, including Vincent van Gogh, Pablo Picasso, Henri Matisse, Leonardo da Vinci, and Claude Monet. The students will work in groups and select their favorite artist. They will create a flyer about the life and work of their favorite artist. Create a flyer to present as an example for your students. Use appropriate font styles, sizes, colors, and images. Include the current date, your name, and e-mail address on the bottom of the flyer.

Learn It Online

WEB INFO

IN BRIEF

KEY TERMS

CHECKPOINT

TEACHING TODAY

EDUCATION ISSUES

INTEGRATION CORNER

SOFTWARE CORNER

IN THE LAB

LEARN IT ONLINE

✱ FEATURES...

Timeline 2004

Guide to WWW Sites

Buyer's Guide 2004

Professional Sites

State/Federal Sites

Interactive Labs

Search Tools

HOME

Web Instructions: To display this page from the Web, start your browser and enter the URL, www.course.com/tdc3. Click Chapter 1 at the top of the Web page and then click Learn It Online on the left sidebar. Click the buttons to display the exercise or the Interactive Lab.

CD-ROM and Network Instructions: If you are running from a CD-ROM: Insert the Shelly Cashman Series Labs with Audio CD-ROM in your CD-ROM drive. If you are running the No-Audio Version from a Hard Disk or Network: Click the Start button on the taskbar, point to Shelly Cashman Series Labs on the All Programs submenu, and then click Interactive Labs.

1. Shelly Cashman Series Using the Mouse Lab

1. Click the button to the left to start the Shelly Cashman Series Using the Mouse Lab.
2. When the Shelly Cashman Series IN THE LAB screen displays, follow the instructions on the screen to start the Using the Mouse Lab.
3. When the Using the Mouse screen displays, read the objectives.
4. If assigned, follow the instructions on the screen to print the questions associated with the Lab.
5. Follow the instructions on the screen to continue in the Lab.
6. When completed, follow the instructions on the screen to quit the Lab.
7. If assigned, submit your answers to the printed questions to your instructor.

2. Shelly Cashman Series Using the Keyboard Lab

Click the button to the left to start and use the Shelly Cashman Series Using the Keyboard Lab.

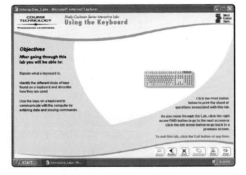

3. Improving Mouse Skills on a Macintosh or PC

Both Macintosh and PC operating systems include simple games, such as Jigsaw Puzzle or Solitaire, which are designed to help users learn mouse skills. To learn more about improving mouse skills, click the button to the left and complete the exercise.

4. Introduction to Macintosh and PCs

Many software packages provide an introductory tour that offers an overview of the program. These tours usually cover any new features and provide tips on using the software; some even use audio and video to enhance the introductory tour. To learn more about taking an introductory tour of your personal computer operating system, click the button to the left and complete the exercise.

Learn It Online

WEB INFO

IN BRIEF

KEY TERMS

CHECKPOINT

TEACHING TODAY

EDUCATION ISSUES

INTEGRATION CORNER

SOFTWARE CORNER

IN THE LAB

LEARN IT ONLINE

✱ FEATURES...

Timeline 2004

Guide to WWW Sites

Buyer's Guide 2004

Professional Sites

State/Federal Sites

Interactive Labs

Search Tools

HOME

5. Who Wants To Be a Computer Genius?

Click the button to the left to find out if you are a computer genius. Directions on how to play the game will display. When you are ready to play, click the PLAY button. Submit your score to your instructor.

6. Crossword Puzzle Challenge

Click the button to the left and complete the puzzle to reinforce skills you learned in this chapter. Directions on how to play the game will display. When you are ready to play, click the SUBMIT button. Submit the completed puzzle to your instructor.

7. Practice Test

Click the button to the left and answer each question. When completed, enter your name and click the Grade Test button to submit the quiz for grading. Make a note of any missed questions. If required, print a copy to submit to your instructor.

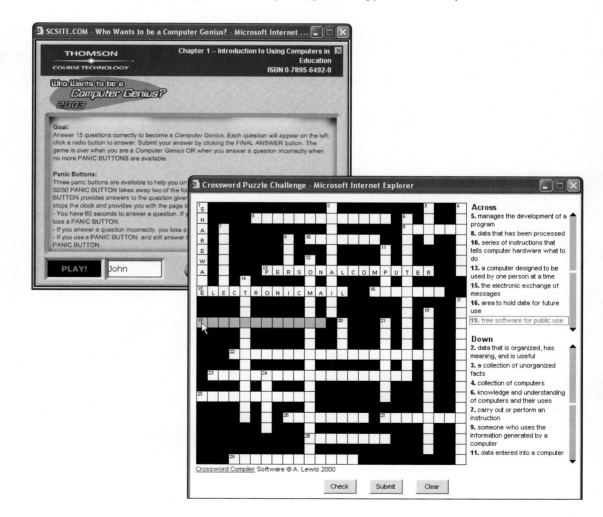

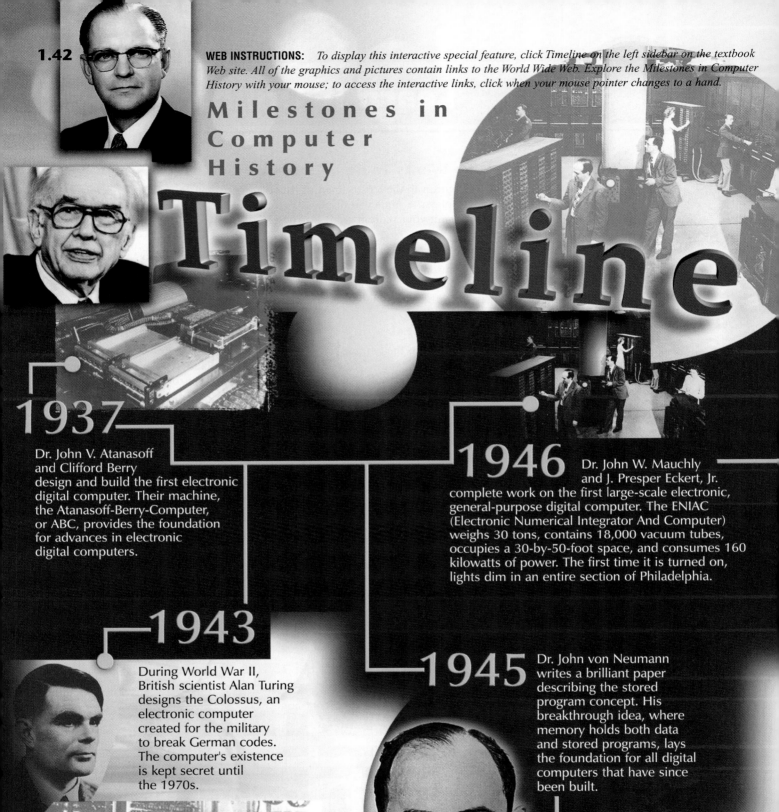

1.42

WEB INSTRUCTIONS: *To display this interactive special feature, click Timeline on the left sidebar on the textbook Web site. All of the graphics and pictures contain links to the World Wide Web. Explore the Milestones in Computer History with your mouse; to access the interactive links, click when your mouse pointer changes to a hand.*

Milestones in Computer History

Timeline

1937

Dr. John V. Atanasoff and Clifford Berry design and build the first electronic digital computer. Their machine, the Atanasoff-Berry-Computer, or ABC, provides the foundation for advances in electronic digital computers.

1946

Dr. John W. Mauchly and J. Presper Eckert, Jr. complete work on the first large-scale electronic, general-purpose digital computer. The ENIAC (Electronic Numerical Integrator And Computer) weighs 30 tons, contains 18,000 vacuum tubes, occupies a 30-by-50-foot space, and consumes 160 kilowatts of power. The first time it is turned on, lights dim in an entire section of Philadelphia.

1943

During World War II, British scientist Alan Turing designs the Colossus, an electronic computer created for the military to break German codes. The computer's existence is kept secret until the 1970s.

1945

Dr. John von Neumann writes a brilliant paper describing the stored program concept. His breakthrough idea, where memory holds both data and stored programs, lays the foundation for all digital computers that have since been built.

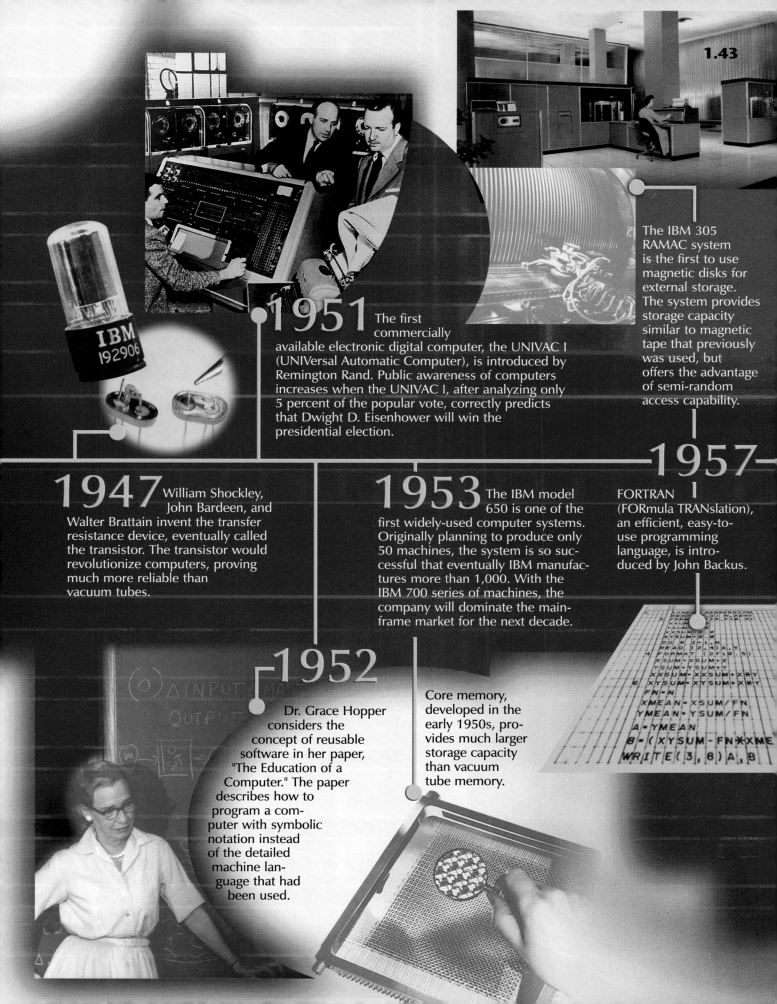

1951 The first commercially available electronic digital computer, the UNIVAC I (UNIVersal Automatic Computer), is introduced by Remington Rand. Public awareness of computers increases when the UNIVAC I, after analyzing only 5 percent of the popular vote, correctly predicts that Dwight D. Eisenhower will win the presidential election.

The IBM 305 RAMAC system is the first to use magnetic disks for external storage. The system provides storage capacity similar to magnetic tape that previously was used, but offers the advantage of semi-random access capability.

1957 FORTRAN (FORmula TRANslation), an efficient, easy-to-use programming language, is introduced by John Backus.

1947 William Shockley, John Bardeen, and Walter Brattain invent the transfer resistance device, eventually called the transistor. The transistor would revolutionize computers, proving much more reliable than vacuum tubes.

1953 The IBM model 650 is one of the first widely-used computer systems. Originally planning to produce only 50 machines, the system is so successful that eventually IBM manufactures more than 1,000. With the IBM 700 series of machines, the company will dominate the mainframe market for the next decade.

1952 Dr. Grace Hopper considers the concept of reusable software in her paper, "The Education of a Computer." The paper describes how to program a computer with symbolic notation instead of the detailed machine language that had been used.

Core memory, developed in the early 1950s, provides much larger storage capacity than vacuum tube memory.

1.44

Computers built with transistors mark the beginning of the second generation of computer hardware.

1958

COBOL, a high-level business application language, is developed by a committee headed by Dr. Grace Hopper. COBOL uses English-like phrases and runs on most business computers, making it one of the more widely-used programming languages.

1960

Dr. John Kemeny of Dartmouth leads the development of the BASIC programming language. BASIC will be widely used on personal computers.

Digital Equipment Corporation (DEC) introduces the first mini-computer, the PDP-8. The machine is used extensively as an interface for time-sharing systems.

1965

1959

More than 200 programming languages have been created.

IBM introduces two smaller, desk-sized computers: the IBM 1401 for business and the IBM 1602 for scientists. The IBM 1602 initially is called the CADET, but IBM drops the name when campus wags claim it is an acronym for Can't Add, Doesn't Even Try.

1964

The number of computers has grown to 18,000.

Third-generation computers, with their controlling circuitry stored on chips, are introduced. The IBM System/360 computer is the first family of compatible machines, merging science and business lines.

1968

Alan Shugart at IBM demonstrates the first regular use of an 8-inch floppy (magnetic storage) disk.

In a letter to the editor titled, "GO TO Statements Considered Harmful," Dr. Edsger Dijsktra introduces the concept of structured programming, developing standards for constructing computer programs.

Computer Science Corporation becomes the first software company listed on the New York Stock Exchange.

	CSC STOCK PRICE NYSE/COMPOSITE Corrected Data for Dividends		
DATE	PRICE	HIGH	LO
1/02/68	2.83	2.97	2
1/03/68	2.60	2.81	2
1/04/68	2.61	2.62	2
1/05/68			
1/08/68	2.54	2.60	
1/09/68	2.55	2.60	
1/10/68	2.46		
		30,100	
		2.51	13,500
		2.48	23,400
		2.49	7,800
		2.50	18,800

IBM

Under pressure from the industry, IBM announces that some of its software will be priced separately from the computer hardware. This unbundling allows software firms to emerge in the industry.

The ARPANET network, a predecessor of the Internet, is established.

1969

Dr. Ted Hoff of Intel Corporation develops a microprocessor, or microprogrammable computer chip, the Intel 4004.

1971

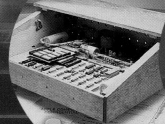

1970

Fourth-generation computers, built with chips that use LSI (large-scale integration) arrive. While the chips used in 1965 contained as many as 1,000 circuits, the LSI chip contains as many as 15,000.

1975

MITS, Inc. advertises the first microcomputer, the Altair. Named for the destination in an episode of *Star Trek*, the Altair is sold in kits for less than $400. Although initially it has no keyboard, no monitor, no permanent memory, and no software, 4,000 orders are taken within the first three months.

1976

Steve Wozniak and Steve Jobs build the first Apple computer. A subsequent version, the Apple II, is an immediate success. Adopted by elementary schools, high schools, and colleges, for many students the Apple II is their first contact with the world of computers.

Ethernet, the first local area network (LAN), is developed at Xerox PARC (Palo Alto Research Center) by Robert Metcalf. The LAN allows computers to communicate and share software, data, and peripherals. Initially designed to link minicomputers, Ethernet will be extended to personal computers.

1.46

VisiCalc, a spreadsheet program written by Bob Frankston and Dan Bricklin, is introduced. Originally written to run on Apple II computers, VisiCalc will be seen as the most important reason for the acceptance of personal computers in the business world.

The first public online information services, CompuServe and the Source, are founded.

1979

The IBM PC is introduced, signaling IBM's entrance into the personal computer marketplace. The IBM PC quickly garners the largest share of the personal computer market and becomes the personal computer of choice in business.

1981

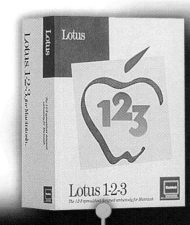

Lotus Development Corpora is founded. Its spreadsheet software, Lotus 1-2-3, which combines spreadsheet, grap and database programs in or package, becomes the best-s program for IBM personal computers.

1983

1980

Alan Shugart presents the Winchester hard drive, revolutionizing storage for personal computers.

1982

3,275,000 personal computers are sold, almost 3,000,000 more than in 1981.

Instead of choosing a person for its annual award, *TIME* magazine names the computer Machine of the Year for 1982, acknowledging the impact of computers on society.

IBM offers Microsoft Corporation cofounder, Bill Gates, the opportunity to develop the operating system for the soon-to-be announced IBM personal computer. With the development of MS-DOS, Microsoft achieves tremendous growth and success.

Hayes introduces the 300 bps smart modem. The modem is an immediate success.

COMPAQ

Compaq, Inc. is founded to develop and market IBM-compatible PCs.

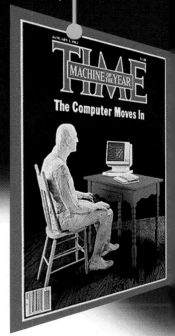

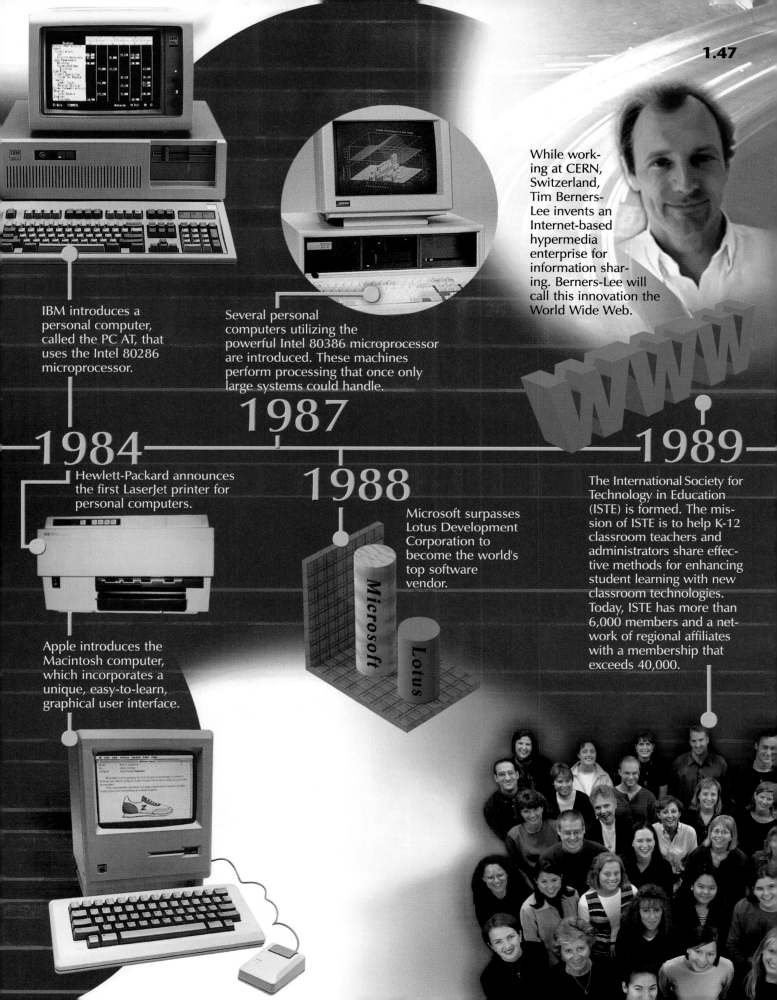

IBM introduces a personal computer, called the PC AT, that uses the Intel 80286 microprocessor.

Several personal computers utilizing the powerful Intel 80386 microprocessor are introduced. These machines perform processing that once only large systems could handle.

While working at CERN, Switzerland, Tim Berners-Lee invents an Internet-based hypermedia enterprise for information sharing. Berners-Lee will call this innovation the World Wide Web.

1987

1984

Hewlett-Packard announces the first LaserJet printer for personal computers.

1989

1988

Microsoft surpasses Lotus Development Corporation to become the world's top software vendor.

Apple introduces the Macintosh computer, which incorporates a unique, easy-to-learn, graphical user interface.

The International Society for Technology in Education (ISTE) is formed. The mission of ISTE is to help K-12 classroom teachers and administrators share effective methods for enhancing student learning with new classroom technologies. Today, ISTE has more than 6,000 members and a network of regional affiliates with a membership that exceeds 40,000.

1.48

Microsoft releases Windows 3.1, the latest version of its Windows operating system. Windows 3.1 offers improvements such as TrueType fonts, multimedia capability, and object linking and embedding (OLE). In two months, 3,000,000 copies of Windows 3.1 are sold.

1992

Several companies introduce computers using the Pentium microprocessor from Intel. The Pentium chip is the successor to the Intel 486 processor. It contains 3.1 million transistors and is capable of performing 112,000,000 instructions per second.

Jim Clark and Marc Andreessen found Netscape and launch Netscape Navigator 1.0, a browser for the World Wide Web.

1991 — 1993 — 1994

AskERIC (Educational Resources Information Center) starts up as a project of the ERIC Clearinghouse on Information and Technology at Syracuse University. Today, the federally funded AskERIC provides an extensive and searchable database of documents and resources; educators can send questions on any educational topic to AskERIC and receive a response within 48 hours.

The International Society for Technology in Education (ISTE) introduces the first edition of "Technology Standards for Teachers," containing 13 indicators.

Marc Andreessen creates a graphical Web browser called Mosaic. This success leads to the organization of Netscape Communications Corporation.

N C S A
MOSAIC
X Window System • Microsoft Windows • Macintosh

The Clinton Administration creates the Telecommunications and Information Infrastructure Assistance Program (TIIAP), which supplies grants to public institutions to fund the installation of advanced communications technologies. Over the next four years, TIIAP awards 378 grants of approximately $118 million in federal grant funds, which are matched by more than $180 million in nonfederal funds.

Microsoft Windows 95 Upgrade
for users of Windows

Microsoft releases Windows 95, a major upgrade to its Windows operating system. Windows 95 consists of more than 10,000,000 lines of computer instructions developed by 300 person-years of effort. More than 50,000 individuals and companies test the software before it is released.

President Clinton launches a $2 billion, five-year, Technology Literacy Challenge — a program designed to catalyze and leverage state, local, and private sector efforts so American schools can provide students with the skills they need to succeed in the next century.

The Summer Olympics in Atlanta makes extensive use of computer technology, using an IBM network of 7,000 personal computers, 2,000 pagers and wireless devices, and 90 industrial-strength computers to share information with more than 150,000 athletes, coaches, journalists, and Olympics staff members, and millions of Web users.

1995

Sun Microsystems launches Java, an object-oriented programming language that allows users to write one application for a variety of computer platforms. Java becomes one of the hottest Internet technologies.

1996

U.S. Robotics introduces PalmPilot, a handheld personal organizer. The PalmPilot's user-friendliness and low price make it a standout next to more expensive personal digital assistants (PDAs).

President Clinton signs the Telecommunications Act of 1996 into law. The act's Universal Service clause requires that schools and libraries are provided affordable telecommunication services.

An innovative technology called webtv combines television and the Internet by providing viewers with tools to navigate the Web.

JAVA™

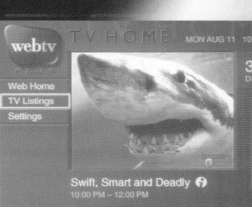

webtv
TV HOME   MON AUG 11 10:32 PM
Web Home
TV Listings
Settings

Swift, Smart and Deadly
10:00 PM – 12:00 PM

2 FOX   5 CBS   11 ABC   15 HBO   54 PBS

webtv
TV Home
Using WebTV
Community
Mail Favorites Explore Search
Around San Francisco Today Mostly Cloudy
EXPLORE entertainment
Your backstage pass to Hollywood
WEB HOME
Home for KellyP

1.50

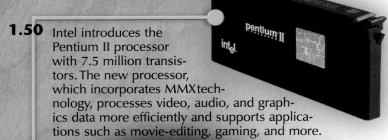

Intel introduces the Pentium II processor with 7.5 million transistors. The new processor, which incorporates MMX technology, processes video, audio, and graphics data more efficiently and supports applications such as movie-editing, gaming, and more.

The Federal Communications Commission (FCC) approves the Education Rate (E-Rate) discount program to provide K-12 schools and all public libraries with discounted telecommunications services. FCC Chairman Hundt describes the E-Rate program as, "the biggest, single national effort to change education in K-12 classrooms in the history of our country."

DVD (Digital Video Disc), the next generation of optical disc storage technology, is introduced. DVD can store computer, audio, and video data in a single format, with the capability of producing near-studio quality. By year's end, 500,000 DVD players are shipped worldwide.

Microsoft ships Windows 98, an upgrade to Windows 95. Windows 98 offers improved Internet access, better system performance, and support for a new generation of hardware and software. In six months, more than 10,000,000 copies of Windows 98 are sold worldwide.

1997 — 1998

Deep Blue, an IBM supercomputer, defeats world chess champion Gary Kasparov in a six-game chess competition. Millions of people follow the nine day-long rematch on IBM's Web site.

The International Society for Technology in Education (ISTE) releases the second edition of "Technology Standards for Teachers," containing 18 indicators organized into three major categories.

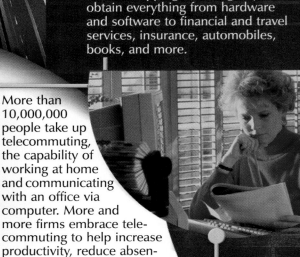

E-commerce, or electronic commerce — the marketing of goods and services over the Internet — booms. Companies such as Dell, E*TRADE, and Amazon.com spur online shopping, allowing buyers to obtain everything from hardware and software to financial and travel services, insurance, automobiles, books, and more.

Fifty million users are connected to the Internet and World Wide Web.

More than 10,000,000 people take up telecommuting, the capability of working at home and communicating with an office via computer. More and more firms embrace telecommuting to help increase productivity, reduce absenteeism, and provide greater job satisfaction.

iste

High school students begin taking online courses at The Florida High School Online.

Apple Computer introduces the iMac, the latest version of its popular Macintosh computer. The iMac abandons such conventional features as a floppy disk drive but wins customers with its futuristic design, see-through case, and easy setup. Consumer demand outstrips Apple's production capabilities, and some vendors are forced to begin waiting lists.

Intel releases its Pentium III processor, which provides enhanced multimedia capabilities.

Microsoft introduces Office 2000, its premier productivity suite, offering new tools for users to create content and save it directly to a Web site without any file conversion or special steps.

Microsoft **Office**2000 **Premium**

1998

1999

Preparing Tomorrow's Teachers to Use Technology (PT3) — The U.S. Department of Education initiates a multiyear, innovative, $125 million grant program to create technology-proficient educators at all levels: multiyear preservice teachers, in-service teachers, and faculty in higher education.

Governments and businesses frantically work to make their computers Y2K (Year 2000) compliant, spending more than $500 billion worldwide. Y2K noncompliant computers cannot distinguish if 01/01/00 refers to 1900 or 2000, and thus may operate using a wrong date. This Y2K bug can affect any application that relies on computer chips, such as ATMs, airplanes, energy companies, and the telephone system.

Intel, with support from Microsoft, launches the Intel Teach to the Future program — a worldwide initiative to help teachers effectively integrate the use of computer technology into classroom curriculum.

Shawn Fanning, 19, and his company, Napster, turn the music industry upside down by developing software that allows computer users to swap music files with one another without going through a centralized file server. The Recording Industry of America, on behalf of five media companies, sues Napster for copyright infringement.

The International Society for Technology in Education (ISTE) releases the National Educational Technology Standards (NETS) for teachers and K-12 students. The National Council for Accreditation of Teacher Education adopts the NETS for teachers (NETS-T) for accrediting teacher education programs.

According to the U.S. Commerce Department, Internet traffic is doubling every 100 days, resulting in an annual growth rate of more than 700 percent. It has taken radio and television 30 years and 15 years respectively, to reach 60 million people. The Internet has achieved the same audience base in 3 years.

2000

E-commerce achieves mainstream acceptance. Annual e-commerce sales exceed $100 billion, and Internet advertising expenditures reach more than $5 billion.

Intel unveils its Pentium 4 chip with clock speeds starting at 1.4 GHz. The Pentium 4 includes 42 million transistors, nearly twice as many as contained on its predecessor, the Pentium III.

Dot-com companies (Internet based) go out of business at a record pace — nearly one per day — as financial investors withhold funding due to the companies' unprofitability.

Telemedicine uses satellite technology and videoconferencing to broadcast consultations and to perform distant surgeries. Robots are used for complex and precise tasks. Computer-aided surgery uses virtual reality to assist with training and planning procedures.

Microsoft releases Microsoft Office 2001 suite for the Macintosh, which includes Word, Excel, Entourage, and PowerPoint.

Apple Computers releases Mac OS X, the latest version of its popular operating system. Apple claims that Mac OS X is the most advanced and easiest-to-use operating system in history.

More than 25 million computer users subscribe to America Online and take advantage of its AOL Anywhere features, including Instant Messenger, e-mail, and customized news and information pages. AOL's merger with Time Warner combines the strengths of the Internet, entertainment, and communications industries.

2001

Microsoft introduces Office XP Professional, which includes voice recognition and speech capabilities. Microsoft claims that Office XP is the ultimate set of business tools and that it is a complete suite of software that is powerful enough to meet all personal and professional computing needs.

Wireless technology, especially handheld computers, achieves significant market penetration. Prices drop, usage increases, and wireless carriers scramble for new services, particularly for a mobile workforce that can access the Internet anywhere at any time.

Microsoft releases Windows XP Professional for business and advanced home computing and Windows XP Home Edition for home use.

Avid readers enjoy e-books, which are digital texts read on compact computer screens. E-books can hold the equivalent of 10 traditional books containing text and graphics. Readers can search, highlight text, and add notes.

DVD writers (DVD+RW) begin to replace CD writers (CD-RW). DVDs can store up to eight times as much data as CDs. Uses include storing home movies, music, photos, and backups. Digital cameras and video editors help the average user develop quality video to store on DVDs.

In January 2002, President Bush signs into law the No Child Left Behind Act — the most sweeping reform of federal education policy in a generation. The act creates strong standards for what every child should know and learn in reading and math in grades 3-8 and states that student progress and achievement will be measured for every child, every year.

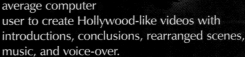

Digital video cameras, DVD writers, easy-to-use video editing software, and improvements in storage capabilities allow the average computer user to create Hollywood-like videos with introductions, conclusions, rearranged scenes, music, and voice-over.

2002

The world of wireless communications, wireless notebook computers, and other wireless devices are breaking down traditional K-12 communication barriers worldwide and are opening new and exciting doors to a wireless world of learning.

Microsoft releases Pocket PC 2002 software that allows PDAs to interface with PCs and Microsoft software.

Handspring revolutionizes handheld devices by offering the first all-in-one device that has a built-in cell phone, Web-browsing, and e-mail features.

1.55

Intel releases its new Centrino mobile technology designed specifically for mobile computing with built-in wireless LAN capability, breakthrough mobile performance, and Intel's first integrated computing technology designed from the ground up for wireless notebook PCs.

Microsoft releases the Class Server Learning Management Platform that makes it easy for school districts to create, deliver, and grade standards-aligned tests and lessons over the Web — helping teachers track and improve student achievement against local curriculum standards, and meet the challenges of No Child Left Behind.

Class Server 3.0
Learning Management Platform

Wireless desktop computer components such as keyboards, mouse devices, home networks, and public Internet access points become commonplace. Latest operating systems include support for both the Wi-Fi (wireless fidelity) and Bluetooth standards. Wireless capabilities are standard on many PDAs and Tablet PCs.

2003

The International Society for Technology in Education (ISTE) announces that by summer of 2003, 48 states will adopt, adapt, align with, or reference one set of its National Educational Technology Standards (NETS).

iste
National Educational Technology Standards (NETS)

Microsoft introduces OneNote 2003, a new program in the Office family that enables users to capture, organize, and reuse notes on notebook computers, desktop computers, or Tablet PCs; potentially changing forever the way professors, instructors, and teachers grade assignments and more.

The Tablet PC is introduced as the next-generation mobile PC. It runs Windows XP Table PC software and is designed like a notebook, is fully wireless, and includes note-taking and other new features.

G5

Apples introduces the Power Mac G5 processor — the first 64-bit processor, which means it breaks the 4 gigabyte barrier and can use up to 8 gigabytes of main memory.

The federal Education Rate, or E-Rate program, invests more than $14 billion, since 1998, to connect libraries and K-12 classrooms to the Internet. As a result, virtually all U.S. students now have access to the Internet from school. FCC Chairman Powell states that one of the more successful broadband projects that exists is the E-Rate program.

2003 ———————— 2004

By the end of 2004, experts predict that more than 1 billion people will send 244 billion e-mail messages monthly.

me@e-mail.com

Microsoft releases the latest version of its flagship Office suite in numerous versions, including a Microsoft Office Student and Teacher Edition that includes Word 2003, Excel 2003, and PowerPoint 2003.

Communications, Networks, the Internet, and the World Wide Web

2

Objectives

After completing this chapter, you will be able to:

- Define communications
- Identify the basic components of a communications system
- Describe how and why network computers are used in schools and school districts
- Explain how the Internet works
- Describe the World Wide Web portion of the Internet
- Explain how Web documents are linked to one another
- Explain the use of Web browser software

- Explain how to use a Web search tool to find information
- Identify several types of multimedia products available on the Web
- Explain how Internet services such as e-mail, newsgroups, chat rooms, and instant messaging work
- Describe the educational implications of the Internet and the World Wide Web
- Describe different ways to connect to the Internet and the World Wide Web

Communications and networks are the fastest growing areas of computer technology. Adding tremendously to this growth is the popularity of the Internet and the World Wide Web (also called the Web), which is a service of the Internet that supports graphics and multimedia. Together, the Internet and the World Wide Web represent one of today's most exciting uses of networks. Already, these networks have changed dramatically the way people gather information, conduct research, shop, take classes, and collaborate on projects.

Businesses encourage you to browse their Web-based catalogs, send them e-mail for customer service requests, and buy their products online. The government publishes thousands of informational Web pages to provide individuals with materials such as legislative updates, tax forms, and e-mail addresses for members of Congress. Colleges give tours of their campuses on the Web, accept applications online, and offer thousands of classes on the Internet.

Communications, networks, and the Internet also have changed dramatically the way teachers instruct and students learn. Today, communications media and networks are breaking down the walls of a classroom, allowing students to view the world beyond where they live and learn. The Internet is expanding beyond the covers of a textbook to include interactive, up-to-date, Web-based content. Never before has any technology opened so many opportunities for learning.

The future will bring even more exciting applications of these technologies. Federal and state governments, private businesses, and organizations are investing billions of dollars in Internet-related hardware and software for K-12 schools. As a result of this substantial investment, most public schools have equipped their classrooms with multimedia computers and provided teachers and students with access to the Internet. This chapter discusses communications, networks, the Internet, and the World Wide Web; explains how they work; and reviews how teachers and administrators can use these technologies to communicate, obtain almost unlimited educational information, and enhance student learning.

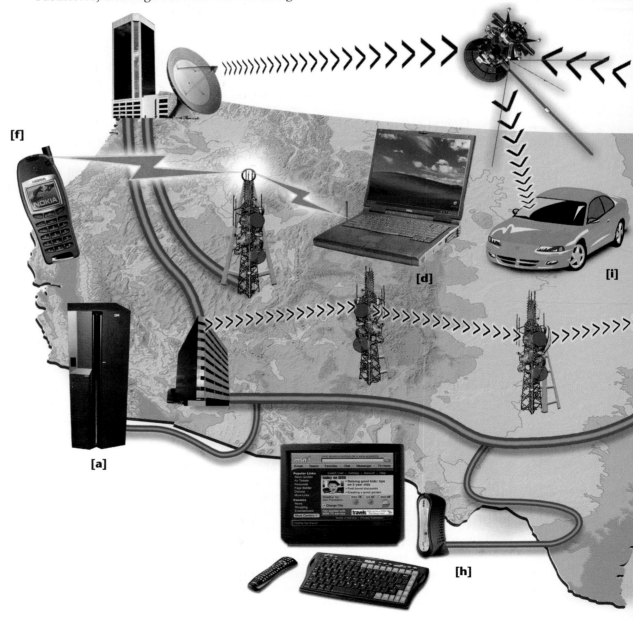

What Is Communications?

Communications, sometimes called **telecommunications**, describes a process in which two or more computers or devices transfer data, instructions, and information. The ability to communicate information instantly and accurately has changed the way people conduct business and interact with each other, and the way students learn. Electronic mail (e-mail), voice mail, fax (facsimile), telecommuting, online services, videoconferencing, the Internet, and the World Wide Web are examples of applications that rely on communications technology.

Communications Networks

Computers were stand-alone devices when first introduced. As computers became more widely used, companies designed hardware and software so computers could communicate with one another. Originally, developers created communication capabilities only for large computers. Today, even the smallest computers and handheld devices can communicate with each other. Figure 2-1 shows a sample communications system, which can contain all types of devices.

FAQ

What are set-top boxes?

A **set-top box**, or Internet appliance [see Figure 2-1], sits on top of or near a television set and allows users to access the Internet and navigate Web pages using a keyboard and a device resembling a remote control.

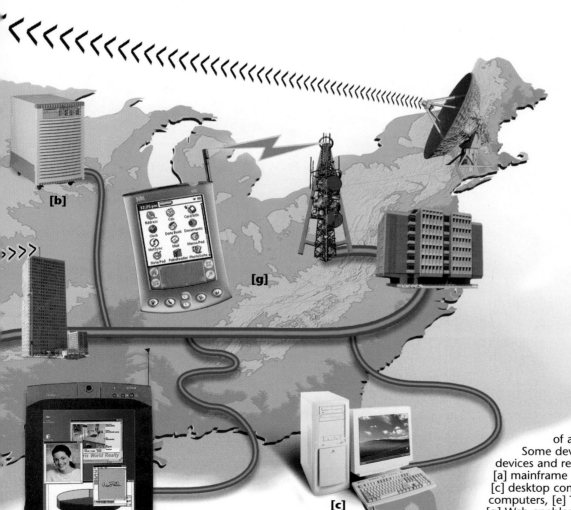

[b]

[g]

[e]

[c]

Figure 2-1 An example of a communications system. Some devices that serve as sending devices and receiving devices are [a] mainframe computers, [b] servers, [c] desktop computers, [d] notebook computers, [e] Tablet PCs, [f] smart phones, [g] Web-enabled PDAs, [h] set-top boxes, and [i] GPS receivers. The communications channel consists of telephone lines, cable television and other underground lines, microwave stations, and satellites.

A communications **network** is a collection of computers and other equipment organized to share data, information, hardware, and software. A basic communications system consists of the following equipment:

- Two computers, one to send and one to receive data

- Communications devices that send and receive data

- A communications channel over which data is sent

This basic model also includes **communications software**, which are programs that manage the transmission of data between computers.

A **communications channel** is the path that data follows as the data is transmitted from the sending equipment to the receiving equipment in a communications system.

Communications channels are made up of **transmission media**, which are the physical materials or other means used to establish a communications channel. The most widely used transmission medium is twisted-pair cable. Standard telephone lines in your home also use twisted-pair cables. **Twisted-pair cable** consists of pairs of plastic-coated copper wires twisted together [Figure 2-2]. Other examples of transmission media include coaxial cable, fiber-optic cable, microwave transmission, communications satellites, and wireless transmissions.

Digital signals are individual electrical pulses that a computer uses to represent data. Telephone equipment originally was designed to carry only voice transmission, which is comprised of a continuous electrical wave called an **analog signal**. For telephone lines to carry data, a communications device called a **modem** converts digital signals into analog signals.

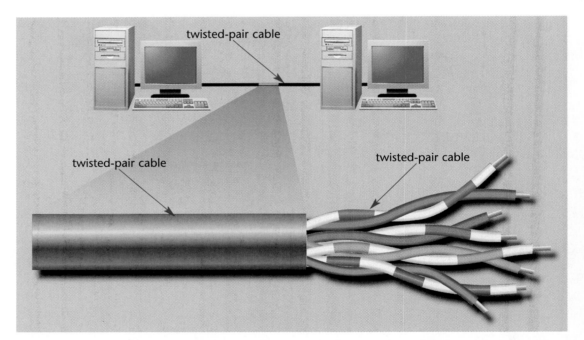

Figure 2-2 Twisted-pair cables often are used to connect personal computers with one another or a personal computer to a regular telephone line. It is inexpensive and easily installed.

The word modem comes from a combination of the words, *modulate*, to change a digital signal into sound or analog signal, and, *demodulate*, to convert an analog signal into a digital signal [Figure 2-3a]. Computers at both the sending and receiving ends of this communications channel must have a modem for data transmission to occur. At the sending computer, a modem converts digital signals from a computer to analog signals for transmission over regular telephone lines. At the receiving computer, a modem converts analog signals back to digital signals.

A number of different kinds of modems are in use today. Most computers purchased for home use include internal modems that can transmit data at rates up to approximately 56,000 bits per second (56 K modem). An **internal modem** is built on a circuit board that is installed inside a computer and attaches to a telephone socket using a standard telephone cord. Many home and small business users now are using cable modems and DSL modems, also called digital modems, which provide significantly higher data access rates than 56 K [Figure 2-3b]. Cable modems provide

WEB INFO

For details about modems, visit the Teachers Discovering Computers Web site, click Chapter 2, click Web Info, and then click Modem.

[a] digital to analog to digital communications channel

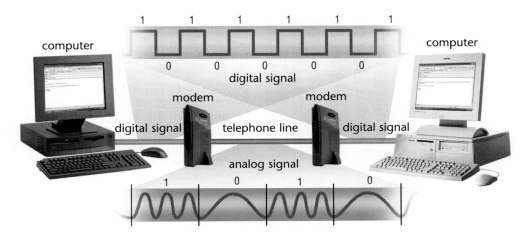

[b] all digital communications channel

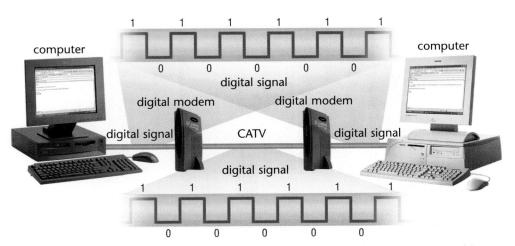

FAQ

Are "digital" modems really modems?

According to the definition of a modem (analog to digital conversion and vice versa), the use of term modem in this context is not correct. However, the industry does refer to DSL and cable modems as digital modems.

Figure 2-3 A modem connects a communications channel, such as a telephone line or a cable television line, to a sending or receiving device such as a computer. Depending on the type of communications channel, a modem may need to convert digital signals to analog signals (and vice versa) before transferring data, instructions, and information to or from a sending or receiving device.

broadband access over a cable television (CATV) network and DSL modems provide broadband access over telephone lines. These newer types of modems are discussed later in this chapter. Networked computers contain a network interface card [Figure 2-4]. **Network interface cards (NICs)** connect computers directly to a school or business network without using a modem. Networks are classified as either local area networks or wide area networks.

1. network interface card installs in expansion slot of computer; cards often have connectors for different types of cables; only one type of cable can be attached at a time
2. twisted-pair cable
3. standard modular connector

Figure 2-4 A network interface card.

LOCAL AREA NETWORKS

A **local area network (LAN)** is a communications network that covers a limited geographical area such as a school, office, building, or group of buildings. A LAN consists of a number of computers connected to a central computer, or server. A **server** manages the resources on a network and provides a centralized storage area for software programs and data. A **wireless LAN (WLAN)** is a LAN that uses no wires. Instead of wires, a WLAN uses wireless media, such as radio waves.

WIDE AREA NETWORKS

A **wide area network (WAN)** covers a large geographical region (such as a city or school district) and uses regular telephone cables, digital lines, microwaves, wireless systems, satellites, or other combinations of communications channels. A WAN can consist of numerous local area networks organized into one larger network. For example, a large school district may establish a WAN that consists of dozens of local area networks, each LAN representing an individual school.

HOME NETWORKS

If you have multiple computers in your home or home office, you can connect all of them together with a **home network** [Figure 2-5]. Some of the many advantages to having a

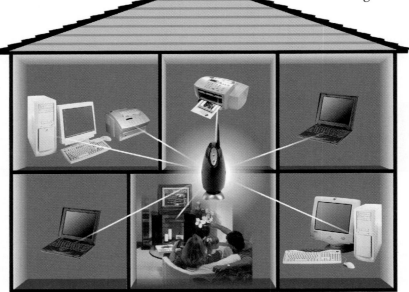

Figure 2-5 An example of a home network.

home network are that all computers in the house can be connected to the Internet at the same time, each computer can access files and programs on the other computers, and all computers can share the same peripherals, such as a scanner, printer, or DVD drive.

Networking the Classroom, School, and District

Due to extensive federal, state, and local funding, virtually all schools and school districts in the United States have networked their computers. Schools have installed networks for three reasons: (1) to share hardware and software resources, (2) to enable communications among schools and other organizations, and (3) to connect students and teachers to the Internet.

A school network server connects all of the computers located within a school. Recall that a *server* is a computer that can store large amounts of data and

information and stores the network software that manages resources on the local area network. Typically, any teachers and students who use the network can access software and data on the server, although school or network administrators can limit access to specific records and software applications.

As an example of how a school district might network its computers, consider the Washington County Public School District, which consists of one high school (Ridgedale High School), two middle schools (Dresden and Fall Hills Middle Schools), and three elementary schools (Acorn, Johnson, and Martin Luther King Elementary Schools).

Martin Luther King Elementary School is a small school with fourteen classrooms. Each classroom has 3 modern Macintosh computers and a printer connected to the school's local area network [Figure 2-6]. Also connected to Martin Luther King Elementary's local area network is a computer lab that contains 24 networked Macintosh computers and 4 additional computers that are used by school

WEB INFO

For more information about school networks, visit the Teachers Discovering Computers Web site, click Chapter 2, click Web Info, and then click School Networks.

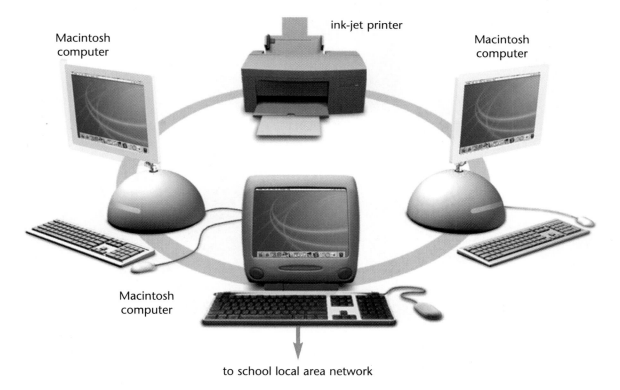

Figure 2-6 In each classroom, three Macintosh computers and a printer are connected to the school's local area network.

administrators and staff. In total, Martin Luther King Elementary School's local area network consists of 70 Macintosh computers and numerous printers all connected to a central server [Figure 2-7].

The local area network at Martin Luther King Elementary and the district's five other school LANs are connected to a large-capacity server and its associated equipment located at the Washington County Public School District's Central Office. Together, these networks form a wide area network that contains more than 600 networked Macintosh computers and PCs [Figure 2-8].

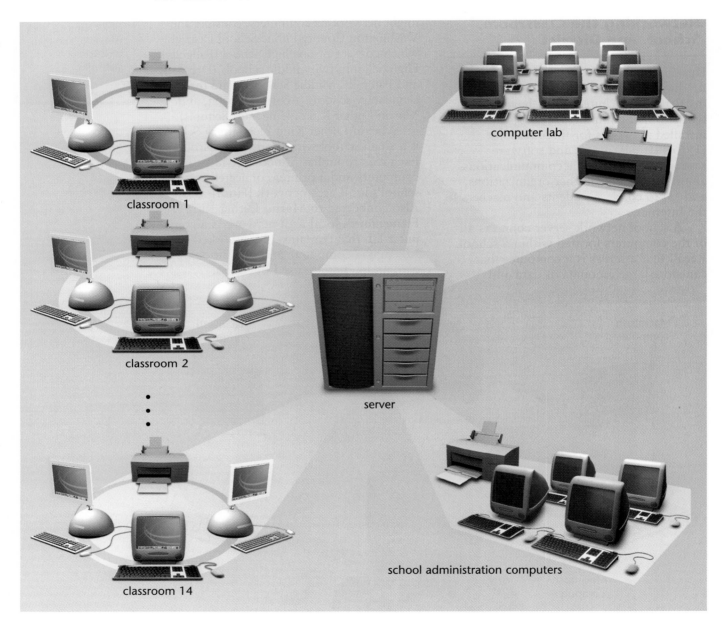

Figure 2-7 The school's local area network consists of computers in 14 classrooms, in the computer lab, and four school administration computers.

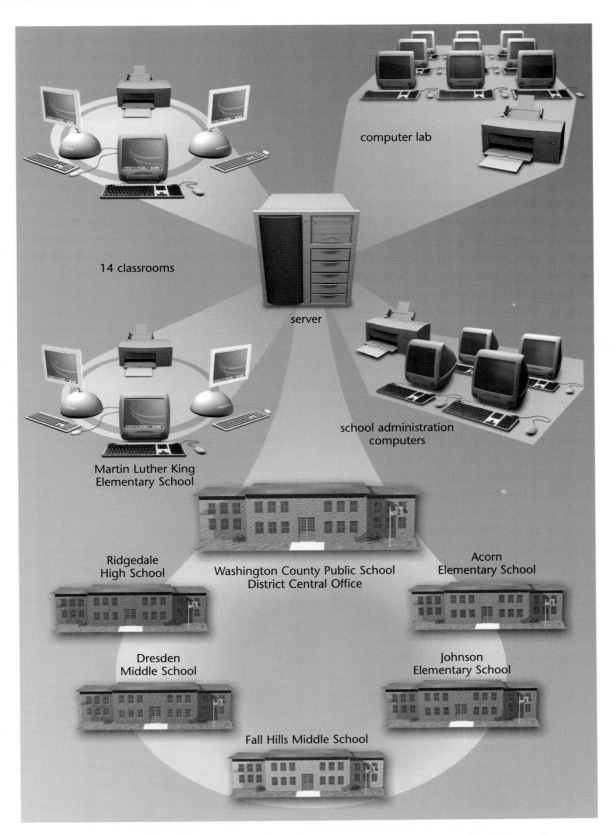

computer lab

14 classrooms

server

school administration
computers

Martin Luther King
Elementary School

Ridgedale
High School

Washington County Public School
District Central Office

Acorn
Elementary School

Dresden
Middle School

Johnson
Elementary School

Fall Hills Middle School

Figure 2-8 The school district's wide area network consists of the local area networks of six member schools all connected to a server located at the district's central office.

WIRELESS SCHOOLS AND CLASSROOMS

Not long ago, you used traditional telephones, connected to the telephone company by cables, to communicate with your friends, family, and fellow teachers. Today, wireless technology allows you to keep in touch with friends and family from anywhere in the world, using a variety of devices: a smart pager, a cellular telephone, a handheld computer, or a notebook computer with high-speed Internet access.

Teachers and students already are part of the wireless revolution that is taking place in education. Numerous colleges, universities, and K-12 schools are installing wireless networks and utilizing wireless notebook computers and other wireless devices. Many experts, including Steve Jobs, CEO of Apple Computers, believe that the future of educational computing, in both K-12 and higher education, will be wireless networks, wireless notebook computers, and other wireless devices.

Today, most major computer manufacturers provide wireless network solutions and devices for K-12 schools [Figure 2-9]. Devices include wireless keyboards, wireless notebook computers, wireless mobile labs, and many other devices. The use of wireless networks and devices in K-12 schools and classrooms is discussed in future chapters and in the special feature, A World Without Wires, which follows Chapter 8.

HIGH SPEED OR BROADBAND ACCESS

Over the past 5 to 10 years, school districts have concentrated on installing local and wide area networks so that their teachers and students will have Internet access in their classrooms or at the point of instruction. Many school networks, however, do not provide their classroom computers with continuous high-speed access to the Internet; access speeds vary greatly. Students and teachers must be provided continuous high-speed access to allow them to find and quickly download complex, content-rich resources. The federal government recognizes this and is spearheading initiatives to provide broadband access to K-12 schools. Networks and media that use **broadband** technologies transmit signals at much faster speeds than traditional network configurations. A recent federal report to the president and Congress stated that the promise of widely available, high quality Web-based education is made possible by technological and communications trends that could lead to important educational applications over the next two or three years.

FAQ

What does bandwidth have to do with Internet Access?

Bandwidth is a measure of how fast data and information travel over transmission channels. Thus, higher-speed broadband Internet connections have a higher bandwidth than dial-up connections.

Figure 2-9 An example of a mobile wireless lab. Instead of taking your students to a school's computer lab, the lab is brought to your students.

The Benefits of Computer Networks in Education

One benefit of networking is that administrators, teachers, and students can share computer hardware, software, and data resources available throughout the school district. For example, administrators can maintain all student records and information securely at one central location. Teachers and administrative staff who have a need for access to student records can access various student information databases from just about any networked computer at any location.

By far, the most important benefit of networking school computers is that administrators, teachers, and students instantly can access the unlimited educational resources available on the Internet and communicate with other educators and students all over the world [Figure 2-10]. In brief, networking provides schools with limitless possibilities for teaching and learning. Without question, the introduction of networks and the Internet into today's schools is having a dramatic impact on the current generation of teachers and students.

Figure 2-10 The Internet is useful as a tool to hold students' attention and even amaze them.

What Is the Internet?

You have learned that a network, such as the one installed at Martin Luther King Elementary School, is a collection of computers and devices connected via communications devices and media. Recall also that the world's largest network is the **Internet,** which is a worldwide collection of networks that link together millions of businesses, governments, educational institutions, and individuals using modems, telephone lines, and other communications devices and media [Figure 2-11]. Each of these networks provides resources and data that add to the abundance of goods, services, and information accessible via the Internet.

Figure 2-11 The world's largest network is the Internet, which is a worldwide collection of networks that link together millions of businesses, governments, educational institutions, and individuals.

Networks that comprise the Internet, also called the **Net,** consist of federal, regional, local, and international networks. Public or private organizations own individual networks that constitute the Internet; no single organization owns or controls the Internet. Each organization on the Internet is responsible only for maintaining its own network.

Today, more than 500 million users around the world connect to the Internet for a variety of reasons. Figure 2-12 on the next page illustrates sites on the Internet that represent some of the following uses:

- Access a wealth of information, news, research, and educational material

- Conduct business or complete banking and investing transactions

- Access sources of entertainment and leisure, such as online games, magazines, and vacation-planning guides

- Shop for goods and services

WEB INFO

For an overview of the Internet, visit the Teachers Discovering Computers Web site, click Chapter 2, click Web Info, and then click Internet.

- Meet and converse with people around the world in discussion groups or chat rooms

- Access other computers and exchange files

- Send messages to or receive messages from other connected users

- Download and listen to music or download and watch movies

- Take a course or access educational materials

To allow you to perform these and other activities, the Internet provides a variety of services, such as the World Wide

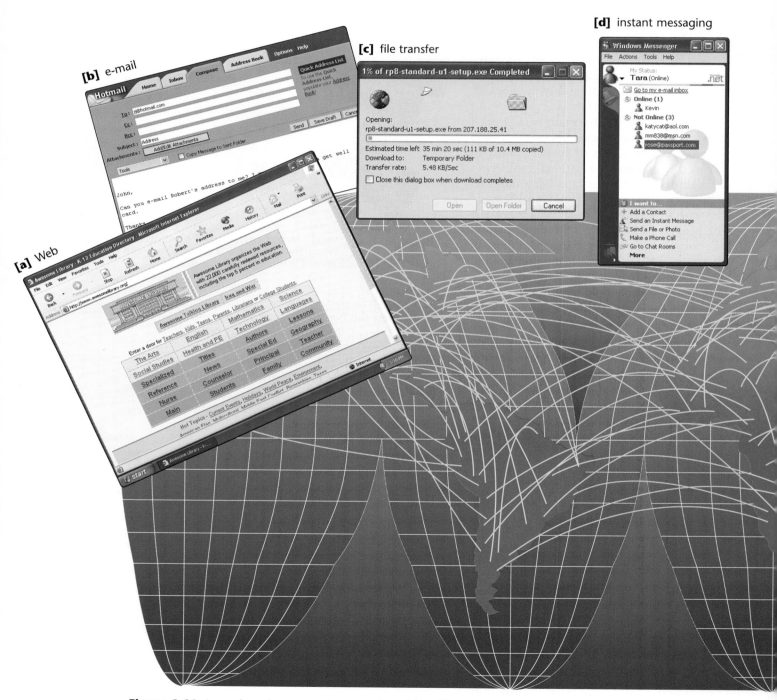

Figure 2-12 A number of reasons why more than 500 million users around the world connect to the Internet.

Web, electronic mail (e-mail), File Transfer Protocol (FTP), newsgroups and message boards, mailing lists, instant messaging, short message service, and chat rooms. These services along with a discussion of the history of the Internet and how the Internet works are explained in the following sections.

History of the Internet

Although the history of the Internet is relatively short, its growth has been explosive. The Internet has it roots in a networking project of the U.S. Department of Defense's **Advanced Research Projects Agency (ARPA)**. ARPA's goal was to build

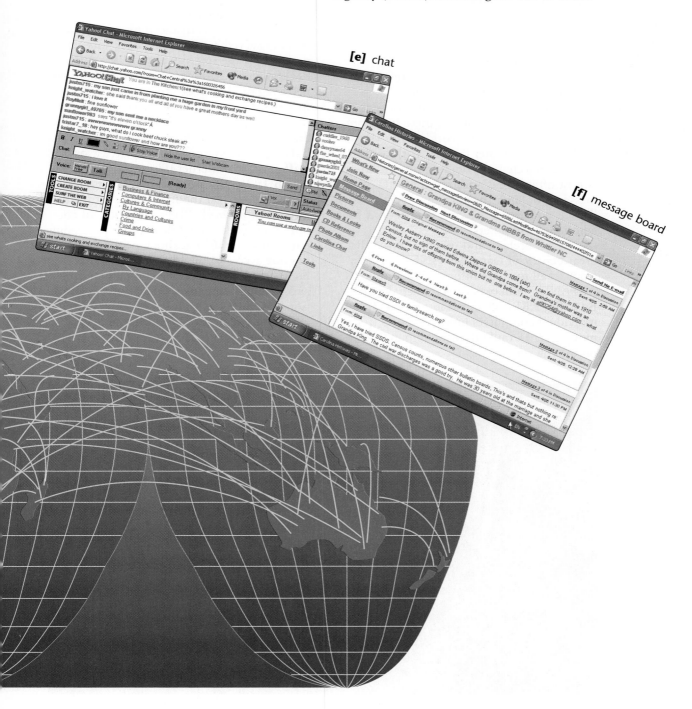

[e] chat

[f] message board

For the history of the Internet, visit the Teachers Discovering Computers Web site, click Chapter 2, click Web Info, and then click History.

a network that (1) would allow scientists at different locations to share information and collaborate on military and scientific projects and (2) could function even if part of the network were disabled or destroyed by a disaster such as a nuclear war. That network, called **ARPANET**, became functional in September 1969, effectively linking together scientific and academic researchers in the United States.

The original ARPANET was a wide area network consisting of four main computers, one each located at the University of California at Los Angeles, the Stanford Research Institute, the University of California at Santa Barbara, and the University of Utah. Each of these four computers served as the network's host. A **host** is the main computer in a network of computers connected by communications links. A host often stores and transfers data and messages on high-speed communications lines and provides network connections for additional computers.

As researchers and others realized the great benefit of using ARPANET's electronic mail to share information and notes, ARPANET underwent phenomenal growth. By 1984, ARPANET had more than 1,000 individual computers linked as hosts (today, more than 35 million host computers exist on the Internet).

To take further advantage of the high-speed communications offered by ARPANET, organizations decided to connect entire networks to ARPANET. In 1986, for example, the **National Science Foundation (NSF)** connected its huge network of five supercomputer centers, called **NSFnet**, to ARPANET. This configuration of complex networks and hosts became known as the Internet.

Because of its advanced technology, NSFnet served as the major backbone network of the Internet until 1995. A **backbone** is a high-speed network that connects regional and local networks to the Internet. Other computers then connect to these regional and local networks to access the Internet. A backbone thus handles the bulk of the communications activity, or **traffic**, on the Internet [Figure 2-13].

In 1995, NSFnet terminated its backbone network on the Internet to return to a research network. Today, a variety of corporations, commercial firms, and other companies operate the backbone networks that provide access to the Internet. These backbone networks, telephone companies, cable and satellite companies, educational institutions, and the government all contribute extensive resources to the Internet. As a result, the Internet is a truly collaborative entity.

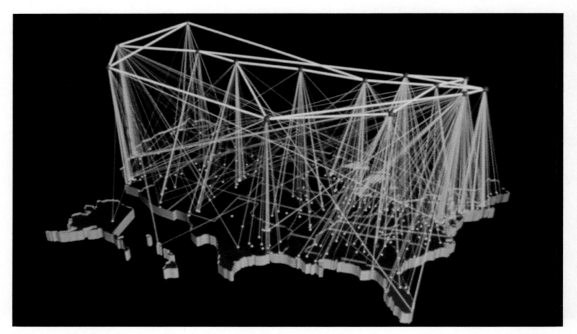

Figure 2-13 This map was prepared by the National Science Foundation and shows the major United States Internet connections.

Over the years, the total number of computers connected to the original network increased steadily and within the last few years, explosively. Today, experts estimate that hundreds of millions of computers distribute information over the Internet, including those at virtually all K-12 schools. More than 95 percent of K-12 classrooms in the United States are now connected to the Internet.

A new Internet, called Internet2, is an ongoing development project that went online in 1999. **Internet2 (I2)** is an extremely high-speed network that will develop and test advanced Internet technologies for research, teaching, and learning. Members of Internet2 include more than 190 universities in the United States, along with 60 companies and the United States government. Eventually it will benefit users of the Internet.

How the Internet Works

Computers connected to the Internet work together to transfer data and information around the world. When a computer sends data over the Internet, the computer's software divides the data into small pieces, called **packets**. The data in a packet might be part of an e-mail message, a file, a document, or a request for a file. Each packet contains the data, as well as the recipient (destination), origin (sender), and sequence information needed to reassemble the data at the destination. Packets travel along the fastest path available to the recipient's computer via hardware devices called **routers** [Figure 2-14].

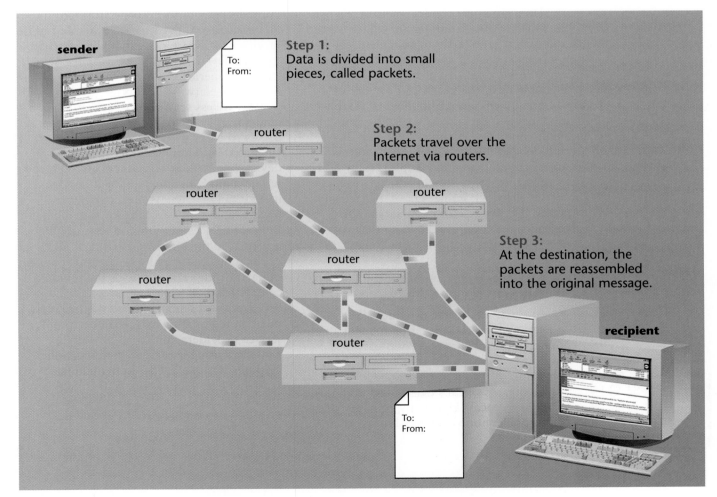

Figure 2-14 How data travels over the Internet.

If the most direct path to the destination is overloaded or not operating, routers send the packets along an alternate path. Although each packet may arrive out of sequence, the destination computer uses the sequence information contained in each packet to reassemble the original message, file, document, or request. **Packet switching** is the technique of breaking a message into individual packets, sending the packets along the best route available, and reassembling the data.

For a technique such as packet switching to work, all of the devices on the network must follow certain standards or protocols. A **communications protocol** specifies the rules that define how devices connect to each other and transmit data over a network. The protocol used to define packet switching on the Internet is **transmission control protocol/Internet protocol (TCP/IP)**.

Data sent over the Internet travels over networks and communications lines owned and operated by many companies. You can connect to these networks in one of several ways. Some users connect to the Internet through an Internet service provider or an online service, using a modem to establish a connection by dialing a specific telephone number. Organizations such as schools and businesses provide Internet access for students and employees by connecting their own network to an Internet service provider. Some school districts and states also provide Internet services for teachers and administrators so they can access the Internet from their homes.

INTERNET SERVICE PROVIDERS VERSUS ONLINE SERVICE PROVIDERS

An **Internet service provider (ISP)** is an organization that has a permanent connection to the Internet and provides temporary connections to individuals and companies for a fee.

Two types of ISPs exist: local and national. A **local ISP** usually provides one or more telephone numbers limited to a small geographic area. A **national ISP** is a larger business that provides local telephone numbers in most major cities and towns nationwide and broadband access in many locations. Because of their size, national ISPs offer more services and generally have a larger technical support staff than local ISPs. If you live in a rural area, the most important consideration when selecting an ISP is to be sure that it provides a local telephone number for Internet access, so you can avoid paying long-distance charges for the time you are connected to the Internet.

Like an ISP, an **online service provider (OSP)** also provides access to the Internet, but such online services have members-only features that offer a variety of special content and services. Typical content and services include news, weather, educational information, financial information, hardware and software guides, games, entertainment, news, and travel information. For this reason, the fees for using an online service usually are slightly higher than fees for an ISP. The most popular online services are America Online (AOL) and Microsoft Network (MSN).

A **wireless service provider (WSP)** is a company that provides wireless Internet access to users with wireless modems or Web-enabled handheld computers or devices. Notebook computers also can use wireless modems. Web-enabled devices include cellular telephones, two-way pagers, and hands-free (voice activated) Internet devices in automobiles. An antenna on the wireless modem or Web-enabled device typically sends and receives signals through the airwaves to communicate with the WSP.

Users and schools access the Internet through regional or national ISPs, online service providers, and wireless service providers using a variety of connection methods [Figure 2-15]. Individual user accounts vary from about $10 to $25 per month for dial-up access and $40 to $55 for higher-speed access.

WEB INFO

For a list of Internet service providers, visit the Teachers Discovering Computers Web site, click Chapter 2, click Web Info, and then click ISP.

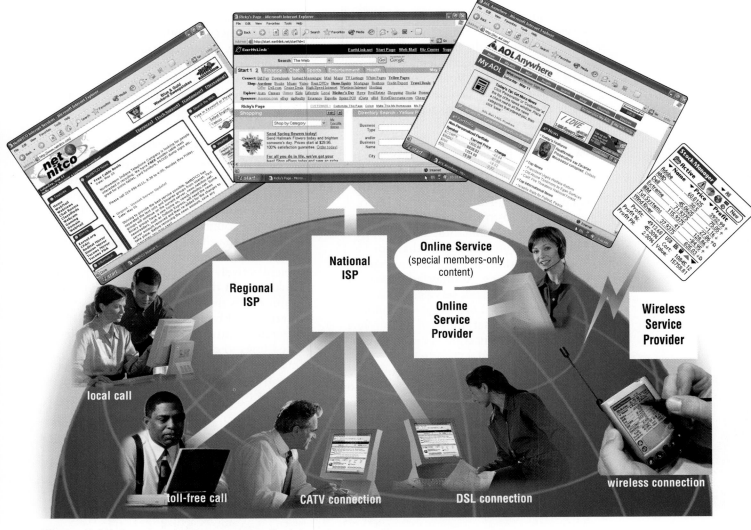

Figure 2-15 Common ways users access the Internet.

CONNECTING TO THE INTERNET

Teachers and students often connect to the Internet through their school network. When connecting from home or from the road while traveling, individuals typically use dial-up access to connect to the Internet. With **dial-up access**, you use your computer and a modem to dial into an ISP or online service over regular telephone lines. The computer at the receiving end, whether at an ISP or online service, also uses a modem. Dial-up access provides an easy way for mobile and home users to connect to the Internet to check e-mail, read the news, and access other information. Because dial-up access uses standard telephone lines, the speed of the connection is limited.

Newer technologies such as cable TV (CATV) and digital subscriber line (DSL) offer home users and small businesses affordable and high-speed alternatives to traditional dial-up access. These new services are not yet available in all areas, especially rural areas.

With more than 100 million homes wired for cable television, it is not surprising that more and more users are getting Internet access from their cable company. Road Runner is a popular high-speed CATV online service provided by AOL Time Warner. CATV uses a high-speed **cable modem** that sends and receives data over the cable television network.

As shown in **Figure 2-16**, CATV service enters your home through a single line and then is split between your televisions and your cable modem, which in turn is connected to your computer. Access speeds with CATV can be significantly faster than using dial-up access, in many cases 20 to 50 times faster. Installation and monthly access fees vary.

Another high-speed alternative to a modem is a **digital subscriber line** (DSL) that transmits data on existing standard telephone lines. DSL can provide Internet access from 25 to 150 times faster than dial-up access. Installation and monthly fees for DSL typically are higher than for CATV. Both DSL and cable modems use broadband technologies. Another advantage of using CATV and DSL services is that they are dedicated lines or always-on connections to the Internet, unlike a dial-up line on which the connection is reestablished each time it is used.

Many hotels and airports provide dial-up or broadband Internet connections usually for a usage or per-day fee. In many public locations, people connect wirelessly to the Internet through a **public Internet access point**. Public Internet access points are appearing in airports, hotels, shopping malls, schools, and coffee shops providing Internet access either for a usage fee or free.

THE INTERNET BACKBONE

The inner structure of the Internet works much like a transportation system. Just as highways connect major cities and carry the bulk of the automotive traffic across the country, the main communications lines that have the heaviest amount of traffic (data packets) on the Internet are collectively referred to as the **Internet backbone**. In the United States, the communications lines that make up the Internet backbone intersect at several different points. National ISPs use dedicated lines to connect directly to the Internet. Smaller, regional networks lease lines from local telephone companies to connect to national networks. These

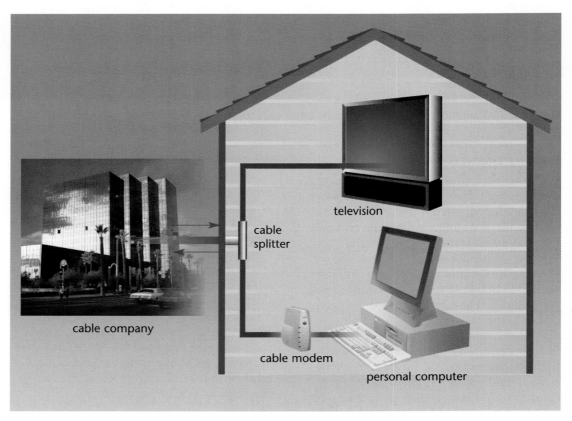

Figure 2-16 A typical cable modem installation.

smaller, slower-speed networks extend from the backbone into regions and local communities like roads and streets. Figure 2-17 illustrates how all of the components of the Internet work together to transfer data over the Internet to and from your computer using a dial-up connection.

INTERNET ADDRESSES

The Internet relies on an addressing system much like that of the postal system to send data to a computer at a specific destination. Each computer's location on the Internet has a specific numeric address consisting of four groups of numbers. Because these all-numeric computer

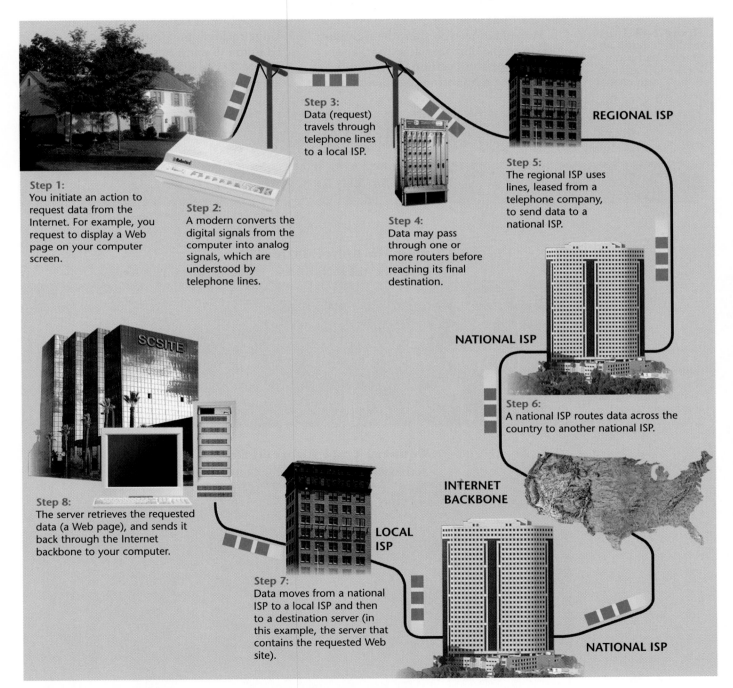

Step 1:
You initiate an action to request data from the Internet. For example, you request to display a Web page on your computer screen.

Step 2:
A modern converts the digital signals from the computer into analog signals, which are understood by telephone lines.

Step 3:
Data (request) travels through telephone lines to a local ISP.

Step 4:
Data may pass through one or more routers before reaching its final destination.

Step 5:
The regional ISP uses lines, leased from a telephone company, to send data to a national ISP.

REGIONAL ISP

Step 6:
A national ISP routes data across the country to another national ISP.

NATIONAL ISP

Step 8:
The server retrieves the requested data (a Web page), and sends it back through the Internet backbone to your computer.

LOCAL ISP

INTERNET BACKBONE

Step 7:
Data moves from a national ISP to a local ISP and then to a destination server (in this example, the server that contains the requested Web site).

NATIONAL ISP

Figure 2-17 How data might travel the Internet using a dial-up connection.

addresses are difficult to remember and use, the Internet supports the use of text-based names that represents the numeric address. The text version of a computer address is called a **domain name**. Figure 2-18 details both the numeric address and the domain name of the Shelly Cashman Series Web site. The components of a domain name are separated by periods, each of which is referred to as a dot.

For domestic Web sites, the rightmost portion of the domain name contains a domain type abbreviation that identifies the type of organization that maintains the Web site. The rightmost portion of a university Web site, for example, would be .edu, which denotes it as a site operated by an educational institution. The domain names for some K-12 school sites include the abbreviation, .k12, followed by the abbreviation for the school's state. For international Web sites, the domain name also includes a country code, such as .us for the United States and .uk for the United Kingdom. Figure 2-19a lists common domain type abbreviations. Figure 2-19b lists several country code abbreviations.

Figure 2-18 The numeric address and domain name for the Shelly Cashman Series® Instructional Web site.

Numeric address	198.80.146.30

Domain name	www.scsite.com	identifies specific computer

identifies type of organization

Domain Abbreviations

Domain Abbreviation	Type of Organization
com	Commercial organizations, businesses, and companies
edu	Educational institutions
gov	Government institutions
mil	Military organizations
net	Network providers
org	Nonprofit organizations
k12	K-12 schools

Figure 2-19a This table lists domain abbreviations commonly used today.

Country Code Abbreviations

Abbreviation	Country
au	Australia
ax	Antarctica
ca	Canada
de	Germany
dk	Denmark
fr	France
jp	Japan
nl	Netherlands
se	Sweden
th	Thailand
uk	United Kingdom
us	United States

Figure 2-19b A partial listing of country code abbreviations.

The World Wide Web

Although many people use the terms World Wide Web and Internet interchangeably, the World Wide Web is just one of the many services available on the Internet. The World Wide Web actually is a relatively new aspect of the Internet. While the Internet has been in existence since the late 1960s, the World Wide Web came into existence in the early 1990s. Since then, however, it has grown phenomenally to become the most widely used service on the Internet.

The **World Wide Web**, or simply **Web**, consists of a worldwide collection of electronic documents that have built-in hyperlinks to other related documents. These **hyperlinks**, also called **links**, allow users to navigate quickly from one Web page to another, regardless of whether the Web pages are located on the same computer or on different computers in different countries. A **Web page** is an electronic document viewed on the Web. A Web page can contain text, graphics, sound, and video, as well as hyperlinks to other Web pages. A **Web site** is a collection of related Web pages. Most Web sites have a starting point, called a **home page**, which is similar to a book cover or table of contents for the site and provides information about the site's purpose and content.

Each Web page on a Web site has a unique address, called a **Uniform Resource Locator** (**URL**). As shown in Figure 2-20, a URL consists of a protocol, domain name, and sometimes the path to a specific Web page. Most Web page URLs begin with **http://**, which stands for **hypertext transfer protocol**, the communications protocol used to transfer pages on the Web. You access and view Web pages using a software program called a Web browser, or browser.

The Web pages that comprise a Web site are stored on a server, called a Web server. A **Web server** is a computer that

For an overview of the World Wide Web, visit the Teachers Discovering Computers Web site, click Chapter 2, click Web Info, and then click WWW.

FAQ

How does a person or company obtain a domain name?

You register for a domain name from a registrar, which is an organization that maintains a master list of names for a particular top-level domain, .com, for example. Some registrars also offer Web site hosting.

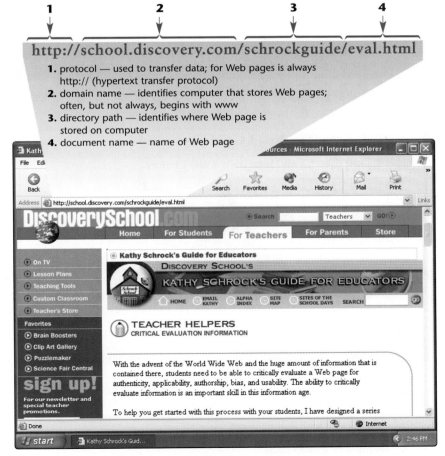

1 2 3 4

http://school.discovery.com/schrockguide/eval.html

1. protocol — used to transfer data; for Web pages is always http:// (hypertext transfer protocol)
2. domain name — identifies computer that stores Web pages; often, but not always, begins with www
3. directory path — identifies where Web page is stored on computer
4. document name — name of Web page

Figure 2-20 The components of a Uniform Resource Locator (URL).

How do I change my Web browser's home page?

To change the home page in Internet Explorer, click Tools on the menu bar, click Internet Options, click the General tab, type or paste the desired Web address, and then click the OK button.

delivers (serves) requested Web pages. For example, when you enter the URL http://www.course.com/tdc.3 in your browser, your browser sends a request to the server whose domain name is course.com. The server then fetches the page named tdc3 and sends it to your browser.

Web servers can store multiple Web sites. For example, many Internet service providers grant their subscribers storage space on a Web server for their personal, school, or company Web site.

HOW A WEB PAGE WORKS

A Web page [Figure 2-21] is a hypertext or hypermedia document residing on an Internet computer that can contain text, graphics, video, and sound. A **hypertext** document contains text hyperlinks to other documents. A **hypermedia** document contains text, graphics, video, or sound hyperlinks that connect to other documents.

Three types of hyperlinks exist. **Target hyperlinks** link to another location in the same document. **Relative hyperlinks** link to another document on the same Internet computer. **Absolute hyperlinks** link to another document on a different Internet computer that could be across the country or across the world.

Hypertext and hypermedia allow students to learn in a nonlinear way. Reading a book from cover to cover is a linear way of learning. Branching off and investigating related topics as you encounter them is a nonlinear way of learning, also known as **discovery learning**. For example, as a student, you might learn about geology and want to learn more about mining. On the Web, you can click different links to access documents about mining, which then might stimulate your interest in old mining towns. You then could take a virtual tour and explore an old mining town, which might inspire you to read about a particular person who made his or her fortune in mining. The discovery learning experience described in this example — in which students branch from one related topic to another in a nonlinear fashion — is powerful and effective.

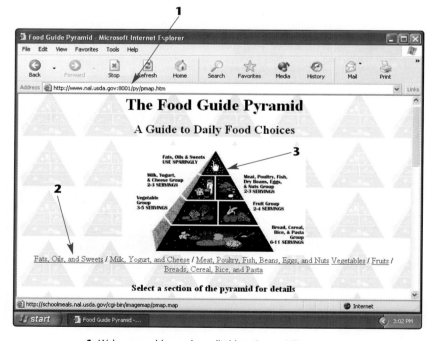

1. Web page address; also called location or URL
2. different color indicates document associated with this hypertext link has been viewed
3. pointer positioned over a hypertext link changes shape to a hand with a pointing finger

Figure 2-21 An example of a Web page.

The Web's capability to support such learning makes it an interesting place to explore and positions it as a valuable tool for teaching and learning. Exploration offers great opportunities for discovery learning. As students' interest inspires them to learn more, the Web allows them to continue to explore for additional sources of information on any given topic. **Web surfing** is displaying pages from one Web site after another and is like using a remote control to jump from one TV channel to another.

A **Webmaster** is the person responsible for developing Web pages and maintaining a Web site. Webmasters and other Web page developers create and format Web pages using **Hypertext Markup Language (HTML),** which is a set of special codes, called **tags,** that define the placement and format of text, graphics, video, and sound on a Web page. Because HTML can be difficult to learn and use, many other user-friendly tools exist for **Web publishing,** which is the development and maintenance of Web pages. Today, many teachers are utilizing user-friendly programs, such as Dreamweaver, FrontPage, Microsoft Word, Microsoft Publisher, Netscape Composer, AppleWorks, and many other programs to publish and maintain their own classroom Web pages [Figure 2-22a]. You will learn how to create your own Web page using Microsoft Word in Chapter 3. You also will learn how to create and integrate curriculum pages into your lesson plans in Chapters 6 and 7.

WEB BROWSER SOFTWARE

As just discussed, you access and view Web pages using a software program called a Web browser. A **Web browser,** or **browser,** is a program that interprets HTML and displays Web pages and enables you to link to other Web pages and Web sites. Figure 2-22b shows the HTML source document used to create the teacher's Web page shown in Figure 2-22a. Your Web browser translates the source document with HTML tags into a functional and beautiful Web page.

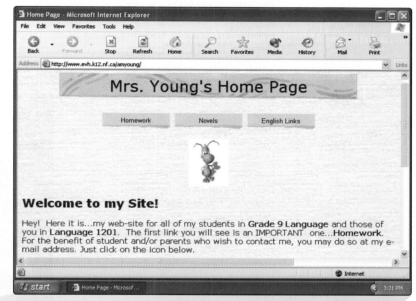

[a] A teacher's classroom Web page.

Figure 2-22 The HTML code [Figure 2-22b] for the top portion of the Web page shown in Figure 2-22a. Web browser software interprets the HTML tags and displays the text, graphics, and hyperlinks.

[b] HTML source document.

To access an interactive tutorial on using Netscape, visit the Teachers Discovering Computers Web site, click Chapter 2, click Web Info, and then click Netscape.

To access an interactive tutorial on using Internet Explorer, visit the Teachers Discovering Computers Web site, click Chapter 2, click Web Info, and then click Explorer.

The first Web browsers used only text commands and displayed only text-based documents. In 1993, Marc Andreessen, a student at the University of Illinois, created a graphical Web browser called Mosaic. **Mosaic** displayed documents that included graphics and used a graphical interface. The graphical interface made it easier and more enjoyable to view Web documents and contributed to the rapid growth of the Web. Andreessen later developed the Netscape Navigator Web browser.

Before you can use a Web browser to view pages on the World Wide Web, your computer has to connect to the Internet through an Internet service provider or online service. When the browser program opens, it retrieves and displays a home page [Figure 2-23]. As discussed earlier, a home page often is used to describe the first page at a Web site. The same term describes the Web page designated as the page to display each time you start your browser. Most browsers utilize the manufacturer's Web page as the default home page, but you may change your browser's home page at any time. Many teachers, for example, set their browsers to display their school's home page when they start their browser.

Once the browser retrieves a Web page using the page's URL, it can take anywhere from a few seconds to several minutes to display the page on your computer screen. The speed at which a Web page displays depends on the speed of the Internet connection and your computer and the amount of graphics on the Web page. To speed up the display of pages, Web browsers let you turn off the graphics and display text only.

Web-enabled mobile devices such as PDAs and smart phones use a special type of browser called a **microbrowser** [Figure 2-24] designed for small screens and limited computing power. Many Web pages are designed specifically for display on mobile devices.

[a] microbrowser for a Web-enabled PDA

[b] microbrowser for a smart phone

Figure 2-23 Web page displayed in Internet Explorer.

Figure 2-24 Web pages displayed in microbrowsers on a PDA and a smart phone.

Browsers display hyperlinks to other documents either as underlined text of a different color or as a graphical image. When you position the mouse pointer over a hyperlink, the mouse pointer changes to a small hand with a pointing finger. Some browsers also display the URL of the hyperlinked document at the bottom of the screen. You can display the document by clicking the hyperlink with a pointing device or by typing the URL in the location or Address text box of the Web browser. To remind you that you have seen a document, some browsers change the color of a text hyperlink after you click it.

Two ways to keep track of Web pages you have viewed are a history list and a favorites or bookmark list. A **history list** records the pages viewed during the time you are online, also known as a session. If you think you might want to return to a page in a future session, you can record its location with a favorite or bookmark. A **favorite** or **bookmark** consists of the title and URL of a page. Bookmark lists, also called **favorites**, are stored on your computer, and may be used in future Web sessions. Favorites, bookmarks and history lists allow you to display a Web page quickly by clicking the name in the list.

SEARCHING FOR INFORMATION ON THE WEB

Searching for information on the Web can be challenging due to the sheer volume of content on the Web. In addition, no central menu or catalog of Web site content and addresses exists. Many companies, however, do provide search tools and maintain organized directories of Web sites to help you locate specific information. **Search tools** enable users to locate information found at Web sites all over the world [Figure 2-25]. Two basic types of search tools exist: search engines and subject directories.

A **search engine** is a specific type of search tool that finds Web sites, Web pages, and Internet files that match one or more keywords you enter. Some search engines look for simple word matches and others allow for more specific searches on a series of words or an entire phrase. Search engines do not actually search the entire Internet (such a search would take an extremely long time). Instead, they search

an index or database of Internet sites and documents. Search tool companies continuously update their databases. Because of the explosive growth of the Internet and because search engines scan different parts of the Internet and in different ways, performing the same search using different search engines often will yield different results.

Many search engines also provide subject directories. A **subject directory** is a type of search tool that allows users to navigate to areas of interest without having to enter keywords. Surfing subject directories is a simple matter of following the links to the specific topic you are looking for. Subject directories are usually organized in categories such as education, sports, entertainment, or business. The special feature, Guide to WWW Sites and Searching Techniques, at the end of this chapter includes extensive information on using search tools starting on page 2.60. Also included is information on and links to a number of popular educational search tools.

MULTIMEDIA ON THE WEB

Most Web pages include more than just formatted text and hyperlinks. In fact, some of the more exciting Web developments involve **multimedia**, which is the combination of graphics, animation, audio, video, and virtual reality (VR). A Web

WEB INFO

To access an interactive tutorial on using bookmarks, visit the Teachers Discovering Computers Web site, click Chapter 2, click Web Info, and then click Bookmarks.

WEB INFO

For links to many popular education-related search engines, visit the Teachers Discovering Computers Web site, click Chapter 2, click Web Info, and then click Education Search Engines.

Figure 2-25 Google is a popular search engine.

page that incorporates color, sound, motion, and pictures with text has much more appeal than one with text on a plain background. Combining text, audio, video, animation, and sound brings a Web page to life, increases the types of information available on the Web; expands the Web's potential uses; and makes the Internet a more entertaining place to explore. Although multimedia Web pages often require more time to open because they contain large files such as video or audio clips, the pages usually are worth the wait.

Most browsers have the capability to display basic multimedia elements on a Web page. Sometimes, however, your browser needs an additional program called a **plug-in**, which extends the capability of the browser.

You can download or copy plug-ins free from many Web sites [Figure 2-26]. In fact, Web pages that use multimedia elements often include links to Web sites containing the required plug-in. Most browsers include commonly used plug-ins, but users often have to update their browsers as new plug-ins become available. Some plug-ins run on mobile devices as well as computers. Others have special versions for mobile devices.

Popular Plug-In Applications

	Plug-In Applications	Description	Web Site
▶ Get Acrobat Reader free!	**Acrobat Reader**	View, navigate, and print Portable Document Format (PDF) files — documents formatted to look on screen just as they look in print	www.adobe.com
INSTALL NOW	**Flash Player**	View dazzling graphics and animation, hear outstanding sound and music, display Web pages across an entire screen	macromedia.com
Liquid Player Six	**Liquid Player**	Listen to and purchase CD-quality music tracks and audio CDs over the Internet; burn CDs; access MP3 files	liquidaudio.com
Q	**QuickTime**	View animation, music, audio, video, and VR panoramas and objects directly in a Web page	apple.com
real ①NE PLAYER	**RealOne Player**	Listen to live and on-demand near-CD-quality audio and newscast-quality video; stream audio and video content for faster viewing; play MP3 files; create music CDs	real.com
INSTALL NOW	**Shockwave Player**	Experience dynamic interactive multimedia, 3-D graphics, and streaming audio	macromedia.com
Windows Media Player	**Windows Media Player**	Listen to live and on-demand audio; play or edit WMA and MP3 files; burn CDs; watch DVD movies	microsoft.com

Figure 2-26 Plug-ins can extend the multimedia capability of Web browsers. Users usually can download them free from the manufacturers' sites.

The following sections discuss multimedia Web developments in the areas of graphics, animation, audio, video, and virtual reality.

GRAPHICS   Graphics were the first medium used to enhance the text-based Internet. The introduction of graphical Web browsers allowed Web page developers to incorporate illustrations, logos, and other images into Web pages. Today, many Web pages use colorful graphical designs and images to convey messages [Figure 2-27].

Two common file formats for graphical images found on the Web are JPEG (pronounced JAY-peg) and GIF (pronounced jiff or giff). Figure 2-28 lists these and other file formats used on the Internet.

The Web contains thousands of image files on countless subjects that you can download at no cost and use for noncommercial purposes. Because some graphical files can be time-consuming to download, some Web sites use thumbnails on their pages. A **thumbnail** is a small version of a larger graphical image that usually you can click to display the full-sized image [Figure 2-29 on the next page].

ANIMATION   Animation is the appearance of motion created by displaying a series of still images in rapid sequence. Animated

Figure 2-27 Many Web pages use colorful graphic designs and images to convey their messages.

Common Graphics Formats Used on the Internet

Acronym	Name	File Extension
BMP	Bit map	.bmp
GIF (pronounced JIFF or GIFF)	Graphics Interchange Format	.gif
JPEG (pronounced JAY-peg)	Joint Photographic Experts Group	.jpg
PCX	PC Paintbrush	.pcx
PNG (pronounced ping)	Portable Network Graphics	.png
TIFF	Tagged Image File Format	.tif

Figure 2-28 Graphics formats used on the Internet.

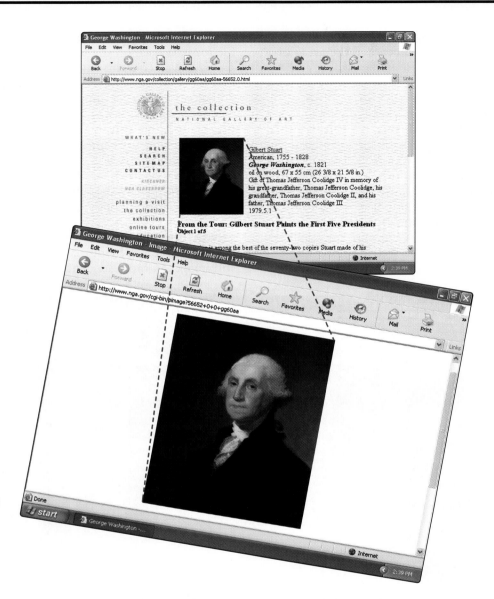

Figure 2-29 After the visitor clicks the thumbnail of the George Washington painting in the top screen, a full-sized image of the painting appears in a separate window.

FAQ

How long does it take to download a single song?

Depending on the speed of your Internet connection and the size of the file, a single song can take from one to eight minutes to download.

graphics make Web pages visually more interesting and draw attention to important information or links. For example, text that is animated to scroll across the screen, called a **marquee** (pronounced mar-KEE), can serve as a ticker to display stock updates, news, school sports scores and events, or weather.

One popular type of animation, called an **animated GIF**, is a group of several images combined into a single GIF file. An abundance of education-related animations are available on the Web, many that you can download or copy at no cost.

AUDIO On the Web, you can listen to prerecorded audio clips and live audio. **Audio** is music, speech, or any other sound. Simple Web audio applications consist of individual sound files that are available for downloading to a computer. Once downloaded, you can play or listen to the contents of these files. Audio files exist in a variety of formats, including MP3, WAV, WMA (Windows Media Audio), MPEG, RealAudio, and QuickTime. Audio files are compressed to reduce their file sizes. For example, the MP3 format reduces an audio file to about one-tenth of its original size, while preserving the original quality of the sound.

Controversy concerning copyright infringement has surfaced due to the ease with which music can be transferred across the Internet. Users can download copyrighted music legally only if the copyright holder of the music has granted permission for users to download and play it. Many music publishers allow users to purchase and download an entire CD of music tracks to their hard disk.

Most current operating systems contain a program, called a **player**, that can play audio files on your computer. Windows Media Player, RealOne Player, and Apple QuickTime are popular players. If your player will not play a particular audio format, you can download the necessary player free from the Web.

More advanced Web audio applications use streaming audio. **Streaming** is the process of transferring data in a continuous and even flow. Streaming is important because most users do not have fast enough Internet connections to download large audio files quickly. **Streaming audio** enables you to listen to the sound file as it downloads to your computer.

Many radio and television stations use streaming audio to broadcast music, interviews, talk shows, sporting events, music videos, news, live concerts, and other segments [Figure 2-30].

VIDEO Video consists of full-motion images that are played back at various speeds. Many Web sites include real-time video to enhance your understanding of information or for entertainment [Figure 2-31].

Figure 2-30 Many radio and television stations use streaming audio to broadcast programs. This figure shows a National Public Radio news report playing in Windows Media Player.

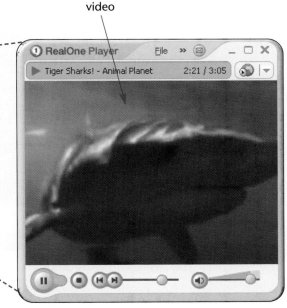

Figure 2-31 A video broadcast from the Animal Planet television channel Web site playing in RealOne Player.

Like audio, simple Web video applications consist of individual video files, such as movies or television clips, that a user must download completely before viewing. Because video segments usually are large and take a long time to download, they often are short.

Streaming video allows you to view longer or live video images as the video file downloads to your computer. Windows Media Player, RealOne Player, and Apple QuickTime also can play downloaded or streaming video files.

Streaming video has the potential to create new possibilities for learning. As the speed of the Internet increases dramatically over the next few years, students from even the most remote schools will have access to thousands of full-motion videos from all over the world.

VIRTUAL REALITY   Virtual reality (VR) is the simulation of a real or imagined environment that appears as a three-dimensional (3-D) space. On the Web, VR involves the display of 3-D images that you can explore and manipulate interactively. Using special VR software, a Web developer can create an entire 3-D site that contains infinite space and depth called a **VR world**. A VR world, for example, might show a room with furniture. You can walk through such a VR room by moving your pointing device forward, backward, or to the side. To view a VR world, you may need to update your Web browser by downloading a VR plug-in program.

Games are a popular use of virtual reality, but VR has many practical applications as well. Companies can use VR to showcase products or create advertisements. Architects create VR models of buildings and rooms to show their clients how a construction project will look before construction begins. Virtual reality also opens up a world of learning opportunities. Science educators, for example, can create VR models of molecules, organisms, and other structures for students to examine [Figure 2-32]. Students also can take virtual tours of historic sites located all over the world. Several schools even use VR to allow parents to take a virtual tour of the school from their home.

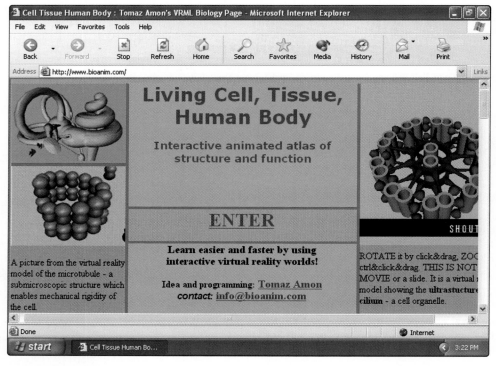

Figure 2-32 This instructional Web site uses VR to teach biology students about cells and body tissue.

Other Internet Services

Although the World Wide Web is the most talked about service on the Internet, many other Internet services are available. These services include e-mail, FTP, newsgroups and message boards, mailing lists, chat rooms, instant messaging, and short message service. Each of these services is discussed in the following sections.

E-MAIL

E-mail (**electronic mail**) is the transmission of messages and files via a computer network. E-mail was one of the original features of the Internet, enabling scientists and researchers working on government-sponsored projects to communicate with their colleagues at other locations. Today, e-mail enables administrators, teachers, and students to communicate with millions of Internet users all over the world. E-mail has become a primary communications method for both personal and business use.

Using an **e-mail program**, you can create, send, receive, forward, store, print, and delete messages. E-mail messages can be simple text or can include attachments such as word processing documents, graphics, audio or video clips, and even family pictures [Figure 2-33].

When you receive an e-mail message, your Internet service provider's software places the message in your personal mailbox. Your **mailbox** is a storage location usually residing on your computer that connects you to the Internet, such as the server operated by your ISP. A **mail server** is a server that contains user's mailboxes and associated e-mail messages. Most ISPs and online services provide an Internet e-mail program and a mailbox on a mail server as a standard part of their Internet access services. You also can use free e-mail services such as Hotmail or Yahoo! Mail.

An **e-mail address** is a combination of a user name and a domain name that identifies the user so he or she can receive messages [Figure 2-34]. Your **user name** is a unique combination of characters that identifies you, and it must differ from other user names located on the same mail server. Your user name sometimes is limited to eight characters and often is a combination of your first and last names, such as the initial of your first name plus your last name. You may choose a nickname or any combination of characters for your user name, but unusual combinations may be harder to remember.

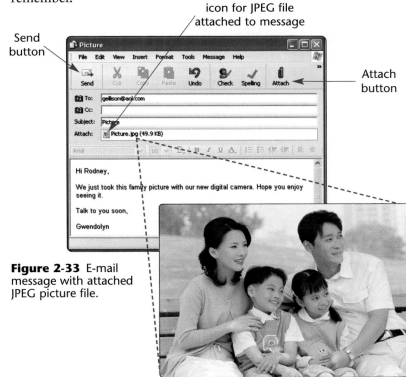

Figure 2-33 E-mail message with attached JPEG picture file.

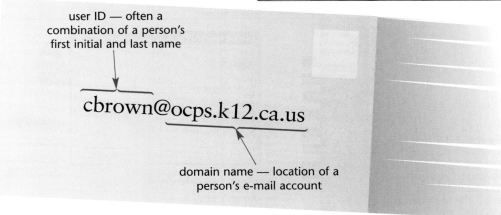

Figure 2-34 An example of an Internet e-mail address. Sometimes, the underscore character or a period separates sections of the user's name; for example, cindy_brown@ocps.k12.ca.us.

Although no complete listing of Internet e-mail addresses exists, several Internet sites list addresses collected from public sources. These sites also allow you to list your e-mail address voluntarily so others may find it. The site might prompt you for other information, such as the high school or college from which you graduated, so others can determine if you are the person they want to reach.

FTP

File Transfer Protocol (FTP) is an Internet standard that allows you to exchange files with other computers on the Internet. For example, if you click a link on a Web page in your browser window that begins to download a file to your hard disk, you probably are using FTP [Figure 2-35].

An **FTP server** is a computer that allows users to upload and download files using FTP. An FTP server contains one or more FTP sites. An **FTP site** is a collection of files including text, graphics, audio, video, and program files. Some FTP sites limit file transfers to individuals who have authorized accounts (user names and passwords) on the FTP server. Many corporations, for example, maintain FTP sites for their employees.

Other FTP sites allow **anonymous FTP**, whereby anyone can transfer some, if not all, available files. Many educational sites, for example, have FTP sites that use anonymous FTP to allow educators to download

lesson plans and other files. Many program files located on anonymous FTP sites are freeware or shareware programs. Many FTP sites allow users to download educational and other application software for a free 30-day evaluation period. This allows teachers, administrators, and other users to evaluate software for content and appropriateness before purchasing.

To view or use an FTP file, first you must **download**, or copy, it to your computer. In most cases, you click the file name to begin the download procedure. Large files on FTP sites often are compressed to reduce storage space and download transfer time. Before you use a compressed file, you must expand it with a decompression program, such as WinZip or Stuffit. Such programs usually are available at the FTP site or are packaged with the file you download.

In some cases, you may want to **upload**, or copy, a file to an FTP site. For example, once you create a personal Web page, you need to upload the Web page from your computer to the Web server that will store your Web page. To upload files from your computer to an FTP site, you use an FTP program. Many Internet service providers include an FTP program when you subscribe to their service. Several FTP programs also are available on the Web. In addition, many operating systems such as Windows XP have built-in FTP capabilities.

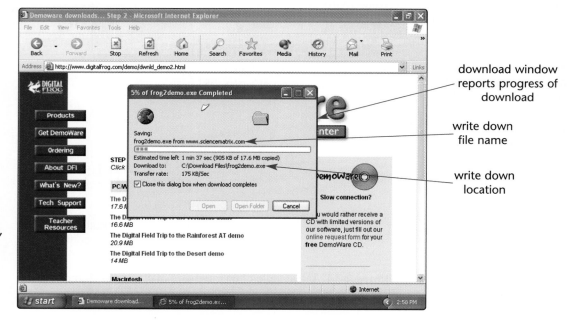

Figure 2-35
To ensure you can find the file when the download is complete, you should write down the file's name and the location on the hard disk on which the file is being saved.

NEWSGROUPS AND MESSAGE BOARDS

A **newsgroup** is an online area in which users conduct written discussions about a particular subject. To participate in a discussion, a user sends a message to the newsgroup and other users in the newsgroup read and reply to the message. The entire collection of Internet newsgroups is called **Usenet**, which contains thousands of newsgroups on a multitude of topics. Some major topic areas include education, news, recreation, business, and computers.

A **news server** is a computer that stores and distributes newsgroup messages. Most universities, corporations, ISPs, online services, and other large organizations have a news server. Some newsgroups require you to enter your user name and password to participate in the discussion. These types of newsgroups are used when the messages on the newsgroup are to be viewed only by authorized members, such as students taking a college course.

To participate in a newsgroup, you must use a program called a **newsreader**, which is included with most browsers. The newsreader enables you to access a newsgroup to read a previously entered message, called an **article** and add an article of your own, called **posting**.

A newsreader also keeps track of which articles you have and have not read.

Newsgroup members often post articles as a reply to another article — either to answer a question or to comment on material in the original article. These replies often cause the author of the original article, or others, to post additional articles related to the original article. The original article and all subsequent related replies are called a **thread** or **threaded discussion**. A thread can be short-lived or continue for some time, depending on the nature of the topic and the interest of the participants.

Using the newsreader, you can search for newsgroups discussing a particular subject, such as a type of musical instrument, brand of sports equipment, or educational topic. If you like the discussion in a particular newsgroup, you can **subscribe** to it, which means your newsreader saves the location so you can access it easily in the future.

A popular Web-based type of discussion group that does not require a newsreader is a message board. **Message boards** also are called discussion boards and typically are easier to use than newsgroups. Many Web sites provide message boards for their users [Figure 2-36].

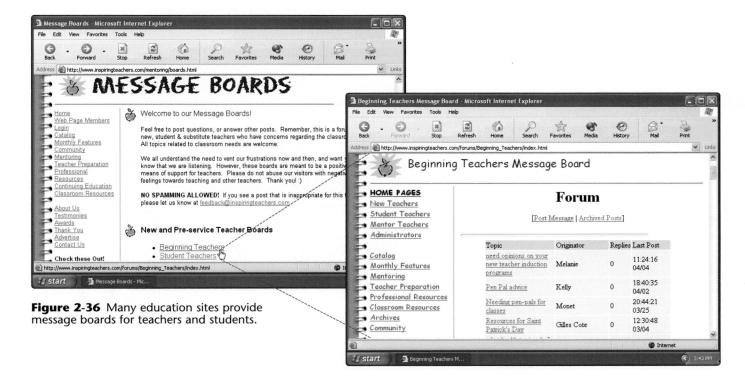

Figure 2-36 Many education sites provide message boards for teachers and students.

MAILING LISTS

A **mailing list** is a group of e-mail names and addresses given a single name. When a user sends a message to a mailing list, every person on the list receives a copy of the message in his or her mailbox. To add your e-mail name and address to a mailing list, you subscribe to it; to remove your name, you **unsubscribe** from the mailing list. **LISTSERV** is a popular software program used to manage many educational mailing lists.

The basic difference between a newsgroup and a mailing list is that users on the mailing list discuss topics using e-mail, whereas newsgroup members use a newsreader for discussions. Thousands of mailing lists exist on a variety of topics in areas of entertainment, business, computers, society, culture, health, recreation, and education. To locate a mailing list dealing with a particular topic, you can use your Web browser to search for mailing lists or LISTSERV.

CHAT ROOMS

A **chat** is a real-time typed conversation that takes place on a computer. **Real time** means that something occurs immediately. With chat, when you enter a line of text on your computer screen, your words immediately display on one or more participant's screens. To conduct a chat, you and the people with whom you are conversing must be online at the same time.

A **chat room** refers to the communications medium, or channel, that permits users to chat with each other. Anyone on the channel can participate in the conversation, which usually deals with a specific topic.

To start a chat session, you must connect to a chat server through a **chat client**, which is a program on your computer. Today's browsers usually include a chat client. If yours does not, you can download a chat client from the Web. Some chat clients are text-based only, while others support graphical and text-based chats. Some chat rooms support voice or video chats that allow users to hear and see each other.

Once you install a chat client, you then can create or join a conversation on a chat server. The channel name should indicate the topic of discussion. The person who creates a channel acts as the channel operator and has responsibility for monitoring the conversation and disconnecting anyone who becomes disruptive. Users can share operator status or transfer operator status to someone else.

Numerous controlled and monitored chat rooms are available for K-12 students and teachers. Several Web sites also exist for the purpose of conducting chats. Some chat sites even allow participants to assume the role or appearance of a character [Figure 2-37].

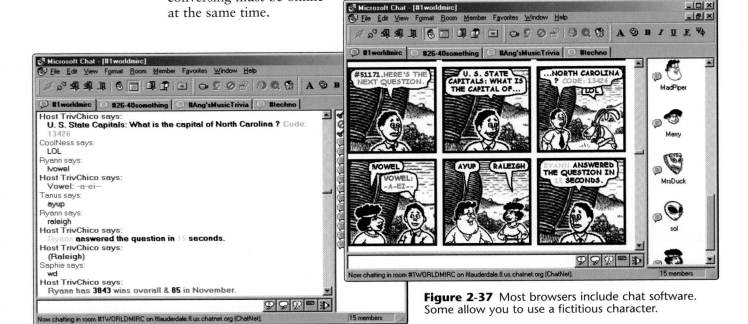

Figure 2-37 Most browsers include chat software. Some allow you to use a fictitious character.

INSTANT MESSAGING

Instant messaging (IM) is a real-time Internet communications service that notifies you when one or more people are online and then allows you to exchange messages or files, or join a private chat room with them [Figure 2-38]. Many IM services also can alert you to information, such as calendar appointments, stock quotes, weather, or sport scores.

People use IM on all types of computers, including handheld computers and Web-enabled devices. While popular with all age groups, instant messaging services such as AOL Instant Messenger have become a staple of teenage life for tens of millions of middle and high school students from all around the world.

SHORT MESSAGE SERVICE

Short message service (SMS) is a means for smart phone, cellular telephone, or PDA users to send and receive brief text messages on their Web-enabled devices. Most SMS messages have a limit of about 160 characters per message. Students and other users around the world send millions of text messages daily.

Netiquette

Netiquette, which is short for **Internet etiquette,** is the code of acceptable behaviors users should follow while on the Internet; that is, the conduct expected of individuals while online. Netiquette includes rules for all aspects of the Internet, including the Web, e-mail, FTP, newsgroups and message boards, chat rooms, and instant messaging. Figure 2-39 on the next page outlines the rules of netiquette.

Internet Security

Any time a school district or business connects its private network to a public network such as the Internet, it must consider security concerns such as unauthorized access to confidential information. To prevent unauthorized access, schools and businesses implement one or more layers of security. A **firewall** is a general

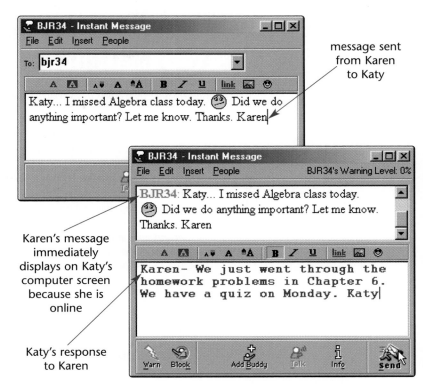

message sent from Karen to Katy

Karen's message immediately displays on Katy's computer screen because she is online

Katy's response to Karen

Figure 2-38 Instant messaging is a very popular means of communications used by today's teenagers.

term that refers to both hardware and software used to restrict access to data on a network. Firewalls deny network access to unauthorized personnel. For example, firewalls restrict students from access to inappropriate materials or sensitive information such as student grades and attendance records.

Even with netiquette guidelines, the Internet still opens up the possibility for inappropriate behaviors and content. For example, amidst the wealth of information and services on the Internet, some content may be inappropriate for certain people. Some Web sites, newsgroups, and chat rooms, for instance, contain content or discussions that are unsuitable for children. Schools need to ensure that students do not gain access to inappropriate or objectionable materials.

To assist schools and parents with these types of issues, many browsers include software that can screen out unacceptable content. You also can purchase stand-alone Internet **filtering software,** which allows parents, teachers, and others to block access to certain materials on the Internet.

WEB INFO

For more information about filtering software, visit the Teachers Discovering Computers Web site, click Chapter 2, click Web Info, and then click Filtering Software.

 **Netiquette**

Golden Rule: *Treat others as you would like them to treat you.*

1. In e-mail, newsgroups, and chat rooms:
   - Keep messages brief using proper grammar and spelling.
   - Be careful when using sarcasm and humor, as it might be misinterpreted.
   - Be polite. Avoid offensive language.
   - Avoid sending or posting **flames**, which are abusive or insulting messages. Do not participate in **flame wars**, which are exchanges of flames.
   - Avoid sending spam, which is the Internet's version of junk mail. **Spam** is an unsolicited e-mail message or newsgroup posting sent to many recipients or newsgroups at once.
   - Do not use all capital letters, which is the equivalent of SHOUTING!
   - Use **emoticons** to express emotion. Popular emoticons include

:)	Smile
:(	Frown
:|	Indifference
:\	Undecided
:o	Surprised

   - Use abbreviations and acronyms for phrases such as

BTW	by the way
FYI	for your information
FWIW	for what it's worth
IMHO	in my humble opinion
TTFN	ta ta for now
TYVM	thank you very much

   - Clearly identify a **spoiler**, which is a message that reveals a solution to a game or ending to a movie or program.

2. Read the **FAQ** (frequently asked questions) document, if one exists. Many newsgroups and Web pages have an FAQ.

3. Use your user name for your personal use only.

4. Do not assume material is accurate or up to date. Be forgiving of other's mistakes.

5. Never read someone's private e-mail.

Figure 2-39 The rules of netiquette.

WEB INFO

For more information about Acceptable Use Policy (AUP), visit the Teachers Discovering Computers Web site, click Chapter 2, click Web Info, and then click AUP.

Schools help protect students from the negative aspects of the Internet by using filtering software, firewalls, and teacher observation. Most schools also use an **Acceptable Use Policy (AUP)**, which is an outline of user standards that reminds teachers, students, and parents that they are guests on the Internet and that they need to use it appropriately. Most schools require students, teachers, and parents to sign AUPs. These and other security issues will be discussed in greater detail in Chapter 8.

The Impact of the Internet and the World Wide Web on Education

More than 500 years ago, Johannes Gutenberg developed a printing press that made the written word accessible to the public and revolutionized the way people shared information. The World Wide Web is the Gutenberg printing press of modern times — opening doors to new learning resources and opportunities and allowing the sharing of information and knowledge such as never before. Just a few years ago, most students were unable to visit the Library of Congress, the White House, the Smithsonian Institution, the National Art Gallery, or the Louvre Museum. Today, students around the world can visit these historic places and thousands of others on the Web, exploring these locales on interactive and sometimes even virtual tours.

Not only does the Internet provide access to extensive text and multimedia resources, it also allows teachers and students to communicate with other teachers and students all over the world. For example, **ePALS** Classroom Exchange is a project designed to enable students to develop an understanding of different cultures through student e-mail exchanges [Figure 2-40]. The mission of ePALS is to have students creatively write in primary and secondary languages, as well as do research and gather information about other cultures and individuals. Project ePALS is adaptable for any grade level in any country.

As the Internet expanded and evolved from a text-based communications system into the powerful multimedia communications system of today, educators quickly recognized the tremendous potential of the Internet — and especially the Web — to revolutionize the classroom. By providing a variety of learning tools, the Internet and the Web are transforming the way teachers instruct and the way students learn basic skills and core subjects. These changes have brought the Web to the forefront of instructional strategies in education in a very short period.

The potential of the Web for improving the way to teach K-12 students is enormous, is still growing, and will continue to expand for many years to come.

Throughout this textbook, hundreds of links and dozens of exercises will help you understand the incredible possibilities the Web offers for K-12 education in general and your classroom in particular.

WEB INFO

For more information about ePALS, visit the Teachers Discovering Computers Web site, click Chapter 2, click Web Info, and then click ePALS.

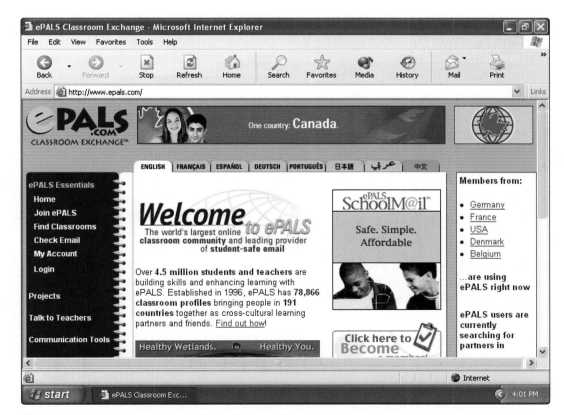

Figure 2-40 An online project, ePals, allows millions of students from all over the world to communicate with each other.

The Future of the Internet and the World Wide Web

What is the future of the Internet and the World Wide Web? Without question, the Web will continue to evolve as a primary communications channel for people around the world. As the Web grows in size and operates at higher speeds, it will continue to have a major influence on restructuring K-12 education. Other predictions regarding the future of the Internet and the World Wide Web and its impact on education include the following:

- In the next few years, the Internet will connect 80 percent of the world's computers.

- By the middle of this decade, more than a billion wireless communication devices will be in use worldwide, and many of these products will have the ability to access the Web wirelessly.

- All K-12 teachers will have access to the Internet in their classrooms.

- Wireless networks, wireless notebook computers, wireless mobile labs, wireless Tablet PCs, and other wireless devices will become commonplace in K-12 education.

- Everyday home and office appliances and other devices that use embedded computers, such as automobiles, will have built-in Internet access capabilities.

- Web search capabilities will be more intelligent and focused.

- Within a few years, the Web will operate at speeds 100 to 1,000 times faster than today.

- Businesses will continue to be the driving force behind the Web's expansion.

- Increased access speeds and greater availability will allow teachers and students to view thousands of full-motion videos over the Web.

- The Web will become an integral part of all education and will revolutionize the way students learn core subjects.

Finally, many experts believe that separate, proprietary networks used for telephone, television, and radio will merge with the Internet. Eventually, a single, integrated network will exist, made up of many different media that will carry all communications traffic.

Guide to World Wide Web Sites and Searching Techniques

At the end of this chapter is a special feature that contains links to and information about more than 150 popular up-to-date Web sites. This special feature also introduces you to using search tools and contains links and information on popular education-specific search tools.

The best way to learn how to use the Internet and the World Wide Web is to log on and explore. Choose a subject and use a search tool to see what is on the World Wide Web. To display this interactive special feature, click Guide to WWW Sites on the left sidebar at the textbook Web site [Figure 2-41]. Click the links to access the various Web sites and search tools.

FAQ

What is Wi-Fi?

Wi-Fi is wireless fidelity and outlines standards for wireless technology. To learn more about Wi-Fi and the wireless revolution, review the special feature, A World Without Wires, which follows Chapter 8.

feature selected   Guide to WWW Sites displays   scroll bar

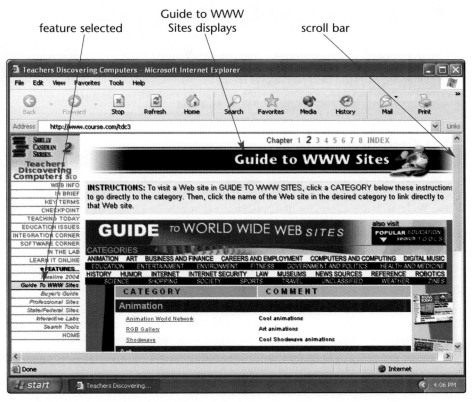

Figure 2-41 Guide to WWW Sites special feature displayed at the textbook Web site.

Summary of Communications, Networks, the Internet, and the World Wide Web

Communications will continue to impact how you work, learn, teach, access information, and use computers. Because of communications technology, individuals, schools, and organizations no longer are limited to local data resources; they can obtain information instantly from anywhere in the world. Communications networks are just one way that school

districts will use communications technology to meet current instructional and management challenges. In just a few years, the Internet and World Wide Web may redefine education, just as it has transformed modern businesses and today's society. As educators all over the world integrate the Internet and the World Wide Web into their classroom curricula, their efforts are effecting an educational revolution in today's schools — one that is having a significant positive impact on the quality of graduating students.

In Brief

Web Instructions: To display this page from the Web, start your browser and enter the URL, www.course.com/tdc3. Click Chapter 2 at the top of the Web page and then click In Brief on the left sidebar. Click the links for current and additional information. To listen to an audio version of this In Brief, click the Audio button to the top left of these instructions.

WEB INFO

IN BRIEF

KEY TERMS

CHECKPOINT

TEACHING TODAY

EDUCATION ISSUES

INTEGRATION CORNER

SOFTWARE CORNER

IN THE LAB

LEARN IT ONLINE

✱ FEATURES...

Timeline 2004

Guide to WWW Sites

Buyer's Guide 2004

Professional Sites

State/Federal Sites

Interactive Labs

Search Tools

HOME

1. What Is Communications?

Communications, sometimes called **telecommunications**, refers to the transmission of data and information between two or more computers using a communications channel. **Electronic mail (e-mail)**, **voice mail**, **facsimile (fax)**, **telecommuting**, **online services**, **videoconferencing**, the **Internet**, and the **World Wide Web** are examples of applications that rely on communications technology.

2. Communications Networks

A communications **network** is a collection of computers and other equipment organized to share data, information, hardware, and software. Networks also require **communications software**.

3. Local and Wide Area Networks

A **local area network** (**LAN**) is a communications network that covers a limited geographical area such as a school, an office, a building, or a group of buildings. A LAN consists of a number of computers connected to a central computer, or server. A **wide area network** (**WAN**) covers a large geographical region (such as a city or school district) and uses regular telephone cables, digital lines, microwaves, wireless systems, and satellites.

4. Benefits of Computer Networks

One benefit of networking is that administrators, teachers, and students can share computer hardware, software, and data resources. The most important benefit of networking school computers is that administrators, teachers, and students instantly can access the unlimited educational resources available on the Internet and communicate with other educators and students all over the world.

5. The Internet

The **Internet** is a worldwide collection of networks that link together millions of businesses, governments, educational institutions, and individuals via modems, telephone lines, and other communications devices and media. Each of these networks provides resources and data that add to the abundance of goods, services, and information accessible via the Internet.

6. How the Internet Works

The Internet operates by dividing data into separate parts, called **packets**, and sending the packets along the best route available to a destination computer. The software used to perform this technique, called **packet switching**, is a communications protocol named **transmission control protocol/Internet protocol** (**TCP/IP**). People can connect to the Internet through an organization such as a school or company, an **online service provider** (**OSP**), or an **Internet service provider** (**ISP**).

7. The World Wide Web

The **World Wide Web**, or simply **Web**, consists of a worldwide collection of electronic documents that have built-in hyperlinks to other related documents. These **hyperlinks**, also called **links**, allow users to navigate quickly from one Web page to another, regardless of whether the Web pages are located on the same computer or on different computers in different countries.

8. How a Web Page Works

A **Web page** is an electronic document viewed on the Web. A Web page is a **hypertext** document (document with text hyperlinks) or **hypermedia** document (document with text, graphics, video, or sound hyperlinks) residing on an Internet computer. The three types of hyperlinks are **target hyperlinks** that move from one location in a document to another location in the same document; **relative hyperlinks** that move from one document to another document on the same Internet

In Brief

WEB INFO

IN BRIEF

KEY TERMS

CHECKPOINT

TEACHING TODAY

EDUCATION ISSUES

INTEGRATION CORNER

SOFTWARE CORNER

IN THE LAB

LEARN IT ONLINE

✱ FEATURES...

Timeline 2004

Guide to WWW Sites

Buyer's Guide 2004

Professional Sites

State/Federal Sites

Interactive Labs

Search Tools

HOME

computer; and **absolute hyperlinks** that move from one document to another document on a different Internet computer. Displaying pages from one Web site after another is called **Web surfing**. Web pages are created using **Hypertext Markup Language (HTML)**, which is a set of special instructions that specifies links to other documents and how the page is displayed.

9. Web Browser Software

Web browser software is a program that interprets and displays Web pages and enables you to link to other Web pages. Each time a browser is started, a **home page** appears. The browser retrieves Web pages using a **Uniform Resource Locator (URL)**, which is an address that points to a specific resource on the Internet. Browsers display hyperlinks either as underlined text of a different color or as graphical images. A linked document can be displayed by clicking the hyperlink or by typing its URL in the location or Address text box.

10. Web Search Tools

Search tools enable users to locate information found at Web sites all over the world. Two basic types of search tools exist: search engines and subject directories. A **search engine** is a specific type of search tool that finds Web sites, Web pages, and Internet files that match one or more keywords you enter. A **subject directory** allows users to navigate to areas of interest without having to enter keywords.

11. Multimedia on the Web

Some of the more exciting Web developments involve multimedia. Most browsers have the capability of displaying basic multimedia elements on a Web page. Sometimes, however, the browser needs an additional program called a **plug-in**, which extends the capability of the browser. Web pages may include the following multimedia elements: **graphics**, **animation**, **audio**, **video**, and **virtual reality (VR)**.

12. Other Internet Services

Although the Web is the most talked about service on the Internet, many other Internet services are available. These services include e-mail, FTP, newsgroups and message boards, mailing lists, chat rooms, instant messaging, and short message service (SMS). **E-mail (electronic mail)** is the transmission of messages and files via a computer network. **File transfer protocol (FTP)** is an Internet standard that allows you to exchange files with other computers on the Internet. A **newsgroup** is an online area in which users conduct written discussions about a particular subject. A **chat** is a real-time typed conversation that takes place on a computer. **Instant messaging (IM)** is a real-time Internet communications service that notifies you when one or more people are online, and then allows you to exchange messages. **Short message service (SMS)** is a means for smart phone, cellular telephone, or PDA users to send and receive brief text messages.

13. Netiquette and Security

Netiquette is the code of acceptable behaviors users should follow while on the Internet. To prevent unauthorized access, schools and businesses implement one or more layers of security. A **firewall** is a general term that refers to both hardware and software used to restrict access to data on a network. Internet **filtering software** allows parents, teachers, and others to block access to certain materials on the Internet.

Key Terms

Web Instructions: To display this page from the Web, start your browser and enter the URL, www.course.com/tdc3. Click Chapter 2 at the top of the Web page and then click Key Terms on the left sidebar. Scroll through the list of terms. Click a term to display its definition and a picture. Click Key Terms on the left to redisplay the Key Terms page. Click the TO WEB button for current and additional information about the term from the Web.

WEB INFO

IN BRIEF

KEY TERMS

CHECKPOINT

TEACHING TODAY

EDUCATION ISSUES

INTEGRATION CORNER

SOFTWARE CORNER

IN THE LAB

LEARN IT ONLINE

＊ FEATURES...

Timeline 2004

Guide to WWW Sites

Buyer's Guide 2004

Professional Sites

State/Federal Sites

Interactive Labs

Search Tools

HOME

absolute hyperlinks [2.22]
Acceptable Use Policy (AUP) [2.36]
Advanced Research Projects Agency
   (ARPA) [2.13]
analog signal [2.04]
animated GIF [2.28]
animation [2.27]
anonymous FTP [2.32]
ARPANET [2.14]
article [2.33]
audio [2.28]

backbone [2.14]
bandwidth [2.07]
bookmark [2.25]
broadband [2.10]
browser [2.23]

cable modem [2.17]
chat [2.34]
chat client [2.34]
chat room [2.34]
communications [2.03]
communications channel [2.04]
communications protocol [2.16]
communications software [2.04]

dial-up access [2.17]
digital signals [2.04]
digital subscriber line (DSL) [2.18]
discovery learning [2.22]
domain name [2.20]
download [2.32]

e-mail address [2.31]
e-mail program [2.31]
electronic mail (e-mail) [2.31]
emoticons [2.36]
ePALS [2.37]

FAQ [2.36]
favorite [2.25]
File Transfer Protocol (FTP) [2.32]
filtering software [2.35]
firewall [2.35]
flames [2.36]
flame wars [2.36]
FTP server [2.32]
FTP site [2.32]

graphics [2.27]

history list [2.25]
home network [2.06]

home page [2.21]
host [2.14]
http:// [2.21]
hyperlinks [2.21]
hypermedia [2.22]
hypertext [2.22]
Hypertext Markup Language
   (HTML) [2.23]
hypertext transfer protocol [2.21]

instant messaging (IM) [2.35]
internal modem [2.05]
Internet [2.11]
Internet2 [2.15]
Internet backbone [2.18]
Internet etiquette [2.35]
Internet service provider (ISP) [2.16]

links [2.21]
LISTSERV [2.34]
local area network (LAN) [2.06]
local ISP [2.16]

mailbox [2.31]
mailing list [2.34]
mail server [2.31]
marquee [2.28]
message boards [2.33]
microbrowser [2.24]
modem [2.04]
Mosaic [2.24]
multimedia [2.25]

national ISP [2.16]
National Science Foundation (NSF)
   [2.14]
Net [2.11]
netiquette [2.35]
network [2.04]
network interface cards (NICs) [2.06]
newsgroup [2.33]
newsreader [2.33]
news server [2.33]
NSFnet [2.14]

online service provider (OSP) [2.16]

packets [2.15]
packet switching [2.16]
player [2.28]
plug-in [2.26]
posting [2.33]
public Internet access point [2.18]

real time [2.34]
registrar [2.21]
relative hyperlinks [2.22]
routers [2.15]

search engine [2.25]
search tools [2.25]
server [2.06]
short message service (SMS) [2.35]
spam [2.36]
spoiler [2.36]
streaming [2.29]
streaming audio [2.29]
streaming video [2.30]
subject directory [2.25]
subscribe [2.33]

tags [2.23]
target hyperlinks [2.22]
telecommunications [2.03]
thread [2.33]
threaded discussion [2.33]
thumbnail [2.27]
transmission control protocol/
   Internet protocol (TCP/IP) [2.16]
transmission media [2.04]
twisted-pair cable [2.04]

Uniform Resource Locator (URL)
   [2.21]
unsubscribe [2.34]
upload [2.32]
Usenet [2.33]
user name [2.31]

video [2.29]
virtual reality (VR) [2.30]
VR world [2.30]

Web [2.21]
Web browser [2.23]
Webmaster [2.23]
Web page [2.21]
Web publishing [2.23]
Web server [2.21]
Web site [2.21]
Web surfing [2.23]
wide area network (WAN) [2.06]
Wi-Fi [2.38]
wireless LAN (WLAN) [2.06]
wireless service provider [2.16]
World Wide Web [2.21]

Checkpoint

WEB INFO

IN BRIEF

KEY TERMS

CHECKPOINT

TEACHING TODAY

EDUCATION ISSUES

INTEGRATION CORNER

SOFTWARE CORNER

IN THE LAB

LEARN IT ONLINE

✱ FEATURES...

Timeline 2004

Guide to WWW Sites

Buyer's Guide 2004

Professional Sites

State/Federal Sites

Interactive Labs

Search Tools

HOME

Web Instructions: To display this page from the Web, start your browser and enter the URL, www.course.com/tdc3. Click Chapter 2 at the top of the Web page and then click Checkpoint on the left sidebar. Click a blank line for the answer. Click the links for current and additional information.

1. Label the Figure

Instructions: Identify the components of a communications system.

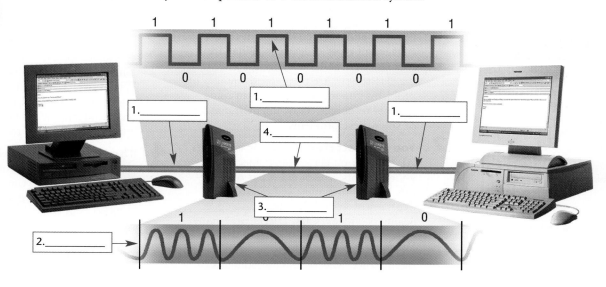

2. Matching

Instructions: Match each term from the column on the left with the best description from the column on the right.

____ 1. e-mail
____ 2. Webmaster
____ 3. network
____ 4. filtering software
____ 5. search tool

a. an individual responsible for developing Web pages and maintaining a Web site
b. a collection of computers and other equipment organized to share data, hardware, and software
c. the transmission of messages and files via a computer network
d. enables users to locate information found at Web sites all over the world
e. allows parents, teachers, and others to block access to certain materials on the Internet

3. Short Answer

Instructions: Write a brief answer to each of the following questions.

1. How are local area networks (LANs) different from wide area networks (WANs)? _____
2. What is a Web page? What purpose do hyperlinks have on a Web page? What is Hypertext Markup Language (HTML)? _____
3. Explain the process of streaming over the Web. How are streaming audio and streaming video similar? For what purposes is streaming used? _____
4. What is a firewall? What is filtering software? What is an Acceptable Use Policy (AUP)? Why is the use of firewalls, filtering software, and AUPs so important for K-12 networks? _____
5. What is a search tool? Name the two basic types of search tools and describe how each of these works. Which would you use to search for links in the category, Education? _____

Teaching Today

Web Instructions: To display this page from the Web, start your browser and enter the URL, www.course.com/tdc3. Click Chapter 2 at the top of the Web page and then click Teaching Today on the left sidebar. Click the links for current and additional information.

WEB INFO

IN BRIEF

KEY TERMS

CHECKPOINT

TEACHING TODAY

EDUCATION ISSUES

INTEGRATION CORNER

SOFTWARE CORNER

IN THE LAB

LEARN IT ONLINE

✱ FEATURES...

Timeline 2004

Guide to WWW Sites

Buyer's Guide 2004

Professional Sites

State/Federal Sites

Interactive Labs

Search Tools

HOME

1. Using the Internet in the classroom has numerous benefits for teachers, who can use it to find current information, online resources for lesson plans and Web-based projects, and interactive content that engages all types of learners. What are some other benefits of using the Internet in the classroom? Are there disadvantages or problems you might encounter in using Internet resources? How might you avoid or solve these problems?

2. You have started using the computer lab to work on classroom projects with your students, which is a great opportunity for all students to get hands-on experiences with different technologies. Scanners, videos, CDs, DVDs, and many other technologies are available from which to choose. Students also can access the Internet. Managing your students in the lab while they explore these different technologies will be a challenge. You decide to design a project so your students will work in groups to research a famous person in history. Do students need guidance on how to use a search engine to perform a proper search? Do they need help to avoid getting lost using the various technologies? Is asking the correct question or questions an important part of the solution for finding the correct answer? What about searching reference materials? Are students using primary and secondary resources? How could you design a plan where the students collaborate to develop effective projects while you still manage a classroom of students working on different projects and technologies? How could you design research projects that go beyond the standard writing of a paper to engage students in using many different types of technologies in a collaborative way?

3. Electronic mail (e-mail) has become a preferred means of communications for many businesses, schools, and individuals. Whether using an internal network or the Internet for e-mail, you should be aware

of netiquette guidelines to help ensure that recipients understand the intent behind your e-mail messages. Some users, for example, add emoticons to an e-mail message to communicate intended emotions (by adding a smiley face to a funny comment, for example). How is using e-mail different from writing a letter? What are the similarities, if any? How might you use e-mail in your classroom with students? What benefits might your students experience from using e-mail?

4. The Internet and Web contain thousands of wonderful sites for educators and students of all ages. Unfortunately, the Web has sites that are inappropriate for children, and some that collect information that invade the privacy of adults and children. The Federal Trade Commission's Children's Online Privacy Protection Act (COPPA) was passed by Congress in October 1998 to protect children from those who would steal personal information. COPPA also provides information on how to locate sites that have been reviewed by experts and rated as safe for children. All teachers, students, and parents should become knowledgeable about the rules and regulations that exist to protect their identity. How can you ensure student privacy on the Internet? As a teacher, what can you do to teach your students about Internet safety, information privacy, and more?

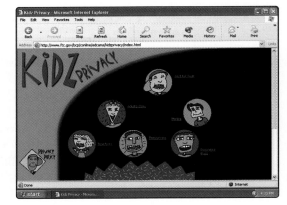

Education Issues

Web Instructions: To display this page from the Web, start your browser and enter the URL, www.course.com/tdc3. Click Chapter 2 at the top of the Web page and then click Education Issues on the left sidebar. Click the links for current and additional information to help you respond to the Education Issues questions.

WEB INFO

IN BRIEF

KEY TERMS

CHECKPOINT

TEACHING TODAY

EDUCATION ISSUES

INTEGRATION CORNER

SOFTWARE CORNER

IN THE LAB

LEARN IT ONLINE

✱ FEATURES...

Timeline 2004

Guide to WWW Sites

Buyer's Guide 2004

Professional Sites

State/Federal Sites

Interactive Labs

Search Tools

HOME

1. Digital Equity

More people are connected to the Internet than ever before, but a large population of users is still not connected. Students do not always have access to technology, the Internet, and World Wide Web and this creates a division between the technology haves and have-nots, known as the digital divide. The National Telecommunications and Information Administration (NTIA) states that the gap between the haves and have-nots is increasing. You design a project that requires your students to work in groups and conduct research on a specific content area. Knowing that only a portion of your students have computers at home, how can you design meaningful homework assignments that take into account students who do not have access to computers or the Internet at home?

2. Online Research Services

When preparing a research report, students often spend a large part of their efforts locating the necessary information. While Internet search tools can help students find relevant information, they often fail to point them to important resources such as journals and books. To ensure that the results of their searches are more comprehensive, some students are turning to Web-based online research services. Visit an online research service to learn about its features. What resources does the service use? How much does it cost? How is using an online research service like using a library? How appropriate is the service for students? Would you want your students using an online research service?

3. Virtual High Schools

Today, many high schools, especially small rural high schools, have difficulty offering classes such as AP biology, Latin, AP calculus, and other similar classes due to budget constraints, classroom overcrowding, lack of qualified teachers, and other important issues. Currently, many school districts and states are addressing these problems by offering a variety of online classes. Most educators agree that the Internet has great potential for education and that online classes need to be part of the K-12 learning environment. Some districts even have opened 100 percent online or virtual high schools, which has generated a heated debate among educators about the effectiveness and even appropriateness of such schools. Do you think 100 percent online high schools are an effective solution? Why or why not? Substantiate your answer.

4. Net Censoring

Each day, schools, organizations, and individuals across the country continue in an ongoing debate about Internet censorship. A number of organizations, including the American Library Association, oppose the use of Internet filtering software programs. Some people feel that schools are censoring out valuable information and that students would be better off with unlimited access, coupled with strict teacher observation and guidelines. Others, however, are very concerned about the use of the Internet in schools and do not want children using the Internet — even if filtering programs and Acceptable Use Policies are in place. Do you think schools should limit or ban Internet usage? How could you use the Internet effectively in your classroom without offending or angering parents?

Integration Corner

Web Instructions: To display this page from the Web, start your browser and enter the URL, www.course.com/tdc3. Click Chapter 2 at the top of the Web page and then click Integration Corner on the left sidebar. Click any Corner and then click the various links for extensive and curriculum-specific information.

WEB INFO

IN BRIEF

KEY TERMS

CHECKPOINT

TEACHING TODAY

EDUCATION ISSUES

INTEGRATION CORNER

SOFTWARE CORNER

IN THE LAB

LEARN IT ONLINE

✱ FEATURES...

Timeline 2004

Guide to WWW Sites

Buyer's Guide 2004

Professional Sites

State/Federal Sites

Interactive Labs

Search Tools

HOME

Integration Corner is designed for teachers and other educators who are looking for innovative ways to integrate technology into their content-specific curriculum. Integration Corner not only provides great Web sites with current information but also shows what other educators are doing in the field of educational technology. These Corners are designed for all educators regardless of their area of interest. Be sure to review information and sites outside of your teaching area because many great integration ideas in one area can be modified easily for use in other curricular areas.

Teachers and administrators will find other colleagues in their areas with whom to connect and share the successes and hurdles of integrating technology in a classroom or an entire school system. Consider this your one stop for integration ideas and resources. Links to educational Web sites are organized in the following 12 Corners, and different Web resources are available for each chapter. Figure 2-44 shows examples of the Web resources provided in the Chapter 2 Elementary Corner.

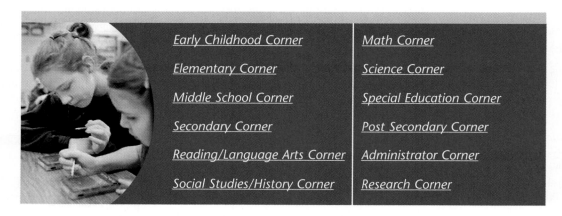

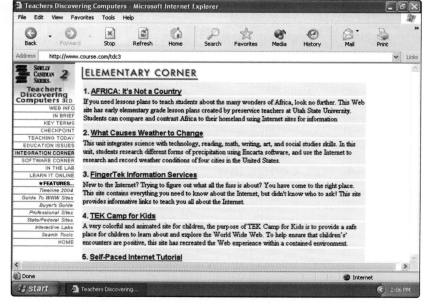

Figure 2-44 Examples of the Web resources provided in the Chapter 2 Elementary Corner.

Software Corner

Web Instructions: To display this page from the Web, start your browser and enter the URL, www.course.com/tdc3. Click Chapter 2 at the top of the Web page and then click Software Corner on the left sidebar. Click the links for additional information and instructions on how to download or receive an evaluation copy.

WEB INFO

IN BRIEF

KEY TERMS

CHECKPOINT

TEACHING TODAY

EDUCATION ISSUES

INTEGRATION CORNER

SOFTWARE CORNER

IN THE LAB

LEARN IT ONLINE

* FEATURES...

Timeline 2004

Guide to WWW Sites

Buyer's Guide 2004

Professional Sites

State/Federal Sites

Interactive Labs

Search Tools

HOME

1. If you have concerns about students accessing inappropriate Web sites while surfing the Internet, take a look at this software program. WebWhacker allows educators to *whack* Web sites and save them to a hard drive or a floppy disk. With WebWhacker, you simply determine how many levels of the Web site you need for your students to access and save the necessary Web pages. Students will not even realize they are not on the Internet right away because the program saves the Web sites exactly as they look, complete with links, buttons, animations, and all other features intact and working. WebWhacker is a super way for you to download information, while keeping your students on task and protecting them from unsuitable Web information.

2. Bailey's Book House, produced by EDMARK, provides seven activities for prekindergarten to second grade students to learn letters and their sounds, words, common adjectives, rhyming, storytelling, and more. Students can enjoy rhymes and give them zany endings just for fun. This software also allows students to create their own storybooks and greeting cards. Bailey's Book House is an excellent tool for teaching important beginning skills to preschoolers.

3. Math Companion is a powerful mathematical activity sheet generator developed for grades K-8 that has been aligned with 110 basic math objectives of the National Council for Teaching Mathematics (NCTM). Math Companion is a super tool for teachers and parents that provides students with many examples of mathematical problems. Math Companion, Volume 1, allows you to create custom activity sheets for word problems, basic math skills, and anagrams. You even can import line art graphics to create color-in activity sheets in minutes! Time, money, place value, fractions, and geometry are all covered in this program. Create games, flash cards, and worksheets using Math Companion, Volume 2. Both of these titles help students master important math skills.

4. Finding information for students to complete research papers and multimedia projects is made easy with the help of reference software; and it is easy to use. Simply type keywords and search. The Encarta Reference Library combines nine great resources that include Encarta Encyclopedia Deluxe, Encarta Interactive World Atlas, Learning Tools, and more. It also includes an almanac, a dictionary, and an authoritative resource on many topics that enhance reports and multimedia presentations in classrooms of all ages.

5. High school science teachers will enjoy using Digital Frog; it explains a frog dissection without the disgusting smell of formaldehyde! Digital Frog uses full color video and detailed animations, including 3-D, to explain the dissection of a frog. Scientific definitions and human comparisons help clarify difficult concepts for students. The program uses narration, color photos, and graphics to explain the entire process.

In the Lab

WEB INFO

IN BRIEF

KEY TERMS

CHECKPOINT

TEACHING TODAY

EDUCATION ISSUES

INTEGRATION CORNER

SOFTWARE CORNER

IN THE LAB

LEARN IT ONLINE

✱ FEATURES...

Timeline 2004

Guide to WWW Sites

Buyer's Guide 2004

Professional Sites

State/Federal Sites

Interactive Labs

Search Tools

HOME

Web Instructions: To display this page from the Web, start your browser and enter the URL, www.course.com/tdc3. Click Chapter 2 at the top of the Web page and then click In the Lab on the left sidebar. Click the links for tutorials, productivity ideas, integration examples, ideas, and more.

PRODUCTIVITY IN THE CLASSROOM

Introduction: All students and teachers need to know how to write a professional cover letter as well as how to develop a resume. Many of the popular word processing applications provide Wizards and Templates that take users through the steps of creating these special documents. Learning how to use these Wizards and Templates will save you time and provide useful guidance.

1 Using a Letter Wizard to Create a Cover Letter

Problem: As a recent graduate from a Master's program in Educational Technology, you are seeking a position as a Technology Coordinator at a local middle school. Open your word processing software and create a cover letter as described below. Use the letter shown in **Figure 2-43** as an example. (*Hint:* If you do not have the suggested font, use any appropriate font.)

Instructions: Perform the following tasks.

1. Create a cover letter using a Letter Wizard. If possible, use a similar letterhead style as shown in **Figure 2-43**. Insert your own name and address when requested by the Wizard.
2. Modify the cover letter so the font is 12-point Times or Times New Roman. Use today's date in the date line. Modify the inside address and message by personalizing the information to your specific situation.
3. Create a numbered list highlighting at least two of your accomplishments.
4. Check the cover letter for spelling and grammar errors.
5. Save the cover letter on a floppy disk. Use an appropriate file name.
6. Print the cover letter.
7. Follow your instructor's directions for handing in the assignment.

2 Using a Resume Wizard to Create a Resume

Problem: You have prepared the cover letter in **Figure 2-43** and now are ready to create a resume similar to the one shown in **Figure 2-44** on page 2.50 to send to the director of technology. You want your information to be clearly presented and to highlight your qualifications. Use a Resume Wizard or Template. (*Hint*: If you do not have the suggested font, use any appropriate font.)

Instructions: Perform the following tasks.

1. Use a Resume Wizard to create a resume. Use your name and address information.
2. Personalize the resume using your specific information.
3. Check the resume for spelling and grammar errors.
4. Save the resume on a floppy disk using an appropriate file name.
5. Print a copy of the resume.
6. Follow your instructor's directions for handing in the assignment.

In the Lab

WEB INFO

IN BRIEF

KEY TERMS

CHECKPOINT

TEACHING TODAY

EDUCATION ISSUES

INTEGRATION CORNER

SOFTWARE CORNER

IN THE LAB

LEARN IT ONLINE

✱ FEATURES...

Timeline 2004

Guide to WWW Sites

Buyer's Guide 2004

Professional Sites

State/Federal Sites

Interactive Labs

Search Tools

HOME

JON MARC BOWERS

692 East First Street
Chapel Hill, NC 27516
(919) 555-4332

August 5, 2004

Ms. Roz Seguero
Director of Technology
Chapel Hill City School District
1452 Fort King Street
Chapel Hill, NC 27514

Dear Ms. Seguero,

I would like to be considered for the position of Technology Coordinator at Blue Ridge Middle School. I believe my training and experience will greatly assist the staff and students to effectively use and integrate technology.

I have been an educator for the past six years and I have organized and led numerous staff development workshops on a variety of software applications. I also have extensively integrated technology throughout my classroom curriculum.

I would like to mention my most important qualifications:

1. Recently completed a Master's degree in Educational Technology
2. Nationally Board Certified Educator 2002
3. Microsoft Office Specialist certified in Microsoft Word, Excel, and PowerPoint

I look forward to meeting with you to discuss this position further. Please contact me at (919) 555-4332 or e-mail me at jmbowers@spms.k12.nc.us.

Sincerely,

Jon Marc Bowers

Figure 2-43

In the Lab

WEB INFO

IN BRIEF

KEY TERMS

CHECKPOINT

TEACHING TODAY

EDUCATION ISSUES

INTEGRATION CORNER

SOFTWARE CORNER

IN THE LAB

LEARN IT ONLINE

✱ FEATURES...

Timeline 2004

Guide to WWW Sites

Buyer's Guide 2004

Professional Sites

State/Federal Sites

Interactive Labs

Search Tools

HOME

Jon Marc Bowers
692 East First Street
Chapel Hill, NC 27516
(919) 555-4332
jmbowers@spms.k12.nc.us

OBJECTIVE: To obtain a position as Technology Coordinator to assist administrators and teachers in learning how to integrate technology effectively throughout their classroom curriculum that will positively impact student achievement.

QUALIFICATIONS
During my tenure at Orange Grove Middle School, I organized and led numerous technology staff development workshops on a variety of software applications including Word, PowerPoint, Excel, Access, HyperStudio, Inspiration, Photoshop, and Dreamweaver. I also created and maintained the school Web site and assisted other teachers in creating, posting, and maintaining their classroom Web pages. I assisted teachers with basic troubleshooting on both hardware and software. As part of my graduate program of study, I completed a 40-hour internship with the district technology coordinator and assisted with installing a new computer lab at a local elementary school.

EDUCATION
2002-2004 Master of Arts, Educational Technology, University of Central Florida, Orlando, FL
1995-1999 Bachelor of Arts, Middle Grades Education, University of North Carolina at Chapel Hill, Chapel Hill, NC

EMPLOYMENT
2004-Present
Math Teacher, Blue Ridge Middle School
Responsible for teaching all aspects of the 7th grade math curriculum for gifted students and regular education students. Develop and teach pre-algebra curriculum in a combination 7th/8th grade class.

1999-2004 Math Teacher, Orange Grove Middle School
Responsible for teaching all aspects of the 7th grade math curriculum including pre-algebra and regular curriculum courses. Team leader for the 7th grade Math department. Organized meetings, reviewed curriculum and served on the textbook adoption committee. Technology committee member for three years and was teacher representative on the School Advisory Counsel. Organized and sponsored the Math Wizards after-school program that provided student tutoring, homework help, and mentoring.

AWARDS and PROFESSIONAL ACTIVITIES
2004 - 1998 Member of the National Council of Teachers of Mathematics
2003 - Teacher of the Year Orange Grove Middle School
2002 - National Board Certification
2000 - Rookie Teacher of the Year

Figure 2-44

INTEGRATION IN THE CLASSROOM

1 As a follow-up activity to career day at your school, you have your students locate job advertisements online. The students select a job they would be interested in and then use a Wizard or Template to write a cover letter. Use the cover letter shown in Figure 2-43 on the previous page as an example of the type of information the students should include in the first two paragraphs. The students also should include a numbered list highlighting two of their accomplishments and then a closing paragraph with contact information. Create a cover letter to use as an example for your students. Include today's date, your name, and address.

2 Using the job they selected from the Internet, the students will create a resume to go along with their cover letter. Create a resume to use as an example for your students. Modify the resume you created. Change the information in the resume to match the cover letter in Integration in the Classroom number 1 above.

3 Your students have just finished reading a book of their choice and they are ready to begin working on their book reports. To make it more interesting, you want the students to select a character from their book, choose a job for the character, and write a cover letter and resume based on the character's life. Choose one of your favorite characters from a book and create a sample cover letter and resume for your students. Use today's date and your name and address as the potential employer.

Learn It Online

Web Instructions: To display this page from the Web, start your browser and enter the URL, www.course.com/tdc3. Click Chapter 2 at the top of the Web page and then click Learn It Online on the left sidebar. Click the buttons to display the exercise or the Interactive Lab.

WEB INFO

IN BRIEF

KEY TERMS

CHECKPOINT

TEACHING TODAY

EDUCATION ISSUES

INTEGRATION CORNER

SOFTWARE CORNER

IN THE LAB

LEARN IT ONLINE

✱ FEATURES...

Timeline 2004

Guide to WWW Sites

Buyer's Guide 2004

Professional Sites

State/Federal Sites

Interactive Labs

Search Tools

HOME

1. Shelly Cashman Series Connecting to the Internet Lab

Click the button to the left to start and use the Shelly Cashman Series Connecting to the Internet Lab.

2. Shelly Cashman Series World Wide Web Lab

Click the button to the left to start and use the Shelly Cashman Series The World Wide Web Lab.

3. Search Engine Tutorial

Click the button to the left to complete an exercise to learn how to conduct Internet searches.

4. Using Bookmarks

Click the button to the left to complete an exercise to learn how to make and organize your bookmarks.

5. Who Wants To Be a Computer Genius?

Click the button to the left to find out if you are a computer genius. Directions on how to play the game will be displayed. When you are ready to play, click the PLAY button. Submit your score to your instructor.

6. Crossword Puzzle Challenge

Click the button to the left to complete the puzzle to reinforce skills you learned in this chapter. Directions on how to play the game will be displayed. When you are ready to play, click the SUBMIT button. Submit the completed puzzle to your instructor.

7. Practice Test

Click the button to the left and answer each question. When completed, enter your name and click the Grade Test button to submit the quiz for grading. Make a note of any missed questions. If required, print a copy to submit to your instructor.

GUIDE TO WORLD WIDE WEB SITES AND SEARCHING TECHNIQUES

The World Wide Web is an exciting and highly dynamic medium that has revolutionized the way people access information. You can display information on virtually any topic you can imagine, if you know the URL. If you do not know the URL, you must use a search tool because the Web has no bibliographic control. Statistics from the NEC Research Institute indicate that every second, 25 new Web pages are added to the more than 10 billion Web pages already on the Internet. Given this, finding the information you want can be a massive chore if you do not know the URL or how to use Web search tools.

To help you locate information, this special feature provides four resources: a topical list of some of the more popular Web sites, an introduction to searching techniques, a list of portals with search capabilities, and an extensive list of popular education search tools.

WEB INSTRUCTIONS: *To gain World Wide Web access to additional and up-to-date information regarding this special feature, start your browser and enter the URL, www.course.com/tdc3. When the Teachers Discovering Computers home page is displayed, click the special feature, Guide to WWW Sites, on the left sidebar.*

Categories

Animation	Fitness	News Sources
Art	Genealogy	Reference
Business and Finance	Government and Politics	Robotics
Careers and Employment	Health and Medicine	Science
Computers and Computing	History	Shopping
Digital Music	Humor	Society
Directories	Internet	Sports
Education	Internet Security	Travel
Entertainment	Kid-Safe Sites	Unclassified
Environment	Law	Weather
	Museums	Zines

CATEGORY/SITE NAME	LOCATION	COMMENT
Animation		
Animation World Network	awn.com	Animation-related publishing group pertaining to all aspects of animation
RGB Gallery	hotwired.lycos.com/rgb	Art animations
Shockwave.com	shockwave.com	Cool Shockwave animations
Art		
fineArt forum	msstate.edu/fineart_online/home.html	Art plus technology net news
Louvre Museum	www.louvre.fr/louvrea.htm	Web version of Louvre Museum in Paris
The Andy Warhol Museum	Warhol.org	Famous American pop artist
WebMuseum: Leonardo da Vinci	ibiblio.org/wm/paint/auth/vinci	Works of the famous Italian artist and thinker
World Wide Arts Resources	wwar.com	Links to many art Web sites
Business and Finance		
All-Biz.com – Small Business Network	all-biz.com	Links to Web business information
BusinessWeek Online	businessweek.com	Online investing
FinanCenter	financenter.com	Personal finance information
Lycos Finance	ragingbull.lycos.com	Lycos's financial portal
Morningstar.com	www.morningstar.com	Mutual fund Web site
MSN Money	money.msn.com	Microsoft's financial portal
PCQuote.com	pcquote.com	Free delayed stock quotes
Quicken.com	quicken.com	Personal financial advice
SiliconInvestor	siliconinvestor.com	Stock chat for technology investors
SmartMoney	smartmoney.com	Live snapshot of the stock market
Stockgroup	stockgroup.com	Investment information and technology solutions
The Wall Street Journal Online	online.wsj.com	Financial news page
Yahoo! Finance	quote.yahoo.com	Free real-time stock quotes
Careers and Employment		
CareerBuilder	careerbuilder.com	Job listings from U.S. newspapers
Careermag.com	careermag.com	Career articles and information
Job Options	joboptions.com	Searchable job database
Monster.com	monster.com	Job finder

For an updated list and Web links, click the special feature, Guide to WWW Sites, on the left sidebar of the textbook home page.

CATEGORY/SITE NAME	LOCATION	COMMENT
Computers and Computing		
Computer companies	Insert name or initials of most computer companies before .com to find their Web sites. Examples: ibm.com, microsoft.com, dell.com	
Computer History Museum	computerhistory.org	Exhibits and history of computing
Expertcity	expertcity.com	Live experts offer technical support
Internet.com	internet.com	E-business and technology network
MIT Media Lab	www.media.mit.edu	Information on computer trends
The Apple Museum	theapplemuseum.com	The history of the Apple computer
The PC Guide	pcguide.com	PC reference information
The Virtual Museum of Computing	vlmp.museophile.com/computing	History of computing and online computer-based exhibits
Virtual Computer Library	www.utexas.edu/computer/vcl	Information on computers and computing
ZDNet	zdnet.com	Downloads and product reviews
Digital Music		
Live Concerts	www.liveconcerts.com	RealMedia streamed concerts
MP3.com	mp3.com	Music files
Sonique	sonique.com	MP3 player and media products
This American Life	thislife.org	Public radio program
Directories		
555-1212.com	555-1212.com	Online directory information service
InfoSpace	infospace.com	Directory and search engine
SuperPages.com	superpages.com	Verizon Information Services
Switchboard.com	switchboard.com	Variety of directories
WhoWhere?	whowhere.lycos.com	Lycos directory
Yahoo! People Search	people.yahoo.com	Yahoo! directory
Education		
CollegeNET	www.collegenet.com	Searchable database of thousands of colleges and universities
EdLinks	webpages.marshall.edu/~jmullens/edlinks.html	Links to many educational Web sites
The Open University	www.open.ac.uk	Independent study courses from the U.K.
UMUC Distance Education	umuc.edu/distance	University of Maryland distance education
WiredScholar	www.wiredscholar.com	Information on financing an education

For an updated list and Web links, click the special feature, Guide to WWW Sites, on the left sidebar of the textbook home page.

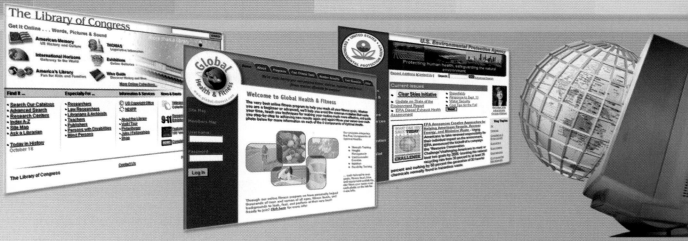

CATEGORY/SITE NAME	LOCATION	COMMENT
Entertainment		
CDNOW	cdnow.com	Search for and buy all types of music
Internet Movie Database (IMDb)	imdb.com	Movies
IUMA (Music Archive)	iuma.com	Underground music database
ABCNEWS Entertainment	abcnews.go.com/sections/entertainment/	ABC's entertainment page
Online Classics	www.onlineclassics.com	Classical music information
Playbill On-Line	playbill.com	Theater news
Rock and Roll Hall of Fame	rockhall.com	Cleveland museum Web site
Environment		
EnviroLink Network	envirolink.com	Environmental information
Greenpeace	greenpeace.org	Environmental activism
EPA	epa.gov	U.S. government environmental news
Fitness		
24 Hour Fitness	24hourfitness.com	A health and fitness community
GlobalFitness.com	global-fitness.com	Health and fitness
Genealogy		
Cyndi's List	cyndislist.com	List of genealogy sites
Mormon Church	familysearch.org	Renowned Internet genealogy service
National Genealogical Society	ngsgenealogy.org	Genealogical information
Government and Politics		
CIA	www.cia.gov	International information about countries
Democratic National Committee	democrats.org	Democratic party news
FedWorld	www.fedworld.gov	Links to U.S. government Web sites
PoliSci.com	polisci.com	Politics on the Web
Republican National Committee	rnc.org	GOP party news
The Library of Congress	www.loc.gov	Variety of U.S. government information
The White House	www.whitehouse.gov	Take a tour and learn about the occupants
U.S. Census Bureau	www.census.gov	Population and other statistics
United Nations	www.un.org	Latest UN projects and information
Health and Medicine		
Centers for Disease Control and Prevention (CDC)	www.cdc.gov	How to prevent and control disease
Cornucopia of Disability Information (CODI)	codi.buffalo.edu	Resource for disability products and services
Mayo Clinic	mayoclinic.com	Diseases and conditions reference
American Medical Women's Association	www.amwa-doc.org	Articles and links to other Web sites

For an updated list and Web links, click the special feature, Guide to WWW Sites, on the left sidebar of the textbook home page.

CATEGORY/SITE NAME	LOCATION	COMMENT
History		
American Memory	rs6.loc.gov/amhome.html	American history
The History Channel	historychannel.com	Search any topic in history
Virtual Library History	www.ukans.edu/history/VL	Organized links to history Web sites
World History Archives	www.hartford-hwp.com/archives	Links to history Web sites
Humor		
Comedy Central	comcentral.com	Comedy TV network online
Late Show with David Letterman	cbs.com/latenight/lateshow/	Letterman's nightly show including archived Top 10 lists
Dilbert.com	dilbert.com	Humorous insights about the workplace
Ucomics.com	ucomics.com	Comic strip gallery
Internet		
Beginners' Central	northernwebs.com/bc	Beginners' guide to the Internet
Glossary of Internet Terms	matisse.net/files/glossary.html	Matisse Enzer's definitions of Internet terms
WWW Frequently Asked Questions	www.boutell.com/faq/oldfaq/index.html	Common Web questions and answers
Internet Security		
F-Secure Security Information Center	f-secure.com/virus-info/	Industry standard information source for new virus hoaxes and false alerts
Internet Security Alliance	www.isalliance.org	A public-private partnership for information sharing and e-security issues
Kid-Safe Sites		
CartoonNetwork.com	cartoonnetwork.com	Interactive site for the cable network
Disney Online	disney.com	Disney's interactive site
FoxKids	foxkids.com	The Fox network's interactive site for children
Nick.com	nick.com	Nickelodeon's site for fun and games
Law		
American Bar Association	www.abanet.org	Source for legal information
Copyright Website	benedict.com	Provides copyright information
FindLaw	findlaw.com	Law resource portal
KuesterLaw	kuesterlaw.com	Technology law resource
Legal Information Institute	www.law.cornell.edu	Cornell Law School legal information

For an updated list and Web links, click the special feature, Guide to WWW Sites, on the left sidebar of the textbook home page.

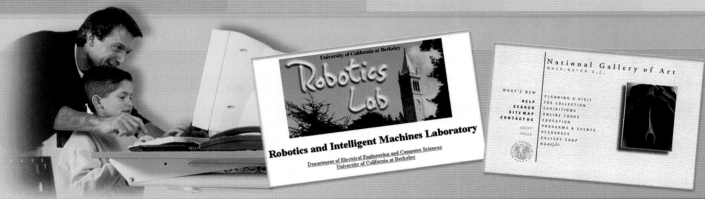

CATEGORY/SITE NAME	LOCATION	COMMENT
Museums		
Smithsonian Institution	www.si.edu	Information and links to Smithsonian museums
The National Gallery of Art, Washington, D.C.	nga.gov	Plan a visit or take an online tour
U.S. Holocaust Memorial Museum	ushmm.org	Dedicated to World War II victims
University of California Museum of Paleontology	www.ucmp.berkeley.edu	Information about dinosaurs and other exhibits
News Sources		
Cable News Network	cnn.com	CNN all-news network
CNET	cnet.com	Technology news
Newsday.com	newsday.com	All the latest information
TIME.com	time.com	Excerpts from Time-Warner magazines
USA TODAY	usatoday.com	Latest U.S. and international news
Wired News	wired.com	Wired magazine online and HotWired network
Reference		
AskERIC	askeric.org	Educational resources
Ask Jeeves	askjeeves.com	Search engine
Bartleby	bartleby.com	Reference books online
Internet Public Library	ipl.org	Literature and reference works
The New York Public Library	www.nypl.org	Extensive reference and research material
Webopedia	webopedia.com	Online dictionary and search engine
What You Need to Know About	about.com	Search engine and portal
Robotics		
Remotebot.net	remotebot.net	Control a robot with your Netscape Web browser; interactive robotic museum
Robotics and Intelligent Machines Laboratory	robotics.eecs.berkeley.edu	Robotics and mechanical and electrical engineering
University of Massachusetts Robotics Information	www-robotics.cs.umass.edu/robotics.html	Robotics resource index page
Science		
American Institute of Physics	www.aip.org	Physics research information
Exploratorium	exploratorium.edu	Interactive science exhibits
Chemistry Information Service	chemie.de	List of chemistry information Web sites
Molecular Expressions: Science, Optics and You	www.micro.magnet.fsu.edu/primer/java/ scienceopticsu/powersof10/index.html	Examine the Milky Way at 10 million light years from the Earth; travel space and more
National Institute for Discovery Science (NIDS)	www.nidsci.org	Research of anomalous phenomena
Solar System Simulator	space.jpl.nasa.gov	JPL's spyglass on the cosmos
The NASA Homepage	www.nasa.gov	Information about U.S. space program
The Nine Planets	www.nineplanets.org	Tour the solar system's nine planets

For an updated list and Web links, click the special feature, Guide to WWW Sites, on the left sidebar of the textbook home page.

2.58

CATEGORY/SITE NAME	LOCATION	COMMENT
Shopping		
ActivePlaza	activeplaza.com	Online shopping mall
Amazon.com	amazon.com	Books and gifts
Barnes & Noble	bn.com	Online bookstore
BizRate	bizrate.com	Rates e-commerce Web sites
BizWeb	bizweb.com	Search for products from more than 46,000 companies
CNET Shopper	shopper.cnet.com	Computer and electronic products
CommerceNet	www.commerce.net	Nonprofit with focus on B2B e-commerce
Consumer World	consumerworld.org	Consumer information
Ebay	ebay.com	Online auctions
CarsDirect.com	www.carsdirect.com/home	Automobile buying Web site
Internet Bookshop	www.bookshop.co.uk	1.4 million titles about more than 2,000 subjects
Lands' End	landsend.com	Classic clothing for the family
Society		
Association for Computing Machinery (ACM)	acm.org	World's first educational and scientific computing society
Center for Applied Ethics	www.ethicsweb.ca/resources	Computer and information ethics resources
Center for Computing and Social Responsibility	www.ccsr.cse.dmu.ac.uk/index.html	Social and ethical impacts of information and communications technologies
Computer Professionals for Social Responsibility	cpsr.org	A public-interest alliance of computer scientists and others concerned about the impact of computer technology on society
Computers and Society	acm.org/sigcas	Special interest group within Association for Computing Machinery (ACM)
Electronic Frontier Foundation	eff.org	Protecting rights and promoting freedom
Electronic Privacy Information Center	epic.org	Links to latest news regarding privacy issues
International Center for Information Ethics (ICIE)	icie.zkm.de	An academic Web site about information ethics
International Federation for Information Processing (IFIP)	www.ifip.or.at/	Computers and social accountability
ISWorld Net Professional Ethics	http://www.iscityu.edu.hk/Research/Resources/ethics/ethics.htm	Practice of ethics in the information systems profession
Privacy.Org	privacy.org	Current privacy issues

For an updated list and Web links, click the special feature, Guide to WWW Sites, on the left sidebar of the textbook home page.

CATEGORY/SITE NAME	LOCATION	COMMENT
Sports		
ESPN SportsZone	msn.espn.go.com/main.html	Latest sports news
NBA Basketball	nba.com	Information and links to team Web sites
NFL Football	nfl.com	Information and links to team Web sites
Sports Illustrated	sportsillustrated.cnn.com	Leading sports magazine
Travel		
CitySearch	citysearch.com	United States and international city guides
InfoHub Specialty Travel Guide	infohub.com	Worldwide travel information
Lonely Planet Online	www.lonelyplanet.com	Budget travel guides and stories
Expedia.com	expedia.com	Complete travel resource
Travelocity.com	www.travelocity.com	Online travel agency
TravelWebSM	travelweb.com	Places to stay
Unclassified		
American Singles.com	americansingles.com	Links to dating resources
Cool Site of the Day	cool.infi.net	Different Web site each day
Famous Name Changes	www.famousnamechanges.com	Names of stars before they were stars
WebPhotos	webphotos.com	Online photo community
Where's George?	wheresgeorge.com	The Great American Dollar Bill Locator
Weather		
Intellicast	intellicast.com	International weather and skiing information
The Weather Channel	weather.com	National and local forecasts
Weather Underground	wunderground.com	Weather maps
Zines		
Rock School	rockschool.com	Everything you need to know about being in a rock band
The AFU & Urban Legends Archive	urbanlegends.com	Urban legends
TruthOrFiction.com	truthorfiction.com	Check out the latest rumors circulating on the Web

For an updated list and Web links, click the special feature, Guide to WWW Sites, on the left sidebar of the textbook home page.

WORLD WIDE WEB SEARCH TOOLS

Successful Searching

Successful searching of the Web involves two key steps:

1. Briefly describe the information you are seeking. Start by identifying the main idea or concept in your topic and determine any synonyms, alternate spellings, or variant word forms for the concept.

2. Use the brief description with a search tool to display links to pages containing the desired information.

The two most common search tools are subject directories and search engines. You use a **subject directory** by clicking through its collection of categories and subcategories until you reach the information you want. You use a **search engine** to search for a keyword. The following sections describe how to use a subject directory and a search engine.

Using a Subject Directory

A subject directory provides categorized lists of links. These categorized lists are arranged by subject and then displayed in a series of menus. Using this type of search tool, you can locate a particular topic by starting from the top and clicking links through the different levels, going from the general to the specific. Each time you click a category link, the search tool displays a page of subcategory links from which you again choose. You continue in this fashion until the search tool displays a list of Web pages on the desired topic. Browsing a subject directory requires that you make assumptions about the topic's hierarchical placement within the categorized list.

For the following example, assume you have been assigned the task of writing a research paper on Mark Twain. The assignment requires that you include at least one Web page citation. This example uses the Yahoo! (yahoo.com) search directory to locate information on Mark Twain.

1 Start your browser and then enter the URL www.yahoo.com in the Address box. When the Yahoo! home page is displayed, scroll down and then point to the Literature link below Arts & Humanities as shown in Figure 1. You point to Literature because that is the category in which Mark Twain made his contributions.

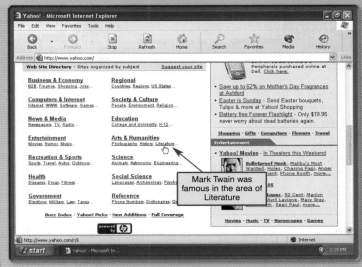

Figure 1 Yahoo! home page.

2 Click Literature. When the Literature page is displayed, point to the Authors link as shown in Figure 2. You point to Authors because Mark Twain was an author. Each time you click a category link, you move closer to the topic.

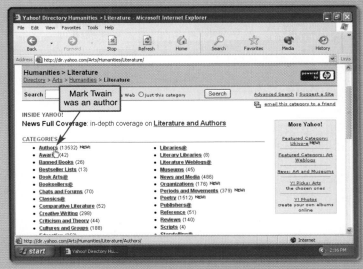

Figure 2 Literature categories.

3 Click Authors. When the Authors page is displayed, scroll down and then point to the letter T in the alphabetical site listings as shown in Figure 3. (You also can find information about Mark Twain by clicking the Literary Fiction link.)

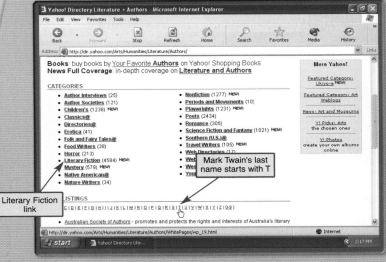

Figure 3 Authors categories.

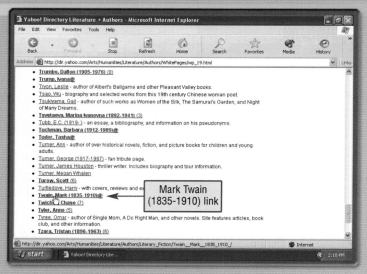

Figure 4 Alphabetical list of authors.

Click the letter T. The browser window displays an alphabetical listing of authors whose last names begin with T, as well as other author-related organizations that begin with T. Scroll down and then point to the Twain, Mark (1835-1910) link as shown in Figure 4.

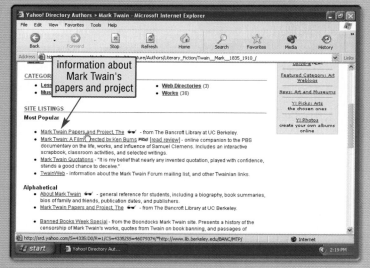

Figure 5 Twain, Mark (1835-1910) categories.

Click Twain, Mark (1835-1910). When the page appears, scroll down and then point to the Mark Twain Papers & Project link as shown in Figure 5.

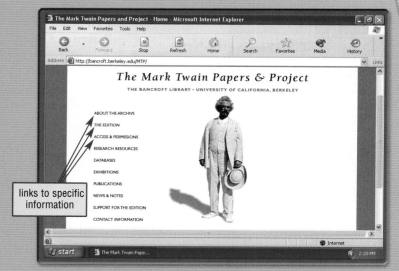

Figure 6 The Mark Twain Papers & Project Web page.

Click the Mark Twain Papers & Project link. When the page appears (Figure 6), click the link one at a time. Use the browser's Back button to return to The Mark Twain Papers & Project page after viewing the page associated with each link.

With just a few clicks, the Yahoo! search directory displays information about Mark Twain. The Mark Twain subcategory page shown in Figure 6 displays several links to his writings, as well as to pages about exhibitions and other resources.

The major problem with a search directory is deciding which categories to choose as you work through the menus of links presented. For additional information on how to use the Yahoo! search directory, click the Help link in the upper-right corner of the Yahoo! home page.

Using a Search Engine

Search engines require that you enter search text or keywords (single word, words, or phrase) that define what you are looking for, rather than clicking through menus of links. Search engines often respond with results that include thousands of links to Web pages, many of which have little or no bearing on the information you are seeking. You can eliminate the superfluous pages by carefully choosing a keyword (or words) that limits the search. The following example uses the Google search engine to search for the phrase, mark twain papers.

1 Start your browser and then enter the URL www.google.com in the Address box. When the Google home page is displayed, type mark twain papers in the Search text box and then point to the Google Search button as shown in Figure 7.

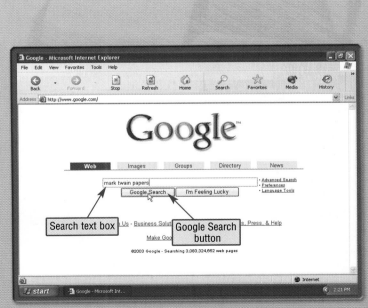

Figure 7 Google home page.

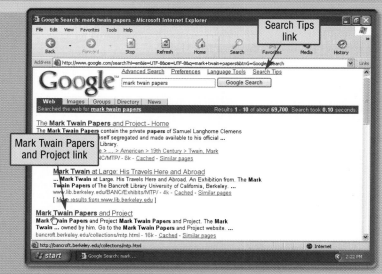

Figure 8 Google search results.

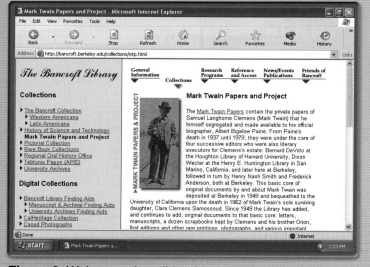

Figure 9 Web page describing Mark Twain and his writings.

2 Click the Google Search button. When the results of the search are displayed, scroll through the links and read the descriptions. Point to the Mark Twain Papers & Project link as shown in Figure 8.

3 Click the Mark Twain Papers and Project link. A Web page appears that contains extensive information about the collected original documents by and about Mark Twain (Figure 9).

The results in Figure 8 include more than 69,000 links to Web pages concerning Mark Twain's papers. Most search engines sequence the results based on how close the keywords are to one another in the Web page titles and their descriptions. Thus, the first few links probably contain more relevant information. For additional information on how to use the Google search engine, click the Search Tips link in the upper-right corner of the Google home page (Figure 8).

Limiting the Search

If you enter a phrase with spaces between the keywords, most search engines return links to pages that include all of the words. Figure 10 lists some common operators, commands, and special characters you can use to refine your search.

Guidelines to Successful Searching

You can improve your Web searches by following these guidelines.

1. Use nouns as keywords, and put the most important terms first.

2. Use the asterisk (*) to find plurals of words. For example: retriev* returns retrieves, retrieval, retriever, and any other variation.

3. Type keywords in lowercase to find both lowercase and uppercase variations.

4. Use quotation marks to create phrases so the search engine finds the exact sequence of words.

5. Use a hyphen alternative. For example, use email OR e-mail.

6. Limit the search by language.

7. Use uppercase characters for Boolean operators in your search statements to differentiate between the words and operators.

8. Before you use a search engine, read its Help.

9. The Internet contains many search engines. If your search is unsuccessful with one search engine, try another.

Popular Search Sites

Most search sites include both a search engine and subject directory. Figure 11 contains a list of popular search sites and their URLs where you can access search engines and subject directories to search the Web. For additional information about search sites, visit www.searchenginewatch.com.

CATEGORY OF OPERATOR	OPERATOR	KEYWORD EXAMPLES	DESCRIPTION
Boolean	AND (+)	art AND music smoking health hazards fish +pollutants +runoff	Requires both words to be in the page. No operator between words or the plus sign (+) are shortcuts for the Boolean operator AND.
	OR	mental illness OR insane canine OR dog OR puppy flight attendant OR stewardess OR steward	Requires only one of the words to be in the page.
	AND NOT (–)	auto AND NOT SUV AND NOT convertible computers – programming shakespeare – hamlet – (romeo+juliet)	Excludes pages with the word following AND NOT. The minus sign (–) is a shortcut for the Boolean operator AND NOT.
Parentheses	( )	physics AND (relativity OR einstein)	Parentheses group portions of Boolean operators together.
Phrase Searching	" "	"harry potter" "19th century literature"	Requires the exact phrase within quotation marks to be in the page.
Wildcard	*	writ* clou*	The asterisk (*) at the end of words substitutes for any combination of characters.

Figure 10 Search engine keyword operators, commands, and special characters.

SEARCH SITE	URL
Google	www.google.com
AllTheWeb	www.alltheweb.com
Yahoo!	www.yahoo.com
MSN Search	search.msn.com
AOL Search	search.aol.com
Ask Jeeves	www.askjeeves.com
HotBot	www.hotbot.com
Lycos	www.lycos.com
LookSmart	www.looksmart.com
AltaVista	www.altavista.com
Netscape Search	search.netscape.com
Overture	www.overture.com
InfoSpace	www.infospace.com

Figure 11 Popular search sites.

Ask Jeeves for Kids

ajkids.com

Ask Jeeves for Kids is a Web site that makes it easy for kids to find answers to questions. When students visit this Web site they can ask a question in plain English. After interacting with the student to confirm the question, Ask Jeeves for Kids displays a single Web site that answers their question.

Awesome Library

awesomelibrary.org

Awesome Library organizes 16,000 carefully reviewed links that are useful for teachers, students (kids or teens), parents, or librarians. This Web site also allows users to browse in 15 different languages.

Ben's Guide to U.S. Government for Kids

bensguide.gpo.gov

This government sponsored site provides learning tools for K-12 students, parents, and teachers. It includes resources on how the United States government works and other related topics.

Blue Web'N

www.kn.pacbell.com/wired/bluewebn

Blue Web'N is a searchable database containing thousands of outstanding Internet learning Web sites categorized by subject area, audience, and type. It also includes lessons, activities, projects, resources, references, tools, and more.

Busy Teachers' WebSite K-12

www.ceismc.gatech.edu/busyt

This Web site is designed to offer teachers direct source materials, lesson plans, and classroom activities. Teachers learning how to use the Internet will have an enjoyable and rewarding experience navigating through this Web site.

Education Index

educationindex.com

This popular and annotated guide to the best education-related Web sites on the World Wide Web is sorted by subject and life stage. You will find what you are looking for quickly and easily.

Education World

www.education-world.com

Visit this complete, online resource guide where educators can access a search engine that identifies educational Web sites. You also will be able to connect to lesson plans, research materials, up-to-date news information from *USA TODAY*, monthly site reviews, employment listings, and articles written by education experts.

Popular Education Search Tools

A number of outstanding search tools are tailored for use by K-12 educators. Figure 12 contains a list of the more popular education search tools. Many of these search tools contain both search engines and subject directories. In addition, a number of these search tools are reviewed by experienced educators to ensure the content and links are appropriate for K-12 students. *For an updated list and Web links, click the special feature, Guide to WWW Sites, on the left sidebar of the textbook home page, and then click the Popular Education Search Tools link or scroll to the end of the extensive list of Web sites.*

Figure 12

EduHound

www.eduhound.com

EduHound is a highly specialized educational directory with built-in resource links for educators, students, and parents. This wonderful Web site seeks to harness the vast informational resources on the World Wide Web, while enabling educators to use the Internet as a classroom tool.

emTech

www.emtech.net

This Web site contains more than 15,000 resources organized by topics for teachers, students, parents, and other education professionals.

FirstGov for Kids

kids.gov

This is the U.S. government interagency Kids' Portal and provides links to federal kids' Web sites along with some of the best kids' sites from other organizations, all grouped by subject. This is an outstanding site for kids to search for government resources.

Great Web Sites for Kids

www.ala.org/alsc/children_links.html

Looking for something fun and educational on the World Wide Web? You are likely to find it on this list of kids' Web sites compiled by the American Library Association.

Kathy Schrock's Guide for Educators

school.discovery.com/schrockguide

Kathy Schrock's Guide for Educators is a categorized list of Web sites that are useful for enhancing curriculum and professional growth. It is updated often to include the best Web sites for teaching and learning.

KidsClick!

sunsite.berkeley.edu/KidsClick!

This Web site for kids is compiled by librarians and contains a database of more than 5,000 sites organized into more than 600 subjects.

Kid's Search Tools

www.rcls.org/ksearch.htm

This site allows kids to search a variety of kid-safe search engines from a single page.

Learning Page

learningpage.com

This site contains a large collection of instructional materials that you can download and print, including lesson plans, books, worksheets, and many other materials.

Figure 12 *(continued)*

Sites for Teachers

www.sitesforteachers.com

Sites for Teachers includes links to Web sites that contain teacher resources and educational materials. Web sites are ranked according to popularity.

STEM-NET Theme Pages for Elementary Students and Teachers

www.stemnet.nf.ca/CITE/themes.html

This Web site contains a general listing of theme-related links on a broad range of educational topics such as the solar system, bats, sea life, weather, inventions, and much, much more.

The Gateway to Educational Materials (GEM)

www.thegateway.org

The Gateway to Educational Materials, sponsored by the U.S. Department of Education, is a consortium effort to provide educators with quick-and-easy access to thousands of educational resources, such as lesson plans and curriculum units found on various federal, state, university, nonprofit, and commercial Web sites.

TekMom's Search Tools for Students

tekmom.com/search

An all-in-one search page for kids' search sites, including links to reference and research resources.

Yahooligans!

www.yahooligans.com

Yahooligans is a browsable, searchable directory of Web sites for kids and teens. Each Web site has been carefully checked by experienced educators to ensure that the content and links are age-appropriate.

Figure 12 *(continued)*

Application Software Productivity Tools for Educators

3

Objectives

After completing this chapter, you will be able to:

- Explain the role of an operating system and list the main operating systems used on today's computers

- Define and describe a user interface and a graphical user interface

- Identify the important features of widely used software applications

- Describe the advantages of software suites

- Explain how to create documents

- Discuss why the use of special needs software is important for K-12 schools

- List and describe learning aids and support tools that help you use and learn software applications

- Explain how to work with different versions of software applications

An essential aspect of building computer literacy is learning about software, which is the series of instructions that tell computer hardware how to perform tasks. Having a solid understanding of software — especially application software — will help you comprehend how administrators, teachers, students, and other individuals use personal computers in today's society. It also will help you use your computer to be more productive, organized, and well-informed.

Application software such as word processing, spreadsheets, and e-mail programs can help you perform tasks such as creating documents, doing research, and managing projects. Before discussing various software applications used by teachers and students, however, this chapter provides a basic overview of the operating system and the user interface used on both Macintosh computers and PCs. As you learned in Chapter 1, the user interface controls how you work with any software, including application software.

Understanding application software also can help advance your personal and professional goals by helping you manage student records, teach students with different academic needs, and work more productively. In addition, this chapter introduces you to the learning aids and tools available to help you and your students learn to use software applications. Finally, you will learn how to work with different versions of the same software on different computers. You can refer back to this chapter as you learn more about how computers are used today and how they can help you in your teaching career.

The Operating System

As with most computer users, you probably are somewhat familiar with application software. To use any application software, however, your computer must be running another type of software — an operating system.

THE ROLE OF THE OPERATING SYSTEM

As described in Chapter 1, software can be categorized into two types: system software and application software. **System software** consists of programs that control the operations of the computer and its devices. As shown in Figure 3-1, system software serves as the interface between

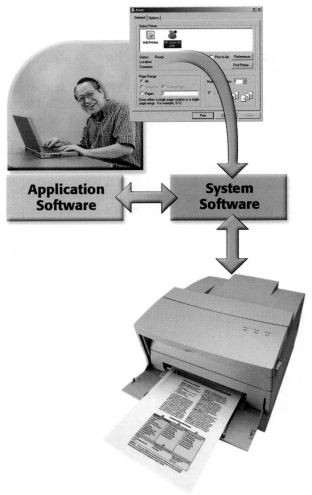

Application Software ⟷ **System Software**

Figure 3-1 System software is the interface between the user, the application software, and the computer's hardware. In this example, a user instructs the word processing software to print, the word processing software sends the print instructions to the system software, and the system software sends the print instructions to the printer.

you (the user), your application software, and your computer's hardware. One type of system software, the **operating system**, contains instructions that coordinate all of the activities of the hardware devices in a computer. The operating system also contains instructions that allow you to run application software.

Before either a Macintosh computer or a PC can run any application software, the operating system must be loaded from the hard disk into the computer's memory. Each time you start your computer, the operating system is loaded, or copied, into memory from the computer's hard disk. After the operating system is loaded, it tells the computer how to perform functions such as processing program instructions and transferring data between input and output devices and memory. The operating system, which remains in memory while the computer is running, allows you to communicate with the computer and other software, such as word processors, grade books, and other application programs. The operating system continues to run until the computer is turned off.

USING DIFFERENT OPERATING SYSTEMS

Each new release of an operating system contains new features that make computers more powerful and easy to use. In addition, the newest operating systems provide enhanced integration with the World Wide Web and increase the multimedia capabilities of computers. Due to budget constraints and other factors, however, schools and home users do not always upgrade their computers every time a new version of an operating system is released. As a result, a number of different versions of operating systems currently are running on school and home computers.

MICROSOFT WINDOWS   Microsoft **Windows**, which often is referred to simply as Windows with a capital W, is the most used operating system in the world. Figure 3-2 shows the latest version, Windows XP. The following is a brief summary of the evolution of the various versions of Microsoft Windows that are in use today.

- Windows 98 — **Windows 98** was an upgrade to Windows 95 and is still a commonly used version of Windows found on many school and home computers. Many schools use a network version of Windows 95/98 called Windows NT.

- Windows 2000 — Microsoft marketed **Windows 2000** in two main versions: Windows Millennium Edition, or Windows Me, for home users; and Windows 2000 Professional, which is a network version for businesses and schools. Windows 2000 is similar in appearance to Windows 98.

- Windows XP — **Windows XP**, released in late 2001, is a significant upgrade to the Windows operating system and is available in two main versions: Windows XP Home edition and Windows XP Professional for businesses and schools [Figure 3-2]. Windows XP also is available in a version specifically tailored for Media Center PCs. Included with all versions of Windows XP are significant multimedia and movie-making enhancements, increased ease of use, and Internet Explorer 6.

- Windows XP Tablet PC Edition — The **Windows XP Tablet PC Edition** includes all the features of Windows XP Professional with additional features that are unique to using a Tablet PC, including the ability to write on the screen using a digital pen, saving handwritten notes, and other features.

MACINTOSH OPERATING SYSTEM OR MAC OS Most users of Macintosh computers will use one of two versions of Mac OS.

- Mac OS, version 9.1 — Many Apple and Macintosh school computers use **Mac OS, version 9.1**.

- Mac OS X — The **Mac OS X** version of the Macintosh operating system, released in 2001, is a significant upgrade to the Macintosh operating system in both appearance and use that is different from previous versions [Figure 3-3]. Included with this version are enhanced speech

recognition, multimedia capabilities, Web functionality, and improved CD R/W capabilities.

OTHER OPERATING SYSTEMS Two other common operating systems are UNIX and Linux.

- UNIX — **UNIX** is a multitasking operating system developed for mainframe computers in the early 1970s by scientists at Bell Laboratories, a subsidiary of AT&T.

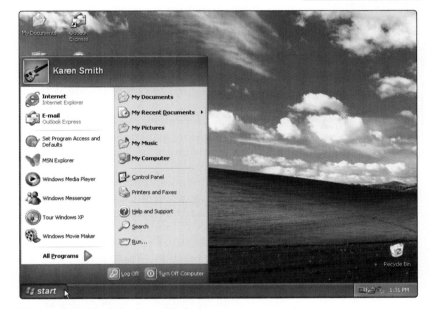

Figure 3-2 The Windows XP desktop.

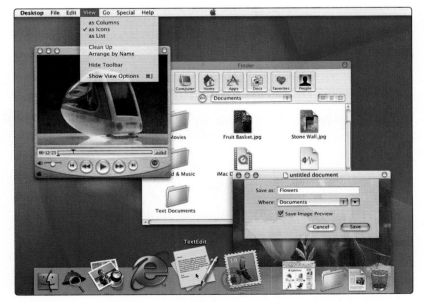

Figure 3-3 Mac OS X displays differently than previous versions of this popular operating system used on Apple Macintosh computers.

Today, versions of UNIX are available for computers of all sizes.

- Linux — **Linux** is a popular, multitasking UNIX-type operating system that is one of the faster growing operating systems in use today. Unlike Windows and Mac OS, both of which are proprietary systems, Linux is **open source software**, which means its code is available free to the public. Many programmers have donated time to make Linux the best possible version of UNIX.

THE ROLE OF THE USER INTERFACE

All software, including the operating system, is designed to communicate with the user in a certain way, through a user interface. A **user interface** controls how you enter data or instructions (input) and how information is presented on the screen (output).

One of the more common user interfaces is a graphical user interface. A **graphical user interface**, or **GUI** (pronounced gooey), combines text, graphics, and other visual cues to make software easier to use. In 1984, Apple introduced a new operating system based on a graphical user interface. Recognizing the value of this easy-to-use interface, many software companies followed suit, developing their own GUI software.

FAQ

Can I simply turn the computer off when I am finished?

No! You must use the operating system's shut-down procedure so various processes are closed in sequence and items in memory are released properly.

Figure 3-4 The five major categories of popular application software. You likely will use software from more than one of these categories.

Application Software

Recall that **application software** consists of programs designed to perform specific tasks for users. Application software, also called an **application program**, can be used for the following purposes:

- As a productivity/business tool
- Supporting school and professional activities
- Assisting with graphics and multimedia projects
- Helping with home and personal activities
- Facilitating communications

The table in Figure 3-4 categorizes popular types of application software by their general use. These five categories are not all-inclusive or mutually exclusive; for example, e-mail can support productivity, a software suite can include Web page authoring tools, and tax preparation software can be used by a business. In the course of a day, week, or month, you are likely to find yourself using software from many of these categories, whether you are at school, home, or work. Even though you may not use all of the applications, you should at least be familiar with their capabilities.

Communications applications such as e-mail, Web browsers, and others were discussed in Chapter 2. This chapter gives a general overview of each of the other four categories and provides specific examples of applications in each category that are used on both PCs and Macintosh computers.

CATEGORIES OF APPLICATION SOFTWARE

Productivity Business	Graphic Design/ Multimedia	School	Home/Personal	Communications
• Word Processing	• Desktop Publishing	• School/Student Management	• Personal Finance	• E-Mail
• Spreadsheet	• Paint/Image Editing	• Grade Book	• Tax Preparation	• Web Browser
• Presentation Graphics	• Multimedia Authoring	• Education/Reference	• Legal	• Chat Rooms
• Database	• Web Page Authoring	• Special Needs	• Entertainment	• Newsgroups
• Personal Information Management				• Instant Messaging
• Software Suite				• LISTSERV

A huge variety of application software such as word processing is available as packaged software that can be purchased from software vendors in retail stores or on the Web. A particular software product, such as Microsoft Word for example, often is called a **software package**. Many application software packages also are available as shareware, freeware, and public-domain software; these packages, however, usually have fewer capabilities than retail software packages.

STARTING A SOFTWARE APPLICATION

To use application software, you must instruct the operating system to start the program. Figure 3-5 illustrates how to start

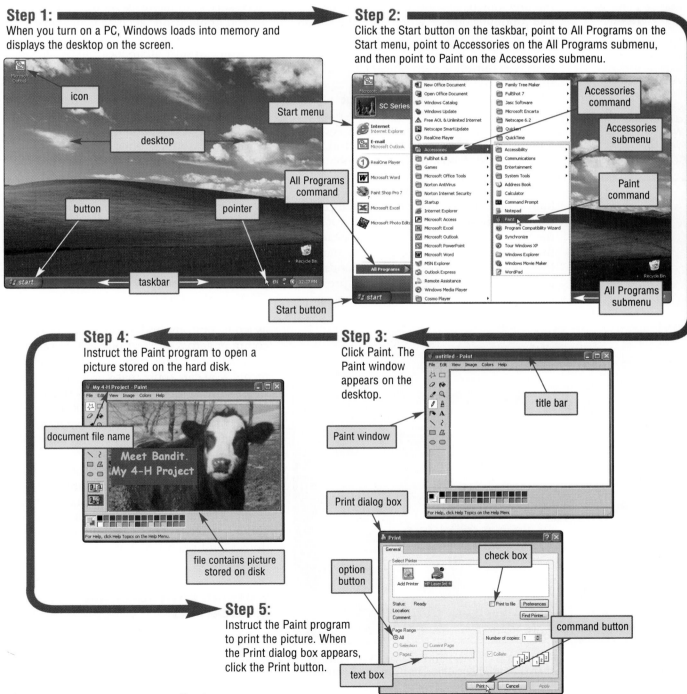

Figure 3-5 How to start an application.

and then interact with the Paint program on a PC using Microsoft Windows XP.

Both Mac OS and Microsoft Windows use the concept of a desktop to make the computer easier to use. The **desktop** is an on-screen work area that uses common graphical elements such as icons, buttons, windows, menus, and dialog boxes to make it easy and intuitive for users to interact with the computer. Step 1 of Figure 3-5 on the previous page shows icons, buttons, and a pointer on the Windows XP desktop.

An **icon** is a small image that represents a program, an instruction, or some other object. A **button** is a graphical element (usually a rectangular or circular shape) that when selected, causes a specific action to take place. To select a button, typically you click it using a pointing device such as a mouse. You also can select a button using the keyboard. Icons, text, or a combination of both are used to identify buttons.

The Windows desktop contains a Start button in its lower-left corner, which can be used to start an application. When you click the Start button, the Start menu appears on the desktop. A **menu** is a list of commands from which you can select. **Commands** are instructions that cause a computer program to perform a specific action. Some menus

WEB INFO

For more information about application software packages, visit the Teachers Discovering Computers Web site, click Chapter 3, click Web Info, and then click Application.

have a **submenu**, which is a list of commands that appears when you select a command on a previous menu. For example, as shown in Step 2 of Figure 3-5, when you click the Start button and point to the All Programs command on the Start menu, the All Programs submenu is displayed. Selecting the Accessories command on the All Programs submenu displays the Accessories submenu. As shown in the Accessories submenu, Windows includes several applications such as Calculator, Paint, and WordPad.

You can start an application by clicking its program name on a menu or submenu. Doing so instructs the operating system to start the application by transferring the program's instructions from a storage medium into memory. For example, if you click Paint on the Accessories submenu, Windows transfers the program instructions from the computer's hard disk into memory.

Once started, an application is displayed in a window on the desktop. A **window** is a rectangular area of the screen that is used to display a program, data, and/or information [see Step 3 of Figure 3-5]. The top of a window has a **title bar**, which is a horizontal space that contains the window's name.

One of the major advantages of a graphical user interface is that elements such as icons, buttons, and menus, usually are common across applications. After you learn the purpose and functionality of these elements, you can apply that knowledge to several software applications. Many of the features just described also are applicable to the desktop of the Macintosh operating system, which is arranged somewhat differently [Figure 3-5].

The features of a user interface make it easier for users to communicate with a personal computer. You will see examples of these features and how they are used as you learn about various software applications used by schools, businesses, and individuals.

WORKING WITH SOFTWARE APPLICATIONS

While using many software applications, you have the ability to create, edit, format, print, and save documents. A **document** is a piece of work created with

menus   icons

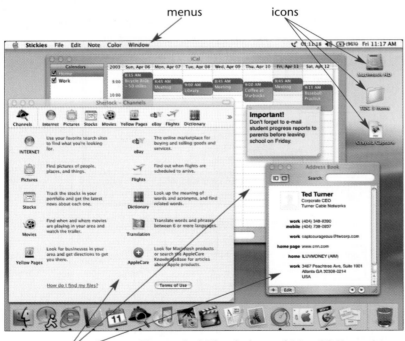

application windows

Figure 3-6 The desktop of Mac OS X consists of an arrangement different from the Windows desktop; however, both operating systems contain similar features.

an application and saved on a disk with a unique file name. Many users think of documents as files created using word processing software. To a computer, however, data is nothing more than a collection of characters, so a spreadsheet or graphic is as much a document as a letter or report. During the process of developing a document, you likely will switch back and forth among the following activities.

Creating involves developing the document by entering text or numbers, designing graphics, and performing other tasks using an input device such as a keyboard or mouse. If you design a map using the graphics tools in Paint, for example, you are creating a document.

Editing is the process of making changes to the document's existing content. Common editing tasks include inserting, deleting, cutting, copying, and pasting items in a document. For example, using Paint, you can **insert**, or add, text to the map, such as the names of key landmarks. When you **delete**, you remove text or objects. To **cut** involves removing a portion of the document and electronically storing it in a temporary storage location called

the **Clipboard**. When you **copy**, a portion of the document is duplicated and stored on the Clipboard. To place whatever is stored on the Clipboard into the document, you **paste** it into the document.

Formatting involves changing the appearance of a document. Formatting is important because the overall look of a document can significantly affect its ability to communicate effectively. For example, you might want to increase the size of the text to improve readability.

One often-used formatting task involves changing the font, font size, or font style of text. A **font** is a name assigned to a specific design of characters. Arial and Times New Roman are examples of fonts. The **font size** specifies the size of the characters in a particular font. Font size is gauged by a measurement system called **points**. A single point is about 1/72 of an inch in height. The text you are reading in this book is 10 point. Thus, each character is about 10/72 of an inch in height. A **font style** is used to add emphasis to a font. Examples of font styles are **bold**, *italic*, and underline. Examples of these and additional formatting features are shown in Figure 3-7.

For more information about fonts, visit the Teachers Discovering Computers Web site, click Chapter 3, click Web Info, and then click Font.

Figure 3-7
Examples of formatting features available with many productivity programs.

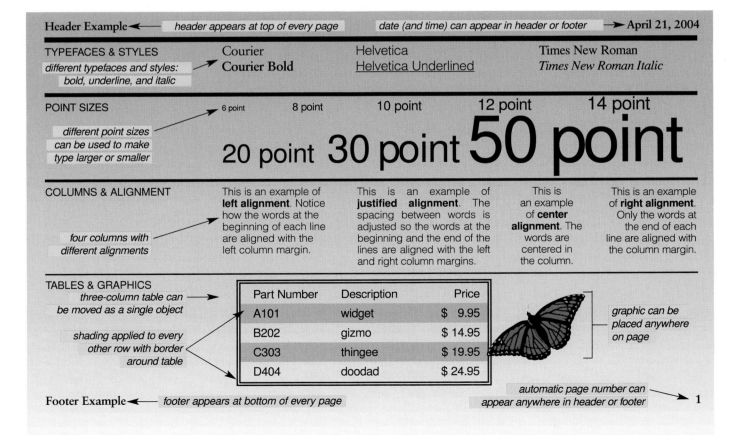

Header Example ◄—	header appears at top of every page	date (and time) can appear in header or footer —►	April 21, 2004

TYPEFACES & STYLES	Courier	Helvetica	Times New Roman
different typefaces and styles: bold, underline, and italic	**Courier Bold**	<u>Helvetica Underlined</u>	*Times New Roman Italic*

POINT SIZES — *different point sizes can be used to make type larger or smaller*

6 point 8 point 10 point 12 point 14 point

20 point 30 point 50 point

COLUMNS & ALIGNMENT	This is an example of **left alignment**. Notice how the words at the beginning of each line are aligned with the left column margin.	This is an example of **justified alignment**. The spacing between words is adjusted so the words at the beginning and the end of the lines are aligned with the left and right column margins.	This is an example of **center alignment**. The words are centered in the column.	This is an example of **right alignment**. Only the words at the end of each line are aligned with the column margin.
four columns with different alignments				

TABLES & GRAPHICS
three-column table can be moved as a single object
shading applied to every other row with border around table

Part Number	Description	Price
A101	widget	$ 9.95
B202	gizmo	$ 14.95
C303	thingee	$ 19.95
D404	doodad	$ 24.95

graphic can be placed anywhere on page

While you are creating, editing, and formatting a document, it is held temporarily in memory. After you have completed these steps, you normally will save your document for future use. **Saving** is the process of copying a document from memory to a storage medium such as a floppy disk or hard disk. You should save the document frequently while working with it so your work will not be lost if the power fails or the computer crashes. Many applications also have an optional **AutoSave** feature that automatically saves open documents at specified time periods.

Any document on which you are working or you have saved exists as a file. A **file** is a named collection of data, instructions, or information, such as a document that you create, a program, or a set of data used by a program. To distinguish among various files, each file has a **file name**, which is a unique set of letters, numbers, and other characters that identifies the file.

After you have created a document, you can print it many times, with each copy looking just like the first. **Printing** is the process of sending a file to a printer to generate output on a medium such as

paper. You also can send the document to others electronically, if your computer is connected to a network.

In some cases, when you instruct a program to perform an activity such as printing, a dialog box displays. A **dialog box** is a special window displayed by a program to provide information, present available options, or request a response using command buttons, option buttons, text boxes, and check boxes [Figure 3-8]. A Print dialog box, for example, gives you many printing options, such as printing multiple copies, using different printers, or viewing the document on the screen exactly as it will look when printed.

Many software applications support voice recognition. **Voice recognition**, also called **speech recognition**, is the computer's capability of distinguishing spoken words. You speak into the computer's microphone and watch your words display on your screen as you talk. You also can edit and format a document by speaking or spelling instructions. Figure 3-9 shows how to dictate words and issue voice commands in Microsoft Word.

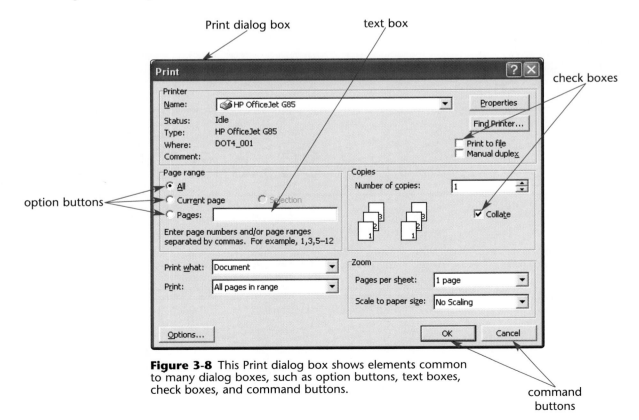

Figure 3-8 This Print dialog box shows elements common to many dialog boxes, such as option buttons, text boxes, check boxes, and command buttons.

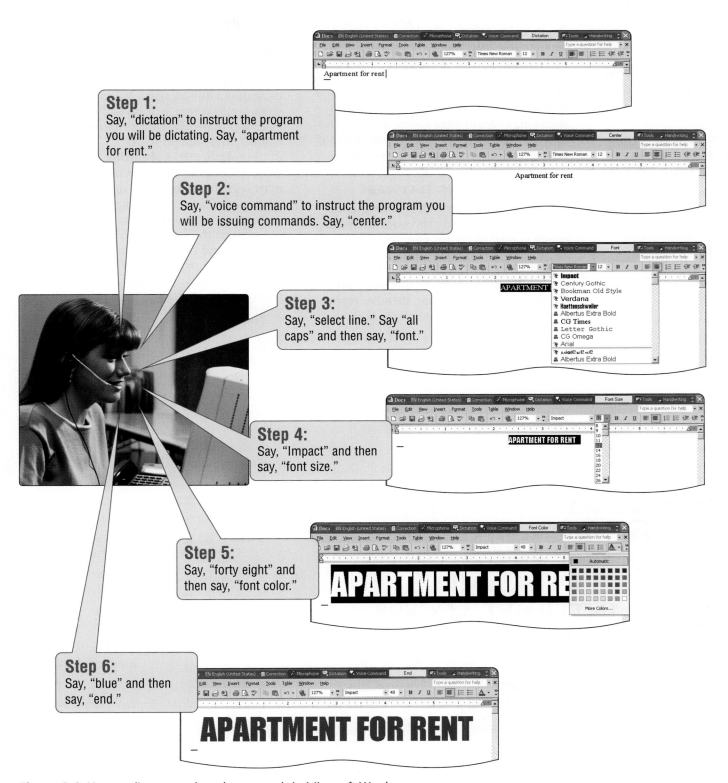

Figure 3-9 How to dictate words and commands in Microsoft Word.

Productivity Software

Productivity software is designed to make people more effective and efficient while performing daily activities. Productivity software includes applications such as word processing, spreadsheet, database, presentation graphics, personal information management, and software suites. The features and functions of each of these applications are discussed in the following sections.

WORD PROCESSING SOFTWARE

One of the more widely used application software is **word processing software,** which is used to create, edit, and format documents that consist primarily of text [Figure 3-10]. Millions of people use word processing software every day to create documents such as letters, memos, reports, fax cover sheets, mailing labels, and newsletters. The more popular word processing programs used in schools today are Microsoft Word, WordPerfect, and the word processing applications included with AppleWorks, ClarisWorks, and Microsoft Works. By acquiring solid word processing skills, teachers can increase their productivity significantly by using word processing software to create written documents, such as lesson plans, handouts, parent communications, and student tests.

In addition to supporting basic text, word processing software has many formatting features to make documents look professional and visually appealing. When developing a newsletter, for example, you can change the font and font size of headlines and headings, change the color of characters, or organize text into newspaper-style columns. Any colors used for characters or other formatting will print as black or gray unless you have a color printer.

Web Info

For more information about Microsoft Works, visit the Teachers Discovering Computers Web site, click Chapter 3, click Web Info, and then click Microsoft Works.

document displays in word processing window

printed document

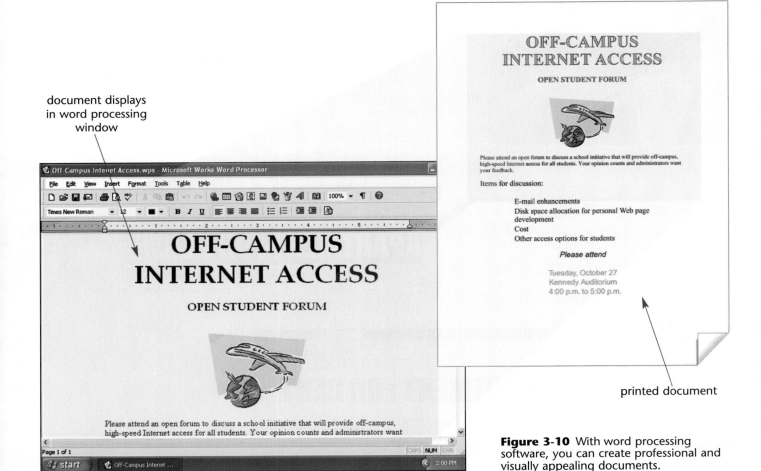

Figure 3-10 With word processing software, you can create professional and visually appealing documents.

Most word processing software also can incorporate many types of graphics. For example, you can enhance a document by adding a **border**, which is a decorative line or pattern along one or more edges of a page or graphic. One type of graphic commonly included with word processing software is **clip art**, which is a collection of drawings, diagrams, and photographs that can be inserted in other documents. **Clip art collections**, which can contain several hundred to several thousand images, usually are grouped by type, such as buildings, nature, or people [Figure 3-11]. If you want to use clip art not included in your word processing software package, you can create clip art and other graphics using Paint or other applications and **import** (bring into) the clip art into a word processing document. Paint and image editing software is discussed later in this chapter. After you insert, or import, a clip art image or other graphic into a document, you can move, resize, rotate, crop, and adjust its color.

All word processing software provides basic capabilities to help you create, edit, and format documents. For example, you can define the size of the paper on which to print, as well as the **margins** — that is, the portion of the page outside the main body of text, on the top, bottom, left, and right sides of the paper. The word processing software automatically readjusts any text so it fits within the new definitions.

With **wordwrap**, if you type text that extends beyond the page margin or window boundary, the word processor automatically positions text at the beginning of the next line. Wordwrap allows you to type words in a paragraph continually without pressing the ENTER key at the end of each line.

In some instances, such as if you create a multipage document, you can view only a portion of a document on the screen at a time. As you type more lines of text than can be displayed on the screen, the top portion of the document moves upward, or scrolls, off the screen. **Scrolling** is the process of moving different portions of the document into view on the screen.

A major advantage of using word processing software is that you can change easily what you have written. You can insert, delete, or rearrange words, sentences, or entire sections. You can use the **find** or **search** feature to locate all occurrences of a particular character, word, or phrase. This feature can be used in combination with the **replace** feature to substitute existing characters or words with new ones. Current word processing software packages even have a feature that automatically corrects errors and makes word substitutions as you type text.

To review the spelling of individual words, sections of a document, or the entire document, you can use a

Figure 3-11 Clip art consists of previously created illustrations that can be added to documents. Clip art collections include graphic images that are grouped by type. These clip art examples are from an animals and nature collection.

WEB INFO

For details about spelling bees, visit the Teachers Discovering Computers Web site, click Chapter 3, click Web Info, and then click Spelling.

spelling checker, also called a **spell checker** [Figure 3-12]. Spelling checker compares the words in the document with an electronic dictionary that is part of the word processing software. You can customize the electronic dictionary by adding words

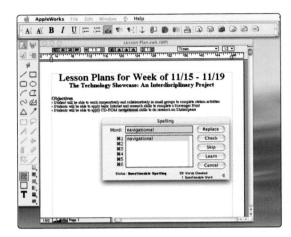

Figure 3-12
Spell checkers are included with most word processors. Shown is the spell checker included with AppleWorks.

such as names of companies, schools, streets, and cities, and personal names so the software can spell check those words as well. Many word processing software packages allow you to check the spelling of a whole document at one time or check the spelling of single words as you type them.

You also can insert headers and footers into a word processing document. A **header** is text you want at the top of each page; a **footer** is text you want at the bottom of each page. Page numbers, as well as company and school names, report titles, or dates are examples of items frequently included in headers and footers.

Many word processing programs make it quick and easy for teachers and students to create personalized templates using special programs called wizards. A **wizard**, or **assistant**, is an automated tool that helps you complete a task by asking you questions and then automatically performing actions based on your answers. Many software applications include wizards. Word processing software, for example, uses wizards to help you create memorandums, meeting agendas, letters, and other professional looking documents. Word processing wizards and templates also can help you create personalized templates for a letterhead, resume, newsletter, certificate, bibliography, tests, and more [Figure 3-13].

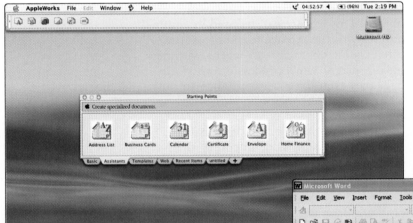

[a] AppleWorks

Figure 3-13 A wizard, called an assistant in AppleWorks, allows teachers and students quickly to create personalized flyers, newsletters, certificates, and more. Figure 3-13a shows some of the assistants available in AppleWorks and Figure 3-13b shows some of the templates available in Microsoft Word.

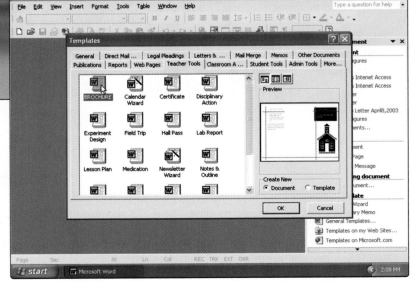

[b] Microsoft Word

In addition to these basic features, most current word processing packages provide many other features, some of which are listed in the table in Figure 3-14.

SPREADSHEET SOFTWARE

Another widely used software application is **spreadsheet software**, which allows you to organize numeric data in rows and columns. These rows and columns collectively are called a **spreadsheet**, or **worksheet**. Manual spreadsheets created using pencil and paper have long been used to organize numeric data. The data in an electronic spreadsheet is organized in the same manner as it is in a manual spreadsheet [Figure 3-15 on the next page].

POPULAR WORD PROCESSING FEATURES

Feature	Description
AutoCorrect	As you type words, the AutoCorrect feature corrects common spelling errors. AutoCorrect also corrects capitalization mistakes.
AutoFormat	As you type, the AutoFormat feature automatically applies formatting to your text. For example, it automatically can number a list or convert a Web address to a hyperlink.
Columns	Most word processing software can arrange text in two or more columns to look similar to a newspaper or magazine. The text from the bottom of one column automatically flows to the top of the next column.
Grammar Checker	You can use the grammar checker to proofread documents for grammar, writing style, and sentence structure errors in a document.
Mail Merge	Create form letters, mailing labels, and envelopes.
Tables	Tables are a way of organizing information into rows and columns. Instead of evenly spaced rows and columns, some word processing packages allow you to draw the tables, any size or shape, directly into the document.
Templates	A template is a document that contains the formatting necessary for a specific document type. Templates usually exist for memos, fax cover sheets, and letters.
Thesaurus	With a thesaurus, you can look up a synonym (word with the same meaning) for a word in a document.
Tracking Changes/ Comments	If multiple users work with a document, the word processing software can highlight or color-code changes made by various users. You also can add comments to a document, without changing the text itself. Comments allow you to communicate with the other users working on the document.
Voice Recognition	With some word processing packages, you can speak into the computer's microphone and watch the spoken words display on your screen as you talk. With these packages, you also can speak commands such as editing and formatting the document.
Web Page Development	Most word processing software supports Internet connectivity, allowing you to create, edit, and format documents for the World Wide Web. You automatically can convert an existing word processing document into the standard document format for the World Wide Web.

Figure 3-14 Some of the features included with word processing software.

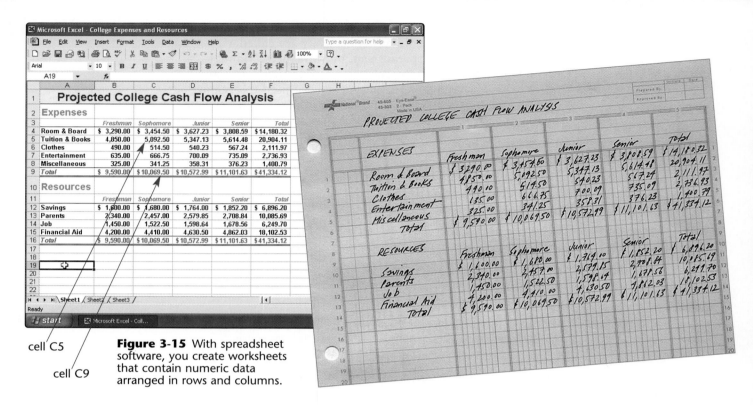

cell C5

cell C9

Figure 3-15 With spreadsheet software, you create worksheets that contain numeric data arranged in rows and columns.

Individuals who frequently work with numbers, such as financial statements and payroll, use spreadsheets. Many teachers interact with spreadsheet programs on a daily basis. Every time teachers enter a student's grade or attendance information into a computer, they are entering information into a special spreadsheet program, called an electronic grade book. K-12 grade book programs are discussed later in this chapter.

As with word processing software, most spreadsheet software has basic features to help you create, edit, and format electronic spreadsheets. These features, as included in several popular spreadsheet packages, are described below. Typically used in schools are spreadsheet software included in Microsoft Works, AppleWorks, and ClarisWorks; and Microsoft Excel that is packaged with Microsoft Office.

Spreadsheet files normally have 256 columns and 65,536 rows. Each column is identified by a letter, and each row is identified by a number. The column letters begin with A and row numbers begin with 1. Only a small fraction of these columns and rows are displayed on the screen at one time. To view different parts of a worksheet, you can scroll to display it on your screen.

The intersection of a column and row is called a **cell**. Cells are identified by the column and row in which they are located. For example, the intersection of column C and row 5 is referred to as cell C5. In Figure 3-15, cell C5 contains the number 5,092.50, which represents Sophomore Tuition & Books expenses.

Cells may contain three types of data: labels (text), values (numbers), and formulas. The text, or **label**, entered in a cell is used to identify the data and help organize the spreadsheet. Using descriptive labels, such as Room & Board, Tuition & Books, and Clothes, helps make a spreadsheet more meaningful.

Many of the spreadsheet cells shown in Figure 3-15 contain a number, or a **value**. Other cells, however, contain formulas that are used to generate values. A **formula** performs calculations on the numeric data in the spreadsheet and displays the resulting value in the cell containing the formula. In Figure 3-15, for example, cell C9 could contain the formula to calculate the projected total expenses for the student's sophomore year.

A **function** is a predefined formula that performs common calculations such as adding the values in a group of cells. For example, instead of using the formula =C4+C5+C6+C7+C8 to calculate the projected total expenses for the student's sophomore year, you should use the function =sum(C4:C8), which adds, or sums, the contents of cells C4, C5, C6, C7, and C8.

Another standard feature of spreadsheet software is the capability of turning numeric data into a **chart** that graphically illustrates the relationship of the numeric data. Visual representation of data in charts often makes it easier to analyze and interpret information. Most charts are variations of three basic chart types — line charts, pie charts, and column charts as shown in Figure 3-16. To improve their appearance, most charts can be displayed or printed in a three-dimensional format.

As with word processing software, you quickly can create professional looking spreadsheets using wizards. Using the wizards in most popular spreadsheet packages is easy and allows you to create grade books, classroom and school schedules, charts, and more. Spreadsheet software also incorporates many of the features of word processing software such as a spelling checker, font formatting, and the capability of converting an existing spreadsheet document into the standard document format for the World Wide Web. Because individual rows, columns, cells, or any combination of cells can be formatted, school districts and businesses often use spreadsheet programs to create their standardized forms.

DATABASE SOFTWARE

A **database** is a collection of data organized in a manner that allows access, retrieval, and use of that data. In a manual system, schools record information on paper and store it in a filing cabinet [Figure 3-17]. In a computerized database, such as the one shown in Figure 3-20 on page 3.17, data is stored in an electronic format on a storage medium. **Database software** allows you to create a computerized database; add, change, and delete data; sort and retrieve data from the database; and create forms and reports using the data in the database.

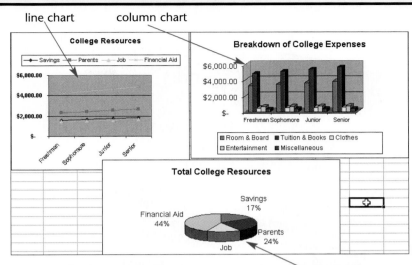

line chart   column chart

pie chart

Figure 3-16 Three basic types of charts provided with spreadsheet software are line charts, column charts, and pie charts. The line chart, column chart, and pie chart shown were created from the data in the worksheet in Figure 3-15.

Figure 3-17 A database is similar to a manual system in which related data items are stored in files.

Database software is used extensively by businesses and other organizations to organize data and information about customers, employees, equipment, product inventory, sales information, and more. Schools use databases to organize data and information about students, staff members, school policies, equipment inventories, book inventories, purchases, and more. Database programs typically used in schools include Microsoft Access, FileMaker Pro, and the database software included in Microsoft Works, AppleWorks, and ClarisWorks.

WEB INFO

For an example of how athletes use databases for training purposes, visit the Teachers Discovering Computers Web site, click Chapter 3, click Web Info, and then click Athlete.

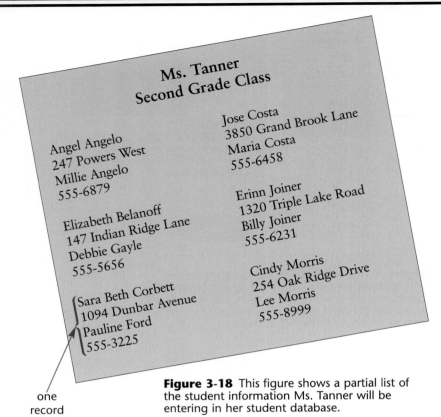

one
record

Figure 3-18 This figure shows a partial list of the student information Ms. Tanner will be entering in her student database.

a collection of related facts called **fields**. For example, a student database file might consist of records containing names, address information, and parental or guardian information. All of the data that relates to one student would be considered a record. Each fact in a record, such as the street address or telephone number, is called a field.

Figures 3-18 through 3-20 present the development of a database containing basic information about students enrolled in Ms. Eileen Tanner's second grade class at Martin Luther King Elementary School. This simple database contains the following information about each student: first name, last name, guardian's address, name, and telephone number.

Before you begin creating a database, make a list of the data items you want to organize [Figure 3-18]. Each set of related information will become a record. Each item will become a field in the database. To identify the different fields, assign each field a unique name that is short, yet descriptive. For example, the field name for a student's last name could be Last Name, the field name for a student's first name could be First Name, and so on. Database programs differ slightly in how they require the user to enter or define

When you use a database, you need to be familiar with the terms file, record, and field. Just as in a manual system, a **database file** is a collection of related data that is organized in records. Each **record** contains

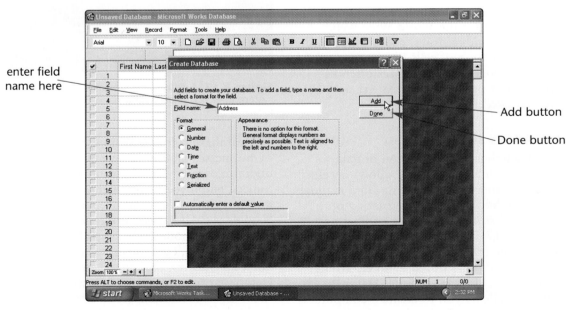

enter field
name here

Add button

Done button

Figure 3-19 To create database fields in Microsoft Works, you simply type in each field name and then click the Add button. After entering all the fields you need and clicking the Done button in the Create Database dialog box, you are ready to enter the data in the new database.

fields. A field entry screen from Microsoft Works is shown in Figure 3-19.

After the database structure is created by defining the fields, data for individual database records can be entered. After data for all records are entered, the database can be used to produce information. Figure 3-20 shows the database after the information about the students has been entered.

As with word processing and spreadsheet software, database software includes wizards that allow teachers and students to create databases for use as address books, directories of parents and students, equipment and book inventories, and so on.

PRESENTATION GRAPHICS SOFTWARE

Using **presentation graphics software,** you can create documents called **presentations,** which you then use to communicate ideas, messages, and other information to a group, such as a class or auditorium of people. The presentations can be viewed as **slides** that are displayed on a large monitor or projected onto a screen.

Slides also can be made into traditional overhead transparencies or printed and given to students as a handout [Figure 3-21 on the next page].

Presentation programs typically used in schools are the presentation software included in AppleWorks, ClarisWorks, and Microsoft PowerPoint packaged with Microsoft Office. As with all of the individual software programs in Microsoft Office, you can purchase and use PowerPoint separately.

Presentation graphics software typically provides an array of predefined presentation formats that define complementary colors for backgrounds, text, and other special effects. Presentation graphics software also provides a variety of layouts for each individual slide so you can create a title slide; a two-column slide; a slide with clip art; and others. Any text, charts, and graphics used in a slide can be enhanced with 3-D and other effects such as shading, shadows, and textures.

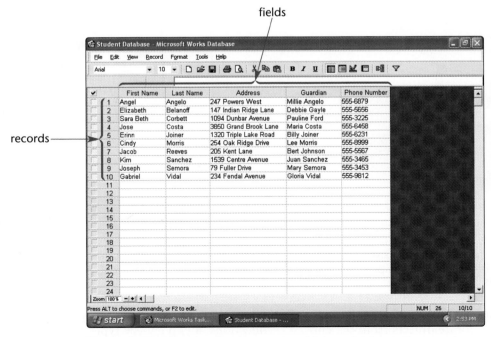

Figure 3-20 After data has been entered into a database, the records can be arranged in any order specified by users. In this example, the records have been organized alphabetically based on students' last names.

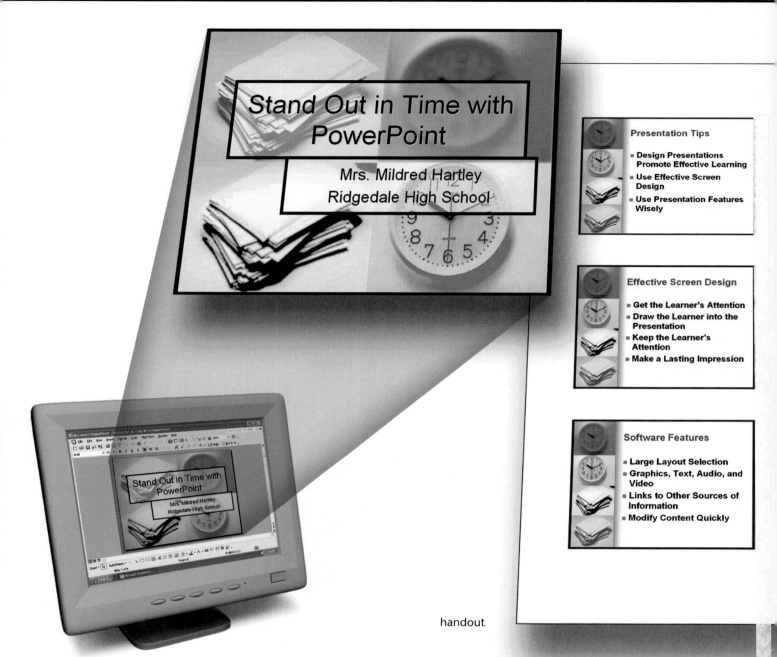

screen display

handout

Figure 3-21 Teachers and students use presentation graphics software to create electronic slides. The slides can be displayed on a computer, projected on a screen, printed and handed out, or made into transparencies.

With presentation graphics software, you can incorporate objects from the clip art/image gallery into your slides to create multimedia presentations. A **clip art/image gallery** includes clip art images, pictures, video clips, and audio clips. A clip art/image gallery can be stored on a hard disk, a CD-ROM, or a DVD-ROM; in other cases, you access the clip art/image

gallery on the Web. As with clip art collections, a clip gallery typically is organized by categories such as academic, business, entertainment, and transportation. For example, the transportation category may contain a clip art image of a bicycle, a photograph of a locomotive, a video clip of an airplane in flight, and an audio clip of a Model T car horn.

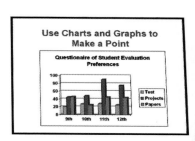

transparency

WEB INFO

For tips on using graphics effectively in a presentation, visit the Teachers Discovering Computers Web site, click Chapter 3, click Web Info, and then click Presentation.

When building a presentation, you also can set the slide timing so the presentation automatically displays the next slide after a predetermined delay. You can apply special effects to the transition between each slide. For example, one slide might slowly dissolve as the next slide comes into view.

To help organize the presentation, you can view small versions of all the slides in a slide sorter. A **slide sorter** presents a screen view similar to how 35mm slides would look on a photographer's light table [Figure 3-22 on the next page]. The slide sorter allows you to arrange the slides in any order or display them one at a time by clicking the mouse or pressing a key on the keyboard.

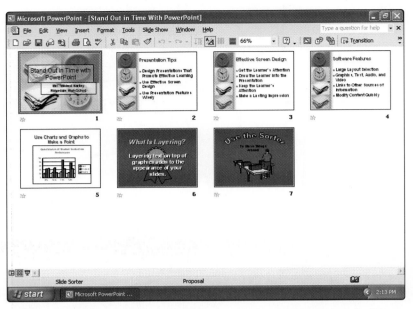

Figure 3-22 This slide sorter screen shows a small version of each slide. Using a pointing device or the keyboard, users can rearrange the order of the slides.

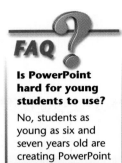

FAQ

Is PowerPoint hard for young students to use?

No, students as young as six and seven years old are creating PowerPoint presentations.

Presentation graphics software also incorporates some of the features provided in word processing software such as spelling checking, formatting, and converting an existing slide show into a format that can be viewed on the World Wide Web.

Presentation graphics programs are important software programs for K-12 schools. Teachers can create and integrate electronic presentations into any classroom curriculum as an exciting alternative to the traditional lecture-only teaching style [Figure 3-23]. Students take great pride in creating their own presentations using presentation graphics software. Later chapters provide real-life examples of how teachers integrate presentation graphics software into their instruction and curriculum. A unique feature of presentation graphics software is that it allows you to create a

Figure 3-23 Electronic slide presentations are an exciting alternative to the traditional lecture-only teaching style.

presentation that presents information in a nonlinear format. When using overhead transparencies, teachers traditionally show one transparency after another in a predetermined order — that is, linear teaching and learning.

With presentation graphics software programs, teachers and students can create presentations easily with links to a variety of information sources. Teachers and students, for example, can create presentations with links to other slides, other presentations, other files and software programs, animations, audio and video clips, and even sites on the World Wide Web [Figure 3-24]. Using these links, teachers and students can branch off in a nonlinear fashion at any point in a presentation, to display or access additional information.

The ability to modify presentation content according to student interest makes presentation graphics software a powerful teaching and learning tool. The In the Lab end-of-chapter section in Chapter 5 discusses using and integrating Microsoft PowerPoint in more depth.

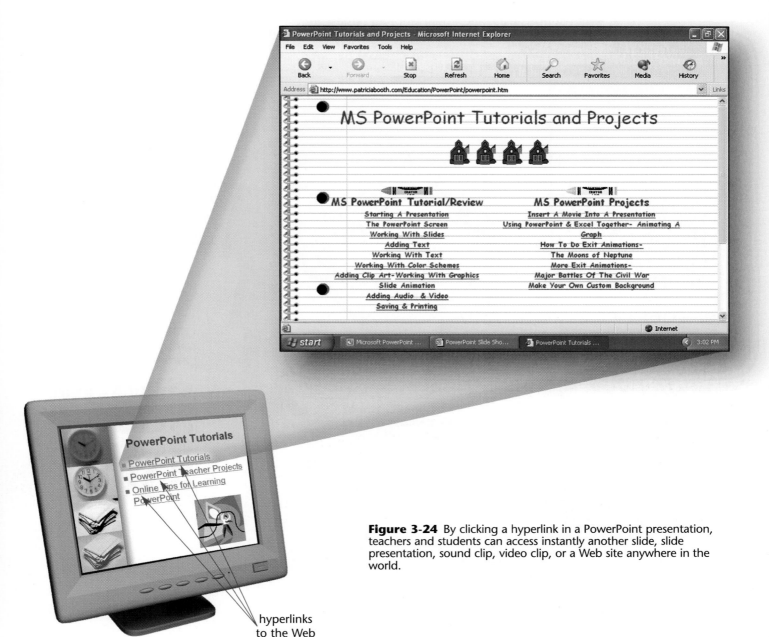

Figure 3-24 By clicking a hyperlink in a PowerPoint presentation, teachers and students can access instantly another slide, slide presentation, sound clip, video clip, or a Web site anywhere in the world.

FAQ

Are PDAs also called Pocket PCs?

Only some of them. A **Pocket PC** is a type of PDA that uses the Pocket PC operating system software developed by Microsoft; only a PDA that uses the Pocket PC software is called a Pocket PC.

PERSONAL INFORMATION MANAGERS

A **personal information manager (PIM)** is a software application installed on PDAs that includes an appointment calendar, address book, notepad, and other features to help you organize personal information such as appointments, task lists, and more, as shown in Figure 3-25. A PIM allows you to take information that you tracked previously in a weekly or daily calendar, and organize and store it on your computer. PIMs can manage many different types of information such as telephone messages, project notes, reminders, task and address lists, and important dates and appointments.

An **appointment calendar** allows you to schedule activities for a particular day and time. With an **address book**, you can enter and maintain names, addresses, and telephone numbers of coworkers, family members, and friends. Instead of writing notes on a piece of paper, you can use a **notepad** to record ideas, reminders, and other important information.

Most PDAs contain many other features and built-in software programs in addition to those shown in Figure 3-25, including e-mail, Web browsing, instant messaging, and more. One of these features allows users to **synchronize**, or transfer, information and programs from the PDA

Address Book/Contacts

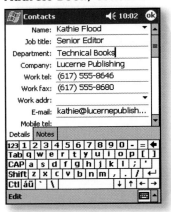

Memos/Notepad

To-Do List

Datebook/Calendar

Calculator

Figure 3-25 Most PDAs come equipped with an address book, to-do list, notepad, calendar, and calculator.

to a personal computer and vice versa. Some PDAs transfer information wirelessly and others connect to the computer with a cable [Figure 3-26]. Many PDAs allow you to transfer information to another PDA by a process called beaming. **Beaming** is a method of transferring data through an infrared port. As with personal computers, PDAs require an operating system. Common PDA operating systems include Palm OS, PocketPC, and Linux.

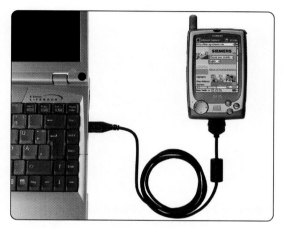

FIGURE 3-26 Most PDAs allow the user to synchronize, or transfer, information and programs from a personal computer to the PDA and vice-versa.

PDA SOFTWARE

In addition to PIMs or installed software, a large selection of software is available for PDAs for a variety of uses including personal productivity, business, communications, medical, scientific, travel, global positioning, entertainment, games, multimedia, and education. You can download PDA applications from the Web [Figure 3-27] or purchase them at computer and electronic stores.

Downloading and installing programs is an easy process. First, you download the software program to your personal computer, and then you install the software on your PDA using your PDA's synchronization software.

Software purchased at stores usually is supplied on a CD-ROM. You use the CD-ROM to install the software on your personal computer and then use the PDA's synchronization software to install the software on your PDA. A significant number of PDA software programs are available as shareware, freeware, or trial editions and can be found at a number of Web sites [Figure 3-28].

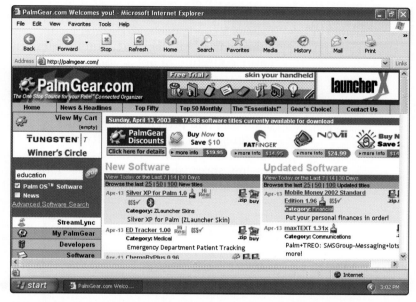

Figure 3-27 PalmGear.com is a popular reseller of PDA software programs.

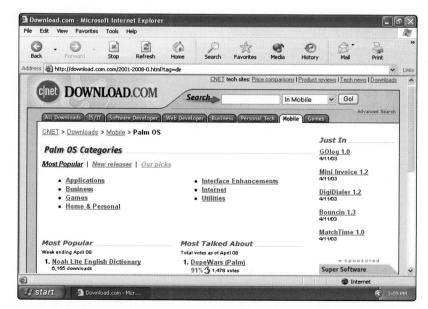

Figure 3-28 Download.com is a popular Web site for downloading shareware and freeware programs, including popular programs for PDAs.

For updated links to these and other PDA software sites, visit the Teachers Discovering Computers Web site, click Chapter 3, click Web Info, and then click PDA Software.

Students and teachers can benefit from PDA software designed for educational uses. Figure 3-29 describes a few of the hundreds of PDA software programs that are designed for teachers and students both in K-12 schools and institutions of higher education.

SOFTWARE SUITES AND INTEGRATED SOFTWARE

A **software suite** is a collection of individual application software packages sold as a single package [Figure 3-30]. When you install the suite, you install the entire collection of applications at once, rather than installing each application individually. At a minimum, suites typically include word processing, spreadsheet, database, and presentation graphics.

Integrated software is software that combines applications such as word processing, spreadsheet, and database into a single, easy-to-use package. Unlike a software suite, however, you cannot purchase the applications in the integrated software package individually. Each application in

an integrated software package is designed specifically to work as part of a larger set of applications (thus the name, integrated).

The applications within the integrated software package typically do not have all the capabilities of stand-alone productivity software applications. Integrated software thus is less expensive than a more powerful software suite. For many school, home, and personal users, however, the capabilities of an integrated software package more than meet their needs. In addition to

Figure 3-30 Microsoft Office is available in versions for both PC and Macintosh computers.

EDUCATION SOFTWARE FOR PDAs

Application	Description	Examples	Web Links
Teacher Management Tools	Manages grading, attendance, rosters, curriculum standards, planning, assessment, reporting, contact information, and more.	• Teachers P.E.T. • eStandards (Media-X) • Tracker and Seeker • Handango Teacher Suite	www.coffeepotsoftware.com/ www.media-x.com/products/estandards/index.php www.schoolid.com/ www.handango.com/
Reference Materials and Other Teaching Applications	Different types of sources for information containing useful facts or information.	• Merriam-Webster® Dictionary • Dictionary ToGo • Formulas for Palm OS®	www.franklin.com www.learningtogo.com/sitemap.php www.standalone.com/palmos/formulas/
ERIC Reference List on PDAs	This bibliography presents information on the educational uses of PDAs with Web links.	• Educational Resources Information Center (ERIC) CRIB	www.eriche.org/crib/PDAcrib.html
Curriculum-Specific Applications	Applications designed to support specific curriculum needs and standards.	• ImagiMath • ImagiProbe • Quizzler • Mental Math Scholastic Wireless	www.imagiworks.com/index5.html www.imagiworks.com/Pages/Products/ImagiProbe.html www.quizzlerpro.com/ www.aaamath.com/men.html teacher.scholastic.com/wireless/

Figure 3-29 Shown are just a few of the hundreds of ideas and software programs that can be used to benefit both students and teachers.

Microsoft Office, popular integrated software packages used in schools include **Microsoft Works** for PCs and **AppleWorks** for Macintosh computers [Figure 3-31].

Figure 3-31 Two popular integrated software packages used on home and school computers. Microsoft Works often is found on PCs and contains word processing, spreadsheet, database, and communications software. AppleWorks is used on Macintosh computers and contains word processing, spreadsheet, database, paint, and presentation software.

Both integrated software and software suites offer two major advantages: lower cost and ease of use. Typically, buying a collection of software packages in a suite costs significantly less than purchasing the application packages separately. Software suites provide ease of use because the applications within a suite normally use a similar interface and have some common features. Thus, once you learn how to use one application in the suite, you are familiar with the other applications in the suite. For example, once you learn how to print using the suite's word processing package, you can apply the same skill to the spreadsheet, database, and presentation graphics software in the suite.

Graphics and Multimedia Software

In addition to productivity software, many individuals also work with software designed specifically for their fields of work. For example, engineers, architects, desktop publishers, and graphic artists often use powerful software that allows them to work with graphics and multimedia. Types of graphics and multimedia software include desktop publishing software, paint/image editing software, multimedia authoring tools, Web page authoring software, and many others. The features and functions of some of these applications are discussed in the following sections.

DESKTOP PUBLISHING SOFTWARE

Desktop publishing (DTP) software allows you to design, produce, and deliver sophisticated documents that contain text, graphics, and brilliant colors. Although many word processing packages have some of the capabilities of DTP software, professional designers and graphic artists use DTP software because it is designed specifically to support **page layout**, which is the process of arranging text and graphics in a document. DTP software is ideal for the production of high-quality color documents such as newsletters, marketing literature, catalogs, and annual reports. In the past, documents of this type were created by slower, more expensive traditional publishing methods such as typesetting. Today's DTP software also allows you to convert a color document into a format for use on the World Wide Web.

Many home, school, and small business users use a much simpler, easy-to-understand DTP software designed for individual desktop publishing projects. Using this DTP software, you can create newsletters, brochures, and advertisements; postcards and greeting cards; letterhead and business cards; banners; calendars; logos; and other such documents. Personal DTP software guides you through the development of these documents by asking a series of questions, offering numerous predefined layouts, and providing standard text you can add to documents. As you enter text, the personal DTP software checks your spelling. You can print your finished publications on a color printer or place them on the Web. Teachers and students use desktop publishing software such as Microsoft Publisher and Adobe PageMaker to lay out school yearbooks and create flyers, certificates, and newsletters [Figure 3-32 on the next page].

Why can I not open some files on the Web including brochures, applications, education articles, and reports?

Many companies and education journals save some documents using the Adobe PDF format. This is so readers do not have to have the same program used to create the document. To view and print a PDF file, simply download the free Adobe Acrobat Reader software from the Adobe Web site (www.adobe.com).

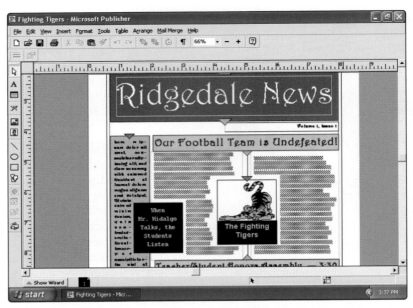

Figure 3-32 Teachers and students use desktop publishing software, such as Microsoft Publisher, to lay out school yearbooks and create flyers, certificates, newsletters, and other types of documents.

WEB INFO

For samples of clip art available on the Internet, visit the Teachers Discovering Computers Web site, click Chapter 3, click Web Info, and then click Clip Art.

PAINT/IMAGE EDITING SOFTWARE

Graphic artists, multimedia professionals, desktop publishers, and many others use paint software and image editing software to create and modify graphics, such as those used in DTP documents and Web pages [Figure 3-33]. **Paint software** allows you to draw pictures, shapes, and other graphics using various tools on the screen such as a pen, brush, eye dropper, and paint bucket. **Image editing software** provides the capabilities of paint software as well as the capability of modifying existing graphics. For example, you can retouch photographs; adjust or enhance image colors; and add special effects such as shadows and glows.

Many home, school, and small business users opt for personal paint/image editing software. Personal paint/image editing software provides a much easier to use interface and usually has simplified capabilities, with functions tailored to the needs of the home and small business user. As with the professional versions, personal paint software includes various simplified tools that allow you to draw pictures, shapes, and other graphics.

Personal image editing software provides the capabilities of paint software, and the capability of modifying existing graphics. One popular type of image editing software, called **photo-editing software**, allows you to edit digital photographs by removing red-eye, adding special effects, or creating electronic photo albums. When the photograph is complete, you can print it on labels, calendars, business cards, and banners; or place it on a Web page.

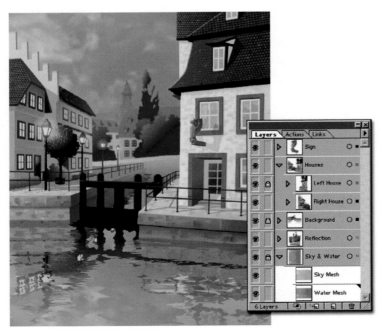

Figure 3-33 With image editing software, artists can create and modify a variety of graphic images.

VIDEO AND AUDIO EDITING SOFTWARE

Video consists of full-motion images played back at various speeds. With video editing software, you can modify a segment of a video, called a clip [Figure 3-34]. For example, you can add and remove clips, or add special effects like sounds, banners, credits, and more. Video editing programs normally allow you either to edit or add audio components. Current PC and Macintosh operating systems include extensive audio and video editing capabilities; you and your students can even make your own movies.

elicit direct student participation. Commercially produced multimedia presentations usually are stored and delivered via a CD-ROM or DVD-ROM, over a local area network, or via the Internet.

Figure 3-34 Users can use video editing software to modify video images.

CLIP ART/IMAGE GALLERY

Although many applications include clip art, you may find that you want a wider selection of graphics. One way to obtain them is to purchase a clip art/image gallery, which is a collection of clip art and photographs. In addition to clip art, many clip art/image galleries provide fonts, animations, sounds, video clips, and audio clips. You can use the images, fonts, and other items from the clip art/image gallery in all types of documents, such as letters, flyers, and class projects [Figure 3-35].

MULTIMEDIA AUTHORING SOFTWARE

Multimedia authoring software is used to create electronic presentations that can include text, graphics, video, audio, and animation. **HyperStudio** is an example of an easy-to-use multimedia authoring software program that allows the author to combine many multimedia elements into a series of interactive cards. The software helps you create presentations by allowing you to control the placement of text and graphics and the duration of sounds, video, and animation. Once created, such multimedia presentations often take the form of interactive computer-based presentations designed to facilitate learning and

Figure 3-35 Clip art/image galleries provide thousands of clip art images and photographs for use in documents such as letters, newsletters, greeting cards, class projects, and presentations.

WEB PAGE AUTHORING SOFTWARE

Web page authoring software is designed specifically to help you create Web pages, in addition to organizing, managing, and maintaining Web sites. As noted in previous sections, many application software packages include Web page authoring features that you can use to create Web pages and Web sites [Figure 3-36].

Figure 3-36 The figure shows you how to convert a word processing document automatically into the standard document format for the World Wide Web by saving it as a Web page. Once saved, the document can be published to the Web and viewed in any Web browser.

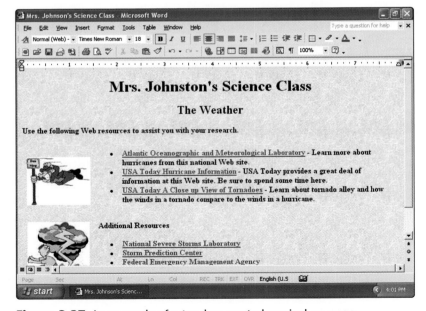

Figure 3-37 An example of a teacher-created curriculum page.

Word processing programs, for example, contain enough features to satisfy the formatting and layout needs of teachers and students for building curriculum pages and other Web documents, as shown in Figure 3-37. A **curriculum page** is a teacher-created document that contains hyperlinks to teacher-selected Web sites that assist in teaching content-specific curriculum objectives.

Web page authoring software features allow you to create sophisticated multimedia Web pages that include graphics, video, audio, animation, and other special effects. Many school technology coordinators use Web page authoring programs, such as **Adobe GoLive, Macromedia Dreamweaver,** and **Microsoft FrontPage,** to create Web pages for schools and school districts. Some teachers and students build their home pages using **Netscape Composer,** which is part of the Netscape Communicator free software package [Figure 3-38]. With Web page authoring software, both new and experienced users can create fascinating Web pages.

The special feature following this chapter provides you with step-by-step instructions for creating a teacher's Web page using Microsoft Word. In addition, the textbook Web site provides downloadable step-by-step instructions for creating a teacher's Web page in the latest version of Netscape Composer.

Software for School Use

Many school districts are undergoing a period of transition in how they maintain student records and other pertinent information. An important factor driving this transition is the installation of networks: many school districts are networking all of their classrooms and schools into local and wide area networks.

Having networks in schools allows schools to manage and maintain information about students and teachers in a centralized way. At the lower end, some schools still maintain all student records manually or in software programs on individual computers. Teachers and other school personnel then periodically input student records manually into student management software that

Figure 3-38 Some teachers and students build their Web pages using Netscape Composer, which is included with Netscape Communicator.

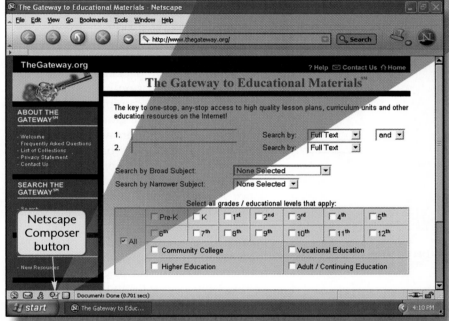

Netscape Composer button

WEB INFO

For tips on using Netscape Composer, visit the Teachers Discovering Computers Web site, click Chapter 3, click Web Info, and then click Composer.

stores grades and attendance records. Software for schools and professional use includes school management software, student management software, grade book software, educational and reference software, and software for students with special needs.

SCHOOL AND STUDENT MANAGEMENT SOFTWARE

Schools that have networked at least one computer in each classroom usually install school and student management software. When standardized throughout the school district, these programs can improve dramatically a school's ability to manage and analyze daily operations, budgets, and student information.

School management software is a centralized program that allows district and school personnel to manage the school district operations, such as budgeting, inventory, technology, and expenses. Most school management software packages allow a school district to keep a database of all district assets, salaries and benefits, and food services inventory; manage other school and department budgets; and track transportation vehicle maintenance and use. Some school management software also includes databases for attendance and other student information and has other functions similar to student management software. **Student management software** is a centralized program that allows administrators, teachers, and other staff to manage and track information about students, which includes attendance and academic records.

For information about grade book programs, visit the Teachers Discovering Computers Web site, click Chapter 3, click Web Info, and then click Grade Books.

Recall from Chapter 1, Washington County Public Schools has networked all of its classroom computers [Figure 3-39]. Teachers throughout the district enter attendance information into the district's student management software program shortly after classes begin. Within a few minutes, district and school administrators know exactly how many students are present. Teachers also enter student grades into the same grade book and attendance program installed on all district computers. Record keeping at Washington County Schools thus is fully automated.

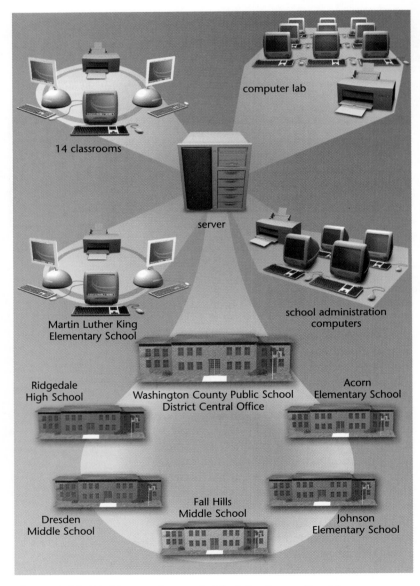

Figure 3-39 Washington County Public Schools uses its wide area network that connects all district classrooms to track student attendance records, grades, and more.

GRADE BOOK SOFTWARE

Grade book software allows teachers to track and organize student tests, homework, lab work, and other scores. Most grade book software allows you to track thousands of students and hundreds of assignments within the same grade book and sort students by name, student number, or current average. Most programs allow teachers to weight various scores automatically, apply grading curves, adjust letter grade cutoffs, or use a customized grading scale, such as Fair, Good, Excellent, and so on. Grades can be displayed and entered as points, percentages, letter grades, or in a customized grading scale.

Grade book software also integrates with other software packages. Schools that use network-based or online testing programs, for example, can import student scores directly into the grade book. Teachers also can import and export grades and rosters to a word processing, spreadsheet, or database program.

At some schools, teachers enter attendance and student grades into the same grade book software, which is installed on all district computers. Not all schools have mandated standard grade book programs for teachers to use, however; so many teachers choose their own grade book programs. Numerous outstanding grade book and attendance programs are available for teachers. Some of these are shareware programs; others have trial versions that you can download from the Web for evaluation purposes. Popular grade book programs include Grade Machine, MicroGrade, GradeQuick, Easy Grade Pro, and Gradebook Plus. You also can create basic grade books using the wizards and templates in Microsoft Excel, AppleWorks, and other programs [Figure 3-40].

EDUCATIONAL AND REFERENCE SOFTWARE

Educational software supports learning objectives and goals. Educational software exists for just about any subject, from learning a foreign language to learning how to cook. Preschool to high school learners can use educational software to assist them with subjects such as reading and math or to prepare them for class or college entrance exams.

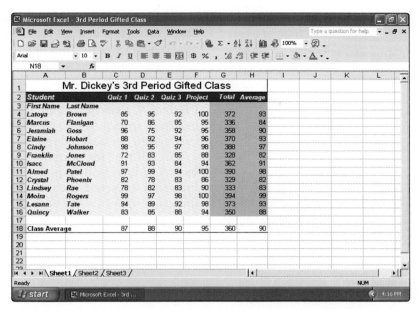

Figure 3-40 An example of a grade book that teachers can create using Microsoft Excel.

Educational software will be covered in greater depth in later chapters. You also can find information about Web links to dozens of popular educational software programs in Software Corner at the end of each chapter.

Reference software provides valuable and thorough information for everyone in an educational setting and in the family. Popular reference software includes encyclopedias, dictionaries, health/medical guides, and travel directories [Figure 3-41]. Chapter 5 covers many types of educational and reference software applications and discusses their features in detail.

FAQ

Are Microsoft Encarta, Britannica Reference Suite, and other popular reference software programs available on CD and DVD?

Yes, and the expanded storage capacity of DVDs allows for these manufactures to add additional, extensive, and high quality video segments, animations, graphics, and more.

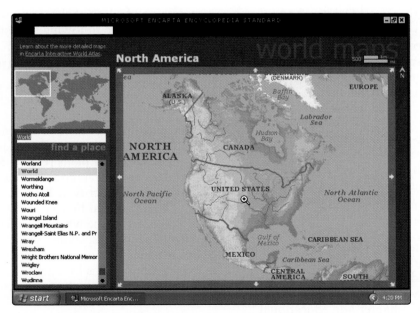

Figure 3-41 Reference software provides valuable and thorough information for all types of users. For example, Microsoft Encarta includes text, pictures, and videos on geography and thousands of other topics.

SPECIAL NEEDS SOFTWARE

Special needs software is designed specifically for students with physical impairments or learning disabilities, to assist them in completing school assignments and everyday tasks [Figure 3-42]. Special needs software includes such programs as speech synthesis software, text enlargement programs, talking calculators, and more.

Figure 3-42 Using assistive technology software, teachers help students with disabilities learn subject-related content.

Speech synthesis software allows students with speech and vocal muscle disorders to participate in classroom discussions. Students assign certain keys to reproduce specific frequently used phrases. They use the phrase keys to type in a response; the word processing software then reads the response in a computerized voice.

Students with visual impairments may use software with text enlargement features, which enable them to see the screen better. Other helpful software applications include an on-screen talking calculator that features big, colorful number buttons and high-quality speech synthesis.

Today, teachers have many software options available to use as tools to enhance teaching and learning of students with special needs. Many software applications discussed in this chapter and educational multimedia applications discussed in Chapter 5 also can assist students with special needs. When students use these

WEB INFO

For more information about a popular and free text-to-speech software program, visit the Teachers Discovering Computers Web site, click Chapter 3, click Web Info, and then click ReadPlease.

software programs in combination with assistive devices such as touch screens and adaptive keyboards, their ability to succeed increases. These and other special input and output devices designed for use by students with special needs are discussed in Chapter 4. Examples of how teachers can integrate special needs software into their curriculum are covered in Chapters 5-7.

Recall that the textbook Web site includes an end-of-chapter section called Integration Corner. Included with Integration Corner for each chapter is Special Education Corner, where you will find dozens of links to special needs software programs and information on how other teachers are integrating technology with special needs students.

Software for Home and Personal Use

Many software applications are designed specifically for home or personal use. Personal software includes personal finance software, tax preparation software, legal software, entertainment software, and more. Most of the products in this category are relatively inexpensive, often priced at less than $50. The features and functions of some of these applications are discussed in the following sections.

PERSONAL FINANCE SOFTWARE

Personal finance software is a simplified accounting program that helps you pay bills; balance your checkbook; track your personal income and expenses, such as credit-card bills; track investments; and evaluate financial plans [Figure 3-43]. Popular personal finance software includes Quicken and Microsoft Money.

Using personal finance software can help you determine where, and for what purpose, you are spending money so you can manage your finances. Reports can summarize transactions by category (such as dining), by payee (such as the electric company), or by period (such as the last two months). Bill-paying features include the ability to print checks on your printer or have an outside service print your checks.

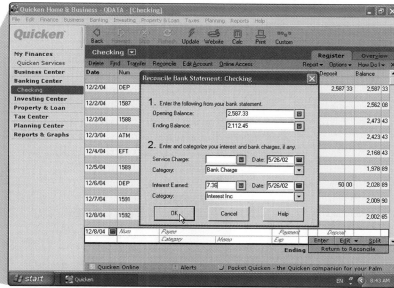

Figure 3-43 Many home users work with personal finance software to assist them with balancing their checkbook and paying bills.

For information about income tax preparation programs, visit the Teachers Discovering Computers Web site, click Chapter 3, click Web Info, and then click Income Tax.

Personal finance software packages usually offer a variety of online services, which require access to the Web. For example, you can track your investments online, compare insurance rates from leading insurance companies, and even do your banking online. With online banking, you can transfer money electronically from your checking to savings or vice versa. To obtain current credit card statements, bank statements, and account balances, you download transaction information from your bank using the Web.

Financial planning features include analyzing home and personal loans, preparing income taxes, and managing retirement savings. Other features in many personal finance packages include home inventory, budgeting, and tax-related transactions.

TAX PREPARATION SOFTWARE

Tax preparation software guides individuals, families, or small businesses through the process of filing federal taxes [Figure 3-44]. Popular tax preparation software includes TurboTax and TaxCut. These software packages offer money-saving tax tips, designed to lower your tax bill. After you answer a series of questions and complete basic forms, the tax preparation

software creates and analyzes your tax forms to search for missed potential errors and deduction opportunities. After the forms are complete, you can print any necessary paperwork. Most tax preparation software packages even allow you to file your tax forms electronically.

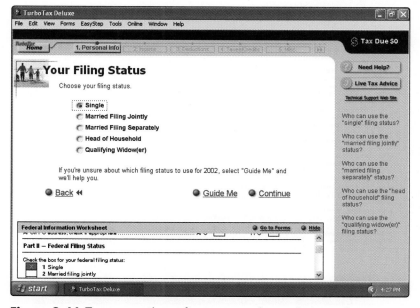

Figure 3-44 Tax preparation software can assist you in preparing your federal and state tax returns efficiently and accurately. You even can file your return electronically using the Internet.

LEGAL SOFTWARE

Legal software assists in the preparation of legal documents and provides legal advice to individuals, families, and small businesses [Figure 3-45]. Legal software provides standard contracts and documents associated with buying, selling, and renting property; estate planning; and preparing a will. By answering a series of questions or completing a form, the legal software tailors the legal document to your needs.

After the legal document is created, you can file the paperwork with the appropriate agency, court, or office; or you can take the document to your attorney for his or her review and signature.

ENTERTAINMENT SOFTWARE

Entertainment software includes interactive games, videos, and other programs designed to support a hobby or just provide amusement and enjoyment. For example, you can use entertainment software to play games, make a family tree, compose music, or fly an aircraft.

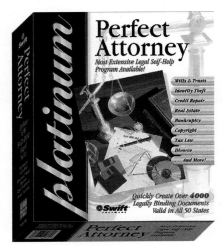

Figure 3-45 Legal software provides legal advice to individuals, families, and small businesses and assists in the preparation of legal documents.

Learning Aids and Support Tools

Learning how to use an application software package effectively involves time and practice. To aid you in that learning process, your school may offer professional development classes or in-service workshops. In addition to these learning opportunities, many software applications and Web sites provide Help, tutorials, and FAQs. Thousands of books also are available to help you learn specific software packages. Many tutorials are packaged with software or are available free on the Web.

USING HELP

Help is the electronic equivalent of a user manual; it usually is integrated into an application software package [Figure 3-46]. Help provides assistance that can increase your productivity and reduce your frustrations by minimizing the time you spend learning how to use an application software package.

In most packages, a function key or a button on the screen starts the Help feature. When you are using an application and have a question, you can use the Help feature to ask a question or access the Help topics by subject, keyword, or alphabetical order. Help displays a list of topics related to the keywords or questions you type.

Additional Help is available at the Microsoft Office Web site.

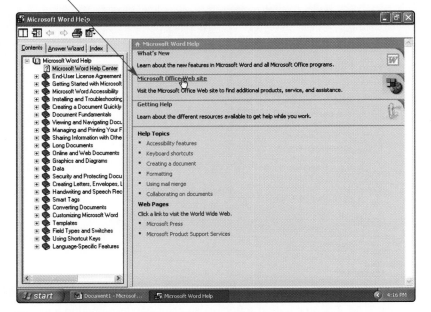

Figure 3-46 Help provides assistance without having to leave your application.

Often Help is **context-sensitive,** meaning that the Help information is related to the current task being attempted. Most Help also points you to Web sites that provide updates and more comprehensive resources to answer your software questions. In many cases, Help has replaced the user manual altogether, and software developers no longer include user manuals along with the software.

OTHER LEARNING RESOURCES

If printed documentation is included with a software package, often it is organized as reference material rather than structured for learning. This makes it helpful once you know how to use a package, but difficult to use when you are first learning. For this reason, many **trade books** are available to help you learn to use the features of software application packages. These books are available where software is sold, in regular bookstores [Figure 3-47], or online. Web pages that contain an **FAQ** (**frequently asked questions**) section about application software abound on the Internet and help you find answers to common questions.

Tutorials are step-by-step instructions using real examples that show you how to use an application. Some tutorials are written manuals; others are software-based or Internet-based, thus allowing you to use your computer to learn about an application software package.

Many colleges and K-12 school districts provide training on many of the applications discussed in this chapter. If you would like more direction than is provided in Help, trade books, FAQs, and tutorials, contact your college or school district for a list of workshops and continuing education courses that they offer.

In addition to those discussed here, many other software programs are available for use in schools, homes, and businesses. In the chapters that follow, you will learn more about other types of educational software, including how-to guides, computer-assisted instructional software, educational games, tutorials, educational simulations, multimedia authoring software, and CD-ROM-based and Web-based multimedia applications.

Figure 3-47 Many bookstores sell trade books to help you learn to use the features of personal computer application packages.

Software Versions and Upgrades

Software programs, including operating systems, usually are designated by a **version** number. A new version of a software product designed to replace an older version of the same product is called an **upgrade.** As software manufacturers develop a newer version of a software package, the newer version usually is assigned higher numbers.

Most manufacturers designate major software releases by increasing the version number by a whole number, for example, version 4.0 to 5.0. To designate minor software improvements, manufacturers usually change the version number by less than a whole number change, such as version 4.0 to 4.2. Some manufacturers use calendar years to designate the latest version. For example, in 2000, Microsoft introduced Microsoft Windows 2000, which was an upgrade to Windows 98. Similar versions of software, however, can have different designations when used on Macintosh computers and PCs. Microsoft Office 2001 for Macintosh computers, for example, is basically the same as Microsoft Office XP for Windows.

USING DIFFERENT SOFTWARE VERSIONS

Because of the cost of software, most schools do not upgrade their software each time a manufacturer releases a new version. When schools purchase new computers, however, the latest versions of operating systems and application software often are preinstalled on the computers.

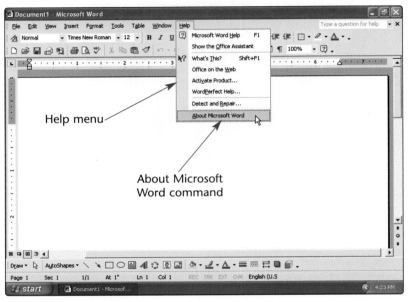

Figure 3-48 To determine the version of a particular software program, on the Help menu click the last command, which normally opens a window that provides information about the software you are using.

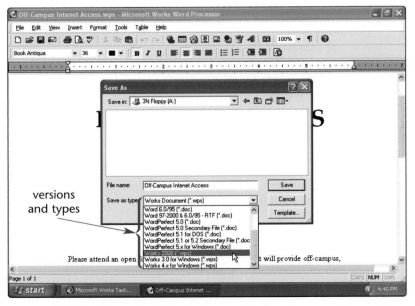

Figure 3-49 Most software applications allow users to save their work in earlier versions of the same software or in a different file format that can be read by another software program.

Teachers and students should know which versions of software applications are installed on their school, classroom, and home computers. Most software includes an About or Information command on the Help menu to indicate the software version [Figure 3-48]. Often, teachers and students have different versions of the same software on their home and classroom computers; a teacher might have PowerPoint 2000 on a two-year old classroom computer and PowerPoint 2003 on a new home computer.

When working with different versions of the same software, two general rules can help make your work easier. First, an older version of a software package may not open a file created in a newer version of the software. Second, newer versions usually open files created in older versions.

To help alleviate this problem, most software programs allow you to save a document in a format compatible with earlier versions of the same software or in a different file format that can be read by another software program [Figure 3-49].

WORKING WITH MACINTOSH COMPUTERS AND PCS

When teachers and students try to move between a Macintosh computer and a PC while working on a document or file, problems can occur. Even experienced users occasionally have problems working with the same document on both Macintosh and PC platforms. Some teachers and students, however, have a PC at home and Macintosh computers in their classrooms or vice versa — and thus have to use files on both platforms.

One source of the problem is that Macintosh computers and PCs format floppy disks differently. While Macintosh computers can access a document or file saved on a PC-formatted disk, PCs normally cannot open files saved on a Macintosh-formatted disk. Working with both a Macintosh and a PC, however, is possible. One solution is to save a document or file created on a PC in a Macintosh or Rich Text format [Figure 3-50]. Another solution is to install and use a software program specifically designed to support PC to Mac and Mac to PC file conversions, such as MacLink Plus Deluxe or MacOpener.

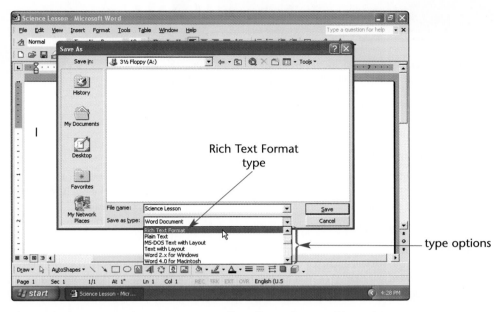

Figure 3-50 Many software programs allow files to be saved in various formats.

If you have to work with files on both computer platforms, you should speak with experienced teachers and other users in similar circumstances; they can help you find a solution for your situation. You also can ask for assistance from your instructor or school technology coordinator.

Creating a Teacher's Web Page

At the end of this chapter is a step-by-step special feature that provides you with instructions on how to create a teacher's Web page using Microsoft Word. You also can download a similar step-by-step project that provides you with instructions on how to create a similar teacher's Web page in Netscape Composer. The special feature that follows Chapter 7 will provide you with additional Web development skills, as you learn how to create and use curriculum pages.

Summary of Application Software Productivity Tools for Educators

In this chapter, you have learned about user interfaces and several software applications used in schools, businesses, and homes. You also have read about some of the learning aids and support tools that are available for application software. Understanding these software applications increases your computer literacy and helps you to understand how personal computers can help in your career as a teacher, in your classroom instruction, and at home. The next chapter introduces you to hardware applications for education; future chapters provide information on additional software applications used by educators and show you how to integrate various software applications into your classroom curriculum.

In Brief 3

Web Instructions: To display this page from the Web, start your browser and enter the URL, www.course.com/tdc3. Click Chapter 3 at the top of the Web page and then click In Brief on the left sidebar. Click the links for current and additional information. To listen to an audio version of this In Brief, click the Audio button to the top left of these instructions.

WEB INFO

IN BRIEF

KEY TERMS

CHECKPOINT

TEACHING TODAY

EDUCATION ISSUES

INTEGRATION CORNER

SOFTWARE CORNER

IN THE LAB

LEARN IT ONLINE

✱ FEATURES...

Timeline 2004

Guide to WWW Sites

Buyer's Guide 2004

Professional Sites

State/Federal Sites

Interactive Labs

Search Tools

HOME

1. Application Software

Application software consists of programs designed to perform specific tasks for users. Packaged software can be purchased from software vendors in retail stores or on the Web. A particular software product such as Microsoft Word often is called a **software package**.

2. Role of the Operating System

System software consists of programs that control the operations of the computer and its devices. One type of system software, the **operating system**, contains instructions that coordinate all of the activities of the hardware devices in a computer. The operating system also contains instructions that allow the computer to run application software.

3. Role of the User Interface

All software, including the operating system, is designed to communicate with the user in a certain way, through a user interface. A **user interface** controls how users enter data or instructions (input) and how information is presented on the screen (output). One of the more common user interfaces is a graphical user interface. A **graphical user interface**, or GUI, combines text, graphics, and other visual cues to make software easier to use. **Mac OS** and **Windows** are popular graphical user interfaces.

4. Starting a Software Application

Mac OS and Windows use the concept of a desktop to make the computer easier to use. The **desktop** is an on-screen work area that uses common graphical elements such as icons, buttons, windows, menus, and dialog boxes. An **icon** is a small picture that represents a program, an instruction, or some other object. A **button** is a graphical element that when selected, causes a specific action to take place. A **menu** is a list of commands from which you can select. **Commands** are instructions that cause a computer program to perform a specific action.

5. Working with Software Applications

A **document** is a piece of work created with an application program and saved on a disk with a unique file name. **Creating** involves developing the document by entering text and performing other tasks using an input device such as a keyboard. **Editing** is the process of making changes to the document's existing content. **Formatting** involves changing the appearance of a document. **Saving** is the process of copying a document from memory to a storage medium. **Printing** is the process of sending a file to a printer to generate output.

6. Productivity Software

Productivity software is designed to help people work more effectively and efficiently while performing daily activities. Productivity software includes applications such as word processing, spreadsheet, database, presentation graphics, personal information management, and software suites.

7. Word Processing Software

The most widely used software is **word processing software**, which is used to create, edit, and format documents that consist primarily of text. The most popular word processing programs used in schools today are Microsoft Word and the word processing applications included with AppleWorks, ClarisWorks, and Microsoft Works.

In Brief

WEB INFO

IN BRIEF

KEY TERMS

CHECKPOINT

TEACHING TODAY

EDUCATION ISSUES

INTEGRATION CORNER

SOFTWARE CORNER

IN THE LAB

LEARN IT ONLINE

✻ FEATURES...

Timeline 2004

Guide to WWW Sites

Buyer's Guide 2004

Professional Sites

State/Federal Sites

Interactive Labs

Search Tools

HOME

8. Spreadsheet Software

Another widely used software application is **spreadsheet software,** which allows you to organize numeric data in rows and columns. These rows and columns collectively are called a **spreadsheet,** or **worksheet.** Individuals who frequently work with numbers (for example, financial statements and payroll) use spreadsheets.

9. Database Software

A **database** is a collection of data organized in a manner that allows access, retrieval, and use of that data. In a computerized database, data is stored in an electronic format on a storage medium. **Database software** allows you to create a computerized database; add, change, and delete data; sort and retrieve data from the database; and create forms and reports using the data in the database.

10. Presentation Graphics Software

Presentation graphics software allows you to create documents called **presentations,** which are used to communicate ideas, messages, and other information to a group, such as a class or auditorium. The presentations can be viewed as **slides** that display on a large monitor or project onto a screen.

11. Software Suites and Integrated Software

A **software suite** is a collection of individual application software packages sold as a single package. Suites typically include word processing, spreadsheet, database, and presentation graphics software applications. **Integrated software** is software that combines applications such as word processing, spreadsheet, and database into a single, easy-to-use package. Unlike a software suite, however, you cannot purchase the applications in the integrated software package individually.

12. Graphics and Multimedia Software

Graphics and multimedia software include desktop publishing, paint/image editing, multimedia authoring, and Web page authoring software. **Desktop publishing (DTP) software** allows you to design, produce, and deliver sophisticated documents that contain text, graphics, and brilliant colors. Paint/image editing software allows you to create and modify graphics such as those used in DTP documents and Web pages. **Multimedia authoring software** is used to create electronic presentations that can include text, graphics, video, audio, and animation. **Web page authoring software** is software designed specifically for creating Web pages and organizing, managing, and maintaining Web sites.

13. Software for School and Professional Use

Software for schools and professional use includes school management software, student management software, grade book software, educational/reference software, and software for students with special needs. **School management software** is a centralized program that allows district and school personnel to manage the school district operations. **Student management software** allows administrators, teachers, and other staff to manage and track information on students. **Grade book software** is a program that allows teachers to track and organize student tests, homework, lab work, and other scores.

14. Educational and Reference Software

Educational software is designed for the learning environment. Educational software exists for just about any subject, from learning a foreign language to learning how to cook. **Reference software** provides valuable and thorough information for everyone in an educational setting and in the family. Popular reference software includes encyclopedias, dictionaries, health/medical guides, and travel directories.

15. Learning Aids and Support Tools

Help is the electronic equivalent of a user manual; it usually is integrated into an application software package. **Trade books** are available to help users learn to use the features of software application packages. These trade books are available where software is sold. **Tutorials** are step-by-step instructions using real examples that show users how to use an application.

Key Terms

Web Instructions: To display this page from the Web, start your browser and enter the URL, www.course.com/tdc3. Click Chapter 3 at the top of the Web page and then click Key Terms on the left sidebar. Scroll through the list of terms. Click a term to display its definition and a picture. Click Key Terms on the left to redisplay the Key Terms page. Click the TO WEB button for current and additional information about the term from the Web.

WEB INFO

IN BRIEF

KEY TERMS

CHECKPOINT

TEACHING TODAY

EDUCATION ISSUES

INTEGRATION CORNER

SOFTWARE CORNER

IN THE LAB

LEARN IT ONLINE

✱ FEATURES...

Timeline 2004

Guide to WWW Sites

Buyer's Guide 2004

Professional Sites

State/Federal Sites

Interactive Labs

Search Tools

HOME

address book [3.22]
Adobe GoLive [3.28]
AppleWorks [3.25]
application software [3.04]
appointment calendar [3.22]
assistant [3.12]
AutoSave [3.08]

beaming [3.23]
border [3.11]
button [3.06]

cell [3.14]
chart [3.15]
clip art [3.11]
clip art collections [3.11]
clip art/image gallery [3.18]
Clipboard [3.07]
commands [3.06]
context-sensitive [3.35]
copy [3.07]
creating [3.07]
curriculum page [3.28]
cut [3.07]

database [3.15]
database file [3.16]
database software [3.15]
delete [3.07]
desktop [3.06]
desktop publishing (DTP)
    software [3.25]
dialog box [3.08]
document [3.06]

editing [3.07]
educational software [3.30]
entertainment software [3.34]

FAQ (frequently asked questions)
    [3.35]
fields [3.16]
file [3.08]
file name [3.08]
find [3.11]
font [3.07]
font size [3.07]
font style [3.07]
footer [3.12]
formatting [3.07]
formula [3.14]
function [3.15]

grade book software [3.30]
graphical user interface [3.04]
GUI [3.04]

header [3.12]
Help [3.34]
HyperStudio [3.27]

icon [3.06]
image editing software [3.26]
import [3.11]
insert [3.07]
integrated software [3.24]

label [3.14]
legal software [3.34]
Linux [3.04]

MAC OS, version 9.1 [3.03]
MAC OS X [3.03]
Macromedia Dreamweaver [3.28]
margins [3.11]
menu [3.06]
Microsoft FrontPage [3.28]
Microsoft Windows [3.02]
Microsoft Works [3.25]
multimedia authoring software
    [3.27]

Netscape Composer [3.28]
notepad [3.22]

open source software [3.04]
operating system [3.02]

page layout [3.25]
paint software [3.26]
paste [3.07]
personal finance software [3.32]
personal information manager (PIM)
    [3.22]
photo-editing software [3.26]
Pocket PC [3.22]
points [3.07]
presentation graphics software
    [3.17]
presentations [3.17]
printing [3.08]
productivity software [3.10]

record [3.16]
reference software [3.31]
replace [3.11]

saving [3.08]
school management software
    [3.29]
scrolling [3.11]
search [3.11]
slide sorter [3.19]
slides [3.17]
software package [3.05]
software suite [3.24]
special needs software [3.32]
speech recognition [3.08]
speech synthesis software [3.32]
spell checker [3.12]
spelling checker [3.12]
spreadsheet [3.13]
spreadsheet software [3.13]
student management software
    [3.29]
submenu [3.06]
synchronize [3.22]
system software [3.02]

tax preparation software [3.33]
title bar [3.06]
trade books [3.35]
tutorials [3.35]

UNIX [3.03]
upgrade [3.35]
user interface [3.04]

value [3.14]
version [3.35]
video [3.27]
voice recognition [3.08]

Web page authoring software
    [3.28]
window [3.06]
Windows 98 [3.02]
Windows 2000 [3.03]
Windows XP [3.03]
Windows XP Tablet PC Edition
    [3.03]
wizard [3.12]
word processing software [3.10]
wordwrap [3.11]
worksheet [3.13]

Checkpoint

Web Instructions: To display this page from the Web, start your browser and enter the URL, www.course.com/tdc3. Click Chapter 3 at the top of the Web page and then click Checkpoint on the left sidebar. Click a blank line for the answer. Click the links for current and additional information.

WEB INFO

IN BRIEF

KEY TERMS

CHECKPOINT

TEACHING TODAY

EDUCATION ISSUES

INTEGRATION CORNER

SOFTWARE CORNER

IN THE LAB

LEARN IT ONLINE

✱ FEATURES...

Timeline 2004

Guide to WWW Sites

Buyer's Guide 2004

Professional Sites

State/Federal Sites

Interactive Labs

Search Tools

HOME

1. Label the Figure

Instructions: Identify each component of the Print dialog box.

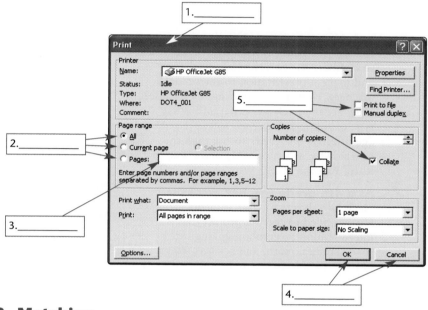

2. Matching

Instructions: Match each term from the column on the left with the best description from the column on the right.

____ 1. Clipboard

____ 2. database

____ 3. field

____ 4. commands

____ 5. cell

a. collection of related facts

b. instructions that cause software to perform specific actions

c. temporary storage location

d. intersection where a column and row meet

e. collection of data stored in files

3. Short Answer

Instructions: Write a brief answer to each of the following questions.

1. What is a graphical user interface? Describe some common features of both the Windows and Macintosh graphical user interface. _____

2. Name and describe four different types of productivity software used by K-12 teachers. Which productivity software program do you use the most? Why? _____

3. What are the advantages of integrated software and software suites? Describe three popular integrated software or software suites used in K-12 schools. _____

4. What is a database? How are databases used in K-12 schools? _____

5. What are the advantages of using presentation graphics software programs? What are the disadvantages? How are teachers and students using presentation graphics programs? _____

Teaching Today

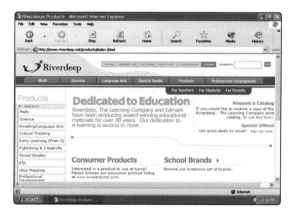

Web Instructions: To display this page from the Web, start your browser and enter the URL, www.course.com/tdc3. Click Chapter 3 at the top of the Web page and then click Teaching Today on the left sidebar. Click the links for current and additional information.

WEB INFO

IN BRIEF

KEY TERMS

CHECKPOINT

TEACHING TODAY

EDUCATION ISSUES

INTEGRATION CORNER

SOFTWARE CORNER

IN THE LAB

LEARN IT ONLINE

✱ FEATURES...

Timeline 2004

Guide to WWW Sites

Buyer's Guide 2004

Professional Sites

State/Federal Sites

Interactive Labs

Search Tools

HOME

1. Your school uses Macintosh computers. Your principal is considering purchasing AppleWorks for all classroom and lab computers. You have never used AppleWorks, however, you are familiar with Microsoft Office 2001 for the Macintosh. Your principal has asked you to compare the two software packages and make a presentation to the school's teachers. How are the packages the same? How are the packages different? What type of support does each software package offer? Is one easier to use than the other? Why or why not? Is one easier to learn than the other? Why or why not?

2. As a 4th grade teacher, you must teach all subjects to your students. You have decided to teach a project that is interdisciplinary, combining language arts, social studies, math, and science. You also have decided to integrate technology throughout the lesson not only to do research but also to help students learn to become better researchers, writers, and presenters. The topic of your project is Ancient Egypt. You start by using the Media Center to gather books, CD-ROMs, reference materials, Web sites, and more. What kind of lesson plan can you develop to encourage your students to create a project for which they use the Internet, reference software, word processing, and presentation graphics software? Where could you locate sample lesson plans to help you get started? Explain your plan to integrate these software applications into an interdisciplinary lesson that includes two or more curriculum areas.

3. Your principal just let you know that you will have students with special needs in your class this year. You are planning to purchase software for your classroom to integrate technology into the curriculum. What software can you purchase that will benefit both your regular students as well as your special-needs students? Explore software products for your grade level. Can you use these products in the classroom described above? What special features do these software packages include for special-needs learners? Will these features be useful with regular education students as well? Why or why not? What special technology tools are offered? Would these tools be useful with regular education students? Why or why not? How can you locate other software companies that sell educational software?

4. Most state Departments of Education negotiate one-year or multi-year contracts with various vendors for educational software products. This enables schools to acquire software products at substantial discounts. Contact a school in your district or access your state's Department of Education Web page and find out about a few of the software products available through the state purchasing program. Compare these prices with purchasing the same software either online or at a local computer store. What kind of discounts are the schools receiving? How many titles are available through the state catalog? What procedures does a teacher have to go through to purchase software not in the catalog?

Education Issues

WEB INFO

IN BRIEF

KEY TERMS

CHECKPOINT

TEACHING TODAY

EDUCATION ISSUES

INTEGRATION CORNER

SOFTWARE CORNER

IN THE LAB

LEARN IT ONLINE

✱ FEATURES...

Timeline 2004

Guide to WWW Sites

Buyer's Guide 2004

Professional Sites

State/Federal Sites

Interactive Labs

Search Tools

HOME

Web Instructions: To display this page from the Web, start your browser and enter the URL, www.course.com/tdc3. Click Chapter 3 at the top of the Web page and then click Education Issues on the left sidebar. Click the links for current and additional information to help you respond to the Education Issues questions.

1. Word Processing

Many teachers believe that word processing software improves the quality of written work by making it easier for students to create and edit documents. Students can use clip art, scanned images, or other computer graphics to enhance their work. Some people argue, however, that word processing software has become a crutch, eliminating the need to learn the rudiments of language. These people believe students are not forced to know basic grammar and spelling rules because word processing software alerts them to errors. How do you think word processing software has influenced written communication? Does it result in better student work or simply more correct yet mediocre work? What word processing features most enhance the quality of written material?

2. Reading Problems

You teach 8th grade, and this year you have the most challenging group of students you have ever had. Many of your students seem completely uninterested in learning or even in coming to school for that matter. As a result, you have continuous discipline problems and spend a lot of time sending students to the principal's office. After a few days, you become convinced that a deeper problem must exist, so you do a little research and find out that many of the students are below the 30th percentile in reading. You wonder how these students got this far without knowing how to read. Traditional reading programs obviously have not worked for these students. Using the Internet and other sources, do research to find out whether reading software programs and educational technology might be able to help them? In your research, investigate alternative techniques using technology that might motivate these students and help them to learn to read. Where could you locate software and innovative teaching strategies that could help you turn these students around?

3. Database Software

Increasingly sophisticated software applications have impacted not only business, entertainment, and recreation, but education as well. Database software can give students the opportunity to record, track, and analyze data on virtually any subject matter. Learning about database software also provides students with knowledge of an important software program that is used extensively in business and on the Web. Does learning and using database software help students develop higher-order thinking and problem-solving skills? What other advantages does using database software offer? What are some disadvantages to using database software in the classroom? How might another application described in this chapter be used to teach higher-order thinking skills or problem solving?

4. Computer Use in the Classroom

With the explosion of educational software, multimedia, and the Internet, educators still are learning the best use for computers in the classroom. Drill and practice? Problem solving? Games? A growing number of educators feel that students should be taught the software applications they will have to know to succeed in the workplace. From the applications presented in this chapter, make a list of five applications you think every student should learn, from more important to less important. Explain your ranking. At what level do you think each application should be taught? Why?

Integration Corner

WEB INFO

IN BRIEF

KEY TERMS

CHECKPOINT

TEACHING TODAY

EDUCATION ISSUES

INTEGRATION CORNER

SOFTWARE CORNER

IN THE LAB

LEARN IT ONLINE

✳ FEATURES...

Timeline 2004

Guide to WWW Sites

Buyer's Guide 2004

Professional Sites

State/Federal Sites

Interactive Labs

Search Tools

HOME

Web Instructions: To display this page from the Web, start your browser and enter the URL, www.course.com/tdc3. Click Chapter 3 at the top of the Web page and then click Integration Corner on the left sidebar. Click any Corner and then click the various links for extensive and curriculum-specific information.

Integration Corner is designed for teachers and other educators who are looking for innovative ways to integrate technology into their content-specific curriculum. Integration Corner not only provides great Web sites with current information but also shows what other educators are doing in the field of educational technology. These Corners are designed for all educators regardless of their interest. Review information and Web sites outside of your teaching area because many great integration ideas in one area easily can be modified for use in other curricular areas.

Teachers and administrators will find other colleagues in their areas with whom to connect and share the successes and hurdles of integrating technology in a classroom or an entire school system. Consider this your one stop for integration ideas and resources. Links to educational Web sites are organized in the following 12 Corners, and different Web resources are available for each chapter. Figure 3-51 shows examples of the Web resources provided in the Chapter 3 Middle School Corner.

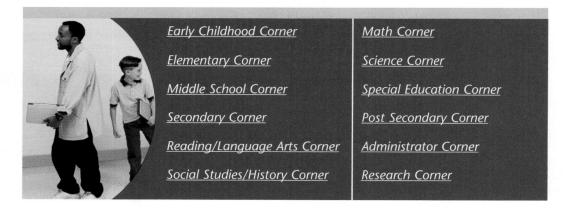

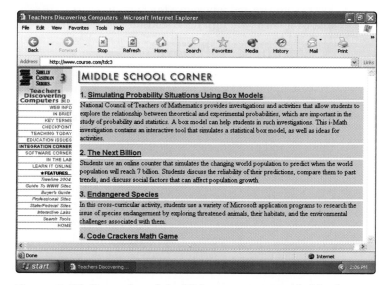

Figure 3-51 Examples of the Web resources provided in the Chapter 3 Middle School Corner.

Software Corner

WEB INFO

IN BRIEF

KEY TERMS

CHECKPOINT

TEACHING TODAY

EDUCATION ISSUES

INTEGRATION CORNER

SOFTWARE CORNER

IN THE LAB

LEARN IT ONLINE

★ FEATURES...

Timeline 2004

Guide to WWW Sites

Buyer's Guide 2004

Professional Sites

State/Federal Sites

Interactive Labs

Search Tools

HOME

Web Instructions: To display this page from the Web, start your browser and enter the URL, www.course.com/tdc3. Click Chapter 3 at the top of the Web page and then click Software Corner on the left sidebar. Click the links for additional information and instructions on how to download or receive an evaluation copy.

1. Teachers of exceptional students will find the PrimeTime Math series excellent support software for math curriculum. PrimeTime Math engages students by providing stories about real-world professionals using math in real-life situations. This software meets the National Council of Teachers of Mathematics (NCTM) standards by building mathematical understanding through use of stories about crimes, medical emergencies, fires, and wilderness search and rescues, while at the same time assisting students in realizing the importance of math in the world in which they live. Daily application is made abundantly clear with the PrimeTime Math series.

2. Adobe Photoshop allows you to edit pictures downloaded from digital cameras and the Internet to create unique cards, T-shirts your students can design, and personalized calendars for classroom instruction and parent communication. After editing your photos for red-eye, improving the color and contrast, or simply adding special effects, you can share your final product with faculty, parents, and students, or even post pictures on the World Wide Web. Using Adobe Photoshop helps your classroom pictures have a professionally finished look without a lot of hassle!

3. Developing students' critical-thinking skills and creating learning opportunities that engage higher-order thinking skills always have been a struggle for teachers. Thinkology by Heartsoft is the first software product developed to help K-3 students master essential critical thinking while having fun! Students are guided through a critical-thinking-skills journey with a cast of clever animated characters. Students watch animated stories and then have 10 different engaging activities to choose from that reinforce the critical-thinking skills learned in the story. Students learn to reason through concepts and are asked questions such as, does this make sense? Thinkology is an excellent addition to any K-3 classroom.

4. Ever had trouble getting young learners to organize their thoughts and develop their great ideas into understandable concepts? Kidspiration is an excellent visual learning tool for teaching K-5 students to organize and express those great ideas through visual learning! Created for inexperienced readers and writers, Kidspiration helps students increase their confidence as they learn to understand concepts, organize information, write stories, and convey and share their thoughts. Brainstorming, visual mapping, thought webs, and other visual tools are used to enhance students' comprehension of concepts and information.

5. Want to make teaching tessellations to your middle and high school students fun and easy? One piece of software that makes the concept of tessellations easier to teach and allows students to practice is Tessellation Exploration by Tom Snyder Productions. The software includes an extensive tutorial on the concept of tessellations. Teachers can use the software as a presentation tool in the classroom to present the concept of tessellations. Next, you can let your students use Tessellation Exploration to construct their own tessellations, by selecting a base shape and moves, such as slides, flips, and turns; students watch their tessellation form before their eyes.

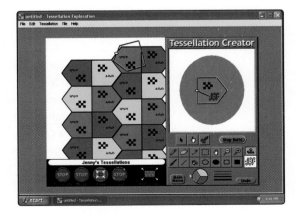

Students also can create slideshows with the tessellations or print them out. This software does a marvelous job of teaching concepts and allowing students to create a tessellation.

In the Lab

WEB INFO

IN BRIEF

KEY TERMS

CHECKPOINT

TEACHING TODAY

EDUCATION ISSUES

INTEGRATION CORNER

SOFTWARE CORNER

IN THE LAB

LEARN IT ONLINE

✱ FEATURES...

Timeline 2004

Guide to WWW Sites

Buyer's Guide 2004

Professional Sites

State/Federal Sites

Interactive Labs

Search Tools

HOME

Web Instructions: To display this page from the Web, start your browser and enter the URL, www.course.com/tdc3. Click Chapter 3 at the top of the Web page and then click In The Lab on the left sidebar. Click the links for tutorials, productivity ideas, integration examples and ideas, and more.

PRODUCTIVITY IN THE CLASSROOM

Introduction: Spreadsheets have many uses for both students and teachers in the classroom. Spreadsheets are a great teacher productivity tool. Grade books, lesson plans, rubrics, classroom inventory, textbook inventory, and many other time saving documents can be created in a spreadsheet. Students can creatively display data using a spreadsheet's charting feature, in addition to sorting and manipulating data, thereby using higher-order thinking skills.

Many of the productivity software suites have spreadsheet programs. Excel is a part of the Microsoft Office suite. Microsoft Works and AppleWorks also have a spreadsheet program. Lotus 1-2-3 and Quattro Pro also are popular spreadsheet programs.

Spreadsheets are not just for math class. It is possible to integrate spreadsheets effectively into many different curriculum areas in ways that excite students and empower their learning.

1 Building a Grade Book Spreadsheet

Problem: Keeping a grade book by hand can be a tedious task. To save time, you have created your grade book in a spreadsheet program so you can calculate percentages and grades quickly as shown in **Figure 3-52**. Open your spreadsheet software and create the grade book as described below. Use the grade book shown in **Figure 3-52** as an example. (*Hint:* Use Help to better understand the steps. If you do not have the suggested font, use any appropriate font.)

Instructions: Perform the following tasks.

1. Create the spreadsheet shown in **Figure 3-52** using the names and numbers as displayed.
2. Calculate the total and average for each student and for the entire class.
3. Personalize the spreadsheet title by inserting your name and curriculum area. Format the spreadsheet title in 16-point Arial black font and centered over columns A through H. Add a solid black border to cells A1:H1.
4. Use the AutoFormat option and select an appropriate table format for cells A2:H16. The numbers appear in the Number format with 0 decimal places.
5. Bold the Class Average label in cell A18 and column headings in row 2. Calculate the class total and class average for each item. The numbers appear in the Number format with a comma separator and 0 decimal places. Add a solid black border to the bottom of cells A18:H18.

	A	B	C	D	E	F	G	H	I
1	**Mr. Radcliff's 4th Period Language Arts Class**								
2	**Student**		*Book Report*	*Vocab Quiz*	*Poem*	*Essay*	*Total*	*Average*	
3	**First Name**	**Last Name**							
4	*Jenny*	*Carlson*	98	100	100	97	395	99	
5	*Leah*	*Chambers*	80	70	85	90	325	81	
6	*Brittany*	*Cook*	70	80	75	75	300	75	
7	*Oliver*	*Flint*	78	80	90	95	343	86	
8	*Maria*	*Gomez*	94	80	85	92	351	88	
9	*Ema*	*Granger*	100	90	95	100	385	96	
10	*Chelsea*	*Jackson*	85	100	75	90	350	88	
11	*Cho*	*Ling*	92	90	85	95	362	91	
12	*Devon*	*McBride*	75	90	85	90	340	85	
13	*Justin*	*Pillman*	95	100	92	95	382	96	
14	*Carlos*	*Ramirez*	93	90	95	95	373	93	
15	*Harry*	*Rollins*	96	90	95	100	381	95	
16	*Juan*	*Sanchez*	88	80	90	85	343	86	
17									
18	**Class Average**		88	88	88	92	356	89	
19									
20									

Figure 3-52

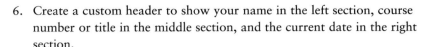

In the Lab

WEB INFO

IN BRIEF

KEY TERMS

CHECKPOINT

TEACHING TODAY

EDUCATION ISSUES

INTEGRATION CORNER

SOFTWARE CORNER

IN THE LAB

LEARN IT ONLINE

✱ FEATURES...

Timeline 2004

Guide to WWW Sites

Buyer's Guide 2004

Professional Sites

State/Federal Sites

Interactive Labs

Search Tools

HOME

6. Create a custom header to show your name in the left section, course number or title in the middle section, and the current date in the right section.
7. Save the spreadsheet on a floppy disk using an appropriate file name.
8. Print the spreadsheet.
9. Follow directions from your instructor for turning in the assignment.

2 Building a Student Council Fund-Raiser Spreadsheet

Problem: You are the teacher sponsor of the student council at your middle school. To raise money, student council members sell various items throughout the day and at special school functions. You want to see which items are the most profitable for the group and what time of day is the most successful, so you keep track of sales for four weeks. Using a spreadsheet program, prepare the spreadsheet and chart shown in **Figures 3-53** and **3-54**. (*Hint:* Use Help to better understand the steps. If you do not have the suggested font or color, use any appropriate font or color.)

Instructions: Perform the following tasks.

1. Create the spreadsheet shown in Figure 3-53 using the numbers as displayed.
2. Calculate the total sales for each period, each item, and for the four weeks.
3. Personalize the spreadsheet title by inserting the name of your school. Add a grey, solid pattern to the foreground of cells A1:E1. Format the title as 16-point Arial bold purple font and centered over columns A through E.
4. Format the subtitle, Student Council Fund-Raisers, as 12-point Arial bold black font and centered over columns A through E. Add a border around cells A2:E2.
5. Use AutoFormat and select an appropriate table format for the remaining portion of the spreadsheet. Display the numbers using the Currency format with 2 decimal places.

	A	B	C	D	E	F
1	Orangewood Elementary School					
2	Student Council Fund-Raisers					
3	*Item*	*Before School*	*Lunch*	*After School*	*Total*	
4	Lollipops	$100.00	$25.00	$175.00	$300.00	
5	Flowers	$175.00	$250.00	$75.00	$500.00	
6	Pizza	$0.00	$0.00	$450.00	$450.00	
7	Pencils	$300.00	$100.00	$50.00	$450.00	
8	Total	$575.00	$375.00	$750.00	$1,700.00	
9						
10						

Figure 3-53

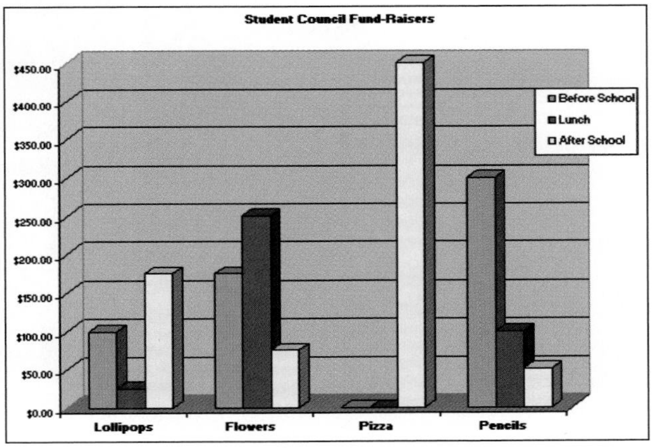

Chart: Student Council Fund-Raisers — 3-D Column chart with legend showing Before School, Lunch, After School for Lollipops, Flowers, Pizza, Pencils.

Figure 3-54

6. Create a custom header to show your name on the left, course number or title in the middle, and the current date on the right of the header.
7. Print the spreadsheet.
8. Create the 3-D Column chart from the spreadsheet data as shown in **Figure 3-54**. Add the title, Student Council Fund-Raisers, to the chart. Include a border and gridlines for the chart.

(continued)

In the Lab

WEB INFO

IN BRIEF

KEY TERMS

CHECKPOINT

TEACHING TODAY

EDUCATION ISSUES

INTEGRATION CORNER

SOFTWARE CORNER

IN THE LAB

LEARN IT ONLINE

✱ FEATURES...

Timeline 2004

Guide to WWW Sites

Buyer's Guide 2004

Professional Sites

State/Federal Sites

Interactive Labs

Search Tools

HOME

2 Building a Student Council Fund-Raiser Spreadsheet *(continued)*

9. Create a custom header to show your name at the left, course number or title in the middle section, and the current date in the right section. Print the 3-D Bar chart.
10. Save the spreadsheet and chart on a floppy disk using an appropriate file name.
11. Follow directions from your instructor for turning in the assignment.

INTEGRATION IN THE CLASSROOM

1 You are working on categorizing with your 3rd grade students. To meet state technology standards for students and to assist them with understanding this concept, you introduce spreadsheets and charts. Together with the class, you create a spreadsheet to show your students' favorite colors. You then create a 3-D Column chart to show their favorite colors graphically. Create a sample spreadsheet and 3-D Column chart to demonstrate the project for the students. Include a custom header to show your name in the left section, course number or title in the middle section, and the current date in the right section.

2 As a part of your Health Education class, you decide to have your students keep track of the total fat grams they consume daily during breakfast, lunch, dinner, and snacks for one week. You encourage students to examine the labels on products and nutrition tables for all foods consumed, including fast food. The students will create a spreadsheet including totals for each day of the week and each meal of the week to determine which days and meals are the healthiest. The students will also include a bar graph to illustrate their data. Create a sample spreadsheet and Bar chart to demonstrate the project for the students. Include a custom header to show your name on the left, course number or title in the middle, and the current date on the right of the header.

3 Now that the students are aware of their total fat grams consumed, you want them to explore exercise options and burning calories. Students will select three types of aerobic exercise that they will participate in for 30 minutes, three times a week. They will need to determine how many calories each type of exercise will burn. (*Hint:* Have the students search the World Wide Web.) The students will prepare a spreadsheet to record the total minutes spent exercising weekly and chart the number of calories each type of exercise burned over a one-week period. Create a sample spreadsheet and Pie chart to demonstrate the project for the students. Include a custom header to show your name on the left, course number or title in the middle, and the current date on the right of the header.

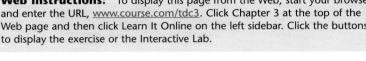

Learn It Online

Web Instructions: To display this page from the Web, start your browser and enter the URL, www.course.com/tdc3. Click Chapter 3 at the top of the Web page and then click Learn It Online on the left sidebar. Click the buttons to display the exercise or the Interactive Lab.

WEB INFO

IN BRIEF

KEY TERMS

CHECKPOINT

TEACHING TODAY

EDUCATION ISSUES

INTEGRATION CORNER

SOFTWARE CORNER

IN THE LAB

LEARN IT ONLINE

* FEATURES...

Timeline 2004

Guide to WWW Sites

Buyer's Guide 2004

Professional Sites

State/Federal Sites

Interactive Labs

Search Tools

HOME

1. Shelly Cashman Series Word Processing Lab

Click the button to the left to start and use the Shelly Cashman Series Word Processing Lab.

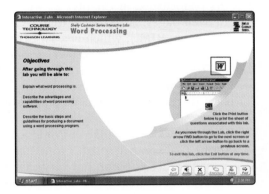

2. Shelly Cashman Series Working with Spreadsheets Lab

Click the button to the left to start and use the Shelly Cashman Series Working with Spreadsheets Lab.

3. Shelly Cashman Series Designing a Database Lab

Click the button to the left to start and use the Shelly Cashman Series Designing a Database Lab.

4. Shelly Cashman Series Evaluating Operating Systems Lab

Click the button to the left to start and use the Shelly Cashman Series Evaluating Operating Systems Lab.

5. Who Wants To Be a Computer Genius?

Click the button to the left to find out if you are a computer genius. Directions on how to play the game will display. When you are ready to play, click the PLAY button. Submit your score to your instructor.

6. Crossword Puzzle Challenge

Click the button to the left and complete the puzzle to reinforce skills you learned in this chapter. Directions on how to play the game will display. When you are ready to play, click the SUBMIT button. Submit the completed puzzle to your instructor.

7. Practice Test

Click the button to the left and answer each question. When completed, enter your name and click the Grade Test button to submit the quiz for grading. Make a note of any missed questions. If required, print a copy to submit to your instructor.

Creating a Teacher's Web Page Using Microsoft Word

As you learned in Chapter 2, Web publishing is the development and maintenance of Web pages. Also, recall that Web pages are created using **Hypertext Markup Language (HTML)**, which is a set of special codes, called **tags**, that define the placement and format of text, graphics, video, and sound on a Web page.

Today, teachers and students do not have to learn HTML to create Web pages and Web sites. Instead, user-friendly programs allow teachers, students, and other users to create their own Web pages easily using basic word processing skills. Numerous software programs specifically designed for creating Web pages, called **HTML editors**, are available. Popular HTML editors used by educators include Adobe GoLive, Microsoft FrontPage, and Macromedia Dreamweaver.

Another popular and very easy to use program for creating Web pages is Netscape Composer, which is included with Netscape Communicator and thus already is installed on many home and school computers. If you do not have Netscape Communicator installed on your home or school computer, you can download a free copy from the Web. Complete step-by-step instructions for completing this project in the latest version of Netscape Composer are available either to download or print from the World Wide Web at: www.course.com/tdc3/sf3.

As you have learned, Microsoft Word is a full-featured word processing program that allows teachers and students to create and revise professional looking documents, such as letters, announcements, newsletters, flyers, brochures, reports, and much more. What you may not know is that Word also provides many tools that you and your students can use to create Web pages quickly and easily.

In this project, you will build a basic teacher's Web page called Mr. Handley's Home Page using Word (Figure 1). Mr. Handley is a history teacher at Ridgedale High School. You may find it helpful to refer back to Figure 1 to see the completed Web page as you work through this project. Included are step-by-step instructions using Word 2002 (part of Office XP) installed on a PC. You also can create this project using Word 2000 installed on a PC or Word installed on a Macintosh computer; however, you may encounter slight variations from the step-by-step instructions in this project.

Although Web pages can be as distinctive and different as the individuals who create them, a relatively small set of basic features are common to many Web pages. The **title** of a Web page is the text that appears on the title bar of the browser window when the page is being displayed; the title also can refer to the first line or main heading of a Web page. The **background** of a Web page is similar to the wallpaper in Windows or the image on the desktop of a Macintosh computer. It provides the backdrop against which other elements are shown. The background can be either a solid color or a small graphic image that is tiled, or repeated, across the entire page.

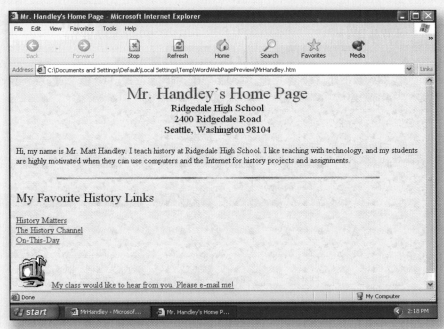

FIGURE 1

Normal text is the text that makes up the main information content of a Web page. Normal text also can be formatted so that it appears bold, italic, underlined, or in different colors. **Headings** are used to set off different paragraphs of text or different sections of a page. Headings usually are formatted in a larger font size than normal text and often are bold. **Horizontal lines**, also called **horizontal rules,** normally display across the page and are used to separate different sections of the page. **Images** are graphics and pictures that are contained on a Web page. Some images are animated and continuously change their appearance. **Links** are areas of the Web page, text or graphics, which when selected cause the browser to display another file or Web page, or play sounds or videos. Finally, many Web pages include an e-mail link to allow users to send an e-mail message from the Web page.

In this project, you will learn how to download graphics from the World Wide Web, open a new Word Web page, select a background image, create a title, insert and format text and headings, insert horizontal lines and graphics, create a linked list of favorite places, create an e-mail link, and save and view Mr. Handley's Home Page in your browser. Chapter 3 described the features of word processing software. This project assumes you possess basic word processing skills such as entering, selecting, and formatting text.

Downloading Image Files

Clip art images are graphical images that are available for you to use on your Web and curriculum pages. Clip art images either may be free or can be purchased. In addition, Microsoft provides more than 120,000 clip art images that are available free from its Design Gallery Live Web site. You also can download free images from hundreds of web sites. This project requires that you download an e-mail image from the World Wide Web. The image will be used to identify the e-mail link. Perform the following steps to download an image file from the World Wide Web.

Steps to Download Image Files

 Start your browser, type the URL `www.course.com/tdc3/sf3` **in the Address text box, and then press the ENTER key.**

Internet Explorer displays the Teachers Discovering Computers Word project Web page.

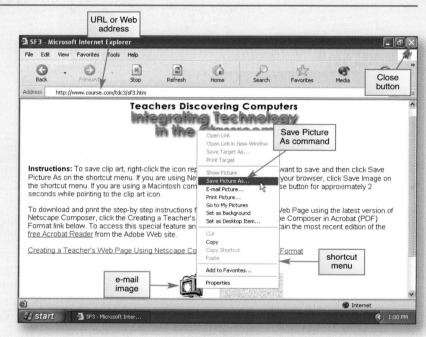

FIGURE 2

Right-click the e-mail image and then point to Save Picture As on the shortcut menu.

The shortcut menu is displayed (Figure 2). If you are using Netscape as your browser, point to the Save Image command. If you are using a Macintosh computer, press the mouse button for approximately two seconds to display the shortcut menu.

Insert a floppy disk in drive A and then click Save Picture As. When the Save As dialog box is displayed, click the Save in box arrow, click 3½ Floppy (A:) in the list, and then click the Save button in the Save As dialog box. Click the Close button in your browser window.

The e-mail image file is saved on your floppy disk.

Starting Microsoft Word and Opening a New Web Page

The following steps show how to start Word and open a new Web page so you can begin developing Mr. Handley's Home Page.

Steps to Start Word and Open a New Web Page

1 **Click the Start button on the Windows taskbar, point to All Programs on the Start menu, and then point to New Office Document on the All Programs submenu.**

The commands on the Start menu and All Programs submenu are displayed above the Start button (Figure 3).

FIGURE 3

2 **Click New Office Document. When Windows displays the New Office Document dialog box, if necessary, click the General tab, click Web Page, and then point to the OK button.**

Windows displays the New Office Document dialog box that allows you to select from hundreds of office documents and templates (Figure 4). Web Page is selected in the General area and document information appears in the Preview area.

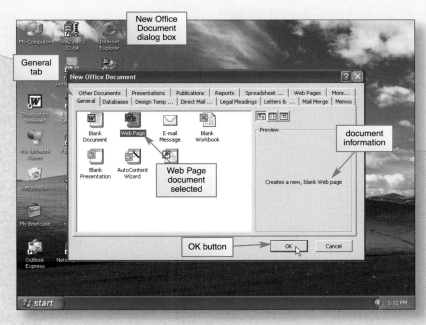

FIGURE 4

3 Click the OK button. If the Word window is not maximized, double-click its title bar to maximize it. If necessary, click the Font Size box arrow on the Formatting toolbar and then click 12 in the Font Size list to change the font size to 12.

Word is opened and displays a new blank Web page (Figure 5). Depending on the computer you are working on, the default font size may display 10 or 12. Font size 12 is required for this Web page.

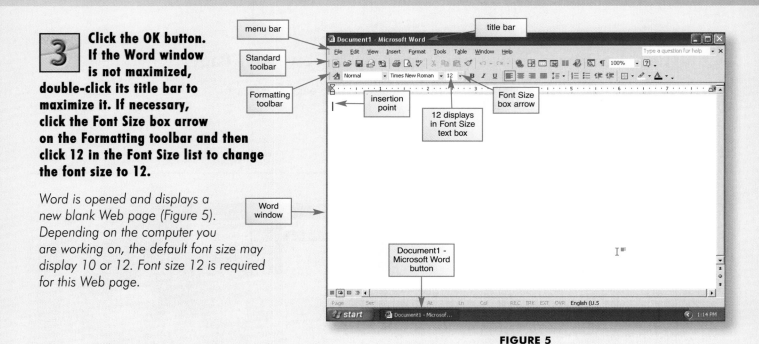

FIGURE 5

Selecting a Background Image

The background of a Web page is created by tiling, or repeating, a small graphic image many times across the page. Users can choose from thousands of graphic images to use for their Web page backgrounds. Background images can be downloaded from dozens of clip art Web sites, including Microsoft's Design Gallery Live Web site, or inserted from clip art CDs. For this project, you will use a textured background image that is available in Word.

Steps to Select a Background

1 Click Format on the menu bar, point to Background, and then point to Fill Effects (Figure 6).

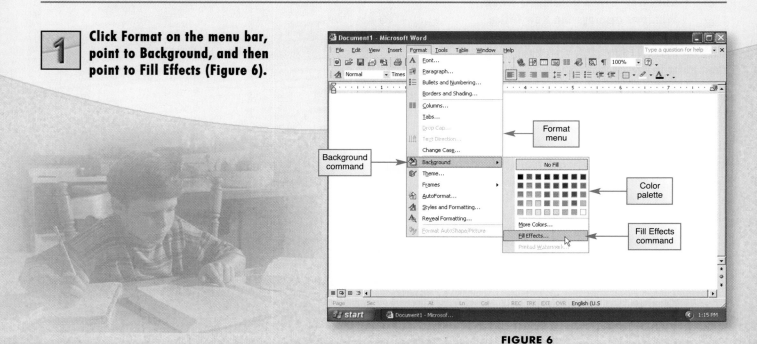

FIGURE 6

Click Fill Effects. When Word displays the Fill Effects dialog box, click the Texture tab. Click the third texture, Parchment, and then point to the OK button.

Word displays the Fill Effects dialog box and the numerous textures that are available in the Texture area. The name and a sample of the selected texture are also displayed (Figure 7).

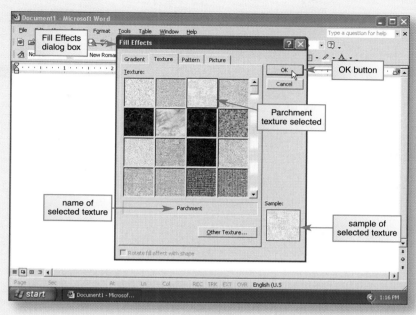

FIGURE 7

Click the OK button.

Word tiles the Parchment texture across the Web page (Figure 8).

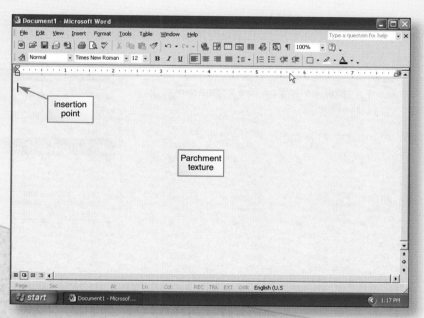

FIGURE 8

Entering and Formatting Text

Entering and formatting text on a Word Web page is the same as entering and formatting text in any other Word document. In the sequence of steps on the next pages, you will enter the title and other information for Mr. Handley's Home Page.

Steps to Enter and Format Text

 Type Mr. Handley's Home Page **and then press the ENTER key. Drag through the text you just entered to select it and then click the Font Size box arrow on the Formatting toolbar.**

Word inserts the title, moves the insertion point to the beginning of the next line, and selects the text (Figure 9). A list of available font sizes displays in the Font Size list.

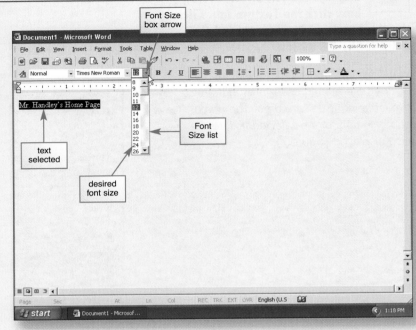

FIGURE 9

 Click 24 and then point to the Center button on the Formatting toolbar.

Word increases the font size of the title to 24 (Figure 10).

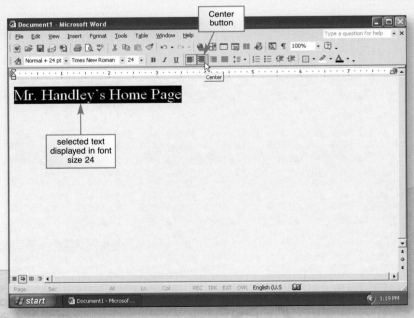

FIGURE 10

3 Click the Center button, click the Font Color box arrow on the Formatting toolbar, and then point to the color Dark Red (row 2, column 1).

Word centers the title text and displays the Font Color palette (Figure 11).

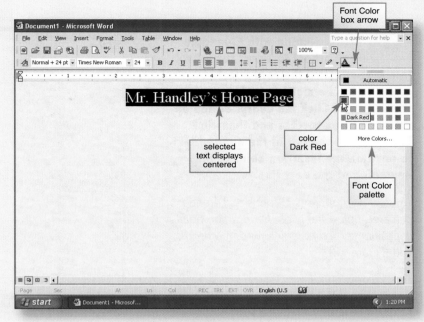

FIGURE 11

4 Click Dark Red and then click below and to the left of the title to position the insertion point at the beginning of the next line.

The text appears in the color dark red and the insertion point is now positioned at the beginning of the next line (Figure 12).

5 Type Ridgedale High School **and then press the** ENTER **key. Type** 2400 Ridgedale Road **and then press the** ENTER **key. Type** Seattle, Washington 98104 **and then press the** ENTER **key.**

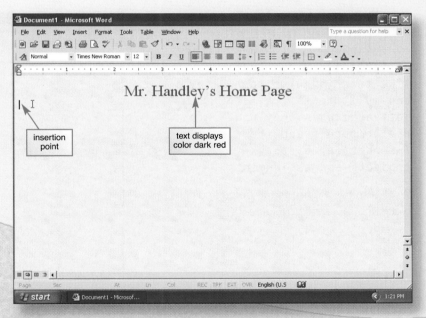

FIGURE 12

6 Drag through the three lines of text beginning with Ridgedale High School to select the school information. Click the Font Size box arrow on the Formatting toolbar and then click 14. Click the Center button on the Formatting toolbar and then click below and to the left of the entered text to position the insertion point at the beginning of the next line.

The text now appears in font size 14 and is centered below the title. The insertion point is positioned at the beginning of the next line (Figure 13).

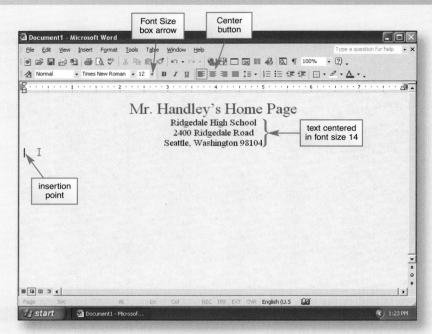

FIGURE 13

7 Press the ENTER key. Type Hi, my name is Mr. Matt Handley. I teach history at Ridgedale High School. I like teaching with technology, and my students are highly motivated when they can use computers and the Internet for history projects and assignments.

Word displays the text in the default color black and font size 12 (Figure 14).

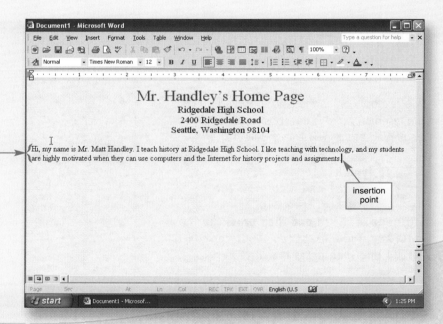

FIGURE 14

Inserting a Horizontal Line and a Heading

Horizontal lines, also called rules, are used to set apart different sections of a Web page. Perform the following steps to insert a horizontal line and then enter a heading.

Steps to Insert a Horizontal Line and a Heading

![1] **Press the ENTER key twice. Click Format on the menu bar and then click Borders and Shading. When Word displays the Borders and Shading dialog box, point to the Horizontal Line button at the bottom of the dialog box (Figure 15).**

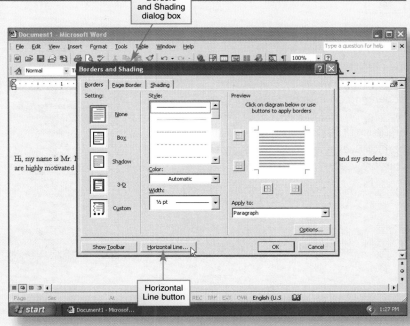

FIGURE 15

![2] **Click the Horizontal Line button. When Word displays the Horizontal Line dialog box, click the horizontal line as shown in Figure 16, and then point to the OK button.**

Word displays the selected horizontal line option with a blue border around it (Figure 16). A number of horizontal lines are available from which to choose. The options on your computer may be different from those shown in Figure 16.

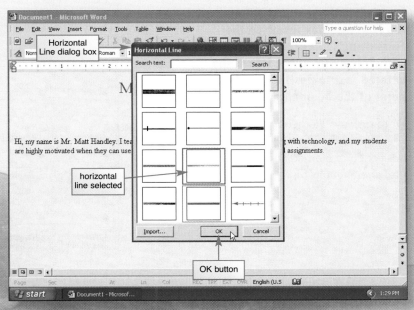

FIGURE 16

3   **Click the OK button.**

Word inserts a horizontal line and the insertion point moves to the beginning of the next line (Figure 17). The horizontal line may display differently than shown depending on the computer you are working on and the version of Word you are using. The horizontal line will display normally when the Web page is viewed in your browser.

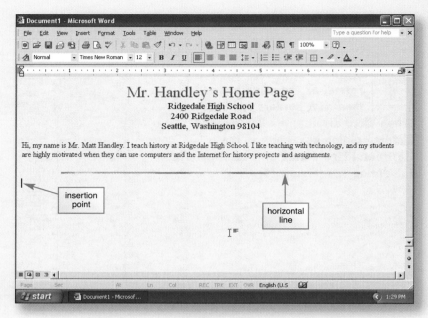

FIGURE 17

4   **Press the ENTER key once. Type** My Favorite History Links **and then press the ENTER key. Select the text just entered, click the Font Size box arrow on the Formatting toolbar, click 18, and then click below and to the left of the entered text to position the insertion point at the beginning of the next line.**

Word displays the heading in font size 18 and the insertion point is positioned at the beginning of the next line (Figure 18).

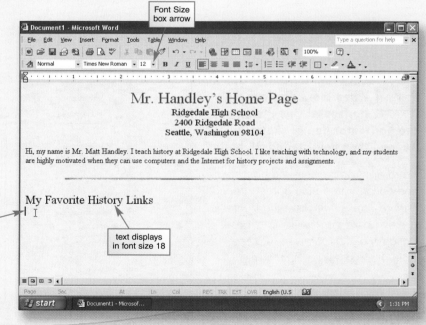

FIGURE 18

Creating Links to Web Sites

Using text and graphic links, you can create links for your students to Web sites on the World Wide Web. Perform the following steps to enter the names of three education-related Web sites and then link each name to its corresponding Web site by entering the Web site's Uniform Resource Locator (URL).

Steps to Create Links to Web Sites

1 **Press the ENTER key. Type** History Matters **and then press the ENTER key. Type** The History Channel **and then press the ENTER key. Type** On-This-Day **and then press the ENTER key.**

2 **Drag through the text, History Matters, and then click the Insert Hyperlink button on the Standard toolbar.**

The History Matters text is selected and Word displays the Insert Hyperlink dialog box (Figure 19).

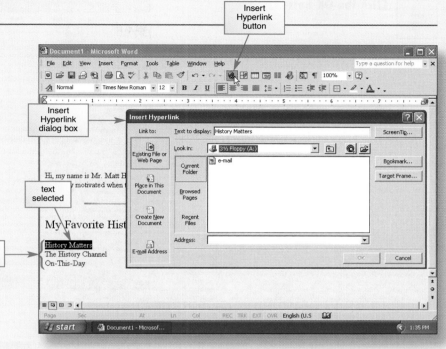

FIGURE 19

3 **If necessary, click the Existing File or Web Page button in the Link to area, and then type** http://historymatters.gmu.edu **in the Address text box. Point to the OK button.**

The URL appears in the Address text box (Figure 20). In Word 2000, you need to type the URL in the Type the file or Web page name text box below the Text to display text box.

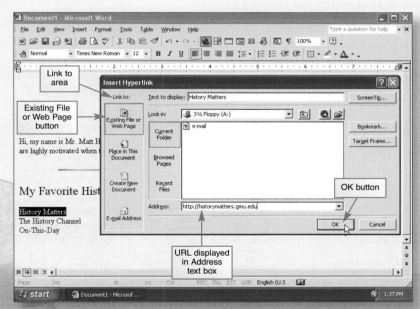

FIGURE 20

Click the OK button.

Word links the text to the entered Web site and the linked text appears underlined and in the default color blue (Figure 21).

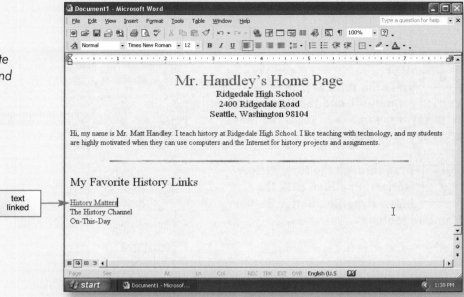

FIGURE 21

Repeat the procedures explained in Steps 2, 3, and 4 for the remaining two named Web sites, using the following URLs:

The History Channel
`http://www.historychannel.com`
On-This-Day
`http://www.on-this-day.com`

The Web page displays with the three links underlined and in the default color blue (Figure 22). The three Web sites are linked to their respective URLs.

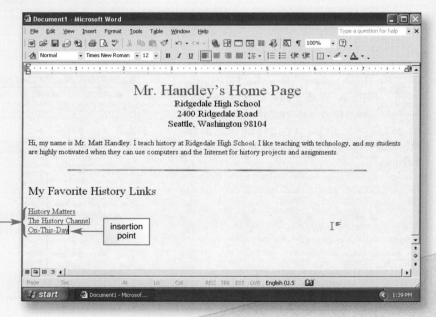

FIGURE 22

Inserting an Image, E-Mail Information, and an E-Mail Link

Adding graphics can enhance a Web page. Thousands of graphic images are available on the World Wide Web or in clip art galleries. Some graphics are animated and thus continuously change their appearance while the Web page is viewed in a browser. Many teachers and other users provide e-mail information and an e-mail link on their Web pages so students or others viewing the page can send e-mail messages directly from the page. Perform the following steps to add an image, e-mail information, and an e-mail link.

Steps to Insert an Image, E-Mail Information, and an E-Mail Link

1 If necessary, position the insertion point at the end of the On-This-Day link and then press the ENTER key twice. Click Insert on the menu bar. Point to Picture and then point to From File on the Picture submenu (Figure 23).

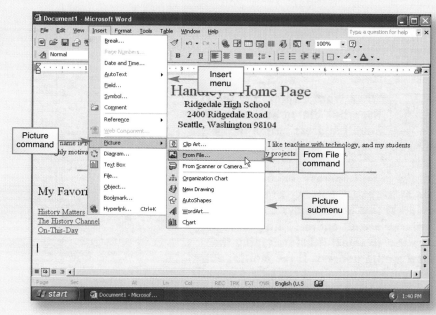

FIGURE 23

2 Click From File. If necessary, click the Look in box arrow, click 3½ Floppy (A:) in the Look in list, and then double-click the e-mail image.

The e-mail image appears and the insertion point is positioned to the right of the e-mail image (Figure 24). The image may not appear as shown or may appear only partially depending on the computer you are working with and the version of Word you are using. The image will display normally when the Web page is viewed in your browser.

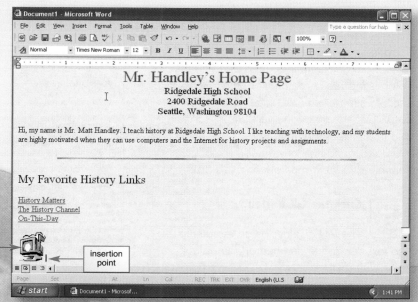

FIGURE 24

Press the SPACEBAR twice and then type My class would like to hear from you. Please email me! **Drag through the text to select it and then click the Insert Hyperlink button on the Standard toolbar.**

When Word displays the Insert Hyperlink dialog box, click the E-mail Address button in the Link to area, type mailto: matthandley@Ridgedale.k12.wa.us **in the E-mail address text box, and then point to the OK button. If the E-mail address text box displays a previously entered e-mail address, drag through the text to select it before typing the new mailto address. If the mailto: entry appears, type the** matthandley **e-mail address after the mailto: entry.**

The e-mail link text is selected on the Web page and the mailto: address appears in the E-mail address text box (Figure 25). The last e-mail address entered will be displayed automatically in the E-mail address text box or it may be blank. It is important that no spaces be typed between mailto: and the e-mail address and that the colon is included. The mailto: entry allows users to send e-mail messages from a Web page. Depending on the version of Word and the computer that you are using, Word may automatically enter the mailto: command in the E-mail address text box.

Click the OK button.

The text displays as an e-mail link. The text displays underlined and in default color blue (Figure 26).

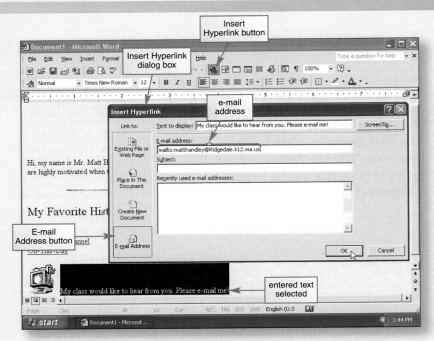

FIGURE 25

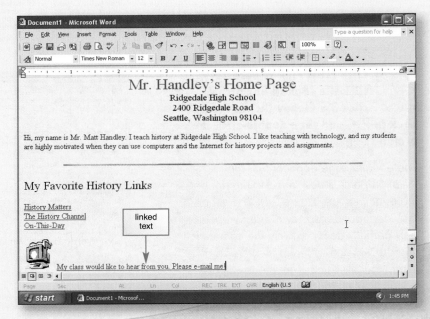

FIGURE 26

Saving and Previewing a Web Page

It is important to preview your Web page in your browser. This allows you to verify that the page appears as you want others to see it; sometimes you may have to make minor adjustments to your page in Word so it is displayed correctly in your browser. If your school uses both Internet Explorer and Netscape, you might want to view your Web page in both browsers. Browser software sometimes displays Web pages differently.

Before you preview Web page you have created, you should save it. Perform the following steps to save Mr. Handley's Home Page and then view it in your browser.

Steps to Save and Preview a Web Page

1 **Click the Save button on the Standard toolbar. When Word displays the Save As dialog box, click the Change Title button. When Word displays the Set Page Title dialog box, type** Mr. Handley's Home Page **in the Page title text box, and then point to the OK button.**

The title of the Web page appears in the Page title text box. This is the title that will be displayed on the title bar when the Web page is viewed in a browser (Figure 27).

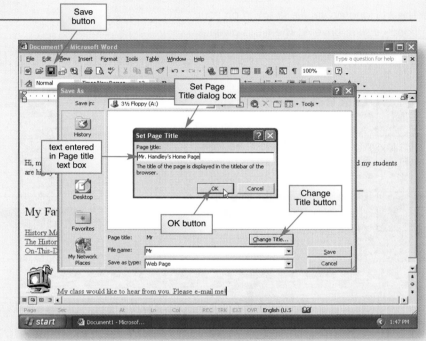

FIGURE 27

2 **Click the OK button and then type** MrHandley **in the File name text box. If necessary, click the Save in box arrow, click 3½ Floppy (A:) in the Look in list, and then point to the Save button in the Save As dialog box (Figure 28).**

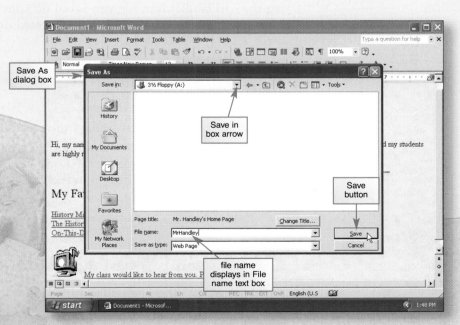

FIGURE 28

3 **Click the Save button in the Save As dialog box. Click File on the menu bar and then point to Web Page Preview (Figure 29).**

The MrHandley.htm file is saved on your floppy disk in drive A. The file is given an .htm extension, which indicates it is a Web page.

4 **Click Web Page Preview.**

Your default browser opens and displays Mr. Handley's Home Page (see Figure 1 on page 3.51).

5 **Close your browser and then close Word by clicking their Close buttons.**

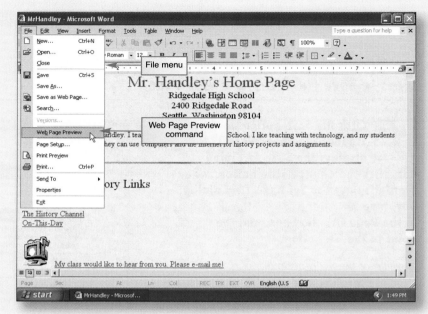

FIGURE 29

Printing and Opening a Web Page in Internet Explorer

Congratulations, you now have created a Web page using Microsoft Word. To print your Web page from your browser, click File on the menu bar and then click Print.

You can display your Web page on another Macintosh computer or PC by opening the MrHandley.htm file you saved on your floppy disk in a browser. Perform the following steps to open a Web page (located on a floppy disk) in Internet Explorer.

TO OPEN A WEB PAGE IN INTERNET EXPLORER

1. Start Internet Explorer.

2. Insert your floppy disk in drive A. Click File on the menu bar and then click Open.

3. When Internet Explorer displays the Open dialog box, click the Browse button.

4. In the Microsoft Internet Explorer dialog box, click the Look in box arrow and then click 3½ Floppy (A:) in the Look in list. Double-click the MrHandley.htm file and then click the OK button in the Open dialog box.

5. Close Internet Explorer.

Additional Web Page Authoring Features

Word has many other Web page authoring features. For example, you and your students can include tables, frames, sounds, videos, pictures, scrolling text, bullets, check boxes, option buttons, list boxes, text boxes, and much more on your Web pages. You also can upload your Web page to the World Wide Web. You will learn how to use additional Word Web page authoring features in the special feature that follows Chapter 7.

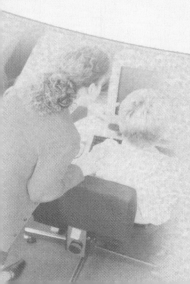

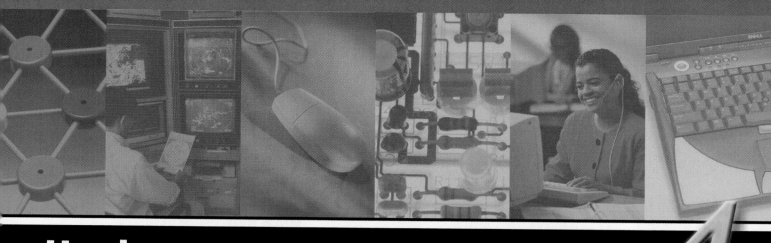

Hardware for Educators

4

Objectives

After completing this chapter, you will be able to:

- Describe the system unit

- Define the term, bit, and describe how a series of bits are used to represent data

- Identify the major components of the system unit and explain their functions

- Explain how the CPU uses the four steps of a machine cycle to process data

- Describe the four types of input and input devices

- List the characteristics of a keyboard and identify various types of keyboards

- Identify various types of pointing devices

- Differentiate among the four types of output

- Identify the different types of output devices

- Explain the differences among various types of printers

- Differentiate between storage and memory

- Identify types of storage media and devices

- Explain how data is stored on floppy disks, hard disks, and CD-ROMs

- Differentiate between CD-ROMs and DVD-ROMs

During your teaching career or personal endeavors, you most likely will decide to purchase a new computer or upgrade an existing one. To be effective in this decision-making process and to be an informed teacher, you should possess a general knowledge of major computer components and how various computer components interact. In addition, the International Society for Technology in Education (ISTE) has developed a series of K-12 national technology standards and skills that K-12 students need to learn throughout their education. One of these technology standards recommends that graduating K-12 students demonstrate a sound understanding of the nature and operation of technology systems. To help you better understand these concepts, this chapter presents a brief look at some of the hardware components used for input, processing, output, and storage. Because Macintosh computers and PCs use similar, and in many cases identical, hardware components, the majority of information presented in this chapter applies to both computer platforms. In instances where Macintosh computers and PCs use slightly different hardware, these differences are explained.

contain almost all of their components in the system unit, including the keyboard and monitor or display. The following explanation of how data is represented in a computer will help you understand how the system unit processes data.

WEB INFO

For more information about the National Educational Technology Standards for Students (NETS-S), visit the Teachers Discovering Computers Web site, click Chapter 4, click Web Info, and then click NETS-S.

The System Unit

The **system unit** is a box-like case that houses the electronic components a computer uses to process data [Figure 4-1]. The system unit is made of metal or plastic and protects the electronic components from damage. On a personal computer, these components and most storage devices reside inside the system unit; other devices, such as a keyboard and monitor usually are located outside the system unit. Notebook computers, PDAs, and other mobile devices

Data Representation

To understand fully how the various components of the system unit work together to process data, you need a basic understanding of how data is represented in a computer. Human speech is **analog,** meaning that it uses continuous signals to represent data and information. Most computers, by contrast, are **digital,** meaning that they understand only two discrete states: on and off. Computers are electronic devices powered by electricity, which has

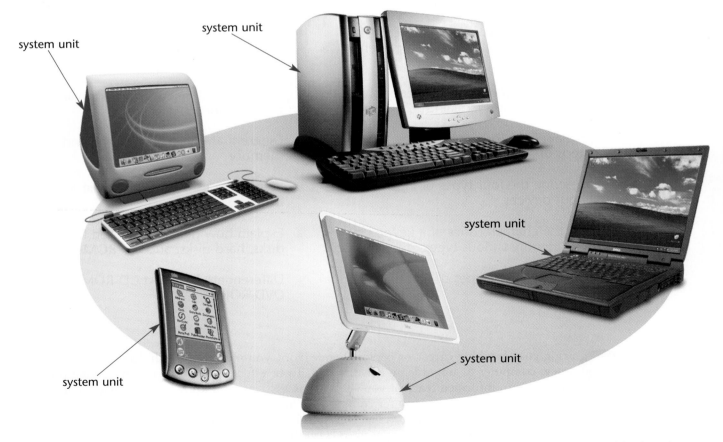

Figure 4-1 On PCs and many Macintosh computers, the system unit usually is separated from the monitor and keyboard. Some system units are located below the monitor on the desktop, while tower units usually are positioned vertically on the floor. The system unit and monitor are combined in some Macintosh computers such as the iMac. On notebook computers and handheld computers, the keyboard is built into the system unit.

only two states: on or off. These two states are represented by electronic circuits using two digits; 0 is used to represent the electronic state of off (absence of an electric charge) and 1 is used to represent the electronic state of on (presence of an electric charge) [Figure 4-2].

BINARY DIGIT (BIT)	ELECTRONIC CHARGE	ELECTRONIC STATE
1		ON
0		OFF

Figure 4-2 A computer circuit represents the binary digits 0 or 1 electronically by the absence or presence of an electronic charge.

When people count, they use the digits 0 through 9, which are digits in the decimal system. Because a computer understands only two states, it uses a number system that has just two unique digits, 0 and 1. This numbering system is referred to as the **binary** system. Using just these two numbers, a computer can represent data electronically by turning circuits off or on.

Each on or off digital value is called a **bit** (short for **bi**nary dig**it**), and represents the smallest unit of data the computer can handle. By itself, a bit is not very informative. When eight bits are grouped together as a unit, they are called a **byte**. A byte is informative because it provides enough different combinations of 0s and 1s to represent 256 individual characters including numbers, uppercase and lowercase letters of the alphabet, and punctuation marks [Figure 4-3].

The combinations of 0s and 1s used to represent characters are defined by patterns called a coding scheme. The most widely used coding scheme to represent data on many personal computers is the **American Standard Code for Information Interchange**, called **ASCII** (pronounced ASK-ee).

Coding schemes such as ASCII make it possible for humans to interact with digital computers that recognize only bits. When you press a key on a keyboard, the keyboard converts that action into a binary form the computer understands. That is, every character is converted to its corresponding byte. The computer then processes that data in terms of bytes, which actually is a series of on/off electrical states. When processing is finished, the computer converts the bytes back into numbers, letters of the alphabet, or

WEB INFO

For more information about the American Standard Code for Information Interchange, visit the Teachers Discovering Computers Web site, click Chapter 4, click Web Info, and then click ASCII.

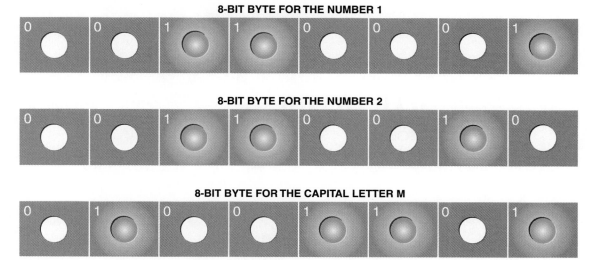

8-BIT BYTE FOR THE NUMBER 1

8-BIT BYTE FOR THE NUMBER 2

8-BIT BYTE FOR THE CAPITAL LETTER M

Figure 4-3 Eight bits grouped together as a unit are called a byte. A byte is used to represent a single character in the computer.

For a more detailed description of motherboards, visit the Teachers Discovering Computers Web site, click Chapter 4, click Web Info, and then click Motherboard.

special characters to be displayed on a screen or printed [Figure 4-4]. All of these conversions take place so quickly that you do not even realize they are occurring.

The Components of the System Unit

The major components of the system unit discussed in the following sections include the motherboard, the CPU and microprocessor, memory, expansion slots and expansion cards, and ports and connectors.

THE MOTHERBOARD

Many of the electronic components in the system unit reside on a circuit board called the **motherboard**. Figure 4-5 shows a photograph of a personal computer motherboard and identifies some of its components, including several different

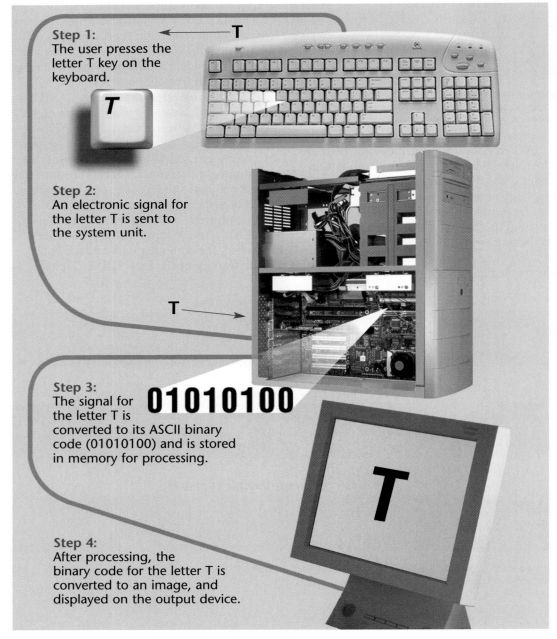

Step 1:
The user presses the letter T key on the keyboard.

Step 2:
An electronic signal for the letter T is sent to the system unit.

Step 3:
The signal for the letter T is converted to its ASCII binary code (01010100) and is stored in memory for processing.

01010100

Step 4:
After processing, the binary code for the letter T is converted to an image, and displayed on the output device.

Figure 4-4 Converting a letter to binary form and back.

Figure 4-5 The motherboard in a personal computer contains many chips and other electronic components.

types of chips. A **chip** is a small piece of semiconducting material usually no bigger than one-half-inch square and is made up of many layers of circuits and microscopic components that carry electronic signals. The motherboard in the system unit contains many different types of chips. Of these, one of the most important is the central processing unit (CPU).

THE CPU AND MICROPROCESSOR

The **central processing unit** (**CPU**) interprets and carries out the basic instructions that operate a computer. The CPU, also called the **processor**, manages most of a computer's operations. Most of the devices that connect to a computer communicate with the CPU to carry out tasks [Figure 4-6].

What is the difference between a chip and an integrated circuit?

A computer chip is a small piece of material, usually silicon, on which integrated circuits are etched. An integrated circuit contains many microscopic pathways that carry electrical current, as well as millions of electronic components.

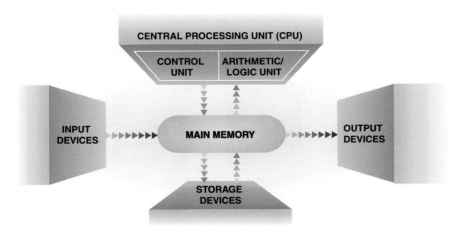

Figure 4-6 Most of the devices connected to a computer communicate with the CPU to carry out a task. The arrows in this figure represent the flow of data, instructions, and information.

In a personal computer, a single chip known as the **microprocessor** contains the CPU [Figure 4-7]. A microprocessor contains a number of components including a control unit, an arithmetic/logic unit, and a system clock. The following sections describe how these components work together to perform processing operations.

Figure 4-7 Most high-performance PCs use Pentium and Athlon processors. Basic PCs have a Celeron processor. High-performance Macintosh computers use the new G5 processor. Many high-performance notebook computers use Centrino mobile technology.

THE CONTROL UNIT   The **control unit**, one component of the CPU, directs and coordinates most of the operations in the computer. The control unit has a role much like a traffic cop. The control unit interprets each instruction issued by a program and then initiates the appropriate action to carry out the instruction. For every instruction, the control unit operates by repeating a set of four basic operations: (1) fetching an instruction, (2) decoding the instruction, (3) executing the instruction, and, if necessary, (4) storing the result [Figure 4-8].

Fetching is the process of obtaining a program instruction or data item from memory. **Decoding** is the process of translating the instruction into commands the computer understands. **Executing** is the process of carrying out the commands. **Storing** is the process of writing the result to memory. Together, these four instructions comprise the **machine cycle** or instruction cycle.

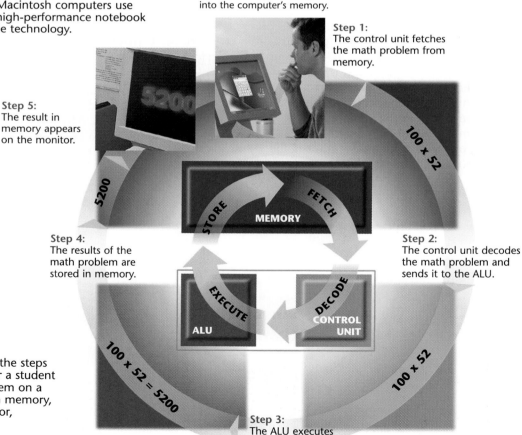

A student enters a math problem into the computer's memory.

Step 1:
The control unit fetches the math problem from memory.

Step 2:
The control unit decodes the math problem and sends it to the ALU.

Step 3:
The ALU executes the math problem.

Step 4:
The results of the math problem are stored in memory.

Step 5:
The result in memory appears on the monitor.

Figure 4-8 This figure shows the steps involved in a machine cycle for a student wanting to solve a math problem on a computer. Once the result is in memory, it can be displayed on a monitor, printed, or stored on a disk.

THE ARITHMETIC/LOGIC UNIT The arithmetic/logic unit (ALU), another component of the CPU, performs the execution part of the machine cycle. Specifically, the ALU performs the arithmetic, comparison, and logical operations.

Arithmetic operations include addition, subtraction, multiplication, and division. **Comparison operations** involve comparing one data item with another to determine if the first item is greater than, equal to, or less than the other. Depending on the result of the comparison, different actions may occur. For example, to determine a student's letter grade, the student's numeric grade is compared with a set of numbers corresponding to various letter grades (say, a numeric grade equal to or greater than 90 equates to a letter grade of A). If the student's numeric grade is equal to or greater than 90, then a letter grade of A is given; if the numeric grade is less than 90, a letter grade of A is not given and more comparisons are performed until a letter grade can be assigned. **Logical operations** work with conditions and logical operators such as AND, OR, and NOT. For example, if you wanted to search a job database for part-time work in the admissions office, you would search for any jobs classified as part-time AND listed under admissions.

THE SYSTEM CLOCK The control unit relies on a small chip called the **system clock** to synchronize, or control the timing of, all computer operations. Just as your heart beats at a regular rate to keep your body functioning, the system clock generates regular electronic pulses, or ticks, that set the operating pace of components in the system unit. Think of the components of the CPU as members of a marching band that take their steps to the beat of the system clock drummer.

Clock speed is the speed at which a processor executes instructions and is measured in megahertz (MHz) and gigahertz (GHz). One **megahertz** equates to one million ticks of the system clock and one **gigahertz** equates to one billion ticks of the system clock. Thus, a computer that operates at 1.7 GHz has 1.7 billion clock cycles, or ticks, in one second. The faster the clock speed, the more instructions the CPU can execute per second.

MEMORY

While performing a processing operation, a processor needs a place to store data and instructions temporarily. A computer uses **memory** to store data and information. The memory chips on the circuit boards in the system unit perform this function.

Memory stores three basic items: (1) the operating system and other system software that control the computer equipment; (2) application software designed to carry out a specific task such as word processing; and (3) the data being processed by the application software.

Recall that a computer stores a character as a series of 0s and 1s, called a byte. Thus, a byte is the basic storage unit in memory. When a computer transfers program instructions and data from a storage device into memory, the computer stores them as bytes. The computer stores each byte in a precise location in memory, called an address. An **address** is simply a unique number identifying the location of the byte in memory. The illustration in Figure 4-9

FAQ

Does the system clock also keep track of the current day and time?

No, a separate battery-backed chip, called the real-time clock, keeps track of the date and time in a computer. The battery continues to run the real-time clock even when the computer is off.

seat #A1   seat #A2   seat #A3   seat #A4   seat #A5   seat #A6

Figure 4-9 This figure shows how seats in a stadium are similar to addresses in memory: (1) a seat holds one person at a time and an address in memory holds a single byte, (2) both a seat and an address can be empty, and (3) a seat has a unique identifying number and so does an address.

shows how seats in a stadium are similar to addresses in memory: (1) a seat holds one person at a time and an address in memory holds a single byte, (2) both a seat and an address can be empty, and (3) a seat has a unique identifying number and so does an address. Thus, to access data or instructions in memory, the computer references the addresses that contain bytes of data.

Because a byte is such a small amount of storage, several terms have evolved to define memory and storage devices [Figure 4-10]. A **kilobyte** of memory, abbreviated **KB** or **K**, is equal to 1,024 bytes, but is usually rounded to 1,000 bytes. A **megabyte**, abbreviated **MB**, is equal to approximately 1 million bytes. A **gigabyte**, abbreviated **GB**, is equal to approximately 1 billion bytes.

The system unit contains two types of memory: volatile and nonvolatile. The contents of **volatile memory** are lost (erased) when the computer's power is turned off. The contents of **nonvolatile memory**, on the other hand, are not lost when power is removed from the computer. RAM (random access memory) is an example of volatile memory; ROM (read-only memory) is an example of nonvolatile memory. The following sections discuss each of these types of memory.

RANDOM ACCESS MEMORY (RAM) The memory chips in the system unit are called **random access memory (RAM)**. When the computer is powered on, certain operating system files (such as the files that determine how your desktop is displayed) are loaded from a storage device such as a hard disk into RAM. As long as the power remains on, these files remain in RAM. Because RAM is volatile, the programs and data stored in RAM are erased when the power to the computer is turned off. Any

programs and data needed for future use must be copied from RAM to a storage device such as a hard disk before the power to the computer is turned off.

The most common form of RAM used in personal computers is **synchronous dynamic RAM**, or **SDRAM**. Today, most RAM is installed by using a **dual inline memory module (DIMM)**. A DIMM is a small circuit board that contains multiple RAM chips [Figure 4-11]. Common DIMM sizes can hold 128 and 256 megabytes of memory. DIMM chips are installed in special sockets on the motherboard and can be removed and replaced easily with larger-capacity RAM chips.

The amount of RAM a computer requires often depends on the types of applications to be used on the computer. Remember that a computer can manipulate

dual inline memory module

memory chip

Figure 4-11 This photo shows a dual inline memory module (DIMM).

Memory and Storage Sizes

Term	Abbreviation	Approximate Memory Size	Exact Memory Amount	Approximate Pages of Text
Kilobyte	KB or K	1 thousand bytes	1,024 bytes	1/2
Megabyte	MB	1 million bytes	1,048,576 bytes	500
Gigabyte	GB	1 billion bytes	1,073,741,824 bytes	500,000
Terabyte	TB	1 trillion bytes	1,099,511,627,776 bytes	500,000,000

Figure 4-10 This table outlines terms used to define storage size.

only data that is in memory. RAM is something like the workspace you have on the top of your desk. Just as a desktop needs a certain amount of space to hold papers, pens, and your computer, a computer needs a certain amount of memory to store an application program and files.

The more RAM a computer has, the more programs and files it can work on at once. Having sufficient RAM (256 megabytes or higher) is important for manipulating graphics; downloading music, video clips, and movies; and creating and editing sound, digital images, and video.

A software package usually indicates the minimum amount of RAM and other system requirements it requires [Figure 4-12]. For an application to perform optimally, you usually need more than the minimum specifications on the software package.

READ-ONLY MEMORY (ROM) Read-only memory (ROM) devices are chips that store information or instructions that do not change. For example, ROM chips contain the sequence of instructions the computer follows to load the operating system and other files when you first turn it on. Manufacturers permanently record instructions and data on ROM chips. Unlike RAM, ROM memory is nonvolatile because it retains its contents even when the power is turned off. Manufacturers install ROM chips in automobiles, home appliances, toys, educational games, and thousands of other items used by people everyday.

EXPANSION SLOTS AND EXPANSION CARDS

An **expansion slot** is an opening, or socket, where a circuit board can be inserted into the motherboard. These circuit boards add new devices or capabilities to the computer such as more memory, higher-quality sound devices, a modem, or graphics capabilities. **Expansion card, adapter card,** or **expansion board** are terms used to describe these types of circuit boards. Sometimes a device or feature is built into the expansion card; other times a cable is used to connect the expansion card to a device outside the system unit, such as a

Figure 4-12 The minimum Macintosh or PC system requirements for many application software programs usually are printed on the side of the box. If the program can be used on both Macintosh computers and PCs, the system requirements usually are listed for both.

scanner. Figure 4-13 shows an expansion card being plugged into an expansion slot on a personal computer motherboard.

Figure 4-13 This figure shows an expansion card being inserted into an expansion slot on the motherboard of a personal computer.

Three types of expansion cards found in most of today's computers are a video adapter, a sound card, and an internal modem. A video adapter, also called a graphics adapter or card, converts computer output into a video signal that is sent through a cable to the monitor, which displays an image on the screen. A sound card is used to enhance the sound-generating capabilities of a personal computer by allowing sound to be input through a microphone and output through speakers. An internal modem is a communications device that enables computers to communicate via telephone lines or other means.

In the past, installing an expansion card in PCs required setting switches and other elements on the motherboard. Many of today's computers support **Plug and Play**, which refers to the computer's capability to configure expansion cards and other devices automatically as they are installed. Having Plug and Play support means a user can plug in a device, turn on the computer, and then use, or play, the device without having to configure the system manually. Macintosh computers have supported Plug and Play for many years,

which is just one of the reasons many K-12 schools purchased Macintosh computers for use in their offices and classrooms.

Notebook and other mobile computers have a special type of expansion slot for installing PC cards. A **PC Card** is a thin credit card-sized device that adds memory, fax/modems, network cards, disk drives, and other capabilities to small computers [Figure 4-14]. A **flash memory card** is a removable memory device that allows users to transfer data and information from a mobile device to a desktop computer. Many mobile and consumer devices, such as PDAs, digital cameras, digital music players, and cellular telephones, use flash memory cards.

Figure 4-14 This picture shows a PC Card in a PC Card slot on a notebook computer.   PC Card

PORTS AND CONNECTORS

Cables often attach external devices such as a keyboard, monitor, printer, mouse, and microphone to the system unit. A **port** is the point of attachment to the system unit. Most computers contain ports on the back of the system unit [Figure 4-15].

Ports use different types of **connectors** that usually are either male or female and come in various sizes and shapes. Male connectors have one or more exposed pins, like the end of an electrical cord you plug into the wall. Female connectors have matching receptacles to accept the pins, like an electrical wall outlet.

WEB INFO

For an overview of how to troubleshoot a Macintosh, visit the Teachers Discovering Computers Web site, click Chapter 4, click Web Info, and then click Troubleshoot.

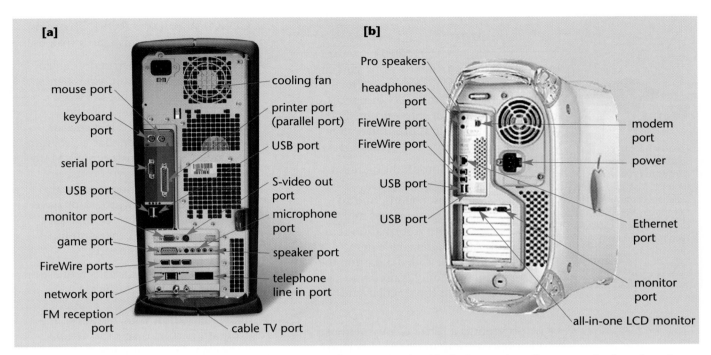

[a]

mouse port

keyboard port

serial port

USB port

monitor port

game port

FireWire ports

network port

FM reception port

cooling fan

printer port (parallel port)

USB port

S-video out port

microphone port

speaker port

telephone line in port

cable TV port

[b]

Pro speakers

headphones port

FireWire port

FireWire port

USB port

USB port

modem port

power

Ethernet port

monitor port

all-in-one LCD monitor

Figure 4-15 Ports are sockets used for cables that connect the system unit with devices such as the mouse, keyboard, and printer. Usually ports are on the back of the system unit and often are labeled and color coded making it easier for users to plug in various cables. Figure 4-15a shows the back of a PC and Figure 4-15b shows the back of a Macintosh computer.

Two newer ports that may one day replace most computer ports are USB and FireWire ports [Figure 4-16]. The **universal serial bus (USB) port** can connect up to 127 different peripheral devices with a single connector type. Personal computers typically contain two to four USB ports in the back; some contain two to four in the front as well. The latest version, called the **USB 2.0 port**, is more advanced and faster, with speeds 40 times faster than the original USB port. The USB 2.0 port is

used for devices that transfer a large amount of data, such as MP3 music players, DVDs, and removable hard disks.

Similar to a USB port, a **FireWire** port can connect multiple devices that require faster data transmission speeds, such as digital video cameras, digital VCRs, color printers, and DVD drives to a single connector. The FireWire port is found on newer PCs and Macintosh computers.

FAQ

Can older USB devices plug into a USB 2.0 port?

Yes, USB 2.0 is backward compatible, which means that it supports older USB devices as well as new USB 2.0 devices.

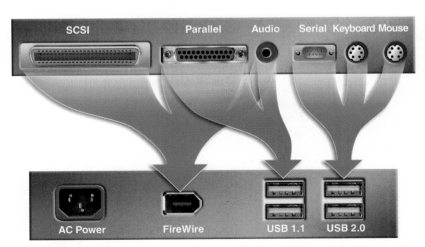

SCSI   Parallel   Audio   Serial Keyboard Mouse

AC Power   FireWire   USB 1.1   USB 2.0

Figure 4-16 Many computer professionals believe USB and FireWire ports someday will replace many other ports.

What Is Input?

Input is any data or instructions you enter into the memory of a computer. Once input is in memory, the CPU can access it and process the input into output. Four types of input are data, programs, commands, and user responses [Figure 4-17].

- **Data** is a collection of unorganized facts that can include words, numbers, pictures, sounds, and so on. A computer manipulates and processes data into information that is useful. Although a single item of data should be called a datum, the term data commonly is used and accepted as both the singular and plural form of the word.

- A **program** is a series of instructions that tells a computer how to perform the tasks necessary to process data into information. Programs are kept on storage media such as a hard disk, CD-ROM, or DVD-ROM. Programs respond to commands issued by a user.

- A **command** is an instruction given to a computer program. Commands can be issued by typing keywords or pressing special keys on the keyboard. A **keyword** is a special word, phrase, or code that a program understands as an instruction. Many programs also allow you to issue commands by selecting graphical objects. Today, most programs have a graphical user interface that uses icons, buttons, and other graphical objects to issue commands.

- Sometimes a program asks a question that requires a **user response**, such as Do you want to save the changes you made? Based on your response, the program performs specific actions. For example, if you answer, Yes, to this question, the program saves your changed file on a storage device.

WEB INFO

To search for a solution to a specific hardware problem for a PC, visit the Teachers Discovering Computers Web site, click Chapter 4, click Web Info, and then click Search.

Figure 4-17
Four types of input are data, programs, commands, and user responses.

DATA

Mary Jones
Tests - 89, 93, 84
Absences - 4

PROGRAMS

GRADE BOOK
WORD PROCESSOR

USER RESPONSES

YES   NO   CANCEL

COMMANDS

What Are Input Devices?

An **input device** is any hardware component that allows you to enter data, programs, commands, and user responses into a computer. Input devices include keyboards, pointing devices, scanners and reading devices, digital cameras, audio and video input devices, and input devices for students with special needs. Many of these input devices are discussed in the following pages.

THE KEYBOARD

One of the primary input devices used with a computer is the keyboard. A **keyboard** is a group of switches resembling the keys on a typewriter that allow users

to enter input. Most keyboards are similar to the ones shown in **Figures 4-18a** and **4-18b**. You enter data, commands, and other input into a computer by pressing keys on the keyboard.

Personal computer keyboards usually contain from 101 to 105 keys; keyboards for smaller computers, such as notebook computers, contain fewer keys. A keyboard includes keys that allow you to type letters, numbers, spaces, punctuation marks, and other symbols such as the dollar sign ($) and the asterisk (*). A keyboard also contains special keys that allow you to enter data and instructions into the computer.

All computer keyboards have a typing area that includes the letters of the alphabet, numbers, punctuation marks, and other basic keys. Because of the layout of

To learn more about keyboards, visit the Teachers Discovering Computers Web site, click Chapter 4, click Web Info, and then click Keyboard.

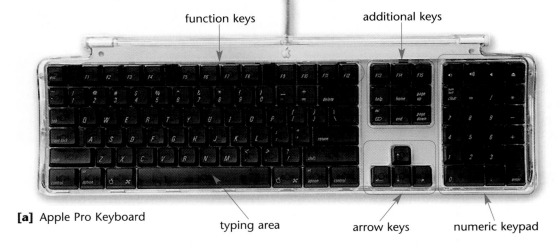

[a] Apple Pro Keyboard

function keys · additional keys · typing area · arrow keys · numeric keypad

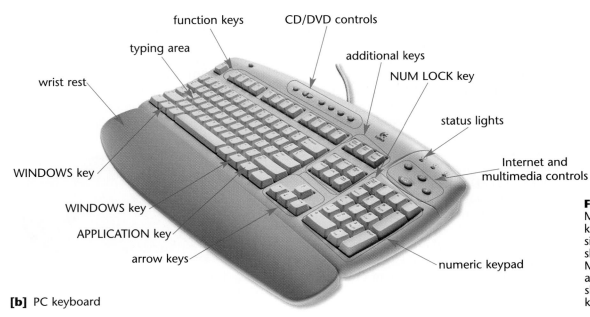

function keys · typing area · CD/DVD controls · additional keys · NUM LOCK key · wrist rest · status lights · WINDOWS key · Internet and multimedia controls · WINDOWS key · APPLICATION key · arrow keys · numeric keypad

[b] PC keyboard

Figure 4-18
Macintosh and PC keyboards are similar. Figure 4-18a shows a typical Macintosh keyboard and Figure 4-18b shows a typical PC keyboard.

FAQ

What is the rationale for the arrangement of keys in the typing area of a keyboard?

Well over 125 years ago, the keys on a QWERTY manual or mechanical typewriter were arranged to reduce the number of key jams. This key layout continues to be widely used.

its typing area, a standard computer keyboard sometimes is called a QWERTY keyboard. Pronounced KWER-tee, this keyboard layout is named after the first six letters on the top-left alphabetic line of the keyboard.

Many desktop computer keyboards also have a numeric keypad located on the right side of the keyboard. A **numeric keypad** is a calculator-style arrangement of keys representing numbers, a decimal point, and some basic mathematical operators. The numeric keypad is designed to make it easier to enter numbers.

Keyboards also contain keys that can be used to position the insertion point on the screen. The **insertion point**, or cursor, is a symbol that indicates where on the screen the next character you type will appear. Depending on the program, the symbol may be a vertical bar, a rectangle, or an underline. These keys, called arrow keys, allow you to move the insertion point right, left, up, or down. Most keyboards also contain keys such as HOME, END, PAGE UP, and PAGE DOWN that you can press to move the insertion point to the beginning or end of a line, page, or document.

Most keyboards also include toggle keys, which can be switched between two different states. The NUM LOCK key, for example, is a toggle key found on computer keyboards. When you press it once, it locks the numeric keypad so you can use it to type numbers. When you press the NUM LOCK key again, the numeric keypad is unlocked so the same keys serve as arrow keys that move the insertion point. The CAPS LOCK key is another example of a toggle key and is used on both PCs and Macintosh computers. Many keyboards have status lights in the upper-right corner that light up to indicate that a toggle key is activated.

Newer keyboards include specialized buttons that allow you to access and use your CD/DVD drive, adjust speaker volume, open your e-mail program, start your Web browser, and more. Most keyboards attach to a serial port on the system unit via a cable. On notebook computers and handheld computers, the keyboard often is built into the top of the system unit [Figure 4-19].

Figure 4-19 On notebook computers and mobile devices, the keyboard often is built into the top of the system unit. Some keyboards can be detached.

A popular keyboard used in K-12 classrooms is a **cordless keyboard**, also called a **wireless keyboard**. A cordless keyboard is a battery-operated device that transmits data using wireless technology, such as radio waves or infrared light waves [Figure 4-20]. Cordless keyboards are available for use on both Macintosh computers and PCs. Some cordless keyboards include a pointing device.

Figure 4-20 Cordless keyboards can be passed easily from student to student while they work on group projects.

POINTING DEVICES

A **pointing device** is an input device that allows you to control a pointer on the screen. In a graphical user interface, a pointer, or mouse pointer, is a small symbol on the monitor's screen. A pointer often takes the shape of a block arrow (⇖), an I-beam (I), or a pointing hand (☝). Using a pointing device, you can position the pointer to move or select items on the screen. For example, you can use a pointing device to move the insertion point; select text, graphics, and other objects; and click buttons, icons, links, and menu commands. Common pointing devices include the mouse, trackball, joystick, wheel, and touch screen.

MOUSE   A mouse is the most widely used pointing device, because it takes full advantage of a graphical user interface. Designed to fit comfortably under the palm of your hand, a **mouse** is an input device used to control the movement of the pointer on the screen and to make selections from the screen. The top of the mouse usually has one or two buttons; some have a small wheel. The mouse used with PCs usually is a two-button mouse [Figure 4-21]; a one-button mouse is used with Macintosh computers [Figure 4-22]. The most common type of mouse is a mechanical mouse. The bottom of a mechanical mouse is flat and contains a multidirectional mechanism, usually a small ball, which senses movement of the mouse.

The mouse often rests on a **mouse pad**, which usually is a rectangular rubber or foam pad that provides better traction for the mouse than the top of a desk. The mouse pad also protects the ball mechanism from a build up of dust and dirt, which could cause it to malfunction.

As you move the mouse across a flat surface such as a mouse pad, the pointer on the screen also moves. For example, when you move the mouse to the left, the pointer moves left on the screen. When you move the mouse to the right, the pointer moves right on the screen, and so on.

By using the mouse to move the pointer on the screen and then pressing, or **clicking**, the buttons on the mouse, you can perform actions such as pressing buttons, making menu selections, editing a document, and moving, or **dragging**, data from one location in a document to another. To press and release a mouse button twice without moving the mouse is called **double-clicking**. Double-clicking can be used to perform actions such as starting a program or opening a document. The function of the buttons on a two-button mouse can be changed to accommodate right- and left-handed individuals.

Other mouse types include an optical mouse and a cordless or wireless mouse. An **optical mouse** has no moving mechanical parts; instead, it uses devices that emit and sense light to detect the mouse's movement. A **cordless mouse** or **wireless mouse** is a battery-powered device that

FAQ

What can I do to reduce chances of experiencing repetitive strain injuries?

Do not rest your wrist on the edge of a desk; use a wrist rest. Keep your forearm at wrist level so your wrist does not bend. Do hand exercises every fifteen minutes. Keep your shoulders, arms, hands, and wrists relaxed while you work. Keep your feet flat on the floor, with one foot slightly in front of the other.

mouse buttons   wheel button

ball mechanism

Figure 4-21 A mouse is used to control the movement of a pointer on the screen and make selections on the screen. Electronic circuits in a mouse translate the movement of the mouse into signals that are sent to the computer. Shown is a typical mouse used with PCs.

Figure 4-22 A Macintosh mouse usually has only one button.

transmits data using wireless technology, such as radio waves or infrared light waves. Many cordless keyboards also contain a wireless mouse.

TOUCHPAD AND POINTING STICK   A **touchpad** is a small, flat, rectangular pointing device that is sensitive to pressure and motion. Most touchpads have one or more buttons near the pad that work like mouse buttons. Touchpads often are found on notebook computers [Figure 4-23]. To avoid using both a keyboard and a mouse with desktop computers, some schools purchase special keyboards that include a touchpad.

A **pointing stick** is a pressure-sensitive pointing device shaped like a pencil eraser that is positioned between keys on the keyboard [Figure 4-24]. Some notebook computers contain both touchpads and pointing sticks.

TRACKBALL   Some users opt for pointing devices other than a mouse, such as a trackball. Whereas a mouse has a ball mechanism on the bottom, a **trackball** is a stationary pointing device with a ball mechanism on its top [Figure 4-25]. The ball mechanism in a larger trackball is about the size of a Ping-Pong ball; notebook computers have small trackballs about the size of a marble. To move the pointer using a trackball, you rotate the ball mechanism with your thumb, fingers, or palm of your hand. Around the ball mechanism, a trackball usually has one or more buttons that work just like mouse buttons. A trackball requires frequent cleaning because it picks up oils from fingers and dust from the environment. If you have limited desk space or use a notebook computer, however, a trackball is a good alternative to a mouse because you do not have to move the entire device.

JOYSTICK AND WHEEL   Users running game software, such as a driving or flight simulation software, may prefer to use a joystick or wheel as their pointing device.

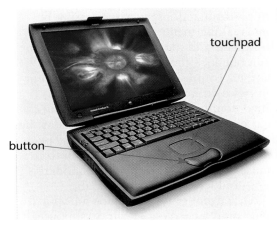

Figure 4-23 Many notebook computers have a touchpad that can be used to control the movement of the pointer.

Figure 4-24 Some notebook computers use a pointing stick to control the movement of the pointer.

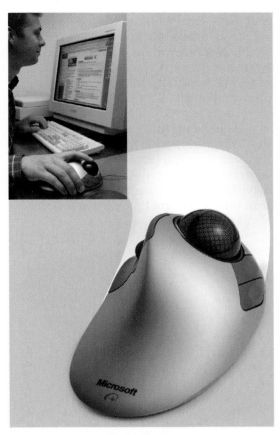

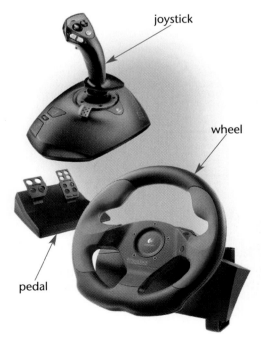

Figure 4-25 A trackball is like an upside-down mouse. You rotate the ball with your thumb, fingers, or palm of your hand to move the pointer.

A **joystick** is a vertical lever mounted on a base [Figure 4-26]. You move the lever in different directions to control the actions of a vehicle or a player. The lever usually includes buttons, called triggers, that you can press to activate certain events. Some joysticks also have additional buttons that you can set to perform other actions.

A **wheel** is a steering-wheel type input device. You turn the wheel to simulate driving a car or other vehicle. Most wheels also include foot pedals for acceleration and breaking action. A joystick and wheel typically attach via a cable to the game port on a sound card or game card, or to a USB port.

TOUCH SCREEN A monitor that has a touch-sensitive panel on the screen is called a **touch screen**. You interact with the computer by touching areas of the screen with your finger. In this case, the screen acts as an input device. To enter data, instructions, and information, you touch words, pictures, numbers, or locations identified on the screen. A touch screen often is used as the input device for a **kiosk**, which is a freestanding computer that provides information to the user [Figure 4-27]. Visitors at museums, for example, can use a kiosk to access and print maps, facts on tours and exhibits, and other information.

joystick

wheel

pedal

Figure 4-27 This kiosk allows you to create personalized greeting cards.

Figure 4-26 Joysticks and wheels are used with game software to control the actions of a vehicle or player.

OPTICAL READERS

An **optical reader** is a device that reads characters, marks, and codes and then converts them into digital data that can be processed by a computer. Three types of optical readers exist. The first is **optical character recognition** (OCR), which is a technology that involves reading typewritten, computer-printed, and in some cases handwritten characters on documents and converting the images into a form that the computer can understand. For example, the portion of a gas bill that you return with your payment usually has your account number, payment amount, and other information printed in optical characters [Figure 4-28].

Optical mark recognition (OMR) devices read hand-drawn marks, such as small circles or rectangles, and are used by many schools and colleges. Students place these marks on a form, such as a test, survey, or questionnaire answer sheet.

A bar code scanner uses laser beams to read bar codes. A **bar code** is an identification code that consists of a set of vertical lines and spaces of different widths. The bar code, which represents data that identifies the item, is printed on a product's package or label and is read by bar code scanners. Bar codes are printed on virtually all items purchased in retail stores.

OPTICAL SCANNERS

An optical scanner, usually called simply a **scanner**, is an input device that electronically can capture an entire page of text or images such as photographs or artwork [Figure 4-29]. A scanner converts the text or image on the original document into digital data that can be stored on a disk and processed by the computer. The digitized data can be printed, displayed separately, or merged into another document for editing. Handheld devices that scan only a portion of a page at a time also are available.

Figure 4-29 A typical optical scanner. Items to be scanned are placed on a piece of glass under the top cover, similar to making a copy on a copier.

WEB INFO

To learn more about optical scanners, visit the Teachers Discovering Computers Web site, click Chapter 4, click Web Info, and then click Scanner.

OCR characters indicate amount due and account number

Figure 4-28
OCR characters frequently are used with turnaround documents. With this bill, you tear off the top portion and return it with your payment.

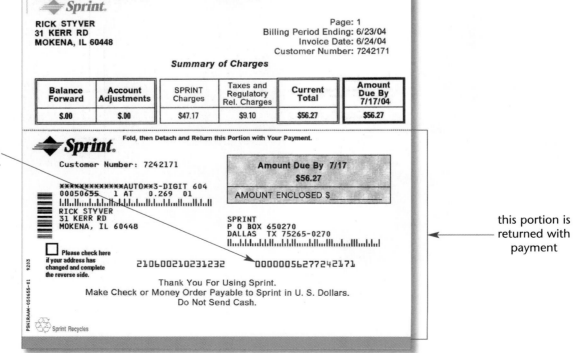

this portion is returned with payment

DIGITAL CAMERAS

A **digital camera** allows you to take pictures and store the photographed images digitally instead of on traditional film [Figure 4-30]. After you have taken a picture or series of pictures, you download, or transfer a copy of, the pictures to your computer. Once the pictures are stored on your computer, they can be edited with photo-editing software, printed, posted on a Web site, and more.

AUDIO AND VIDEO INPUT

Although characters (text and numbers) still are the primary forms of input into a computer, individuals increasingly are using other types of input such as images, audio, and video. In the previous sections, you learned about a variety of ways to input image data. The next sections discuss methods used to input audio and video data into a computer. Audio and video data often are stored on a computer's hard disk.

Audio input is the process of recording music, speech, or sound effects. Most personal computers sold today are equipped with a sound card necessary to record high-quality sound. Recorded sound is input via a device such as a microphone, tape player, or audio CD player, which plugs into a port on the sound card.

With a microphone plugged into the microphone port on the sound card, you can record sounds using the computer. After you save the sound as a file, you can play it, add it to a document, or edit it using audio-editing software.

Another use for a microphone is speech recognition. **Speech recognition**, also called **voice recognition**, is the capability of a computer to distinguish spoken words. Speech recognition programs do not understand speech; they only recognize a vocabulary of certain words. The vocabulary of speech recognition programs can range from two words (such as Yes and No) to more than two million words. Experts agree that voice recognition eventually will be added to all software programs.

Video input or video capture is the process of entering a full-motion recording into a computer. To capture video, you plug a video camera, VCR, or a similar device into a video capture card, which converts the

Figure 4-30
A digital camera is used to take pictures and store the images on a computer.

analog video signal into a digital signal that a computer can understand. After the device is connected to the card, you can begin recording. After the video is saved, you can play the video, copy it onto a videotape, or edit it using video-editing software.

Recent advances in audio and video technologies are allowing users to create and edit audio and video clips easily. The creation, use, and integration of audio and video in K-12 education is becoming popular. Creating and editing audio and video on both Macintosh computers and PCs will be covered in greater detail in the next chapter and in the special feature, Digital Imaging and Video Technology, which follows Chapter 5.

INPUT DEVICES FOR HANDHELD COMPUTERS

Increasingly more people, including many teachers and students, are using a variety of mobile devices such as PDAs, smart phones, and mobile computers such as the Tablet PC. A large variety of input alternatives are available for these devices and computers. Figure 4-31 on the next page provides examples of devices that can be used to input data into a PDA.

Additional input devices used in businesses, homes, and schools are described in Chapters 5 through 7, and in Digital Imaging and Video Technology (the special feature that follows Chapter 5), and A World Without Wires (the special feature that follows Chapter 8).

To learn more about digital cameras, visit the Teachers Discovering Computers Web site, click Chapter 4, click Web Info, and then click Digital Cameras.

For an explanation of speech recognition, visit the Teachers Discovering Computers Web site, click Chapter 4, click Web Info, and then click Speech Recognition.

telephone kit

digital camera

voice recorder

memory card

stylus

Graffiti characters

handwriting recognition characters

stylus

on-screen keyboard

stylus

visor

transfer data from
desktop computer

cradle

mini keyboard

Figure 4-31 Users have many options to input data into a PDA.

WEB INFO

To learn more about alternative keyboards, visit the Teachers Discovering Computers Web site, click Chapter 4, click Web Info, and then click Alternative Keyboards.

INPUT DEVICES FOR STUDENTS WITH SPECIAL NEEDS

The growing presence of computers in everyone's lives has generated an awareness of the need to address computing requirements for those with physical limitations. Today, the Americans with Disabilities Act (ADA) requires that all schools ensure that students with all types of special needs are not excluded from participation in, or denied access to, educational programs or activities. In addition to speech recognition, which is ideal for students who are visually impaired, other input devices are available.

Students with limited hand mobility who want to use a keyboard have several options. One option is to use a keyguard. A keyguard, when placed over the keyboard, prevents students from inadvertently pressing keys and provides a guide so students strike only one key at a time [Figure 4-32]. Keyboards with larger keys also are available. Another option is a screen-displayed

Figure 4-32 A keyguard.

keyboard, in which a graphic of a standard keyboard is displayed on the student's screen. Students then use a pointing device to press the keys on the screen-displayed keyboard. A touch window is a device that attaches to the front of a monitor that allows students to select items by touching the screen instead of using a keyboard [Figure 4-33].

Figure 4-33 A touch window allows students who are physically challenged to make inputs into a computer by touching the screen instead of using the keyboard.

A variety of pointing devices are available for students with motor disabilities. Small trackballs that can be controlled with a thumb or one finger can be attached to a table, mounted to a wheelchair, or held in a student's hand. Students with limited hand mobility can use a head-mounted pointer to control the pointer or insertion point. Learning how to integrate software programs and hardware devices into your curriculum that allow students with special needs to use computers as tools for learning will be covered in Chapters 6 and 7.

What Is Output?

Output is data that has been processed into a useful form called information. That is, a computer processes input into output. Computers generate several types of output, depending on the hardware and software being used and the requirements of the user. Four common types of output are text, graphics, audio, and video [Figure 4-34].

What can I do to ease eyestrain while using my computer?

Blink your eyes every five seconds. Use a glare screen. Adjust the room lighting. Use larger fonts or zoom the display. Take an eye break every 10 to 15 minutes. If you wear glasses, ask your doctor about computer glasses.

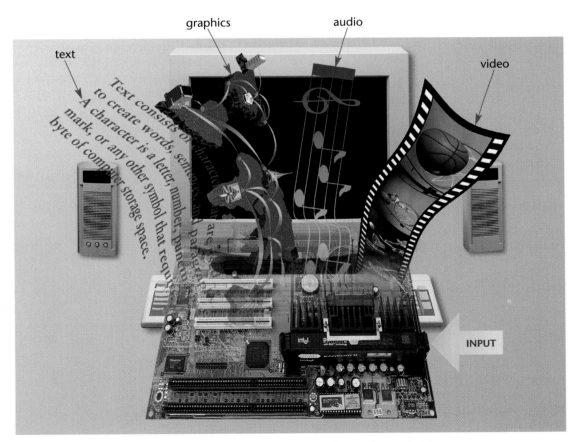

Figure 4-34 Four common types of output are text, graphics, audio, and video.

- **Text** consists of characters that are used to create words, sentences, and paragraphs. A character is a letter, number, punctuation mark, or any other symbol that requires one byte of computer storage space.

- **Graphics** are digital representations of nontext information, such as images, drawings, charts, pictures, and photographs. Displaying a series of still graphics creates an animation, a graphic that has the illusion of motion. Many of today's software programs support graphics; others are designed specifically to create and edit graphics. Graphics programs, called image editors, allow you to alter graphics by including enhancements such as blended colors, animation, and other special effects.

- **Audio** is any music, speech, or other sound that is stored and produced by the computer. Recall that sound waves, such as the human voice or music, are analog. To store such sounds, a computer converts them from a continuous analog signal into a digital format.

- **Video** consists of photographic images that are played back at speeds that provide the appearance of full motion in real-time. Video often is captured with a video input device such as a video camera or VCR.

often is called **soft copy**, because the information exists electronically and is displayed for a temporary period.

Monitors for personal computers are available in a variety of sizes, with the more common being 15, 17, 19, and 21 inches. The size of a monitor is measured diagonally, from corner to corner. Most monitors are referred to by the diagonal measurement of the large glass tube inside the monitor, which is larger than the actual viewing area provided by the monitor (known as the viewable size). For example, a monitor listed as a 17-inch monitor may have a viewable size of only 15.7 inches.

Determining what size monitor to use depends on your intended use. A larger monitor allows you to view more information at once, but usually is more expensive. If you work on the Web or use multiple applications at one time, however, you may want to invest in at least a 17-inch monitor.

Like a television set, the core of most monitors is a large glass tube called a **cathode ray tube** (CRT) [Figure 4-35]. The screen, which is the front of the tube, is coated with tiny dots of phosphor material that glow when electrically charged. The CRT moves an electron beam back and forth across the back of the screen, causing the dots to glow, which produces an image on the screen.

{"image_id":"1"}

What Are Output Devices?

An **output device** is any computer component capable of conveying information to a user. Commonly used output devices include monitors, printers, data projectors, facsimile machines, multifunction devices, speakers, and headsets. Each of these output devices is discussed in the following pages.

MONITORS AND DISPLAY DEVICES

A **display device** is an output device that displays text, graphics, and video information. A **monitor** is a display device that is housed in a plastic or metal case. Information shown on a display device

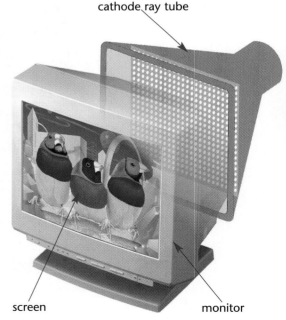

Figure 4-35 The core of most personal computer monitors is a cathode ray tube.

Each dot, called a **pixel** (short for picture element), is a single point in an electronic image [Figure 4-36]. Monitors consist of hundreds, thousands, or millions of pixels arranged in rows and columns that can be used to create pictures. The pixels are so close together that they appear connected.

Figure 4-36 A pixel is a single dot of color, or point, in an electronic image.

Many types of specialized monitors exist, including large display monitors and LCD monitors and displays.

LARGE DISPLAY MONITORS **Large display monitors** are large monitors that allow an audience or a group of students in a classroom to view images and multimedia displayed on a computer. These large monitors are available in screen sizes from 27 inches to 36 inches. Many teachers connect large screen televisions to their computers, while other teachers use large display monitors that are designed specifically for use with computers in schools [Figure 4-37]. Connecting a desktop computer to a standard large screen television requires an

inexpensive converter. Some notebook computers now contain the necessary components to be connected directly to a traditional television using a standard S-video cable.

Some of the new large classroom monitors designed specifically for schools use high-definition television technology. **High-definition television (HDTV)** is a type of television set that works with digital broadcasting signals, supports a wider screen, and displays at a higher resolution than a standard television set.

For even larger displays, some businesses and a few schools are using gas plasma monitors, which can measure more than 50 inches wide. A **gas plasma monitor** is a flat-panel display that uses gas plasma technology, which substitutes a layer of gas for the liquid crystal material in an LCD monitor. Gas plasma monitors are very expensive [Figure 4-38].

Figure 4-38 Large gas plasma monitors can measure more than 50 inches wide.

Using large display monitors can significantly impact student learning by allowing teachers to integrate technology at the point of instruction. The benefits of using large display monitors in classrooms will be detailed in Chapters 6 and 7.

Figure 4-37 Large classroom monitors are available in sizes up to 36 inches.

Figure 4-39 An LCD monitor is much thinner and lighter than a CRT monitor.

FLAT PANEL MONITORS AND DISPLAYS   A **flat panel monitor**, also called an **LCD monitor**, is a desktop monitor that uses liquid crystal instead of a cathode-ray tube to present information on a screen [Figure 4-39]. Flat panel monitors are available in 15, 17, 18, 20, 21, and 23 inches and consume less than one-third the power of CRT monitors. Even though they are more expensive than CRT monitors, flat panel monitors are very popular because they take up less space and produce crisp, bright images. Mobile computers, such as notebook computers and Tablet PCs, and mobile devices, such as PDAs and smart phones, use LCD monitors [Figure 4-40].

Another popular mobile device that uses an LCD display is an electronic book. An **electronic book (e-book)** is a small, book-sized computer that allows users to read, save, highlight, bookmark, and add notes to online text [Figure 4-41]. You download new book content to your e-book from the World Wide Web. To obtain the same functionality of an e-book device for your personal computer, notebook computer, Tablet PC, or PDA, you can download and install free e-book reader software programs, such as Microsoft Reader and Adobe Acrobat eBook Reader, from the Web. Many experts are predicting that e-book technology may one day replace traditional printed books in many areas, including education.

MONITOR QUALITY   The quality of a CRT monitor depends largely on its resolution, dot pitch, and refresh rate. The **resolution**, or sharpness and clarity, of a monitor is related directly to the number of pixels it

Figure 4-40 Notebook computers and Tablet PCs have color LCD screens. Many PDAs and newer smart phones have color displays.

Figure 4-41 Electronic books, which are about the size of a paperback book, use an LCD display. Users can download new book content from Web sites to their e-books, other mobile devices, notebook computers, and personal computers.

can display. Resolution is expressed as two separate numbers: the number of columns of pixels and the number of rows of pixels a monitor can display. For example, a screen with a 800 × 600 (pronounced 800 by 600) resolution can display 800 columns and 600 rows of pixels (or a total of 480,000 pixels). Most monitors can display up to 1280 × 1024 pixels with 800 × 600 typically the standard. A monitor with a higher resolution displays a greater number of pixels, which provides a smoother but smaller image.

Another factor that determines monitor quality is **dot pitch**, which is the distance between each pixel on a monitor. The smaller the distance between the pixels, the sharper the displayed image. To minimize eye fatigue, you should use a monitor with a dot pitch of .28 millimeters or smaller.

Recall that an electron beam moving back and forth behind the screen causes pixels on the screen to glow — thus creating an image. These pixels, however, only glow for a small fraction of a second before beginning to fade. The monitor thus redraws the picture many times per second so that the image does not fade. The speed that the monitor redraws images on the screen is called the **refresh rate**.

Some monitors display an **ENERGY STAR** label, which identifies the monitor as an energy-efficient product as defined by the Environmental Protection Agency (EPA). Monitors usually are equipped with controls to adjust the brightness, contrast, positioning, height, and width of images. Finally, many monitors sit on a tilt-and-swivel base so you can adjust the angle of the screen to minimize neck strain and reduce glare from overhead lighting.

PRINTERS

A **printer** is an output device that produces text and graphical information on a physical medium such as paper or transparency film. Printed information is called **hard copy** because it is a more permanent form of output than that presented on a monitor. Users can print a hard copy of a file in either portrait or landscape orientation. A page with **portrait orientation** is taller than it is wide, with information printed across the shorter width of the paper. A page with **landscape orientation** is wider than it is tall, with information printed across the widest part of the paper.

Because printing requirements vary greatly among users, manufacturers offer printers with varying speeds, capabilities, and printing methods. Generally, printers can be grouped into two categories: impact and nonimpact.

IMPACT PRINTERS An **impact printer** forms marks on a piece of paper by striking a mechanism against an ink ribbon that physically contacts the paper. Because of the striking activity, impact printers generally are noisy. Impact printers usually are inexpensive and print relatively quickly, but they do not provide high print quality.

One commonly used type of impact printer is a dot-matrix printer. A **dot-matrix printer** produces printed images when tiny pins on a print head mechanism strike an inked ribbon [Figure 4-42].

Dot-matrix printers typically use 8½-by-11-inch continuous-form paper, in which each sheet of paper is connected.

Is a flat display the same as a flat-panel display?

No. A flat display refers to a CRT monitor that has a flat screen. A flat-panel display has a shallow depth and uses liquid crystal technology.

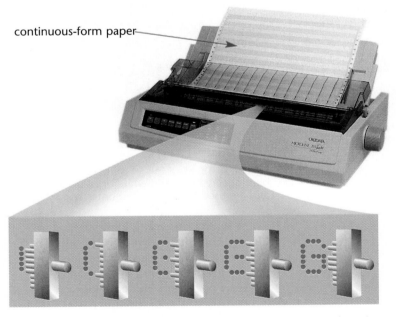

continuous-form paper

Figure 4-42 A dot-matrix printer produces printed images when tiny pins strike an inked ribbon.

NONIMPACT PRINTERS A **nonimpact printer** forms marks on a piece of paper without actually striking the paper. Because these printers do not strike the paper, they are much quieter than impact printers. Two common types of nonimpact printers are ink-jet and laser printers.

Because of their reasonable cost and print quality, ink-jet printers often are used in homes and schools [Figure 4-43]. An **ink-jet printer** is a type of nonimpact printer that forms marks by spraying tiny drops of liquid ink onto a piece of paper. Ink-jet printers can produce high-quality text and graphics in both black-and-white and color on a variety of media such as paper, envelopes, labels, or transparencies. Many ink-jet printers can print photo-quality images on standard-weight paper; others require a heavier weight premium paper. Ink-jet printers use small ink cartridges that are replaced easily or may be refilled using inexpensive ink-jet refill kits. In addition, many ink-jet printers include software to help you create items such as announcements, banners, cards, and so on.

WEB INFO

For more information about ink-jet printers, visit the Teachers Discovering Computers Web site, click Chapter 4, click Web Info, and then click Ink-Jet Printer.

Figure 4-43 Most ink-jet printers can print high-quality black-and-white or color documents and are used extensively in homes and schools.

A **laser printer** is a high-speed, high-quality nonimpact printer. Operating in a manner similar to a copy machine, a laser printer uses powdered ink, called toner, which is packaged in a cartridge. When electrically charged, the toner sticks to a special drum inside the printer and then is transferred to the paper through a combination of pressure and heat [Figure 4-44]. When the toner runs out, you simply replace the cartridge.

Figure 4-44 A laser printer operates similarly to a copy machine. Electrically charged toner sticks to a special drum inside the printer and then is transferred to the paper through a combination of pressure and heat.

Laser printers, similarly to ink-jet printers, usually use individual sheets of letter and legal-size paper stored in a removable tray that slides into the printer case. Most printers also have a manual feed slot where you can insert individual sheets, transparencies, and envelopes.

Although laser printers cost more than ink-jet printers, laser printers quickly print very high-quality black-and-white text and graphics. Although color laser printers are available, they are expensive and rarely found in K-12 schools.

Other nonimpact printers include photo printers, thermal printers, portable printers, label and postage printers, plotters, and large-format printers.

DATA PROJECTORS

A **data projector** projects the image that displays on a computer screen onto a large screen, so that an audience, such as a classroom or school assembly, can see the image clearly [Figure 4-45]. Data projectors range in size from large devices attached to a ceiling or wall in an auditorium to smaller, portable devices. Three types of smaller units are LCD projection panels, LCD projectors, and DLP (digital light processing) projectors. An LCD projection panel uses liquid crystal display technology and is designed to be placed on

Figure 4-45 Data projectors produce sharp, bright images.

top of an overhead projector. An LCD projector, which also uses liquid crystal display technology, attaches directly to a computer and uses its own light source to display the information shown on the computer screen. A digital light processing (DLP) projector uses tiny mirrors to reflect light, producing crisp, bright, colorful images that remain in focus and can be seen clearly even in a well-lit room.

FACSIMILE (FAX) MACHINE

A **facsimile (fax) machine** is a device that transmits and receives documents over telephone lines. The documents can contain text, graphics, or photos, or can be handwritten. When a document is sent or received via a fax machine, these documents are known as faxes. A fax machine scans the original document, converts the image into digitized data, and transmits the digitized image [Figure 4-46]. A fax machine at the receiving end reads the incoming data, converts the digitized data into an image, and prints or stores a copy of the original image.

The fax machine described above is a stand-alone fax machine. You also can add fax capability to your computer via a fax modem. A fax modem is a communications device that allows you to send and receive electronic documents as faxes. A fax modem transmits electronic documents, such as a word processing letter or digital photo. A fax modem is like a regular modem except that it transmits documents to a fax machine or to another fax modem. When you receive a fax on your computer, you can view the document on the screen or print it using special fax software.

Figure 4-46 A stand-alone fax machine.

MULTIFUNCTION DEVICES

A **multifunction device** (**MFD**) is a single piece of equipment that provides the functionality of a printer, fax machine, copier, and scanner [Figure 4-47]. The features of multifunction devices vary widely. For example, some use color ink-jet printer technology, while others include a black-and-white laser printer. Small businesses, home offices, and school administrative offices use multifunction devices because they take up less space and cost less than a separate printer, scanner, copy machine, and fax machine. Quality multifunction devices are available for less than $150.

Figure 4-47 This multifunctional device is a color printer, scanner, fax, and copy machine all in one device.

AUDIO OUTPUT

Audio output is any music, speech, or other sound produced by a computer and is widely available on the Internet. You can listen to music on your computer by simply inserting an audio compact disc (CD) into the CD-ROM drive. You can hear sounds of video clips while viewing them on the monitor. Two commonly used devices for audio output are speakers and headsets.

Many computers have a small internal speaker, but they usually produce low-quality sound. For this reason, many personal computers are sold with stereo speakers. **Speakers** can be separate devices that can be placed on either side of the monitor or they can be built into the monitor or the system unit. Stereo speakers are connected to ports on the sound card. Most speakers have tone and volume controls.

When using speakers, anyone within listening distance can hear the output. Speakers are not always practical in classrooms and computer labs. Often, teachers and students use headsets that can be plugged into a port on the sound card [Figure 4-48]. By using headsets, students will not be disturbed by sounds on nearby computers.

Figure 4-48 Headsets are used to prevent students from being disturbed by sounds coming from nearby computers.

OUTPUT DEVICES FOR STUDENTS WITH SPECIAL NEEDS

For students with special needs, many options with respect to output devices are available. Students who are hearing-impaired, for example, can instruct programs to display words and visual signals instead of sounds. Students who are visually impaired can change screen settings to magnify text, change colors, and so on, to make the words easier to read. Instead of viewing the monitor, students who are visually impaired also can use speech output, where the computer reads the information that displays on the screen. Another alternative is a Braille printer, which outputs information in Braille onto paper [Figure 4-49]. Learning

Figure 4-49 A Braille printer.

WEB INFO

For more information about Braille printers, visit the Teachers Discovering Computers Web site, click Chapter 4, click Web Info, and then click Braille Printer.

how to integrate software programs and hardware devices into your curriculum that allow students with special needs to use computers as tools for learning will be covered in Chapters 6 and 7.

What Is Storage?

Storage refers to the media on which data, instructions, and information are kept, as well as the devices that record and retrieve these items. To understand storage, you should understand the difference between how a computer uses memory and how it uses storage. As discussed earlier in this chapter, random access memory, called RAM, temporarily stores data and programs that are being processed. You also will recall that RAM is volatile because data and programs stored in memory are lost when the power is turned off or a power failure occurs.

Storage stores data, instructions, and information when they are not being processed. Think of storage as a filing cabinet used to hold file folders, and memory as the top of your desk [Figure 4-50]. When you need to work with a file, you remove it from the filing cabinet (storage) and place it on your desk (memory). When you are finished with the file, you return it to the filing cabinet (storage). Storage is non-volatile, which means that data and instructions in storage are retained even when power is removed from the computer.

Storage Media and Devices

A **storage medium** (media is the plural), also called **secondary storage**, is the physical material on which data, instructions, and information are kept. One commonly used storage medium is a **disk**, which is a round, flat piece of plastic or metal on which items such as data, instructions, and information can be encoded. A **storage device** is the mechanism used to record and retrieve these items to and from a storage medium.

Storage devices can function as sources of input and output. For example, each time a storage device transfers data, instructions, and information from a storage medium into memory — a process called reading — it functions as an input source. When a storage device transfers these items from memory to a storage medium — a process called writing — it functions as an output source.

The size, or capacity, of a storage device, is measured by the amount of bytes (characters) it can hold. Storage capacity usually is measured in megabytes or gigabytes. Some devices can hold thousands of bytes, while others can store trillions of bytes. For example, a typical floppy disk can store 1.44 MB of data and a typical hard disk can store 80 GB of data.

Storage requirements among users vary greatly. A teacher, for example, might have a list of names, test scores, and average grades for 30 students that requires several hundred bytes of storage. Users of larger computers, such as banks or libraries, might need to store trillions of bytes worth of historical or catalog records. To meet the needs of a wide range of users, numerous types of storage media and storage devices exist, many of which are discussed in the following sections.

Figure 4-50 Think of storage as a filing cabinet used to hold file folders and memory as the top of your desk. When you need to work with a file, you remove it from the filing cabinet (storage) and place it on your desk (memory). When you are finished with the file, you return it to the filing cabinet (storage).

FLOPPY DISKS

A **floppy disk** or **diskette** is a portable, inexpensive storage medium that consists of a thin, circular, flexible plastic disk with a magnetic coating enclosed in a square-shaped plastic shell [Figure 4-51]. In the early 1970s, IBM introduced a new type of storage medium, called the floppy disk. Because these early, 8-inch-wide disks had flexible plastic covers, many users referred to them as floppies or floppy diskettes. The next generation of floppies looked much the same, but were only 5.25-inches wide. Today, the most widely used floppy disk is 3.5-inches wide. The flexible cover of the earlier floppy disks has been replaced with a rigid plastic outer cover. Thus, although today's 3.5-inch disks are not at all floppy, users still refer to them as floppy disks.

CHARACTERISTICS OF A FLOPPY DISK
A floppy disk is a type of a magnetic disk, which means it uses magnetic patterns to store data, instructions, and information on the disk's surface. Most magnetic disks are read/write storage media; that is, you can access (read) data from and place (write) data on a magnetic disk any number of times.

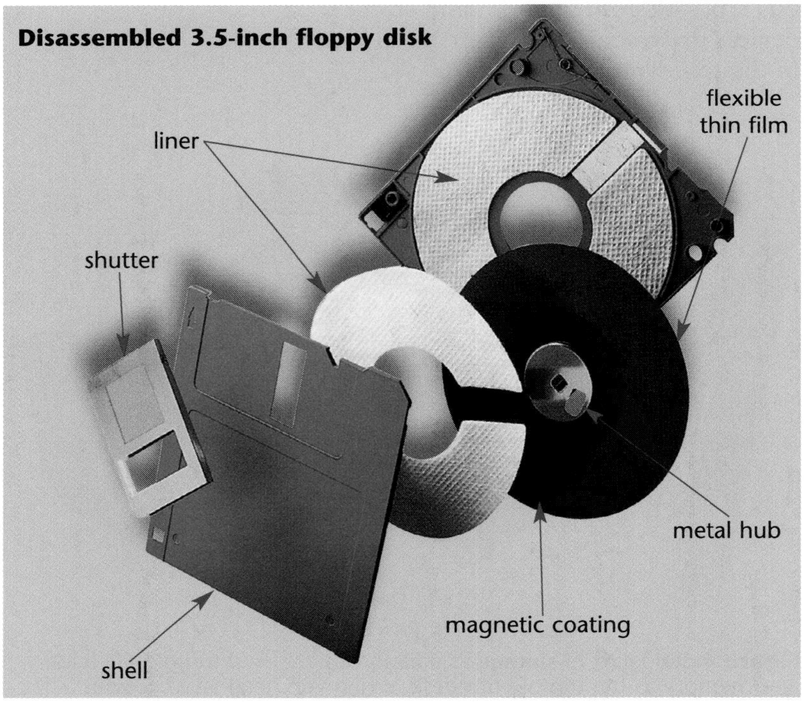

A new blank floppy disk has no data, instructions, or information stored on it. Before a computer can write on a new floppy disk, it must be formatted. **Formatting** is the process of preparing a disk (floppy disk or hard disk) for reading and writing by organizing the disk into storage locations called tracks and sectors [Figure 4-52]. A **track** is a narrow storage ring around the disk — similar to the annual rings on a tree. A **sector** is a pie-shaped section of the disk, which breaks the tracks into small arcs.

Most disks are preformatted by the disk manufacturer for use on either a PC or a Macintosh computer. In some cases, however, you must format the disks yourself. Because a Macintosh formats disks differently than PCs, a Macintosh formatted disk cannot normally be used in a PC. Macintosh computers, however, can read PC formatted disks.

To protect them from accidentally being erased, floppy disks have a write-protect notch. A write-protect notch is a small hole in the corner of the disk. By sliding a small tab, you either can cover or expose the notch. On a floppy disk, if the write-protect notch is closed, or covered, the disk drive can write on the floppy disk. If the write-protect notch is exposed, or open, the disk drive cannot write on the floppy disk; it can, however, read from the disk. Some floppy disks have a second hole on the opposite side of the disk that does not have a small tab; this hole identifies the disk as a high-density floppy disk.

A high-density (HD) floppy disk, the most widely used 3.5-inch floppy disk, can store 1.44 MB of data — the equivalent of approximately 700 pages of 2,000 characters each. With reasonable care, floppy disks can last for many years — providing an inexpensive and reliable form of storage. When handling a floppy disk, you should avoid exposing it to heat, cold, magnetic fields, and contaminants such as dust, smoke, or salt air.

A **floppy disk drive** is a device that can read from and write on a floppy disk. Personal computers usually have a floppy disk drive installed inside the system unit.

Disassembled 3.5-inch floppy disk

liner
flexible thin film
shutter
metal hub
magnetic coating
shell

Figure 4-51 In a 3.5-inch floppy disk, the thin circular flexible film is enclosed between two liners. A piece of metal called a shutter covers an opening to the recording surface in the rigid plastic shell.

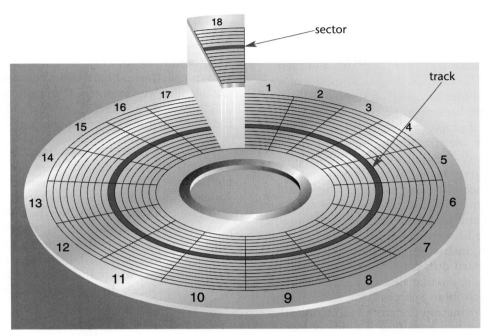

For a discussion of backup procedures, visit the Teachers Discovering Computers Web site, click Chapter 4, click Web Info, and then click Backup.

Figure 4-52 A track is a narrow recording band that forms a full circle on the surface of a disk. The disk's storage locations then are divided into pie-shaped sections, which break the tracks into small arcs called sectors.

Modern PCs usually have one installed floppy disk drive that is called drive A. Older Macintosh computers also have one installed floppy disk drive and the drive is referred to simply as the floppy disk drive.

All newer Macintosh desktop computers (eMac, iMac, and PowerMac G4) and all newer Macintosh and most PC notebook computers do not come equipped with an internal floppy disk drive. External floppy disk drives can be attached to Macintosh computers using a USB port.

HIGH-CAPACITY REMOVABLE DISKS

Several manufacturers make high-capacity disk drives that use disks with capacities of 100 MB or greater. With these high-capacity disks, you can store large files containing graphics, audio, or video; transport a large number of files from one computer to another; or make a backup of all of your important files. A **backup** is a duplicate of a file, program, or disk that can be used if the original is lost, damaged, or destroyed.

One popular high-capacity drive is the Zip drive. A **Zip drive** is a special high-capacity disk drive developed by Iomega Corporation. These drives use a special 3.5-inch Zip disk, which can store 100 to 750 MB of data. Some personal computers are equipped with a built-in Zip drive. You

also can add an external Zip drive either to a Macintosh computer or PC [Figure 4-53]. Just like floppy disks, Macintosh computers format Zip disks differently than PCs. Macintosh formatted Zip disks normally cannot be used in a PC. Many modern Macintosh computers, however, can read and write on PC-formatted Zip disks.

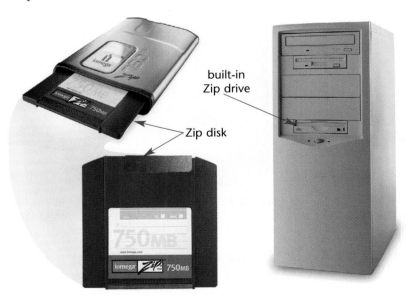

Figure 4-53 Some computers are equipped with a built-in Zip drive. You also can add an external Zip drive to a PC or Macintosh computer.

HARD DISKS

When personal computers were introduced, software programs and their related files required small amounts of storage and files fit easily on floppy disks. As software became more complex and included graphical user interfaces and multimedia, file sizes and storage requirements increased. Today, hard disks, which provide for larger storage capacities and much faster access times than floppy disks, are the primary media for storing software programs and files. Current personal computer hard disks can store from 30 GB to 100 GB of data, instructions, and information.

A **hard disk** usually consists of several inflexible, circular disks, called platters, on which items such as data, instructions, and information are stored electronically. A **platter** in a hard disk is made of aluminum, glass, or ceramic and is coated with a material that allows data to be magnetically recorded on its surface. Although removable hard disks do exist, the hard disks in most personal computers are housed permanently inside the system unit and are enclosed in an airtight, sealed case to protect the platters from contamination [Figure 4-54].

WEB INFO

For more information about hard disks, visit the Teachers Discovering Computers Web site, click Chapter 4, click Web Info, and then click Hard Disk.

hard drive installed in system unit

Figure 4-54 The hard disk in a personal computer normally is housed permanently inside the system unit.

Like a floppy disk, a hard disk is a magnetic disk that stores data, instructions, and information using magnetic patterns. Hard disks also are read/write storage media; that is, you can both read from and write on a hard disk any number of times.

WEB INFO

For more information about CD-ROMs, visit the Teachers Discovering Computers Web site, click Chapter 4, click Web Info, and then click CD-ROM.

Before you can write data, instructions, or information on a hard disk, the hard disk must be formatted. Hard disk manufacturers typically format hard disks before they are installed in computers. Typically, a hard disk is designated drive C on PCs and as the HD Disk on Macintosh computers.

EXTERNAL AND REMOVABLE HARD DISKS

Two types of portable hard disks are external hard disks and removable hard disks. An **external hard disk** is a separate hard disk that connects to a USB or FireWire port by a cable [Figure 4-55a]. External hard disks can store 120 GB or higher. Removable external hard disks use cartridges that you insert and remove from an external hard disk drive [Figure 4-55b].

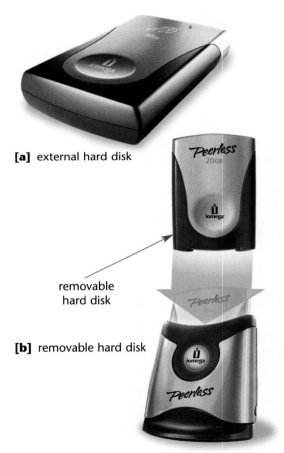

[a] external hard disk

removable hard disk

[b] removable hard disk

Figure 4-55 Examples of large-capacity portable hard disks.

Other portable external hard drives, called **USB drives**, are mini external hard drives that you can carry on your key chain and plug into a USB or FireWire port. These small and durable portable hard drives hold 64, 128, 256, and 512 MB or more and provide a moderately priced solution you can use to transfer files and programs between home and school computers. Because these are Plug and Play devices, they are easy to use [Figure 4-56].

cover with key chain ring   portable hard drive

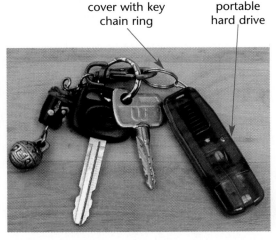

Figure 4-56 The TwinTech Industry portable hard drive is a small and durable hard disk that can be carried on a key chain.

CDs AND DVDs

CDs and DVDs are a type of optical storage media that consists of a flat, round, portable, plastic disc with a protective metal coating. These discs usually are 4.75 inches in diameter and less than one-twentieth of an inch thick. (Recall from Chapter 1 that the term *disk* is used for magnetic media and *disc* is used for optical media.)

CDs and DVDs primarily store music, movies, digital photographs, and software programs. Just about every personal computer today includes some type of CD or DVD drive [Figure 4-57]. Some CD and DVD drives are read only, meaning you cannot write (save) on the media. Others are read/write, which allows users to save on the disc just as they save on a hard disk.

On personal computers, the drive designation of a CD or DVD drive usually follows alphabetically after that of the hard disk. For example, if your hard disk is drive C, then the CD or DVD drive usually will be drive D. When you place a CD or DVD in a Macintosh computer, an icon that looks like a CD appears on the computer desktop.

CHARACTERISTICS OF CDs AND DVDs

CDs and DVDs are optical media that store data, information, music, and video in microscopic pits on the bottom portion of the disc. A high-powered laser light creates the pits. A lower-powered laser light reads items from the disc by reflecting light through the bottom of the disc, which usually is either gold or silver in color. The reflected light is converted into a series of bits the computer can process. Most manufacturers place a silk-screened label on the top of the disc.

Push the button to slide out the tray.

Insert the disc, label side up.

Push the same button to close the tray.

Figure 4-57 To use CD and DVD drives, you push a button to slide out a tray, insert the disc with the label side up, and then push the same button to close the tray.

WEB INFO

For more information about DVD-ROMs, visit the Teachers Discovering Computers Web site, click Chapter 4, click Web Info, and then click DVD-ROM.

CARE OF CDs AND DVDs Manufacturers guarantee that a properly cared for CD or DVD will last five years, but could last up to 100 years. Figure 4-58 outlines some guidelines for the proper care of CDs and DVDs. Never bend a disc. Exposing discs to extreme temperatures or humidity could cause them to warp. Stacking discs, touching the underside of discs, or exposing them to any type of contaminant may scratch a disc. If a disc becomes warped or if its surface is scratched, data on the disc may be unreadable. Always place a CD or DVD in its protective case, called a jewel box or disc storage case, when you are finished using it.

CDs and DVDs are available in a variety of formats. The following sections discuss many of these formats.

CD-ROM Compact disc read-only memory (CD-ROM) (pronounced SEE-DEE-rom), is a type of optical disc that uses the same laser technology as audio CDs for recording music. Unlike an audio CD, a CD-ROM can contain text, graphics, animation, and video, as well as sound. The contents of standard CD-ROMs are written, or **recorded**, by the manufacturer and only can be read and used; that is, they cannot be erased or modified — hence, the name read-only.

Because audio CDs and CD-ROMs use the same laser technology, you can use your CD-ROM drive to listen to an audio CD while working on your computer.

A CD-ROM can hold 650 MB of data, instructions, and information — about 450 times the capacity of a high-density

Figure 4-58 Some guidelines for the proper care of CDs and DVDs.

3.5-inch floppy disk. Because CD-ROMs have such high storage capacities, they are used to store and distribute today's complex software, such as programs for children, education, games, and reference [Figure 4-59]. Most of today's software programs are sold on CD; some programs even require that the disc be in the drive each time you use the program.

PICTURE CDs A Kodak **Picture CD** is a type of compact disc that stores digital versions of a single roll of film using a .jpg file format. Many film developers offer Picture CD service when consumers drop off film to be developed. In addition to printed photographs and negatives, you also receive a Picture CD containing your pictures. The additional cost for a Picture CD is about $10 per roll of film.

Standard CD-ROM drives can read a Picture CD. Using photo editing software and the photographs on the Picture CD, you can remove red eye, crop the photographs, enhance colors, and edit just about any aspect of the photograph. In addition, you can print photos from a Picture CD on glossy paper with an ink-jet printer. Many stores have kiosks at which you can print pictures from a Picture CD [Figure 4-60].

CD-R AND CD-RW Many computers today include either a CD-R or a CD-RW drive as standard equipment. Unlike standard CD-ROM drives, these new drives allow you to record your own data onto a CD-R or CD-RW disc.

Figure 4-59 CD-ROMs are used to store and distribute multimedia software including programs for children, education, games, and reference.

Step 1:
Drop off the film to be developed. Mark the Picture CD box on the film-processing envelope.

Step 2:
When you pick up prints and negatives, a Picture CD contains digital images of each photograph.

Step 3:
At home, print images from the Picture CD on your ink-jet or photo printer. At a store, print images from the Picture CD at a kiosk.

Figure 4-60 How a Picture CD works.

A **compact disc-recordable (CD-R)** is a compact disc onto which you can record your own information, such as text, graphic, and audio. With a CD-R, you can write on part of the disc at one time and another part at a later time. You can write on each part only one time, and you cannot erase the disc's content. To write on a CD-R disc, you must have CD-R software and a CD-R drive.

A **compact disc-rewriteable (CD-RW)** is an erasable disc you can write on multiple times. With CD-RW, the disc acts like a floppy or hard disk. You can easily write and rewrite data multiple times. To write on a CD-RW disc, you must have CD-RW software and a CD-RW drive.

A popular use of CD-RW and CD-R discs is to create audio CDs. The steps in Figure 4-61 illustrate techniques for

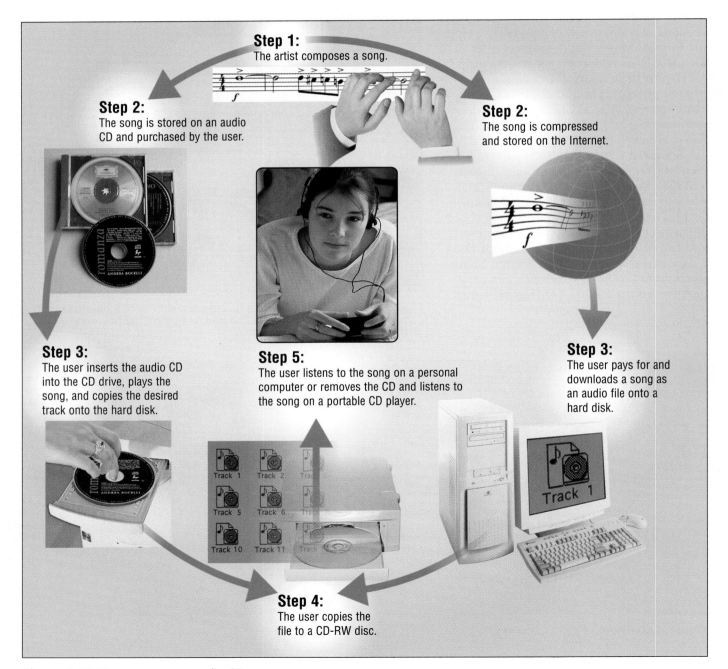

Step 1:
The artist composes a song.

Step 2:
The song is stored on an audio CD and purchased by the user.

Step 2:
The song is compressed and stored on the Internet.

Step 3:
The user inserts the audio CD into the CD drive, plays the song, and copies the desired track onto the hard disk.

Step 5:
The user listens to the song on a personal computer or removes the CD and listens to the song on a portable CD player.

Step 3:
The user pays for and downloads a song as an audio file onto a hard disk.

Track 1   Track 2

Track 5   Track 6

Track 10   Track 11

Track 1

Step 4:
The user copies the file to a CD-RW disc.

Figure 4-61 How to create an audio CD.

copying the song(s) from an existing CD or downloading the song(s) from the Web, in most cases for a fee.

DVD-ROM AND DVD+RW Although CDs have large storage capacities, even these are not large enough for many of today's complex programs. Some software, for example, is sold on five or more CDs. To meet the tremendous storage requirements of today's software, the digital video disc read-only memory (DVD-ROM) format was developed.

A **digital video disc read-only memory (DVD-ROM)** is an extremely high capacity CD capable of storing from 4.7 GB to 17 GB, more than enough to hold a telephone book containing every resident in the United States [Figure 4-62]. Not only is the storage capacity greater than a CD, but the quality of a DVD far surpasses that of a CD. In order to read a DVD-ROM, you must have a **DVD-ROM drive**. Many computers now are sold with DVD-ROM drives that will read both CDs and DVDs.

DVDs are available in a variety of formats, including one which stores motion pictures. To view a DVD movie, you insert the DVD movie disc into a DVD player connected to your television or into a computer's DVD-ROM drive. Many computers that contain a DVD-ROM drive allow you to connect your computer directly to your television. Users also can purchase recordable (DVD-R) and rewrite-able (DVD+RW) versions of DVDs, which are similar to CD-R and CD-RW in the way they operate.

As the cost of DVD technologies becomes more reasonable, many industry professionals believe that DVDs will eventually replace CDs, VCRs, and VHS tapes in our businesses, homes, and schools.

Many new computers come with a standard combination DVD-ROM/CD-RW drive or optional DVD-R/CD-RW. The DVD-R/CD-RW drive is called a SuperDrive on newer Macintosh computers.

Chapter 5 and the Digital Imaging and Video Technology special feature that follows Chapter 5 discuss in detail the processes of creating, editing, and using CD-R, CD-RW, and DVD+RW technology at home and in education.

FAQ

Is it legal to copy songs onto a CD?

It is legal to copy songs from an audio CD that you purchase, as long as you use the copied music for your own personal use. It is not legal to download copyrighted music unless the song's copyright holder has granted permission; normally you must pay a fee to download songs legally.

DVD-ROM drive

DVD-ROM

Figure 4-62 A DVD-ROM is an extremely high capacity compact disc capable of storing 4.7 GB to 17 GB.

MINIATURE MOBILE STORAGE MEDIA

PDAs, digital cameras, music players, and smart phones do not have a great deal of internal storage. They often use some form of mobile storage media to store digital images, music, or documents [Figure 4-63].

Many types of mobile storage media are available, with capacities ranging from 16 MB to 2 GB or more. Many miniature storage media are no bigger than a postage stamp. The table in Figure 6-64 summarizes the storage capacities and uses of popular miniature storage media.

Buyer's Guide

At the end of this chapter is a special feature that introduces you to purchasing, installing, maintaining, and troubleshooting a desktop or notebook computer.

A World Without Wires

A revolution in wireless technology and wireless devices is rapidly changing the way people work, play, and learn. To learn more about this wireless revolution and its potential impact on society and education, review the A World Without Wires special feature that follows Chapter 8.

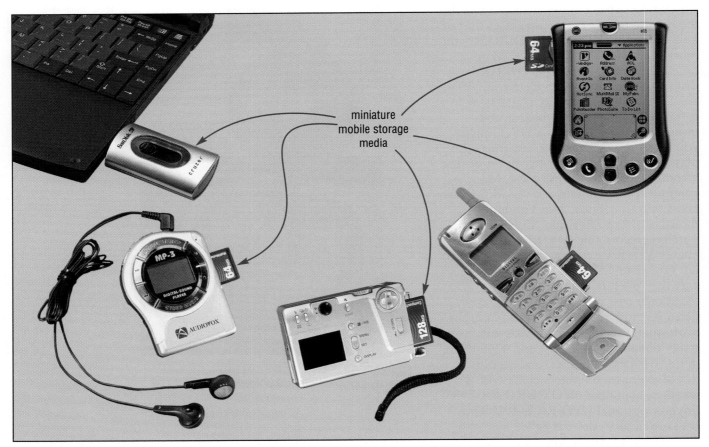

Figure 4-63 Notebook computers, PDAs, music players, digital cameras, and smart phones use miniature mobile storage media.

MINIATURE MOBILE STORAGE MEDIA

Device Name	Storage Capacity	Type	Use
CompactFlash 	16 MB to 1 GB	Flash memory card	Digital cameras, PDAs, notebook computers, printers, music players, cellular telephones
Smart Media 	16 MB to 128 MB	Flash memory card	Digital cameras, PDAs, photo printers, cellular telephones
Secure Digital 	16 MB to 256 MB	Flash memory card	Digital cameras, PDAs, music players, cellular telephones, digital video cameras, car navigation systems, e-books
Memory Stick 	16 MB to 128 MB	Flash memory card	Digital cameras, notebook computers, photo printers
Microdrive 	1 GB	Magnetic media	Digital cameras, PDAs, music players, notebook computers, video cameras
USBDrive 	32 MB to 2 GB	Flash memory card	Plugs into any USB port to function as a mini hard disk

FIGURE 4-64 Popular miniature mobile storage media.

FAQ

Are mobile storage media also called smart cards?

No, a smart card, which is similar in size to a credit or ATM card, stores data on a thin microprocessor embedded in the card. Smart cards contain a processor and have input, process, output, and storage capabilities. Mobile storage media only have storage capabilities.

Summary of Hardware for Educators

In this chapter, you learned about the various hardware components used in schools, businesses, and homes. First, you learned about some of the major components of the system unit. Next, you learned how to identify several types of input devices and how they operate. Third, you reviewed various output devices and learned how to identify and use them. Finally, you learned about storage devices. You now should have a good understanding of the information processing cycle and how various hardware devices are used in education.

In Brief

Web Instructions: To display this page from the Web, start your browser and enter the URL, www.course.com/tdc3. Click Chapter 4 at the top of the Web page and then click In Brief on the left sidebar. Click the links for current and additional information. To listen to an audio version of this In Brief, click the Audio button at the top left of these instructions.

WEB INFO

IN BRIEF

KEY TERMS

CHECKPOINT

TEACHING TODAY

EDUCATION ISSUES

INTEGRATION CORNER

SOFTWARE CORNER

IN THE LAB

LEARN IT ONLINE

✱ FEATURES...

Timeline 2004

Guide to WWW Sites

Buyer's Guide 2004

Professional Sites

State/Federal Sites

Interactive Labs

Search Tools

HOME

1. The System Unit

The **system unit** is a box-like case that houses the electronic components a computer uses to process data. The system unit is made of metal or plastic and protects the electronic components from damage. The major components in the system unit include the motherboard, the CPU and microprocessor, memory, expansion slots and expansion cards, and ports and connectors.

2. Bits and Bytes

Most computers are **digital**, meaning that they understand only two discrete states: on and off. In order to store and process data, a computer must convert the data into a form it understands. Each on or off digital value is called a **bit** (short for **bi**nary digi**t**), and represents the smallest unit of data the computer can handle. When eight bits are grouped together as a unit, they are called a **byte**.

3. CPU and Microprocessor

The **central processing unit** (**CPU**) interprets and carries out the basic instructions that operate a computer. The CPU manages most of a computer's operations. A chip known as the **microprocessor** contains the CPU. A microprocessor contains a number of components including a control unit, an arithmetic/logic unit, and a system clock.

4. Memory

Computers use **memory** to store data and information temporarily. Several terms have evolved to define memory and storage devices. A **kilobyte** (**KB or K**) of memory is equal to 1,000 bytes, a **megabyte** (**MB**) is equal to one million bytes, and a **gigabyte** (**GB**) is equal to one billion bytes. Two common types of memory are RAM and ROM. **RAM** is an example of volatile memory and **ROM** is an example of nonvolatile memory.

5. Types of Input

Input is entering data, programs, commands, and user responses into memory. **Data** is a collection of unorganized facts that include words, numbers, pictures, and sounds. A **program** is a series of instructions that tells a computer how to perform tasks. A **command** is an instruction given to a computer program. **User response** is a user's input to a question from a program.

6. Keyboards

A **keyboard** is a group of switches resembling the keys on a typewriter that allow users to enter input. You enter data, commands, and other input into a computer by pressing keys on the keyboard. A keyboard contains keys that allow you to type letters, numbers, spaces, punctuation marks, and other symbols.

7. Pointing Devices

A **pointing device** is an input device that allows you to control the movement of the pointer on the screen and to make selections from the screen. Common pointing devices include the mouse, trackball, and joystick. A **mouse** is an input device that usually has one or two buttons and a ball mechanism on the bottom. A **trackball** is a stationary pointing device with a ball mechanism on its top. A **joystick** is a vertical lever mounted on a base.

8. Audio and Video Input

Audio input is the process of recording music, speech, or sound effects. Recorded sound is input via a device such as a microphone, tape player, or audio CD player. **Video input** is the process of entering

In Brief

WEB INFO

IN BRIEF

KEY TERMS

CHECKPOINT

TEACHING TODAY

EDUCATION ISSUES

INTEGRATION CORNER

SOFTWARE CORNER

IN THE LAB

LEARN IT ONLINE

✳ FEATURES...

Timeline 2004

Guide to WWW Sites

Buyer's Guide 2004

Professional Sites

State/Federal Sites

Interactive Labs

Search Tools

HOME

a full-motion recording into a computer. To capture video, you plug a video camera, a VCR, or a similar device into a video capture card.

9. Types of Output

Output is data that has been processed into a useful form called information. Four common types of output are text, graphics, audio, and video. Text consists of characters that are used to create words, sentences, and paragraphs. Graphics are digital representations of nontext information, such as images and drawings. Audio is music, speech, or other sound that is stored and produced by the computer. Video consists of photographic images that are played back on a computer at speeds that provide the appearance of full motion in real-time.

10. Output Devices

An **output device** is any computer component capable of conveying information to a user. Commonly used output devices include monitors, printers, data projectors, facsimile machines, multifunction devices, speakers, and headsets.

11. Monitors

A **monitor** is a display device that conveys text, graphics, and video information visually and is housed in a plastic or metal case. Monitors for personal computers are available in a variety of sizes, with the more common being 15, 17, 19, and 21 inches. Like a television set, the core of a monitor is a large glass tube called a **cathode ray tube** (**CRT**). The quality of a monitor depends largely on its resolution, dot pitch, and refresh rate.

12. Printers

A **printer** is an output device that produces text and graphical information on a physical medium such as paper or transparency film. Printers are grouped in two categories: impact and nonimpact. The more commonly used type of impact printer is a dot-matrix printer. A **nonimpact printer** forms marks on a piece of paper without actually striking the paper. Two common types of nonimpact printers are ink-jet and laser printers.

13. Storage

Storage refers to the media on which data, instructions, and information are kept, as well as the devices that record and retrieve these items. Storage is nonvolatile, which means that data and instructions in storage are retained even when power is removed from the computer. A **storage medium** is the physical material on which data, instructions, and information are kept. One commonly used storage medium is a **disk**, which is a round, flat piece of plastic or metal on which items such as data, instructions, and information can be encoded.

14. Floppy Disks

A **floppy disk**, or **diskette**, is a portable, inexpensive storage medium that consists of a thin, circular, flexible plastic disk with a magnetic coating enclosed in a square-shaped plastic shell. Floppy disks are read/write magnetic storage media; that is, you can access (read) data from and place (write) data on a floppy disk any number of times.

15. Hard Disks

Hard disks provide for larger storage capacities and much faster access times than floppy disks and are the primary media for storing software programs and files. A **hard disk** usually consists of several inflexible, circular disks, called platters, on which items such as data, instructions, and information are stored electronically.

16. CDs and DVDs

CDs and DVDs are a type of optical storage media that consists of a flat, round, portable, plastic disc with a protective metal coating. CDs and DVDs are available in a variety of formats.

Key Terms

Web Instructions: To display this page from the Web, start your browser and enter the URL, www.course.com/tdc3. Click Chapter 4 at the top of the Web page and then click Key Terms on the left sidebar. Scroll through the list of terms. Click a term to display its definition and a picture. Click Key Terms on the left to redisplay the Key Terms page. Click the TO WEB button for current and additional information about the term from the Web.

WEB INFO

IN BRIEF

KEY TERMS

CHECKPOINT

TEACHING TODAY

EDUCATION ISSUES

INTEGRATION CORNER

SOFTWARE CORNER

IN THE LAB

LEARN IT ONLINE

✷ FEATURES...

Timeline 2004

Guide to WWW Sites

Buyer's Guide 2004

Professional Sites

State/Federal Sites

Interactive Labs

Search Tools

HOME

adapter card [4.09]
address [4.07]
American Standard Code for
   Information Interchange (ASCII)
   [4.03]
analog [4.02]
arithmetic/logic unit (ALU) [4.07]
arithmetic operations [4.07]
audio [4.22]
audio input [4.19]
audio output [4.28]

backup [4.31]
bar code [4.18]
binary [4.03]
bit [4.03]
byte [4.03]

cathode ray tube (CRT) [4.22]
central processing unit (CPU)
   [4.05]
chip [4.05]
clicking [4.15]
clock speed [4.07]
command [4.12]
compact disc read-only memory
   (CD-ROM) [4.34]
compact disc-recordable (CD-R)
   [4.36]
compact disc-rewriteable (CD-RW)
   [4.36]
comparison operations [4.07]
connectors [4.10]
control unit [4.06]
cordless keyboard [4.14]
cordless mouse [4.15]

data [4.12]
data projector [4.26]
decoding [4.06]
digital [4.02]
digital camera [4.19]
digital video disc read-only memory
   (DVD-ROM) [4.37]
disk [4.29]
diskette [4.30]
display device [4.22]
dot-matrix printer [4.25]
dot pitch [4.25]
double-clicking [4.15]
dragging [4.15]
dual inline memory module (DIMM)
   [4.08]
DVD-ROM drive [4.37]

electronic book (e-book) [4.24]
ENERGY STAR [4.25]
executing [4.06]
expansion board [4.09]

expansion card [4.09]
expansion slot [4.09]
external hard disk [4.32]
facsimile (fax) machine [4.27]
fetching [4.06]
FireWire port [4.11]
flat panel monitor [4.24]
floppy disk [4.30]
floppy disk drive [4.30]
formatting [4.30]

gas plasma monitor [4.23]
gigabyte (GB) [4.08]
gigahertz (GHz) [4.07]
graphics [4.22]

hard copy [4.25]
hard disk [4.32]
high-definition television (HDTV)
   [4.23]

impact printer [4.25]
ink-jet printer [4.26]
input [4.12]
input device [4.13]
insertion point [4.14]

joystick [4.17]

keyboard [4.13]
keyword [4.12]
kilobyte (K or KB) [4.08]
kiosk [4.17]

landscape orientation [4.25]
large display monitors [4.23]
laser printer [4.26]
LCD monitor [4.24]
logical operations [4.07]

machine cycle [4.06]
megabyte (MB) [4.08]
megahertz (MHz) [4.07]
memory [4.07]
microprocessor [4.06]
monitor [4.22]
motherboard [4.04]
mouse [4.15]
mouse pad [4.15]
multifunction device (MFD) [4.28]

nonimpact printer [4.26]
nonvolatile memory [4.08]
numeric keypad [4.14]

optical character recognition (OCR)
   [4.18]
optical mark recognition (OMR)
   [4.18]
optical mouse [4.15]
optical reader [4.18]
output [4.21]

output device [4.22]
PC Card [4.10]
Picture CD [4.35]
pixel [4.23]
platter [4.32]
Plug and Play [4.10]
pointing device [4.15]
pointing stick [4.16]
port [4.10]
portrait orientation [4.25]
printer [4.25]
processor [4.05]
program [4.12]

random access memory (RAM)
   [4.08]
read-only memory (ROM) [4.09]
recorded [4.34]
refresh rate [4.25]
resolution [4.25]

scanner [4.18]
secondary storage [4.29]
sector [4.30]
soft copy [4.22]
speakers [4.28]
speech recognition [4.19]
storage [4.29]
storage device [4.29]
storage medium [4.29]
storing [4.06]
synchronous dynamic RAM
   (SDRAM) [4.08]
system clock [4.07]
system unit [4.02]

text [4.22]
touchpad [4.16]
touch screen [4.17]
track [4.30]
trackball [4.16]

universal serial bus (USB) port
   [4.11]
USB 2.0 port [4.11]
USB drives [4.32]
user response [4.12]

video [4.22]
video input [4.19]
voice recognition [4.19]
volatile memory [4.08]

wheel [4.17]
wireless keyboard [4.14]
wireless mouse [4.15]

Zip drive [4.31]

Checkpoint

Web Instructions: To display this page from the Web, start your browser and enter the URL, www.course.com/tdc3. Click Chapter 4 at the top of the Web page and then click Checkpoint on the left sidebar. Click a blank line for the answer. Click the links for current and additional information.

WEB INFO

IN BRIEF

KEY TERMS

CHECKPOINT

TEACHING TODAY

EDUCATION ISSUES

INTEGRATION CORNER

SOFTWARE CORNER

IN THE LAB

LEARN IT ONLINE

★ FEATURES...

Timeline 2004

Guide to WWW Sites

Buyer's Guide 2004

Professional Sites

State/Federal Sites

Interactive Labs

Search Tools

HOME

1. Label the Figure

Instructions: Identify these areas or keys on a typical desktop computer keyboard.

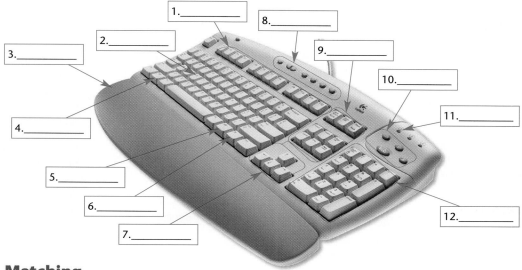

1. _____
2. _____
3. _____
4. _____
5. _____
6. _____
7. _____
8. _____
9. _____
10. _____
11. _____
12. _____

2. Matching

Instructions: Match each term from the column on the left with the best description from the column on the right.

____ 1. byte
____ 2. scanner
____ 3. output
____ 4. Zip drive
____ 5. chip

a. small piece of <u>semiconducting material</u> usually no bigger than one-half-inch square
b. <u>eight bits</u> grouped together as a unit
c. data that has been processed into a useful form, called <u>information</u>
d. an <u>input device</u> that can capture an entire page of text electronically
e. a special high-capacity floppy disk drive developed by <u>Iomega Corporation</u>

3. Short Answer

Instructions: Write a brief answer to each of the following questions.

1. What are the components of the <u>system unit</u>? What is the purpose of the central processing unit and system clock? _____
2. How are <u>RAM and ROM</u> similar? How are they different? What terminology is used to describe the storage capacity of RAM chips? _____
3. How is a computer <u>keyboard</u> like a typewriter? What keys can be found on most keyboards but not on traditional typewriters? What is the purpose of these keys? _____
4. How are impact printers different from nonimpact printers? What are examples of each type of printer? Which <u>type of printer</u> is used commonly in schools? _____
5. How does <u>formatting</u> prepare a floppy disk for storage? What is the storage capacity of a 3.5-inch high-density floppy disk? _____

Teaching Today

WEB INFO

IN BRIEF

KEY TERMS

CHECKPOINT

TEACHING TODAY

EDUCATION ISSUES

INTEGRATION CORNER

SOFTWARE CORNER

IN THE LAB

LEARN IT ONLINE

✱ FEATURES...

Timeline 2004

Guide to WWW Sites

Buyer's Guide 2004

Professional Sites

State/Federal Sites

Interactive Labs

Search Tools

HOME

Web Instructions: To display this page from the Web, start your browser and enter the URL, www.course.com/tdc3. Click Chapter 4 at the top of the Web page and then click Teaching Today on the left sidebar. Click the links for current and additional information.

1. **Teachers are always** looking for new technology tools to integrate in their classrooms. Math teachers have known for years that graphing calculators are excellent tools for teaching math. Students can use them not only to solve math problems, but also to see the solutions more graphically. Providing graphing calculators also can help students solve problems relating to other areas such as geometry, algebra, astronomy, radioactivity, lasers, art, video production, and many others. Use the Internet to research other ways to integrate graphic calculators into other non-math teaching areas. Write a list of ideas that you discover in your research.

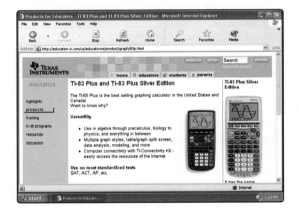

2. **Because of their low cost**, floppy disks are still the most widely used portable storage media in schools and universities today. They are not the best storage medium in all situations, however. Because they can hold only 1.44 MB of information, they do not have the capacity to store large graphic files. If your students create multimedia projects, or projects that contain a large number of graphics, a floppy disk might not provide sufficient storage space. Also, some schools feel that floppy disks pose a security risk because of viruses and do not allow students to

use them. In light of these disadvantages, do floppy disks still have a roll in the classroom? What are the advantages of using floppy disks? What other portable storage media could you and your students use in your classroom?

3. **While teachers can sometimes** select application software packages for use in the classroom, they often do not choose the type of computers used at their schools. Suppose you want to purchase an educational software package that reinforces your specific content objectives. How can you determine if your classroom computers will support the software? Where should you look to find the software's system requirements? How would you determine if your computer meets those requirements? For example, how could you determine if your computer had enough memory, a fast enough processor, or enough hard disk space?

4. **Last year, you received a color ink-jet printer** — a Hewlett-Packard DeskJet 952C — for your classroom. Until recently, the printer worked flawlessly. Lately, however, when you print a document, the ink is smearing and the print quality is poor. No one at your school can provide technical assistance or support. Where else might you find technical support? Does the manufacturer (Hewlett-Packard, in this example), provide technical support? Via what methods can you contact the manufacturer or access technical support information — telephone, e-mail, fax, the Web, or all of these? Which type of support would you prefer? Visit Hewlett-Packard's Web site and use its Web-based technical support to determine how to fix the printer problem. How does Web-based support differ from face-to-face support or support via telephone? What are some advantages and disadvantages of Web-based support?

Education Issues

Web Instructions: To display this page from the Web, start your browser and enter the URL, www.course.com/tdc3. Click Chapter 4 at the top of the Web page and then click Education Issues on the left sidebar. Click the links for current and additional information to help you respond to the Education Issues questions.

WEB INFO

IN BRIEF

KEY TERMS

CHECKPOINT

TEACHING TODAY

EDUCATION ISSUES

INTEGRATION CORNER

SOFTWARE CORNER

IN THE LAB

LEARN IT ONLINE

✳ FEATURES...

Timeline 2004

Guide to WWW Sites

Buyer's Guide 2004

Professional Sites

State/Federal Sites

Interactive Labs

Search Tools

HOME

1. Reading Comprehension

Over the last five years, reading scores have continued to drop in one of your local school districts. Knowing that reading is one of the more crucial life skills that all students must have to be successful, the district competed for and received a $1.3 million dollar grant to help students become better readers. The grant focuses on integrating e-books in the classroom as a way to fuel students' enthusiasm for reading, which will improve reading literacy throughout the district. Some teachers agree that if properly integrated, e-books can increase reading comprehension and scores. Others do not think e-books will be effective and would like to stay with traditional methods of teaching reading. What do you think? Can e-books be used to help teach students to be better readers? Should there be a mix? Are lesson plans available that support using e-books? Defend your opinion.

EBooks:
A Paper Tiger?
Survey: Few Believe eBooks
Will Replace Paper Versions

By Hillel Italie
The Associated Press

NEW YORK, Sept. 21 — Book buyers who also use the Internet don't believe electronic books will replace the paper kind, according to a survey published today. And a substantial number said they weren't even aware of the new medium.

The publishing industry has invested millions in new technology over the past couple of years, but of 1,140 book buyers questioned, only four said e-books would replace the paper format. (rocketbook.com)

2. The Paperless Classroom

A major expense for schools and businesses is the cost of paper. As computers became popular in business, people predicted the paperless office where nearly all documents would exist only electronically. Yet, much to the dismay of environmentalists, studies show that many of today's offices use more paper than in the past. Why do you think computerized offices use more paper than ever before? What about schools? Will there ever be a paperless school or classroom? Would you want to teach in a paperless classroom? What impact might the increased use of computers and the World Wide Web have on paper usage in your classroom? Do you think students who take classes online use less or more paper? Why? What could you do to decrease the amount of paper used? Will you let your students print information they find on the Web on your classroom printer?

3. Disk Drives

This past summer, your school purchased and set up three new iMac computers in each classroom. Last year your classroom was equipped with older Macintosh computers on which you had installed many educational software programs. Many of these software packages are stored on floppy disks, as are many of your classroom management tools and files. Your new Macintosh computers, however, do not have floppy disk drives. What will you do? Can you still use the educational software or your files?

4. Obsolete Equipment

Many businesses, government agencies, and parents donate obsolete computer equipment to schools. Although fully operational, this equipment often is not capable of running multimedia software due to slow processors, lack of memory, lack of hard disk space, and the lack of a CD-ROM drive. Some teachers feel that any kind of computer is better than no computer. Do you agree or disagree? Does a use exist for these types of computers in the classroom or in a school lab? How could you use one in your classroom? Should schools continue to accept older computers? Why or why not?

Integration Corner

Web Instructions: To display this page from the World Wide Web, start your browser and enter the URL, www.course.com/tdc3. Click Chapter 4 at the top of the Web page and then click Integration Corner on the left sidebar. Click any Corner and then click the various links for extensive and curriculum-specific information.

WEB INFO

IN BRIEF

KEY TERMS

CHECKPOINT

TEACHING TODAY

EDUCATION ISSUES

INTEGRATION CORNER

SOFTWARE CORNER

IN THE LAB

LEARN IT ONLINE

✱ FEATURES...

Timeline 2004

Guide to WWW Sites

Buyer's Guide 2004

Professional Sites

State/Federal Sites

Interactive Labs

Search Tools

HOME

Integration Corner is designed for teachers and other educators who are looking for innovative ways to integrate technology into their content-specific curriculum. Integration Corner not only provides great Web sites with current information but also shows what others educators are doing in the field of educational technology. These Corners are designed for all educators regardless of their interest. Review information and Web sites outside of your teaching area because many great integration ideas in one area easily can be modified for use in other curricular areas.

Teachers and administrators will find other colleagues in their areas with whom to connect and share the successes and hurdles of integrating technology in a classroom or an entire school system. Consider this your one stop for integration ideas and resources. Links to educational Web sites are organized in the following 12 Corners, and different Web resources are available for each chapter. Figure 1-65 shows examples of the Web resources provided in the Chapter 4 Secondary Corner.

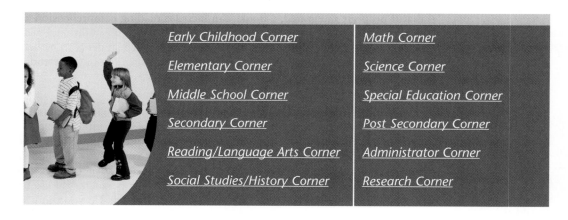

Early Childhood Corner   *Math Corner*

Elementary Corner   *Science Corner*

Middle School Corner   *Special Education Corner*

Secondary Corner   *Post Secondary Corner*

Reading/Language Arts Corner   *Administrator Corner*

Social Studies/History Corner   *Research Corner*

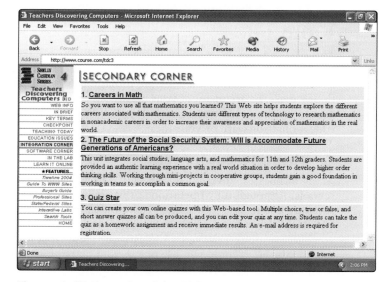

Figure 4-65 Examples of the Web resources provided in the Chapter 4 Secondary Corner.

Software Corner

Web Instructions: To display this page from the World Wide Web, start your browser and enter the URL, www.course.com/tdc3. Click Chapter 4 at the top of the Web page and then click Software Corner on the left sidebar. Click the links for additional information and instructions on how to download or receive an evaluation copy.

WEB INFO

IN BRIEF

KEY TERMS

CHECKPOINT

TEACHING TODAY

EDUCATION ISSUES

INTEGRATION CORNER

SOFTWARE CORNER

IN THE LAB

LEARN IT ONLINE

✱ FEATURES...

Timeline 2004

Guide to WWW Sites

Buyer's Guide 2004

Professional Sites

State/Federal Sites

Interactive Labs

Search Tools

HOME

1. The Graph Club, by Tom Snyder Productions, is an easy-to-use graphing tool every elementary classroom should have! You can create activities where your students conduct research and graph their findings. The Graph Club allows students to construct and interpret pie, line, picture, and bar graphs. Students learn to use graphs to analyze data and solve problems, as well as write about graphs they create. Graphs can be printed by the page or even made in poster size for classroom use. The Graph Club is an innovative way to help your students understand and interpret graphs and is an excellent resource for standardized test preparation.

2. Millie's Math House is an excellent program for prekindergarten through second grade students. Seven activities provide students the opportunity to learn shapes, sizes, patterns, sequencing, and numbers. Students learn to count and practice addition and subtraction while making silly looking bugs and jelly bean cookies or even building mouse houses! This program is interactive and provides feedback, making Millie's Math House a great way to keep students interested while they learn.

3. Your students can learn to interact and write stories about Timmy & His Friends with Make-A-Story. Students choose different characters, settings and actions, and then they can hear the stories read aloud in English or a foreign language. Students can work through eighteen exciting activities to gain an appreciation of different cultures while comparing those cultures through number and word activities, stories, songs, games, and crafts. This is excellent software for developing cross-curricular activities for language arts, math, social studies, and creativity.

4. Teachers and students need to work successfully on research reports and multimedia projects. Grolier Multimedia Encyclopedia can assist your students in creating awesome multimedia presentations with 15,500 images, full audio features, and more than 150 videos and panoramas of amazing sites. Research reports will be a snap for students with more than 60,000 articles and the Millennium feature, which chronicles important world events for the last 1,000 years as well as Internet links. Grolier Multimedia Encyclopedia is an excellent resource for any classroom.

5. With Geometer's Sketchpad, by Key Curriculum Press, your students can explore and analyze geometric figures and concepts they are learning in the classroom. While preserving the geometric relationships of the shapes, students can manipulate the geometric figures created in Geometer's Sketchpad. Use Geometer's Sketchpad for presentations or allow your students to work alone or in groups. This software is extremely versatile and can be used from grades 5 through college. The software comes with an instructional video and documentation. The documentation includes tutorials and sample classroom activities. Extensive Internet resources also are available.

In the Lab

Web Instructions: To display this page from the World Wide Web, start your browser and enter the URL, www.course.com/tdc3. Click Chapter 4 at the top of the Web page and then click In The Lab on the left sidebar. Click the links for tutorials, productivity ideas, integration examples and ideas, and more.

WEB INFO

IN BRIEF

KEY TERMS

CHECKPOINT

TEACHING TODAY

EDUCATION ISSUES

INTEGRATION CORNER

SOFTWARE CORNER

IN THE LAB

LEARN IT ONLINE

✱ FEATURES...

Timeline 2004

Guide to WWW Sites

Buyer's Guide 2004

Professional Sites

State/Federal Sites

Interactive Labs

Search Tools

HOME

PRODUCTIVITY IN THE CLASSROOM

Introduction: Database software allows you to create, store, sort, and retrieve data. Databases enable computer users to manipulate large amounts of data to produce different results. A classic example of a database is your local telephone directory.

Many database programs have wizards that walk you through creating a database, often called a database table. When you first create a database, it may look very similar to a spreadsheet in layout and design. This often is referred to as Datasheet view or List view. In this view, you can see a number of the records in the database at one time. The rows in the database are called records. Records can contain information about a person, product, or event. The columns in the database are called fields. Fields contain a specific piece of information within a record. Most database applications have a Design view, also called Form view, where information is added one record at a time and only one record is displayed at a time. Be sure to use the Help feature of your database software to learn more about the different views and features.

To learn new skills, or to improve your current skills, click the following links: Microsoft Access, FileMaker Pro, Microsoft Works, and AppleWorks.

1 Creating and Formatting a Student Information Database

Problem: At the beginning of every school year, students are asked to fill out information cards. To save time and to begin teaching the students about databases, create a database that contains the fields shown in Figure 4-66. Then have the students enter their information into the database, keeping it updated throughout the year. This allows you always to have the most current information available.

Open your database software and create the Student Information Database. Use the field names shown in Figure 4-66. (*Hint:* Use Help to better understand the steps.)

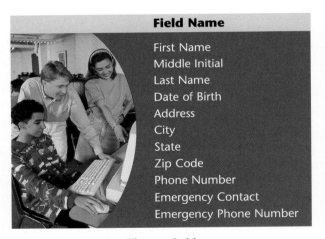

Field Name

First Name
Middle Initial
Last Name
Date of Birth
Address
City
State
Zip Code
Phone Number
Emergency Contact
Emergency Phone Number

Figure 4-66

Instructions: Perform the following tasks.

1. Create the database using the field names listed in Figure 4-66.
2. Determine the proper field widths and types so the information displays properly.
3. Enter student information to create 10 records. Enter your name for the first record.
4. Save the database on a floppy disk using an appropriate file name.
5. Print the database as a table or list.
6. Create a cover sheet using word processing software that includes your name, the current date, and the course title.
7. Follow the directions from your instructor for handing in this assignment.

In the Lab

WEB INFO

IN BRIEF

KEY TERMS

CHECKPOINT

TEACHING TODAY

EDUCATION ISSUES

INTEGRATION CORNER

SOFTWARE CORNER

IN THE LAB

LEARN IT ONLINE

＊FEATURES...

Timeline 2004

Guide to WWW Sites

Buyer's Guide 2004

Professional Sites

State/Federal Sites

Interactive Labs

Search Tools

HOME

2 Creating and Formatting a Hardware Inventory Database

Problem: At the end of every school year, you must turn in your classroom technology inventory. Creating the inventory by hand is time-consuming and tedious. Entering the information into a database will allow you to update the information quickly and generate the necessary reports. Create a database that contains information regarding the technology in your classroom. The contents of the database are shown in Figure 4-67. (*Hint:* Use Help to understand the steps better.)

Technology Inventory Information

Manufacturer	Hardware	Serial Number	Year	Used By
Compaq	15" Monitor	023BA64WF389	2003	Students
Compaq	System Unit	CM29M-KY9KJ-TPBXJ-GRCCC-WVQRD	2003	Students
Compaq	17" Monitor	036ZV21LP912	2003	Students
Compaq	System Unit	CM21X-NY6NJ-PTAYK-BNUIU-MCWRD	2003	Students
Sony	15" Flat Screen Monitor	977AX56VR311	2003	Students
Dell	System Unit	00JKXW-KR2RR-JJ8870	2002	Students
Dell	Notebook Computer	6D3CJC58380WB	2002	Teacher
Compaq	Presario Notebook Computer	6D3CJC58380WB	2001	Students
Apple	iBook	CJ54404K39X	2003	Students
Apple	iMac	XA6352RG7Y7	2002	Students
Hewlett-Packard	Printer	SBG94AGWQK	2001	Teacher
Compaq	Printer	1M05DG2VXBP	2002	Students
Apple	Printer	CC552AAQ69O	2002	Students
Visioneer	Scanner	052C00900D1	2002	Students
Kodak	Digital Camera	144527D3	2003	Students

Figure 4-67

Instructions: Perform the following tasks.

1. Create the database using the five fields in Figure 4-67. Format the fields so the information is displayed properly.
2. Enter the data for the first 15 records from Figure 4-67 into the database.
3. Personalize the database by adding three additional records — the manufacturer, type of hardware, serial number (create a number if necessary), year purchased, and who uses the hardware item.
4. Save the database on a floppy disk using an appropriate file name.
5. Print the database as a table or list.
6. Create a cover sheet using word processing software that includes your name, the current date, and the course title.
7. Follow the directions from your instructor for handing in this assignment.

In the Lab

WEB INFO

IN BRIEF

KEY TERMS

CHECKPOINT

TEACHING TODAY

EDUCATION ISSUES

INTEGRATION CORNER

SOFTWARE CORNER

IN THE LAB

LEARN IT ONLINE

✱ FEATURES...

Timeline 2004

Guide to WWW Sites

Buyer's Guide 2004

Professional Sites

State/Federal Sites

Interactive Labs

Search Tools

HOME

INTEGRATION IN THE CLASSROOM

1 Your science class is studying the <u>solar system</u>. The class is divided into groups and each group will gather the facts about their assigned planet. You have the students create a class database with the following fields: planet name, distance from the sun, number of moons, average temperature in Fahrenheit, length of year, size, atmosphere, and gravity at the surface. The students enter their findings and then compare and contrast the planets based on the different characteristics. Create a sample database selecting one planet and enter the appropriate information to demonstrate the project for the students. Include a header with your name and a footer with the current date.

2 Your third grade class is taking a field trip to the zoo. You want the students to have the opportunity to learn about animals in a creative way. Students will gather information about their <u>animals</u> from books, the Internet, and multimedia CD-ROMs. With the help of a parent volunteer, the students will enter their information into a simple database. You have selected the following fields for the database: animal name, country or origin, habitat, food, weight/size, and number of babies. Create a sample database selecting at least two zoo animals and enter the appropriate information to demonstrate the project for the students. Include a header with your name and a footer with the current date.

3 In math class, you have students work in groups to invest $5,000 in a six-month certificate of deposit (CD). Students will use the Internet to gather information from local <u>banks and credit unions</u> and make a list of the current interest rates, minimum investment amounts, and total amounts earned in six months. The students then will create a database showing the name of the financial institution, its address and telephone number, the interest rate, the total value of the CD in six months, and the amount of interest earned. Create a sample database to demonstrate the project for the students. Include a header with your name and a footer with the current date.

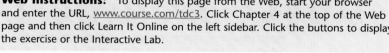

Learn It Online

Web Instructions: To display this page from the Web, start your browser and enter the URL, www.course.com/tdc3. Click Chapter 4 at the top of the Web page and then click Learn It Online on the left sidebar. Click the buttons to display the exercise or the Interactive Lab.

WEB INFO

IN BRIEF

KEY TERMS

CHECKPOINT

TEACHING TODAY

EDUCATION ISSUES

INTEGRATION CORNER

SOFTWARE CORNER

IN THE LAB

LEARN IT ONLINE

＊FEATURES...

Timeline 2004

Guide to WWW Sites

Buyer's Guide 2004

Professional Sites

State/Federal Sites

Interactive Labs

Search Tools

HOME

1. Shelly Cashman Series Understanding the Motherboard

Click the button to the left to start and use the Shelly Cashman Series Understanding the Motherboard Lab.

2. Shelly Cashman Series Configuring Your Display

Click the button to the left to start and use the Shelly Cashman Series Configuring Your Display Lab.

3. Shelly Cashman Series Maintaining Your Hard Drive

Click the button to the left to start and use the Shelly Cashman Series Maintaining Your Hard Drive Lab.

4. Troubleshooting Hardware Problems

Teachers need to develop troubleshooting skills so they can identify and fix basic computer-related hardware problems. Click the button to the left and complete this exercise to learn more about fixing basic hardware problems.

5. Who Wants To Be a Computer Genius?

Click the button to the left to find out if you are a computer genius. Directions on how to play the game will display. When you are ready to play, click the PLAY button. Submit your score to your instructor.

6. Crossword Puzzle Challenge

Click the button to the left and complete the puzzle to reinforce skills you learned in this chapter. Directions on how to play the game will display. When you are ready to play, click the SUBMIT button. Submit the completed puzzle to your instructor.

7. Practice Test

Click the button to the left and answer each question. When completed, enter your name and click the Grade Test button to submit the quiz for grading. Make a note of any missed questions. If required, print a copy to submit to your instructor.

Buyer's Guide 2004

HOW TO PURCHASE, INSTALL, AND MAINTAIN A PERSONAL COMPUTER

(a) desktop computer

(b) notebook computer

(c) Tablet PC

(d) PDA

Should I buy a desktop or mobile computer?

For what purposes will I use the computer?

Should the computer I buy be compatible with the computers at school or work?

Should I buy a Mac or PC?

FIGURE 1

At some point, perhaps while you are taking this course, you may decide to buy a personal computer. The decision is an important one, which will require an investment of both time and money. As with many buyers, you may have little computer experience and find yourself unsure of how to proceed. You can get started by talking to your friends, coworkers, and instructors about their computers. What type of computers did they buy? Why? For what purposes do they use their computers? You also should answer the following four questions to help narrow your choices to a specific computer type before reading the Buyer's Guide guidelines for purchasing a desktop computer, notebook computer, Tablet PC, or PDA.

1 **Do you want a desktop or mobile computer?**
A desktop computer (Figure 1a) is designed as a stationary device that sits on or below a desk or table in a location such as a home, office, or dormitory room. A desktop computer must be plugged into an electrical outlet to operate. A mobile computer or device, such as a notebook computer (Figure 1b), Tablet PC (Figure 1c), or PDA (Figure 1d), is smaller, more portable, and has a battery that allows you to operate it for a period without an electrical outlet.

Desktop computers are a good option if you work mostly in one place and have plenty of space in your work area. Desktop computers generally give you more performance for your money and are easier to upgrade than mobile computers.

Increasingly more desktop computer users are buying notebook computers to take advantage of their portability to work in the library, while traveling, and at home. The past disadvantages of notebook computers, such as lower processor speeds, poor-quality monitors, weight, short battery life, and significantly higher prices, have all but disappeared when compared with desktop computers.

If you are thinking of using a mobile computer to take notes in class, then consider a Tablet PC with handwriting and drawing capabilities. Typically, note-taking involves writing text notes and drawing charts, schematics, and other illustrations. By allowing you to write and draw directly on the screen with a digital pen, a Tablet PC eliminates the distracting sound of the notebook keyboard tapping and allows you to capture drawings. Some notebook computers can convert to Tablet PCs (see Figure 11 on page 4.61).

A PDA is a lightweight mobile device that fits easily in your pocket, which makes it ideal if you require a mobile computing device as you move from place to place. PDAs provide personal organizer functions, such as a calendar, appointment book, address book, and thousands of other applications. Some PDAs also function as cellular telephones. The small size of the processor, screen, and keyboard, however, limit a PDA's capabilities when compared with a desktop or notebook computer. For this reason, most people who purchase PDAs also have a desktop or notebook computer to handle heavy-duty applications.

Drawbacks of mobile computers and devices are that they tend to have a shorter useful lifetime than desktop computers, cost more than desktop computers, and lack the high-end capabilities. Their portability makes them susceptible to vibrations, heat or cold, and accidental drops, which can cause components such as hard disks or monitors to fail. Also, because of their size and portability, they are easy to lose and are a prime target of thieves.

2 **For what purposes will you use the computer?** Having a general idea of the purposes for which you want to use your computer will help you decide on the type of computer to buy. At this point in your research, it is not necessary to know the exact application software titles or version numbers you might want to use. Knowing that you plan to use the computer primarily to create word processing, spreadsheet, database, and presentation documents, however, will point you in the direction of a desktop or notebook computer. If you plan to use a mobile device to get organized, then a PDA may be your best choice. If you want the portability of a PDA, but need more computing power, then a Tablet PC may be the best alternative. You also must consider that some application software runs only on a Mac, while others run only on a PC with the Windows operating system. Still other software may run only on a PC running the UNIX or Linux operating systems.

3 **Should the computer be compatible with the computers at school or work?** If you plan to bring work home, telecommute, or take distance education courses, then you should purchase a computer that is compatible with those at school or

work. Compatibility is primarily a software issue. If your computer runs the same operating system version, such as Windows XP, and the same application software, such as Office XP, then your computer will be able to read documents created at school or work and vice versa. Incompatible hardware can become an issue if you plan to connect directly to a school or office network using a cable or wireless technology. You usually can obtain the minimum system requirements from the Information Technology (IT) department at your school or workplace.

4 **Should the computer be a Mac or PC?** If you ask a friend, coworker, or instructor, which is better — a Mac or a PC — you may be surprised by the strong opinion expressed in the response. No other topic in the computer industry causes more heated debate. The Mac has strengths, especially in the areas of graphics, movies, photos, and music. The PC, however, has become the industry standard with 95 percent of the market share. Figure 2 compares features of the Mac and PC in several different areas. Overall, the Mac and PC have more similarities than differences, and you should consider cost, compatibility, and other factors when choosing whether to purchase a Mac or PC.

Area	Comparison
Cost and availability	Macs are priced slightly higher than PCs. Mac peripherals also are more expensive. The PC offers more available models from a wide range of vendors. You can custom build, upgrade, and expand a PC for less money than a Mac.
Exterior design	The Mac has a more distinct and stylish appearance than most PCs.
Free software	Although free software for the Mac is available on the Internet, significantly more free software applications are available for the PC.
Market share	The PC dominates the personal computer market. While the Mac sells well in education, publishing, Web design, graphics, and music, the PC is the overwhelming favorite of businesses.
Operating system	Both Mac OS X and Windows XP are stable. Users claim that Mac OS X provides a better all-around user experience than Windows XP. The PC supports other operating systems, such as Linux and UNIX.
Program control	Both have simple and intuitive graphical user interfaces. The Mac relies more on the mouse and less on keyboard shortcuts than the PC. The mouse on the Mac has one button, whereas the mouse on a PC has a minimum of two buttons.
Software availability	The basic application software most users require, such as the Office suite, is available for both the Mac and PC. More specialized software, however, often is available only for PCs. Many programs are released for PCs long before they are released for Macs.
Speed	PC processor speeds are faster than Mac processor speeds and offer more from which to choose.
Viruses	Dramatically fewer viruses attack Macs. Mac viruses also generally are less infectious than PC viruses.

FIGURE 2 Comparison of Mac and PC features.

After evaluating the answers to these four questions, you should have a general idea of how you plan to use your computer and the type of computer you want to buy. After you have decided on the type of computer you want, you can follow the guidelines presented in this Buyer's Guide to help you purchase a specific computer of that type, along with software, peripherals, and other accessories.

This first set of guidelines will help you purchase, install, and maintain a desktop computer. Many of the guidelines presented also apply to the purchase of a mobile computer or device, such as a notebook computer, Tablet PC, or PDA. Later in this Buyer's Guide, sections on purchasing a notebook computer, PDA, or Tablet PC address additional considerations specific to those computer types.

HOW TO PURCHASE A DESKTOP COMPUTER

If you have decided that a desktop computer is most suited to your computing needs, the next step is to determine specific software, hardware, peripheral devices, and services to purchase, as well as where to buy the computer.

1 **Determine the specific software you want to use on your computer.** Before deciding to purchase a particular program, be sure it contains the features necessary for the tasks you want to perform. Rely on the computer users in whom you have confidence to help you decide on the software to use. The minimum requirements of the application software you select may determine the operating system (Windows XP, Linux, UNIX, Mac OS X) you need. If you have decided to use a particular operating system that does not support application software you want to use, you may be able to purchase similar application software from other manufacturers.

Many Web sites and trade magazines, such as those listed in Figure 3, provide reviews of software products. These Web sites frequently have articles that rate computers and software on cost, performance, and support.

Your hardware requirements depend on the minimum requirements of the application software you will run on your computer. Some application software requires more memory and disk space than others, as well as additional input, output, and storage devices. For example, suppose you want to run software that can copy one CD's or DVD's contents directly to another CD or DVD, without first copying the data to your hard disk. To support that, you should consider a desktop computer or a high-end notebook computer, because the computer will need two CD or DVD drives: one that reads from a CD or DVD, and one that reads from and writes on a CD or DVD. If you plan to run software that allows your computer to work as an

entertainment system, then you will need a CD or DVD drive, quality speakers, and an upgraded sound card.

Type of Computers	Web Site	URL
PC	Computer Shopper	shopper.cnet.com
	PC World Magazine	pcworld.com
	BYTE Magazine	byte.com
	PC Magazine	zdnet.com/reviews
	Yahoo! Computers	computers.yahoo.com
	Microsoft Network	eshop.msn.com
	Dave's Guide to Buying a Home Computer	css.msu.edu/PC-Guide/
Mac	ZDNet News	zdnet.com/mac
	Macworld Magazine	macworld.com
	Apple	apple.com
	Switch to Mac Campaign	apple.com/switch

For an updated list with Web sites and their URLs, visit www.course.com/tdc3 and then click Buyer's Guide on the left sidebar.

FIGURE 3   Hardware and software reviews.

2 **Look for bundled software.** When you purchase a computer, it may come bundled with several programs. Some sellers even let you choose which application software you want. Remember, however, that bundled software has value only if you would have purchased the software even if it had not come with the computer. At the very least, you probably will want word processing software and a browser to access the Internet. If you need additional applications, such as a spreadsheet, a database, or presentation graphics, consider purchasing a software suite, such as Microsoft Works, Microsoft Office, Apple Works, or Sun StarOffice, which include several programs at a reduced price.

3 **Avoid buying the least powerful computer available.** After you know the application software you want to use, you then can consider the following important criteria about the computer's components: (1) processor speed, (2) size and types of memory (RAM) and storage, (3) types of input/output devices, (4) types of ports and adapter cards, and (5) types of communications devices. The information in Figure 4 can help you determine what system components are best for you.

Computer technology changes rapidly, meaning a computer that seems powerful enough today may not serve your computing needs in a few years. In fact, studies show that many users regret not buying a more powerful computer. To avoid this, plan to buy a computer that will last you for two to three years. You can help delay obsolescence by purchasing the fastest processor, the most memory, and the largest hard disk you can afford. If you must buy a less powerful computer, be sure you can upgrade it with additional memory, components, and peripheral devices as your computer requirements grow.

4 **Consider upgrades to the mouse, keyboard, monitor, printer, microphone, and speakers.**
You use these peripheral devices to interact with your computer, so you should make sure they are up to your standards. Review the peripheral devices listed in Figure 4 and then visit both local computer dealers and large retail stores to test the computers on display. Ask the salesperson what

input and output devices would be best for you and whether you should upgrade beyond what comes standard. A few extra dollars spent on these components when you initially purchase a computer can extend its usefulness by years.

5 **Determine whether you want to use telephone lines or broadband (cable or DSL) to access the Internet.** If your computer has a modem, then you can access the Internet using a standard telephone line. Ordinarily, you call a local or toll-free 800 number to connect to an ISP (see Guideline 6 on page 4.57). Using a dial-up Internet connection is relatively inexpensive but slow.

CD/DVD Drives: Most computers come with a 32X to 48X speed CD-ROM drive that can read CDs. If you plan to write music, audio files, and documents on a CD or DVD, then you should consider upgrading to a CD-RW. An even better alternative is to upgrade to a DVD+RW/CD-RW combination drive. It allows you to read DVDs and CDs and to write data on (burn) a DVD or CD. A DVD has a capacity of at least 4.7 GB versus the 650 MB capacity of a CD.

Card Reader: A card reader is useful for transferring data directly from a removable flash memory card, such as the ones used in your camera or music player. Make sure the card reader can read the flash memory cards that you use.

Digital Camera: Consider an inexpensive point-and-shoot digital camera. They are small enough to carry around, usually operate automatically in terms of lighting and focus, and contain storage cards for storing photographs. A 1.3- to 2.2-megapixel camera with an 8 MB or 16 MB storage card is fine for creating images for use on the Web or to send via e-mail.

Digital Video Capture Device: A digital video capture device allows you to connect your computer to a camcorder or VCR and record, edit, manage, and then write video back to a VCR tape, a CD, or a DVD. The digital video capture device can be an external device or an adapter card. To create quality video (true 30 frames per second, full-sized TV), the digital video capture device should have a USB 2.0 or FireWire port. You will find that a standard USB port is too slow to maintain video quality. You also will need sufficient storage: an hour of data on VCR tape requires about 5 GB of disk storage.

Floppy Disk Drive: Make sure the computer you purchase has a standard 3.5-inch, 1.44 MB floppy disk drive. A floppy disk drive is useful for backing up and transferring files.

Hard Disk: It is recommended that you buy a computer with 40 to 60 GB if your primary interests are browsing the Web and using e-mail and Office suite-type applications; 60 to 80 GB if you also want to edit digital photographs; 80 to 100 GB if you plan to edit digital video or manipulate large audio files even occasionally; and 100 to 160 GB if you will edit digital video, movies, or photography often or store audio files and music or consider yourself to be a power user.

Joystick/Wheel: If you use your computer to play games, then you will want to purchase a joystick or a wheel. These devices, especially the more expensive ones, provide for realistic game play with force feedback, programmable buttons, and specialized levers and wheels.

Keyboard: The keyboard is one of the more important devices used to communicate with the computer. For this reason, make sure the keyboard you purchase has 101 to 105 keys, is comfortable, easy to use, and has a USB connection. A wireless keyboard should be considered, especially if you have a small desk area.

Microphone: If you plan to record audio or use speech recognition to enter text and commands, then purchase a close-talk headset with gain adjustment support.

Modem: Most computers come with a modem so that you can use your telephone line to dial out and access the Internet. Some modems also have fax capabilities. Your modem should be rated at 56 Kbps.

Monitor: The monitor is where you will view documents, read e-mail messages, and view pictures. A minimum of a 17-inch screen is recommended, but if you are planning to use your computer for graphic design or game playing, then you may want to purchase a 19-inch or 21-inch monitor. The LCD flat panel monitor should be considered, especially if space is an issue.

FIGURE 4 Hardware guidelines. *(continued)*

(continued from previous page)

Mouse: As you work with your computer, you use the mouse constantly. For this reason, spend a few extra dollars, if necessary, and purchase a mouse with an optical sensor and USB connection. The optical sensor replaces the need for a mouse ball, which means you do not need a mouse pad. For a PC, make sure your mouse has a wheel, which acts as a third button, in addition to the top two buttons on the left and right. An ergonomic design is also important because your hand is on the mouse much of the time when you are using your computer. A wireless mouse should be considered to eliminate the cord and allow you to work at short distances from your computer.

Network Card: If you plan to connect to a network or use broadband (cable or DSL) to connect to the Internet, then you will need to purchase a network card. Broadband connections require a 10/100 PCI Ethernet network card.

Printer: Your two basic printer choices are ink-jet and laser. Color ink-jet printers cost on average between $50 and $300. Laser printers cost from $300 to $2,000. In general, the cheaper the printer, the lower the resolution and speed, and the more often you are required to change the ink cartridge or toner. Laser printers print faster and with a higher quality than an ink-jet, and their toner on average costs less. If you want color, then go with a high-end ink-jet printer to ensure quality of print. Duty cycle (the number of pages you expect to print each month) also should be a determining factor. If your duty cycle is on the low end — hundreds of pages per month — then stay with a high-end ink-jet printer rather than purchasing a laser printer. If you plan to print photographs taken with a digital camera, then you should purchase a photo printer. A photo printer is a dye-sublimation printer or an ink-jet printer with higher resolution and features that allow you to print quality photographs.

Processor: For a PC, a 2.0 GHz Intel or AMD processor is more than enough processor power for home and small office/home office users. Game, large business, and power users should upgrade to faster processors.

RAM: RAM plays a vital role in the speed of your computer. Make sure the computer you purchase has at least 256 MB of RAM. If you have extra money to invest in your computer, then consider increasing the RAM to 512 MB or more. The extra money for RAM will be well spent.

Scanner: The most popular scanner purchased with a computer today is the flatbed scanner. When evaluating a flatbed scanner, check the color depth and resolution. Do not buy anything less than a color depth of 48 bits and a resolution of 1200 x 2400 dpi. The higher the color depth, the more accurate the color. A higher resolution picks up the more subtle gradations of color.

Sound Card: Most sound cards today support the Sound Blaster and General MIDI standards and should be capable of recording and playing digital audio. If you plan to turn your computer into an entertainment system or are a game user, then you will want to spend the extra money and upgrade the sound card.

Speakers: Once you have a good sound card, quality speakers and a separate subwoofer that amplifies bass frequencies can turn your computer into a premium stereo system.

Video Graphics Card: Most standard video cards satisfy the monitor display needs of home and small office/home office users. If you are a game user or a graphic designer, you will want to upgrade to a higher quality video card. The higher refresh rates will further enhance the display of games, graphics, and movies.

PC Video Camera: A PC video camera is a small camera used to capture and display live video (in some cases with sound), primarily on a Web page. You also can capture, edit, and share video and still photos. The camera sits on your monitor or desk. Recommended minimum specifications include 640 x 480 resolution, a video with a rate of 30 frames per second, and a USB 2.0 or FireWire connection.

Wireless LAN Access Point: A Wireless LAN Access Point allows you to network several computers, so they can share files and access the Internet through a single cable modem or DSL connection. Each device that you connect requires a wireless card. A Wireless LAN Access Point can offer a range of operation up to several hundred feet, so be sure the device has a high-powered antenna.

Zip Drive: Consider purchasing a Zip or Peerless disk drive to back up important files. The Zip drive, which has a capacity of up to 750 MB, is sufficient for most users. An alternative to purchasing a backup drive is to purchase a CD-RW or DVD+RW and burn backups of key files on a CD or DVD.

FIGURE 4 Hardware guidelines.

DSL and cable connections provide much faster Internet connections, which are ideal if you want faster file download speeds for software, digital photos, and music. As you would expect, they also are more expensive. DSL, which is available through local telephone companies, also may require that you subscribe to an ISP. Cable is available through your local cable television provider and some online service providers (OSPs). If you subscribe to cable, then you would not use a separate Internet service provider or online service provider.

6 **If you are using a dial-up or wireless connection to connect to the Internet, then select an ISP or OSP.** You can access the Internet via telephone lines in one of two ways: via an ISP or an OSP. Both provide Internet access for a monthly fee that ranges from $6 to $25. If you are using DSL, you will have to pay additional costs for a residential DSL line. Local ISPs offer Internet access to users in a limited geographic region, through local telephone numbers. National ISPs provide access for users nationwide (including mobile users), through local and toll-free telephone numbers and cable. Because of their size, national ISPs generally offer more services and have a larger technical support staff than local ISPs. OSPs furnish Internet access as well as members-only features for users nationwide. Figure 5 lists several national ISPs and OSPs. Before you choose an ISP or OSP, compare such features as the number of access hours, monthly fees, available services (e-mail, Web page hosting, chat), and reliability.

7 **Use a worksheet to compare computers, services, and other considerations.** You can use Figure 6 to compare prices for either a PC or a Mac. Most companies advertise a price for a base computer that includes components housed in the system unit (processor, RAM, sound card, video card), disk drives (floppy disk, hard disk, CD-ROM, CD-RW, DVD-ROM, and DVD+RW), a keyboard, mouse, monitor, printer, speakers, and modem. Be aware, however, that some advertisements list prices for

Company	Service	URL
America Online	OSP	aol.com
AT&T WorldNet	ISP	www.att.net
CompuServe	OSP	compuserve.com
EarthLink	ISP	earthlink.net
Juno	OSP	juno.com
MSN	OSP	msn.com
NetZero	OSP	netzero.com
Prodigy	ISP/OSP	www.prodigy.net

For an updated list with Web sites and their URLs, visit www.course.com/tdc3 and then click Buyer's Guide on the left sidebar.

FIGURE 5 National ISPs and OSPs.

computers with only some of these components. Monitors and printers, for example, often are not included in a base computer's price. Depending on how you plan to use the computer, you may want to invest in additional or more powerful components. When you are comparing the prices of computers, make sure you are comparing identical or similar configurations.

Computer Cost Comparison Worksheet

Items to Purchase	Desired System (PC)	Desired System (Mac)	Local Dealer #1 Price	Local Dealer #2 Price	Online Dealer #1 Price	Online Dealer #2 Price	Comments
OVERALL SYSTEM							
Overall System Price	< $1,500	< $1,500					
HARDWARE							
Processor	Pentium 4 at 2.0 GHz	PowerPC G4 at 800 MHz					
RAM	256 MB	256 MB					
Cache	256 KB L2	256 KB L2					
Hard Disk	80 GB	80 GB					
Monitor	17 Inch	17 Inch					
Video Graphics Card	64 MB	64 MB					
Floppy Disk Drive	3.5 Inch	3.5 Inch					
CD/DVD Bay 1	48x CD-ROM	32x/10x/40x CD-RW/DVD					
CD/DVD Bay 2	32x/10x/40x CD-RW/DVD	NA					
Speakers	Stereo	Stereo					
Sound Card	Sound Blaster Compatible	Sound Blaster Compatible					
USB Ports	2	2					
FireWire Port	2	2					
Network Card	Yes	Yes					
Fax/Modem	56 Kbps	56 Kbps					
Keyboard	Standard	Apple Pro Keyboard					
Pointing Device	IntelliMouse	IntelliMouse or Apple Pro Mouse					
Microphone	Close-Talk Headset with Gain Adjustment	Close-Talk Headset with Gain Adjustment					
Printer	Color Ink-Jet	Color Ink-Jet					
Printer Cable	Yes	Yes					
Backup	250 MB Zip	250 MB Zip					
SOFTWARE							
Operating System	Windows XP Home Edition	Mac OS X					
Application Software	Office XP Small Business Edition	Office v.X for Mac					
Antivirus	Yes - 12 Mo. Subscription	Yes - 12 Mo. Subscription					
OTHER							
Card Reader	MemoryStick Dual Reader	MemoryStick Dual Reader					
Digital Camera	2-Megapixel	2-Megapixel					
Internet Connection	1-Year Subscription	1-Year Subscription					
Joystick	Yes	Yes					
PC Video Camera	With Microphone	With Microphone					
Scanner							
Surge Protector							
Warranty	3-Year On-Site Service	3-Year On-Site Service					
Wireless card	Internal	Internal					
Wireless LAN Access Point	LinkSys	Apple AirPort					
Total Cost			$ -	$ -	$ -	$ -	

FIGURE 6 A worksheet is an effective tool for summarizing and comparing the prices and components of different computer vendors.

8 **If you are buying a new computer, you have several purchasing options: buying from your school bookstore, a localcomputer dealer, a local large retail store, or ordering by mail via telephone or the Web.** Each purchasing option has certain advantages. Many college bookstores, for example, sign exclusive pricing agreements with computer manufacturers and, can offer student discounts. Local dealers and local large retail stores, however, more easily can provide hands-on support. Mail-order companies that sell computers by telephone or online via the Web often provide the lowest prices, but extend less personal service. Some major mail-order companies, however, have started to provide next-business-day, on-site services. Most major companies offer special prices and services for educators (Figure 7). A credit card usually is required to buy from a mail-order company. Figure 8 lists some of the more popular mail-order companies and their Web site addresses. Finally, check your Sunday newspaper for advertisements from major retailers, such as Circuit City, Sears, Staples, and Best Buy. These advertisements frequently offer sale prices, closeout specials, and rebates of $200 or more. In addition, some prices include a free printer. Monitor, or other components.

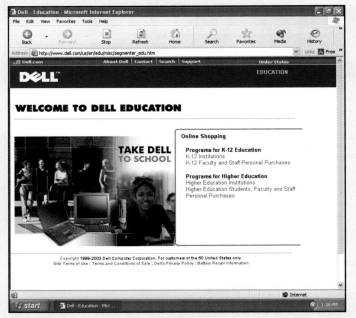

FIGURE 7 Many major computer companies offer special prices and services for educators.

9 **If you are buying a used computer, stay with name brands such as Dell, Gateway, Hewlett-Packard, and Apple.** Although brand-name equipment can cost more, most brand-name computers have longer, more comprehensive warranties,

are better supported, and have more authorized centers for repair services. As with new computers, you can purchase a used computer from local computer dealers, local large retail stores, or mail order via the telephone or the Web. Classified ads and used computer sellers offer additional outlets for purchasing used computers. Figure 9 lists several major used computer brokers and their Web site addresses.

Type of Computer	Company	URL
PC	CompUSA	shopper.cnet.com
	dartek.com	thenew.hp.com
	Dell	compusa.com
	Gateway	www.dartek.com
	HP	dell.com
	Micron	gateway.com
	Shopper.com	micron.com
Macintosh	The Apple Store	store.apple.com
	ClubMac	clubmac.com
	MacConnection	macconnection.com
	MacExchange	macx.com

For an updated list with Web sites and their URLs, visit www.course.com/tdc3 and then click Buyer's Guide on the left sidebar.

FIGURE 8 New computer mail-order companies.

Company	URL
Amazon.com	amazon.com
American Computer Exchange	www.amcoex.com
eBay	ebay.com
Off Lease Computer Supermarket	off-leasecomputers.com
U.S. Computer Exchange	uscomputerexchange.com

For an updated list with Web sites and their URLs, visit www.course.com/tdc3 and then click Buyer's Guide on the left sidebar.

FIGURE 9 Used computer mail-order companies.

10 **If you have a computer and are upgrading to a new one, then consider selling or trading in the old one.** If you are a replacement buyer, your older computer still may have value. If you cannot sell the computer through the classified ads, via a Web site, or to a friend, then ask if the computer dealer will buy your old computer. An increasing number of companies are taking trade-ins. Do not expect too much money for your old computer, however.

11 **Be aware of hidden costs.** Before purchasing, be sure to consider any additional costs associated with buying a computer, such as an additional telephone line, a cable or DSL modem, an uninterruptible power supply (UPS), computer furniture, floppy disks and paper, and computer training classes you may want to take. Depending on where you buy your computer, the seller may be willing to include some or all of these in the computer purchase price.

12 **Consider more than just price.** The lowest-cost computer may not be the best long-term buy. Consider such intangibles as the vendor's time in business, the vendor's regard for quality, and the vendor's reputation for support. If you need to upgrade your computer often, you may want to consider a leasing arrangement, in which you pay monthly lease fees, but can upgrade or add on to your computer as your equipment needs change. No matter what type of buyer you are, insist on a 30-day, no-questions-asked return policy on your computer.

13 **Avoid restocking fees.** Some companies charge a restocking fee of 10 to 20 percent as part of their money-back return policy. In some cases, no restocking fee for hardware is applied, but it is applied for software. Ask about the existence and terms of any restocking policies before you buy.

14 **Consider purchasing an extended warranty or service plan.** If you use your computer for business or require fast resolution to major computer problems, consider purchasing an extended warranty or a service plan through a local dealer or third-party company. Most extended warranties cover the repair and replacement of computer components beyond the standard warranty. Most service plans ensure that your technical support calls receive priority response from technicians. You also can purchase an on-site service plan that states that a technician will come to your home, work, or school within 24 hours. If your computer includes a warranty and service agreement for a year or less, think about extending the service for two or three years when you buy the computer.

CENTURY COMPUTERS
Performance Guarantee
(See reverse for terms & conditions of this contract)

Invoice #: 1984409	Effective Date: 10/12/04
Invoice Date: 10/12/04	Expiration Date: 10/12/09

Customer Name: Leon, Richard
Date: 10/12/04
Address: 1123 Roxbury
           Sycamore, IL 60178
Day phone: (815) 555-0303
Evening Phone: (728) 555-0203

System & Serial Numbers
IMB computer
S/N: US759290C

John Smith
Print Name of Century's Authorized Signature

10/12/04
Date

15 **Use a credit card to purchase your new computer.** Many credit cards offer purchase protection and extended warranty benefits that cover you in case of loss of or damage to purchased goods. Paying by credit card also gives you time to install and use the computer before you have to pay for it. Finally, if you are dissatisfied with the computer and are unable to reach an agreement with the seller, paying by credit card gives you certain rights regarding withholding payment until the dispute is resolved. Check your credit card terms for specific details.

HOW TO PURCHASE A NOTEBOOK COMPUTER

If you need computing capability when you travel or to use in lectures or meetings, you may find a notebook computer to be an appropriate choice. The guidelines mentioned in the previous section also apply to the purchase of a notebook computer. The following are additional considerations unique to notebook computers.

1 **Purchase a notebook computer with a sufficiently large active-matrix screen.**
Active-matrix screens display high-quality color that is viewable from all angles. Less expensive, passive-matrix screens sometimes are difficult to see in low-light conditions and cannot be viewed from an angle. Notebook computers typically come with a 12.1-inch, 13.3-inch, 14.1-inch, 15-inch, or 16.1-inch display. For most users, a 14.1-inch display is satisfactory. If you intend to use your notebook computer as a desktop computer replacement, however, you may opt for a 15-inch or 16.1-inch display. Notebook computers with these larger displays weigh seven to ten pounds, however, so if you travel a lot and portability is essential, you might want a lighter computer with a smaller display. The lightest notebook computers, which weigh less than 3 pounds, are equipped with a 12.1-inch display. Regardless of size, the resolution of the display should be at least 1024 ◊ 768 pixels. To compare the monitor size on various notebook computers, visit the company Web sites in Figure 10.

Type of Notebook	Company	URL
PC	Acer	www.acer.com
	Dell	dell.com
	Fujitsu	fujitsu.com
	Gateway	gateway.com
	HP	hp.com
	IBM	ibm.com
	NEC	nec.com
	Sharp	sharp.com
	Sony	sony.com
	Toshiba	toshiba.com
Mac	Apple	apple.com

For an updated list with Web sites and their URLs, visit www.course.com/tdc3 and then click Buyer's Guide on the left sidebar.

FIGURE 10 Companies that sell notebook computers.

2 **Experiment with different keyboards and pointing devices.** Notebook computer keyboards are far less standardized than those for desktop computers. Some notebook computers, for example, have wide wrist rests, while others have none. Notebook computers also use a range of pointing devices, including pointing sticks, touchpads, and trackballs. Before you purchase a notebook computer, try various types of keyboards and pointing devices to determine which is easiest for you to use. Regardless of the pointing device you select, you also may want to purchase a regular mouse to use when you are working at a desk or other large surface.

3 **Make sure the notebook computer you purchase has a CD and/or DVD drive.**
Loading and installing software, especially large Office suites, is much faster if done from a CD, CD-RW, DVD, or DVD+RW. Today, most notebook computers come with an internal or external CD-ROM drive. Some notebook computers even come with a CD drive and a CD-RW drive or a DVD drive and a CD-RW or DVD+RW/CD-RW drive. Although DVD drives are more expensive, they allow you to play CDs and DVD movies using your notebook computer and a headset.

4 **If necessary, upgrade the processor, memory, and disk storage at the time of purchase.**
As with a desktop computer, upgrading your notebook computer's memory and disk storage usually is

less expensive at the time of initial purchase. Some disk storage is custom designed for notebook computer manufacturers, meaning an upgrade might not be available in the future. If you are purchasing a lightweight notebook computer, then it should include at least a 1.4 GHz processor, 256 MB RAM, and 40 GB of storage.

5 **The availability of built-in ports on a notebook computer is important.** A notebook computer does not have a lot of room to add adapter cards. If you know the purpose for which you plan to use your notebook computer, then you can determine which ports you will need. Most notebooks come with common ports, such as a mouse port, IrDA port, serial port, parallel port, video port, and USB port. If you plan to connect your notebook computer to a TV, however, then you will need a PC-to-TV port. If you want to connect to networks at school or in various offices, make sure the notebook computer you purchase has a built-in network card. If your notebook computer does not come with a network card built-in, then you will have to purchase an external network card that slides into an expansion slot in your notebook computer, as well as a network cable. If you expect to connect an iPod portable digital music player to your notebook computer, then you will need a FireWire port.

6 **If you plan to use your notebook computer for note-taking at school or in meetings, consider a notebook computer that converts to a Tablet PC.** Some computer manufacturers have developed convertible notebook computers that allow the screen to rotate 180 degrees on a central hinge and then fold down to cover the keyboard and become a Tablet PC (Figure 11). You then can use a pencil-like device to input text or drawings into the computer by writing on the screen.

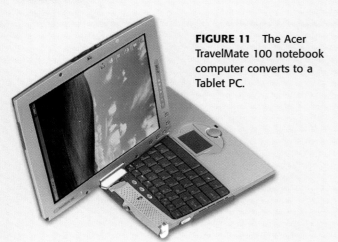

FIGURE 11 The Acer TravelMate 100 notebook computer converts to a Tablet PC.

7 **Consider purchasing a notebook computer with a built-in wireless card to connect to your home network.** Many users today are setting up wireless home networks. With a wireless home network, the desktop computer functions as the server and your notebook computer can access the desktop computer from any location in the house to share files and hardware, such as a printer, and browse the Web. If your notebook computer does not come with a built-in wireless card, you can purchase an external one that slides into your notebook computer. Most home wireless networks allow connections from distances of 150 to 800 feet. Consider purchasing your new notebook computer with Intel Centrino mobile technology so you can connect wirelessly to the Internet from tens of thousands of worldwide locations using the Wi-Fi standard.

8 **If you are going to use your notebook computer for long periods without access to an electrical outlet, purchase a second battery.** The trend among notebook computer users today is power and size over battery life, and notebook computer manufacturers have picked up on this. Many notebook computer users today are willing to give up longer battery life for a larger screen, faster processor, and bigger storage. For this reason, you need to be careful in choosing a notebook computer if you plan to use it without access to electrical outlets for long periods, such as an airplane flight. You also might want to purchase a second battery as a backup. If you anticipate running your notebook computer on batteries frequently, choose a computer that uses **lithium-ion batteries** (they last longer than nickel cadmium or nickel hydride batteries).

9 **Purchase a well-padded and well-designed carrying case.** An amply padded carrying case will protect your notebook computer from the bumps it will receive while traveling. A well-designed carrying case will have room for accessories such as spare floppy disks, CDs and DVDs, a user manual, pens, and paperwork (Figure 12).

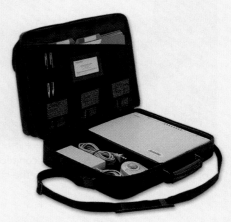

FIGURE 12 Well-designed carrying case.

10 **If you travel overseas, obtain a set of electrical and telephone adapters.** Different countries use different outlets for electrical and telephone connections. Several manufacturers sell sets of adapters that will work in most countries (Figure 13).

FIGURE 13 Set of electrical and telephone adapters for travel abroad.

11 **If you plan to connect your notebook computer to a video projector, make sure the notebook computer is compatible with the video projector.** You should check, for example, to be sure that your notebook computer will allow you to display an image on the computer screen and projection device at the same time (Figure 14). Also, ensure that your notebook computer has the ports required to connect to the video projector.

FIGURE 14 A notebook computer connected to a video projector to project what displays on the screen.

12 **For improved security, consider a fingerprint scanner.** More than 25 million notebook computers are stolen or lost each year. If you have critical information stored on your notebook computer, then consider purchasing one with a fingerprint scanner to protect the data if your computer is stolen or lost. Fingerprint security offers a level of protection that extends well beyond the standard password protection.

HOW TO PURCHASE A TABLET PC

The Tablet PC (Figure 15) combines the mobility features of a traditional notebook computer with the simplicity of pencil and paper, because you can create and save Office-type documents by writing and drawing directly on the screen with a digital pen. Tablet PCs use the Windows XP Tablet PC Edition operating system, which expands Windows XP Professional by including digital pen and speech capabilities. A notebook computer and a Tablet PC have many similarities. For this reason, if you are considering purchasing a Tablet PC, review the guidelines for purchasing a notebook computer, as well as the guidelines that follow.

Company	URL
Acer	www.acer.com/us
Fujitsu	fujitsu.com
Hewlett-Packard	hp.com
Microsoft	microsoft.com/windowsxp/tabletpc
VIA Technologies	via.com
ViewSonic	viewsonic.com

For an updated list with Web sites and their URLs, visit www.course.com/tdc3 and then click Buyer's Guide on the left sidebar.

FIGURE 16 Companies involved with Tablet PCs.

FIGURE 15 The lightweight Tablet PC, with its handwriting capabilities, is the latest addition to the family of mobile computers.

1 **Make sure the Tablet PC fits your mobile computing needs.** The Tablet PC is not for every mobile user. If you find yourself in need of a computer in class or you are spending more time in meetings than in your office, then the Tablet PC may be right for you. Before you invest in a Tablet PC, however, determine the programs you plan to use. You should not buy a Tablet PC simply because it is a new and interesting type of computer. For additional information about the Tablet PC, visit the Web sites listed in Figure 16. You may have to use the search capabilities on the home page of the companies listed to locate information about the Tablet PC.

2 **Decide whether you want a convertible or pure Tablet PC.** Convertible Tablet PCs have an attached keyboard and look like a notebook computer. You rotate the screen and lay it flat against the computer for note-taking. The pure Tablet PCs are slim and lightweight, weighing less than four pounds. They have the capability of easily docking at a desktop to gain access to a large monitor, keyboard, and mouse. If you spend a lot of time attending lectures or meetings, then the pure Tablet PC is ideal. Acceptable specifications for a Tablet PC are shown in Figure 17 on the next page.

3 **Be sure the weight and dimensions are conducive to portability.** The weight and dimensions of the Tablet PC are important because you carry it around like a notepad. The Tablet PC you buy should weigh four pounds or less. Its dimensions should be approximately 12 inches by 9 inches by 1.5 inches.

4 **Port availability, battery life, and durability are even more important with a Tablet PC than they are with a notebook computer.** Make sure the Tablet PC you purchase has the ports required for the applications you plan to run. As with any mobile computer, battery life is important, especially if you plan to use your Tablet PC for long periods without access to an electrical outlet. A Tablet PC must be durable because if you use it for what it was built for, then you will be handling it much like you handle a pad of paper.

Tablet PC Specifications	
Dimensions	12" x 9" x 1.5"
Weight	Less than 4 Pounds
Processor	Pentium III at 2.0 GHz
RAM	128 MB
Hard Disk	20 GB
Display	10.4" XGA TFT 16-Bit Color
Digitizer	Electromagnetic Digitizer
Battery	4-Cell (3-Hour)
USB	2
FireWire	1
Docking Station	Grab and Go with CD, Keyboard, and Mouse
Bluetooth Port	Yes
802.11b Card	Yes
Network Card	10/100 Ethernet
Modem	56 Kbps
Speakers	Internal
Microphone	Internal
Operating System	Windows XP Tablet PC Edition
Application Software	Office XP Small Business Edition
Antivirus Software	Yes - 12 Month Subscription
Warranty	1-Year Limited Warranty Parts and Labor

FIGURE 17 Tablet PC specifications.

FIGURE 18 A Tablet PC lets you handwrite notes and draw on the screen using a digital pen.

Mouse Unit	Digital Pen
Point	Point
Click	Tap
Double-click	Double-tap
Right-click	Tap and hold
Click and drag	Drag

FIGURE 19 Standard point-and-click of a mouse unit compared with the gestures made with a digital pen.

5 **Experiment with different models of the Tablet PC to find the digital pen that works best for you.** The key to making use of the Tablet PC is to be comfortable with its handwriting capabilities and on-screen keyboard. Not only is the digital pen used to write on the screen (Figure 18), but you also use it to make gestures to complete tasks in a manner similar to the way you use a mouse. Figure 19 compares the standard point-and-click of a mouse unit with the gestures made with a digital pen. Other gestures with the digital pen replicate some of the commonly used keys on a keyboard.

6 **Check out the comfort level of handwriting in different positions.** You should be able to handwrite on a Tablet PC with your hand resting on the screen. You also should be able to handwrite holding the Tablet PC in one hand, as well as with it on your lap.

7 **Make sure the LCD display device has a resolution high enough to take advantage of Microsoft's ClearType technology.** Tablet PCs use a digitizer under a standard 10.4-inch motion-sensitive LCD display to make the digital ink on the screen look like real ink on paper. The Tablet PC also uses ClearType technology that makes the characters crisper on the screen so your notes are easier to read and cause less fatigue to the eyes. To ensure you get the maximum benefits from the new ClearType technology, make sure the LCD display has a resolution of 800 x 600 in landscape mode and a 600 x 800 in portrait mode.

8 **Test the built-in Tablet PC microphone and speakers.** With many application software packages that recognize human speech, such as Microsoft Office XP, it is important that the Tablet PC's built-in microphone operates at an acceptable level. If the microphone is not to your liking, you may want to purchase a close-talk headset with your Tablet PC. Increasingly more users are sending information as audio files, rather than relying solely on text. For this reason, you also should check the speakers on the Tablet PC to make sure they meet your standards.

9 **Consider a Tablet PC with a built-in PC video camera.** A PC video camera adds streaming video and still photography capabilities to your Tablet PC, while still allowing you to take notes in lectures or in meetings.

10 **Review the docking capabilities of the Tablet PC.** The Windows XP Tablet PC Edition operating system supports a grab-and-go form of docking, so you can pick up and take a docked Tablet PC with you, just as you would pick up a notepad on your way to a meeting. Two basic types of docking stations are available. One type of docking station (Figure 20) changes the Tablet PC into a desktop computer. It uses the Tablet PC as a monitor. The station has a CD or DVD drive, full-sized keyboard, mouse, and other accessories. Another type of docking station lets you dock your PC to your desktop computer and use Windows XP Dual Monitor support. **Windows XP Dual Monitor support** allows you to work on one monitor, while using the Tablet PC monitor to display often-used applications, such as your calendar or address book.

11 **Wireless access to the Internet and your e-mail is essential with a Tablet PC.** Make sure the Tablet PC has wireless networking, so you can access the Internet and your e-mail anytime and anywhere. Your Tablet PC also should include standard network connections, such as dial-up and Ethernet connections.

12 **Review available accessories to purchase with your Tablet PC.** Tablet PC accessories include docking stations, mouse units, keyboards, security cables, additional memory and storage, protective handgrips, screen protectors, and various types of digital pens. You should review the available accessories when you purchase a Tablet PC.

FIGURE 20 A Tablet PC docked to create a desktop computer with the Tablet PC as the monitor.

HOW TO PURCHASE A PDA

If you need to stay organized when you are on the go, then a lightweight, palm-sized or pocket-sized mobile device, called a PDA, may be the right choice. PDAs typically are categorized by the operating system they run. Although several are available, the two primary operating systems are Palm OS (Figure 21) or a Windows-based operating systems, such as Pocket PC 2002 (Figure 22).

FIGURE 21 Sony's NR70V PDA with Palm OS. The NR70V lets you take pictures with its digital camera, listen to MP3 files, display videos and images, plus keep your datebook and contact list organized.

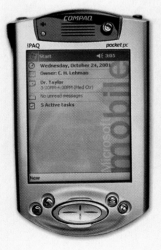

FIGURE 22 Compaq's iPaq H3970 with Pocket PC 2002 includes Bluetooth wireless connectivity. The iPaq plays MP3 music or audio programs from the Web, as well as records and plays back voice notes or meeting notes.

This section lists guidelines you will want to consider when purchasing a PDA. You also should visit the Web sites listed in Figure 23 to gather more information about the type of PDA that best suits your computing needs.

Web Site	URL
Compaq	welcome.hp.com/country/us/eng/prodserv/handheld.html
Handspring	handspring.com
Microsoft	pocketpc.com
Palm	palm.com
PDA Buyers Guide	pdabuyersguide.com
Shopper.com	shopper.cnet.com
Sony	sonystyle.com
Wireless Developer Network	wirelessdevnet.com

For an updated list with Web sites and their URLs, visit www.course.com/tdc3 and then click Buyer's Guide on the left sidebar.

FIGURE 23 Reviews and information about PDAs.

① Determine the programs you plan to run on your PDA. All PDAs can handle basic organizer-type software such as a calendar, address book, and notepad. The availability of other software depends on the operating system you choose. The depth and breadth of software for the Palm OS is significant, with more than 11,000 basic programs and more than 600 wireless programs. PDAs that run Windows-based operating systems, such as Pocket PC 2002, may have fewer programs available, but the operating system and application software are similar to those with which you are familiar, such as Word and Excel.

② Consider how much you want to pay. The price of a PDA can range from $100 to $800, depending on its capabilities. In general, Palm OS devices are at the lower end of the cost spectrum and Pocket PC and other Windows-based devices are at the higher end. For the latest PDA prices, capabilities, and accessories, visit the Web sites listed in Figure 23.

③ Determine whether you need wireless access to the Internet and e-mail or mobile telephone capabilities with your PDA. Some PDAs offer wireless access to the Internet, instant messaging, and e-mail, for a monthly network connection fee. To run the wireless features, the functionality of the PDAs often is stripped down to conserve battery power. Some wireless PDAs, such as Handspring's Treo 270, come with a mobile telephone built-in (Figure 24). These features and services allow PDA users to access real-time information from anywhere to help make decisions while on the go.

4 **Make sure your PDA has enough memory.**
Memory (RAM) is not a major issue with low-end PDAs with monochrome displays and basic organizer functions. Memory is a major issue, however, for high-end PDAs that have color displays and wireless features. Without enough memory, the performance level of your PDA will drop dramatically. If you plan to purchase a high-end PDA running the Palm OS operating system, the PDA should have at least 16 MB of RAM. If you plan to purchase a high-end PDA running the Pocket PC 2002 operating system, the PDA should have at least 48 MB of RAM.

FIGURE 24 The Handspring Treo 270 running Palm OS has a full-color display and can be used as a telephone, an organizer, or to access e-mail and the Web.

5 **Practice with the touch screen, handwriting recognition, and built-in keyboard before deciding on a model.** To enter data into a PDA, you use a keyboard or a pen-like stylus to handwrite on the screen. The keyboard either is mounted on the front of the PDA or it slides out. The Handspring Treo shown in Figure 24, comes with a small, built-in keyboard that works like a mobile telephone keypad. With handwriting recognition, the PDA translates your handwriting into a computerized font. You also can use the stylus as a pointing device to select items on the screen and enter data by tapping an on-screen keyboard. By practicing data entry before buying a PDA, you can learn if one PDA may be easier for you to use than another. You also can buy third-party software to improve a PDA's handwriting recognition.

6 **Decide whether you want a color display.**
Pocket PC devices usually come with a color display that supports as many as 65,536 colors. Palm OS devices also have a color display, but the less expensive ones have a monochrome display in 4 to 16 shades of gray. Having a color display does result in greater on-screen detail, but it also requires more memory and uses more power. Resolution also influences the quality of the display.

7 **Compare battery life.** Any mobile device is useful only if it has the power required to run. Palm OS devices with monochrome screens typically have a much longer battery life than Pocket PC devices with color screens. To help alleviate this problem, many Palm OS and Pocket PC devices have incorporated rechargeable batteries that can be recharged by placing the PDA in a cradle or connecting it to a charger.

8 **Even with PDAs, seriously consider the importance of ergonomics.** Will you put the PDA in your pocket, a carrying case, wear it on your belt? How does it feel in your hand? Will you use it indoors or outdoors? Many screens are unreadable outdoors. Do you need extra ruggedness, such as would be required in construction, in a manufacturing plant, or in a warehouse?

9 **Check out the accessories.** Determine which accessories you want for your PDA. PDA accessories include carrying cases, portable mini- and full-sized keyboards, removable storage, modems, synchronization cradles and cables, car chargers, wireless communications, global positioning system modules, digital camera modules, expansion cards, dashboard mounts, replacement styli, and more.

10 **Decide whether you want additional functionality.** In general, off-the-shelf Pocket PC devices have broader functionality than Palm OS devices. For example, voice-recording capability, e-book players, MP3 players, and video players are standard on most Pocket PC devices. If you are leaning towards a Palm OS device and want these additional functions, you can purchase additional software or expansion modules to add them later.

11 **Determine whether synchronization of data with other PDAs or personal computers is important.** Most PDAs come with a cradle that connects to the USB or serial port on your computer so you can synchronize data on your PDA with your desktop or notebook computer. Increasingly more PDAs are Bluetooth and/or 802.11b enabled, which gives them the capability of synchronizing wirelessly. Most PDAs today also have an infrared port that allows you to synchronize data with any device that has a similar infrared port, including desktop and notebook computers or other PDAs.

HOW TO INSTALL A COMPUTER

It is important that you spend time planning for the installation of your computer. Follow these steps to ensure your installation experience will be a pleasant one and that your work area is safe, healthy, and efficient.

1 **Read the installation manuals before you start to install your equipment.** Many manufacturers include separate installation manuals with their equipment that contain important information. You can save a great deal of time and frustration if you make an effort to read the manuals before starting the installation process.

2 **Do some additional research.** To locate additional instructions or advice about installing your computer, review the computer magazines or Web sites listed in Figure 25 to search for articles about installing a computer.

Web Site	URL
Getting Started/Installation	
HelpTalk Online	www.helptalk.com
Ergonomics	
Apple Ergonomics	apple.com/about/ergonomics/
Ergonomic Computing	www.ergonomic-computing.co.uk/
Healthy Choices for Computer Users	www-ehs.ucsd.edu/ergo/ergobk /vdt_bk.pdf
HealthyComputing.com	healthycomputing.com
IBM Healthy Computing	www.pc.ibm.com/ww/healthycomputing
Video Display Terminal Health and Safety Guidelines	uhs.berkeley.edu/Facstaff/Ergonomics

For an updated list with Web sites and their URLs, visit www.course.com/tdc3 and then click Buyer's Guide on the left sidebar.

FIGURE 25 Web references on setting up and using your personal computer.

3 **Set up your computer in a well-designed work area and remain aware of health issues as you work.** Ergonomic studies have shown that using the correct type and configuration of chair, keyboard, monitor, and work surface will help you work comfortably and efficiently and help protect your health. For your computer work space, experts recommend an area of at least two feet by four feet. You also should set up a document holder that keeps documents at the same height and distance as your computer screen to minimize neck and eye discomfort. Finally, use nonglare light bulbs that illuminate your entire work area to reduce eyestrain. Figure 26 illustrates additional guidelines for setting up your work area. Figure 27 provides computer user health guidelines.

4 **Install your computer in a work space where you can control the temperature and humidity.** You should keep the computer in an area with a constant temperature between 60°F and 80°F. High temperatures and humidity can damage electronic components. Be careful when using space heaters, for example, as the hot, dry air they generate can cause disk problems.

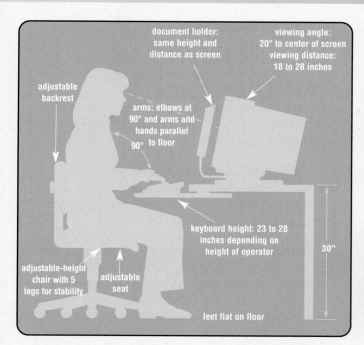

FIGURE 26 A well-designed work area should be flexible to allow adjustments to the height and build of different individuals. Good lighting and air quality also are important considerations.

Computer User Health Guidelines

1. Work in a well-designed work area, as shown in Figure 26.

2. Alternate work activities to prevent physical and mental fatigue. If possible, change the order of your work to provide some variety.

3. Take frequent breaks. Every 15 minutes, look away from the screen to give your eyes a break. At least once per hour, get out of your chair and move around. Every two hours, take at least a 15-minute break.

4. Incorporate hand, arm, and body stretching exercises into your breaks. During your lunch break, try to get outside and walk.

5. Make sure your computer monitor is designed to minimize electro-magnetic radiation (EMR).

6. Try to eliminate or minimize surrounding noise that contributes to stress and tension.

7. If you frequently use the telephone and the computer at the same time, consider using a telephone headset. Cradling the telephone between your head and shoulder can cause muscle strain.

8. Be aware of symptoms of repetitive strain injuries: soreness, pain, numbness, or weakness in neck, shoulders, arms, wrists, and hands. Do not ignore early signs; seek medical advice.

FIGURE 27 Following these health guidelines can help computer users maintain their health.

5 **Set up your work space near an available electrical outlet and set aside a proper location for the electrical wires.** Your computer and peripheral devices, such as the monitor and printer, require an electrical outlet. To maintain safety and simplify the connections, purchase a surge protector to connect the computer and peripheral devices to the electrical outlet. Place the electrical wires in a location where they are not a fire risk and you can avoid tripping on them. After you turn your computer off, turn the master switch on the surge protector off.

6 **Have a telephone outlet and telephone or cable connection near your work space so you can connect your modem and/or place calls while using your computer.** To plug in your modem to access the Internet, you will need a telephone outlet or cable connection close to your computer. Having a telephone nearby also helps if you need to place business or technical support calls while you are working on your computer. Often, if you call a vendor about a hardware or software problem, the support person can talk you through a correction while you are on the telephone. To avoid data loss, however, do not place floppy disks on the telephone or near any other electrical or electronic equipment.

7 **If you plan to set up a wireless network, choose an area that is free from potential signal interference.** Low-level basement areas, doors, trees, and walls, for example, can affect the signals between wireless devices. The signal pattern for most wire-less antennae is circular, with the strongest signal closest to the antenna. The best advice is to give the antenna ample room and determine its placement by trial and error.

8 **Install bookshelves.** When you set up your work space, install bookshelves above and/or to the side of your computer area to keep manuals and other reference materials handy.

9 **Obtain a computer tool set.** Computer tool sets include screwdrivers and other tools you might need to work on your computer, such as an antistatic wristband to prevent static electricity from damaging the computer's circuitry. Computer dealers, office supply stores, and mail-order companies sell these tool sets. To keep all the tools together, get a tool set that comes in a zippered carrying case.

10 **Save all the paperwork that comes with your computer.** Keep the documents that come with your computer in an accessible place, along with the paperwork from your other computer-related purchases. To keep different-sized documents together, consider putting them in a manila file folder, large envelope, or sealable plastic bag.

11 **Record the serial numbers of all your equipment and software.** Write the serial numbers of your equipment and software on the outside of the manuals packaged with these items. As noted in the next section, you also should create a single, comprehensive list that contains the serial numbers of all your equipment and software.

12 **Complete and mail your equipment and software registration cards or register online.** When you register your equipment and software, the vendor usually enters you in its user database. Being a registered user not only can save you time when you call with a support question, it also makes you eligible for special pricing on software upgrades.

13 **Keep the shipping containers and packing materials for all your equipment.** Shipping containers and packing materials will come in handy if you have to return your equipment for servicing or must move it to another location.

14 **Identify device connectors.** At the back or front of your computer, you will find a number of connectors for your printer, monitor, mouse, telephone line, and so forth (Figure 28). If the manufacturer has not identified them for you, use a marking pen to write the purpose of each connector on the back or front of the computer case, or photograph or draw the connectors and label them in a notebook.

15 **Keep your computer area clean.** Avoid eating and drinking around your computer. Also avoid smoking, because cigarette smoke can damage floppy disk drives and floppy disk surfaces.

16 **Check your home or renter's insurance policy.** Some renter's insurance policies have limits on the amount of computer equipment they cover. Other policies do not cover computer equipment at all if it is used for business. In this instance, you may want to obtain a separate insurance policy.

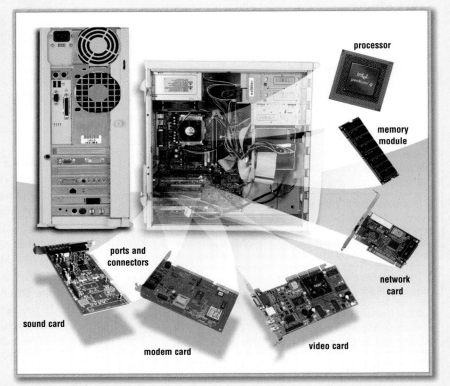

FIGURE 28 Adapter cards have a connector that is positioned in the back of the computer when the card is inserted in an expansion slot on the motherboard.

OUTLINE FOR COMPUTER OWNER'S NOTEBOOK

1. List of Vendors
   Vendor
   Product(s)
   City/State
   URL
   E-mail address
   Telephone number
   Technical support telephone
      number

2. Internet and online services
   information
   Service provider name
   URL
   E-mail address
   Logon telephone number
   Alternate logon telephone
      number
   Technical support telephone
      number
   User ID
   Password

3. Serial numbers
   Product
   Manufacturer
   Serial number

4. Hardware purchase history
   Product
   Manufacturer
   Vendor
   Cost
   Date purchased
   Warranty information

5. Software purchase history
   Product
   Manufacturer
   Vendor
   Cost
   Date purchased
   Date installed/uninstalled
   Product keys/registration
      numbers

6. Trouble log
   Date
   Time
   Problem
   Resolution

7. Support calls
   Date
   Time
   Company
   Contact
   Problem
   Comments

8. Vendor paperwork

FIGURE 29 To keep important information about your computer on hand and organized, use an outline such as this sample outline.

HOW TO MAINTAIN YOUR COMPUTER

Even with the most sophisticated hardware and software, you may need to do some type of maintenance to keep your computer working properly. You can simplify and minimize the maintenance by following the steps listed in this section.

1 **Start a notebook or file using a simple outline that includes information about your computer.** Keep a notebook that provides a single source of information about your entire computer, including hardware, software, and network connectivity. Each time you make a change to your computer, such as adding or removing hardware or software or altering computer parameters, record the change in your notebook. Include the following items in your notebook:

- Vendor support numbers from your user manuals

- Serial numbers of all equipment and software

- User IDs, passwords, and nicknames for your ISP or OSP, network access, Web sites, and so on

- Vendor and date of purchase for all software and equipment

- Trouble log that provides a chronological history of equipment or software problems

- Notes on any discussions with vendor support personnel

Figure 29 provides a suggested outline for the contents of your Computer Owner's Notebook.

2 **Before you work inside your computer, turn off the power and disconnect the equipment from the power source.** Working inside your computer with the power on can affect both you and the computer adversely. In addition, before you touch anything inside the computer, you should touch an unpainted metal surface, such as the power supply. Doing so will help discharge any static electricity that could damage internal components. As an added protection, for less than $10 buy an antistatic wristband from an electronics or computer store to prevent static electricity from damaging the computer's circuitry while you replace components. Do not twist, bend, or force components into place. Gently work around existing cables.

3 **Keep the area surrounding your computer dirt and dust free.** Reducing the dirt and dust around your computer will reduce the need to clean the inside of your computer. If dust builds up inside the computer, remove it carefully with compressed air and a small vacuum. Do not touch the components with the vacuum.

FIGURE 30 The Disk Defragmenter utility defragments the hard disk by reorganizing the files so they are in contiguous (adjacent) clusters, making disk operations faster.

4 **Back up important files and data.** Use a utility program included with the operating system or from a third-party to create a recovery or rescue disk to help you restart your computer if it crashes. Regularly copy important data files on disks, tape, or another computer.

5 **Protect your computer from viruses.** You can protect your computer from viruses by installing an antivirus program and then periodically updating the program by connecting to the manufacturer's Web site. Also, never open a file from an unknown source, particularly those received as e-mail attachments.

6 **Keep your computer tuned.** Most operating systems include several computer utilities that provide basic maintenance functions. In Windows, for example, these utilities are available via the System Tools submenu on the Accessories submenu. One important utility is the Disk Defragmenter, which allows you to reorganize files so they are in contiguous (adjacent) clusters, making disk operations faster (Figure 30). Some programs allow you to schedule maintenance tasks for times when you are not using your computer. If necessary, leave your computer on at night so it can run the required maintenance programs. If your operating system does not provide the tools, you can purchase a stand-alone utility program to perform basic maintenance functions.

7 **Learn to use diagnostic tools.** Diagnostic tools help you identify and resolve problems, thereby helping to reduce your need for technical assistance. Diagnostic tools help you test components, monitor resources such as memory and processing power, undo changes made to files, and more. As with basic maintenance tools, most operating systems include diagnostic tools; you also can purchase or download many stand-alone diagnostic tools.

8 **Conserve energy wherever possible.** A simple way to conserve energy is to avoid animated screen savers, which use additional power and prevent your computer from going into hibernation. Fortunately, many of the recent computer, monitor, and printer models go into a very low power mode when not in use for a few minutes. If your printer does not go into a very low power mode, then keep it turned off until you need to print a document or report. Finally, shut your computer system down at night and turn off the main switch on your surge protector.

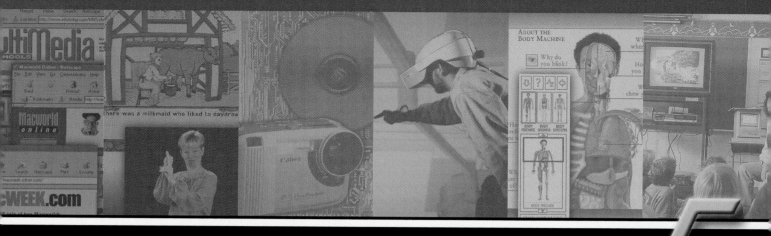

Integrating Multimedia and Educational Software Applications

5

Objectives

After completing this chapter, you will be able to:

- Define multimedia

- Describe types of media used in multimedia applications

- Explain the different uses of multimedia applications

- Discuss multimedia applications on the Web

- Identify various K-12 software applications

- Specify what is meant by an interactive multimedia application

- Examine the uses of multimedia authoring software programs

- Explain why multimedia applications are important for education

Today, multimedia plays an increasingly important role in education, business, and entertainment. Multimedia involves the use of computers to present text, graphics, video, animation, and sound in an integrated way. Unlike television, which combines and presents these media elements in a set order, most multimedia applications are interactive. An interactive multimedia application allows you to choose the material you want to view, define the order in which it is presented, and receive feedback on your actions. **Interactivity**, which is one of the essential features of multimedia applications, also allows for individualized instruction and exploration, both of which enrich the educational experience.

This chapter introduces you to many basic multimedia concepts, discusses educational applications of multimedia, and describes various media components used in multimedia applications. First, you learn about the different types and uses of multimedia applications. Next, the chapter provides examples of a few of the hundreds of outstanding multimedia education software applications that are available for teaching and learning, many of which are inexpensive. You then learn how to create, design, and present multimedia presentations. Finally, the chapter reinforces the potential of these multimedia software applications to change dramatically the way students learn.

What Is Multimedia?

Have your students watched the space shuttle blast into orbit, viewed the Mona Lisa in the Louvre Museum, traveled to Egypt, or visited this nation's capital and explored its history [Figure 5-1]?

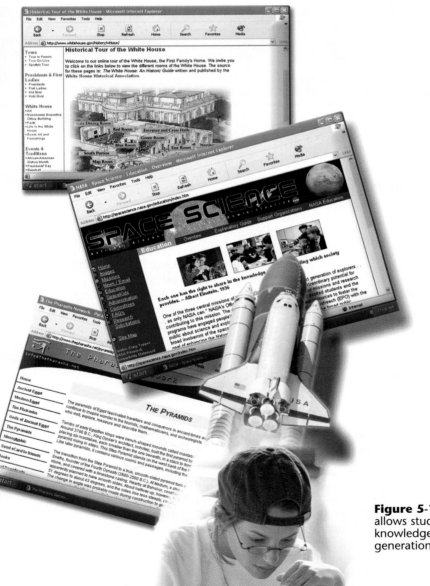

With multimedia, your students can interact with and become part of these learning adventures and much more without ever physically setting foot outside of the classroom. Never before have students been able to explore the world in so many visual and interactive ways. Interactive multimedia is changing the way people work, learn, and play. Extensive research conducted over a period of more than 20 years clearly confirms that the effective integration of interactive multimedia applications into the classroom curriculum can revolutionize the way students learn core and other subjects.

Multimedia is the combination of the following elements: text, color, graphics, animation, audio, and video. **Multimedia software** refers to any computer-based presentation or application software that uses multimedia elements. **Interactive multimedia** describes a multimedia application that accepts input from the user by means of a keyboard, voice, or a pointing device such as a mouse; and performs an action in response. Most interactive multimedia applications allow you to move through information at your own pace. As you progress through the application or complete certain tasks, you receive feedback in the form of a sound, points, or other response.

The multimedia application shown in Figure 5-2, for example, allows students to interact with and learn about the

Figure 5-1 Interactive multimedia allows students to explore the world's knowledge in ways unheard of just a generation ago.

human body. The ability of users to interact with a multimedia application is perhaps its most unique and important feature — a feature that has the potential to change dramatically the way K-12 students learn. Interactive multimedia allows students to define their own learning paths, investigate topics in depth, and get immediate feedback from drill-and-practice or exploration activities. Multimedia applications also tend to engage and challenge students, thus encouraging them to think creatively and independently.

With many multimedia applications, you navigate through the content by clicking links with a pointing device such as a mouse. Recall from Chapter 2 that Web pages use links to allow users to navigate quickly from one document to another. In a multimedia application, a **link** serves a similar function, allowing users to access information quickly and navigate from one topic to another in a nonlinear fashion. For example, while reading about Marco Polo, you might click the keyword, Travels, to display a map of his journeys or listen to a reading from his travel journals.

In a multimedia application, any clickable object — text, graphics, animation, and even videos — can function as a link. Figure 5-3 shows the main menu of a multimedia application that uses text, graphics, and animations as links to additional sources of information. The following sections provide an introduction to the different media elements contained in multimedia applications.

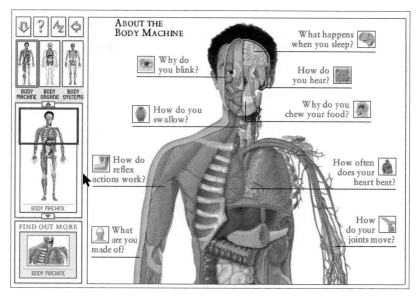

Figure 5-2 The Ultimate Human Body by DK Multimedia is a popular educational program that allows students to interact with and learn about the human body. Clicking the heart, for example, allows students to see and hear a human heart in action.

barometer image link

Figure 5-3
The bottom screen shows the main menu for a popular nature encyclopedia. The menu provides text, buttons, and graphics that allow students or teachers quickly to choose a particular topic. Every object on the main menu is a link to discovery learning. The upper right screen shows what happens when a user clicks the barometer. An enlarged barometer now provides numerous additional links to other multimedia sources of information.

WEB INFO

For more information about multimedia applications, visit the Teachers Discovering Computers Web site, click Chapter 5, click Web Info, and then click Multimedia Applications.

TEXT

Text consists of characters that are used to create words, sentences, and paragraphs and is a fundamental element used in all multimedia applications. Multimedia applications not only use ordinary text to convey basic information, they also use a variety of textual effects to emphasize and clarify information. A different font size, color, or style, for example, often is used to emphasize certain words or phrases. Many multimedia applications use text-based menus that allow you to select and display information on a certain topic [Figure 5-4].

GRAPHICS

Recall from Chapter 4 that a **graphic** is a digital representation of nontext information such as a drawing, chart, or photograph. A graphic, also called a picture or image, contains no movement or animation.

In multimedia applications, graphics serve several functions. For one, graphics can illustrate certain concepts more vividly than text. A picture of Saturn, for example, clearly depicts the planet's rings in a way that text cannot. Graphics also play an important role in the learning process: many individuals — who are **visual learners** —

learn concepts faster or retain a higher percentage of material if they *see* the information presented graphically. Graphics also serve as navigational elements in many software packages. Multimedia applications, for one, often use graphics as buttons that link to more information. The graphical user interfaces used on Macintosh computers, PCs, and graphical Web browsers also demonstrate the importance of graphics when using computers.

If you are creating a multimedia application, you can obtain graphics in several ways. You can purchase a **clip art collection**, which is a set of previously created digital graphics that you can insert into a document. Many clip art collections are grouped by themes, such as Academic, Maps, and People [Figure 5-5]. You also can create your own graphics using a paint or drawing program. Many presentation graphics and multimedia authoring software packages, for example, include drawing tools for creating graphics as shown in Figure 5-6. As you will learn later in the chapter, you can obtain photographs for use in a multimedia application by using a color scanner to digitize photos; taking photographs with a digital camera; or using a collection of photographs on a CD or DVD.

WEB INFO

For more information about free clip art, visit the Teachers Discovering Computers Web site, click Chapter 5, click Web Info, and then click Clip Art.

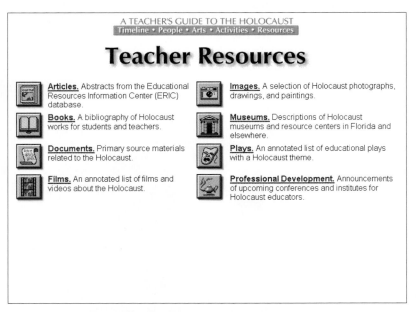

Figure 5-4 The main menu from A TEACHER'S GUIDE TO THE HOLOCAUST CD provides text and buttons that allow teachers quickly to access the listed topic.

Figure 5-5 Most computer stores carry a variety of clip art collections to assist users in creating multimedia projects.

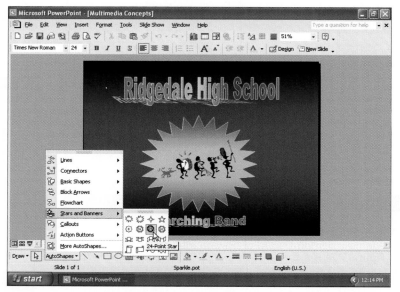

Figure 5-6 Microsoft PowerPoint provides an AutoShapes palette on the Drawing toolbar that allows you to draw a 24-point star or other shapes to include in a multimedia presentation. This type of graphic image is a resizeable, movable object that can be colored in many different ways or combined with other clip art, graphics, or text.

ANIMATION

Displaying a series of still graphics creates an **animation**, which is a graphic that has the illusion of motion. Animations range in scope from a basic graphic with a simple motion (for example, a blinking icon) to a detailed image with complex movements (such as a simulation of how an avalanche starts). As with graphics, animations can convey information more vividly than text alone. An animation showing the up-and-down movement of pistons and engine valves, for example, provides a better illustration of the workings of an internal combustion engine than a written explanation, as shown in Figures 5-7a through 5-7c.

The use of animation has improved the quality of educational software dramatically and made Web sites more interesting for users. You can create your own detailed and highly dynamic animations using a graphics animation software package. In addition, you can obtain previously created animations from a CD, DVD, or on the Web.

AUDIO

Audio is any digitized music, speech, or sound that is stored on and produced by a computer. As with animation, audio allows developers to provide information in a way that brings a concept or concepts to life. The vibration of a human heartbeat or the melodies of a symphony, for example, are concepts difficult to convey without the use of sound. Using audio in a multimedia application to supplement text and graphics enhances understanding. An actor's narration added to the text of a Shakespearean play, for example, reinforces a student's grasp of the passage [Figure 5-8].

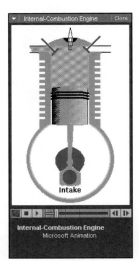

[b] Piston down motion

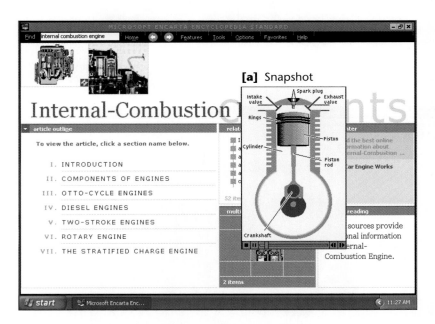

[a] Snapshot

Figure 5-7 Microsoft's Encarta Encyclopedia contains numerous media animations, including a demonstration of how an internal-combustion engine works. Figure 5-7a is a snapshot of the initial screen, Figure 5-7b shows that the piston has moved down during the intake stroke, and Figure 5-7c shows the piston moving up during the compression stroke.

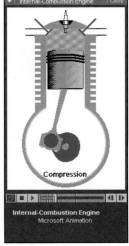

[c] Piston up motion

play button

Figure 5-8 Interactive encyclopedias offer students many opportunities to hear the words and passages of great historical events and literary works, such as Shakespeare's *Macbeth*. By clicking the play button, students hear passages from *Macbeth*.

You can obtain audio files for use in multimedia applications in several different ways. One method is to capture sounds digitally using a microphone, tape or audio CD player, or any other audio input device that is plugged into a port on a sound card or a USB or FireWire port.

Musical Instrument Digital Interface (**MIDI**) is the electronic music industry's standard that defines how digital musical devices represent sounds electronically. Software programs that conform to the MIDI standard allow you to compose and edit music and other sounds. For example, you can change the speed, add notes, or rearrange the score to produce an entirely new sound. Most sound cards support the MIDI standard, so you can play and manipulate sounds on a computer that were created originally on another computer. As with graphics and animations, you also can purchase audio clips on a CD, DVD, or download them from thousands of Web sites.

VIDEO

Video consists of photographic images that are played back at speeds of 15 to 30 frames per second and provide the appearance of full motion in real-time. The integration of video into classroom curricula has significantly influenced the way that students learn core subjects. Videos can reinforce lectures and readings, provide a common base of knowledge, and show things that students would not otherwise experience. For example, after reading the text of one of Martin Luther King's speeches, students can watch a video of King delivering that same speech to an enthusiastic crowd.

To use video in a multimedia application, you first must capture, digitize, and edit the video segment using special video production hardware and software. As described in Chapter 4, video often is captured digitally with a video input device such as a video camera or VCR.

Due to the size of video files, incorporating video into a multimedia application often is a challenge. Video files require tremendous amounts of storage space: a three-minute segment, or **clip**, of high-quality video can take an entire gigabyte of storage. To decrease the size of the files, video often is compressed.

Video compression works by taking advantage of the fact that only a small portion of the image changes from frame to frame. A video compression program thus might store the first reference frame and then, assuming that the following

WEB INFO

For an overview of digital video software, visit the Teachers Discovering Computers Web site, click Chapter 5, click Web Info, and then click Digital Video.

FAQ

Is there more than one MPEG standard?

Yes, the latest standard is called MPEG 4.

frames will be almost identical to it, store only the changes from one frame to the next. Prior to viewing, video compression software decompresses the video segment. The **Moving Pictures Experts Group** has defined a popular standard for video compression and decompression, called **MPEG** (pronounced em-peg). These standardized compression methods reduce the size of video files up to 95 percent, while retaining near-television quality.

Video compression and other improvements in video technology have allowed video to play a more important role in multimedia applications. Technologies such as streaming video also have made video a viable part of multimedia on the Web.

Multimedia Applications

A **multimedia application** involves the use of multimedia technology in education, business, and entertainment [Figure 5-9]. Businesses use multimedia, for example, in interactive advertisements and for job- and skill-training applications. Teachers use multimedia applications to deliver classroom presentations that enhance student learning. Students, in turn, use multimedia applications to learn by reading, seeing, hearing, and interacting with the subject content. Multimedia also is used in a huge variety of computer games and other types of entertainment.

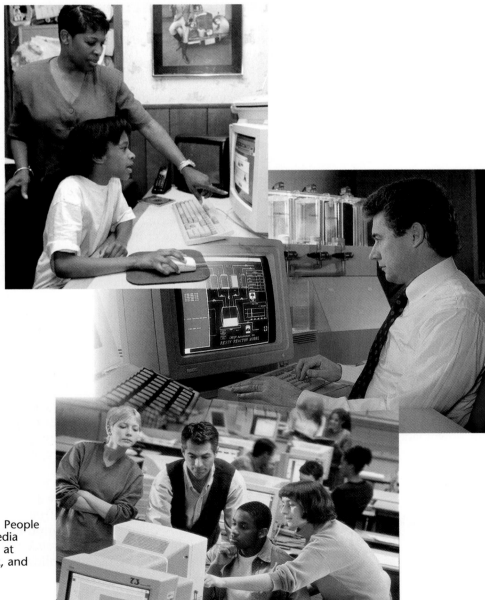

Figure 5-9 People use multimedia applications at home, work, and school.

Another important application of interactive multimedia is to create **simulations**, which are computer-based models of real-life situations. Multimedia simulations often replace costly and sometimes hazardous demonstrations and training in areas such as chemistry, biology, medicine, and aviation.

The following sections provide a more detailed look at different types of well-known multimedia applications, including computer-based training, electronic books and references, how-to guides, newspapers, and magazines. These sections also address the use of multimedia in entertainment, virtual reality, information kiosks, and the importance of multimedia on the World Wide Web. After learning about the various types of well-known multimedia applications, you will learn about specific K-12 educational software applications used to improve teaching and learning by virtually all schools.

COMPUTER-BASED TRAINING (CBT)

Computer-based training (CBT) is a tool which allows individuals to learn by using and completing exercises using instructional software on computers. Computer-based training is popular in business and industry to teach new skills or enhance the existing skills of employees. Athletes, for example, use multimedia computer-based training programs to practice baseball, football, soccer, tennis, and golf skills, while airlines use multimedia CBT simulations to train employees. Schools use CBT to train teachers how to teach students math, reading, computer skills, and many other subjects. Interactive CBT software called **courseware** usually is available on CD, DVD, or the Web.

One important advantage of computer-based training is that it allows for flexible, on-the-spot training. Businesses and schools, for example, can set up corporate training or teacher professional development labs so employees can update their skills without leaving the workplace [Figure 5-10]. Installing CBT software on an employee's computer or on the company network provides even more flexibility — allowing employees to update their job skills right at their desks, at home, or while traveling.

Figure 5-10 Teachers can learn innovative uses of technology, teaching strategies, and various subject-related software packages in a school district's professional development center.

Computer-based training provides a unique learning experience because learners receive instant feedback — in the form of positive response for correct answers or actions, additional information on incorrect answers, and immediate scoring and results. Testing and self-diagnostic features allow instructors to verify that an individual has mastered curriculum objectives and identify students who need additional instruction or practice. Computer-based training is especially effective for teaching software skills if the CBT is integrated with the software application because it allows students to practice using the software as they learn.

ELECTRONIC BOOKS AND REFERENCES

Imagine a library in your hands and in the hands of your student. Read your favorite *Harry Potter* novel, delete it, and download the complete works of Hemingway. The electronic book has arrived. Many analysts predict that electronic books will revolutionize the publishing industry and impact education in many positive, imaginative, and yet-to-be determined ways.

WEB INFO

For more information about electronic books, visit the Teachers Discovering Computers Web site, click Chapter 5, click Web Info, and then click Electronic Books.

You learned in Chapter 4 that an **electronic book**, or **e-book**, is a small, book-sized computer that allows users to read, save, highlight, bookmark, and add notes to online text [Figure 5-11]. In addition, you learned that to obtain the same functionality of an e-book device for your personal computer, notebook computer, Tablet PC, or PDA, you can download and install free e-book reader software programs, such as Microsoft Reader and Adobe Acrobat eBook Reader, from the Web. Electronic books have many of the elements of a regular book, including pages of text and graphics. You generally turn the pages of an electronic book by clicking icons. A table of contents, glossary, and index also are available at the click of a button. To display a definition or a graphic, play a sound or video sequence, or connect to a Web site, you simply click a link (often a bold or underlined word).

Figures 5-11 E-books are small handheld computers that can hold thousands of pages of text.

Microsoft developed a technology called **ClearType** to improve the quality of reading materials on LCD screens, such as e-books. ClearType changes the brightness and contrast of pixels surrounding each letter to give the letter more of a printed appearance. The goal of ClearType is to make on-screen reading as natural as reading from printed materials.

E-book content is obtainable in a number of ways, from purchasing unlimited use or time-based permits, in which the e-book content disappears after the amount of time purchased has expired, to obtaining free e-book content.

For example, **Project Gutenberg** makes thousands of literary and reference books and materials available free to everyone [Figure 5-12]. The e-book revolution is just beginning to impact the way people live, teach, and learn; stay abreast of new and exciting ways to use and integrate e-book applications in teaching and learning.

Another popular type of electronic book is an electronic reference text, such as a multimedia encyclopedia on CD or DVD. An **electronic reference text** is a digital

Figure 5-12 Geoffrey Chaucer's *The Canterbury Tales* is among the thousands of public domain reference and literacy works available from Project Gutenberg (www.gutenberg.net).

version of a reference text, which uses text, graphics, sound, animation, and video to explain a topic or provide additional information. The multimedia encyclopedia, Microsoft Encarta, for example, includes the complete text of a multivolume encyclopedia. In addition to text-based information, Microsoft Encarta includes thousands of photos, animations, audio, and detailed illustrations. This array of multimedia information is accessible via menus and links.

Electronic reference texts, such as multimedia encyclopedias, also are available on the Web. Figure 5-13 lists a cross section of electronic reference texts that are available for home and school use.

In addition to education, health and medicine are areas in which electronic references play an important role. For example, instead of using volumes of books, health professionals and students rely on electronic references for articles, photographs, illustrations, and animations that cover hundreds of health and first aid topics. Physical education, science, and medical students, for example, use the reference, A.D.A.M. (Animated Dissection of Anatomy for Medicine) [Figure 5-14], to learn about the human body. Practicing physicians also use the software to communicate information to their patients.

Electronic Reference Texts

Name	Publisher	URL	Description
Encarta Encyclopedia Reference Library	Microsoft	www.microsoft.com	Combines nine great resources, including Encarta Encyclopedia Deluxe, Encarta Interactive World Atlas, Learning Tools, and more. Also includes translation dictionaries, homework tools, dynamic multimedia, live streaming video, and updates.
Encarta Encyclopedia Deluxe	Microsoft	www.microsoft.com	Contains more than 60,000 articles, hundreds of photos, illustrations, maps, live streaming video, a natural language search function, a dynamic timeline, virtual tours, 360-degree views, and text-to-speech capabilities.
Children's Encyclopedia	Dorling-Kindersley	www.dk.com	Delivers an interactive experience for younger students that combines fascinating and educational interactive reference materials that support learning by stimulating children's natural desire to explore.
Encyclopedia Britannica	Riverdeep	www.riverdeep.com	Contains 75,000 articles, more than 21,000 images, 1,300 clickable maps and 25 timelines with 6,900 hotlinks, videos, audio clips, and more.
American Sign Language for Kids	Multimedia	www.m-2k.com	Uses text, QuickTime video, animations, and illustrations to teach 2,600 signs; includes learning games and fingerspelling.

Figure 5-13 These electronic reference texts use multimedia to clarify topics for students and supply additional information about thousands of subjects.

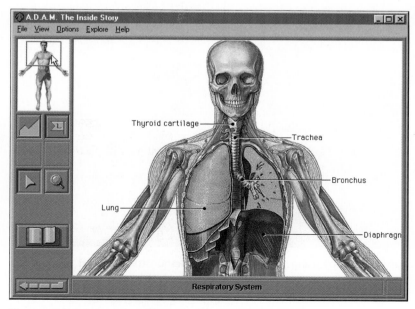

Figure 5-14 Interactive CDs or DVDs such as A.D.A.M. can be used to study the respiratory system and other systems of the body.

HOW-TO GUIDES

Today, many interactive multimedia applications are available to help individuals in their daily lives. These multimedia applications fall into the broad category of how-to guides. **How-to guides** are multimedia applications that include step-by-step instructions and interactive demonstrations to teach you practical new skills [Figure 5-15]. Similar to computer-based training applications used by schools and businesses, how-to guides allow you to acquire new skills, become more productive, and try out your skills in a risk-free environment. The skills you learn with a how-to guide, however, usually apply to enhancing talents outside of your job.

How-to guides can help you buy a home or a car; design a garden; plan a vacation; repair your home, car, or computer; and more. Landscaping how-to guides, for example, allow you to design a landscape; place trees, shrubs, and flowers; and then add features such as pathways, fences, and retaining walls to complete the design [Figure 5-16]. Many gardening how-to guides allow you to explore a database of plants with color photographs and the growth attributes of each one. Multimedia how-to guides are available on CD, DVD, and the Web.

MULTIMEDIA NEWSPAPERS AND MAGAZINES (E-ZINES)

A **multimedia newspaper** and a **multimedia magazine** are digital versions of a newspaper or magazine distributed on CD, DVD, or via the World Wide Web. Many popular magazines and most newspapers have companion Web sites that provide multimedia versions of some or all of their printed content [Figure 5-17]. An **electronic magazine**, or **e-zine**, is a digital publication available on the Web.

WEB INFO

To view an online how-to guide, visit the Teachers Discovering Computers Web site, click Chapter 5, click Web Info, and then click Guide.

How-to Guides on CD/DVD

Name	Publisher	URL	Description
3D Home Design Suite Professional 5	Broderbund	www.broderbund.com	Customize your current floor plans or plan a new home. Software has 2-D and 3-D editing tools.
Cosmopolitan Virtual Makeover	Virtual Makeover	www.virtualmakeover.com	Input your photograph and change your image by experimenting with 600 hairstyles, 680 captivating cosmetic colors, and hundreds of accessories in 360 views. You can save, print, and send e-mail attachments.
Master Landscape & Home Design	Punch! Software	www.punchsoftware.com	Design a garden or entire yard by using scanned photos of your own property; choose trees, shrubs, flowers, and vines. You also can view sample gardens, and then view the plants as they grow and change with the seasons.
MasterCook Deluxe	SierraHome Network	www.sierra.com/home.do	Prepare more than 4,000 dishes based on nutritional value and ingredients on hand. Watch instructional videos and adjust the portions to the number of servings needed.
Teach Yourself PC Maintenance	Learn2.com, Inc.	www.tutorials.com/	Learn computer concepts and terms and learn how to install drives and accessory hardware; such as memory, modems, maintenance tools how to clean your keyboard and more from interactive tutorials.

Figure 5-15 These how-to guides teach useful skills by using videos, interactive demonstrations, and animations.

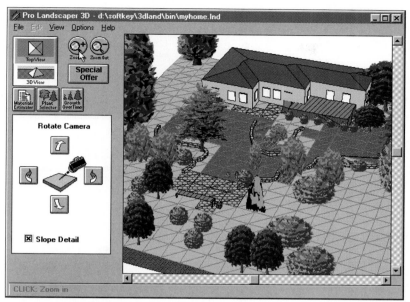

Figure 5-16 This how-to landscaping guide shows a 3-D view of a house with plants, trees, patio, and garden area.

Multimedia Newspapers and Magazines

Name	URL
Independent Newspapers (South Africa)	iol.co.za
Kyodo News (Tokyo)	home.kyodo.co.jp
National Geographic	nationalgeographic.com
Newsweek	newsweek.msnbc.com
The Daily Telegraph (London)	www.telegraph.co.uk
The Globe and Mail (Canada)	globeandmail.ca
The New York Times	nytimes.com
The Wall Street Journal	wsj.com
Time	time.com
USA TODAY	usatoday.com
Washington Post	washingtonpost.com

Figure 5-17 This list contains only a few of the hundreds of multimedia newspapers and magazines from dozens of countries that use video and audio clips, animations, and other interactive multimedia tools to bring the world to homes and classrooms.

Multimedia newspapers and magazines usually include the sections and articles found in print-based versions, such as departments, editorials, and more. Unlike printed publications, however, electronic magazines use many types of media to convey information. Audio and video clips can be included to showcase recent album releases or movies; animations can depict weather patterns or election results.

Some multimedia magazines exist only in their digital format, whereas others are simply electronic versions of existing print magazines. Today, many print-based journals and magazines have companion Web sites that provide some or all of the magazine's printed content. Up-to-the-minute news, interactive polls, and multimedia elements such as audio and video clips enhance the content found in the printed magazine [Figure 5-18 on the next page].

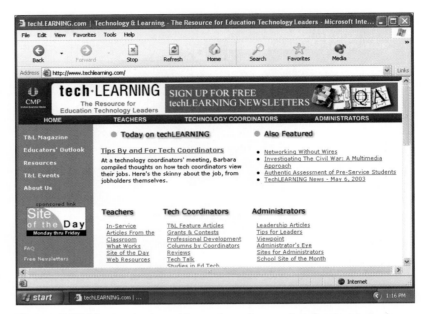

Figure 5-18 Many print-based journals and magazines have companion Web sites. *Technology & Learning* uses its Web site to provide the latest updates on educational technology and issues. Many online journals and magazines are searchable, allowing you to locate specific articles or information.

ENTERTAINMENT AND EDUTAINMENT

As described, multimedia combines the media elements of television *and* interactivity — thus making it ideal for entertainment. Multimedia **computer games**, for example, use a combination of graphics, sound, and video to create a realistic and entertaining game situation. Often, the game simulates a real or fictitious world, in which you play the role of a character and have direct control of what happens in the game [Figure 5-19].

The music industry also sells interactive multimedia applications on CDs and DVDs. Some interactive music CDs, for example, let you play musical instruments along with your favorite musician, read about the musician's life and interests, and even create your own version of popular songs. Like interactive games, these applications give you a character role and put you in control of the application. Many multimedia applications are used for **edutainment**, which is an experience meant to be both educational and entertaining [Figure 5-20].

Figure 5-19 Entertainment applications, rich in multimedia content, provide fun for both children and adults.

Entertainment Applications

Name	Publisher	URL	Description
Backyard Baseball	Infogames Entertainment	www.funkidsgames.com	Select players from 30 Major League Baseball teams or create your own team colors, ballpark, and strategy. Play online with other Windows users.
Dogz	Nintendo of America, Inc.	www.nintendo.com	Use voice recognition to train your Dogz to sit, fetch, or roll over; create custom scenes with the Play Scene Editor.
Motocross Madness	Microsoft	www.microsoft.com	Perform stunts on your motorbike while you race up to eight opponents online via the MSN Gaming Zone.
Empire in Arms	Matrix Games	www.matrixgames.com	Play this game of grand strategy alone or with up to six other players via e-mail or on the Internet.
The Sims	Electronic Arts	www.thesims.com	Develop characters in a neighborhood, build their homes, and display your creations on the World Wide Web with these open-ended games.

Edutainment Applications

Name	Publisher	URL	Description
Carmen Sandiego	Riverdeep Interactive Learning	www.carmensandiego.com	Discover geography by searching for lawbreakers in various locales using foreign languages and Internet links to maps and satellite pictures. The police chief gives updates using real-time video.
Harry Potter	Warner Brothers	www.harrypotter.com	Read extensive information on *Harry Potter* books at this official Harry Potter Web site where you can attend the Hogswarts School of Witchcraft and Wizardry, receive Quidditch training, and much more.
SimCity4	Electronic Arts	www.simcity.ea.com	Explore SimCity, one of the more widely used student edutainment games. With *SimCity*, you can create an entire city from the ground up.
Reader Rabbit	Riverdeep Interactive Learning	www.readerrabbit.com	Try out top-selling programs that teach young children problem solving, decision making, and logic skills. Offers help and prints reports.
The New Way Things Work	DK Multimedia	www.dk.com	Discover how hundreds of machines work by viewing animations, illustrations, and videos.

Figure 5-20 Edutainment applications offer teachers and students both education and entertainment.

VIRTUAL REALITY

Virtual reality (VR) is the use of a computer to create an artificial environment that appears and feels like a real environment and allows you to explore space and manipulate the setting. In its simplest form, a virtual reality application displays a view that appears to be a three-dimensional view of a place or object, such as a landscape, a building, a molecule, or a red blood cell, which users can explore. Architects use this type of software to show clients how a proposed construction or remodeling will appear.

Advanced forms of VR software require you to wear specialized headgear, body suits, and gloves to enhance the experience of the artificial environment [Figure 5-21]. The headgear displays the artificial environment in front of your eyes. The body suit and gloves sense your motion and direction, allowing you to move through and pick up and hold items displayed in the virtual environment. Experts predict that body suits eventually will provide tactile feedback so you can experience the touch and feel of the virtual world.

Your first encounter with VR is likely to be a Web-based virtual reality game. In such games, as you walk around the game's electronic landscape, the site notes your movements and changes your view of the landscape accordingly. Other VR Web sites allow you to take VR tours of a city, view hotel accommodations, or interact with local attractions. The United States Senate Web site provides a virtual tour of

Figure 5-21 A virtual reality body suit allows VR software to interpret the body movements of the wearer. The software then manipulates the image in the virtual environment and displays it in the headset.

the U.S. Capitol building. Students can take a guided tour or venture out on their own to tour the Capitol [Figure 5-22].

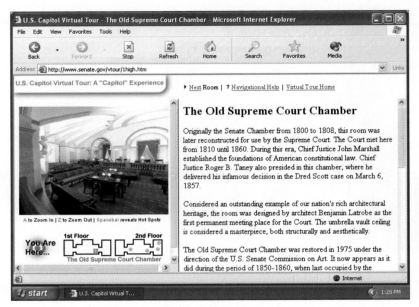

Figure 5-22 The Web allows students to take virtual tours of many historic locations all over the world. At this government Web site, students can take a guided tour of The Old Supreme Court Chamber.

WEB INFO

To take a virtual tour of a museum, visit the Teachers Discovering Computers Web site, click Chapter 5, click Web Info, and then click Tour.

Companies use VR for more practical, commercial applications as well. Office furniture companies have created virtual showrooms in which customers wander among and inspect available products. Automobile and airplane manufacturers are using virtual prototypes to test new models and shorten product design time. Telecommunications firms and others are using computer-based VR applications for employee training. As computing power and the use of the Web increase, practical applications of VR continue to emerge for education, business, and entertainment.

INFORMATION KIOSKS

An **information kiosk** is a computerized information or reference center that allows you to select various options to browse through or find specific information. A typical information kiosk is a self-service structure equipped with computer hardware and software. Kiosks often use touch screen monitors or keyboards for input devices and have all of the data and information needed for the application stored directly on the computer.

Information kiosks provide information in public places where visitors or customers have common questions. Locations such as shopping centers, hotels, airports, colleges and universities for example, use kiosks to provide information on available services, product locations, maps, and other information [Figure 5-23]. Museums and libraries use kiosks to allow visitors to find the location of a specific exhibit. Kiosks providing Internet access also are expected to be popular in the near future.

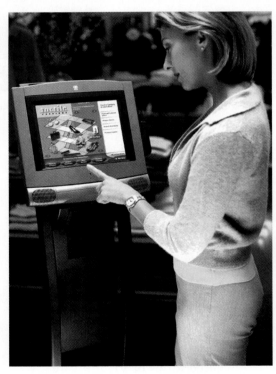

Figure 5-23 Using information kiosks in airports, travelers can check on hotel location and availability, confirm car rentals, read about local attractions, and more. Some kiosks even print local maps and directions to specific sites.

MULTIMEDIA AND THE WORLD WIDE WEB

As you have learned while you have explored the multitude of Web sites provided at this textbook's Web site, multimedia applications play an important role on the World Wide Web. In fact, much of the information on the Web today relies on multimedia. Using multimedia brings a Web page to life, increases the types of information available on the Web, expands the Web's potential uses, and makes the Internet a more entertaining and educational place to explore.

As described in Chapter 2, the Web uses many types of media to deliver information and enhance a user's Web experience [Figure 5-24]. Graphics, animations, audio, and video reinforce text-based content and provide updated information. Many of the multimedia applications described previously, including computer-based training, newspapers, e-zines, games, and virtual reality, are deliverable via the Web.

WEB-BASED TRAINING (WBT) AND DISTANCE LEARNING

Web-based training (WBT) is an approach to computer-based training that uses the technologies of the Internet and the World Wide Web. As with CBT, Web-based training typically consists of self-directed, self-paced instruction on a topic. Because it is delivered via the Web, however, WBT has the advantage of being able to offer up-to-date content on any type of computer platform. As a result, Web-based training already has replaced many traditional computer-based training applications.

Over the past few years, the number of organizations using Web-based training has exploded. Today, almost every major corporation in the United States provides employees with some type of Web-based training to teach new skills or upgrade their current skills.

Web-based training also is available for individuals at home or at work. Many school districts are using the Web to deliver all types of training to their teachers. This media offers anytime, anyplace training.

Today, anyone with access to the Web can take advantage of hundreds of multimedia tutorials offered online. Such tutorials cover a range of topics, from how to change a flat tire to using and integrating Microsoft Office in the classroom [Figure 5-25]. Many of these Web sites are free; others ask you to register

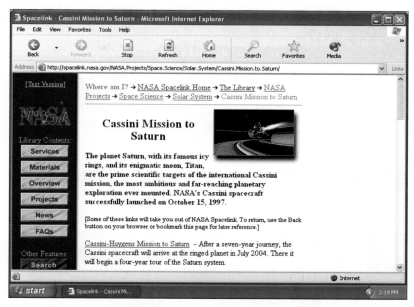

Figure 5-24 A NASA Web server offers textual and graphical information about the mission to Saturn.

and pay a fee to take the complete Web-based training course.

Distance learning, also called **distance education**, **Web-based education**, and **distributed learning**, is the delivery of education from one location to another; the learning takes place at a remote location. Most colleges and universities now offer numerous distance learning courses,

Figure 5-25 An example of the thousands of tutorials that are available on the Web.

usually in the form of Web-based or Web-enhanced courses [Figure 5-26]. A **Web-based course**, often called an **online course**, is a course that is taught mostly or completely on the Web, rather than in a traditional classroom. A **Web-enhanced course** is a traditional classroom course that uses the Web to enhance the content of the course.

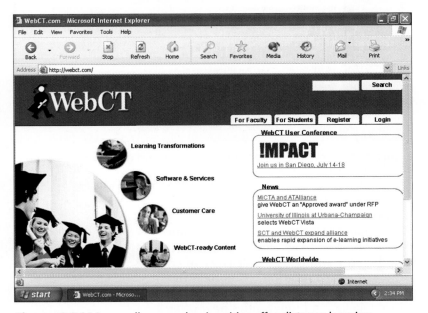

Figure 5-26 Many colleges and universities offer distance learning classes.

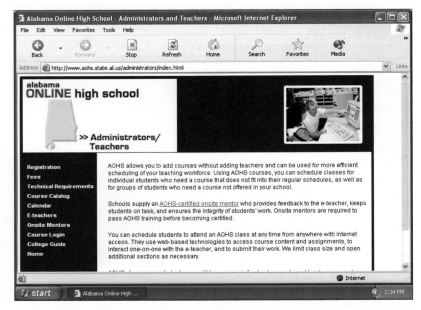

Figure 5-27 The Alabama Online High School enables principals to enroll students in online classes; for example, an individual student who needs a course that does not fit into his or her regular schedule or group of students who need a course not offered in their school.

COLLEGES AND UNIVERSITIES Web-based courses offer many advantages for students that live far from a college or university campus, work full-time, or have scheduling conflicts; it allows them to attend class from home or other locations at any time that fits their schedule. The availability of Web-based courses has exploded in the past few years; experts estimate that more than 3 million students will take an online course this year. Many colleges and universities now offer advanced degrees, including doctorate degrees in which all required courses are offered online. Other colleges and universities offer advanced degrees in which the majority of required courses are offered online. In addition, a number of fully accredited universities no longer provide traditional courses; 100 percent of their courses and degrees are provided online.

HIGH SCHOOLS Most, if not all states, now are providing Web-based or online courses for their high school students [Figure 5-27]. Web-based courses help prevent overcrowding and provide instruction for homebound students. Web-based courses also allow less-populated districts and schools in rural areas to share teachers. By using the Web, these schools can offer specialized classes in French, Latin, calculus, and many other core and advanced subjects. By pooling resources and linking students from more than one school into a Web-based course, school districts can expand the number and type of classes they offer.

Many teachers now are Web-enhancing their classes [Figure 5-28]. By **Web-enhancing** their classes, teachers provide their students with resources to enrich their learning experience. Parents also can access the Web sites to check on homework assignments, activities, student expectations, and more. Another benefit of using the Web in the classroom is having students interact with subject area experts. The Smithsonian Institute, for example, permits teachers and students to interact with the actual scientists who work for the Smithsonian via the Web. Many scientists want to increase educational opportunities for students, who someday may decide to become scientists.

PROFESSIONAL DEVELOPMENT TRAINING

Until recently, in-service professional development training for teachers and administrators has remained basically unchanged for decades. Traditional in-service training involves teachers being trained in classrooms or labs and normally is conducted before or after school, on weekends, during in-service days, or during the summer. Schools often have to provide costly substitutes when teachers are required to be out of the classroom to participate in extensive professional development training.

The traditional model of professional development training is undergoing a revolution — a Web-based or online revolution. Professional development training programs are being redefined in many school districts and state programs. States and school districts are adopting online training as a way to train their teachers in many areas, from technology, to English as a second language, to meeting recertification requirements, to a series of online courses leading to alternative certification. As a result of this professional development revolution, hundreds of thousands of K-12 teachers and administrators now are involved in some type of online professional development training; and this is only the beginning. By 2006 the majority of in-service professional development training for teachers and administrators could be done online.

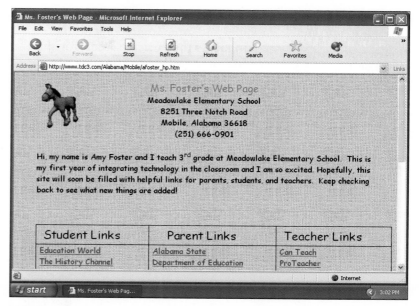

Figure 5-28 Many K-12 teachers provide extensive resources and more for their students by Web-enhancing their classes.

Many companies now work with school districts to provide graduate courses and online professional development training for teachers and administrators [Figure 5-29]. Online professional development training can be self-paced or instructor-led. Most online professional development training available for teachers is self-paced. In **self-paced training,** teachers

Figure 5-29 The Teacher Education Institute provides graduate courses and instructor-led online professional development courses for teachers and administrators.

Figure 5-30 Many school districts provide extensive online professional development opportunities for their teachers and administrators.

typically sign up for a specific course or module, and after completing all the requirements they receive credit for the training. Some self-paced training provides access to a Help desk or instructors that can provide assistance. In contrast, **instructor-led training** involves continuous interaction with an instructor and the courses are more structured, often including schedules and assignment due dates. A number of school districts and even some states have developed online portals for their teachers to enroll in professional development courses, access resources, and receive assistance [Figure 5-30].

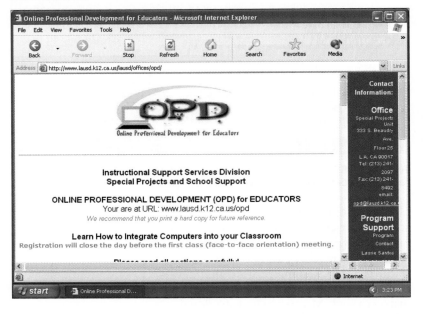

K-12 Educational Software Applications

As described in previous sections, multimedia is important not only for business and entertainment, but also for education. An **educational software application** refers to computer software products used to support teaching and learning of subject-related content. Interactive multimedia applications enrich the learning process by providing individualized instruction and exploration; allowing students to examine their skills in a risk-free environment; and providing instant feedback, testing, and review. Many educational software applications now are correlated to state standards [Figure 5-31].

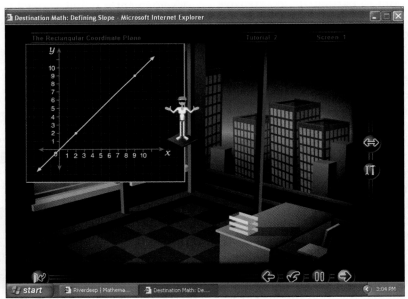

Figure 5-31 Destination Math is an example of an interactive multimedia math problem that provides students with nontraditional ways to master math skills correlated to state standards.

The number and quality of educational software applications designed specifically for the K-12 learning environment have increased dramatically in the past few years. Educational software applications are available in many different designs, forms, and curriculum levels as shown in Figures 5-32a and 5-32b.

The next sections discuss computer-assisted instruction, drill-and-practice, educational games, tutorials, educational simulations, integrated learning systems, and curriculum-specific software applications. Information in Chapters 6 and 7 will provide you with ways to integrate these types of software programs into your classroom curriculum.

COMPUTER-ASSISTED INSTRUCTION (CAI)

Computer-assisted instruction (CAI) has been used in education for more than two decades. Computer-assisted instruction is software designed to help teach facts, information, and/or skills associated with subject-related materials. For practical purposes, using a computer to enhance instruction could be called computer-assisted instruction. Most educators, however, do not feel that computer-assisted instruction accurately describes the many different computer-based educational software programs available today. With the growth of educational technology, the teaching profession has seen the emergence of other names used to refer to education software, such as computer-based instruction (CBI), computer-based learning (CBL), and computer-aided learning (CAL). For the purposes of this textbook, educational software applications refer to computer software products that support teaching and learning of subject-related content [Figure 5-33 on the next page].

DRILL-AND-PRACTICE SOFTWARE

Drill-and-practice software is software that first supplies factual information and then through repetitive exercises allows students to continue to work on specific materials to remember or memorize the information. Another name is **skills-reinforcement software**. Drill-and-practice software is effective for learning basic skills and for remediation.

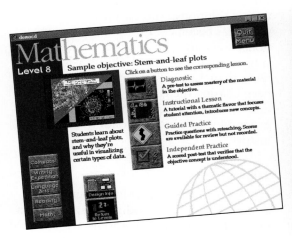

[a] Math program

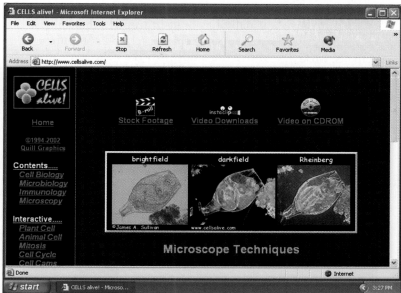

[b] Science Web site

Figure 5-32 Multimedia applications are great tools to help teach difficult math and science concepts. The interactive math program shown in Figure 5-32a allows teachers to pretest students' knowledge before they enter a particular level of instruction. Science Web sites, such as the biology site shown in Figure 5-32b, help students learn basic science concepts before entering the lab so they can focus on the actual hands-on experiment when in the lab.

WEB INFO

For links to popular
education-related
computer-based
applications, visit the
Teachers Discovering
Computers Web site,
click Chapter 5, click
Web Info, and then
click Educational
Applications.

WEB INFO

To access an
interactive tutorial
on using PowerPoint,
visit the Teachers
Discovering
Computers Web site,
click Chapter 5, click
Web Info, and then
click PowerPoint.

Figure 5-34 For
more than a decade,
students of all ages
have been chasing
the elusive Carmen
Sandiego and her
counterparts, while
learning about
geography, cultures,
astronomy, music,
history, and more.

Figure 5-33 An educational multimedia application designed to teach
young learners basic reading skills.

Remediation is reviewing content many
times until a student grasps the concepts
being taught. One of the important features
of drill-and-practice software and other
educational software is that students
receive instant feedback on correct and
incorrect answers. Using drill-and-practice
can increase students' performance in areas
that are weak. Drill-and-practice software
usually has built-in features that once a
student masters a level, the computer will
move the student to the next level automatically. Drill-and-practice software is effective when used with students who require
extra assistance in content instruction.

EDUCATIONAL GAMES

Today, the majority of educational
games are available on CDs, DVDs, and on
the Web. **Educational games** usually include
a set of rules, and students can compete
against other students or the game itself.
Games can be an effective way to teach
information through repetition and practice.

Many students find educational games a
fun way to learn. Various educational games
create problem-solving environments forcing
students to use higher-order thinking skills
to find solutions. The Carmen Sandiego
series has become a front-runner in educational software games that contain nonlinear
subject-related content [Figure 5-34]. For
more than 12 years, young people have
been chasing the fleeting Carmen Sandiego
and her counterparts, while learning about
geography, cultures, astronomy, music, and
history.

TUTORIALS

A **tutorial** is a teaching program
designed to help individuals learn to use a
product or concepts. Tutorials are designed
to tutor, or instruct. Many software products contain built-in tutorials to teach the
user how to use the software. Developers
create educational tutorials that use the
computer to provide an entire instructional
area and are created so students can work

their way through the tutorial to learn content without any help or other materials. The teaching solutions provided by tutorials range from a structured linear approach with specific content objectives to a nonlinear approach that offers alternative paths through the lesson based on students' responses, called **branching**. Branching reflects classroom learning theory by allowing students to excel at their own pace, providing feedback and remediation when needed. Figure 5-35 provides some of the features of effective educational tutorials.

EDUCATIONAL SIMULATIONS

An **educational computer simulation** is a computerized model of real life that represents a physical or simulated process. These programs are unique because the user can cause things to happen, change the conditions, and make decisions based on the criteria provided to simulate real-life situations. These interactive programs model some event, reality, real-life circumstances, or phenomenon. Simulations offer learners the opportunity to manipulate variables that effect the outcomes of the experience. Using simulation is not a new teaching strategy. As you learned earlier in this chapter, business and industry have been using simulation for many years.

Interest is growing in programs such as SimCity, Sim Theme Park, and Sim Coaster that let students design, interact, and provide more accurate explanations and examples of real life. **SimCity** is a very popular simulation program for education [Figure 5-36]. Students design cities, communities, neighborhoods, and businesses, including infrastructure, such as telephone lines, buildings, and more. As the cities grow in size and complexity, natural disasters and other realistic problems occur continuously requiring students to use all available city resources, including financial resources, to keep the cities running.

The availability of educational computer simulations on the Web is experiencing dramatic growth. A student can learn how a building is demolished, dissect a frog, see a real human heart in action, and more.

Tutorial Features

- User-friendly
- Easy to navigate
- Available on both platforms
- Student-centered interactivity throughout software
- Learner control over delivery of content
- Active instructional techniques
- Innovative learning strategies
- Real-life learning experiences
- Motivational and appropriate for grade level
- Contains valid testing
- Appropriate sequence and scope of content
- Evaluated by educators

Figure 5-35 Features of effective educational tutorials.

Figure 5-36 SimCity, a popular simulation program, creates a real-life environment for development of problem-solving skills.

INTEGRATED LEARNING SYSTEMS

An **integrated learning system (ILS)** is a sophisticated software package usually developed by an established educational software corporation as a complete educational software solution in one package. These software solutions provide individual student diagnostic data through pretests, instruction based on the diagnostic data, continuous monitoring of student performance with automatic adjustments in instruction when needed, a variety of formats for teaching content, and multi-levels of content. Most integrated learning systems also offer a comprehensive management solution for maintaining the software and for tracking student use and progress. Although expensive, integrated learning systems are praised as a comprehensive software solution for low-achieving schools. Integrated learning systems are appealing to school administrators, school boards, and principals because they offer a full, flexible solution in one package.

A new type of software application has evolved that is similar to an ILS, called an open learning system or an advanced learning system [Figure 5-37]. An **open learning system** or an **advanced learning system** is an integrated learning system that includes software titles from leading publishers. What makes this type of learning system different from a traditional ILS is the number of different software titles and activities these packages include. In addition, many ILS applications prescribe the solution for the student while the new open learning systems make the teacher the key player in determining and prescribing the appropriate assessment, choosing the ideal activities, matching the software to objectives and standards, and integrating the software into their curriculum.

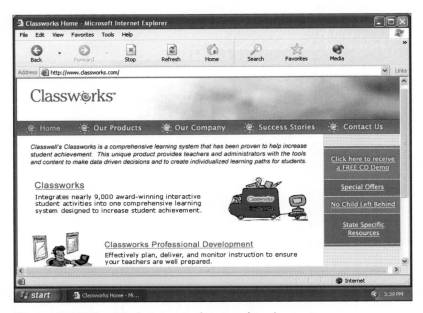

Figure 5-37 ClassWorks is a popular open learning system.

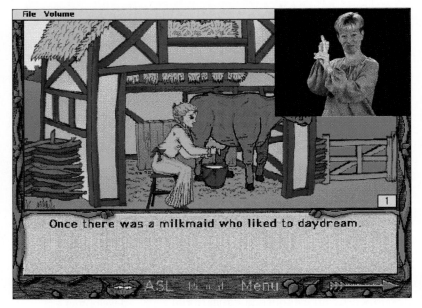

Figure 5-38 The *Aesop's Fables* multimedia application provides access to the visual language through sign language and the printed word for students who are hearing impaired. In the corner of the screen, a teacher signs all the printed words on the screen.

APPLICATIONS FOR STUDENTS WITH DISABILITIES

Educational software applications offer unique advantages to students with physical or learning disabilities. Students who are visually impaired, for example, benefit from the audio capabilities of multimedia applications, as well as the use of graphics and large font sizes. Visual materials such as graphics, animation, and video also make learning easier for students who are hearing impaired. Many educational software companies offer multimedia products with closed captioning or sign language to enhance the learning experience for hearing-impaired students [Figure 5-38].

For students with learning disabilities, the ability to work at their own pace is a major benefit of interactive multimedia applications. Students are able to interact with the software, practice, and review at their own pace, which alleviates the pressure to keep up with peers.

CURRICULUM-SPECIFIC EDUCATIONAL SOFTWARE

Today, hundreds of high quality interactive and multimedia educational programs are available for use by K-12 educators. Most of these programs are available on CD and DVD, or are installed on school networks; others are available on the Web. Many of these educational software applications are designed for curriculum-specific teaching and learning and can be organized in categories as described below. These major categories are by no means all-inclusive, as many software programs are available for K-12 educators that can be used in dozens of curricular areas.

CREATIVITY Creativity applications often allow students to start with a blank canvas, allowing them to use imagination and ingenuity. Students can control the design of their projects completely, using the tools provided by the software application. Some applications provide students with ideas and premade backgrounds and images. Students typically have complete control over the design, graphics, and path they create. A number of popular software programs are available that fit in this category [Figure 5-39]. Creativity software applications include HyperStudio, Inspiration, Kidspiration, Ultimate Writing and Creativity Center, Storybook Weaver, Create Together, Microsoft Publisher, Paint Shop Pro, Photoshop, Disney's Magic Artist, KidWorks, MovieWorks Deluxe, Kid Pix, and Jump Start Artist.

CRITICAL THINKING Critical-thinking applications stimulate students to use critical-thinking skills in a variety of ways [Figure 5-40]. Students often are presented with a problem and a variety of ways to solve the problem. They must use critical-thinking skills to obtain the correct solution to the problem. Critical-thinking software applications include I SPY Treasure Hunt, GeoSarfari Series, the Carmen Sandiego series of software titles, The Way Things Work, Thinkin' Things collection, Zoombinis collection, SimCity, and Thinkology.

WEB INFO

To learn more about integrated learning systems, visit the Teachers Discovering Computers Web site, click Chapter 5, click Web Info, and then click Integrated Learning System.

[a] Carmen Sandiego

Figure 5-40
Dozens of critical-thinking applications are available for students of all ages. Figure 5-40a displays the Carmen Sandiego series of titles that cover geography, math, language arts, history, and more. Figure 5-40b shows a popular program called The Way Things Work.

Figure 5-39 Jump Start Artist is an example of creativity software that helps young students express themselves artistically.

[b] The Way Things Work

EARLY LEARNING   Early learning **applications** are designed to provide students in grades PK-3 with a developmental head start in reading, language arts, math, science, and other curricular areas [Figure 5-41]. Students are presented with engaging graphics, a variety of paths, and a wide variety of activities. These fun and interactive programs include Kidspiration, Millie's Math House, Living Books Library, Sammy's Science House, the JumpStart series of software titles, Reader Rabbit's Reading, and many more outstanding programs.

Figure 5-41 Early learning software applications are designed primarily for grades PK-3, and provide students with a developmental head start. Displayed is a popular program called Kidspiration.

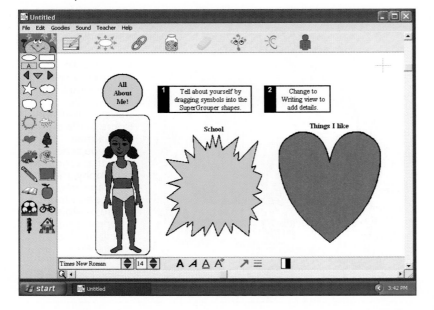

ESL/FOREIGN LANGUAGE   ESL and foreign language **applications** provide K-12 students with assistance in learning English and other languages [Figure 5-42]. These applications enable students to practice their skills in a nonthreatening environment. These language-specific programs include English Express Deluxe, The Heartsoft BestSellers ESL Version, EduOle, Instant Immersion English, Instant Immersion Spanish, Learn to Speak French, Learn to Speak Spanish, and dozens of other language programs designed for students in all grades. You also can download free translation software that lets your computer talk from the ReadPlease Web site. Other translation software allows you and your students to translate English to Spanish, French, German, and other languages.

LANGUAGE ARTS   Language arts **applications**, available for all grade levels, support student learning throughout the reading and writing process [Figure 5-43]. These applications try to engage students, encouraging them to learn critical skills in a fun and creative environment. Popular language arts programs include Ultimate Writing and Creativity Center, Student Writing Center, Clicker 4, the Reader Rabbit series, Vocabulary Development, the High School Reading Comprehension Series, Reading Blaster, and dozens more.

Figure 5-43 Language arts software is available for all grade levels. Shown is Reader Rabbit 1, a software designed for first graders.

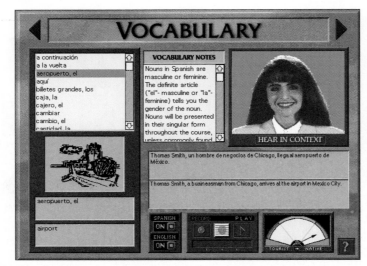

Figure 5-42 ESL and foreign language applications include software programs for Spanish, English, French, and many other languages. Shown is the popular Learn to Speak Spanish program.

MATH AND SCIENCE Math applications help students master basic and complex mathematics and are available for all grade levels [Figure 5-44]. Many applications provide students with skill practice and problem-solving activities. **Science applications** are available for all grade levels and assist students in learning a wide variety of science concepts [Figure 5-45]. Multimedia science applications can assist students in mastering difficult or abstract concepts by providing visual representations. Math programs include the Math Advantage series, Geometer's Sketchpad, Math Blaster, Math WorkShop Deluxe, MathXpert, the Mighty Math series, Math Munchers, Math Companion, Tessellation Exploration, Wild West Math, and many more.

Science applications include Thinkin' Science, Virtual Labs, The Ultimate Human Body, I Love Science, Discovery Channel School series, Magic School Bus series, A.D.A.M. Essentials High School Suite, Pinball Science, GeoSafari, Earth Quest, Science Court, and numerous others.

[a] Math Advantage - Algebra

[b] MathXpert

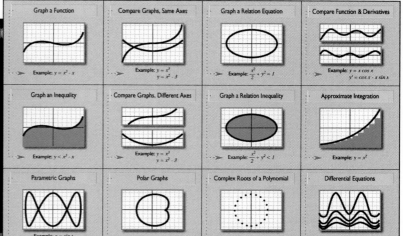

Figure 5-44 Math software engages and motivates students to learn basic and complex concepts. Figure 5-44a shows a Math Advantage Algebra 1 title, and Figure 5-44b displays MathXpert software. MathXpert is designed for high school students and covers hundreds of math concepts including graphing.

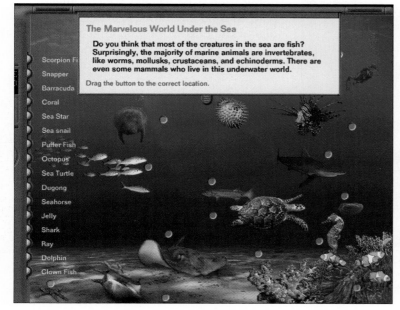

Figure 5-45 Science software allows all students to explore and interact with science concepts. Shown is the GeoSafari Knowledge Pad program on marine animals.

SOCIAL STUDIES   Social studies software applications encourage higher-order thinking skills, provide reinforcement of facts, and allow students to define their own path [Figure 5-46]. Special-education teachers also can use these applications for teaching language skills. A few social studies programs include the Carmen Sandiego series, Oregon Trail, Amazon Trail, TimeLiner, the American History Series, the U.S. Geography series, Chronicle Encyclopedia of History, and Life in Colonial America.

Figure 5-46 Interactive multimedia software, such as the Chronicle Encyclopedia of History, allows students to understand social studies concepts.

Figure 5-47 The basic software that comes with scanners allows users to edit scanned images and save the images in different file formats.

Creating and Presenting Multimedia Applications

Creating or developing multimedia applications involves producing various media elements, defining the elements' relationships to each other, and then sequencing them in an appropriate order. Individuals often use multimedia authoring software to help complete these tasks. Many options are available for you and your students to present multimedia applications.

OBTAINING GRAPHICS FOR A MULTIMEDIA APPLICATION

Graphics, including illustrations, photos, and animations, are essential elements in any multimedia application. Teachers and students easily can add color images and photos to multimedia applications using color scanners and digital cameras.

The basic software that comes with scanners [Figure 5-47] allows users to conduct basic editing of scanned images and also save scanned images in different file formats. A **color scanner** converts images into a digitized format for use in multimedia applications [Figure 5-48]. Sophisticated image editing programs are available for users who require a wider variety of image-editing possibilities.

Another easy and effective way to obtain color photographs for a multimedia application is by using a digital camera [Figure 5-49]. As discussed in Chapter 4, **digital cameras** work much like regular cameras, except they use a small reusable disk or internal memory to store digital

Figure 5-48 A color scanner can convert images into digitized format for multimedia applications and is easy to use.

photographs. You easily can transfer photographs taken with a digital camera to a computer's hard disk and then incorporate them into a multimedia document or presentation.

Figure 5-49 An easy and effective way to obtain digitized color photographs is by using a digital camera. Once the photographs are input into a computer, they can be incorporated into a multimedia application.

Digital images related to virtually any topic or area of interest can be downloaded from the Web, often without cost. For example, you can choose from thousands of clip art images and digital photos from the Microsoft Office Design Gallery Live Web site [Figure 5-50]. In addition, you can purchase CDs or DVDs that contain thousands of digital images from retail stores or Web sites. After you have obtained the graphics you want, you can incorporate them into your multimedia applications or presentations.

MULTIMEDIA AND WEB AUTHORING SOFTWARE

Multimedia authoring software, also called an **authoring tool,** allows an individual to create an interactive multimedia presentation that includes text, graphics, sound, animation, or video. A multimedia presentation, however, is more than just a combination of these elements. Multimedia authoring software lets you create the application or presentation by controlling the placement of text and graphics and the duration of sounds, video, and animations.

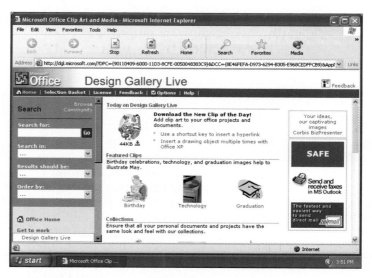

Figure 5-50 The Web comprises many sites from which teachers and students can download graphic images for use in multimedia applications.

Recall that a multimedia application also is interactive, meaning you can decide the amount and order of the material it contains. Multimedia authoring software allows you to create interactivity by defining places in the program that respond to user input. In a multimedia application, for example, you might include a screen where users can click buttons to play a video or skip the video and move to the next screen.

Multimedia developers in corporations and businesses use multimedia authoring software programs such as **ToolBook, Authorware,** and **Director.** Developers use these high-end programs to produce many of the hundreds of educational multimedia applications used in schools today.

Very few teachers use ToolBook or Authorware to develop their own multimedia applications, as these high-end programs are expensive and more tailored to a commercial environment. Many easy-to-use and less expensive authoring programs, however, are widely available and currently are used by K-12 teachers and students in schools all over the world. Two of the more popular multimedia authoring tools used in K-12 schools are Microsoft PowerPoint and HyperStudio.

While not considered a true multimedia authoring software program, Microsoft **PowerPoint** does allow teachers and students to create multimedia presentations that can incorporate text, graphics, animation, audio, video, links, and most important, interactivity. You can learn how to use and integrate Microsoft PowerPoint in your classroom by completing the In the Lab activities at the end of this chapter.

A popular multimedia authoring program used by teachers, students, and businesses is HyperStudio [Figure 5-51]. **HyperStudio** is an easy-to-use multimedia authoring software program that allows the author to combine all of the multimedia elements described in this chapter into a series of interactive cards. Millions of students around the world have used HyperStudio to develop inter-active multimedia projects.

WEB INFO

To learn more about interactive white-boards, visit the Teachers Discovering Computers Web site, click Chapter 5, click Web Info, and then click Interactive Whiteboards.

Figure 5-51 HyperStudio is a popular K-12 multimedia authoring program.

Other popular multimedia authoring and Web development programs used by teachers and students include Adobe GoLive, Macromedia Dreamweaver, Stagecast Creator, SiteCentral, Mediator 7, MovieWorks, Create Together, Netscape Composer, Microsoft FrontPage, MP Express, and Leonardo's Multimedia Toolbox. In addition, both Windows and Mac OS operating systems provide extensive resources that allow you and your students to create your own movies, burn CDs, and create other multimedia products.

PRESENTING MULTIMEDIA

Presenting your multimedia presentations and having your students present their multimedia projects may require a projection system so your students can see and hear the presentations and projects clearly. For most classroom presentations, a large monitor or large-screen television is a practical solution. Other solutions include using data projectors and electronic whiteboards.

LARGE MONITORS OR TELEVISIONS The most practical and least expensive way for you and your students to present multimedia in your classroom is to connect your classroom computer or a notebook computer to a large-screen monitor or a large-screen television. Many school districts provide their teachers with a large-screen monitor or a 27- or 32-inch television for classroom presentations. These large-screen monitors or televisions often are mounted on rolling carts so teachers can use them in more than one classroom [Figure 5-52].

Figure 5-52 Using a large-screen monitor or television connected to a computer is a common way to project computer images in a classroom so all students can view multimedia presentations or interactive software programs. These systems also can be used to show videotapes using a VCR.

Connecting most desktop computers to a television requires a special converter that converts the digital signal of a computer to the analog signal required by most televisions. AVerMedia sells an affordable PC/Mac-to-TV converter for less than $100 that allows you to project any computer application onto a big-screen TV. Some notebook computers now have the converter hardware and software built in and as a result can be connected directly to a television using a cable often supplied with the notebook computer.

DATA PROJECTORS   Recall that a **data projector** is a device that projects the image that appears on a computer screen onto a large screen so an audience, such as a classroom or school assembly, can see the image clearly [Figure 5-53]. Data projectors are expensive and thus are not a practical option for every classroom. Most schools have at least one data projector that can be used by teachers; however, schools normally use data projectors when making presentations to a large group of students, teachers, or parents.

INTERACTIVE WHITEBOARDS   A teaching tool becoming increasingly popular with educators is the **interactive whiteboard**, also called an **electronic whiteboard**, which turns a computer and data projector into a powerful tool for teaching and learning. One interactive whiteboard, called a **SMART Board**, produced by Smart Technologies, is more than a presentation system [Figure 5-54]. With a computer image projected onto the SMART Board, you can press on its large, touch-sensitive surface to access and control any computer application. In addition, you can write notes, draw diagrams, and highlight information. You then can save and print your notes and hand them out to students or make them available on your school's network. Another option is the InterWrite SchoolBoard from the GTCO CalComp.

Figure 5-53 Data projectors are used to project a computer's image and other multimedia capabilities onto a large screen.

Figure 5-54 An electronic whiteboard is an interactive presentation system that turns a computer and data projector into a powerful tool for teaching and learning.

Why Are Multimedia and Educational Software Applications Important for Education?

Multimedia applications are changing the traditional dynamics of learning in classrooms. As previously noted, interactivity is one of the major features of multimedia applications. The ability of users to interact with a multimedia application is perhaps the single most critical feature of multimedia and has enormous potential to improve learning in K-12 schools.

As mentioned earlier, extensive research conducted over a period of more than 20 years has shown that, when properly evaluated and integrated into teaching at the point of instruction, multimedia applications are highly effective teaching tools. Studies indicate that students retain approximately 20 percent of what they see; 30 percent of what they hear; and 50 percent of what they see *and* hear. When a student has a chance to hear, see, *and* interact with a learning environment, he or she can retain as much as 80 percent of the information. Multimedia applications provide that interactive learning environment, which makes them powerful tools for teaching and learning [Figure 5-55].

One of the better reasons for teachers to utilize multimedia software in the classroom is that it appeals to a variety of learning styles. Helping every student learn in his or her own, unique way, insures success for all students. Multimedia software applications assist teachers in meeting this need by combining interactive software integrated with teaching strategies to enhance the learning process. Furthermore, multimedia software is engaging and motivational.

Another important reason for students' increased retention is that they become active participants in the learning process instead of passive recipients of information. Interactive multimedia applications engage students by asking them to define their own paths through an application, which often leads them to explore many related topics.

Many teachers have noted that students are motivated by and enjoy the process of creating their own interactive multimedia applications using multimedia authoring software. Many students enjoy conducting research and writing when their writing projects involve the creation of a multimedia application — and they will more readily practice those skills. Further, the completion of a multimedia project is a self-esteem and confidence booster for many students.

WEB INFO

To learn more about learning styles, visit the Teachers Discovering Computers Web site, click Chapter 5, click Web Info, and then click Learning Styles.

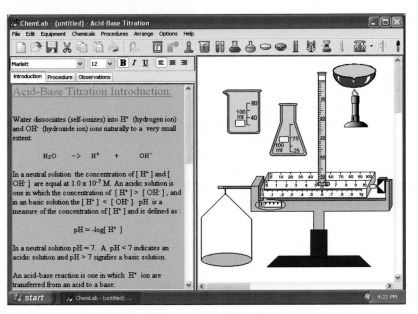

Figure 5-55 Multimedia supports learning; interactive students become active learners.

Teachers can use multimedia software both as a productivity tool and as an integration tool. You can use a multimedia software application such as PowerPoint to introduce new concepts, present lectures, and to demonstrate to students effective screen design and presentation techniques. Additionally, teachers can create a multimedia presentation to present a new concept and then provide students access to the presentation so they can easily review new information and interact directly with the software.

When teachers effectively use multimedia software as a productivity tool, they are modeling for their students how to use this powerful software. This can be the first step in learning to integrate multimedia software effectively into the curriculum. Teachers can have students evidence their learning by creating their own multimedia presentations and presenting them to the class.

For multimedia applications to reach their full potential in the classroom, teachers must evaluate multimedia applications for content and appropriateness. Chapter 7 provides additional guidance on evaluating educational software and Web resources for the classroom.

Copyright is an important matter for you and your students to understand when using and creating multimedia applications. Copyright issues, including fair use guidelines, are covered in detail in Chapter 8. Finally, to reap the full benefits of multimedia at home, you should consider investing in a high-speed DSL or cable connection to the Internet.

Digital Imaging and Video Technology

Using today's technologies, you and your students easily can learn how to create and edit digital graphics and video. Following this chapter is a special feature that introduces you to the world of digital imaging and video technology.

Summary of Integrating Multimedia and Educational Software Applications

This chapter examined how to use, and more important, integrate multimedia and educational software applications in your classroom curriculum. First, you learned about the different elements used in multimedia applications, the variety of multimedia applications, and the growing popularity of distance learning. Next, you learned about educational software applications and how to create and present multimedia applications. Finally, the chapter reviewed the value of multimedia in education. Effectively integrated multimedia education software applications have the potential to impact education in many dramatic ways.

In Brief

Web Instructions: To display this page from the Web, start your browser and enter the URL, www.course.com/tdc3. Click Chapter 5 at the top of the Web page and then click In Brief on the left sidebar. Click the links for current and additional information. To listen to an audio version of this In Brief, click the Audio button at the top left of these instructions.

WEB INFO

IN BRIEF

KEY TERMS

CHECKPOINT

TEACHING TODAY

EDUCATION ISSUES

INTEGRATION CORNER

SOFTWARE CORNER

IN THE LAB

LEARN IT ONLINE

✱ FEATURES...

Timeline 2004

Guide to WWW Sites

Buyer's Guide 2004

Professional Sites

State/Federal Sites

Interactive Labs

Search Tools

HOME

1. What Is Multimedia?

Multimedia is the combination of the following elements: text, color, graphics, animation, audio, and video. **Multimedia software** refers to any computer-based presentation or application software that uses multimedia elements. **Interactive multimedia** describes a multimedia application that accepts input from the user by means of a keyboard, voice, or a pointing device such as a mouse; and performs an action in response.

2. Media Elements

Text consists of characters that are used to create words, sentences, and paragraphs and is a fundamental element used in all multimedia applications. A **graphic** is a digital representation of nontext information such as a drawing, chart, or photograph. Displaying a series of still graphics creates an **animation**, which is a graphic that has the illusion of motion. **Audio** is any digitized music, speech, or other sound that is stored and produced by the computer. **Video** consists of photographic images that are played back at speeds of 15 to 30 frames per second and give the appearance of full motion in real-time.

3. Multimedia Applications

A **multimedia application** involves the use of multimedia technology for education, business, and entertainment. Businesses use multimedia, for example, in interactive advertisements and for job- and skill-training applications. Another important application of interactive multimedia is to create **simulations**, which are computer-based models of real-life situations. Multimedia applications include computer-based training, electronic books and references, how-to guides, and magazines. Multimedia also is used in entertainment, virtual reality, information kiosks, and on the Web.

4. Computer-Based Training

Computer-based training (CBT) is a tool by which individuals learn by using and completing exercises using instructional software on computers. Computer-based training is popular in business and industry to teach new skills or enhance the existing skills of employees. Computer-based training is effective especially for teaching software skills if the CBT is integrated with the software application, because it allows students to practice as they learn.

5. Electronic Books

An **electronic book**, or **e-book**, is a small, book-sized computer that allows users to read, save, highlight, bookmark, and add notes to online text. Electronic books have many of the elements of a regular book, including pages of text and graphics. Generally, you turn the pages of an electronic book by clicking icons. **How-to guides** are multimedia applications that include step-by-step instructions and interactive demonstrations to teach you practical new skills. A **multimedia magazine** is a digital version of a magazine, which is distributed on CD or via the World Wide Web.

6. Entertainment

Multimedia combines the media elements of television and interactivity, making it ideal for entertainment. Multimedia **computer games** use graphics, sound, and video to create a realistic and entertaining game situation. Many multimedia applications are used for **edutainment,** which is an experience meant to be both educational and entertaining. **Virtual reality (VR)** is the use of a computer to create an artificial environment that appears and feels like a real environment and allows a user to explore space and manipulate the setting. As computing power and the use of the Web

In Brief

WEB INFO

IN BRIEF

KEY TERMS

CHECKPOINT

TEACHING TODAY

EDUCATION ISSUES

INTEGRATION CORNER

SOFTWARE CORNER

IN THE LAB

LEARN IT ONLINE

✱FEATURES...

Timeline 2004

Guide to WWW Sites

Buyer's Guide 2004

Professional Sites

State/Federal Sites

Interactive Labs

Search Tools

HOME

increase, practical applications continue to emerge for education, business, and entertainment. An **information kiosk** is a computerized information or reference center that provides information in public locations.

7. World Wide Web

Multimedia applications also play an important role on the **World Wide Web,** which is the part of the Internet that supports multimedia. The Web uses many types of media to deliver information and enhance a user's Web experience. **Web-based training (WBT)** is an approach to computer-based training that uses the technologies of the Internet and the World Wide Web.

8. K-12 Educational Software Applications

Multimedia is important not only for business and entertainment, but also for education. An **educational software application** refers to computer software products used to support teaching and learning of subject-related content. Educational software applications are available in several different designs, forms, and curriculum levels. Educational applications include computer-assisted instruction, drill-and-practice software, educational games, tutorials, educational simulations, integrated learning systems, and Web-based education.

9. Drill-and-Practice, Games, and Tutorials

Drill-and-practice software first supplies factual information and then through repetitive exercises allows students to continue to work on the specific materials to remember the information. **Educational games** usually include a set of rules, and students can compete against other students or the game itself. Games can be an effective way to teach information through repetition and practice. A **tutorial** is a teaching program designed to help individuals learn to use a product or concepts.

10. Simulations and Integrated Learning Systems

An **educational computer simulation** is a computerized model of real life that represents a physical or simulated process. An **integrated learning system (ILS)** is a sophisticated software package usually developed by an established educational software corporation as a complete educational software solution in one package.

11. Web-Based Education

Many colleges and universities and some high schools offer Web-based or Web-enhanced courses. A **Web-based course** is a course that is taught mostly or completely on the Web, rather than in a traditional classroom. A **Web-enhanced course** is a course that uses the Web to enhance the content of a traditional classroom course.

12. Creating Multimedia Applications

Creating or developing multimedia applications involves producing various media elements, defining the elements' relationships to each other, and then sequencing them in an appropriate order. **Multimedia authoring software** allows an individual to create an interactive multimedia presentation that includes text, graphics, sound, animation, or video. Two of the more popular multimedia authoring tools used in K-12 schools are Microsoft PowerPoint and HyperStudio.

13. PowerPoint and HyperStudio

Microsoft **PowerPoint** allows teachers and students to create multimedia presentations that can incorporate text, graphics, animation, audio, video, links, and interactivity. **HyperStudio** is an easy-to-use multimedia authoring software program that allows the author to combine all of the multimedia elements described in this chapter into a series of interactive cards.

Key Terms

WEB INFO

IN BRIEF

KEY TERMS

CHECKPOINT

TEACHING TODAY

EDUCATION ISSUES

INTEGRATION CORNER

SOFTWARE CORNER

IN THE LAB

LEARN IT ONLINE

✳ FEATURES...

Timeline 2004

Guide to WWW Sites

Buyer's Guide 2004

Professional Sites

State/Federal Sites

Interactive Labs

Search Tools

HOME

Web Instructions: To display this page from the Web, start your browser and enter the URL, www.course.com/tdc3. Click Chapter 5 at the top of the Web page and then click Key Terms on the left sidebar. Scroll through the list of terms. Click a term to display its definition and a picture. Click Key Terms on the left to redisplay the Key Terms page. Click the TO WEB button for current and additional information about the term from the Web.

advanced learning system [5.24]
animation [5.06]
audio [5.06]
authoring tool [5.29]
Authorware [5.29]

branching [5.23]

ClearType [5.10]
clip [5.07]
clip art collection [5.04]
color scanner [5.28]
computer-assisted instruction (CAI) [5.21]
computer-based training (CBT) [5.09]
computer games [5.14]
courseware [5.09]
creativity applications [5.25]
critical-thinking applications [5.25]

data projector [5.31]
digital cameras [5.28]
Director [5.29]
distance education [5.17]
distance learning [5.17]
distributed learning [5.17]
drill-and-practice software [5.21]

early learning applications [5.26]
e-book [5.10]
educational computer simulation [5.23]

educational games [5.22]
educational software application [5.20]
edutainment [5.14]
electronic book [5.10]
electronic magazine [5.12]
electronic reference text [5.10]
electronic whiteboard [5.31]
ESL and foreign language applications [5.26]
e-zine [5.12]

graphic [5.04]
graphics [5.28]

how-to guides [5.12]
HyperStudio [5.30]

information kiosk [5.16]
instructor-led training [5.20]
integrated learning system (ILS) [5.23]
interactive multimedia [5.02]
interactive whiteboard [5.31]
interactivity [5.01]

language arts applications [5.26]
link [5.03]

math applications [5.27]
Moving Pictures Experts Group (MPEG) [5.08]
multimedia [5.02]
multimedia application [5.08]
multimedia authoring software [5.29]
multimedia magazine [5.12]

multimedia newspaper [5.12]
multimedia software [5.02]
Musical Instrument Digital Interface (MIDI) [5.07]

online course [5.18]
open learning system [5.24]

PowerPoint [5.30]
Project Gutenberg [5.10]

remediation [5.22]

science applications [5.27]
self-paced training [5.19]
SimCity [5.23]
simulations [5.09]
skills-reinforcement software [5.21]
SMART Board [5.31]
social studies software applications [5.28]

text [5.04]
ToolBook [5.29]
tutorial [5.22]

video [5.07]
video compression [5.07]
virtual reality (VR) [5.15]
visual learners [5.04]

Web-based course [5.18]
Web-based education [5.17]
Web-based training (WBT) [5.17]
Web-enhanced course [5.18]
Web-enhancing [5.19]

Checkpoint

Web Instructions: To display this page from the Web, start your browser and enter the URL, www.course.com/tdc3. Click Chapter 5 at the top of the Web page and then click Checkpoint on the left sidebar. Click a blank line for the answer. Click the links for current and additional information.

WEB INFO

IN BRIEF

KEY TERMS

CHECKPOINT

TEACHING TODAY

EDUCATION ISSUES

INTEGRATION CORNER

SOFTWARE CORNER

IN THE LAB

LEARN IT ONLINE

✱ FEATURES...

Timeline 2004

Guide to WWW Sites

Buyer's Guide 2004

Professional Sites

State/Federal Sites

Interactive Labs

Search Tools

HOME

1. Label the Figure

Instructions: Identify the multimedia devices.

1._____   2._____

3._____   4._____

2. Matching

Instructions: Match each term from the column on the left with the best description from the column on the right.

____ 1. text
____ 2. graphic
____ 3. animation
____ 4. audio
____ 5. video

a. a graphic that has the illusion of motion
b. photographic images played back at speeds of 15 to 30 frames per second to provide the appearance of motion in real-time
c. digitized music, speech, or other sounds stored and produced by a computer
d. characters used to create words, sentences, and paragraphs; a fundamental element in multimedia
e. digital representation of nontext information such as a drawing, chart, or photograph

3. Short Answer

Instructions: Write a brief answer to each of the following questions.

1. What is interactive multimedia software? Why is interactive multimedia software important for K-12 education? _____
2. Name four media components of multimedia software? Briefly describe each. _____
3. What are the differences between electronic reference books and how-to guides? Which one is used more often in education? Why? _____
4. What is virtual reality? How do teachers, students, and others use virtual reality? Is virtual reality available on the Web? _____
5. What is meant by educational software applications? Briefly describe four different categories of educational software applications. _____

Teaching Today

Web Instructions: To display this page from the Web, start your browser and enter the URL, www.course.com/tdc3. Click Chapter 5 at the top of the Web page and then click Teaching Today on the left sidebar. Click the links for current and additional information.

WEB INFO

IN BRIEF

KEY TERMS

CHECKPOINT

TEACHING TODAY

EDUCATION ISSUES

INTEGRATION CORNER

SOFTWARE CORNER

IN THE LAB

LEARN IT ONLINE

✱ FEATURES...

Timeline 2004

Guide to WWW Sites

Buyer's Guide 2004

Professional Sites

State/Federal Sites

Interactive Labs

Search Tools

HOME

1. **Many schools are using multimedia** applications and the Web to help students better understand the past or gain a greater appreciation of other cultures. For example, using a multimedia application called Oregon Trail, students learn about westward expansion by experiencing the hardships and making decisions similar to those facing nineteenth-century settlers. At the Web site for Educational Web Adventures, students can participate in adventures such as Tracking The Tiger Trade, in which they go undercover to Asia to explore the illegal trade of tiger parts, or Amazon Interactive, a project focusing on the people and geography of the Ecuadorian Amazon. Are these kinds of multimedia applications and Web adventures appropriate for all grade levels? How does their use compare with traditional approaches to instruction and learning? How do you think students feel about using these types of resources? How could you best use these types of resources in your classroom? What supplemental materials would you need?

2. **You think your Physical Education students** would learn more and be more motivated if you integrated multimedia into your curriculum. You have heard from other teachers that a wide variety of Health, Nutrition, and Physical Education software is available. Where might you locate a list of such multimedia software titles that meet the standards for the district and that can assist you in teaching your students? Where might you locate such a list on the Web? Do any of the lists you find provide other teachers' reviews of the software? Do any of these resources provide information about incorporating other technologies in the curriculum? In what other ways could you use multimedia to motivate your students to learn? What other actions might you take to ensure that you make an informed decision about choosing multimedia software that is most effective for you and your students?

3. **You have been teaching** your students about famous eighteenth- and nineteenth-century artists. As a final activity, you want to take your students on a field trip to an art museum. The nearest museum, however, is three hours away, so the trip requires bus transportation. Due to the cost of the proposed field trip, your principal has asked you to explore other possibilities. What other options do you have? Could you take your class on a virtual field trip to an art museum? How would you and your students feel about taking that type of field trip? What are some advantages of a virtual field trip? What are some disadvantages?

4. **You are teaching geography** to your class. For their final project, the students are to select an area they would like to visit and then prepare a multimedia presentation describing the country or region, its culture, major landmarks, and famous sites. To gather information, the students will use multimedia reference books and visit geography Web sites. Using the Web for your research, list five or six reference books and Web sites that you might suggest as resources. What other multimedia resources could your students use? How do multimedia resources support student learning?

Education Issues

Web Instructions: To display this page from the Web, start your browser and enter the URL, www.course.com/tdc3. Click Chapter 5 at the top of the Web page and then click Education Issues on the left sidebar. Click the links for current and additional information to help you respond to the Education Issues questions.

WEB INFO

IN BRIEF

KEY TERMS

CHECKPOINT

TEACHING TODAY

EDUCATION ISSUES

INTEGRATION CORNER

SOFTWARE CORNER

IN THE LAB

LEARN IT ONLINE

✴ FEATURES...

Timeline 2004

Guide to WWW Sites

Buyer's Guide 2004

Professional Sites

State/Federal Sites

Interactive Labs

Search Tools

HOME

1. Virtual Dissection

Most people remember dissecting a frog in their high school biology class — the odor of formaldehyde, the nervous laughter, and the unsuspecting classmate who finds a webbed foot in his lunch bag. For many students, conventional dissections are being replaced by virtual dissections using multimedia applications. Students use computers to view color graphics of a frog's anatomy and videos of biological systems, and to take interactive quizzes. Although these multimedia programs on CD and Web activities are supported by animal rights activists and squeamish students, many biol-

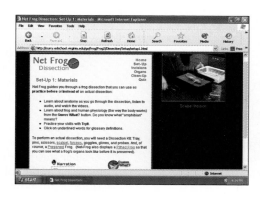

ogy teachers believe there is no substitute for genuine dissection. Should multimedia applications replace traditional dissection? Why or why not? Who should make the choice between virtual and traditional dissection? Why? On what basis should the choice be made?

2. Bringing the Past to the Present

A simulation on a popular multimedia application lets students assume the role of a prominent Civil War general in an actual battle. Students direct and position their army. Confrontations are accompanied by video of battle reenactments. Critics argue that the use of these kinds of multimedia applications lack the insight and detail of a traditional textbook. Supporters claim that, by being immersed in the battle, students gain a better understanding of the Civil War. What place do multimedia applications have in learning history? Why? What are the advantages and disadvantages of multimedia applications compared with traditional textbooks? In what historical studies, if any, would multimedia applications be particularly appropriate? Why?

3. Information Overload

The amount of information available to people is growing every day — as scientists uncover new facts; physicians develop improved treatments; technology firms design unprecedented products; and journalists record history in the making. Technologies such as multimedia CDs, DVDs, and multimedia on the World Wide Web make this vast — some say overwhelming — amount of information easily available to teachers and students. As a result of this potential information overload, experts worry that students might be spending more time sifting through information than actually applying and utilizing information. What do you think? Can there ever be too much information? Why or why not? How could too much information adversely affect teachers and students? What can be done about information overload? How can teachers help students avoid this?

4. Multimedia Realism — Dealing with Tragedy

As a teacher, you are faced with helping your students deal with various types of issues. Most issues are easy to deal with and you know where to go to get advice and help. Helping students cope with tragedy, disaster, and loss is probably the most difficult. On September 11, 2001, the tragic events that unfolded in New York, Washington, D.C., and Pennsylvania affected parents, children, friends, fellow Americans, and people around the world. Many agencies and Web sites exist that can provide you with information to help your students deal with this and other types of tragedies. Should you talk to your students about these issues? Where do you locate resources? How do people learn from a tragedy such as this one? Do you turn this into a teachable moment? Or do you ignore the issue? What precautions should you take to ensure that the information you provide is age appropriate?

Integration Corner

WEB INFO

IN BRIEF

KEY TERMS

CHECKPOINT

TEACHING TODAY

EDUCATION ISSUES

INTEGRATION CORNER

SOFTWARE CORNER

IN THE LAB

LEARN IT ONLINE

✱ FEATURES...

Timeline 2004

Guide to WWW Sites

Buyer's Guide 2004

Professional Sites

State/Federal Sites

Interactive Labs

Search Tools

HOME

Web Instructions: To display this page from the Web, start your browser and enter the URL, www.course.com/tdc3. Click Chapter 5 at the top of the Web page and then click Integration Corner on the left sidebar. Click any Corner and then click the various links for extensive and curriculum-specific information.

Integration Corner is designed for teachers and other educators who are looking for innovative ways to integrate technology into their content-specific curriculum. Integration Corner not only provides great Web sites with current information, but also shows what other educators are doing in the field of educational technology. These Corners are designed for all educators regardless of their area of interest. Review information and Web sites outside of your teaching area because many great integration ideas in one area easily can be modified for use in other curricular areas.

Teachers and administrators will find other colleagues in their areas with whom to connect and share the successes and hurdles of integrating technology in a classroom or an entire school system. Consider this your one stop for integration ideas and resources. Links to educational Web sites are organized in the following 12 Corners, and different Web resources are available for each chapter. Figure 5-56 shows examples of the Web resources provided in the Chapter 5 Special Education Corner.

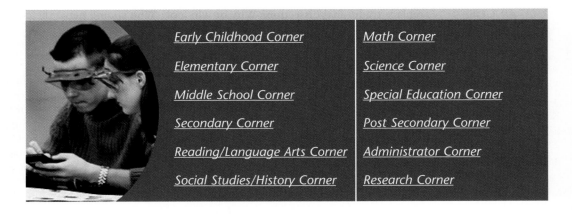

Early Childhood Corner   Math Corner

Elementary Corner   Science Corner

Middle School Corner   Special Education Corner

Secondary Corner   Post Secondary Corner

Reading/Language Arts Corner   Administrator Corner

Social Studies/History Corner   Research Corner

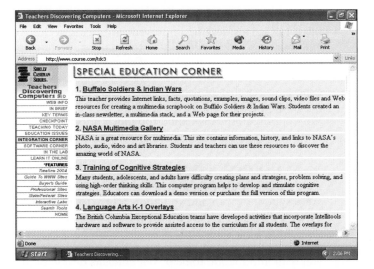

Figure 5-56 Examples of the Web resources provided in the Chapter 5 Special Education Corner.

Software Corner

WEB INFO

IN BRIEF

KEY TERMS

CHECKPOINT

TEACHING TODAY

EDUCATION ISSUES

INTEGRATION CORNER

SOFTWARE CORNER

IN THE LAB

LEARN IT ONLINE

✱ FEATURES...

Timeline 2004

Guide to WWW Sites

Buyer's Guide 2004

Professional Sites

State/Federal Sites

Interactive Labs

Search Tools

HOME

Web Instructions: To display this page from the Web, start your browser and enter the URL, www.course.com/tdc3. Click Chapter 5 at the top of the Web page and then click Software Corner on the left sidebar. Click the links for additional information and instructions on how to download or receive an evaluation copy.

1. HyperStudio is the leading K-12 hypermedia authoring software program that allows students to create multimedia projects and presentations while providing an opportunity for curriculum integration. If you have wanted to use multimedia with your students, HyperStudio is the perfect software for you and your students. HyperStudio incorporates the use of text, sound, graphics, animation, movies, and more to create interactive student projects. The Internet, digital cameras, CDs, DVDs, and other technologies also can be used with HyperStudio to create incredible projects. Teachers can use HyperStudio as an instructional tool through the presentation of lessons, as well as having students create their own presentations and small-group projects. Knowledge Adventure, the distributor of HyperStudio, provides an extensive Web site full of great resources!

2. What if you could have 180 top software titles from leading software publishers such as Tom Snyder Productions, Knowledge Adventure, Davidson & Associates, and Scholastic Software at your fingertips with more than 8,500 activities to support your curriculum? That might be an unbelievable undertaking, but what if you also had a customized system that could set the appropriate learning paths for your students? ClassWorks Gold is an open learning system that manages your favorite software titles and integrates them into the K-8 math and language arts curriculum with a cross-curricular approach. ClassWorks is a new approach to learning that lets teachers customize the individual student's learning paths. ClassWorks has an elaborate assessment system for reporting all student data. ClassWorks provides a great way to learn!

3. Research confirms that the full integration of multimedia math programs can improve retention of math concepts and thus math scores. Developed by educators, the Math Blaster Series from Knowledge Adventure offers interactive multimedia programs for almost all age levels from pre-kindergarten to high school. Math Blaster helps students master math concepts and prepare for state and national testing. Key features include the SmartPoints reward system that motivates and helps students to achieve their personal best. Key skills covered include adding and subtracting, multiplying, understanding and using fractions, reading and understanding number patterns, reading and analyzing charts, sorting complex sets, solving problems, and enhancing logic skills.

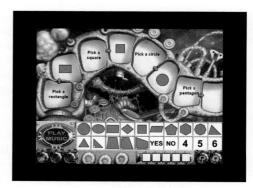

Math Blaster Ages 7-9

4. WebCT, the world's leading provider of integrated e-learning systems for higher education, includes one of the world's top course management systems. WebCT is a powerful and comprehensive courseware tool used by colleges and K-12 institutions to offer online courses, professional development, and alternative types of training solutions. WebCT automates many tasks including scoring true/false, multiple choice, and short answer exams and tracking student progress and activity. Teachers and students can interact and collaborate online using WebCT's bulletin board and internal e-mail system. Students also may upload their own Web pages into a special area within a course. WebCT provides teachers and school districts with a secure and efficient way of offering online courses to students.

In the Lab

WEB INFO

IN BRIEF

KEY TERMS

CHECKPOINT

TEACHING TODAY

EDUCATION ISSUES

INTEGRATION CORNER

SOFTWARE CORNER

IN THE LAB

LEARN IT ONLINE

✱ FEATURES...

Timeline 2004

Guide to WWW Sites

Buyer's Guide 2004

Professional Sites

State/Federal Sites

Interactive Labs

Search Tools

HOME

Web Instructions: To display this page from the Web, start your browser and enter the URL, www.course.com/tdc3. Click Chapter 5 at the top of the Web page and then click In The Lab on the left sidebar. Click the links for tutorials, productivity ideas, integration examples and ideas, and more.

PRODUCTIVITY IN THE CLASSROOM

Introduction: Chapter 5 introduces multimedia software applications and the positive impact they have on learning. Most schools today have a variety of multimedia applications, including Microsoft PowerPoint. Both teachers and students can use PowerPoint to create effective and interesting presentations. Students also can use PowerPoint as an authoring tool to create original stories and book reports. PowerPoint is an excellent tool for creating excitement, interest, and motivation in learning.

After working through these In the Lab activities, return to this section to learn new skills, or to improve your current skills by clicking the following links: Learning Microsoft PowerPoint; PowerPoint FAQ; PowerPoint Tips for Windows and Mac OS.

1 Back to School Open House

Problem: To prepare for Parent Night at your school's Open House, your principal has asked all of the teachers at your school to create a short multimedia presentation outlining classroom rules, homework policies, and necessary student supplies specific to your class. You decide to create your presentation in Microsoft PowerPoint. You create the presentation shown in Figure 5-57. (*Hint:* Use Help to understand the steps better.) If you do not have a suggested template or font, use any appropriate template or font.

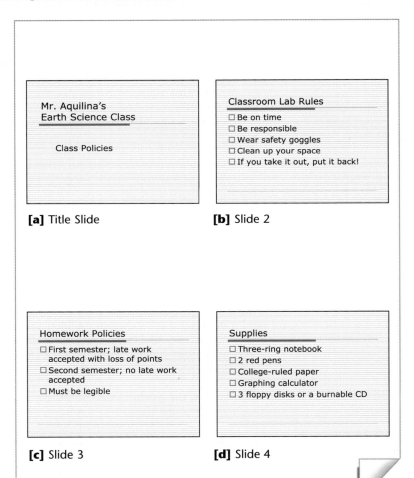

[a] Title Slide

[b] Slide 2

[c] Slide 3

[d] Slide 4

Figure 5-57

In the Lab

Instructions: Perform the following tasks.

1. Create a new presentation using the Profile design template. If you do not have the suggested design template, use any appropriate design.
2. Create the title slide shown in Figure 5-57a using your name in place of Mr. Aquilina and the subject you teach, or intend to teach, in place of Earth Science. Increase the font size of the paragraph, Class Policies, to 36-point.
3. Create the three bulleted list slides shown in Figures 5-57b through 5-57d, personalizing the lists to your specific subject area or grade level.
4. Click the Spelling button on the Standard toolbar. Correct any errors.
5. Save the presentation on a floppy disk using an appropriate file name.
6. Print the presentation.
7. Follow the directions from your instructor for handing in this assignment.

2 Adding Clip Art and Animation Effects to a Presentation

Problem: You decide to enhance your open house presentation from In the Lab 1 by adding clip art and slide transitions as shown in Figure 5-58. You also decide to change to the Ocean design template. (*Hint:* Use Help to understand the steps better.) Use any appropriate clip art image.

Instructions: Use the presentation created in In the Lab 1 for this assignment. Perform the following tasks.

1. Open the Parent Night Open House presentation.
2. Change the design template to the Ocean design template.
3. Insert appropriate clip art on three slides.
4. Resize the clip art as necessary. Resize and relocate the text boxes as needed.
5. Apply the Dissolve slide transition effect to Slides 2, 3, and 4.
6. Save the presentation on a floppy disk.

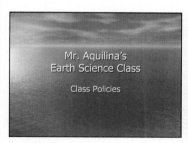

[a] Title Slide

[b] Slide 2

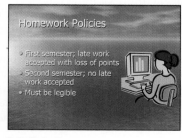

[c] Slide 3

[d] Slide 4

Figure 5-58

WEB INFO

IN BRIEF

KEY TERMS

CHECKPOINT

TEACHING TODAY

EDUCATION ISSUES

INTEGRATION CORNER

SOFTWARE CORNER

IN THE LAB

LEARN IT ONLINE

✱ FEATURES...

Timeline 2004

Guide to WWW Sites

Buyer's Guide 2004

Professional Sites

State/Federal Sites

Interactive Labs

Search Tools

HOME

In the Lab

WEB INFO

IN BRIEF

KEY TERMS

CHECKPOINT

TEACHING TODAY

EDUCATION ISSUES

INTEGRATION CORNER

SOFTWARE CORNER

IN THE LAB

LEARN IT ONLINE

✱ FEATURES...

Timeline 2004

Guide to WWW Sites

Buyer's Guide 2004

Professional Sites

State/Federal Sites

Interactive Labs

Search Tools

HOME

7. Print the presentation as a handout with four slides per page.
8. Follow directions from your instructor for handing in the assignment.

3 Classroom Presentation

Problem: On the first day of school, you want to welcome your students to class and have them participate in an introduction activity. You decide to create a PowerPoint presentation to introduce yourself and provide examples of the type of information they might want to share in the activity.

Instructions: Create a PowerPoint presentation similar to the presentation illustrated in Figure 5-58 on the previous page. Use an appropriate template, attractive font style, size, and clip art images. Include the current date, your name, and e-mail address on the title slide. After you have created the presentation, save the presentation on a floppy disk using an appropriate file name. Print the presentation and then follow your instructor's directions for handing in the assignment.

INTEGRATION IN THE CLASSROOM

1 Your fourth grade students are learning about the life cycle of a butterfly. The students will work in groups to create a research project about one species of butterfly. They will start by gathering the following information: species scientific name; common name; range; four interesting facts; stages in the life cycle; eating habits and favorite flowers or plants; one predator and one defense against predators. Students also will locate at least two images of the butterfly. Then they will create a multimedia presentation using PowerPoint that contains a title slide and at least four additional slides. Students will use bulleted lists to present their findings. They also will include at least two images of their butterfly in their presentation, as well as other suitable clip art. Select a species of butterfly and create a sample presentation. Enter the appropriate information to demonstrate the project for the students. Include the name of the butterfly you select, your name, and the current date on your title slide.

2 Your middle school geography class is studying different countries. For a culminating project, each student selects a country and researches its economy, land formations, temperature and climate, population, and places of interest or historic significance. The students then create PowerPoint presentations to share their research with the class. The presentation should consist of a title slide and at least three other slides containing bulleted lists and images. Students need to include sound, transitions, graphic images, and Internet hypertext links in their presentations. The last slide of each presentation should list references. Prepare a PowerPoint presentation to present as an example for your students. Create a title slide and at least three additional slides with bulleted lists, graphic images, sounds, and transitions. Include your name, the current date, and the name of the country on the title slide. Include a list of references on the last slide.

3 William Shakespeare continues to influence modern theater. You want your high school drama students to understand the contributions of the past to theater and drama today. Students will be divided into four groups. Each group will research one of the following topics: the style and construction of the Globe Theater; forms of entertainment; customs of the theater; and costuming during the time of Shakespeare. Groups will create PowerPoint presentations to present their findings. The presentation should consist of a title slide, slides with bulleted lists, and images. Students also may include Internet hypertext links. Prepare a presentation to present to the students as an example. Create a title slide and at least three additional slides with bulleted lists and graphic images. Include your name, the current date, and the topic on the title slide.

Learn It Online

Web Instructions: To display this page from the Web, start your browser and enter the URL, www.course.com/tdc3. Click Chapter 5 at the top of the Web page and then click Learn It Online on the left sidebar. Click the buttons to display the exercise or the Interactive Lab.

WEB INFO

IN BRIEF

KEY TERMS

CHECKPOINT

TEACHING TODAY

EDUCATION ISSUES

INTEGRATION CORNER

SOFTWARE CORNER

IN THE LAB

LEARN IT ONLINE

✱ FEATURES...

Timeline 2004

Guide to WWW Sites

Buyer's Guide 2004

Professional Sites

State/Federal Sites

Interactive Labs

Search Tools

HOME

1. Shelly Cashman Series Understanding Multimedia

Click the button to the left to start and use the Shelly Cashman Series Understanding Multimedia Lab.

2. Shelly Cashman Series Scanning Documents

Click the button to the left to start and use the Shelly Cashman Series Scanning Documents Lab.

3. Virtual Reality on the Web

Web-based virtual reality applications have the potential to impact K-12 education positively. To learn more about virtual reality, click the button to the left, and complete the exercise.

4. Searching for Sound Files

Sound clips also can enhance multimedia presentations. An abundance of free sound clips are available on the Web. To learn how to find and download free sound clips from the Web, click the button to the left.

5. Multimedia on the Web

The World Wide Web offers high-quality multimedia products for teachers and students. To learn more about these products and see the various media elements used in a sophisticated Web site, click the button to the left.

6. Who Wants To Be a Computer Genius?

Click the button to the left to find out if you are a computer genius. Directions on how to play the game will display. When you are ready to play, click the PLAY button. Submit your score to your instructor.

7. Crossword Puzzle Challenge

Click the button to the left to complete the puzzle to reinforce skills you learned in this chapter. Directions on how to play the game will be displayed. When you are ready to play, click the SUBMIT button. Submit the completed puzzle to your instructor.

8. Practice Test

Click the button to the left and answer each question. When completed, enter your name and click the Grade Test button to submit the quiz for grading. Make a note of any missed questions. If required, print a copy to submit to your instructor.

Digital Imaging and Video Technology

Everywhere you look, people are capturing moments they want to remember. They take pictures or make movies of their vacations, birthday parties, activities, accomplishments, sporting events, weddings, and more. Because of the popularity of digital cameras and digital video cameras, increasingly more people desire to capture their memories digitally, instead of on film. With digital technology, picture takers have the ability to modify and share the digital images and videos they create. When you use special hardware and/or software, you can copy, manipulate, print, and distribute digital images and videos using your personal computer and the Internet. Amateurs can create professional quality results by using more sophisticated hardware and software.

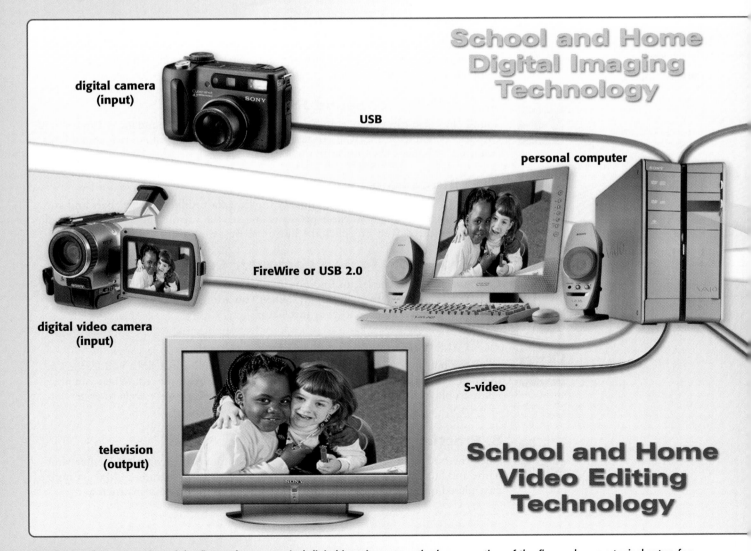

School and Home Digital Imaging Technology

digital camera (input)

USB

personal computer

digital video camera (input)

FireWire or USB 2.0

S-video

television (output)

School and Home Video Editing Technology

FIGURE 1   The top portion of the figure shows a typical digital imaging setup; the lower portion of the figure shows a typical setup for editing video.

Digital photography and recordings deliver significant benefits over film-based photography and movie making. With digital cameras, no developing is needed. Instead, the images reside on storage media such as a hard disk, DVD, or flash memory card. Unlike film, storage media can be reused, which reduces costs, saves time, and provides immediate results. Digital technology allows greater control over the creative process, both while taking pictures and video and in the editing process. You can check results immediately after capturing a picture or video to determine whether it meets your expectations. If you are dissatisfied with a picture or video, you can erase it and recapture it again and again.

As shown in the top portion of Figure 1, a digital camera functions as an input device when it transmits pictures through a cable to a personal computer via a USB port or FireWire port. Using a digital camera in this way allows you to edit the pictures, save them on storage media, and print them on a photographic-quality printer via a parallel port or USB port.

The lower portion of Figure 1 illustrates how you or your students might use a digital video camera with a personal computer. The process typically is the same for most digital video cameras. You capture the images or video with the video camera. Next, you connect the video camera to your personal computer using a FireWire or USB 2.0 port, or you place the storage media used on the camera in the computer. The video then is copied or downloaded to the computer's hard disk. Then, you can edit the video using video editing software. If desired, you can preview the video on a television during the editing process. Finally, you save the finished result to the desired media, such as a VHS tape or DVD+RW, or perhaps e-mail the edited video. In this example, a VCR and a DVD player also can be used to input video from a VHS tape or a DVD.

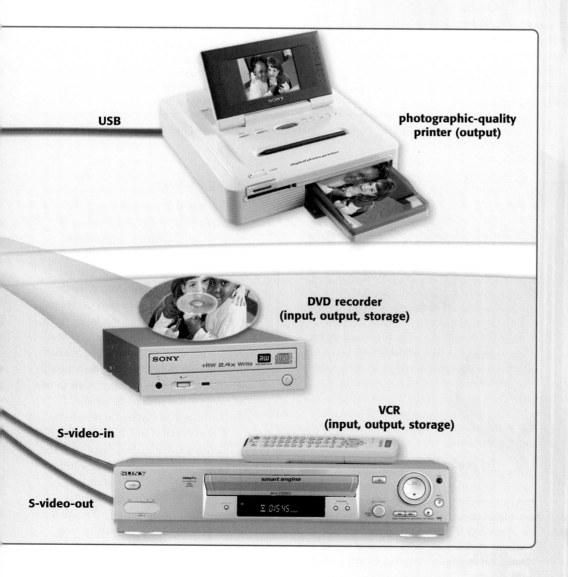

USB

photographic-quality printer (output)

DVD recorder (input, output, storage)

VCR (input, output, storage)

S-video-in

S-video-out

DIGITAL IMAGING TECHNOLOGY

Digital imaging technology involves capturing and manipulating still photographic images in an electronic format. The following sections outline the process of using digital imaging technology.

Selecting a Digital Camera

A **digital camera** is a type of camera that stores photographed images electronically instead of on traditional film. Digital cameras are divided into three categories (Figure 2) based mainly on image resolution, features, and of course, price. The image resolution is measured in pixels (short for picture element). The image quality increases with the number of pixels. The image resolution usually is measured in **megapixels** (million of pixels), often abbreviated as **MP**. Features of digital cameras include red-eye reduction, zoom, autofocus, flash, self-timer, and manual mode for fine-tuning settings. Figure 3 summarizes the three categories of digital cameras.

TYPES OF DIGITAL CAMERAS

Type	Maximum Resolution	Comment	Price
Low-end point and shoot	Less than 2 MP	Fully automatic; fits in your pocket; usually limited to 4-by-6-inch printed output; ideal for Web pages, e-mail attachments, and newsletters	Less than $200
High-end point and shoot	Greater than 2 MP and less than 5 MP	Includes more advanced features that allow for creative control of the camera's settings; makes up to 8-by-10-inch printed pictures; capable of taking pictures at lower resolutions	$200 to $1,000
Professional	Greater than 5 MP	Based on 35mm and APS SLR cameras; includes three image sensors for capturing great color and resolution; has much greater control over exposure and lenses	$1,000 and up

FIGURE 3   Digital cameras often are categorized by image resolution, features, and price.

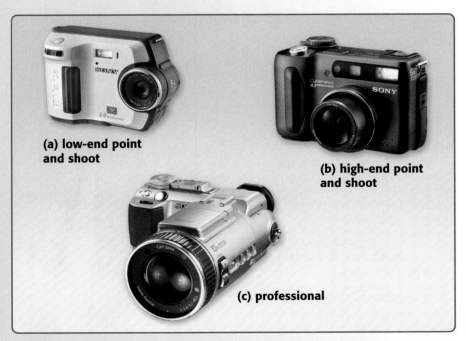

(a) low-end point and shoot

(b) high-end point and shoot

(c) professional

FIGURE 2   The low-end point and shoot digital camera (a) requires no adjustments before shooting. The high-end point and shoot digital camera (b) offers improved quality and features that allow you to make manual adjustments before shooting. The professional digital camera (c) offers better color and resolution and greater control over exposure and lenses.

Taking Pictures

Digital cameras provide you with several options that are set before a picture is taken. Three of the more important options are the resolution, compression, and image file format in which the camera should save the picture. While a camera may allow for a very high resolution for a large print, you may choose to take a picture at a lower resolution if the image does not require great detail or must be a small size. For example, you may want to use the image on a Web page where smaller image file sizes are beneficial.

Compression results in smaller image file sizes. Figure 4 illustrates the image file sizes for varying resolutions and compressions under standard photographing conditions using a 4 megapixel digital camera. Figure 4 also shows the average picture size for a given resolution. The camera may take more time to save an image at lower compression, resulting in a longer delay before the camera is ready to take another picture. A higher compression, however, may result in loss of some image quality. If a camera has a 16 MB flash memory card, you can determine the number of pictures the card can hold by dividing 16 MB by the file size. Flash memory cards are available in sizes from 16 MB to 1 GB.

IMAGE FILE SIZE WITH A 4 MEGAPIXEL DIGITAL CAMERA

Resolution in Pixels	COMPRESSION			Picture Size in Inches
	Low	Medium	High	
2272 x 1704	2 MB	1.1 MB	556 KB	11 by 17
1600 x 1200	1 MB	558 KB	278 KB	8 by 10
1024 x 768	570 KB	320 KB	170 KB	4 by 6
640 x 480	249 KB	150 KB	84 KB	3 by 5

FIGURE 4 Image file sizes for varying resolutions and compressions under standard shooting conditions using a 4 megapixel digital camera.

Most digital cameras also allow you to choose an image file format. Two popular file formats are TIFF and JPEG. The TIFF file format saves the image uncompressed. All of the image detail is captured and stored, but the file sizes can be large. The JPEG file format is compressed. The resolution of the image may be the same as a TIFF file, but some detail may be lost in the image.

Finally, before you take the photograph, you should choose the type of media on which to store the resulting image file. Some cameras allow for a choice of locations, such as a CompactFlash card or Memory Stick, while others allow for only one type of storage media. One major advantage of a digital camera is that you easily can erase pictures from its media, freeing up space for new pictures.

Transfering and Managing Image Files

The method of transferring images from the camera to the personal computer differs greatly depending on the capabilities of both. Digital cameras use a variety of storage media (Figure 5). If your camera uses a flash memory card such as a CompactFlash, SmartMedia, Secure Digital (SD), or Memory Stick, then you can remove the media from the camera and place it in a slot on the personal computer or in a device connected to the personal computer for reading the cards (Figure 6). Your camera also may connect to the personal computer using a USB, USB 2.0, or FireWire port. When you insert the memory card or connect the camera, software on the personal computer guides you through the

process of transferring the images to the hard disk. Some operating systems and software recognize a memory card or camera as though it is another hard disk on the computer. This feature allows you to access the files, navigate them, and then copy, delete, or rename the files while the media is still in the camera.

Microdrive

SD Card

Memory Stick

FIGURE 5 Microdrives, SD Cards, and Memory Sticks are popular storage devices for digital cameras.

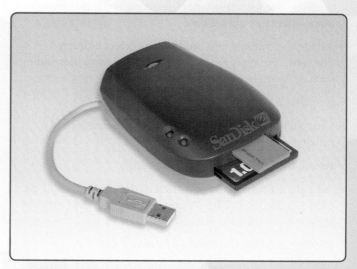

FIGURE 6 Using a USB or FireWire connection, you can add a card reader to your personal computer.

After you transfer the files to the hard disk on your personal computer, you should organize the files by sorting them or renaming them so that information, such as the subject, date, time, and purpose, is saved along with the image. Finally, before altering the images digitally or using the images for other purposes, you should back up the images to another location, such as a CD or DVD, so the original image is recoverable.

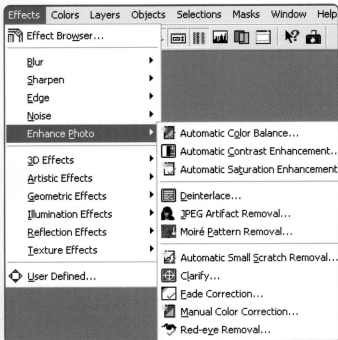

FIGURE 7   The ability to use effects separates digital photography from film photography.

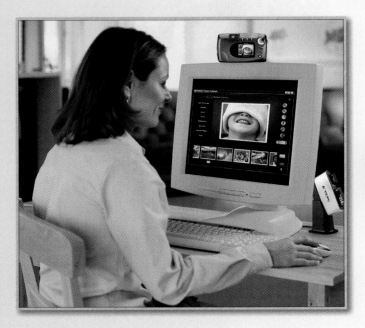

Editing Images

Image editing software allows you to edit digital images. The following list summarizes the more common image enhancements or alterations:

- Adjust the contrast and brightness; correct lighting problems; or help give the photograph a particular feeling, such as warm or stark

- Remove red-eye

- Crop an image to remove unnecessary elements and resize it

- Rotate the image to change its orientation

- Add elements to the image, such as descriptive text, a date, a logo, or decorative items; create collages or add missing elements

- Replace individual colors with a new color

- Add special effects, such as texture or motion blurring to enhance the image

Figure 7 shows some of the effects available in Jasc's Paint Shop Pro on the Enhance Photo submenu.

Printing Images

After an image is digitally altered, it is ready to be printed. You can print images on a personal color printer, or send them to a professional service that specializes in digital photo printing.

When printing the images yourself, make sure that the resolution used to create the image was high enough for the size of the print you want to create. For example, if the camera used a resolution of 640 ◊ 480 pixels, then the ideal print size is a wallet size. If you print such an image at a size of 8-by-10 inches, then the image will appear **pixilated**, or blurry. Use high-quality photo paper for the best results. A photo printer gives the best results when printing digital photography.

Many services print digital images, either over the Internet or through traditional photo developing locations and kiosks (Figure 8), such as those found in drug stores or shopping marts. Some services allow you to e-mail or upload the files to the service, specify the size, quality, and quantity of print, and then they send the prints to you via the postal service. Other services allow you to drop off flash memory cards, CDs, or floppy disks at a photo shop and allow you to pick up the prints, just as you do with traditional photo developing shops.

Distributing Images Electronically

Rather than printing images, you often need to use the images electronically. Depending on the electronic use of the image, the image may require additional processing. If you plan to use the images on a Web site or want to e-mail a photo, you probably want to use a lower-resolution image. Image editing software allows you to lower the resolution of the image, resulting in a smaller file size. You also should use standard file formats when distributing an electronic photo. The JPEG format is viewable using most personal computers or Web browsers.

You can store very high resolution photos on a DVD or a CD. **DVD and CD mastering software** (Figure 9) allows you to create slide show presentations on a recordable DVD or CD that can play in many home DVD players or personal computer DVD drives.

Finally, you should back up and store images that you distribute electronically with the same care as you store your traditional film negatives.

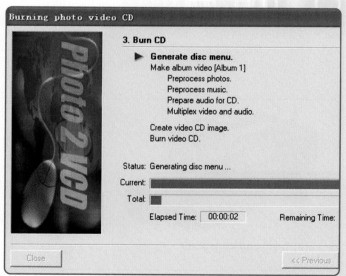

FIGURE 8 A Kodak PictureMaker kiosk allows you to print digital images in high resolution on photo paper.

FIGURE 9 Photo2VCD and similar software applications allow you to create your own photo slide shows on DVD or CD.

DIGITAL VIDEO TECHNOLOGY

Digital video technology allows you and your students to input, edit, manage, publish, and share your videos using a personal computer. With digital video technology, you can transform home videos into Hollywood-style movies by enhancing the videos with scrolling titles and transitions, cutting out or adding scenes, and adding background music and voice-over narration. The following sections outline the process of using digital video technology.

Selecting a Video Camera

Video cameras record in either analog or digital format. **Analog formats** include 8mm, Hi8, VHS, VHS-C, and Super VHS-C. The latter three formats use the types of tapes similar to those used in a standard VCR. **Digital formats** include Mini-DV, MICROMV, Digital8, and DVD. Consumer digital video cameras are by far the most popular type among consumers. They fall into three general categories: high-end consumer, consumer, and webcasting and monitoring (Figure 10). Digital video cameras provide more features than analog video cameras, such as a higher level of zoom, better sound, or more control over color and lighting.

Recording a Video

Video cameras are easier to use than digital cameras. Video cameras, for example, do not require you to set the resolution, compression, or file format before recording. Most video cameras do, however, provide you with a choice of recording programs sometimes called automatic settings. Each recording program includes a different combination of camera settings, so you can adjust the exposure and other functions to match the recording environment. Usually, several different programs are available, such as point and shoot, point and shoot with manual adjustment, sports, portrait, spot lit scenes, and low light. You also have the ability to select special digital effects, such as fade, wipe, and black and white. If you are shooting outside on a windy day, then you can enable the wind screen to prevent wind noise. If you are shooting home videos, then the point-and-shoot recording program is sufficient.

Transfering and Managing Videos

After recording the video, the next step is to transfer the video to your personal computer. Most video cameras connect directly to a USB 2.0 or FireWire port on your personal computer (Figure 11). Transferring video with a digital camera is easy because the video already is in a digital format that the computer can understand.

An analog camcorder or VCR requires additional hardware to convert the analog signals into a digital counterpart before the video can be manipulated on a personal computer. The additional hardware includes a special video capture card using a standard RCA video cable or an S-video cable (Figure 12). **S-video** cables provide greater quality. When you use video capture hardware with an analog video, be sure to close all open programs on your computer because capturing video requires a great deal of processing power.

(a) high-end consumer

(b) consumer

(c) webcasting and monitoring

FIGURE 10   The high-end consumer digital video camera (a) can produce professional-grade results. The consumer digital video camera (b) produces amateur-grade results. The webcasting and monitoring digital video camera (c) is appropriate for webcasting and security monitoring.

When transferring video, plan to use approximately 15 to 30 gigabytes of hard disk storage space per hour of digital video. A typical video project requires about four times the amount of raw footage as the final product. Therefore, at the high end, a video that lasts an hour may require up to 120 gigabytes of storage for the raw footage, editing process, and final video. This storage requirement can vary depending on the software you use to copy the video from the video camera to the hard disk and the format you select to save the video. For example, Microsoft claims that the latest version of its Windows Movie Maker can save 15 hours of video in 10 gigabytes when creating video for playback on a computer, but saves only 1 hour of video in 10 gigabytes when creating video for playback on a DVD or VCR. Macintosh users have made more than one million movies using iMovie. You can download the latest version of iMovie from Apple.

FIGURE 11 A digital video camera is connected to the personal computer via a FireWire or USB 2.0 port and the video. No additional hardware is needed.

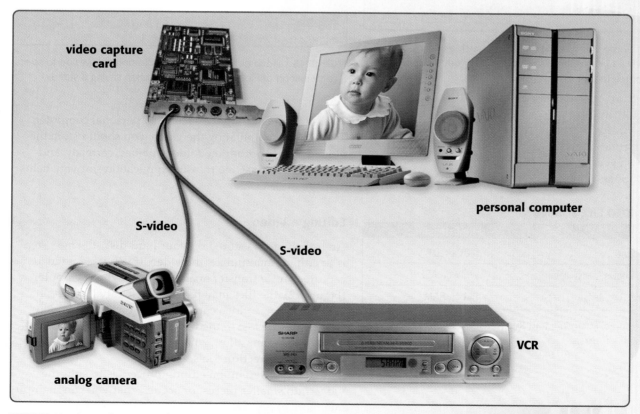

FIGURE 12 An analog camcorder or VCR is connected to the personal computer via an S-video port on a video capture card.

The video transfer requires application software on the personal computer. Windows XP includes the Windows Movie Maker software (Figure 13) that allows you to transfer the video from your video camera. Depending on the length of video and the type of connection used, the video may take a long time to download. Make certain that no other programs are running on your personal computer while transferring the video.

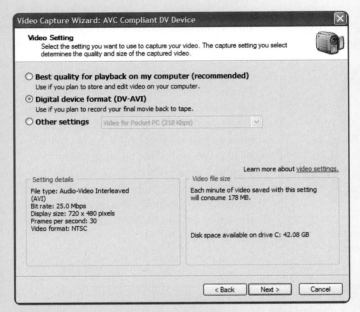

FIGURE 13 Some video editing software, such as Microsoft Windows Movie Maker, allows you to transfer your video from any video source to a hard disk.

When transferring video, the software may allow you to choose a file format and a codec to store the video. A video **file format** holds the video information in a manner specified by a vendor, such as Apple or Microsoft. Some of the more popular file formats are listed in Figure 14.

POPULAR VIDEO FILE FORMATS

File Format	File Extensions
Apple QuickTime	.MOV or .QT
Microsoft Windows Media Video	.WMV or .ASF
RealNetworks RealMedia	.RM or .RAM

FIGURE 14 Apple, Microsoft, and RealNetworks offer the more popular video file formats.

File formats support codecs to encode the audio and video into the file formats. A particular file format may be able to store audio and video in a number of different codecs. A **codec** specifies how the audio and video is compressed and stored within the file. Figure 15 shows some options available for specifying a file format and codec in the Microsoft Windows Movie Maker. The file format and codec you choose often is based on what you plan to do with the movie. For example, if you plan to stream video over the Web using RealNetworks software, the best choice for the file format is the RealMedia format, which uses the RealVideo codec.

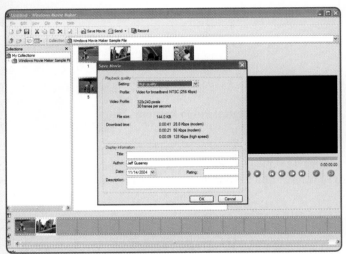

FIGURE 15 Video editing software applications allow you to specify a combination of file format and codec when saving a video.

After transferring the video to a personal computer, and before manipulating the video, you should store the video files in appropriate folders, named correctly, and backed up. Most video transfer application software helps manage these tasks.

Editing a Video

After the video is stored on your hard disk, the next step is to edit, or manipulate, the video. If you used a video capture card to transfer analog video to your computer (Figure 12), the files may require extra initial processing. When you use a video capture card, some of the video frames may be lost in the transfer process. Some video editing programs allow you to fix this problem with **frame rate correction** tools.

The first step in the editing process is to split the video into smaller pieces, or **scenes**, that you can manipulate more easily. This process is called **splitting**. Most video software automatically splits the video into scenes, thus saving you the time. After splitting, you should cut out unwanted scenes or portions of scenes. This process is called **pruning**.

After you create the scenes you want to use in your final production, you edit each individual scene. You can change the size of, or crop, scenes. That is, you may want to cut out the irrelevant top or side of a scene. You also can resize the scene. For example, you may be creating a video that will display in a Web browser. Making a smaller video, such as 320 x 200 pixels instead of 640 x 480 pixels, results in a smaller file that transmits faster over the Internet.

If video has been recorded over a long period, using different cameras or under different lighting conditions, the video may need color correction. **Color correction tools** (Figure 16) analyze your video and match brightness, colors, and other attributes of video clips to create a smooth look to the video.

FIGURE 16 Color correction tools in video editing software allow a great deal of control over the mood of your video creation.

You can add logos, special effects, or titles to scenes. You can place a school or personal logo in a video to identify yourself or the school producing the video. Logos often are added on the lower-right corner of a video and remain for the duration of the video. Special effects include warping, changing from color to black-and-white, morphing, or zoom motion. **Morphing** is a special effect in which one video image is transformed into another image over the course of several frames of video, creating the illusion of metamorphosis. You usually add titles at the beginning and end of a video to give the video context. A training video may have titles throughout the video to label a particular scene, or each scene may begin with a title.

The next step in editing a video is to add audio effects, including voice-over narration and background music. Many video editing programs allow you to add additional tracks, or layers, of sound to a video in addition to the sound that was recorded on the video camera. You also can add special audio effects.

The final step in editing a video is to combine the scenes into a complete video (Figure 17). This process involves ordering scenes and adding transition effects between scenes (Figure 18). Video editing software allows you to combine scenes and separate each scene with a transition. **Transitions** include fading, wiping, blurry, bursts, ruptures, erosions, and more.

Distributing the Video

After editing the video, the final step is to distribute it or save it on a desired media. You can save video in a variety of formats. Using special hardware, you can save the video on standard video tape. A **digital-to-analog converter** is necessary to allow your personal computer to transmit video to a VCR. A digital-to-analog converter may be an external device that connects to both the computer and the input device, or may be a video capture card inside the computer.

FIGURE 17   Scenes, shown on the right, are combined into a sequence on the bottom of the screen.

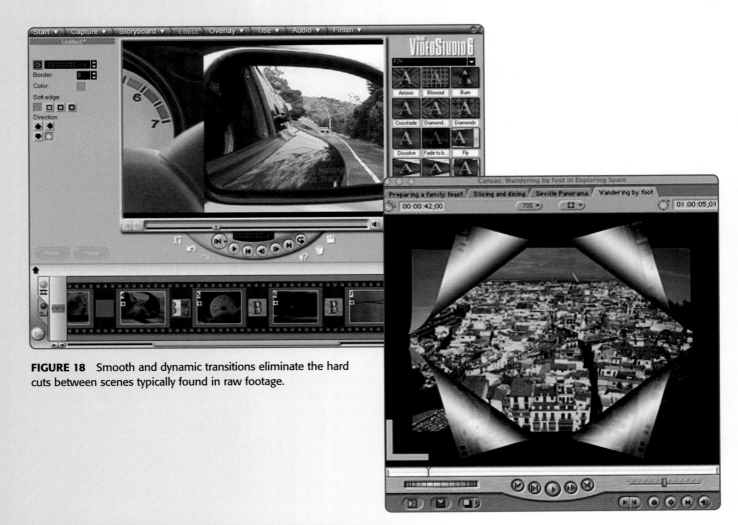

FIGURE 18   Smooth and dynamic transitions eliminate the hard cuts between scenes typically found in raw footage.

Video also can be stored in digital formats in any of several DVD formats, on CD-R, or on video CD (VCD). DVD or CD creation software, which often is packaged with video editing software, allows you to create, or master, DVDs and CDs. You can add interactivity to your DVDs. For example, you can allow viewers to jump to certain scenes using a menu (Figure 19). VCD is a CD format that stores video on a CD-R that can be played in many DVD players.

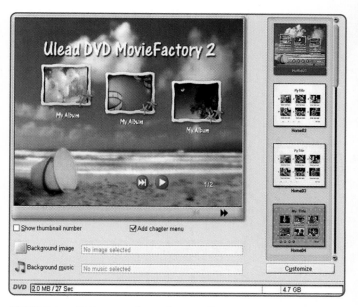

FIGURE 19 DVD mastering software allows you to create interactive menus on your DVD.

You also can save your video creation in electronic format for distribution over the Web or via e-mail. Your video editing software must support the file format and codec you want to use. For example, RealNetworks' Helix media delivery system allows you to save media files in RealVideo file formats.

Professionals use hardware and software that allow them to create a film version of digital video that can be played in movie theaters. This technology is becoming increasingly popular and has been used in the recent *Star Wars* movies. Some Hollywood directors believe that eventually all movies will be recorded and edited digitally.

After creating your final video for distribution or your personal video collection, you should back up the final video file. You can save your scenes for inclusion in other video creations or create new masters using different effects, transitions, and ordering of scenes.

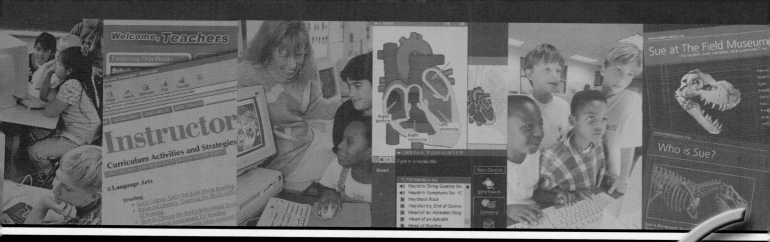

Technology and Curriculum Integration

6

Objectives

After completing this chapter, you will be able to:

- Define curriculum and explain curriculum standards and benchmarks

- Explain technology integration, or curriculum integration

- Describe the use of computers in computer labs versus classroom instruction

- Identify ways in which technology can positively influence learning

- Identify ways to plan for technology integration

- Explain various planning tools and instructional models

- Describe the steps of the ASSURE Model

- Identify ways to get started using technology at a new school

- Describe the use of learning centers

Throughout this textbook, you have learned about computers and other educational technologies, and you have seen the impact technology has on people's lives, schools, and classrooms. Every day, computers help many individuals accomplish job-related tasks more efficiently and effectively. For educators, computers and other technologies serve as the tools needed to implement new and evolving teaching strategies.

The first four chapters of this textbook focused on building computer and information literacy skills. Chapter 5 introduced you to integrating multimedia and education software into your curriculum. This chapter provides you with a basic understanding of how to integrate technology across the curriculum. As you learned in Chapter 1, integration literacy is the ability to use computers and other technologies combined with a variety of teaching and learning strategies to enhance students' learning. Integration literacy means that teachers can determine how to match appropriate technologies to learning objectives, goals, and outcomes. Integration literacy relies on a solid foundation of computer and information literacy, both of which are essential for helping you integrate technology into your classroom curriculum.

What Is Curriculum?

Education can be defined as all of the experiences a learner has under the supervision and guidance of teachers. Education literature defines the term, curriculum, in many ways. Often curriculum is defined simply as that which is taught. For the purpose of this textbook, **curriculum** is defined as different subject matter, such as mathematics, science, English, history and in terms of different grade levels [Figure 6-1].

Many countries have Departments of Education or educational organizations that serve as the governing association for educational regulations and reform. Agencies in the United States include the federal Department of Education (DOE), and each state has its own Department of Education [Figures 6-2a and 6-2b].

The federal Department of Education is the governing body for public education in the United States. State Departments of Education provide their school districts with policies, directives, and updates to state public education issues. In addition, state DOEs provide access to up-to-date statistics, information about standards and accountability, teacher certification,

scholarships, grants and funding sources, resources, and more.

State Departments of Education also provide their school districts with documents that describe curriculum goals and objectives for learning. These documents often are called **curriculum frameworks** or **curriculum guides**. While curriculum frameworks usually include subject-specific goals and standards, they often include direction for specific content areas, benchmarks, activities, and forms of evaluation.

School curriculum frameworks include not only recommendations, but examples that teachers can use to develop curriculum-based lesson plans. They usually are organized by subject and grade level. Curriculum frameworks may include specific curriculum standards and learning goals to assist teachers in meeting curriculum objectives.

Many school districts are drafting their own interpretations of state curriculum standards to improve learning and meet the needs of students. Many districts also are creating guides to help teachers teach curriculum objectives by providing examples and mastery-level checklists with learning goals. These usually have to be included with a teacher's lesson plans to

WEB INFO

For more information about curriculum, visit the Teachers Discovering Computers Web site, click Chapter 6, click Web Info, and then click Curriculum.

WEB INFO

For more information about mastery-level checklists, visit the Teachers Discovering Computer Web site, click Chapter 6, click Web Info, and then click Mastery Checklist.

Figure 6-1 Integrating technology in the classroom helps teachers achieve the learning outcomes defined by the curriculum.

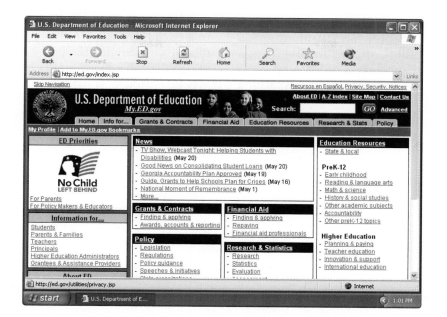

[a]

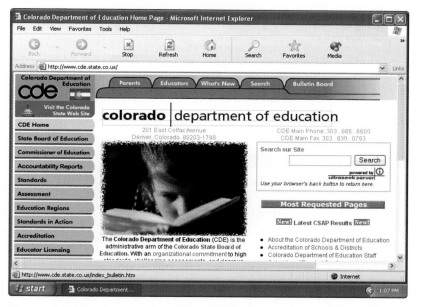

[b]

Figure 6-2 This figure shows the home page of [a] the U.S. Department of Education; and [b] the Colorado Department of Education. The U.S. government and state education agencies provide parents, educators, and students with a multitude of resources and information.

WEB INFO

To access the U.S. Department of Education Web site, visit the Teachers Discovering Computers Web site, click Chapter 6, click Web Info, and then click Department of Education.

FAQ

Does the No Child Left Behind Act (NCLB) require state curriculum standards?

Yes, NCLB requires each state to establish its own standards of what students should know and be able to do in the core content subjects.

make sure students are mastering the skills necessary to be promoted to the next level. Some states and districts are incorporating **Grade Level Expectations (GLEs)** into their curricula. The purpose of GLEs is to show the content and skills that students are expected to master for each subject area and assist teachers in making sure students meet the content standards for a particular subject area.

CURRICULUM STANDARDS AND BENCHMARKS

A **curriculum standard**, also called a **curriculum goal**, defines what a student is expected to know at certain stages of education. Curriculum standards for K-12 education are a collection of general concepts that school districts expect students to learn as they progress through grade levels. Curriculum standards vary from state to state and usually cover core subjects, such as language arts, mathematics, science, social studies, physical education, art, health, and foreign languages. A **benchmark**, or **learning objective**, is a specific, measurable learning outcome or indicator that usually is tied to a curriculum standard. Figure 6-3 lists a sample curriculum standard and appropriate, measurable benchmarks for language arts for different grade levels.

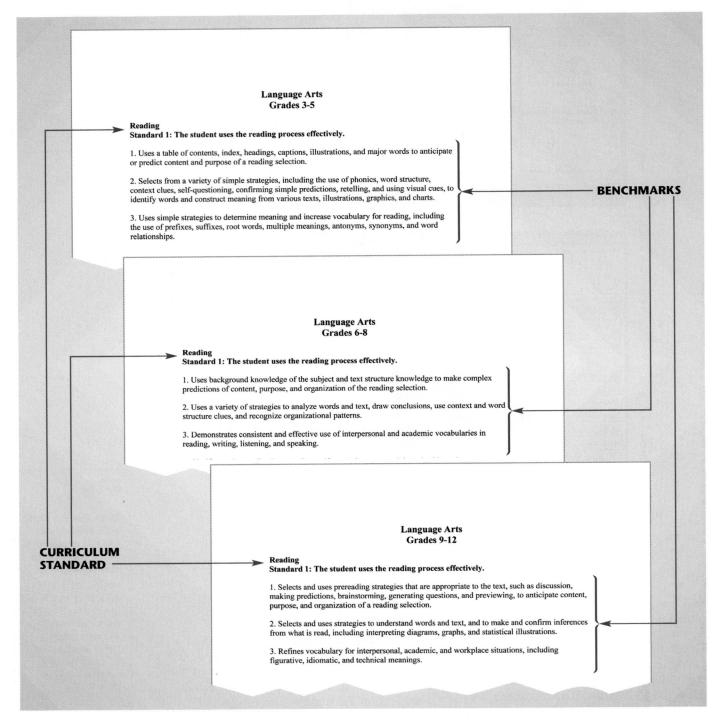

Language Arts
Grades 3-5

Reading
Standard 1: The student uses the reading process effectively.

1. Uses a table of contents, index, headings, captions, illustrations, and major words to anticipate or predict content and purpose of a reading selection.

2. Selects from a variety of simple strategies, including the use of phonics, word structure, context clues, self-questioning, confirming simple predictions, retelling, and using visual cues, to identify words and construct meaning from various texts, illustrations, graphics, and charts.

3. Uses simple strategies to determine meaning and increase vocabulary for reading, including the use of prefixes, suffixes, root words, multiple meanings, antonyms, synonyms, and word relationships.

BENCHMARKS

Language Arts
Grades 6-8

Reading
Standard 1: The student uses the reading process effectively.

1. Uses background knowledge of the subject and text structure knowledge to make complex predictions of content, purpose, and organization of the reading selection.

2. Uses a variety of strategies to analyze words and text, draw conclusions, use context and word structure clues, and recognize organizational patterns.

3. Demonstrates consistent and effective use of interpersonal and academic vocabularies in reading, writing, listening, and speaking.

CURRICULUM STANDARD

Language Arts
Grades 9-12

Reading
Standard 1: The student uses the reading process effectively.

1. Selects and uses prereading strategies that are appropriate to the text, such as discussion, making predictions, brainstorming, generating questions, and previewing, to anticipate content, purpose, and organization of a reading selection.

2. Selects and uses strategies to understand words and text, and to make and confirm inferences from what is read, including interpreting diagrams, graphs, and statistical illustrations.

3. Refines vocabulary for interpersonal, academic, and workplace situations, including figurative, idiomatic, and technical meanings.

Figure 6-3 Each curriculum standard in the Florida Sunshine Standards has one or more measurable benchmarks. The first curriculum standard for reading in language arts, for example, is the same across grades, but the benchmarks increase in difficulty from grades 3 to 12.

What Is Technology Integration?

Defining curriculum is easy when compared with defining technology integration. First, **integration** by itself is defined as bringing different parts together to combine into a whole. Therefore, **technology integration,** also called **curriculum integration,** is the combination of all technology parts, such as hardware and software, together with each subject-related area of curriculum to enhance learning. Furthermore, technology integration is using technology to help meet the curriculum standards and learner outcomes of each lesson, unit, or activity.

Mastering technology integration is not easy. Extensive formal training and practical experiences are imperative for successful integration of technology at all levels of K-12 education. Technology cannot enhance learning unless teachers know how to use and integrate technology into curriculum-specific or discipline-specific areas.

First and foremost, teachers must remember that technology is only a tool to enhance or support instructional strategies. Educators should take steps to integrate technology throughout classroom experiences — and find ways to use technology to teach curriculum-specific content while establishing connections between those subjects and the real world [Figure 6-4]. This chapter will assist you in learning the basics necessary to integrate technology into your classroom and provide the understanding needed to promote integration literacy.

A critical issue related to technology integration is that technology should not drive the curriculum. The curriculum, rather, should drive the technology; that is, teachers should use the appropriate technologies to enhance learning at the appropriate times [Figure 6-5]. In the next section, you will learn the pros and cons of using computers located in a centralized computer lab or in individual classrooms.

CLASSROOM INTEGRATION VERSUS TRADITIONAL COMPUTER LABS

Educational technologists have become the advocates of integrating computers into

Figure 6-4 When a teacher integrates virtual reality technology in his or her classroom curriculum, students are introduced to many unique and positive learning experiences.

Figure 6-5 Many Web sites provide teachers with curriculum integration activities and strategies.

content areas. For years, teachers and administrators have focused their efforts on getting technology or computer labs into schools. A **computer lab**, or **technology lab**, usually is a designated classroom filled with computers and technology for groups of students to use [Figure 6-6]. Lab computers usually are connected to the school's local area network (LAN) and provide many resources in a centralized area.

Figure 6-7 This teacher knows that by using computers at the point of instruction he can enhance the students' learning experiences.

Figure 6-6 At many schools, computer labs give students access to computers and other technologies.

Teachers can schedule time in computer labs for an entire class period and use the labs for many purposes such as whole-group instruction, small-group activities, or individual student-centered learning. In addition to computer labs, school media centers contain computers and also can be scheduled for use by classroom teachers. Computer labs are a popular approach to getting technology into K-12 schools. The primary reason administrators usually opt for computer labs first is due to cost and location. When computers are installed in the same location, they are easier to maintain and connect to a school network. Popular uses for networked school computer labs are for students to work through tutorial software and integrated learning systems software, which you learned about in Chapter 5.

Computer labs clearly provide solutions to some educational dilemmas and are an excellent addition to any school. Research shows that computers and related technologies, however, are more effective when integrated into subject content and

placed in the classroom — at the point of instruction. **Point of instruction** is having the technology in the classroom at the teachers' and students' fingertips [Figure 6-7].

If technology is readily available, teachers and students will use the technology more. An example would be an elementary teacher teaching a lesson on frogs. Students want to see and learn more about frogs, so they start asking questions. Teachers can turn to the technologies in their classrooms, such as multimedia software programs or the Web, to show how a frog jumps, where frogs live, and more.

Convenience is important and so is the availability of the technology at the time of instruction. Many educators refer to this as a teachable moment. When students are interested and ready to learn more about a topic, teachers have a **teachable moment**, which is an open window of opportunity for the information to be comprehended in greater detail by students [Figure 6-8]. Computers, when placed in the hands of teachers and students, provide unique, effective, and powerful opportunities for many different types of teaching and learning by engaging the students in learning experiences.

Figure 6-8 A teacher often can identify a teachable moment just by looking in the faces of excited students who are motivated to learn!

The Classroom in Action

To illustrate the benefits of having technology at the point of instruction, this section takes you into Mr. Balado's fourth-grade classroom at Martin Luther King Elementary School. Just as Mr. Balado finished reading his class a fictional story about a little boy and his secret dinosaur, several students raised their hands to ask questions. "Is the dinosaur a T-Rex?"

asked one student. Another student inquired, "Did people and dinosaurs live at the same time?" "How did dinosaurs grow so big?" asked a third. Mr. Balado smiled, because he expected these types of questions and knew they would open the door to a wonderful opportunity for learning. The questions clearly lead to a teachable moment, which he could maximize by using the classroom technologies.

Mr. Balado's classroom contains five multimedia student computers networked to the school's local area network and the World Wide Web. In addition, Mr. Balado has an instructional computer with access to the Web and connected to a large screen television [Figure 6-9]. Displaying the computer's image onto the larger screen of the television or a projection system is an excellent way to allow all students to see what displays on the computer's monitor, to see and hear interactive multimedia applications, and to interact with the Web and educational software, while at the same time asking questions. These questions create enthusiasm and a desire for additional knowledge among the students.

Are data projection systems still too expensive for the individual classroom?

No, they have come down significantly in price and some districts are making them standard equipment in all new classroom construction and adding them to existing classrooms.

Figure 6-9 Teachers easily can connect a computer to a television to display a computer monitor's image to the entire class.

Mr. Balado already had planned and prepared for the integration of various technologies into his interdisciplinary lesson. First, he had searched the Web for sites that would be appropriate for the fourth-grade curriculum and would provide detailed information and research about different dinosaur species and their environments, anatomy, behavior, and more. Locating the Web sites in advance allowed him to identify several excellent sites and eliminated the need to waste time searching for Web sites during class instruction time. In addition, Mr. Balado evaluated all of the Web sites in advance for their content and appropriateness for his fourth-grade students. Evaluation of technology resources is an important element in technology integration and is covered in detail in Chapter 7.

While interacting with the Web sites, students asked more questions such as, How fast can dinosaurs run? Did some dinosaurs fly? How did they have babies? Are all fossils dinosaurs? How long ago did they live? and How are dinosaurs named? This was all part of Mr. Balado's instructional plan, and his students' questions continued as Mr. Balado actively engaged them in exploration and discovery learning at selected dinosaur Web sites. The students were genuinely excited while exploring the Web sites of famous natural history

museums; they were discovering new concepts while Mr. Balado guided their learning [Figure 6-10].

With computers placed in his classroom at the point of instruction, Mr. Balado had his students' full attention as together they explored interesting Web sites while traveling through interactive virtual tours as paleontologists. **Virtual tours** allow you to walk through doorways, down halls, and let you see everything in a three-dimensional world via a computer as if you were there. Mr. Balado's students no longer were only hearing a story read to them about a fictional dinosaur; they now were seeing, hearing, and interacting with the dinosaurs and other times and places. After they looked at many dinosaur facts and pictures, Mr. Balado sent his students to their desks to write their own stories about dinosaurs, paleontology, and prehistoric times.

Integrating Technology into the Curriculum

As this example illustrates, computers and other technologies can provide unique, effective, and powerful opportunities for many different types of teaching and learning. Educators recognize that technology can serve as an extremely powerful tool that can help alleviate some of the problems of today's schools. Motivating students to learn is one area that all educators constantly are trying to achieve. Technology has the potential to increase student motivation and class attendance. Using these technology tools with students with varying abilities has helped to address different learning styles and reach diverse learners. With the right approach, educators can integrate technologies such as computers, CDs, DVDs, application software, multimedia applications, electronic books and references, handheld computers, and communications applications into almost any classroom situation. For technology to enhance student learning, however, it must be integrated into the curriculum.

The key to successful technology integration is identifying what you are trying to accomplish within your curriculum. First, you must consider what the learning

WEB INFO

To take a virtual tour of a museum, visit the Teachers Discovering Computers Web site, click Chapter 6, click Web Info, and then click Virtual Tour.

UCMP Home Page - Microsoft Internet Explorer

File   Edit   View   Favorites   Tools   Help

Back   Forward   Stop   Refresh   Home   Search   Favorites   Media

Address   http://www.ucmp.berkeley.edu/   Links

UNIVERSITY OF CALIFORNIA, BERKELEY

MUSEUM of PALEONTOLOGY

LEARN ABOUT US AT UCMP

EXPLORE OUR COLLECTIONS

DISCOVER THE

Done   Internet

start   UCMP Home Page - M...   1:27 PM

Figure 6-10 The Web provides vast amounts of information that allows students and teachers to discover innovative ways to enhance learning.

goals and standards are and then you must identify an appropriate technology tool that will help you accomplish your goals. While this process sounds simple, complete integration of technology in all subject areas is complex and takes a great deal of planning. A later section of this chapter will discuss how to plan for technology integration.

After you have determined specific learning goals and objectives and identified technologies appropriate for areas of the curriculum, you then can begin to develop innovative ways to teach a diverse population of learners with different learning styles [Figure 6-11]. A **learning style** refers to how individuals learn, including how they prefer to receive, process, and retain information. Learning styles vary among individuals. For example, some people learn better alone, while others learn better in groups. Many different types of learning styles exist and most individuals learn using a combination of several styles. The use of technologies such as multimedia and the Web can help address learning styles typically neglected by traditional teaching methods.

By engaging students in different ways, technology encourages them to take a more active role in the learning process. To learn more about learning styles and theories, read the special feature that follows this chapter: Learning Theories and Educational Research.

Changing Instructional Strategies

When students play a more active role in the learning process, the teacher's role must change. Teachers are transitioning from the conventional lecture-practice-recall teaching methods — often called the sage on the stage — to a classroom in which teachers engage students in activities that allow them opportunities to construct knowledge — a new role called the guide on the side. That is, teachers are beginning to shift from being the dispenser of knowledge to being the facilitator of learning. Rather than dictating a learning process, a **facilitator of learning** motivates students to want to learn, guides the student learning process, and promotes a learning atmosphere and an appreciation for the subject.

Several assumptions must be considered as teachers become facilitators of learning. The first is that students can accomplish learning and that the teachers' role is to assist their students in this process. A second assumption is that academic work extends beyond the mere storage of

WEB INFO

To discover more about learning styles, visit the Teachers Discovering Computers Web site, click Chapter 6, click Web Info, and then click Learning Styles.

Figure 6-11 Technology is a tool that creates valuable learning experiences for many different types of learners.

information. Instead, teachers want their students to be able to assimilate information and become problem solvers.

As teachers become facilitators of learning and incorporate technology into their instructional strategies, they will progress through several developmental stages. **Wellivers Instructional Transformation Model**, for example, describes five hierarchical stages of technology integration through which all teachers must progress to integrate technology effectively [Figure 6-12].

Barriers to Technology Integration

With all change comes barriers, and technology integration is no exception. Bill Gates stated in a speech, "In all areas of the curriculum, teachers must teach an information-based inquiry process to meet the demands of the Information Age. This is the challenge for the world's most important profession. Meeting this challenge will be impossible unless educators are willing to join the revolution and embrace the new technology tools available." Even after several years, these words still are true.

For more than two decades, several barriers have hindered technology integration in many schools. Such barriers include a lack of teacher training, lack of administration support, limited time for teacher planning, computer placement in remote locations making access difficult, budget constraints, and a basic resistance to change by many educators.

WEB INFO

For more information about barriers to technology integration, visit the Teachers Discovering Computers Web site, click Chapter 6, click Web Info, and then click Barriers.

Wellivers Instructional Transformation Model

1. **Familiarization** — teachers become aware of technology and its potential uses.

2. **Utilization** — teachers use technology, but minor problems will cause teachers to discontinue its use.

3. **Integration** — technology becomes essential for the educational process and teachers are constantly thinking of ways to use technology in their classrooms.

4. **Reorientation** — teachers begin to rethink the educational goals of the classroom with the use of technology.

5. **Revolution** — the evolving classroom becomes completely integrated with technology in all subject areas. Technology becomes an invisible tool that is seamlessly woven into the teaching and learning process.

Figure 6-12 Wellivers Instructional Transformation Model describes five hierarchical stages for technology integration, through which all teachers must progress to integrate technology effectively (Welliver, 1990).

Every educator looks at the integration of technology — and its challenges — from a different perspective. Technology coordinators view the problems of insufficient hardware, software, and training as major obstacles. Teachers consider the lack of time to develop technology-based lessons a concern. Administrators identify teachers' lack of experience using technology in instruction as yet another challenge. Teachers and administrators, however, can and are beginning to overcome these barriers with effective leadership, proper training, planning, and a commitment to enhancing teaching and learning using technology [Figure 6-13].

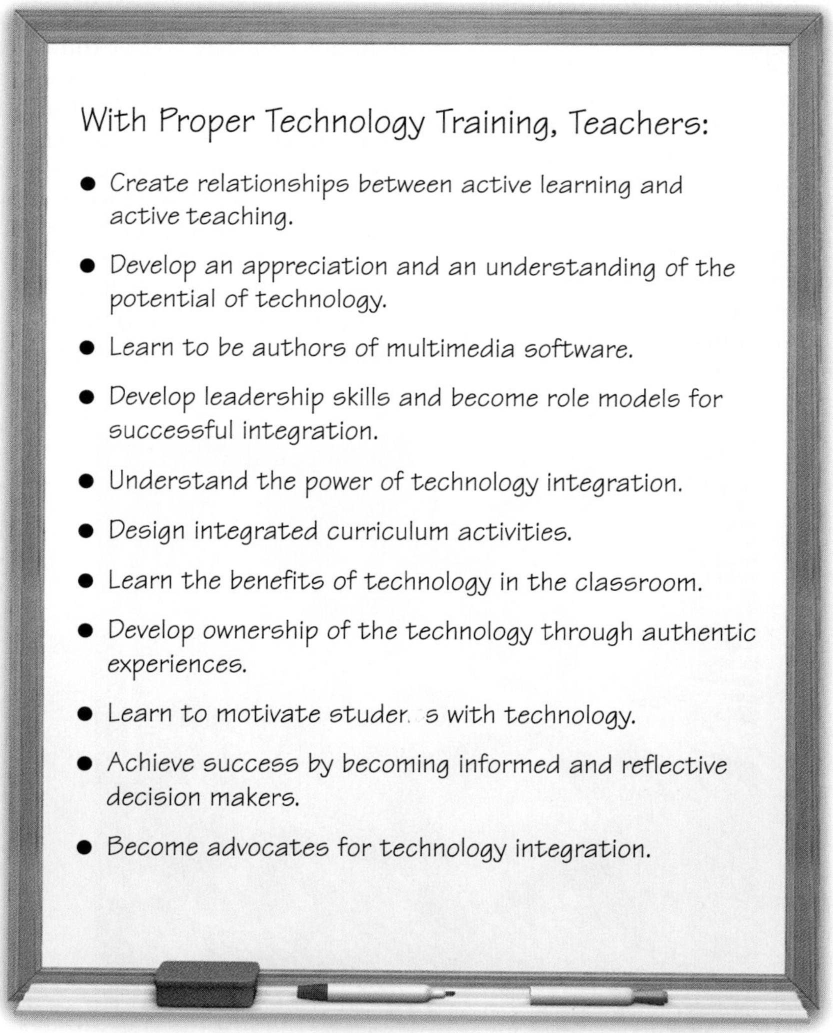

Technology Integration and the Learning Process

Before teachers can begin to develop integration skills, they must realize and understand how the integration of technology can enhance teaching and learning. Research shows that using technology in the classroom motivates students, encourages them to become problem solvers, and creates new avenues to explore information. Teachers also have found that using computers or computer-related technologies can capture and hold students' attention. Interactive technologies, such as software applications, multimedia

WEB INFO

For more information about technology training, visit the Teachers Discovering Computers Web site, click Chapter 6, click Web Info, and then click Technology Training.

With Proper Technology Training, Teachers:

- Create relationships between active learning and active teaching.

- Develop an appreciation and an understanding of the potential of technology.

- Learn to be authors of multimedia software.

- Develop leadership skills and become role models for successful integration.

- Understand the power of technology integration.

- Design integrated curriculum activities.

- Learn the benefits of technology in the classroom.

- Develop ownership of the technology through authentic experiences.

- Learn to motivate students with technology.

- Achieve success by becoming informed and reflective decision makers.

- Become advocates for technology integration.

Figure 6-13 With proper training and planning, educators can overcome many of the barriers to effective technology integration.

software, reference guides, tutorials, animations, simulations, and the Web, are especially engaging as they allow students to determine the flow of information, review concepts, practice skills, do in-depth research, and more.

Technologies that provide interactivity, learner control, and student engagement are a natural choice for improving instruction. When used properly, technology is extremely beneficial in the learning process.

THE LEARNING PROCESS

For learning to take place, learners must be engaged in the process of education. One way to engage learners is to motivate them through authentic learning experiences. **Authentic learning** experiences are instructional activities that demonstrate real-life connections by associating the concept being taught with a real-life activity or event [Figure 6-14]. For authentic learning to take place, teachers must involve students in the process of gathering, analyzing, and using information to make informed decisions that relate to real life.

When possible, teachers should promote **active learning**, which is a type of learning that occurs when students become engaged in inquiring, investigating, solving problems, and formulating and answering their own questions. Active learning also involves the process of students discussing, brainstorming, explaining, and debating issues with each other and with their teacher, both to determine solutions as well as identify their own questions. Active learning promotes the retention of information, motivates students to extend their learning, and gives students a sense of ownership of the information they are presenting. Active learning is especially appropriate when teaching to a wide variety of learning styles.

A lesson on the human digestive system, for example, presents concepts that are difficult for students to understand. Students have never seen the digestive system, nor can they feel or touch it. For students to understand these new concepts, they must have background information, or a knowledge base on which to build. Providing a knowledge base on which students can build is called **anchored instruction**. Through anchored instruction, learning and teaching activities are designed around an anchor (or situation) that provides a scenario or problem enhanced with curriculum materials that

WEB INFO

For more information about authentic learning experiences, visit the Teachers Discovering Computers Web site, click Chapter 6, click Web Info, and then click Authentic Learning.

Figure 6-14 Learners are motivated to learn through authentic real-life experiences.

allow exploration by the learner. Anchored instruction also includes the component of **problem-based instruction,** in which students use the background (anchor) information to begin to solve and understand complex problems or concepts.

Providing students with opportunities to expand their knowledge base allows them to experience visionary exploration or discovery learning. Recall from Chapter 2 that **discovery learning** is a nonlinear learning process that occurs when you investigate related topics as you encounter them. Discovery learning also is an inquiry-based method of teaching and learning where students interact with their surroundings by exploring and manipulating objects, investigating and solving problems through inquiry, or performing hands-on exercises and experiments. When students discover and explore concepts on their own, they are more likely to understand and retain information. Discovery learning also helps students become better thinkers.

TECHNOLOGY AND THE LEARNING PROCESS

Technology can provide numerous tools to support many types of instruction and learning. To teach students about the human heart, for example, a teacher could integrate a multimedia educational software application such as Body Works or Microsoft Encarta into the lesson. **Body Works** is a multimedia product for teaching related concepts about the human body. As you learned in the previous chapter, **Microsoft Encarta** is an interactive multimedia encyclopedia. These multimedia applications provide working visual models of how the various parts of the human heart interact [Figure 6-15]. These multimedia applications thus allow students to see and experience clearly things they could never experience by reading a textbook. Multimedia applications such as these also allow students to build a **cognitive scaffold,** which is a mental bridge to build an understanding of complicated concepts.

Another benefit of integrating educational multimedia applications is that they encourage students to think not only in words and pictures, but also in colors, sounds, animations, and more. When people think, their thoughts are

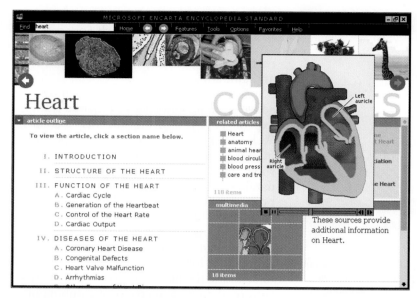

Figure 6-15 Microsoft Encarta is an educational software program that allows students to interact with a myriad of subjects. In this example, students see and hear how the human heart works.

filled with sounds, images, colors, and movements. A young child, for example, will describe a fire engine by indicating its color and demonstrating the sounds and movements of fire engines going to a fire [Figure 6-16]. Most traditional instruction, however, uses words and pictures only, often in two-color textbooks.

Figure 6-16 Everyone thinks in colors, images, sounds, and animations. A young child, for example, will describe a fire engine by imitating the sounds of a siren, indicating its color, and visualizing the sounds and movements of fire engines going to a fire.

Multimedia tools allow students to have learning experiences in which concepts are brought to life with a variety of representations — sounds, colors, pictures, and animations.

Technology helps teachers promote active learning and create authentic learning experiences by allowing students to conduct Web-based research, explore concepts in a multimedia presentation, create a slide show for a history presentation, create a database of results from a group science project, and so on. Technology also provides opportunities for anchored instruction. Students can watch a Web-based video clip of a Himalayan mountain-climbing expedition, for example, and then move on to examine the history of Tibet, the Sherpa culture, the physical effects of climbing in high altitudes, or how avalanches start.

Computers, multimedia, and especially the Web create numerous opportunities for discovery learning. Many students may never be able to visit an extraordinary museum such as the Smithsonian Institution. The Web, however, can transport them to a world beyond their own, filled with infinite amounts of information — visually, audibly, and even virtually. Using discovery learning, you can break down classroom walls with technology, the Web,

and most importantly — imagination. Properly integrated technology allows students to understand concepts more clearly and learn no matter who or where they are.

The Internet and the World Wide Web have been called the **educational equalizer** — that is, they give students of all backgrounds, socioeconomic levels, learning styles, geographic locations, academic levels, and learning abilities access to the same information. **Figure 6-17** illustrates how the Web brings these elements together to provide valuable learning experiences.

The Web allows students to experience educational opportunities previously not available. Students can publish their work, meet students with similar interests across the globe, and participate in shared learning experiences with classrooms worldwide. The Internet and Web also support projects in which students interact with authors, elected officials, or scientists conducting research. E-mail and Web-based projects are ideal for teacher-monitored school projects that involve language arts, cultural learning, history, geography, social studies, science, or communications with friends around the world [**Figure 6-18**].

As illustrated by these examples, computers can provide many unique,

WEB INFO

For more ideas about how to use e-mail in the classroom, visit the Teachers Discovering Computers Web site, click Chapter 6, click Web Info, and then click E-Mail Projects.

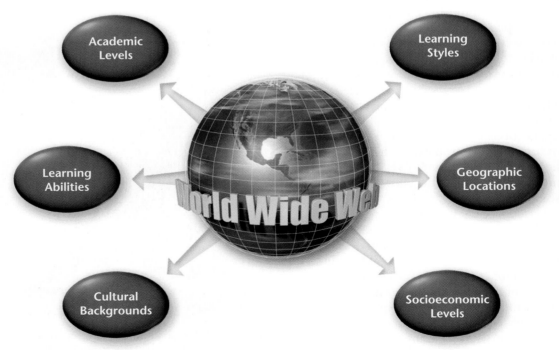

Figure 6-17 The Web has the capability of transporting students to a world beyond their own, filled with an infinite amount of information.

Figure 6-18 Using computers and the World Wide Web, students can join various projects to learn about other cultures and communicate with other students around the world.

WEB INFO

To learn more about cooperative learning, visit the Teachers Discovering Computers Web site, click Chapter 6, click Web Info, and then click Cooperative Learning.

effective, and powerful opportunities for teaching and learning. Such opportunities include skill-building practice, interactive learning, and linking learners to instructional technology resources. In addition, computers support communications beyond classroom walls, thus enabling schools and communities to provide an environment for cooperative learning and the development of innovative opportunities for learning.

Cooperative learning refers to a method of instruction where students work collaboratively in groups to achieve learning objectives and goals. Instead of working alone on activities and projects, students share ideas, learn teamwork skills, and begin to help one another to accomplish tasks or achieve learning goals. Cooperative classroom activities are student-centered, with the teacher serving as a facilitator and the students as information seekers. **High-order thinking skills** are the abilities to solve problems, engage in critical thinking, and interpret and solve complex issues. Teachers need to create activities for students to promote the use of high-order thinking skills throughout their educational experiences [Figure 6-19].

By promoting new and enhanced learning experiences, properly integrated technology offers limitless possibilities for instruction and learning. Computers, multimedia, the Web, and other technologies help students to understand concepts

more clearly and help teachers develop unique activities that maximize every teachable moment. Students become knowledge seekers and active learners who acquire knowledge and find different ways to interpret what they discover. Finally, technology can help improve students' abilities as independent thinkers and encourage them to become life-long learners.

Figure 6-19 Computers support communications beyond classroom walls thus providing an environment that allows for cooperative learning, development of high-order thinking skills, and solving complex problems.

Strategies for Integrating Technology into Teaching

The best strategy for curriculum integration is to put the technology into the hands of trained teachers, make it easily accessible, and let them decide how best to use it in their classrooms at the point of instruction. Teachers then can use an array of teaching strategies to develop a learning environment in which students are encouraged to be independent learners and take responsibility for their own learning.

The main goal of such teaching strategies is to provide a consistent application of technology tools to support instructional curriculum areas. Also, it is important to give every student the opportunity to work with computers and related technologies. When proper strategies are used for technology integration, students enjoy learning to use technology as well as the content in the subject-related curriculum areas.

Already, many experienced educators are integrating technology into subject-specific instruction — and have seen the benefits technology integration can bring to the learning experience. One critically important element in effective technology integration is continuous planning. For technology integration to be successful, careful planning is required at all levels, which involves district-level planning, school-level planning, and classroom-level planning. Each level must plan systematically so that technology is integrated effectively and seamlessly into all facets of education.

The Role of the School District

Effective curriculum integration cannot take place if support for technology integration does not come from several sources within the school district. School district administrators must plan carefully for every aspect of curriculum integration, from purchase to installation to teacher and staff training and technical support. Almost every school district has a detailed technology plan for technology integration. A **technology plan** is an outline that specifies the school district's procedures for purchasing equipment and software, and training teachers to use and then integrate technology into their classroom curriculum. Because of emerging and changing technologies, many school districts update their technology plans every one to three years. Many individual school technology committees review their technology plans every year to make sure they meet their district's plans.

To prepare educators to use the technology once it is implemented, administrators provide technology training with mentorship programs and follow-up staff development after training [Figure 6-20]. A **mentorship program** teams new teachers with experienced teachers to encourage new teachers to learn to integrate technology resources. Collaboration is promoted by sharing planning time and e-mail with other teaching professionals inside and outside the district. Experienced teachers guide new teachers by providing information and suggestions. In-house workshops

WEB INFO

For more information about technology strategies, visit the Teachers Discovering Computers Web site, click Chapter 6, click Web Info, and then click Strategies.

WEB INFO

To view a school district's technology plan, visit the Teachers Discovering Computers Web site, click Chapter 6, click Web Info, and then click Technology Plan.

Figure 6-20
Mentorship programs allow teachers to learn computer and technology integration concepts from experienced teachers in a nonthreatening environment.

are provided so teachers learn to use and integrate the available technologies in their schools and classrooms.

Today, many federal, public, and state grant funding sources now are requiring that the majority of funding be spent on teacher training. This increase in funding should increase the number of teachers using and integrating technology.

In addition, numerous Web sites are dedicated to mentoring new and experienced teachers in everything from how to get started with technology to classroom management. These sites provide wonderful resources for teachers and offer an avenue for teachers to find advice and support. Mentors can help new teachers become more effective in the classroom.

Planning for Technology Integration in the Classroom

Teachers must plan carefully for the use and integration of computers and technologies in the classroom. Just as planning is essential to effective instruction, it is required for effective use and integration of technology in the classroom. One important consideration is deciding on the most appropriate technology to achieve the desired learner outcomes. Teachers must plan how they will teach the curriculum, what areas they need to cover for content, and where they can use technology to meet learning objectives.

Another important consideration in the planning stage is preparing the classroom environment [Figure 6-21]. The way in which you integrate technology into the curriculum will depend largely on how many computers are in your classroom or in your school. Whether you use one computer, two computers, or thirty computers, you must plan how and when you will use those computers and how you will enable your students to use those computers. The amount of planning will vary according to the arrangement of computers in your classroom and school and the scope of your lesson. Chapter 7 discusses these and other planning issues.

ONE-COMPUTER CLASSROOM

In classrooms with only one computer, teachers must plan to maximize the effectiveness of that one computer. In such classrooms, the computer most commonly is used for classroom presentations and demonstrations. To allow students to view the presentation or demonstration, teachers easily can project the monitor's content on a large screen television or a large display monitor. Using a television with a 27-inch or 32-inch screen usually is sufficient. If you do not have a large screen television in your classroom, the school's media center should be able to provide one. Televisions normally are available, as long as you plan ahead.

For more information about curriculum planning with technology, visit the Teachers Discovering Computers Web site, click Chapter 6, click Web Info, and then click Curriculum Planning.

For additional strategies and applications for one-computer classrooms, visit the Teachers Discovering Computers Web site, click Chapter 6, click Web Info, and then click One Computer.

Figure 6-21 Teachers must prepare their classrooms carefully for the integration of computers and other technologies.

For more information about wireless mobile labs, visit the Teachers Discovering Computers Web site, click Chapter 6, click Web Info, and then click Wireless Labs.

Another option is to project the image onto a projection screen or classroom wall using a data projector or interactive whiteboard, described in Chapter 5. Schools normally have only a few of these devices, and you will have to plan ahead to schedule them for use in your classroom.

A good instructional strategy for the classroom computer is to introduce students to various types of software and create learning paths before taking the class to the computer lab. Using this instructional strategy optimizes the time students spend on computers while in the lab. Rather than spending time learning basic software skills, students can devote time to interacting with the computer to experience discovery learning.

In addition, teachers in a one-computer classroom can use the computer for the same purposes as described in the next sections on two or more computer classrooms. Many ways exist to enhance teaching and learning in the one-computer classroom. With only one computer available, however, additional planning may be required.

TWO-COMPUTER CLASSROOM

In classrooms with two computers, teachers must develop a strategy to manage their use. One computer could be used mainly for research on the Internet, presentations, Web-based projects, and e-mail. The other computer might be used as a writing center or for students to create multimedia projects.

Regardless of how you use the computers, you should develop a strategy for how you will allocate computer use and how students' computer time will be managed. Questions that can assist with planning are:

- Will both computers have the same hardware, software, and network access?

- Will one or both computers be connected to the Web?

- Will students rotate through using one or both computers on a daily basis?

- How much time will each student be allowed on each computer?

- Is it better to have the students work together on projects?

- How are you going to observe your students using the Internet?

- How will you evaluate student learning?

MORE THAN TWO COMPUTERS

Teachers who have several computers may find that arranging their classrooms in a single learning center or several learning centers, through which groups of students can rotate as they complete projects or activities, provides an environment for productive use of the computers [Figure 6-22]. Other technologies also can be organized into learning centers, such as a video center in which students can use digital video cameras to record and watch themselves performing plays, telling stories, or role-playing; a CD/DVD center where students can conduct research and learn new skills by interacting with instructional CDs and DVDs; a listening or reading center; a multimedia production center where students can create their own multimedia presentations, and much more.

Figure 6-22 By networking computers with Internet access, teachers can set up learning centers for students to work on projects.

Before setting up a computer center or centers, teachers should ask the planning questions previously cited, in addition to considering how many computers will be in each center and what other technologies, if any, might be included in the center. As indicated, the technologies a teacher utilizes will depend on the learning objectives. Furthermore, part of preparing the classroom environment and determining learning objectives is being aware of the prerequisite skills necessary for students to be successful.

USING A COMPUTER LAB

Because few classrooms include a computer for every student, using a computer lab allows teachers to provide learning opportunities that are not possible in a one-, two-, or even five-computer classroom. The most important advantage of using a computer lab is that all students are provided hands-on experience with using computer technology. Computer labs can be used successfully by teachers for tutorials, remediation, cooperative learning, computer skill instruction (such as word processing, spreadsheets, and databases), Internet research, whole class instruction, and integrated learning systems (ILS).

Computer labs have an added benefit of allowing students to interact with technology and software that is student centered. Taking your class to a computer lab, however, requires careful planning to use the allocated time efficiently and effectively. Managing instruction in a lab environment also requires that teachers carefully plan their learning strategies for this multi-computer environment.

The advantage of using a computer lab for instructional purposes is that all students have access to computers, the Internet, and software. Many times, other available technologies allow students to work on projects and develop additional technology skills, such as video production and much more. Figure 6-23 lists some suggestions to help make your time in the computer lab a successful learning experience.

USING A WIRELESS MOBILE LAB

Today's wireless technology represents an evolution of products and services for businesses and education. Many innovative technologies have evolved and are being used in K-12 and higher education classrooms; these technologies provide teachers with new and exciting integration possibilities. One use of wireless technology is a **wireless mobile lab,** also called a **computer lab on wheels.** A wireless mobile lab is a portable cart with wireless notebook computers that can be transported from one classroom to another [Figure 6-24]. As you learned in previous chapters, wireless communications make technology more accessible and flexible. The wireless mobile lab uses all the advantages of wireless technology, bringing technology to the students without

Figure 6-24 A wireless mobile lab transports computers to the students instead of the students going to a computer lab.

- Work with the computer lab teacher; you will need his or her help and expertise.

- Teach the lesson yourself or encourage the curriculum resource teacher to teach with you.

- Set up clear lab management rules.

- Provide well-thought-out lessons, with clear instructions.

- Make sure to use the available software, Internet, and other technologies to support your curriculum.

- Always, always have a back-up plan for unexpected technology problems.

- Alternate between whole-group, small-group, and individual instruction and assignments.

Figure 6-23 Suggestions that will assist teachers in the computer lab to make the instructional lessons a successful learning experience for students.

having to take them to a dedicated computer or technology lab. The computers can be moved almost anywhere and shared among classrooms. These mobile labs allow for expanded network capabilities and offer many instructional opportunities for teachers.

Wireless mobile labs consist of wireless notebook computers that can be purchased in sets of 8, 10, 16, 24, and 36. The notebook computers are stored and transported in a special cart. The cart serves many proposes, such as moving the computers from classroom to classroom, storing the computers at night, charging the computers, and keeping them secure. The charging capabilities are very unique and each company that has developed mobile labs has its own unique configuration and ways you can charge the computers and external batteries.

Teachers and students both benefit from this access to technology. By bringing technology to the classroom at the point of instruction, wireless mobile labs effectively integrate technology into the classroom. Because of the many possibilities that wireless mobile labs can and are providing, many experts believe that wireless mobile labs eventually will replace many traditional, wired computer labs.

WEB INFO

For another example of how to use a KWL chart, visit the Teachers Discovering Computers Web site, click Chapter 6, click Web Info, and then click KWL Chart.

Planning Lessons with Technology

One of the more important parts of technology planning is developing classroom lessons and activities that utilize technology. Most students begin school having some knowledge about computers. As students use computers in the classroom, however, they gain a familiarity with computers. Many educators have stated that, by using computers and related technologies, students are given new reasons to get excited and motivated about learning and, at the same time, have the opportunity to develop their own computer literacy. Students should, at some point, be taught basic computer concepts and operations, but they will learn many basic computer skills just from everyday use.

When planning lessons that use technology, teachers must consider the skills and knowledge level required for students to start and complete the lesson successfully. If technology is part of the lesson, teachers need to consider student technology skills. Many different tools are available to assess students' skill levels, such as a skill assessment survey. A **skill assessment survey** is designed to identify individual students' academic and technology skill levels and then create a starting point for developing instructional strategies.

KWL CHARTS

Another simple and effective tool to help in the planning process is a KWL chart. A **KWL chart** is an instructional planning chart to assist a teacher in identifying curriculum objectives by stating what students already **K**now, what they **W**ant to Know, and what they Will **L**earn as shown in **Figure 6-25**. A KWL chart is a very helpful planning tool in determining skill and knowledge levels of students before beginning almost any project. Once a teacher has established the learner objectives, the KWL chart can be used as a survey tool to determine what students already know about a topic and what technology skills they will need for a project. The teacher and students then can determine what they will learn from the project and the technologies best suited to mastering the learning objectives.

As the project progresses, students are encouraged to list the objectives and skills learned on the KWL chart. Not only will students be learning subject-related matter, they will be learning new and different types of technology skills when using technology to accomplish tasks.

An alternative version of the KWL chart is a KWHL chart. A **KWHL chart** also is an instructional planning tool, but adds an additional component — How students will learn. This additional component creates an opportunity for students and teachers to plan for how the learning experiences will occur.

A great way to create active learning opportunities for your students is to let them create KWL and KWHL charts when you start a new topic or when they begin

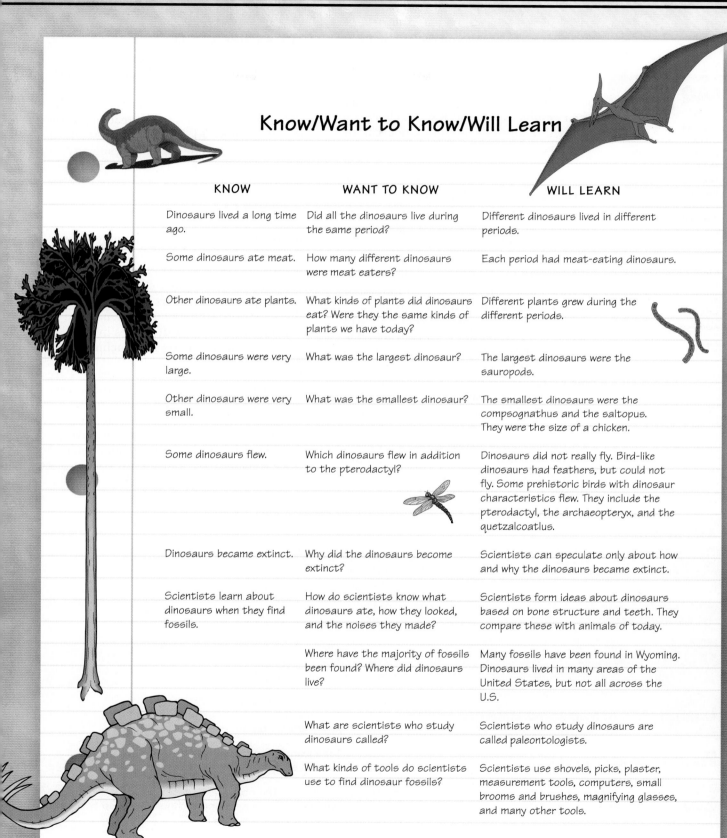

Know/Want to Know/Will Learn

KNOW	WANT TO KNOW	WILL LEARN
Dinosaurs lived a long time ago.	Did all the dinosaurs live during the same period?	Different dinosaurs lived in different periods.
Some dinosaurs ate meat.	How many different dinosaurs were meat eaters?	Each period had meat-eating dinosaurs.
Other dinosaurs ate plants.	What kinds of plants did dinosaurs eat? Were they the same kinds of plants we have today?	Different plants grew during the different periods.
Some dinosaurs were very large.	What was the largest dinosaur?	The largest dinosaurs were the sauropods.
Other dinosaurs were very small.	What was the smallest dinosaur?	The smallest dinosaurs were the compsognathus and the saltopus. They were the size of a chicken.
Some dinosaurs flew.	Which dinosaurs flew in addition to the pterodactyl?	Dinosaurs did not really fly. Bird-like dinosaurs had feathers, but could not fly. Some prehistoric birds with dinosaur characteristics flew. They include the pterodactyl, the archaeopteryx, and the quetzalcoatlus.
Dinosaurs became extinct.	Why did the dinosaurs become extinct?	Scientists can speculate only about how and why the dinosaurs became extinct.
Scientists learn about dinosaurs when they find fossils.	How do scientists know what dinosaurs ate, how they looked, and the noises they made?	Scientists form ideas about dinosaurs based on bone structure and teeth. They compare these with animals of today.
	Where have the majority of fossils been found? Where did dinosaurs live?	Many fossils have been found in Wyoming. Dinosaurs lived in many areas of the United States, but not all across the U.S.
	What are scientists who study dinosaurs called?	Scientists who study dinosaurs are called paleontologists.
	What kinds of tools do scientists use to find dinosaur fossils?	Scientists use shovels, picks, plaster, measurement tools, computers, small brooms and brushes, magnifying glasses, and many other tools.

Figure 6-25 A KWL chart is an instructional planning tool that assists teachers in creating specific curriculum objectives based on the knowledge of their students.

to work on their own projects. You can conduct this exercise as a large group activity in which the whole class participates, or you can break up the class in small groups and then let the groups share their results. KWL and KWHL charts can be used in all subjects from kindergarten to university-level classes.

Instructional Models

Before you start a lesson, you plan the lesson, which is a process that involves using an instructional design or model. Effective teaching with technology also involves using an instructional model. An **instructional model** is a systematic guide for planning instruction or a lesson. When using technology, an instructional model and planning take on a more important role. Which technology you use is not the critical issue; what is important is that you use the technology effectively and the technology is appropriate to the learning objective. Many instructional models are available from which you can choose. For the purpose of this textbook, the popular educational instructional model called the ASSURE Model is described.

THE ASSURE MODEL

The **ASSURE Model** developed by Heinich, Molenda, Russell, and Smaldina is a procedural guide for planning and delivering instruction that integrates technologies and media into the teaching process [Figure 6-26]. The ASSURE Model is a well-known guide for developing any instructional lessons. The following is a description of the steps of the ASSURE Model and an explanation of how to use the model in your classroom.

ANALYZE THE LEARNER Knowing your learner's skill level is important. Some students may come into your classroom with academic and computer skills that others do not possess. Teachers should plan for this situation. Know your audience and consider the diverse differences in the student population you are teaching.

STATE OBJECTIVES Student objectives are statements of the type of skills and knowledge you expect students to be able to demonstrate at the end of instruction. When you have clear student objectives, you can select your materials and determine the focus and purpose of your project more wisely. Be sure to match student objectives to curriculum goals.

ASSURE MODEL

Analyze the Learner	• Who are the learners? • What are their skill levels? • What are their learning styles?
State Objectives	• What do you want the learners to gain knowledge of? • What are the specific learner outcomes?
Select Methods, Media, and Materials	• What methods of instruction do you plan to use? • What media are appropriate? • What materials will you need?
Utilize Methods, Media, and Materials	• How will you use the methods and media? • How will you use the materials? • What is your instructional strategy?
Require Learner Participation	• What will the learners be required to do? • Will the learners engage in active or passive learning?
Evaluate and Revise	• Did the lesson meet the objectives? • How will you evaluate content and technologies used? • How will you revise and improve?

Figure 6-26 The steps of the ASSURE Model, which is an instructional model used by educators to develop technology-enriched lessons.

SELECT METHODS, MEDIA, AND MATERIALS

Selection of methods, media, and materials includes three steps, which are (1) decide on the method of instruction, (2) choose the media format that is appropriate for the method, and (3) select, modify, update, or design materials for the instruction. Media and materials include all items you choose to meet the curriculum goals, such as print, technology, information resources, and related components. Media can take many forms, including CD, DVD, the Internet or the Web, a video, an overhead projector, a graphing calculator, special technology devices for learning, or any combination of these and other items [Figure 6-27]. The first step is to decide which method best meets your needs, such as lecture, discovery, tutorials, or demonstration. Next, you need to decide on the media, how you are going to use the media, and what you want the learners to do. Again, refer back to your objectives to assist you in determining this step. Make sure those materials are available and list what you are planning to use. Finally, determine if you need to modify any of the media or materials or design new media or materials.

UTILIZE METHODS, MEDIA, AND MATERIALS

Teachers should preview all media and materials they are planning to use, including videos, multimedia applications, and Web sites. While a software company may advertise that a particular software product contains the correct content for your objectives, you, as the teacher, must evaluate the content of all software. Next, you will need to prepare the classroom environment. Use these questions to guide you in making preparations:

- What equipment or devices are required to use the media?

- Do you need to reserve extra equipment that you may not have in your classroom?

- How do you prepare your classroom to use the equipment?

- How do you prepare the students to use the media and materials?

Figure 6-27 Teachers must choose which media to use and when it is appropriate to use the technology.

WEB INFO

For assistance with creating lesson plans, visit the Teachers Discovering Computers Web site, click Chapter 6, click Web Info, and then click Lesson Plans.

REQUIRE LEARNER PARTICIPATION As previously discussed, the most effective learning situations are those that require active learning and ask learners to complete activities that build mastery toward the learning objectives. Classroom lessons should motivate students to be active learners who are involved in the process of learning, such as practicing, performing, solving, building, creating, and manipulating. As you develop these lessons, you must decide what information to include in the activities. If students are doing a research project using the Web, for example, they need guidelines of what to incorporate and how you will assess the outcome of the project. Chapter 7 discusses assessment tools in more detail.

EVALUATE AND REVISE At the end of a project, it is important to evaluate all aspects of the lesson or instruction. **Evaluation** is the method of appraising or determining the significance or worth of an item, action, or outcome. This **evaluation process** includes assessing learner outcomes, reviewing, critiques of the learners' work or works based on specific standards, and evaluating reviews of the media and materials used. Teachers should conduct thoughtful reflection on all aspects of the instructional process. **Reflective evaluation** is thinking back on the components of the teaching and learning process and determining the effectiveness of the learner outcomes and the use of technology during the process. Figure 6-28 lists a number of questions that teachers should consider during the evaluation and revision phase.

Critical Questions to Ask During the Evaluate and Revise Phase of the ASSURE Model

- Did students learn what you wanted them to learn?
- Can students demonstrate understanding of the content?
- Was the chosen technology effective?
- Were the learning objectives met using the technology?
- Should learning objectives be taught in a different format?
- Would these learning objectives be better taught without technology or with another technology?
- Can students work cooperatively with a partner on this lesson?
- Would parts of the content be better understood if students worked individually?
- What would you change?
- What would you keep the same?
- How will you revise this lesson?

Figure 6-28 Technology can create powerful opportunities for many different types of teaching and learning; however, teachers must evaluate and revise the use of technology.

Students also should be asked to reflect on their learning experiences, their perceptions on the content learned, and their evaluation of the learning process. Emerging technologies will expand teachers' potential to communicate effectively, to convey ideas, and to amuse, encourage, and educate students. As you revise your lesson plans, you will need to evaluate and consider using new and emerging technologies.

The ASSURE Model is an example of one popular educational model that teachers can use to plan for technology integration into instruction. As you can see, planning is important on all levels — from the district, to the classroom, to planning individual lessons. As a new teacher, planning for technology integration will present its challenges. The next section provides information on where to go for guidance and materials to help you plan for technology integration in your classroom.

Getting Started at a New School

Suppose you are a new teacher and it is the first day of preplanning week for teachers. You are excited to get that first glimpse of your new classroom. When you finally do, you discover you have two new networked computers and a color ink-jet printer in your classroom. Fortunately, you learned about Macintosh computers and PCs during your teacher education courses. While you feel comfortable using computers, you immediately wonder how to get started and begin to consider ways to integrate these computers into your classroom curriculum [Figure 6-29]. As you start to plan for technology integration, you will need to consider many issues related to technology information and support, technology training, hardware, software, other technologies, and technology supplies.

INFORMATION ABOUT TECHNOLOGY

One of the first items to investigate is who else in the school is using technology in their classrooms. Individuals to consult are your principal, media specialist, technology committee members, or other teachers, especially those who teach the same grade level and subjects that you teach. Any of these educators usually will know who else actively is integrating technology in their classrooms. Check to see if your school has a mentorship program.

Ascertain if your school has a technology committee and who the members are. You can get this information from your principal or assistant principal. Consult your teacher's manual for a list of various school committees and their members. A **technology committee** consists of teachers, administrators, and staff who consider, investigate, advise, and make recommendations to the principal and technology coordinator about technology-related issues. A **teacher's manual** is a booklet that contains information, rules and regulations, rights and responsibilities, and policies and procedures that will provide answers to many of your questions.

Finally, you should determine where you should go to get technology support. The principal, media specialist, school or district technology coordinator, and other teachers who use technology either can offer you support or guide you to where you can find support.

Figure 6-29 New teachers need to ask a lot of questions about how to get started using and integrating technology in their new classrooms.

TECHNOLOGY TRAINING

Take time to find out if your school offers any professional development or inservice training for using and integrating technology. Most schools and school districts offer free training for teachers. **Inservice** means training teachers after they have entered the profession of teaching. Your principal, curriculum coordinator, technology coordinator, or district instructional technology coordinators are able to provide information on inservice training opportunities. Sometimes, school secretaries also will be up-to-date on this information.

For information about technology workshops, talk with your principal, curriculum coordinator, other teachers, or district technology coordinator. Let these people know you are interested in any technology or other training that becomes available. If you have students with learning disabilities in your classroom, check with the district exceptional student education program specialist about training opportunities. Many school districts post the dates and times of inservice training and workshops on the district's Web site and on teacher bulletin boards.

HARDWARE

Determining how you can obtain additional hardware or upgrade your classroom computers is another item to consider. As soon as you can, join your school's technology committee. Technology committees help make the decisions on what new technologies will be purchased, where these new technologies will be placed, and establishes how the technology plan for the school is implemented. You also may need to look into educational grants for additional funds. Your principal and curriculum coordinator usually receive notification of grant opportunities. Let them know you are interested in writing a grant and they will provide you with the information. If your district has a person responsible for grant writing for the district or county, he or she can serve as a good source of information. Additionally, you will find numerous grant opportunities on the Internet. Chapter 7 provides more information on locating and writing educational grants.

For more information about grant opportunities, visit the Teachers Discovering Computers Web site, click Chapter 6, click Web Info, and then click Grants.

A question to consider is what type of equipment you can purchase if you receive grant funds. Before you write a grant, determine what kind of equipment you can purchase. Your principal, technology coordinator, curriculum coordinator, or members of the technology committee should be able to provide you with this information. If your school is networked, also check with the network administrator at the district level.

SOFTWARE

With hardware requirements decided, you will need to determine what kind of software is available to you and where you can find it. First, you should check your classroom computer for software that already is installed. To learn more about the software available at your school or on the school's network, ask the school media specialist, curriculum coordinator, technology facilitator, or the district technology coordinator. If you are a special education teacher, you might check with your district exceptional student education coordinator, who should know what software is available for students with disabilities.

Next, determine the procedure for purchasing additional software. The school secretary or other teachers can direct you to the right person for this information. If your school is networked, it is important to check with the network coordinator before purchasing software so you can avoid buying software that already may be installed on the network or may conflict with the network. Many schools install computer-assisted instructional software programs on their network servers for use by all teachers.

Finally, you need to determine if your school district or state Department of Education has an adopted state bid list for purchasing software. Many states contract with companies to purchase specific software applications at reduced prices and these are included on a **state bid list**. Be sure to find out if your state has a special catalog of software titles that they have adopted [Figure 6-30]. Curriculum coordinators, technology coordinators, or media specialists are good sources for this information. Your district office should maintain this information as well.

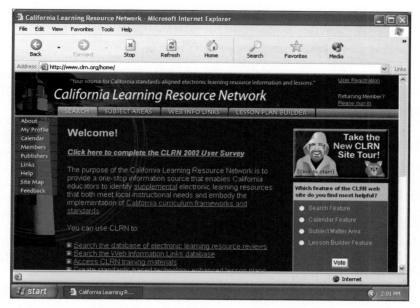

Figure 6-30 Many states provide online access to state-approved electronic learning resources.

OTHER TECHNOLOGIES

Consider other technologies and where you can find them, such as a VCR, digital camera, scanner, data projector, or a presentation television. Your media specialist usually handles scheduling and distribution of VCRs and other equipment [Figure 6-31]. Reserve early because a sign-up sheet and allocation usually is based on a first-come, first-served basis. Ask about the length of time that you are allowed to keep checked-out equipment.

You also should ask where you can find a listing of educational software programs offered throughout the school district for use in the classroom. The media specialist usually has a list of software programs and CD and DVD titles for teachers to use in the classroom. A listing of instructional television programs and

FAQ

Can teachers borrow technologies for their classrooms from other locations?

Yes, public libraries, universities, some businesses, and curriculum resource centers will let teachers check out all types of technologies for use in their classroom.

Figure 6-31 A school's media center can be scheduled for teachers and students. The media specialist usually assists teachers with checking out all types of technologies.

broadcast times, and any videotapes the school has or that are available to the school through interlibrary loan programs usually is maintained by the media specialist. He or she can inform you of the procedures for checking out CDs, DVDs, VCRs, and other equipment.

TECHNOLOGY SUPPLIES

A basic, but often overlooked, question to consider is how you can obtain additional supplies for use with computers and other technologies. If the bulb in your overhead projector burns out, for example, or you need paper or ink cartridges for your printer, to whom do you speak about replacing it? Generally, the media specialist can replace burned-out bulbs and solve other supply problems with projectors. The school secretary or the bookkeeper usually handles orders for general supplies. Talk to the school secretary. He or she will direct you to the appropriate person.

Now that you have some basic knowledge of where to go for guidance and materials to help you integrate technology into your classroom, consider how one teacher is putting it all together.

WEB INFO

To learn how to order technology and other school supplies online, visit the Teachers Discovering Computers Web site, click Chapter 6, click Web Info, and then click Supplies.

Putting It All Together

As described earlier in this chapter, Mr. Balado is well aware that technology can make a difference in his fourth grade students' learning — and he has been using technology to enhance his classroom lessons. After the students completed their writing activity, Mr. Balado planned a highly integrated classroom strategy of teaching the science curriculum to his fourth graders. As part of the integrated learning environment, he provided carefully planned centers, which enabled him to divide his classroom for group activities and inquiry learning through these interdisciplinary lessons.

CREATING AN INTEGRATED LEARNING ENVIRONMENT

Centers, or learning centers, give you the opportunity to break your classroom into many different types of learning environments without ever leaving the room. Just as an office building has different offices in which work is accomplished, learning centers allow students to rotate around the classroom to complete projects or activities [Figure 6-32]. Mr. Balado had an instructional plan for how the students would work through the centers in his

Figure 6-32 Learning centers are a great way to organize a classroom to optimize learning opportunities.

classroom. In Mr. Balado's Paleontology Exploration, students took on the role of explorer and learned what it would be like to have a career in paleontology.

He had five computers in his classroom for student use and 26 students. He divided the students into groups of two and three; these students would work together throughout the levels of the project. Mr. Balado then assigned each group a dinosaur to research.

Students were excited and surprised because most did not even know how to pronounce the name of some of their dinosaurs. Their assignment was to find out what the names of their dinosaurs meant and uncover as many facts as they could about their dinosaurs. Instead of writing a report, students would create a research-based interactive multimedia project, models, and more.

Mr. Balado gave each group the same guidance and questions to think about for their projects, such as, What do paleontologists and scientists really do? Where would I travel? What kind of education would I need? Like actual paleontologists, Mr. Balado also instructed his students to conduct research on their dinosaurs by answering questions such as, What did your dinosaur look like? In what period did your dinosaur live? What did your dinosaur eat? How big was it and how much did it weigh? He also asked each of them to gather all the information they felt was important for them and others in the class to understand their Paleontology Exploration.

He then asked them to formulate their own additional questions and find answers to them. Mr. Balado knew that good questioning skills lead to concrete learning opportunities. Many educators teach their students to use an **essential questioning technique**, which is looking for the most important or fundamental part of a topic. In this process, students develop their own questions, find their own answers, and develop their own meaning from the information they collect. By using this essential questioning technique, students discover insight and are motivated to learn more. After a student has learned how to ask the appropriate questions, they have learned how to learn.

THE CLASSROOM CENTERS

For his lesson on paleontology, Mr. Balado set up seven learning centers in his classroom, which included the discovery computer center, the Web search center with a computer connected to the Internet, the modeling center, the great explorers library center, the science center, the scanning center with a computer set up for scanning pictures and other objects, and the multimedia project center.

The discovery computer center included two computers and a number of different CDs Mr. Balado checked out from the media center that covered paleontology and dinosaurs. He purchased two CDs at his own expense. At the Web search center was one computer that students could use to investigate various Web sites for which Mr. Balado had provided links on his curriculum Web page. To locate these Web sites and other available media, Mr. Balado worked with the media specialist at his school. Once he had collected and evaluated a list of sites for the students to conduct their dinosaur research, Mr. Balado created a curriculum page so students would not be wasting time surfing the Web without supervision [Figure 6-33]. Mr. Balado was quite aware of the dangers of inappropriate or inaccurate information available at some Web sites.

For more information about creating learning centers, visit the Teachers Discovering Computers Web site, click Chapter 6, click Web Info, and then click Learning Centers.

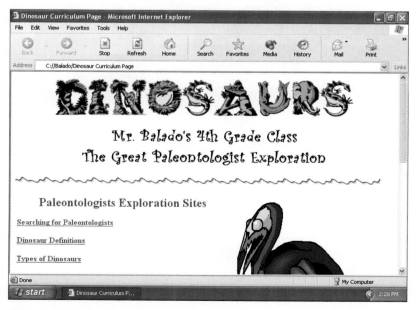

Figure 6-33 Teacher-created curriculum pages allow students to link directly to appropriate Web sites.

WEB INFO

For more information about the benefits of technology integration, visit the Teachers Discovering Computers Web site, click Chapter 6, click Web Info, and then click Benefits.

In the modeling center were all types of modeling tools, modeling clay, paper, rocks, and all types of different-shaped items. This center was for students to create a model of their dinosaurs and other objects related to the project. At the next center, the great explorers library center, as shown in Figure 6-34, Mr. Balado provided a collection of books, journals, and magazines for students to use to research dinosaurs and become great research explorers. The media specialist was instrumental in locating books and print materials through the interlibrary loan program, which was established in the state to assist teachers in obtaining resources from media centers throughout the state.

The scanning center had a computer set up with a flatbed scanner so students could scan pictures from books, magazines, and other sources for use in their projects. The science center, or as the students liked to call it, the Mr. Fossil and Mrs. Bones Dig Site center, had real fossils, rocks, sand, dig tools, and different types of bones made from plastic that Mr. Balado obtained from a dinosaur education package. Mr. Balado

set up this center like a real dig site. He wanted to give his students authentic hands-on experience in what it takes to work as paleontologists.

The last center was the multimedia project center, which had one computer set up for students to create their projects in either PowerPoint or HyperStudio. Because the school had site licenses, PowerPoint and HyperStudio were installed on all of the classroom computers so students could work on their projects as they progressed through the various centers.

THE RESULTS OF TECHNOLOGY INTEGRATION

Students worked though the centers and created some of the more interesting and creative projects Mr. Balado had ever seen. One group had located a picture of a dinosaur in the woods, so for their model, they decided to create a dinosaur and the woods in which it lived.

Most students could describe in detail all of the information they had learned about their dinosaurs — and all of the groups had given their dinosaurs a nickname. The projects were outstanding; most of them contained many pictures and dinosaur stories with actual research and details about the dinosaur and the field of paleontology [Figure 6-35].

Mr. Balado knew that his students were involved actively in their own learning and had interacted with numerous resources,

Figure 6-34 This learning center contains a variety of print resources for students to use to develop their research projects.

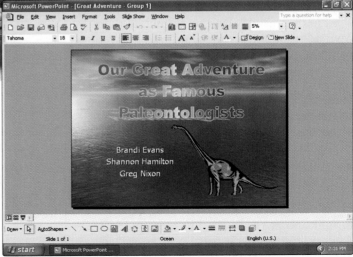

Figure 6-35 Using PowerPoint, students can create multimedia projects.

Web sites, and software programs. By engaging in active learning at each center and using higher-order thinking skills, Mr. Balado's students, with his assistance, created their own questions, found their own answers, and created their own multimedia projects. As a result of this process, Mr. Balado's students created new paths of knowledge for themselves that enhanced their learning.

As Mr. Balado and his students learned, technology can make a difference in the classroom if used appropriately and integrated into the curriculum. In addition, Mr. Balado noticed that his students' self-esteem, self-confidence, and writing skills improved as a result of creating their own projects [Figure 6-36].

Figure 6-36 Students feel an amazing sense of pride and ownership when they complete their own projects.

Learning Theories and Educational Research

At the end of this chapter is a special feature that provides information on educational learning theories and theorists. This special feature introduces you to educational terms, learning theories, educational research, and learning strategies that you should understand and apply to your own instructional strategies. All teaching strategies have learning theories and educational research embedded within the instructional framework. Learning theories help teachers form instructional strategies and technology integration techniques by providing a basic framework for teaching and learning. Teachers learn to combine the different strategies and integration methods that are most suitable and appropriate for teaching their students.

Summary of Technology and Curriculum Integration

As you have learned in this chapter, the best strategy for technology integration is to place technology into the hands of trained teachers, make it easily accessible, and let them decide how best to use it in their classrooms at the point of instruction. Teachers are the content experts who should evaluate all resources used in classrooms. This chapter first discussed curriculum and technology issues as they apply to technology integration and then provided teachers with ideas, an instructional model, and effective planning strategies. The chapter then provided an introduction to the concept of technology integration that will help you build your integration literacy skills. Finally, this chapter showed you how one teacher, Mr. Balado, fully integrated technology into an interdisciplinary lesson. In Chapter 7, you will build upon the skills you have learned in this chapter and increase your integration literacy skills by learning implementation strategies and integration activities that are curriculum directed.

In Brief

Web Instructions: To display this page from the Web, start your browser and enter the URL, www.course.com/tdc/3. Click Chapter 6 at the top of the Web page and then click In Brief on the left sidebar. Click the links for current and additional information. To listen to an audio version of this In Brief, click the Audio button at the top left of the instructions.

WEB INFO

IN BRIEF

KEY TERMS

CHECKPOINT

TEACHING TODAY

EDUCATION ISSUES

INTEGRATION CORNER

SOFTWARE CORNER

IN THE LAB

LEARN IT ONLINE

✷ FEATURES...

Timeline 2004

Guide to WWW Sites

Buyer's Guide 2004

Professional Sites

State/Federal Sites

Interactive Labs

Search Tools

HOME

1. Curriculum, Curriculum Standards, and Benchmarks

Curriculum is defined as all of the experiences a learner has under the supervision and guidance of teachers. A **curriculum standard**, also called a **curriculum goal**, defines what a student is expected to know at certain stages of education. A **benchmark**, or **learning objective**, is a specific, measurable learning objective that usually is tied to a curriculum standard.

2. Technology Integration

Technology integration is the combination of all technology parts, such as hardware and software, together with each subject-related area of curriculum to enhance learning. Technology integration is using technology to help meet the curriculum standards and learner outcomes of each lesson, unit, or activity.

3. Technology Integration in the Curriculum

The key to successful technology integration is identifying what you are trying to accomplish within your curriculum. Teachers must consider what the learning goals and standards are, identify an appropriate technology, and develop innovative ways to teach a diverse population of learners with different learning styles. A **learning style** refers to how individuals learn, including how they prefer to receive information, express themselves, and process information.

4. Changing Instructional Strategies

As students begin to play a more active role in the learning process, the teacher's role must change. Teachers are transitioning from the conventional lecture-practice-recall teaching methods to being the facilitator of learning. Rather than dictating a learning process, a **facilitator of learning** motivates students to want to learn, guides the student learning process, and promotes a learning atmosphere and an appreciation for the subject.

5. Barriers to Technology Integration

With all change comes barriers, and technology integration is no exception. Barriers include a lack of teacher training, lack of administration support, limited time for teacher planning, computer placement in remote locations making access difficult, budget constraints, and a basic resistance to change by many educators.

6. Technology Integration and the Learning Process

For learning to take place, learners must be engaged in the process of education. **Authentic learning** experiences are instructional activities that demonstrate real-life connections by associating the concept being taught with a real-life activity or event. **Active learning** is a learning process in which students become engaged in inquiring, investigating, solving problems, and formulating and answering questions on their own.

7. Strategies for Integrating Technology into Teaching

The best strategy for curriculum integration is to put the technology into the hands of trained teachers, make it easily accessible, and let them decide how best to use it in their classrooms at the point of instruction. When proper strategies are used for technology integration, students enjoy learning to use technology as well as learning content in subject-related curriculum areas.

In Brief

WEB INFO

IN BRIEF

KEY TERMS

CHECKPOINT

TEACHING TODAY

EDUCATION ISSUES

INTEGRATION CORNER

SOFTWARE CORNER

IN THE LAB

LEARN IT ONLINE

✱ FEATURES...

Timeline 2004

Guide to WWW Sites

Buyer's Guide 2004

Professional Sites

State/Federal Sites

Interactive Labs

Search Tools

HOME

8. The Role of the School District

School district administrators must plan carefully for every aspect of curriculum integration, from purchase, to installation, to teacher and staff training. Almost every school district has a detailed technology plan for curriculum integration. A **technology plan** is an outline that specifies the school district's procedures not only for purchasing equipment and software, but also for training teachers to use and then integrate technology into their classroom curriculum.

9. Technology Integration Plans for the Classroom

Teachers must plan carefully for the use and integration of computers and technologies in the classroom. They must plan how they will teach the curriculum, what areas they need to cover for content, and where they can use technology to meet learning objectives. Whether teachers use one computer, two computers, or thirty computers, however, they must plan how and when to use the computers and how they will enable students to use the computers.

10. Lesson Plans that Incorporate Technology

When planning lessons that use technology, teachers must consider the skills and knowledge level required for students to start and complete the lesson successfully. A **KWL chart** is a helpful planning tool in determining the skill and knowledge level of students prior to beginning almost any project. An **instructional model** is a systematic guide for planning instruction or a lesson. The **ASSURE Model** is a procedural guide for planning and delivering instruction that integrates technologies and media into the teaching process.

11. Technology Integration at a New School

Teachers need to consider many issues related to technology information and support, technology training, hardware, software, other technologies, and technology supplies. A **teacher's manual** is a booklet that contains information, rules and regulations, rights and responsibilities, and policies and procedures that will provide answers to many questions.

12. Learning Centers

Creating an integrated learning environment with centers is a great way to put it all together. **Centers,** or **learning centers,** give teachers the opportunity to break their classrooms into many different types of learning environments without ever leaving the room. Technology can make a difference in the classroom if used appropriately and integrated into the curriculum.

Key Terms

WEB INFO

IN BRIEF

KEY TERMS

CHECKPOINT

TEACHING TODAY

EDUCATION ISSUES

INTEGRATION CORNER

SOFTWARE CORNER

IN THE LAB

LEARN IT ONLINE

＊FEATURES...

Timeline 2004

Guide to WWW Sites

Buyer's Guide 2004

Professional Sites

State/Federal Sites

Interactive Labs

Search Tools

HOME

Web Instructions: To display this page from the Web, start your browser and enter the URL, www.course.com/tdc3. Click Chapter 6 at the top of the Web page and then click Key Terms on the left sidebar. Scroll through the list of terms. Click a term to display its definition and a picture. Click Key Terms on the left to redisplay the Key Terms page. Click the TO WEB button for current and additional information about the term from the Web.

active learning [6.12]
anchored instruction [6.12]
ASSURE Model [6.22]
authentic learning [6.12]

benchmark [6.04]
Body Works [6.13]

centers [6.28]
cognitive scaffold [6.13]
computer lab [6.06]
computer lab on wheels [6.19]
cooperative learning [6.15]
curriculum [6.02]
curriculum frameworks [6.02]
curriculum goal [6.03]
curriculum guides [6.02]
curriculum integration [6.05]
curriculum standard [6.03]

discovery learning [6.13]

education [6.02]
educational equalizer [6.14]

essential questioning technique [6.29]
evaluation [6.24]
evaluation process [6.24]

facilitator of learning [6.09]

Grade Level Expectations (GLEs) [6.03]

high-order thinking skills [6.15]

inservice [6.26]
instructional model [6.22]
integration [6.05]

K-12 curriculum [6.02]
KWHL chart [6.20]
KWL chart [6.20]

learning centers [6.28]
learning objective [6.04]
learning style [6.09]

mentorship program [6.16]
Microsoft Encarta [6.13]

point of instruction [6.06]
problem-based instruction [6.13]

reflective evaluation [6.24]

skill assessment survey [6.20]
state bid list [6.26]
student objectives [6.22]

teachable moment [6.06]
teacher's manual [6.25]
technology committee [6.25]
technology integration [6.05]
technology lab [6.06]
technology plan [6.16]

virtual tours [6.08]

Wellivers Instructional Transformation Model [6.10]
wireless mobile lab [6.19]

Checkpoint

Web Instructions: To display this page from the Web, start your browser and enter the URL, www.course.com/tdc3. Click Chapter 6 at the top of the Web page and then click Checkpoint on the left sidebar. Click a blank line for the answer. Click the links for current and additional information.

WEB INFO

IN BRIEF

KEY TERMS

CHECKPOINT

TEACHING TODAY

EDUCATION ISSUES

INTEGRATION CORNER

SOFTWARE CORNER

IN THE LAB

LEARN IT ONLINE

* FEATURES...

Timeline 2004

Guide to WWW Sites

Buyer's Guide 2004

Professional Sites

State/Federal Sites

Interactive Labs

Search Tools

HOME

1. Label the Figure

Instructions: Identify the five hierarchy stages of the Wellivers Instructional Transformation Model.

Wellivers Instructional Transformation Model

1. _____ is when teachers become aware of technology and its potential uses.

2. _____ is when teachers use technology, but minor problems will cause teachers to discontinue its use.

3. _____ is when technology becomes essential for the educational process and teachers are constantly thinking of ways to use technology in their classrooms.

4. _____ is when teachers begin to rethink the educational goals of the classroom with the use of technology.

5. _____ is the evolving classroom that becomes completely integrated with technology in all subject areas. Technology becomes an invisible tool that is seamlessly woven into the teaching and learning process.

2. Matching

Instructions: Match each term from the column on the left with the best description from the column on the right.

_____ 1. ASSURE Model

_____ 2. authentic learning

_____ 3. curriculum standards

_____ 4. mentorship program

_____ 5. KWL chart

a. lessons connected to real-life events

b. instructional planning tool to assist teachers in identifying curriculum objectives

c. procedural guide for planning and delivering instruction that integrates technology

d. collection of general concepts that school districts expect their students to learn

e. new teachers team with experienced teachers

3. Short Answer

Instructions: Write a brief answer to each of the following questions.

1. What is the difference between a curriculum standard and a benchmark? Are both curriculum standards and benchmarks measurable? Why or why not? _____

2. What are learning styles? How can a teacher be a facilitator of learning and at the same time address various students' learning styles? _____

3. Name five barriers to technology integration. In your opinion, which barrier is the most important? Why? _____

4. Name three people who can help teachers find information on available technologies in their schools. Describe other sources that can assist teachers in locating technology resources. _____

5. Name three areas teachers must address when planning for technology integration in a one-computer classroom. Can these same planning strategies also work for a two-computer classroom? _____

Teaching Today

Web Instructions: To display this page from the Web, start your browser and enter the URL, www.course.com/tdc3. Click Chapter 6 at the top of the Web page and then click Teaching Today on the left sidebar. Click the links for current and additional information.

WEB INFO

IN BRIEF

KEY TERMS

CHECKPOINT

TEACHING TODAY

EDUCATION ISSUES

INTEGRATION CORNER

SOFTWARE CORNER

IN THE LAB

LEARN IT ONLINE

✱ FEATURES...

Timeline 2004

Guide to WWW Sites

Buyer's Guide 2004

Professional Sites

State/Federal Sites

Interactive Labs

Search Tools

HOME

1. After using technology in your classroom, you are beginning to understand that using technology is different from integrating technology. You would like to begin integrating technology into your social studies curriculum. Where do you begin? Are resources available on the Internet that can help you? Where can you locate examples of <u>lesson plans</u> that integrate technology but still support your curriculum? Can you modify these lessons to use in your classroom?

2. Your school is located in a rural area, and technology funds are limited. You have used technology with students before and were encouraged by the results. You have one computer in your classroom and would really like to provide your students with greater access to technology. You have decided to explore possible <u>grant opportunities</u>. Your district is small, however, and does not have any grant programs. Very few businesses in your community offer grant opportunities. Where can you learn about other grant opportunities? Are grants available that are specific to your circumstances for which you can apply? What are some other funding options? What other organizations in your community could you contact?

3. You would like to integrate technology into your math curriculum, but you do not know where to start. You want to provide the students with authentic learning activities and you need ideas. You consider talking to a math teacher who integrates technology, but you do not know anyone. You have heard of a Web site where teachers can receive <u>mentoring</u> from other teachers and ask for advice and ideas. What are some advantages to finding assistance online? What are some disadvantages? Could you use this type of assistance for any subject? Why or why not? Could your students benefit from this

type of interaction? Why or why not? How can you locate more resources such as this for yourself and for your students?

4. As a teacher of students with special learning needs, you are very concerned about finding software that appeals to different learning styles. You would like to find a <u>Web resource</u> that will give you information about what learning styles are addressed by specific software products. Does it exist? How can this information assist regular education teachers? How could you evaluate software packages to see what learning styles they appeal to? Are learning styles important to consider when making software purchases? Why or why not?

Education Issues

Web Instructions: To display this page from the Web, start your browser and enter the URL, www.course.com/tdc3. Click Chapter 6 at the top of the Web page and then click Education Issues on the left sidebar. Click the links for current and additional information to help you respond to the Education Issues questions.

WEB INFO

IN BRIEF

KEY TERMS

CHECKPOINT

TEACHING TODAY

EDUCATION ISSUES

INTEGRATION CORNER

SOFTWARE CORNER

IN THE LAB

LEARN IT ONLINE

✷ FEATURES...

Timeline 2004

Guide to WWW Sites

Buyer's Guide 2004

Professional Sites

State/Federal Sites

Interactive Labs

Search Tools

HOME

1. Bilingual Education

A recent survey of state education agencies indicates that more than 4 million students with limited proficiency in English are enrolled in public schools and that this number is growing — dramatically, in many locations — every year. This trend poses unique challenges for educators who want to ensure that these students have the same opportunities as English-proficient students. In transitional bilingual education programs, instruction is provided for some subjects in the students' native language and part of the school day is spent on developing English skills. Bilingual education's critics argue that this approach keeps students in a cycle of native-language dependency that ultimately prevents them from making significant progress in English-language-acquisition and leads to lower test scores. These critics argue that these students must spend 100 percent of their time on task in English in order to master proficiency in English. What do you think? What Web site resources provide teachers with practical material for culturally diverse classrooms? What other technologies and teaching strategies can you use to enhance student learning?

2. Integrated Learning System

Your school district has spent a significant amount of money on a comprehensive integrated learning system that is available for all teachers to use throughout the district. This software generates tests and automatically tracks student progress. The software also includes thousands of interactive student assignments, data-driven decision-making capabilities, and the ability to create customized learning paths for your students so they can progress through the content at their own pace and path. What are some of the benefits of this type of software? What are some disadvantages? Does this type of software appeal to different learning styles? How could students with learning disabilities use this type of software?

3. Levels of Integration

It is the second month of the semester, and you are teaching seventh-grade science. The parents of one of your students contact you. They are upset because when their son was in elementary school, the majority of teachers were using technology in their classrooms. At your middle school, however, their son has not had the same opportunities. The parents are very concerned about the lack of technology. What can you do about this situation? To whom can you refer the parents? Do greater barriers to technology integration exist in middle schools than in elementary or high schools? Why or why not? How could you integrate technology into your seventh-grade science curriculum?

4. Integrating the Internet

In your school district, Internet access is available in all classrooms. Most teachers use the Internet for research. You would like to integrate the Internet in a meaningful way; however, you need some ideas about how to start. Where can you find suggestions on how to integrate the Internet into your classroom? What kinds of projects are the best to start with? What are other appropriate uses for the Internet, besides conducting research? Does your district offer training on Internet technology integration issues or just on how to use technology? How can you integrate the Internet to stimulate authentic learning? Is it appropriate to integrate the Internet for every subject area? Why or why not?

Integration Corner

WEB INFO

IN BRIEF

KEY TERMS

CHECKPOINT

TEACHING TODAY

EDUCATION ISSUES

INTEGRATION CORNER

SOFTWARE CORNER

IN THE LAB

LEARN IT ONLINE

✱ FEATURES...

Timeline 2004

Guide to WWW Sites

Buyer's Guide 2004

Professional Sites

State/Federal Sites

Interactive Labs

Search Tools

HOME

Web Instructions: To display this page from the Web, start your browser and enter the URL, www.course.com/tdc3. Click Chapter 6 at the top of the Web page and then click Integration Corner on the left sidebar. Click any Corner and then click the various links for extensive and curriculum-specific information.

Integration Corner is designed for teachers and other educators who are looking for innovative ways to integrate technology into their content-specific curriculum. Integration Corner not only provides great Web sites with current information but also shows what other educators are doing in the field of educational technology. These Corners are designed for all educators regardless of their area of interest. Review information and Web sites outside of your teaching area because many great integration ideas in one area easily can be modified for use in other curricular areas.

Teachers and administrators will find other colleagues in their areas with whom to connect and share the successes and hurdles of integrating technology in a classroom or an entire school system. Consider this your one stop for integration ideas and resources. Links to educational Web sites are organized in the following 12 Corners, and different Web resources are available for each chapter. Figure 6-37 shows examples of the Web resources provided in the Chapter 6 Post Secondary Corner.

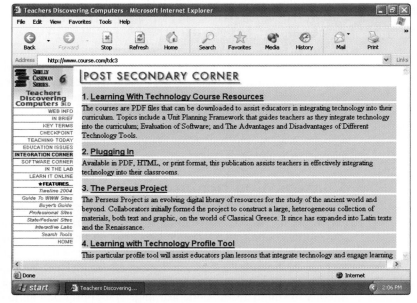

Figure 6-37 Examples of the Web resources provided in the Chapter 6 Post Secondary Corner.

Software Corner

Web Instructions: To display this page from the Web, start your browser and enter the URL, www.course.com/tdc3. Click Chapter 6 at the top of the Web page and then click Software Corner on the left sidebar. Click the links for additional information and instructions on how to download or receive an evaluation copy.

WEB INFO

IN BRIEF

KEY TERMS

CHECKPOINT

TEACHING TODAY

EDUCATION ISSUES

INTEGRATION CORNER

SOFTWARE CORNER

IN THE LAB

LEARN IT ONLINE

✱ FEATURES...

Timeline 2004

Guide to WWW Sites

Buyer's Guide 2004

Professional Sites

State/Federal Sites

Interactive Labs

Search Tools

HOME

1. Teaching students the concepts of pre-algebra and algebra can be a challenge. One software program that will help you meet this challenge is Mighty Math Astro Algebra from Riverdeep. Your students will be captains of a space ship and help the Algebra Alliance solve problems. Each new mission increases in complexity, and you can track student progress. The Grapher allows students to graph ordered pairs, equations, and inequalities. The VariaBlox feature allows students to use virtual manipulatives to solve mathematical problems. The AstroNet provides definitions, explanations, examples, and more. Mighty Math Astro Algebra is engaging and appeals to auditory, visual, and kinesthetic learners.

2. Let your students become scientists through interactive explorations with Science Plus Interactive Explorations. This software allows you and your students to have a virtual laboratory right in your own classroom, providing them with the resources to solve complex scientific problems in a real laboratory. Students investigate authentic, real-world problems, such as studying the temperatures of the volcanoes in Hawaii, researching soil chemistry and acid rain, designing the perfect toboggan ride, and much more. Dozens of explorations provide students with the opportunity to apply real-world solutions to scientific problems through the power of interactive laboratory simulations.

3. Reader Rabbit's Reading Series from The Learning Company provides a playful and engaging way for elementary students to develop essential building blocks to learn to read. The program includes activities to help recognize words and phonics; learn to read, decode, and spell; and develop and enhance vocabulary skills, visual memory, and concentration. It contains four activities, each of which has four levels of difficulty. The activities in Reader Rabbit's Reading 2 for Grades 1-3 contain more than 1,000 practice words and give students many opportunities to practice identifying consonant blends and short and long vowel sounds. A score chart tracks the number of correct responses and attempts, and displays the percentage of correct answers for each of the four levels. Included with the software is a teacher resource binder that includes a comprehensive user's guide, 17 detailed lesson plans, dozens of bonus ideas, Internet resources, a scope and sequence chart, and more.

4. Help your students learn continents, countries, states, capitals, borders, physical features, historical facts, and cultural monuments with games, software (most of it free), and educational activities from Owl & Mouse Educational Software. Your students can learn geography with a free interactive map that teaches the locations of the major cultural monuments of the world. Use the world geography interactive map to teach the physical features of the world including rivers, mountains, lakes, deserts, and rainforests. Your students can learn the countries of different continents and their capitals with fun and educational map puzzle games, too.

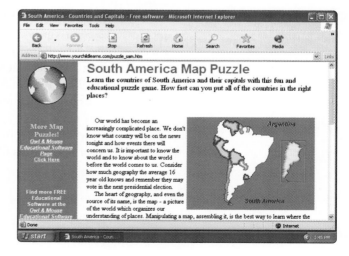

In the Lab 6

WEB INFO

IN BRIEF

KEY TERMS

CHECKPOINT

TEACHING TODAY

EDUCATION ISSUES

INTEGRATION CORNER

SOFTWARE CORNER

IN THE LAB

LEARN IT ONLINE

✱ FEATURES...

Timeline 2004

Guide to WWW Sites

Buyer's Guide 2004

Professional Sites

State/Federal Sites

Interactive Labs

Search Tools

HOME

Web Instructions: To display this page from the Web, start your browser and enter the URL, www.course.com/tdc3. Click Chapter 6 at the top of the Web page and then click In The Lab on the left sidebar. Click the links for tutorials, productivity ideas, integration examples and ideas, and more.

PRODUCTIVITY IN THE CLASSROOM

Introduction: Desktop publishing provides teachers with effective and efficient ways to communicate with students, parents, faculty, and others in a professional manner. Many word processing applications, such as Microsoft Word, AppleWorks, and Microsoft Works, provide templates enabling users to create newsletters and many other documents with ease. Many excellent desktop publishing software applications also are available. Microsoft Publisher and Adobe PageMaker are two popular programs used by educators. Exciting and innovative ways exist that allow teachers to integrate desktop publishing effectively into the curriculum. Students enjoy creating professional looking documents and finding creative ways to exhibit what they have learned.

1 Creating and Formatting a Parent Newsletter

Problem: As a kindergarten teacher, you believe it is important to send home monthly newsletters to keep parents informed of what is happening in the classroom. Open your word processing or desktop publishing software application and create a newsletter as described below. Use the newsletter shown in **Figure 6-38** as an example. If you are using a template, modify the newsletter design to accommodate the template. If you are using Microsoft Word, consider using tables, columns, section breaks, and text boxes to create the newsletter. (*Hint:* Use Help to understand the steps better.)

Instructions: Perform the following tasks.

1. Personalize the newsletter by inserting your name instead of Ms. Erhart's name and the grade level or subject you teach. Format the first and second heading lines in 16-point Times or Times New Roman font centered on the page.

2. Personalize the newsletter by using the current month and year. Enter the month and year right-aligned in 16-point Times or Times New Roman font.

3. Choose an appropriate picture, image, or clip art graphic, and then insert it on the page left-aligned.

4. Create an opening paragraph with at least three lines of text. Format the heading line in 14-point Times or Times New Roman font. Format the text in 12-point Times or Times New Roman font.

5. Create the body of the newsletter in two columns. Format section headings centered in uppercase 12-point Times or Times New Roman bold font. Format the text in 12-point Times or Times New Roman font.

6. Create a closing paragraph at the bottom of the newsletter. Format the text in 12-point Times or Times New Roman font.

7. Choose an appropriate picture, image, or clip art graphic and then insert it on the bottom-right side of the newsletter.

8. Save the document on a floppy disk with a file name of your choice. Print the document and then follow your instructor's directions for handing in the assignment.

In the Lab

WEB INFO

IN BRIEF

KEY TERMS

CHECKPOINT

TEACHING TODAY

EDUCATION ISSUES

INTEGRATION CORNER

SOFTWARE CORNER

IN THE LAB

LEARN IT ONLINE

✱ FEATURES...

Timeline 2004

Guide to WWW Sites

Buyer's Guide 2004

Professional Sites

State/Federal Sites

Interactive Labs

Search Tools

HOME

Ms. Erhart's Kindergarten Class Newsletter

February

Winter Wonders

January passed quickly for our class! February holds many fun activities and lots of good learning. Please be sure to join us for our Valentine's Day party and mark February 23 on your calendar for our special Black History event!

COME OUT AND READ

Our class is hosting a Come Out and Read night! Students can wear pajamas and get comfy on big pillows as they enjoy a good book with a parent or sibling. We also will have a special storyteller coming in to share some exciting stories with the group. Be sure to join us for the fun!

WHAT'S HAPPENING IN CLASS

We continue to focus on letter recognition and letter sounds during February. We also are studying the seasons and reading stories about winter. These are the stories we will use in class. Check them out from the library to reinforce these concepts at home!

A Snowy Day, by Ezra Jack Keats
The Mitten, by Jan Brett
Little Polar Bear, by Hans de Beer
Mama, Do You Love Me?, by Barbara M. Joosse

BLACK HISTORY MONTH

February is Black History Month, and students will learn about the contributions of inspirational African-Americans. To continue our focus on reading during February, we will be using the following books:

The Story of Ruby Bridges, by Robert Coles
Under the Quilt of Night, by Deborah Hopkinson
Sweet Clara and the Freedom Quilt, by Deborah Hopkinson
Martin's Big Words: The Life of Dr. Martin Luther King, Jr., by Doreen Rappaport
Amazing Grace, by Mary Hoffman

The class will work together and create an exciting presentation for their families on February 23! Look for more information in our next newsletter.

Reading is such an important skill, and together we can prepare your children to be successful readers and lifelong learners. Please do not hesitate to contact me if you have any questions or comments. Remember, you are always welcome to come into our classroom and be a part of the learning experience!

Figure 6-38

In the Lab

WEB INFO

IN BRIEF

KEY TERMS

CHECKPOINT

TEACHING TODAY

EDUCATION ISSUES

INTEGRATION CORNER

SOFTWARE CORNER

IN THE LAB

LEARN IT ONLINE

✱ FEATURES...

Timeline 2004

Guide to WWW Sites

Buyer's Guide 2004

Professional Sites

State/Federal Sites

Interactive Labs

Search Tools

HOME

2 Creating and Formatting a Department Newsletter

Problem: You are a member of your high school's Foreign Language department. Your responsibility is to communicate information to the rest of the Foreign Language department. You decide the easiest way to share new information is by creating a newsletter. Use the newsletter shown in Figure 6-39 as an example. (*Hint:* Use Help to understand the steps better.)

Instructions: Format the first and second heading lines in 14-point Arial bold font. Insert your name in place of Mr. Schatz in 12-point Times or Times New Roman bold font. Enter the current month and year in 14-point Arial bold font. Create the body of the newsletter in three columns. Personalize the information in the newsletter to reflect the grade level or subject that you teach. Format the section headings in 12-point Arial bold font. Format the text in 12-point Arial font. Format the country names in 11-point Arial bold font. Enter the Web site titles in 11-point Arial font. Format the Web site addresses in 10-point Arial font. Enter the quote in 12-point Times or Times New Roman italic font. Insert appropriate pictures, images, or clip art graphics.

After you have typed and formatted the newsletter, save the newsletter on a floppy disk with a file name of your choice. Print the newsletter and then follow your instructor's directions for handing in the assignment.

FOREIGN LANGUAGE DEPARTMENT NEWSLETTER
From Mr. Schatz

September

A New Beginning

This year's focus for the Foreign Language department is to integrate technology effectively in the classroom curriculum to enhance student learning and achievement. We have many exciting resources that will help us as we all endeavor to excite our students and improve their learning.

Fall Activities

Our multicultural festival is scheduled for late October. Each language class will prepare a food native to their country and create a PowerPoint presentation on the culture, customs, and favorite cities.

Virtual Field Trips

Be sure to attend this month's department meeting to learn more about virtual field trips and other great Web resources for our foreign language classes! Below are just a few examples:

France:
Musée des arts et métiers
http://www.arts-et-metiers.net/

Spain:
El Alcazar
http://www.GreatBuildings.com/buildings/The_Alcazar.html

If your plan is for one year, plant rice;
If your plan is for ten years, plant trees;
If your plan is for a hundred years, Educate children.
Confucius

Grant Funding

Our department received a grant intended to help students' reading and writing of foreign languages. Please provide me with a list of the software and additional reading materials you would like for your classroom. Each teacher can spend up to $600!!

Handhelds in the Classroom

We have an exciting opportunity to provide our students with access to handheld computers to enhance learning in the foreign language classrooms. We will be discussing methods of effective integration of handheld computers at our next department meeting on September 30. Be sure to attend to learn more!

Figure 6-39

In the Lab

3 Creating and Formatting a State Organization Newsletter

Problem: You are the secretary for your subject area state organization. It is your responsibility to create a newsletter summarizing your state convention, providing information for the following year's convention, and any other pertinent information.

Instructions: Create a newsletter similar to the newsletter illustrated in **Figure 6-39**. Use an appropriate layout, and then select font types and styles, font sizes, and clip art images for the newsletter. Include the current date, your name, and e-mail address. Save the newsletter on a floppy disk using an appropriate file name. Print the newsletter and then follow your instructor's directions for handing in the assignment.

INTEGRATION IN THE CLASSROOM

1 In honor of <u>Black History Month</u>, you have planned a cross-curricular project. You will divide students into groups and assign each group one of the following curricular areas: science, society and culture, math, art, music, or literature. Each group will choose one famous African-American to research that has made a significant contribution in the group's assigned field. Students then will create a newsletter outlining their findings. They will discuss the person's place of birth, family history, educational background, interests, and contributions to their particular field. Students will include at least one image in the newsletter. Select a famous African-American and create a sample newsletter for your students. Include your name and the current date in your sample newsletter.

2 Your high school Spanish class is studying cities in Spain. To reinforce reading and writing Spanish while learning about the country, students will create a newsletter written in Spanish. Students will work in groups and research three different cities in Spain. They will access and read <u>online newspapers</u> from the cities they select, gather <u>travel and tourist information</u>, obtain appropriate graphics that illustrate aspects of their chosen cities, and then create a newsletter in Spanish that presents the information they learned. Students will present their newsletter to the class and distribute a copy of it to each class member. Create a sample newsletter for your students. If you are not fluent in Spanish, select another foreign language. If you are not fluent in a foreign language, research three cities in Spain and create a newsletter presenting travel and tourist information written in English. Include your name, the current date, Web resources, and graphics in your sample newsletter.

3 While teaching the <u>American Revolution</u>, you team up with an English teacher to provide your students with a constructivist learning activity. Students will select one event that led up to the American Revolution and create a newsletter using information and images they locate from print resources and the Internet. Students will conduct their research in the history classroom and the English teacher will assist students with the layout, design, and writing techniques. Using the ideas and techniques you have learned in this section, create a sample newsletter for your students. Include your name, the current date, the course number, and course title in your sample newsletter.

Learn It Online

Web Instructions: To display this page from the Web, start your browser and enter the URL, www.course.com/tdc3. Click Chapter 6 at the top of the Web page and then click Learn It Online on the left sidebar. Click the buttons to display the exercise or the Interactive Lab.

WEB INFO

IN BRIEF

KEY TERMS

CHECKPOINT

TEACHING TODAY

EDUCATION ISSUES

INTEGRATION CORNER

SOFTWARE CORNER

IN THE LAB

LEARN IT ONLINE

✶ FEATURES...

Timeline 2004

Guide to WWW Sites

Buyer's Guide 2004

Professional Sites

State/Federal Sites

Interactive Labs

Search Tools

HOME

1. Shelly Cashman Series Setting Up to Print Lab

Click the button to the left to start and use the Shelly Cashman Series Setting Up to Print Lab.

2. Shelly Cashman Series Working at Your Computer Lab

Click the button to the left to start and use the Shelly Cashman Series Working at Your Computer Lab.

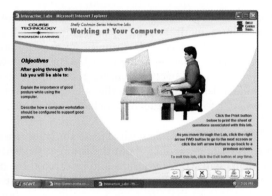

3. Teaching Style

When integrating technology into the curriculum, you use different teaching strategies. Click the button to the left to complete an online assessment to learn more about your teaching style, learning style, and classroom strategies.

4. One-Computer Classroom

Click the button to the left to complete an exercise to find information about how to use and integrate one computer into your classroom instruction.

5. Who Wants To Be a Computer Genius?

Click the button to the left to find out if you are a computer genius. Directions on how to play the game will display. When you are ready to play, click the PLAY button. Submit your score to your instructor.

6. Crossword Puzzle Challenge

Click the button to the left to complete the puzzle to reinforce skills you learned in this chapter. Directions on how to play the game will display. When you are ready to play, click the SUBMIT button. Submit the completed puzzle to your instructor.

7. Practice Test

Click the button to the left and answer each question. When completed, enter your name and click the Grade Test button to submit the quiz for grading. Make a note of any missed questions. If required, print a copy to submit to your instructor.

LEARNING THEORIES AND EDUCATIONAL RESEARCH

A great deal of discussion has taken place about the definition of learning by educational theorists, researchers, and practitioners; yet, no universal definition of learning has been accepted. As a result, numerous definitions exist, and they vary greatly in describing the exact nature of learning. For this textbook, **learning** is defined as the process of gaining knowledge or skills acquired through instruction or study, or to modify behavior through exposure to a type of conditioning or form of gaining experience. A **theory** is a scientific set of principles presented to clarify or explain a phenomenon. **Learning theories** provide frameworks for interpreting the conditions and observations of teaching and learning and provide the bridge between education and research.

Educational research builds the foundation for the development of sound instructional strategies; however, it takes practice and moving the theory into practice to create the bridge that evolves into technology integration. Each new lesson you present to your students should be based on learning theory and educational research. These learning theories have been shown to enhance learning and increase motivation and student achievement. Which learning theory you use depends on what you want to teach and how you want to teach it. This special feature highlights some of the theories and theorists that will help you better integrate technology into your curriculum. For more information about specific learning theories and researchers, including reference materials, access the Web Info annotations located in the margins throughout this special feature. To display a Web Info, access the textbook Web site, click Chapter 6, click Web Info, and then click the desired Web Info segment. The section on the next page discusses the constructivism learning theory.

CONSTRUCTIVISM

Web Info

For more information about Constructivism, visit the Teachers Discovering Computers Web site, click Chapter 6, click Web Info, and then click Constructivism.

Extensive research has been conducted to assist educators in better understanding which instructional strategies will increase students' motivation to learn and determine their comprehension of a subject. Many researchers agree that traditional teacher-directed or lecture-based instruction often is limited in its effectiveness to reach today's learners. Teacher-directed instruction, however, still is used in many classrooms because of its ability to deliver information quickly; yet, students' understanding and comprehension can be low when this is the only teaching method.

Confucius once said, "I hear and I forget. I see and I remember. I do and I understand." Constructivists agree that students learn by doing. When students actively participate in the learning process by using critical-thinking skills to analyze a problem, they will create, or construct, their own understanding of a topic or problem. **Constructivist** theory, or **constructivism,** is based on a type of learning in which the learner forms, or constructs, much of what he or she learns or comprehends (Figure 1). The following sections describe four leading theorists of constructivism.

Figure 1 Leading theorists of constructivism include Jean Piaget, Seymour Papert, Jerome Bruner, Lev Vygotsky, and John Dewey.

Jerome Bruner

An American psychologist and educator, Jerome Bruner (1915 –) proposed that learning is an active process in which the learner constructs new ideas or concepts based on his or her current or past knowledge (Figure 2). Bruner believes that constructivist learners are active learners; they are actively engaged in the learning process. Constructivism emphasizes an integrated curriculum where students learn a subject in various ways or through many different activities.

Technology offers many strategies for the constructivist learning environment. When using the constructivist approach, students may complete a variety of activities while learning about a topic. For example, if students are studying endangered species, they may research this topic by using books in the media center and informational Web sites. They can then use an AlphaSmart to write up their findings in a word processing document, study vocabulary words with electronic flash cards, create a drawing about endangered species in a paint program, build a model with clay, and even learn songs about saving endangered animals or species.

Web Info

For more information about Jerome Bruner, visit the Teachers Discovering Computers Web site, click Chapter 6, click Web Info, and then click Bruner.

Figure 2 Jerome Bruner's constructivist theory stresses that teachers actively should engage their students in their own learning.

Bruner's constructivist theory provides a framework for instruction based on the study of cognition. The theoretical concept of **cognition** suggests that an individual progresses through different intellectual stages. These stages, based on child development research conducted by researchers such as Jean Piaget, are discussed in the next section. In constructivist theory, the learner selects and changes information to understand and make decisions, relying on high-order thinking skills to solve a problem. An individual creates in his or her mind mental models that provide meaning and association to experiences that allow the individual to go beyond the given information. Bruner felt the teacher's role should be to encourage students through exploration and inquiry; in other words, learning should be discovery (Figure 3).

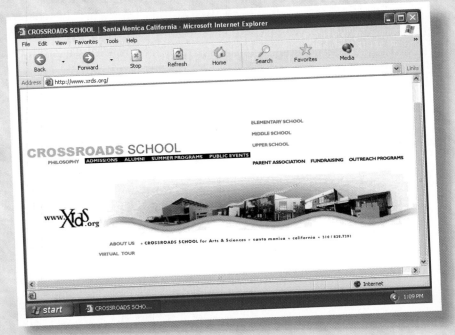

Figure 3 Many schools, such as CROSSROADS SCHOOL for Arts & Sciences, believe students should discover their own learning paths through active learning in areas such as intuition, imagination, artistic creativity, and physical expression.

As far as instruction is concerned, teachers should try to encourage students to discover concepts by themselves. Teachers should engage students by providing activities that guide students and create opportunities for discussion or for using the Socratic method of learning. The **Socratic method** is when students learn how to analyze problems, think critically about one's own point of view and the opinions of others, to articulate and defend their position. This method assists students in solving problems through questioning and answering techniques and engages them in discussion. The task of the teacher is to take the materials to be learned and translate the information into a form appropriate for the learners' current level of understanding. Bruner felt that the curriculum should be organized in a spiral manner so that students continually build upon what they already have learned; this is called the **spiral curriculum**.

Jean Piaget

The theories of Jean Piaget (1896 – 1980) profoundly influenced the constructivist movement (Figure 4). Piaget was a psychologist who developed the cognitive learning theory after he observed children for many years. Piaget perceived that children think very differently from adults. He felt children were active learners and did not need motivation from adults to learn. Piaget believed that children were constructing new knowledge as they moved through different cognitive stages, building on what they already knew. Furthermore, children interpret this knowledge differently as they progressed through different stages. Piaget defined four cognitive stages (Figure 5 on the next page).

Web Info

For more information about Jean Piaget, visit the Teachers Discovering Computers Web site, click Chapter 6, click Web Info, and then click Piaget.

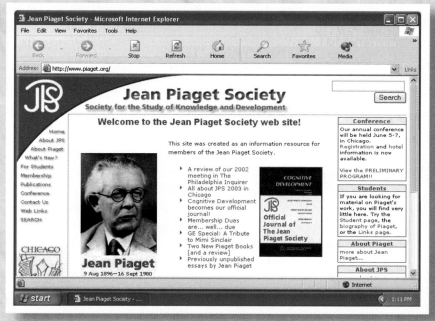

Figure 4 Jean Piaget was a psychologist who developed his learning theory after many years of observing children.

The first stage is called **sensorimotor**, when learning takes place primarily through the child's senses and motor actions. In the second stage, called **preoperational**, children begin to use symbols and images. Children use language symbols and play pretend games. An object such as a cardboard box can be a container, but it also can represent a house.

Next, children move from the two egocentric stages into the third stage called concrete operational. In this stage, beginning about age 7, children begin to think logically. This is the stage when children are beginning to learn many facts. They also can begin to understand other points of view besides their own. Piaget called his last cognitive stage formal operations. During this stage, which begins at about age 12, children transition from concrete thinking to more abstract. They can formulate a hypothesis and understand cause and effect. Children or adolescents begin to formulate their own beliefs and morals.

COGNITIVE STAGES	AGES (Approximate)	CHARACTERISTICS OF LEARNING
Sensorimotor	Birth to 2 years	Imitation, learn through senses and motor activities, do not understand the world around them, and egocentric
Preoperational	2 to 6/7 years	Egocentric, pretend play, drawing ability, speech and communication development, concrete thinking, and intuitive reasoning
Concrete operational	6/7 to 11/12 years	Classification, logical reasoning, problem solving, and beginnings of abstract thinking
Formal operations	11/12 years through adulthood	Comparative reasoning, abstract thinking, deductive logic, and test hypotheses

Figure 5 Piaget's four cognitive stages.

While they are learning, children create what Piaget called schema. **Schema** is their cognitive understanding or development at any given time. Piaget concluded that children assimilate new knowledge as they experience new things and learn new information, which is **assimilation**. Children fit this information or these experiences in their lives to change their knowledge base to make sense of their environment and the world around them, this process Piaget called **accommodation**. Piaget felt that children are working cognitively toward equilibrium as they move through the four different cognitive stages.

Through the insightful work of Piaget and others, researchers believe it is important to provide a rich learning environment for children to explore. Children learn by actively investigating a topic (Figure 6). Piaget's theories support the use and integration of technology because of the opportunities technology supplies to reach a diverse population of learners with different learning styles. Using Web Quests, scavenger and treasure hunts, curriculum pages, and many other educational technologies, teachers can create student-centered activities that actively engage students in the learning process.

Figure 6 Student learning comes alive when teachers integrate the Internet and multimedia software into their classroom curriculum.

Lev Vygotsky

Lev Vygotsky (1896 – 1934), a Russian educational psychologist, also was interested in children's cognitive development (Figure 7). He developed what is known as **social constructivist theory**. While his ideas overlap in many ways with the traditional constructivists' point of view, Vygotsky believed that learning was influenced significantly by social development. He theorized that learning took place within the context of a child's social development and culture. For instance, when children vocalize, they learn that sounds have meanings and sounds become language. They learn that spoken language becomes the inner language that children use to think or develop cognitively. They also learn that gestures have meaning and are used to communicate and interact with others.

Web Info

For more information about Lev Vygotsky, visit the Teachers Discovering Computers Web site, click Chapter 6, click Web Info, and then click Vygotsky.

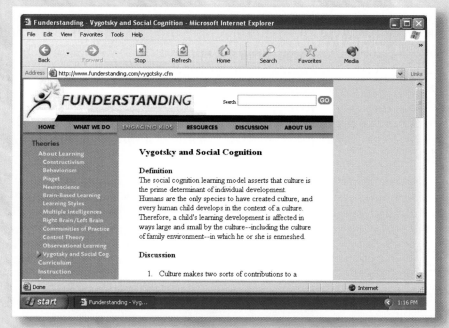

Figure 7 Len Vygotsky was a Russian psychologist who believed that learning is influenced significantly by social development.

As stated earlier, Piaget believed children progressed through different stages of cognitive development and that achieving higher levels of thinking was not accomplished easily. Lev Vygotsky believed that a child's social environment could positively or negatively affect the child's cognitive development. Vygotsky proposed that children have a **zone of proximal development**, which is the difference between the problem-solving ability that a child has learned and the potential that the child can achieve from collaboration with a more advanced peer or expert, such as a teacher.

If some form of expertise challenges a child, then greater cognitive development can occur. Vygotsky theorized that if a 9-year-old child worked on a problem with an adult or another child that was advanced, the 9-year-old would be able to learn the concept or ideas that were more complex than the 9-year-old could understand on his or her own; this is known as **collaborative learning**. With practice, the child then would be able to apply the new cognitive skills to other situations. Vygotsky felt students should work collaboratively to share their different perspectives with each other; then they could negotiate a solution and come to a much deeper understanding of a problem or tasks (Figure 8).

Furthermore, Vygotsky proposed that teachers should discover the level of each child's cognitive/social development, and build or construct their learning experiences from that point. He referred to this process as **scaffolding**. In education, a scaffold is altering of the **schemata**, which is an organized way of creating or providing a cognitive mental framework for understanding and remembering information. As teachers and other students provide information and different perspectives for each other, these sources can become a scaffold, a temporary source of knowledge. Then students assimilate this knowledge and build their own, thus removing the need for a scaffold.

Building on constructivism theory and Vygotsky's scaffolding, the Cognition and Technology Group at Vanderbilt (CTGV) developed anchored instruction. **Anchored instruction** is a model for technology-based learning and is a form of instruction where the student already has learned concepts and information, forming a basis for other information to connect to and build upon, which is called the **anchor**. The CTGV wanted to create complex, realistic problems that students could explore and then develop potential solutions. When challenged with a problem, anchored instruction motivates students to build new ideas and anchor them to what they already have learned.

Figure 8 Vygotsky believed students should work collaboratively to share their different perspectives with each other. Here students use handheld computers to work together to solve math problems.

John Dewey

John Dewey (1859 – 1952) has influenced American education significantly (Figure 9). He was an educational psychologist, philosopher, and political activist who was an advocate for child-centered instruction. He believed that learning should engage and expand the experiences of the learners. He encouraged educators to reflect on their strategies and create activities that combine concrete and practical relevance to students' lives.

Like Vygotsky, Dewey believed that education was a social process. He viewed school as a community that represented a larger picture. In 1896, Dewey began the University Elementary School, or Laboratory School. Many educators called this school the Dewey School. The school prospered and earned national attention. Dewey felt that school should be viewed as an extension of society and students should play an active role in it, working cooperatively with each other. Dewey viewed learning as student-directed with a teacher serving as a guide for resources. He believed students learn by doing and should be allowed to construct, create, and actively inquire. Dewey theorized that this type of learning truly prepared students to function well in society.

Web Info

For more information about John Dewey, visit the Teachers Discovering Computers Web site, click Chapter 6, click Web Info, and then click Dewey.

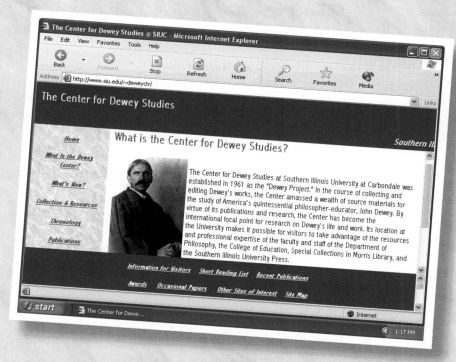

Figure 9 John Dewey, an educational psychologist and philosopher, believed that learning should engage and expand the experiences of the learners.

Dewey was part of a movement in the early 1900s that was called progressive education. **Progressive education** focused on educating the whole child, physically, mentally, and socially, and not on just the dispensation of facts and information. John Dewey's name also has been linked to other early movements, such as **pragmatism**. Pragmatists believed that the truth of a theory could be determined only if a theory worked. In other words, theory is valuable only for its practical application.

Dewey founded several schools in addition to his Laboratory School. He advocated educational reform, pursued philosophy, and supported many political issues, such as women's suffrage. Through his observations, he proposed that education begins with experience. He has been called, by some, the Father of American Education. His influence can be seen in American classrooms today — children are exploring the curriculum, conducting science experiments, using manipulatives for math, and searching the Internet for information.

BEHAVIORISM

As you have learned, constructivism focuses on students being engaged in discovery learning through activities, which accelerate the process of learning. Another popular education theory is behaviorism. **Behaviorism** is a theory that centers on learning, but only as it relates to behavior, not the internal cognitive processing of information. Teachers have implemented these theories for some time. After all, a teacher cannot communicate information very well if he or she cannot control student behavior. Teachers always have used positive and negative rewards. For some students, this type of conditioning works very well. Behaviorists such as Pavlov, Skinner, and Gagne have contributed a great deal to the understanding of human behavior, and their contributions are described in the following sections.

Web Info

For more information about Behaviorism, visit the Teachers Discovering Computers Web site, click Chapter 6, click Web Info, and then click Behaviorism.

Ivan Pavlov

Ivan Pavlov (1849 – 1936) became famous for his behavioral experiments with dogs and won the Nobel Prize in Physiology in 1904 (Figure 10). Pavlov used conditioning to teach dogs to salivate when he rang a bell. When he provided the motivation (food), he achieved his desired effect (salivation). Eventually, the dogs associated the bell with food and they began to salivate when Pavlov rang the bell. This process was termed **classic conditioning** and refers to the natural reflex that occurs in response to a stimulus. Pavlov was a scientist, and he conducted these experiments to study digestion, but as a result, other behaviorists studied his work as an example of stimulus response. Some behaviorists felt this technique of stimulus response had human applications as well.

Web Info

For more information about Ivan Pavlov, visit the Teachers Discovering Computers Web site, click Chapter 6, click Web Info, and then click Pavlov.

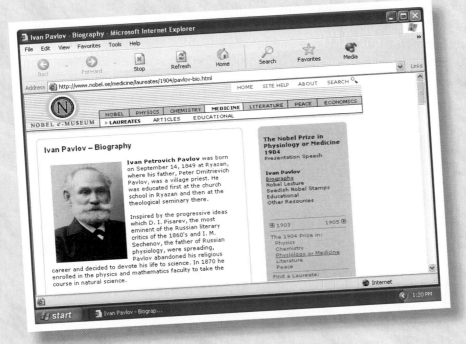

Figure 10 Ivan Pavlov's research into the physiology of digestion led him to create a science of conditioned reflexes that won him the Nobel Prize in 1904.

B.F. Skinner

B.F. Skinner (1904 – 1990) describes another form of conditioning that is labeled as behavioral or operant conditioning (Figure 11). **Operant conditioning** describes learning that is controlled and results in shaping behavior through the reinforcement of stimulus response patterns. Skinner conducted experiments with pigeons and rewarded them when he saw them behaving in a desired manner. When a stimulus response pattern occurs, such as a pigeon turning (a stimulus) then a reward is given (response). Eventually, Skinner was able to teach pigeons to dance using this technique. Ultimately, he taught pigeons to engage in complex tasks such as bowling in a specially constructed bowling alley.

Skinner believed that people shape their behavior based on the rewards or positive reinforcement they receive. Skinner believed human behavior, even the language development of children, is based on stimulus response theory. He observed that when children made attempts at sounds, parents smiled and reinforced that behavior. Eventually, the child learns to say the word correctly as parents and others reinforce his or her efforts.

Figure 11 B.F. Skinner made many contributions to the field of psychology, including the theory of behavioral or operant conditioning.

Web Info

For more information about B.F. Skinner, visit the Teachers Discovering Computers Web site, click Chapter 6, click Web Info, and then click Skinner.

In his experiments, Skinner found that reinforcement was a powerful motivator. He conducted experiments with people as well and he even used his own infant daughter. Skinner felt that when a child produces a desirable behavior and is rewarded for it, that behavior will be repeated. In contrast, if a response is negative, the behavior will be extinguished. Many classroom management techniques are based on these principles. Figure 12 compares classical and operant conditioning.

CLASSICAL CONDITIONING Pavlov	OPERANT CONDITIONING Skinner
Classical conditioning introduces the stimulus and then reinforces the response. A neutral stimulus (the bell) becomes analogous with a reflex (salivation).	Operant conditioning begins with a response (behavior) and then is reinforced with a stimulus (reward). A bond becomes established between the operant (behavior) and the reward.

Figure 12 Classical versus operant conditioning.

Many forms of computer-based instruction and educational software are based on Skinner's operant conditioning. They provide positive reinforcement when a desired behavior occurs and negative reinforcement when the student does not provide the desired behavior. For instance, when the correct answer is given, the software program provides positive verbal and visual feedback for the student's correct response. As Figure 13 shows, even young children enjoy learning and getting positive feedback.

Figure 13 Many software and hardware developers are designing products to reinforce learning for younger students.

Robert Gagne

Web Info

For more information about Robert Gagne, visit the Teachers Discovering Computers Web site, click Chapter 6, click Web Info, and then click Gagne.

Robert Gagne (1916 – 2002), a psychologist and educator, developed his learning theories based partially from the behaviorist's and information-processing point of view. Gagne is known for his contributions in the area of cognitive learning hierarchies, which involves the development of skills based on a building-block principle. Gagne identified five major categories of learning: cognitive strategies, verbal information, intellectual skills, motor skills, and attitudes. He made an enormous contribution to learning theory and instructional systems design. While in the Air Force, he began to develop some of his ideas for his comprehensive learning theory. He incorporated characteristics of both behavior modification theory as well as performance education.

Gagne developed three principles that he viewed as integral for successful instruction: (1) providing instruction on the set of component tasks that build toward a final task, (2) ensuring that each component task is mastered, and (3) sequencing the component tasks to ensure optimal transfer to the final task. In other words, a teacher must teach alphabet recognition so that his or her students can read words. Once students can read words, they can read a sentence, and then two sentences, and then a paragraph, etc. This process reflects a hierarchy of components.

Careful planning must take place so that learning is optimal and instruction can be broken down into carefully planned lessons. Gagne believed that a variety of internal and external conditions must be present for learning to occur and he also believed that learning results in observable behavior. The internal conditions can be described as states that include attention, motivation, and recall. The external conditions are the factors surrounding a person, such as timing and place. The observable behavior is the result of the internal process of learning. Further, Gagne discussed that learners must go through a hierarchy of skills from simple to complex and identified five areas of learning outcomes (Figure 14).

CATEGORIES OF LEARNING	EXAMPLES OF OUTCOMES
1. Verbal information	Learner can state what has been learned
2. Intellectual skills: composed of concrete and defined concepts	Learner can discriminate between facts, can identify colors, and can follow directions
3. Cognitive strategies	Learner reads books
4. Motor skills	Learner can use a mouse or joystick
5. Attitudes	Learner prefers reading to watching TV

Figure 14 Gagne's five areas of learning outcomes.

Gagne sought to understand what conditions were necessary for students to learn. Instruction is an external condition for learning that leads to the internal process of learning. To maximize the potential for the internal process of learning to occur, Gagne identified **nine events of instruction** (Figure 15).

NINE EVENTS OF INSTRUCTION

1. Gain attention of the learners
2. Inform learners of the objective
3. Stimulate recall of prior learning
4. Present the stimulus or lesson
5. Provide learning guidance and instruction

6. Elicit performance
7. Provide feedback
8. Assess performance
9. Enhance retention and transfer

Figure 15 Gagne's nine events of instruction can help teachers develop technology-enriched lesson plans.

OTHER EDUCATIONAL THEORISTS

In addition to constructivists and behaviorists, many other leading researchers and theorists have impacted education in positive and important ways. Two of these important researchers and their contributions are described below.

Howard Gardner

Many researchers have focused on understanding and defining intelligence. They believe that intelligence is a key to understanding how students learn. **Intelligence** is the ability to gain knowledge, apply knowledge, manipulate one's environment, and think abstractly. Howard Gardner (1943 –) developed what he called the theory of multiple intelligences (Figure 16 on the next page).

Gardner, a professor at Harvard University, has conducted years of research on normal and gifted students and also studied adults with brain damage. In those who had been injured, he wanted to correlate what part of the brain had been injured and how the physical injury affected learning and other physical abilities. Through his research, he concluded that individuals use eight different intelligences to perceive and understand the world. Gardner's eight intelligences and suggested integration strategies are described in Figure 17 on page 6.61.

Web Info

For more information about Howard Gardner, visit the Teachers Discovering Computers Web site, click Chapter 6, click Web Info, and then click Gardner.

Figure 16 Howard Gardner is a professor at Harvard Graduate School of Education and is best known for his theory of multiple intelligences.

Gardner believes that individuals may have all of the intelligences, yet one, two, or more intelligences may be more dominant than others. The intelligences also are influenced by biological predisposition and learning opportunities in an individual's cultural context. The teacher-directed learning style appeals strongly to the linguistic-verbal and logical-mathematical intelligences. Gardner suggests that instructional methods should support a variety of other activities that will appeal to other intelligences, sush as physical education, role-playing, arts, cooperative learning, reflections, and creative play.

A variety of assessment methods should be incorporated for students to reflect their learning more accurately. An important observation Gardner made was identifying that educators need to take into account the differences in students' multiple intelligences and use them as a guide to personalize instruction and assessment, which results in the ability to design appropriate instructional strategies.

INTELLIGENCE	DESCRIPTION	TECHNOLOGY INTEGRATION
Linguistic–verbal	Ease in using language; think in words; sensitivity to rhythm and order; enjoy writing, reading, telling stories, and doing crossword puzzles	Word processing programs, prompted programs, label-making programs, word game programs, and programs that require the student to read and answer questions
Logical–mathematical	Ability to engage in inductive and deductive reasoning; use numbers effectively and to categorize, infer, make generalizations, and test hypotheses	Database programs, spreadsheet programs, problem-solving software, simulations that allow students to experiment with problems and observe results, strategy game formats, and probeware
Spatial–visual	Ability to visualize objects and special dimensions, think in images and pictures, like to draw and design, and enjoy puzzles	Draw and paint programs; graphic production software; reading programs that use visual clues such as color coding, desktop publishing, hypermedia, multimedia, concept mapping, and atlas programs
Body–kinesthetic	Ability to move the body with skill and control, expertise in using the body to express ideas and feelings	Software requiring alternate input such as joystick, mouse, touch window, or graphics tablet; keyboarding/word processing programs; graphics programs that produce blueprints for making 3-D models; and software that includes animated graphics
Musical	Ability to recognize patterns and sounds; sensitivity to pitch and rhythm; the capacity to perceive, express, transform or discern musical forms; think in tones, and learn through rhythm and melody	Programs that combine stories with songs; reading programs that associate letters/sounds with music; programs that use music as a reward; programs that allow students to create their own songs, hypermedia, and multimedia
Interpersonal	Ability to understand and communicate effectively with others, understand them, and interpret their behavior	Telecommunications programs, programs that address social issues, programs that include group participation or decision-making, programs that turn learning into a social activity, and games that require two or more players
Intrapersonal	An awareness of oneself, goals, and emotions; the capacity for self-knowledge of one's own feelings; and the ability to use that knowledge for personal understanding	Tutorial software, programs that are self-paced, instructional games in which the opponent is the computer, programs that encourage self-awareness or build self-improvement skills, and programs that allow students to work independently
Naturalist	An awareness of the natural world around them; can identify people, plants, and other environmental features; can develop a sense of cause and effect in relation to natural occurrences such as weather; can formulate and test hypotheses	Problem-solving software, simulations that allow students to experiment with problems and observe results, strategy game formats, database software, concept mapping software, and weather probeware

Figure 17 Using Gardner's eight multiple intelligences and technology integration, teachers can find ways to reach all students.

Benjamin Bloom

Benjamin Bloom (1913 – 1999), an educational psychologist, focused his research on students' cognitive learning domain (Figure 18). Bloom and a group of psychologists sought to classify learning behaviors to understand better how knowledge is absorbed. Bloom classified learning into three domains: cognitive, affective, and psychomotor. Bloom defined the **cognitive domain** as a student's intellectual level, in other words, what a student knows and how he or she organizes ideas and thoughts. He defined the **affective domain** as a student's emotions, interests, attitude, attention, and awareness. Finally, he categorized the **psychomotor domain**, which includes a student's motor skills and physical abilities. All of these domains can overlap in learning activities and are integrated throughout learning experiences.

Bloom wanted to develop a practical means for classifying goals and objectives. Many instructors today develop their goals and objectives with these three domains in mind. Educators are responsible for planning curriculum activities with the objectives that support what students already should know and what they should learn. Teachers create their instructional plans from state standards and learning theories, and then design their daily activities for their classrooms. The knowledge a teacher wants his or her students to gain from a lesson can be arranged from simple to complex. Within the cognitive domain, Bloom identified six levels

Web Info

For more information about Benjamin Bloom, visit the Teachers Discovering Computers Web site, click Chapter 6, click Web Info, and then click Bloom.

Figure 18 Benjamin Bloom's research focused on developing student problem-solving abilities and high-order thinking skills. He was the creator of the concepts of Mastery Learning and Bloom's Taxonomy.

that can be used to acquire knowledge about a topic. The levels move from simple to complex and are designed to increase a student's comprehension. These levels commonly are referred to as **Bloom's Taxonomy** (Figure 19).

Many teachers may not realize they are creating instructional plans that only challenge students within the first two levels. For instance, if students are learning about computers and then are asked to name only the parts and describe what they do, the activity has stayed in the Knowledge and Comprehension levels. If students are asked to propose how computers have changed their lives, the assignment has moved to the Analysis level.

Bloom's Taxonomy has been linked to mastery learning. **Mastery learning** is defined as a model for learning in which students continue to gain information and knowledge, working through modules or teacher instruction until they have mastery of content. Mastery is determined by the length of time it takes a student to learn. All students can learn given the correct conditions for learning and sufficient time. Bloom believed and demonstrated through his research that all children can learn. The critical ingredient is changing instructional methods so students can master the content.

COMPETENCIES	SKILLS
Knowledge: Learner can recall information	Arrange, repeat, recall, define, list, match, name, order, write
Comprehension: Learner can explain and predict	Discover, classify, explain, discuss, give examples, identify, explain, translate
Application: Learner can solve problems and use information	Apply, demonstrate, solve, write, discover, experiment, interpret, show, present
Analysis: Learner can see patterns, organize parts, recognize hidden meanings	Analyze, experiment, examine, compare, contrast, associate, dissect, conclude, test
Synthesis: Learner can use previous ideas to createnew ones, relate ideas from several areas	Collect, assemble, compose, develop, design, invent, create, plan, revise, write, theorize
Evaluation: Learner can compare and discriminate between ideas, judge, and value ideas	Compare, assess, contrast, criticize, evaluate, judge, value, predict, estimate, appraise

Figure 19 The six levels of Bloom's Taxonomy move from simple to complex.

Web Info

For more information about Bloom's Taxonomy, visit the Teachers Discovering Computers Web site, click Chapter 6, click Web Info, and then click Bloom's Taxonomy.

THE CLASSROOM IN ACTION

This section explores how one teacher puts learning theories into action. Nirsa Gautier, a fourth grade teacher, was busy working on a simple spelling rule that her class was having difficulty remembering. Suddenly, she thought of a great idea that might enhance her lesson and assist her students' learning using Bloom's Taxonomy.

Mrs. Gautier stopped her spelling lesson and drew a ladder on the whiteboard (Figure 20). She listed the six thinking levels on the ladder and then explained each level in simple terms. She told her students that for them to be successful thinkers, they needed to progress to each level. The new class goal was to get to the highest level!

Mrs. Gautier then went back to the spelling lesson. She asked her students to identify what thinking level they were operating at on the *thinking ladder*. Some of the students were able to tell her immediately that they were at the Knowledge level. She explained that they could not move to higher levels of thinking success without mastering this basic knowledge. Now she had their attention! The class all agreed they had to remember the rule to move up the ladder.

Mrs. Gautier asked her students to work in groups collaboratively for five minutes to help each other remember the rule. She knew this was a great constructivist learning strategy. After five minutes, she randomly called on students to see if their group strategy had worked. To her amazement, every student she called on knew the rule! She congratulated the class on a job well done and then challenged them to move up to the next level of the thinking ladder.

After this experience, Mrs. Gautier created a large thinking ladder using a word processing program and placed it in the center of the classroom for her students to view. She wanted to make sure that she was integrating the thinking ladder learning strategy into every class lesson. Mrs. Gautier printed the thinking levels on cardstock, glued magnets on the back and placed each thinking level on a rung of the ladder. This gave the students colorful visual cues as they moved along the thinking continuum to a higher thinking level. Mrs. Gautier also created a PowerPoint presentation using pictures that illustrated how the students move up the thinking ladder to thinking success (Figure 21). In the presentation, she explained in more detail each thinking level and how to apply it when the students read, solve problems, and answer questions. Mrs. Gautier had her students discuss which questions were more difficult to answer.

Figure 20 Mrs. Gautier's thinking ladder is based on Bloom's Taxonomy.

The students began to realize that high-level thinking involves more time and thought. Consequently, Mrs. Gautier also realized that she must give her students more time to think before answering questions. She decided to call this *think time*.

To encourage high-order thinking skills, Mrs. Gautier had her students develop questions based on a reading selection. The students responded in their journals and wrote three questions for the selection. Each question had to come from a different thinking level. She found that by asking students to write or construct their own thinking questions from different levels, they first must be able to think on that level. She then would have a student ask a question, another student answer the question, and a third student identify the thinking level. Mrs. Gautier found that often students created better thinking questions than she did! Additionally, many of the students were thrilled to know that they were able to answer questions that required high-level thinking. They liked the challenge.

Mrs. Gautier works her thinking ladder into every subject. When the students create multimedia research projects, she makes sure to include an aspect of each thinking level in the assessment rubric used for evaluation. This guides the students to find information, analyze and evaluate what they read, and then apply it in a meaningful way. After introducing Bloom's Taxonomy in the class, Mrs. Gautier noticed a real excitement as students began to strive to move up the ladder of thinking success.

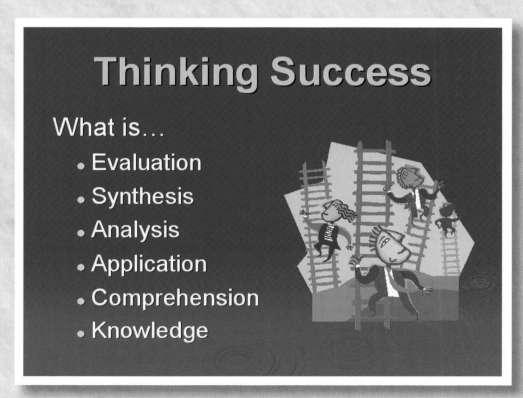

Figure 21 Mrs. Gautier uses PowerPoint to teach her students how to use high-order thinking skills to move up the thinking ladder.

Teaching students thinking skills using Bloom's Taxonomy revolutionized the way Mrs. Gautier teaches and the way her students learn. Her students became more focused because not only were they thinking, but they consciously were developing the thinking process! They became more confident, taking more responsibility for their learning, and realizing that they must do the thinking in order to learn.

SUMMARY OF LEARNING THEORIES AND EDUCATIONAL RESEARCH

Learning is a complex task. Understanding how students learn is an internal process that is difficult to observe. Educators can provide instruction and information, and assess how much information has been retained. Educational research and learning theories are important because they help educators to understand how students learn. From learning theories and research, teachers can improve their instruction, the way they provide information to learners, and they also can improve teaching and learning environments.

Integrating technology into teaching is a very powerful way to weave these learning theories throughout the curriculum. Multimedia technology appeals to a variety of learning styles and learning intelligences (Gardner). Students are more actively engaged in their learning when teachers effectively integrate technology (Bruner). Technology is effective with group projects, working in teams (Vygotsky and Dewey), and problem-solving activities requiring high-order thinking skills that allow students to build new ideas from their current knowledge base (Bloom). Teachers even have used computer time effectively as part of a behavior management system (Pavlov and Skinner).

Learners are dynamic and no two will be the same. In this regard, theorists help teachers understand how to adapt instruction, information, and the environment for different learners. So, much is to be gained by understanding learning theories and what each theorist has contributed. Their ideas can help educators piece together the complex task of teaching all learners.

Integrating learning theories and technology into classroom instructional strategies can make a difference in student motivation and also can increase student achievement in your classroom!

For information on the references used in the creation of this special feature, see Appendix C or access this special feature's Web Info segments.

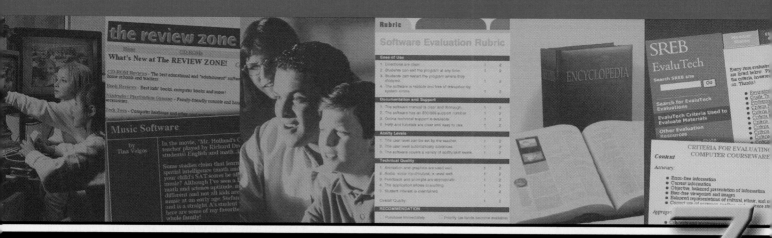

Evaluating Educational Technology and Integration Strategies

Objectives

After completing this chapter, you will be able to:

- Identify sources of information for evaluating technology

- Describe the considerations and tools used to evaluate software applications

- List and explain the key criteria used to evaluate Web resources

- Describe the tools for evaluating the effectiveness of technology

- Describe the methods used to evaluate student projects

- Identify different technology integration strategies by classroom layout

- Define and describe the value of a curriculum page

- Describe ways to integrate technology into specific curriculum subject areas

- Identify possible sources of funding for classroom technology

As you learn about the various types of emerging technology and methods of integrating them into your classroom curriculum, undoubtedly, you will be called upon to evaluate the appropriateness of this technology and the effectiveness of its integration into the learning process. This chapter presents an overview of how to evaluate the many different types of technologies that are available today. It also offers specific strategies for how to integrate technology in your classroom based on the number of computers available to you and your students. Also provided are several subject-specific examples of curriculum integration activities, such as creating and using curriculum pages. Finally, this chapter suggests several ways you can raise funds to pay for state-of-the-art technology in your classroom to enhance the teaching and learning experience.

Evaluating Educational Technology

Evaluating the appropriateness and effectiveness of educational technology is an important aspect of integrating current technology into the classroom. To **evaluate** an item is to determine its value or judge its worth. Evaluating educational technology involves determining if the technology is appropriate and enhances the teaching and learning process. To be considered **appropriate**, educational technology must be suitable for the educational situation and promote learning at the correct levels of ability and academic achievement.

Evaluating educational technology before instruction begins, during the instructional period, and after instruction has taken place is important. [Figure 7-1]. Before using software or sites on the World Wide Web, for example, teachers should determine if this technology meets their curriculum needs and if the product or content is developmentally and age appropriate for their classroom learning situation. Information from many sources helps teachers evaluate the appropriateness of educational technologies.

SOURCES OF INFORMATION

Finding the right educational technology can be difficult, especially for new users of technology, because each year, developers create hundreds of new educational software packages and Web sites for K-12 classroom use [Figure 7-2]. To avoid confusion in this important task, teachers may rely on a variety of resources to help them identify and evaluate the appropriateness of educational technologies. These resources include material from school districts, state Departments of Education, hardware and software catalogs, recommendations from other teachers, and Web sites.

SCHOOL DISTRICTS AND STATE DEPARTMENTS OF EDUCATION Many school districts compile software evaluations that provide guidance on subject-specific software. In addition, many state Departments of Education provide lists of software that are recommended and evaluated by educators. Teachers can access these lists and evaluations at state-sponsored Web sites or they may request them in printed form.

To assist you in locating these sources of information from your school district and state Department of Education, contact your technology coordinator, principal, media specialist, technology committee, or other teachers.

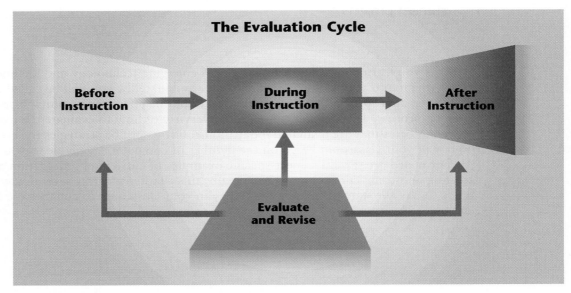

Figure 7-1 Successful technology integration requires evaluation during all phases of instruction.

Figure 7-2 Numerous high-quality educational software packages are available for classroom use.

PROFESSIONAL EDUCATIONAL ORGANIZATIONS Many local, state, regional, national, and international educational organizations provide extensive information on how to evaluate educational resources [Figure 7-3]. Many of these groups provide Web sites with information and feedback on software program levels, content, and pricing.

CATALOGS Often, companies list their hardware and software suited for educational use in catalogs. These catalogs are a valuable resource to help identify technologies for your classroom. In addition to providing information about existing and new products, many software firms also provide information about how their products relate to curriculum and learning standards. You may order free catalogs from most companies by calling a toll-free number or completing an online form at the company's Web site.

RECOMMENDATIONS OF COLLEAGUES
A good way to identify software and other technology that has potential for your classroom is to talk to other educators. Colleagues can offer advice about outstanding products as well as about those to avoid — advice that often is based on first-hand experience.

PUBLISHED EVALUATIONS Departments of Education, professional organizations, and other educational groups publish evaluations of new products. Numerous software developers include evaluations completed by educators on their Web sites. Many educational publications and journals also have sections dedicated to reviews of educational technologies. In addition, many online publications, journals, and other Web sites provide educators with comprehensive evaluations and reviews of educational software and hardware [Figure 7-4].

TECHNOLOGY CONFERENCES Every year, dozens of national and state organizations host educational technology conferences [Figure 7-5]. A **technology conference** is a meeting dedicated to providing a vast array of information and resources for teachers. This gathering may be large or small and includes workshops and presentations by educators and vendors on hundreds of technology topics. In addition, software and hardware vendors usually have booths staffed by representatives to provide teachers with demonstrations and information about their products.

To preview Tom Synder software products, visit the Teachers Discovering Computers Web site, click Chapter 7, click Web Info, and then click Tom Synder.

How can teachers find out about educational technology conferences in their state or across the country?

Access T.H.E. Journal's conference calendar at: www.theconference-calendar.com and search by month, year, state, and country.

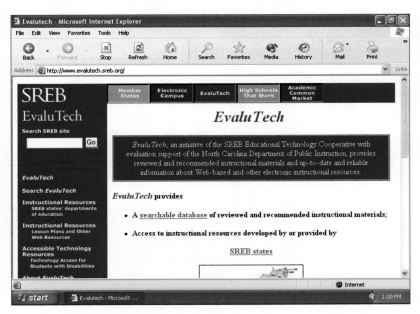

Figure 7-3 Many local, state, regional, national, and international educational organizations maintain Web sites that provide teachers with evaluations of educational technologies.

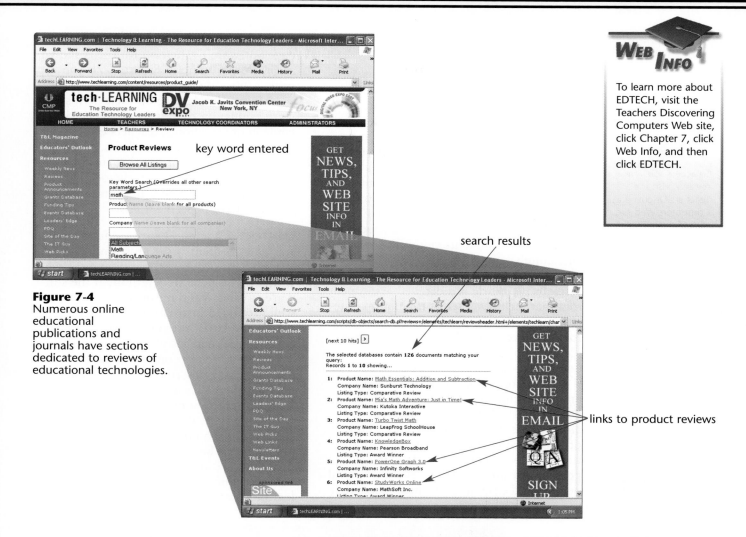

To learn more about EDTECH, visit the Teachers Discovering Computers Web site, click Chapter 7, click Web Info, and then click EDTECH.

key word entered

search results

links to product reviews

Figure 7-4
Numerous online educational publications and journals have sections dedicated to reviews of educational technologies.

THE WEB By far, the Web is the most comprehensive source of tools and resources to help you evaluate educational technology. Teachers may visit thousands of Web sites dedicated to educational topics. Mailing lists, forums, newsgroups, discussion groups, and bulletin boards available on the Web also provide vast sources of information. One of the larger well-known mailing lists is EDTECH. The **EDTECH** mailing list allows educators from many different areas — teachers, administrators, technology coordinators, media specialists, and university faculty — to exchange information, comments, and ideas on educational issues.

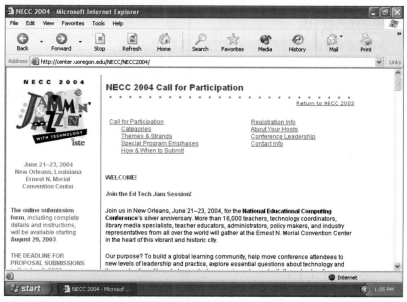

Figure 7-5 Technology conferences provide teachers with valuable resources, information, and opportunities to discuss educational technology issues with other educators and vendors.

To access software reviews, visit the Teachers Discovering Computers Web site, click Chapter 7, click Web Info, and then click Software Reviews.

For more examples of Web site evaluation rubrics for students, visit the Teachers Discovering Computers Web site, click Chapter 7, click Web Info, and then click Rubrics.

EVALUATING SOFTWARE APPLICATIONS

When you identify a software package that potentially is suited to your curriculum needs, you should evaluate the software for appropriateness, review the accuracy of the content, and consider its relevance to the curriculum standards and goals. A cost-effective way to evaluate software is to download a free trial copy from some of the many software companies that offer these trial versions at their Web or FTP sites [Figure 7-6]. Use it for the specified period to determine its suitability for your curriculum.

A rubric is a great tool for evaluating software. A **rubric** is a detailed assessment tool that includes a set of evaluation criteria that specifies the required achievements for each level of quality, which usually is identified by numbers or levels, or by points earned.

Software evaluation rubrics help you and your students evaluate educational software. A **software evaluation rubric** is an assessment tool that provides a number of important evaluation criteria, including content, documentation and technical support, ability and academic levels, technical quality, and ease of use to help assess the quality of software or other items. A two-page Software Evaluation Rubric is shown in **Figure 7-7a** and in **Figure 7-7b** (on page 7.08).

Many schools develop their own software evaluation rubrics for teachers to use, while in other schools, teachers create their own software evaluation rubrics. The Web is a great resource for locating rubrics. Many different software evaluation rubrics are available on the Web for you to use or alter to fit your specific needs.

CONTENT When evaluating educational software, content is the most important area to consider. When examining software content, you need to determine if the software is valid. **Valid** means the software has well-grounded instructional properties, meets standards, provides appropriate content, and teaches what is intended.

Most software companies and distributors provide a description of the content and learning skills addressed for their software packages; some software firms even match the skills the software teaches with specific curriculum standards and learning objectives. When evaluating the contents of a software application, always relate them to your school's and state's specific learning standards and curriculum goals.

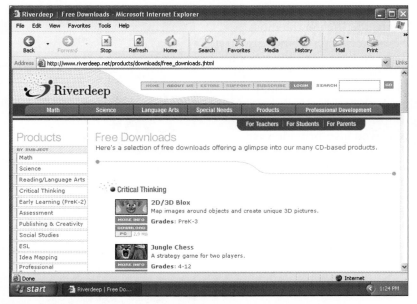

Figure 7-6 Many software companies allow you to download free evaluation copies of their software.

Rubric

Software Evaluation Rubric

Application Title: _____ Subject Area:_____

Version: _____ Producer/Publisher:_____

Purchased From: _____ Date Published: _____

Curriculum Goal(s): _____

Learning Objective(s):_____

Prerequisite Skills: _____

Configuration

Hardware/System Requirements:_____
_____

Type of Drive Required: DVD _____ CD_____3½-inch Floppy _____

Hard Disk Space Required: _____ Memory Required:_____

<u>Program Categories</u>: (Check all that apply)

☐ Presentation ☐ Remediation ☐ Word Processing

☐ Authoring ☐ Simulation ☐ Database

☐ Problem Solving ☐ Tutorial ☐ Spreadsheet

Other:_____

Skill/Ability/Grade Levels: _____

Content Standards: _____
_____

Technology Standards:_____
_____

Use the following system to rate the software

1 = Strongly disagree 2 = Disagree NA = Not applicable
3 = Agree 4 = Strongly agree

Content

	1	2	3	4	NA
1. The content is accurate and factual.	1	2	3	4	NA
2. The content is educationally appropriate.	1	2	3	4	NA
3. The content is free of errors.	1	2	3	4	NA
4. The content meets learning goals and objectives.	1	2	3	4	NA
5. The content is valid.	1	2	3	4	NA
6. The content is free of stereotypes and racial bias.	1	2	3	4	NA
7. The content meets district and state standards.	1	2	3	4	NA

Figure 7-7a A software evaluation rubric helps teachers evaluate educational software packages.

Rubric

Software Evaluation Rubric

Ease of Use

1. Directions are clear.	1	2	3	4	NA
2. Students can quit the program at any time.	1	2	3	4	NA
3. Students can restart the program where they stopped.	1	2	3	4	NA
4. The software is reliable and free of disruption by system errors.	1	2	3	4	NA

Documentation and Support

1. The teacher/instructor manual is clear and thorough.	1	2	3	4	NA
2. The software has an 800/888 support number.	1	2	3	4	NA
3. Online technical support is available.	1	2	3	4	NA
4. Help and tutorials are clear and easy to use.	1	2	3	4	NA

Ability Levels

1. The user level can be set by the teacher.	1	2	3	4	NA
2. The user level automatically advances.	1	2	3	4	NA
3. The software covers a variety of ability/skill levels.	1	2	3	4	NA

Assessment

1. Software has built-in assessment and reporting tools.	1	2	3	4	NA
2. Assessment methods are appropriate and suited to learning objectives.	1	2	3	4	NA
3. Software documents and records student progress.	1	2	3	4	NA
4. Teachers easily can assess students' progress by evaluating progress reports.	1	2	3	4	NA

Technical Quality

1. Animation and graphics are used well.	1	2	3	4	NA
2. Audio (voice input/output) is used well.	1	2	3	4	NA
3. Feedback and prompts are appropriate.	1	2	3	4	NA
4. The application allows branching.	1	2	3	4	NA

Recommendation

☐ Purchase Immediately   ☐ Do Not Purchase

Comments: _____

_____

Evaluator: _____ Date: _____

Figure 7-7b *(continued)*

DOCUMENTATION AND TECHNICAL SUPPORT

When evaluating software, consider the technical support and documentation the software offers. **Documentation** is any printed or online information that provides assistance in installing, using, maintaining, and updating the software. You should review the documentation for readability and depth of coverage. **Technical support** is a service that hardware and software manufacturers and third-party service companies offer to customers to provide answers to questions, repairs, and other assistance. Companies usually provide technical support over the telephone or via the Web [Figure 7-8]. Some firms even provide on-site support.

In addition to reviewing the available documentation and technical support, you also should determine if any other kinds of support are available, such as clear, easy-to-use aids and tutorials. Some software companies, for example, provide instructor resource guides and lesson plans to assist in integrating their software into curriculum areas.

ABILITY LEVELS AND ASSESSMENT

Educators need to evaluate whether the software can be used with more than one ability or academic level. An **ability level** refers to a student's current competency level or the skill level he or she can achieve for a specific learning objective. The **academic level** is based on the grade level with increments to determine if a student is performing at the appropriate level. Several software applications, such as math and reading software, adjust the academic level as students successfully move through specific skills. Numerous software applications allow you to set the academic, or ability levels at which you require students to work. Assessment is discussed starting on page 7.12.

TECHNICAL QUALITY AND EASE OF USE

Technical quality refers to how well the software presents itself and how well it works. Items to evaluate are the clarity of the screen design; appropriateness of feedback and student prompts; and use of graphics, animations, sound, and other media elements.

Ease of use, or user-friendliness, refers to anything that makes the software easy to use. Software should be easy for both

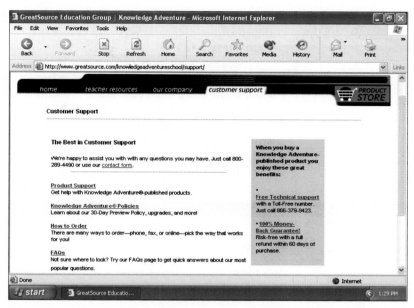

Figure 7-8 Many software manufacturers provide technical support for their products via the Web.

teachers and students to use, while at the same time maintaining the students' interest.

Student opinions also play an important role in successfully integrating new technology. After you complete your evaluation, you may want to obtain feedback from students by allowing them to use and test the software. If students have a difficult time working through exercises, they may dislike the program and get frustrated. If students dislike the software, they will not enjoy using it even though they may learn. This dislike will limit the effectiveness of the software in classroom use. Make sure the software is easy to use and appropriate for your students' grade and ability levels.

EVALUATING WEB RESOURCES

The Web is an incredible resource for teachers. Not all of the information on the Web, however, is placed there by reliable sources. Web page authoring software has made it easy for anyone to create, or publish, a Web page or Web site that contains personal opinions, ideas, theology, and philosophy. In contrast, before a book is published, the content is reviewed for accuracy and objectivity and the author's credentials are verified. Once published, the book's copyright date and table of contents allow users to determine the

For more details about evaluating Web sites, visit the Teachers Discovering Computers Web site, click Chapter 7, click Web Info, and then click Web Site Evaluation.

currency of the information and the book's depth of coverage. A Web site offers no such safeguards.

Because Web sites often contain inaccurate, incomplete, or biased information, evaluating Web resources presents a unique challenge. Teachers must know how to evaluate Web sites and teach their students how to do the same. When evaluating a Web site as an instructional source, you should consider criteria such as

Figure 7-9 Information documenting the authority of a Web site often is found at the bottom of the Web site's home page.

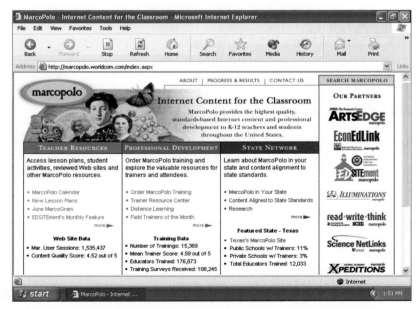

Figure 7-10 Teachers can consider this Web site authoritative because it was created by a number of major organizations and corporations.

authority, affiliation, content, audience, and Web design.

AUTHORITY   When evaluating Web sites, **authority** refers to the credibility of the person or persons who author and create the site. Determining authority is the first place to start in the evaluation process [Figure 7-9]. If the author is not a credible source for information, then the information on the site may be unreliable. A Web site on asteroids by a distinguished astronomy professor, for example, has more authority than an astronomy Web site created by an amateur stargazer. When reviewing a Web site, answer the following questions.

- Is the author clearly identified? If you cannot identify the creator of the Web page, you may want to avoid this Web site.

- Examine the credentials of the author of the Web site. What evidence indicates that the author qualifies to publish on this topic? The authority of the Web page shown in **Figure 7-10**, for example, is based on the credibility of several organizations and corporations.

- Has the author listed his or her occupation, years of experience, position, education, or other credentials? If you do not see this information immediately, refer to the bottom of the home page, which often provides additional information about the author and his or her affiliation. Can the author be contacted for clarification? Listing an e-mail address and other pertinent information is important for establishing authority.

AFFILIATION   **Affiliation** refers to the professional organization, school, school district, university, company, or government office with which a particular Web site is associated. A simple way to determine a site's affiliation is to examine the URL and domain name to identify what type of organization maintains the Web page. A site with a .com domain, for example, is operated by a commercial business; an .edu domain is controlled by an educational institution [Figure 7-11].

Well-known sources of information such as the U.S. government, universities, school districts, newspapers, and non-profit organizations usually have reliable facts on their Web sites. Also, it is good to examine the credentials and reputation of the organization or organizations affiliated with the Web site.

PURPOSE AND OBJECTIVITY Purpose is the reason the Web site was created or the intent of the Web site. As you evaluate a Web site, you must ascertain if it is being provided as a public service, if it is free from bias, and why the author or creator is providing this information.

Objectivity is the process of determining or interpreting the intent or purpose of the Web page and if it is free of bias, such as advertising. If the purpose is not clearly stated, you must attempt to determine the purpose or intent of the Web page. Is the primary intent to provide information or sell a product? Does the author want to make a political point or have fun? Determining the purpose or intent of the Web site plays a critical role in the evaluation process.

CONTENT AND LEARNING PROCESS Content is the information a Web page provides. Web pages use a variety of media to convey facts, opinions, and news. As you evaluate the content of a Web page, consider the following questions.

- Is the content valid and appropriate? Is the content popular or academic, satiric or serious?
- Does the information on the page relate to your curriculum and instructional standards?
- What topics are covered? Is the information clearly labeled and well-organized?
- For what level is the information written? How thorough is the information?
- Do the links within the site add value and assist you in meeting your instructional goals?

As you evaluate the content of a Web page or Web site, keep the learning objectives and curriculum standards of the classroom in mind. Also, take the time to check the links to ensure they work and are appropriate for your intended audience.

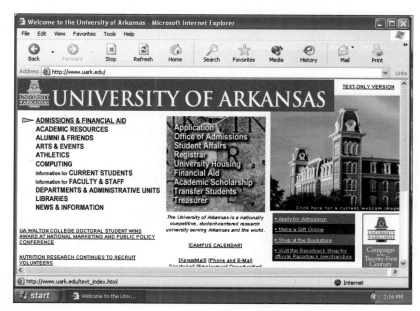

Figure 7-11 This Web site's affiliation is identifiable easily as the University of Arkansas.

Learning process is when the content engages students to use high-order thinking skills to go beyond the simple acquisition of knowledge and become active learners. This is accomplished when the content challenges students to think, compare, reflect, hypothesize, and discuss.

AUDIENCE AND CURRENCY The audience is the individual or group intended to view and use the Web page. You should review the Web page to determine if it is suitable for an audience such as your students. Is the content appropriate for your students? Can you use this Web page in your classroom? Again, keep your learning objectives in mind as you examine the Web page. Currency is the measure of how up-to-date, or timely, the Web page content is and how often it is updated. A good Web page will state clearly when the page was last revised or updated.

DESIGN The design of a Web site is the way it is arranged — that is, the way it uses instructional design principles to deliver content to the user. A well-designed Web site makes it easy and enjoyable for viewers to access the site's content and information. A poorly designed site where links or elements are organized in a confusing way can frustrate viewers because they cannot find the information they want.

An effective Web page loads in a reasonable amount of time, has a pleasing visual appearance, is easy to navigate, and

To learn the 10 Cs for evaluating Internet resources, visit the Teachers Discovering Computers Web site, click Chapter 7, click Web Info, and then click 10 Cs.

links are well organized, clearly marked, work properly, and lead to related materials.

Both in and out of the classroom, teachers and students should evaluate sites critically to maximize the value of the Web. To assist in the evaluation of Web sites, teachers often find rubrics useful.

A **Web evaluation rubric** is a detailed scoring guide for assessing the value of Web sites. As shown in the example in Figure 7-12, Web evaluation rubrics typically provide a number of important evaluation criteria for specific areas such as content, learning process, and authority of the author, and then present rating levels with specific standards for each. Students also benefit from using rubrics. Figure 7-13 shown on page 7.14 illustrates a user-friendly, engaging Student Web Site Evaluation Form. No matter which method you choose, the key is to have a predetermined way of effectively evaluating Web sites.

Evaluating the Effectiveness of Technology Integration

Integrating technology effectively into the curriculum requires planning, time, dedication, and resources. Because it is important to determine whether integration strategies are working, teachers, schools, and school districts should take steps to evaluate the effectiveness of their technology integration.

Evaluating the effectiveness of technology can be challenging; no simple way exists to evaluate what works in all situations — all students, all technology, all schools, and all classrooms. Nor do any standard types of evaluation show the relationship between the technology and student achievement. Educators should not rely on the assumption that technology tools are having some impact. Instead, teachers and administrators must locate or develop techniques to measure the effectiveness of integrating technology.

The first step in evaluating educational technology's impact on student achievement is to develop indicators that measure a student's performance, skills acquired, and academic and ability levels obtained. Test scores are not the only, or even the

To explore technology assessment further, visit the Teachers Discovering Computers Web site, click Chapter 7, click Web Info, and then click Assessing Technology.

best, indicators of the successful integration of technology. The types of learning best supported by technology are those not easily measured by traditional assessments such as standardized tests.

Due to the nature of technology and the way the learning environment is changing, educators must create and use different types of evaluation tools.

ASSESSMENT TOOLS FOR EVALUATING THE EFFECTIVENESS OF TECHNOLOGY INTEGRATION

Evaluating the effectiveness of educational technology can help you assess whether the technology is appropriate for the learner, meets learning objectives, and enhances the learning process. Traditionally, teachers use many different evaluation techniques in the final stage of instruction or when assessing **student performance**. To ensure that students meet the learning objectives, teachers generally use the traditional means of testing to assess student performance. **Assessment** is any method used to understand the current knowledge a student possesses; it can range from a teacher's subjective judgment based on a single observation of a student's performance to a state-mandated standardized test.

Reliable assessment information provides accurate estimates of student performance, permits appropriate generalizations about the students' skills and abilities, and enables teachers or other decision-makers to make appropriate decisions. **Traditional assessments** include testing in the form of multiple choice, fill-in-the blank, true/false, short answer, and essay questions.

Traditional forms of assessment also can be used to evaluate the effectiveness of technology. Just as technology opens many new and exciting doors for teaching and learning, technology also opens new doors for evaluating student performance. When integrating technology, some teachers and schools move toward a nontraditional approach of student assessment, known as alternative assessment. **Alternative assessment** uses nontraditional methods to determine whether students have mastered the appropriate content and skill level. Educators may adopt several approaches to alternative assessment, such as authentic, project-based, and portfolio assessment.

Rubric

Web Evaluation Rubric

Title of Web site: _____

Curriculum Area: _____

URL: _____

Learning Objectives that will be supported by this site: _____

_____

	Level 1	Level 2	Level 3	Level 4	Level
Authority	No author is listed and no e-mail contact is provided.	No author is listed but an e-mail contact is provided.	An author is listed with no credentials and you cannot tell if the author is the creator of the material.	An author is listed with appropriate credentials, and is the creator of the material.	
Affiliation	It is unclear what institution supports this information.	A commercial Internet provider supports the site, but it is unclear if the author has any connection with a larger institution.	The site is supported by a larger institution, but some bias is apparent in the information from the institution.	The site is supported by a reputable institution without bias in the information.	
Purpose	The purpose is unclear or cannot be determined.	The Web site has more than one purpose and meets only a few of my objectives.	The purpose is somewhat clear and meets most of my objectives.	The purpose of the Web site is clear and meets my objectives.	
Objectivity	The Web page is a virtual soapbox.	The Web site contains some bias and a great deal of advertising.	The Web site contains some advertising and minimal bias.	The Web site contains little advertising and is free of bias.	
Content	The information on the Web site does not relate to my objectives.	The information relates to my objectives, but many of the links do not work.	The information relates to my objectives, links work, but the site is not well-organized.	The information relates to my objectives, the links work, and the site is well-organized.	
Learning Process	The information will not challenge learners to think, reflect, discuss, compare, or classify.	The information will not challenge learners to think but does provide interesting facts for resource information.	The information at this Web site will provide some challenges for the learner to think but does not relate to my objectives.	The information will challenge learners to use high-order thinking skills, effectively engage the learner, and meet my learning objectives.	
Audience	The Web pages are not appropriate for my audience.	The Web pages are written above the level of my audience, but some of the information is useful.	The Web pages are written at an appropriate level for my audience and some of the information is useful.	The Web pages are written at an appropriate level and the information is suitable for my classroom.	
Currency	Information on the site has not been revised in the last 18 months, or no date can be located.	Information on the site has not been updated in the last year, but the information still is of good quality.	Information has been updated in the last six months and seems to reflect currency.	Information has been updated in the last three months.	
Design	The Web site design is inappropriate for my audience.	The Web site loads slowly and the general appearance is poor.	The Web site loads well, but the site is not easy to navigate.	The Web site loads well, is easy to navigate, visually pleasing, and easy to read.	
				Total	

Figure 7-12 A rubric is helpful in evaluating the educational value of Web sites.

Rubric

Student Web Site Evaluation Form

Student team members: _____

DESIGN			
Can move easily from page to page	☺	😐	☹
Good use of graphics (pictures and color)	☺	😐	☹

CONTENT			
Information is useful	☺	😐	☹
Content is as good or better than that of similar sites	☺	😐	☹

TECHNICAL ELEMENTS			
Pages load quickly (within 15 seconds)	☺	😐	☹
All links work	☺	😐	☹

CREDIBILITY			
Contact person is stated with his or her e-mail address	☺	😐	☹
The name of the host school or organization is given	☺	😐	☹
Date this site was last updated is provided	☺	😐	☹

page 1 of 1

Figure 7-13 Young students enjoy rubrics that are fun and user-friendly when evaluating Web sites.

AUTHENTIC ASSESSMENT   Authentic assessment, project-based assessment, and portfolio assessment refer to alternative ways to evaluate students' performances to determine how well and in what ways they meet learning objectives and standards.

Authentic assessment can be formal or informal and aims to present the student with tasks that mirror the priorities and challenges typical of their instructional activities. Students answer open-ended questions, create questions, conduct hands-on experiments, do research, write, revise and discuss papers, and create portfolios of their work over time. Authentic assessment is based on a method of learning called authentic learning. **Authentic learning** presents learning experiences that demonstrate real-life connections between students' lessons and the world in which they live.

Authentic assessment measures this learning by evaluating a student's ability to master practical learning standards. Using authentic assessment, for example, a student may be asked to explain historical events, generate scientific hypotheses, solve math problems, create portfolios or presentations, or converse in a foreign language.

Authentic assessment helps students not only understand concepts and subject matter, but also helps them develop real-world skills, which they can apply outside the classroom and beyond the school environment. For example, teachers may look for evidence of good collaboration skills, the ability to solve complex problems and make thoughtful decisions, and the ability to develop and make effective presentations. Authentic assessments reflect student learning over time and provide a better view of student performance, instead of performance based on just one item or one test. A teacher then has documentation of the student's progress throughout the entire project, which provides the teacher with evidence of growth and learning. This type of authentic assessment often is called project-based assessment.

PROJECT-BASED ASSESSMENT **Project-based assessment** is an innovative approach to assessment that focuses on assessing student projects. It is based on a type of authentic learning called project-based learning. **Project-based learning** is a model for teaching and learning that focuses on creating learning opportunities for students by engaging them in real-world projects where they have an active role in completing meaningful tasks, constructing their own knowledge, solving problems, or creating realistic projects. Project-based learning transforms the teacher into the facilitator and the students into the doers or participants in the task at hand. When using any type of authentic learning technique, many teachers use a checklist, rating scale, or a rubric to evaluate the learning process.

PORTFOLIO ASSESSMENT Another popular form of alternative assessment is portfolio assessment. **Portfolio assessment** evaluates student assignments or projects over a period of time. Portfolios are an effective way to match assessment with learning goals. Some educators call this **embedded assessment** because assessment tasks are a part of the learning process. Through the process of creating their own assignments, students improve their abilities to assess their strengths and weaknesses and are able to apply these skills to other areas of study to become better learners. Because students work on long-term assignments, they usually have the opportunity to fix or learn from their mistakes and do a better job on future portfolio assignments.

For portfolio assessment to be successful, students must learn how to interact effectively with their teachers to ensure that they fully understand the teacher's assessment of each portfolio assignment.

Only then will they be able to progress in creating better subsequent assignments.

When students receive guidance and support from their teachers and parents and gain an understanding of themselves as learners, they can experience amazing growth and powerful learning opportunities. The disadvantage of portfolio assessment is that creating and assessing portfolios takes longer to evaluate than a quick test and requires a great deal of work by both the student and the teacher. The results reveal, however, that portfolio assessment is well worth the investment.

In this digital age, electronic portfolios are starting to become more commonplace in K-12 and higher education. An **electronic portfolio**, or **e-folio**, is an electronically-stored portfolio that contains student assignments or projects. Electronic portfolios offer a powerful way for students to create a variety of projects that contain multimedia, text, images, sound, pictures, graphics, and even video based on predetermined criteria that teachers can evaluate to assess learning.

CHECKLISTS, RATING SCALES, AND RUBRICS A **checklist** is a predetermined list of performance criteria used in project-based and portfolio assessment. Figure 7-14 on the next page shows a Project Evaluation Checklist. After a student has met a criterion, the criterion is marked as complete. Checklists usually consist of yes and no questions used to determine if the item or items are present. Checklists usually allow you or your students to keep track of the listed items.

The benefit of a checklist for an assessment tool is that you can measure or use this tool quickly and students understand very quickly if an item is or is not met. When creating your own checklist, you should include items you feel are important. Another effective option is to have your students create their own checklists.

A **rating scale** is a more complex form of checklist that lists a numerical value, or rating, for each criterion. Assessment involves rating each student on his or her achievement for each criterion and specifying the total based on all criteria.

Another very popular form of alternative assessment is the rubric. As you recall, a rubric is a detailed assessment tool that makes it easy for teachers to assess the

WEB INFO

To learn more about portfolio assessment, visit the Teachers Discovering Computers Web site, click Chapter 7, click Web Info, and then click Portfolios.

FAQ

Are any schools using only electronic portfolios or e-folios to evaluate student work?

Yes, a few K-12 schools and many teacher education programs are using only electronic portfolios to evaluate student work.

Checklist

Project Evaluation Checklist

Date:_____

Student Name:_____

Project Title:_____

	YES	NO
CONTENT		
The project meets all learning objectives.	☐	☐
The project is original and creative.	☐	☐
Understanding of the content is evident.	☐	☐
Use of higher-order thinking skills is evident.	☐	☐
Information is accurate and the subject is appropriate.	☐	☐
Information is presented in a logical sequence.	☐	☐
A variety of reliable sources are used.	☐	☐
Sources are properly cited.	☐	☐
Words are spelled correctly and sentences are grammatically correct.	☐	☐
LAYOUT		
The project is visually appealing.	☐	☐
The project is easy to navigate.	☐	☐
The text is easy to read and follow.	☐	☐
Multimedia features are used effectively.	☐	☐
Color and design scheme are appropriate.	☐	☐
ORGANIZATION		
Students completed a project storyboard.	☐	☐
Planning is apparent.	☐	☐
Project flows smoothly.	☐	☐
Project has sense of completeness.	☐	☐

Figure 7-14 Teachers often use alternative assessment tools such as checklists and rating scales to evaluate student performance.

quality of an item, such as a learning project. Rubrics help students understand how teachers will evaluate their projects by providing a range of criteria with information about how to meet each one. Rubrics describe specific and measurable criteria for several levels of quality against which teachers can evaluate completed projects.

Rubrics can help students and teachers define the value or quality of completed assignments. Rubrics also help students critique and revise their own assignments before handing them in. In addition, rubrics help students make sure they have included all required elements and have met each criteria for grading. Although a rubric is similar to a checklist and a rating scale, it describes in greater detail the criteria and components that must be achieved.

TEACHER OBSERVATION When evaluating technology integration or curriculum integration, one of the more widely used authentic assessment techniques is teacher observation. **Teacher observation** as shown in Figure 7-15 is the result of teachers actively observing their students during the learning process.

Teachers notice whether students are highly motivated during the learning process when technology is used, observe how long the students work on a given objective, and observe the length of time students continue working on a task to master its content and skills. Teacher observation is a powerful assessment tool, and often it is used in combination with other assessment tools. All of these tools can be used to evaluate individual and group student projects.

EVALUATING TECHNOLOGY-BASED STUDENT PROJECTS

Today, skills in technology are essential for students to learn. Technology-based student projects help facilitate integrating technology and multimedia into the curriculum. In the process, students learn how to use, manage, and understand technology and how it is used to synthesize and present information on a variety of subjects. Although it might seem like a good idea, you should avoid teaching technology as a separate subject. Instead, you should integrate it into a specific area of your curriculum.

Figure 7-15 This teacher knows that teacher observation is critical when integrating technology.

Some software programs, such as those provided with integrated learning systems (ILS), such as ClassWorks, automatically track student progress. Others, such as Inspiration, HyperStudio, and PowerPoint do not provide assessment components. These multimedia authoring applications, however, are ideal for students to use to create projects that are innovative and motivational. Teachers who use these software programs for technology-based student projects need to develop effective assessment tools to measure their achievements.

Before a teacher presents a project's requirements to students, he or she should create an assessment rubric. Figure 7-16 on the next page illustrates a Student Multimedia Project Evaluation Rubric that guides students on how they will be evaluated on projects. Rubrics are excellent for evaluating all types of student projects. They provide an authentic assessment of project-based learning activities. To determine the criteria to include in the rubric, ask yourself what the students should learn and how this learning will be evidenced in their projects. In the rubric, be sure to specify what students need to include in their projects and clearly inform the students how they will be evaluated.

Checklists, rating scales, and teacher observation also are valid assessment tools for technology-based student projects. Your goals and objectives should define and guide the selection and creation of your assessment tool.

FAQ

Is teacher observation really a powerful tool?

Yes! It is probably one of the most powerful tools that teachers use. A teacher needs to be aware of everything going on in the classroom, whether or not it relates to technology.

Rubric

Student Multimedia Project Evaluation Rubric

Group Members: _____

Project Title: _____

	Beginning		Developing		Accomplished			Exemplary	

Development Process

	Beginning		Developing		Accomplished			Exemplary	
Students used quality reference materials and timely Web sites in gathering information.	0 1	2	3	4 5	6	7	8	9	10
Students completed project outline/storyboard.	0 1	2	3	4 5	6	7	8	9	10
Students obtained permission to use any copyrighted materials.	0 1	2	3	4 5	6	7	8	9	10

Content

Understanding of topic is evident.	0 1	2	3	4 5	6	7	8	9	10
Information is presented in a clear manner, is appropriate, and accurate.	0 1	2	3	4 5	6	7	8	9	10
Content relates to the learning objectives.	0 1	2	3	4 5	6	7	8	9	10
Students used higher-order thinking skills when analyzing and synthesizing content.	0 1	2	3	4 5	6	7	8	9	10
The information is appropriate.	0 1	2	3	4 5	6	7	8	9	10
The information is presented in an original manner and demonstrates logical conclusions.	0 1	2	3	4 5	6	7	8	9	10
Important ideas related to topic are included and an understanding of important relationships is evident.	0 1	2	3	4 5	6	7	8	9	10
Includes properly cited sources.	0 1	2	3	4 5	6	7	8	9	10

Design

The information is presented in a logical, interesting sequence.	0 1	2	3	4 5	6	7	8	9	10
Colors, images, animation, and sound enrich the content.	0 1	2	3	4 5	6	7	8	9	10
The project is interesting and holds your attention.	0 1	2	3	4 5	6	7	8	9	10
Text is easy to read and students have followed rules of good screen design.	0 1	2	3	4 5	6	7	8	9	10
Accurate spelling and grammar are used throughout.	0 1	2	3	4 5	6	7	8	9	10

Presentation

The student maintains eye contact with class.	0 1	2	3	4 5	6	7	8	9	10
The student speaks clearly and is easily heard.	0 1	2	3	4 5	6	7	8	9	10
The presentation is an appropriate length.	0 1	2	3	4 5	6	7	8	9	10

Total Possible _____   **Total** _____

Figure 7-16 A rubric guides students in determining how they will be evaluated on projects. This rubric, for example, is designed to evaluate students' multimedia projects.

EVALUATING CONTENT   Your goals and objectives will help determine the content to include in student projects and how to assess this content. This should be the most important part of the project. For technology-based student projects, content may include factual information about a historical figure, the key points included in a multimedia presentation, biology lab data in a spreadsheet, and other pertinent information. In addition, evaluation of the content also should include a review of punctuation, grammar, spelling, coverage of material, presentation of the material in a logical order, and specific information such as a title, references, and information about the author.

EVALUATING PLANNING   Effective teaching involves planning. Students also must plan a project before creating it, if it is to be effective. When assigning technology-based projects, establish how you want students to plan and what tools they will use. A software planning tool such as **Inspiration** helps students and teachers quickly develop and communicate ideas using flowcharts, concept maps, and story webs through visual learning techniques [Figure 7-17]. **Visual learning techniques** are methods that present ideas and information through graphical webs. Inspiration lets you build visual diagrams to work through the process of thinking, organizing thoughts, revealing patterns, and prioritizing information.

   Flowcharts are diagrams that show the step-by-step actions that must take place by plotting a sequence of events. Flowcharts are useful in helping students outline the individual tasks that must be performed to complete an action, a story, or an experiment and the sequence in which they must be performed. A **concept map** or **story web** helps students use flowcharting to understand the attributes and relationships of the main subject and provides a visual tool for brainstorming and planning [Figure 7-18]. Another useful planning tool is a **storyboard**, which is a drawing that allows students to design and lay out a project or assignment before creating it on a computer.

EVALUATING CREATIVITY   When evaluating student projects, teachers should consider students' originality, imaginative and

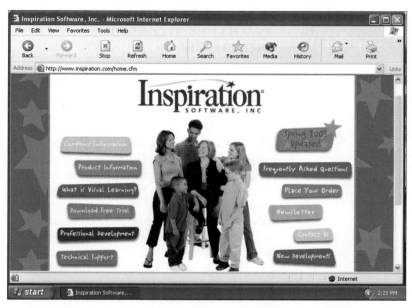

Figure 7-17 Inspiration is an excellent tool for teaching students how to organize their thoughts and ideas.

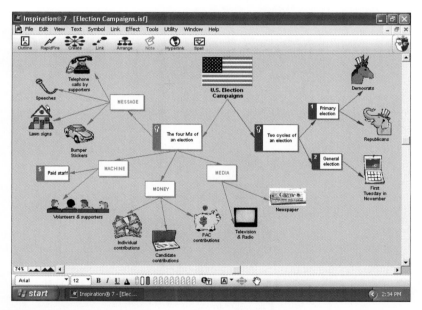

Figure 7-18 Using Inspiration software, students create a concept map to plan an undertaking such as this project on election campaigns.

innovative approach, and artistic abilities — all aspects of **creativity**. Creative student projects should be interesting and unique. Students should demonstrate an understanding of how to use the special effects offered by multimedia authoring software to enhance their projects, instead of distracting from its content. Color, clip art, and artwork should strengthen content, not distract from it.

PUTTING IT ALL TOGETHER — EVALUATING TECHNOLOGY INTEGRATION

Mrs. Vicki Osborne teaches social studies and other subjects at Fall Hills Middle School. She has one computer in her classroom and 26 students. Her middle school is on a **block schedule**, which is an alternative way of scheduling classes. This means the social studies class meets every other day for 90 minutes. Because it is a presidential election year, Mrs. Osborne would like her social studies students to research one of the presidential candidates and then prepare a multimedia presentation to convey their findings to the class.

She has six objectives for the lesson. The students will (1) work cooperatively in groups with three or four students in each group; (2) use reference materials and Web resources to research the candidate; (3) identify three major campaign issues for their candidate; (4) provide personal facts about the candidate, such as education, occupation prior to politics, and military service; (5) create a multimedia project to present their research with either PowerPoint or HyperStudio; and (6) use correct grammar, spelling, and punctuation in their presentation. She will use a rubric to evaluate the students' projects.

Mrs. Osborne began her social studies lesson by displaying her PowerPoint slides on a 32-inch television for easy viewing by all students. The first step was to brainstorm with her students about the lesson and create a concept map about the election process and the candidates [Figure 7-19]. She also passed out a copy of her evaluation rubric, discussed the rubric with her students, and answered their questions. Students then were divided into groups to complete their first task.

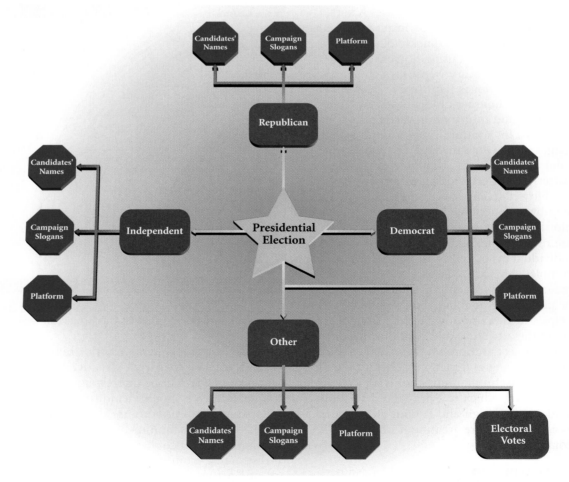

Figure 7-19 Mrs. Osborne and her students create a concept map showing their ideas on the election process and candidates.

Students were required to create a flowchart or storyboard of their projects on paper before they began working on the computers. Mrs. Osborne then approved their flowchart drawings and storyboards. When the groups were ready to begin creating their projects on the computer, Mrs. Osborne borrowed an additional computer from another teacher and arranged for two groups to use computers in the media center. This allowed four groups to work on computers at the same time. Groups rotated through the four computers in 40-minute blocks [Figure 7-20].

When the groups finished their projects, Mrs. Osborne had each group present their project to the class in the media center. She also invited the principal, a local politician, the media specialist, and another social studies class to participate in the presentations. The students were very proud of their projects and enjoyed showing them to their peers, teachers, and school administrators. The school newspaper highlighted some of the projects. To make this an authentic learning experience, Mrs. Osborne's students created voting boxes and placed them all over the school, so the students at Fall Hills Middle School could vote. After the actual presidential election three weeks later, her students planned to compare the school election results with the results of the actual election.

To integrate technology successfully, teachers must continuously evaluate educational technology before instruction begins, during the instructional period, and after instruction has taken place. Technology not only changes the learning process but also changes the teaching and evaluation processes. Teachers have the responsibility to evaluate and update assignments and activities continuously — on a daily, weekly, monthly, or semester basis — depending on the project or assignment.

To make learning more effective, often only minor changes and improvements are necessary. In other instances, however, teachers need to implement major revisions to reflect content, curriculum, or technology changes. The next few sections introduce you to other integration strategies, such as using technology in various classroom configurations and developing curriculum pages.

Integration Strategies

To help meet the constant challenge of motivating students to learn, teachers must change their traditional roles and become facilitators of learning. Technology plays a key role in easing this change because it allows teachers to use technology tools to enhance the learning environment,

FAQ

Are there other software programs that teachers and students can use to create concept maps or flowcharts?

Yes, concept maps, flowcharts, and diagrams easily can be created in most word processors, such as Microsoft Word, by using the drawing tools on the Drawing toolbar.

Figure 7-20 Centers allow students to work collaboratively in groups on subject-directed projects.

motivate students, guide students in an active learning process, and encourage them to learn. The most effective way to integrate technology is to place the technology at the point of instruction — the classroom. Because of the ever-increasing need to motivate students to learn, teachers have a mandate to use the powerful tools of technology to enhance the learning environment.

Many different technologies, availability of computer labs, and different kinds and numbers of computers in the classroom are found in schools today [Figure 7-21]. The following instructional strategies describe techniques to integrate technology into a one-computer classroom, a multi-computer classroom, and a computer lab.

ONE-COMPUTER CLASSROOM

Most classrooms are equipped with one multimedia computer and are referred to as a **one-computer classroom**. Many ways exist in which to integrate educational technology with only one computer in the classroom. As you learned in Chapter 6, the most common practice is to use the computer for classroom presentations and demonstrations. By projecting the computer's image on a projection screen or large-screen television, you can use the computer to supplement and enhance your traditional lectures to accomplish whole-class instruction of learning objectives. You also can use the computer to introduce new concepts, prepare students for a lesson, describe background information for assignments, and explain evaluation criteria.

Figure 7-21 Technology can be integrated into many different classroom environments.

Another strategy permits students to work on the computer in small groups to foster collaboration and cooperative learning opportunities. Students also may use the computer to present their assignments, projects, and research activities to the entire class. In addition, you can use the computer to maintain records, create presentations and projects, do research, and communicate with other teachers [Figure 7-22].

To integrate technology in a one-computer classroom follow these guidelines.

- Obtain Internet access. Use the Web's many educational resources, such as audio, video, and multimedia applications to enhance instruction and learning.

- Utilize educational multimedia application software. Both teachers and students can make use of the abundance of educational software available on CDs, DVDs, and school networks.

- Enhance lectures and presentations. Connect the computer to a television monitor, and use the computer to enhance lectures, create and give presentations, and take students on virtual Web tours.

- Use the computer as a teaching assistant. Tutor individual students by having them use drill and practice software, tutorials, simulations, and problem-solving software.

- Foster group and cooperative learning. Students can use the computer as an informational resource or a creation tool for group projects, such as multimedia presentations.

- Write an ongoing story. Begin a story on the computer, which serves as a creative writing center, and allow student authors to add to it daily. Before you begin, explain the rules for acceptable behavior, the types of content to be included in the story, and the types of entries that are satisfactory.

Figure 7-22 Teachers benefit from using a classroom computer to maintain grades and other important files.

- Start a class newsletter. Allow students to write articles and use word processing or desktop publishing software to create a class newsletter. For example, as an adjunct to a history class, students can collaborate to create a newsletter with sections on various aspects related to that period of history [Figure 7-23].

Figure 7-23 Students gain real-world skills by creating a class or school newsletter.

- Maintain a student database. Instead of having students fill out emergency information forms, let them enter the information into a database on the computer. Students also may enter information on a variety of content-related subject areas, such as information on science projects, vocabulary words, historical places, and so on.

- Utilize the computer as a teacher productivity tool. The computer is an excellent medium on which to create tests and lesson plans, maintain grades and attendance records, write letters to parents, and create achievement certificates. Purchasing gradebook or student information management software helps to streamline many daily management responsibilities.

- Use other low-cost input devices, such as AlphaSmarts and PDAs, for students to create first drafts, take notes in class, and enter data into their documents. Later, the data can be downloaded into the computer. This is a super time-saver and is ideal for student projects.

- Optimize computer lab time. Use the computer to introduce students to various types of software and thus create learning paths before taking students to the school's computer lab. This will optimize the time students spend on computers while in the computer lab.

- New emerging technologies allow you to create an exciting learning environment; for example, you can roll a complete computer lab into your classroom. If your school has a wireless mobile lab, schedule to utilize the lab. This is a great way to move the technology you need into your one-computer classroom.

MULTICOMPUTER CLASSROOM

Having two or more computers in your classroom fosters additional learning opportunities that allow flexibility in computer usage and make technology integration an integral part of the curriculum. Remember, one-computer classroom strategies also apply to a classroom with two or more computers.

One way to use two or more computers is to set up the computers as separate learning centers for student use. Teachers can divide the centers by subject area and then create activities that continuously change to match the curriculum or lessons being taught. A math center, for example, may include CDs, DVDs, and network-based tutorials to reinforce math skills. A language arts center may include word processing software for creative writing projects; HyperStudio, PowerPoint, and Photoshop to create multimedia presentations; as well as reading and spelling software skill programs.

A social science center may allow students to use the Web as a research tool and correspond with other classrooms via the Internet to learn more about the culture, language, history, and geography of other regions. Multimedia CDs such as the Carmen Sandiego series help reinforce mapping and geography skills in relation to other curriculum areas.

Learning centers are an effective way to create a flexible learning environment with many options for students. Teachers can integrate technologies into learning centers to create specialized centers such as a video center, a listening center, and a digital camera center.

To illustrate how one teacher is integrating technology into a science curriculum, consider the middle school classroom of Miss Julie Davis. At the beginning of class, she takes her students for a nature walk on school property to learn about trees, plants, changing seasons, and photosynthesis. During the nature walk, students notice a lot of trash on the school grounds. Students take their PDAs and Tablet PCs to enter data on a form Miss Davis created for them to fill-out during their excursion. This way, the students enter their thoughts, explorations, and findings while they are in the environment, and not later, when they may have forgotten important information and findings.

She lets her students use a digital camera to take pictures of the trash, plants, trees, and other items of interest [Figure 7-24]. In a follow-up discussion in class, the

WEB INFO

For more information about AlphaSmarts, visit the Teachers Discovering Computer Web site, click Chapter 7, click Web Info, and then click AlphaSmarts.

students decide the trash is a form of pollution — and they should do something to make the school cleaner. Miss Davis recognizes this as a teachable moment and asks essential questions to start the students thinking. She asks, "Can we make a difference? How can we help prevent pollution, starting at school?" The students begin brainstorming. Following the discussion, Miss Davis shows the students a short CNN video on global warming.

The next day, Miss Davis continues the learning process by dividing the students into groups to begin their research projects on waste, environmentally hazardous materials, trees, plants, and air associated with the environment. Next, the students begin working on their KWLQS charts. A **KWLQS chart** is similar to the KWL chart discussed in Chapter 6, with the additions of Q, which stands for further questioning, and S, which stands for sharing (referring to the fact that students will share their projects with their fellow students). Miss Davis and the students decide to create a survey to examine all the environmental issues at the school. Most students are aware that the school has trash to dispose of, but most of them have never focused on the hazardous products, such as cleaners, that need to be disposed. Previously, none of the students had thought about the school's various types of trash, or whether the school recycles, or whether the methods used for disposing of hazardous waste could harm the environment. Miss Davis places the students in groups and assigns each group different environmental issues to research.

Miss Davis is fortunate to have four multimedia computers in her classroom. Two of the computers are used as Web research centers, while the other two are set up as creation centers. To complete group projects, students rotate through the Web centers and use her curriculum pages to locate resources from agriculture, environmental protection, and other related Web sites [Figure 7-25]. Then they use the creation centers to develop presentations that suggest ways to protect the environment. The students incorporate their digital pictures into multimedia presentations.

While completing the projects, the students learn about citizenship and that

Figure 7-24 Using a digital camera, students can take pictures to enhance their electronic projects.

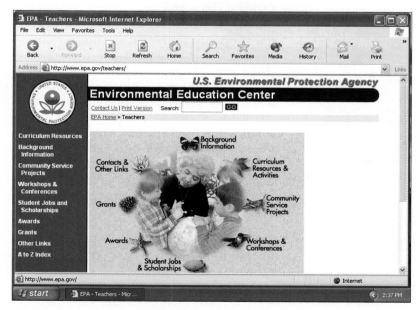

Figure 7-25 Students easily can locate information dealing with pollution, global warming, and other environmental issues on the Web.

everyone is responsible for protecting the environment. They then decide to start a school-wide cleanup project. The class creates flyers using Microsoft Publisher and posts them throughout the school so all the students and teachers will be aware of the environment. They also create a Web page, sharing what they have learned with the community.

As this example illustrates, using computers and other technologies in the classroom promotes active learning, involves the students, and provides a sense of ownership, or authentic learning, of the information being presented. Having two or more computers in the classroom — especially used as learning centers — requires more planning and attention to detail than having just one computer. Before setting up a learning center or centers, teachers should consider how many computers will be in each center and what other technologies, if any, may be included in the center. After the centers are set up, teachers can work on managing and planning activities, scheduling rotation times through each center for the students as they complete projects and activities. Teachers may create a sign-up list or use a timing device so all students have a fair amount of time on the computers.

COMPUTER LABS

Computer labs offer teachers instructional opportunities that are not possible in a one-, two-, or even a five-computer classroom. The most important advantage of using a computer lab or a wireless mobile lab is that all students have hands-on experience using computer technology. Teachers may successfully use computer labs for drill and practice, remediation, collaborative learning, computer skill instruction (for example, word processing), Internet research, whole class instruction, and tutorials.

Students often learn technology skills or subject-specific skills in isolation from the rest of the curriculum while in school computer labs. The labs, however, can also support the technology integration that teaches curriculum goals and objectives. They are not just a place to teach keyboarding, remedial math, and science drills. A lab with multimedia computers, scanners, and Web access makes it possible to integrate computer-related skills into subject-directed curriculum areas. Teachers, for example, can integrate specific software applications into subject-area content.

Teacher-created activities, such as Web scavenger hunts, also teach computer skills, while giving students direction. A **Web scavenger hunt** is an inquiry-oriented activity in which students explore the resources of the Web using discovery learning to find the answers to teacher-created questions [Figure 7-26]. While searching for the answers, students use high-order thinking skills. When teachers plan creative instructional activities in advance, the computer lab, along with other technologies and the Internet, can bring authentic excitement and enthusiasm to students who otherwise might be uninterested in their daily school work.

Curriculum Integration Activities

Many teachers already use computers and technology in their classrooms and computer labs to help meet curriculum standards. For curriculum integration to be effective, however, the curriculum should drive the technologies used in the classroom; that is, teachers should use the applicable technologies to enhance learning at the appropriate times.

As teachers use technology in the classroom, they are finding many different ways to integrate it into curriculum-specific learning objectives. Learning to integrate technology effectively, however, requires planning and practice. The more practice you have in teaching with and integrating technology, the more you will discover innovative ways to use technology to facilitate all types of instruction.

CURRICULUM PAGES

One of the bigger technology integration challenges that teachers face today is determining exactly how to use the Internet in their classrooms. Teachers who integrate the Internet successfully are using it in ways that engage students in problem solving, locating research information, and developing high-order thinking skills. Supervising students and controlling Web activities with curriculum pages is crucial to success in classroom use of the Internet. Recall

WEB INFO

For a tutorial on creating Web treasure hunts, visit the Teachers Discovering Computers Web site, click Chapter 7, click Web Info, and then click Treasure Hunt.

WEB INFO

To learn more about curriculum pages and projects for the one-computer classroom, visit the Teachers Discovering Computers Web site, click Chapter 7, click Web Info, and then click WebQuest.

Roller Coaster Scavenger Hunt

To learn more about the forces behind the fun, visit the Amusement Park Physics Web site at:

www.learner.org/exhibits/parkphysics

1. Do roller coasters have engines? _____

2. What drives a roller coaster? _____

3. What is the difference between running wheels and friction wheels?_____
   _____

4. How do roller coasters stop?_____

5. What is centripetal force? _____

6. What is gravitational force? _____

7. What were the forerunners of present-day roller coasters? _____

8. What type of materials did they use? _____

9. What was the first American roller coaster introduced?_____

10. What year and where did the nation's first theme park open? _____

11. What was the name of the first tubular steel coaster and what year was it introduced?
    _____

12. Have you been on a roller coaster before?_____

   If yes, what was the name of it, where was it, and what did you like most about it?
   _____
   _____

   If no, would you go on one now that you know more about them? Why?
   _____
   _____

   On the back of this paper, list four additional facts that you have learned.
   Good Luck!

Figure 7-26 A scavenger hunt is a great way to have students explore the resources of the Web while using their higher-order thinking skills at the same time.

from Chapter 3 that a **curriculum page** is a teacher-created document that contains hyperlinks to teacher-selected Web sites that assist in teaching content-specific curriculum objectives. In addition, curriculum pages should support learning objectives by providing students with quality Web resources, links to additional information, and opportunities to learn more. Because your curriculum page contains links that you have already researched and evaluated, students waste no time needlessly surfing instead of learning. A curriculum page can be a useful tool to ensure students spend your precious class time linking quickly to Web sites that you know will provide valuable information that is relevant to your lesson. Curriculum pages are easy to create and are a valuable teaching tool for students to use when accessing the World Wide Web.

Simple curriculum pages contain hyperlinks to teacher-selected sites. More detailed curriculum pages provide hyperlinks to sites and instructions for constructive and purposeful activities that students may complete when they get to the selected Web sites. Using curriculum pages with these types of activities helps students find answers to teacher-created questions and helps them create and answer their own questions. Figure 7-27 shows examples of teacher-created curriculum pages.

CREATING LESSON PLANS

Planning is one of the most important variables for good instruction, and curriculum integration demands a great deal of planning. When first introducing technology into the classroom, many teachers try to incorporate technology into their existing lesson plans and activities. Because of the nature of the new technology tools, however, and because teaching and learning

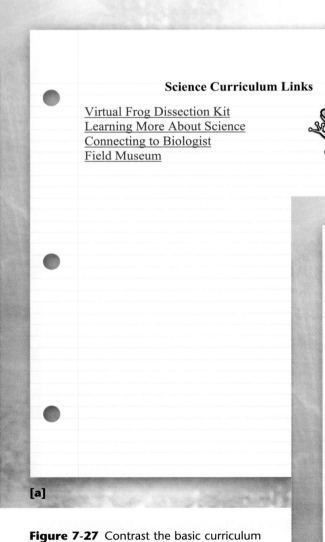

Science Curriculum Links

Virtual Frog Dissection Kit
Learning More About Science
Connecting to Biologist
Field Museum

[a]

Student Assignments, April 10-14
As usual, each date is the due date of the assignment.

Monday, April 10 – Go to the following Web site:
Physics in Today's Classroom. Select physics below the topic Science and answer the following question: How does air temperature affect the speed of sound? Give an example.

Tuesday, April 11 – Go to the following Web site:
The Amazon. Select The Amazon, select data, and select Comparison of a Peruvian and an American city by rooftop views. Answer the question at the bottom of the Web page.

Wednesday, April 12 – Go to the following Web site:
Kathy Schrock's Guide. Your quest is to locate the document Gettysburg Address and information about the speech. Answer the following questions: Who gave this speech, and to whom, why, and when? Discuss the three striking phrases from the speech and their impact upon you.

Thursday, April 13 – Go to the following Web site:
Math and Science Corner. Select option #15. Answer the following questions: What is a Platonic solid? What are the five Platonic solids? How many sides does each have?

Friday, April 14 – Go to the following Web site:
Newton Projects. Go to Season 13, Science Try Its. Conduct the experiment below Move the Cups. What happened to your cups? What science principle explains what happened to the cups? (Hint: Scroll to bottom of page for answer.) Now go to Season 14, Science Try Its. Conduct the experiment below Try it! Outta sight! What happened during this experiment? Why did the penny disappear?

Figure 7-27 Contrast the basic curriculum page [a] with the curriculum page that, in addition to hyperlinks, provides activities for students to complete at the selected Web site [b].

[b]

approaches must change, most teachers learn quickly this initial approach is only partially effective. To be successful in integrating technology, teachers must rethink and redesign activities and create new teaching and learning strategies as they progressively integrate technology across their curriculum. In other words, new technology tools require new instructional lessons.

Teachers do not have to rely solely on their own resourcefulness to create technology-enriched lesson plans and activities. Today, teachers may receive online advice from other educators by joining educational mailing lists, forums, newsgroups, discussion groups, and bulletin boards. Teachers also may refer to **AskERIC**, which is a federally funded Internet-based service providing educational information to teachers, media specialists, administrators, parents, and other interested persons throughout the world [Figure 7-28]. In addition to providing a question-and-answer service, the AskERIC Web site also provides a virtual library, lesson plans, and searchable database that contains more than one million abstracts of documents and journal articles on educational research.

Numerous lesson plans and activities at thousands of educational Web sites are available for teachers to use [Figure 7-29]. Many such sites provide search engines to locate curriculum-specific lesson plans and

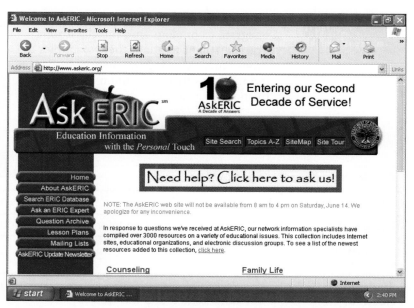

Figure 7-28 Teachers who need educational information, simply can AskERIC by submitting their questions to an Ask an ERIC Expert.

activities for almost any K-12 curriculum area.

The following sections describe one interdisciplinary and seven subject-specific teacher-created curriculum integration activities. Each of these lesson plans are centered on a focus question and use a combination of learning processes and teaching strategies to assist in the delivery of the instructional process. The purpose of these curriculum integration activities is to

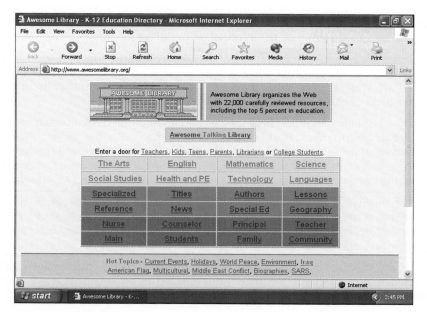

Figure 7-29 Teachers can locate an almost unlimited supply of lesson plans and activities at thousands of Web sites.

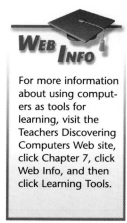

WEB INFO

For more information about using computers as tools for learning, visit the Teachers Discovering Computers Web site, click Chapter 7, click Web Info, and then click Learning Tools.

provide a basic understanding of how to integrate technology into the classroom. You may want to adapt these examples to subject areas covered in your classroom or use them in other curriculum areas for thematic instruction.

LANGUAGE ARTS INTEGRATION Language arts curriculum usually includes instruction in reading, writing, listening, viewing, speaking, and literature. Figure 7-30 shows a curriculum integration activity, called *Oh Where, Oh Where Can Information Be Found?*, that integrates technology into the subject areas of research and writing.

Language Arts

Curriculum Area:	Language Arts
Subject Area:	Research and Writing
Lesson Title:	Oh Where, Oh Where Can Information Be Found?
Suggested Grade Level:	8-12
Equipment Needed:	Technology: One or more computers, television monitor or projection system, access to a computer lab, Internet, and the Web
	Software: Inspiration, word processor, PowerPoint or HyperStudio, multimedia encyclopedias such as, Encarta, Microsoft Bookshelf, and Grolier's Encyclopedia
	Other: Access to media center
Focus Question:	How can media be used effectively in research?
Learning Objectives:	■ Students will determine content for their projects by using a variety of research resources, including indexes, magazines, newspapers, and journals.
	■ Students will use a variety of tools, including electronic card catalogs and computer catalogs and the Internet to gather information for research topics.
	■ Students will create a multimedia research report using PowerPoint, Microsoft Word, AppleWorks, or HyperStudio.
Instructions:	Using Inspiration and a computer connected to a television monitor, brainstorm the various media resources available to conduct research. Compare and contrast the type of information found in each of the different resources identified and create a concept map listing student ideas. Be sure to compare currency of information on the Internet versus information found in print media and have students explain how to determine if the information found on the Internet is accurate.
	Introduce the task by asking the focus question. Allow several students to respond. Divide students into groups of three or four and have groups select a topic to research. Distribute a predetermined assessment rubric, review the elements and information that the multimedia research report must contain, and discuss the evaluation process.
	Students create an outline describing how they will go about finding information on their chosen topic and how each group member will contribute to the success of the project. After the outline has been approved, the students may begin the project using the Web, print media, CDs and DVDs, and the media center as resources for finding their information. Using the computers in the classroom and the computer lab, students will create a multimedia project to present their findings.
Evaluation of Content:	Students will be evaluated on the content of their multimedia research projects using the predetermined assessment rubric. They also will be evaluated throughout the project by a review of their planning outline, by teacher observation, and by how effectively they used media resources to conduct their research.
Evaluation of Curriculum Integration:	Using observation, teachers will evaluate the extent to which technology helped students master the objectives. Teachers also will determine if the selected technology met a variety of learning styles and whether students were able to acquire the needed technology skills while creating their multimedia projects.

Figure 7-30 A sample lesson plan for *Oh Where, Oh Where Can Information Be Found?*

SOCIAL STUDIES INTEGRATION Social studies curriculum usually encompasses instruction in history, geography, civics, and economics. Figure 7-31 shows a curriculum integration activity, called *What Wonderful Webs We Weave*, that integrates technology into the subject area of ancient Egypt.

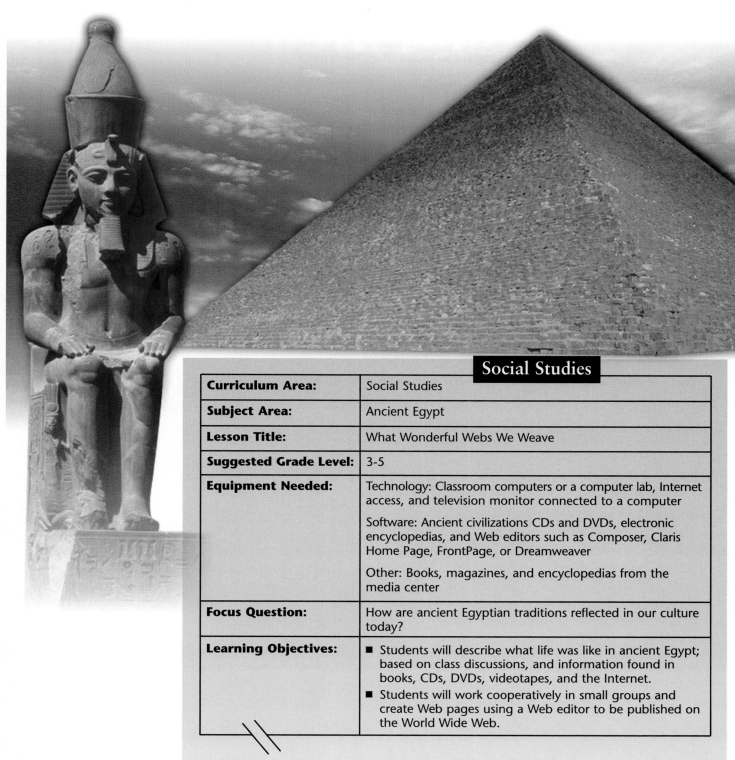

Social Studies

Curriculum Area:	Social Studies
Subject Area:	Ancient Egypt
Lesson Title:	What Wonderful Webs We Weave
Suggested Grade Level:	3-5
Equipment Needed:	Technology: Classroom computers or a computer lab, Internet access, and television monitor connected to a computer
	Software: Ancient civilizations CDs and DVDs, electronic encyclopedias, and Web editors such as Composer, Claris Home Page, FrontPage, or Dreamweaver
	Other: Books, magazines, and encyclopedias from the media center
Focus Question:	How are ancient Egyptian traditions reflected in our culture today?
Learning Objectives:	■ Students will describe what life was like in ancient Egypt; based on class discussions, and information found in books, CDs, DVDs, videotapes, and the Internet.
	■ Students will work cooperatively in small groups and create Web pages using a Web editor to be published on the World Wide Web.

Figure 7-31 A sample lesson plan for *What Wonderful Webs We Weave.*

(continued)

Instructions:	Introduce the activity to students by asking the focus question, then use student responses to create a KWLQS chart about ancient Egypt. As a class, decide on five or six broad topics of study relating to ancient Egypt; mummies, pyramids, Pharaohs, etc. Connect a classroom computer to a television monitor and view teacher-created Web curriculum pages about ancient Egypt. Discuss what makes a Web site interesting, attractive, and relevant. Distribute an evaluation rubric for the students' Web page project. Review the rubric with the students so they will understand how their Web page will be evaluated. Next, divide students into small groups of three to four. Have each group select one of the broad topics the class listed. Allow students to research their particular topic. They may use the CDs, DVDs, Web sites, books, magazines, and encyclopedias from the media center, and the Internet.
	After students have finished their research, they will complete a planning worksheet. Students will plan their content, Web page layout, background, attention-getting titles, animated GIFs, pictures, and links to related Web sites. After students have created their Web pages on paper, they may create them using a Web editor. When the Web pages are complete, they can be posted on your school's server or on a free Web server site.
Evaluation of Content:	Teacher observation along with the project rubric will be used to evaluate this activity. Additionally, students' planning worksheets will be used for assessment purposes. Quality of research, the information drawn from Web sites, and the extent to which the students answered the focus question also will be assessed.
Evaluation of Curriculum Integration:	Learning to access, analyze, and apply information from different resources is a necessary skill for students and will be observed. How well students locate information, determine what information is valuable, and apply that information will be examined. Student motivation and enthusiasm when creating a Web page also will assist with evaluating the technology.

Figure 7-31 (continued)

MATHEMATICS INTEGRATION

Mathematics curriculum usually includes instruction in basic number concepts, measurements, geometry, algebra, calculus, and data analysis. Figure 7-32 shows a curriculum integration activity, called *The Business of Professional Sports*, that integrates technology into the subject areas of measurement, problem solving, and geometry.

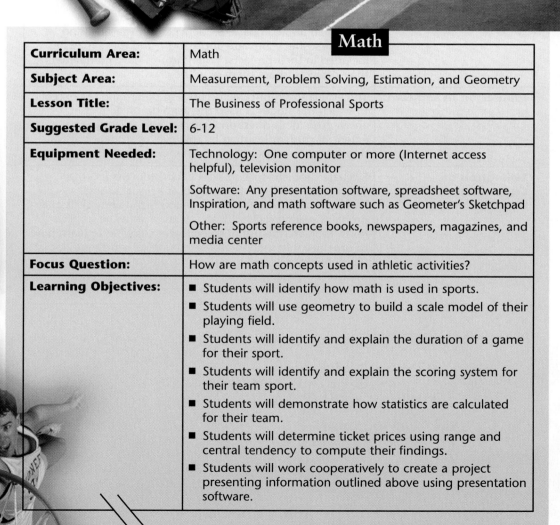

Math	
Curriculum Area:	Math
Subject Area:	Measurement, Problem Solving, Estimation, and Geometry
Lesson Title:	The Business of Professional Sports
Suggested Grade Level:	6-12
Equipment Needed:	Technology: One computer or more (Internet access helpful), television monitor Software: Any presentation software, spreadsheet software, Inspiration, and math software such as Geometer's Sketchpad Other: Sports reference books, newspapers, magazines, and media center
Focus Question:	How are math concepts used in athletic activities?
Learning Objectives:	■ Students will identify how math is used in sports. ■ Students will use geometry to build a scale model of their playing field. ■ Students will identify and explain the duration of a game for their sport. ■ Students will identify and explain the scoring system for their team sport. ■ Students will demonstrate how statistics are calculated for their team. ■ Students will determine ticket prices using range and central tendency to compute their findings. ■ Students will work cooperatively to create a project presenting information outlined above using presentation software.

Figure 7-32 A sample lesson plan for *The Business of Professional Sports.*

(continued)

Instructions:	Have the students list all the team sports they know. Create a concept map using Inspiration, projected to the class on the television monitor with Math as the center. Brainstorm with the class on how math is used in each of the sports they named, and then add these ideas to your concept map. Allow students to select their favorite team sport and then group students according to interest. Distribute an assessment rubric and discuss how it will be used to evaluate students' projects.
	Students will use the learning objectives to determine what type of project they would like to create. Allow them to use the Internet for research, as well as any resources from the media center including newspapers to calculate statistics. Provide each group with a designated time to use the computer. When groups are not using the computer, they may be using other resource materials to develop their projects.
	Coordinate with the media specialist to allow students access to other computers, or schedule time in the computer lab when the groups are working on their presentations. Have students use Geometer's Sketchpad to enter data and evaluate team statistics. Create graphs in Sketchpad and compare. Students create graphs using any spreadsheet software application, and these may be included in their projects. When groups have completed their projects, share them with the class.
Evaluation of Content:	The evaluation rubric will be used to determine the extent to which the students used the learning objectives to answer the focus question. Teachers will determine the extent of student learning by the level of student motivation and a demonstrated understanding of statistics.
Evaluation of Curriculum Integration:	Evaluate problem-solving skills when students use the concept map with brainstorming as a visual model. Furthermore, assess students gaining technology skills and problem-solving skills with the types of software applications. Evaluate the use of spreadsheet software to learn how to organize information and see graphical representation of that information. Evaluate student presentations to determine if this process reinforces skills in communication, organization, problem solving, and critical-thinking skills.

Figure 7-32 *(continued)*

SCIENCE INTEGRATION
Science curriculum usually contains instruction in physical sciences, earth and space sciences, and life sciences. Figure 7-33 shows a curriculum integration activity, called *Let's Think As a Scientist*, that integrates technology into the subject area of physical science.

Science

Curriculum Area:	Science
Subject Area:	Physical Sciences
Lesson Title:	Let's Think As a Scientist
Suggested Grade Level:	K-12
Equipment Needed:	Technology: One computer and a television monitor Software: Thinkin' Science. This lesson can be adapted with other software-specific products. Other: Student computers if available
Focus Question:	Why is it necessary for scientists to have good observation skills?
Learning Objectives:	■ Students will practice observation and memory skills. ■ Students will demonstrate understanding of content. ■ Students will interpret data. ■ Students will determine cause and effect between two events.
Instructions:	Begin this activity with a whole class discussion; use the focus question to guide the conversation. Thinkin' Science explores the earth, life, and physical sciences. Connect the computer to a television monitor or large screen. For this activity, go to Animal Tracking. Students will need to observe animals and then apply problem-solving skills. Students will explore animal behavior and then interpret data that is presented. Guide students by asking questions and drawing their attention to important events. To provide further practice of observation skills, and to increase visual memory, use the activity, *What Did You See?* The students will be presented with a scene. The scene will disappear and students will have to recreate the scene. All students should tell you what needs to be placed in the scene. After you have used the software with the whole class, you may set it up in a learning center. *Note:* Software comes with a Teacher's Guide and reproducible activity sheets. You may place these in the learning center to support the students.
Evaluation of Content:	Students will be quizzed on content provided to determine if memorization and observation skills were mastered. The number of correctly answered questions from each student will determine attainment of content.
Evaluation of Curriculum Integration:	Thinkin' Science is an excellent multimedia application providing positive continuous feedback for students and is interactive. Teacher observation will be used to measure student attention and motivation. Both of these are used as assessment tools. An additional evaluation will be how many students utilize the software in the learning center.

Figure 7-33 A sample lesson plan for *Let's Think As a Scientist*.

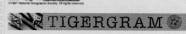

PHYSICAL EDUCATION AND HEALTH INTEGRATION Physical education and health curriculum usually includes instruction in basic health and physical education literacy. Figure 7-34 shows a curriculum integration activity, called *Eating Healthy!*, that integrates technology into the subject area of nutrition.

Physical Education and Health

Curriculum Area:	Physical Education and Health
Subject Area:	Nutrition
Lesson Title:	Eating Healthy!
Suggested Grade Level:	2-4, could be adapted for any grade level
Equipment Needed:	Technology: three computers, at least one with Internet access Software: PowerPoint or HyperStudio, database and drawing programs such as ClarisWorks, AppleWorks, Microsoft Works, and MS Paint Other: Books, nutrition brochures (from hospitals/health departments) and the Dole 5 A Day Web site (www.dole5aday.com)
Focus Question:	How do food choices affect your overall health?
Learning Objectives:	■ Students will be able to use the Internet to take the Dole 5 A Day Challenge. ■ Students will create five recipes that include five servings of fruits/vegetables. ■ Students will enter one of their recipes into a class cookbook database. ■ Students will work cooperatively to locate facts about their assigned fruit/vegetable using the Dole Fruit and Vegetable Encyclopedia and other resources. ■ Students will be able to use PowerPoint or HyperStudio to create and present a multimedia project on their fruit/vegetable.
Instructions:	Individually, students will go to the Dole 5 A Day Web site to take the 5 A Day Challenge and to discover how food choices affect their health. Students will be given time to browse the Web page to learn more about why it is so important to eat at least five fruits/vegetables per day. Students will use the information from the Web site and nutrition brochures to create five recipes for their 5-day menu. Students will select their favorite recipe and add it to the class cookbook database. Students will create a creative cookbook cover using a desktop publishing or draw program. They will print copies of the recipes to share with their families. Students will work in groups of two or three to create a multimedia presentation on an assigned fruit/vegetable. Students will use books, nutrition brochures, and the Dole 5 A Day Web site to collect the information that they need to complete their projects.
Evaluation of Content:	Each student's menu item will be evaluated using a rubric (spelling and grammar included). Group projects also will be evaluated using a rubric (spelling and grammar included). Teachers will observe students as they work to determine whether students understand how food choices affect their overall health.
Evaluation of Curriculum Integration:	The effectiveness of the technology will be evaluated by testing students' content retention in a culminating quiz. Effectiveness will be apparent in student presentations. Students will gain valuable experience exploring Internet resources and learning how to use them to complete an assignment.

Figure 7-34 A sample lesson plan for *Eating Healthy!*

ARTS INTEGRATION   Arts curriculum usually incorporates instruction in the visual and performing arts of drawing, painting, dance, music, and theater. Figure 7-35 shows a curriculum integration activity, called *The Theory of Color*, that integrates technology into the subject area of color theory.

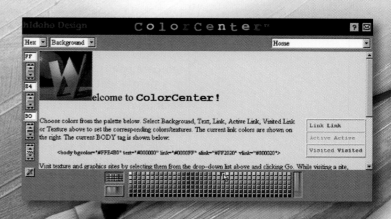

Art	
Curriculum Area:	Art (integrates Math)
Subject Area:	Color-Theory — Reinforcing Basic Reading, Writing, and Math Skills
Lesson Title:	The Theory of Color
Suggested Grade Level:	4-6, easily adapted to higher levels
Equipment Needed:	Technology: Requires access to a student computer lab. Requires computer connected to large monitor or TV. Software: PowerPoint and any paint program
Focus Question:	How does the world around you reflect colors?
Learning Objectives:	■ Increase understanding of color theory. ■ Increase use of reading, math, and writing in the art classroom. ■ Demonstration of abstract conceptualization of written materials. ■ Demonstrate skills in computer paint accessories.

Figure 7-35 A sample lesson plan for *The Theory of Color*.

(continued)

Instructions:	Students are given a brief introduction explaining the goals of the lessons. They are told that an important part of the lesson is their own reading and writing skills. A simple pretest is given to allow students to demonstrate any preexisting knowledge of the content area.
	Color mixing: Using basic math skills and written directions, students prepare a series of diagrammatic color charts that teach basic color mixing and theory. The blank charts are prepared with the paint software. The color formulas will be written in a mathematical or fractional way (e.g., Orange = ½ Yellow + ½ Red). Students will use eyedroppers to mix tempera paints to the proper proportion and paint samples as a permanent record in their portfolios.
	Relating reading and color theory: Based on the belief that children should be taught to visualize color as described in books or stories, children will read a series of excerpts from stories that include written descriptions of colors. Students will create color samples that show an understanding of the written excerpt and the colors described.
	Relating color to written descriptions: In contrast to the previous activity, students will be given blank lined pages for writing text. Each blank paragraph will have a preprinted block of color. Students will be directed to create brief descriptive paragraphs that relate to each of the attached colors.
	Integrating technology: This lesson will be spread over time to allow adequate computer access time. Students will engage in a computer-oriented lesson that integrates what they have learned about colors with both reading and technology.
	Students will create a drawing with the paint program. The requirement for this piece of art will be that it clearly shows three primary colors, three secondary colors, one tint, and one shade.
Evaluation of Content:	A critique rubric will be used that the students easily can understand. Students will engage in critiques of each other's work. Critiques will be consolidated and students and instructors jointly will discuss the results of the exercises. The teacher also will assign individual student work. This will be based on the rubric to ensure consistency and reliability of results. Final results are compared with the pretest, where marked improvement in the students' understanding of color and color theory should be identified.
Evaluation of Curriculum Integration:	As a first-time computer graphics assignment, teacher observation should be used to determine the quality of the projects. Higher levels of complexity or variance in the final projects can be evaluated.

Figure 7-35 *(continued)*

COLOR MATTERS®

WELCOME! CLICK TO ENTER...

EXCEPTIONAL EDUCATION INTEGRATION
Exceptional education curriculum, or **special education curriculum,** usually contains instruction in all curriculum areas with adaptations made for students with unique characteristics or special needs. These students include those who are gifted, learning disabled, physically disabled, emotionally disabled, or mentally disabled. Instruction for regular-education students and exceptional-educational students is merging as teachers find that many of the technology resources and integration activities dramatically enhance the instruction of students with special needs. Teachers easily can modify many of the integration activities illustrated in Figure 7-30 through Figure 7-35 on pages 7.30 through 7.38 to meet the needs of exceptional educational students. Figure 7-36 shows a curriculum integration activity, called *Rainforests Are In Trouble,* that integrates technology into the subject area of current events and can be used for students with special needs.

Special Education

Curriculum Area:	Science, Social, Studies, Math and Language Arts for special education students.
Subject Area:	Current Events
Lesson Title:	Rainforests Are In Trouble
Suggested Grade Level:	3-5 (This lesson has been developed for grade levels 3 to 5 special education students. This lesson can be used with 3rd to 12th grade with appropriate adaptations.)
Equipment Needed:	Technology: Computer and a television monitor or large screen, Internet access and use the Welcome to the Amazon Web site
	Software: Microsoft Encarta or other electronic encyclopedias, Tom Synder's Rainforest Researchers or Rainforest CDs
	Other: *The Lost Compound* video, 3×5 index cards, notebooks, pencils, pens
Focus Question:	Why are rainforests worth saving?
Learning Objectives:	■ Students will collect information about the rainforests.
	■ Students will take a Web expedition to the Amazon using the Internet.
	■ Students will understand current research efforts on tropical rainforests, learn adaptations of organisms, demonstrate knowledge gained of tropical rainforest issues, and explore plant life cycles.
	■ Students will create a multimedia research report.

Figure 7-36 A sample lesson plan for *Rainforests Are In Trouble.*

(continued)

Instructions:	Start the activity by asking students what they know about the troubles in rainforests and why rainforests are worth saving. Then create a KWHL chart with the students. Students will work in groups of four. They will be given a list of Web sites about rainforests. They will access at least three different sites and take notes (3x5 index cards) about five different aspects of the rainforests. If an e-mail address is listed, students will write a short note asking a specific question they want to know about the rainforest. Students will work with their same partners and venture into the Amazon Web site. While there, they enter the options available at the Web site: Research, The Team, Map, About Netspedition, Equipment, and Venezuela and document a brief description of each. Next, the team will give a brief description about one of the butterfly surveys, indicating date, location, and what types of butterflies were caught. The team then will access the log book and choose one specific day on the calendar. They will record the date, location, temperature, a description of one of the photographs, a description of the author's feelings, and the name of the person entering the information. Students still work in their cooperative teams taking turns at the computer. If computer access for inputting data is difficult, use other input devices such as PDAs and AlphaSmarts. Each student plays the role of a scientific expert, chemist, ecologist, botanist, or taxonomist using one of four unique student reference books. Teams watch the video on *The Lost Compound* and use on-screen instructions to guide them in analyzing information, collaborating, and making decisions. Students will create research projects on the computer with drawings, maps, etc.
Evaluation of Content:	The projects the students complete will indicate whether the students grasped the concepts indicated by the above objectives. In addition, PowerPoint or HyperStudio can be completed by individual students on a particular species or rainforest to present to the class. This project could be used as an additional or follow-up assignment.
Evaluation of Curriculum Integration:	Teacher observation will help to verify if the technology assisted in meeting various learning styles and needs of special education students. Teacher observation will determine if technology assisted in student attention and motivation. Students will be evaluated on time on task and length of time students work to master content and technology skills. An additional evaluation will be looking at each student and his or her individual needs throughout the lesson.

Figure 7-36 (continued)

INTERDISCIPLINARY INTEGRATION An **interdisciplinary curriculum** usually includes two or more academic disciplines or curriculum areas to form a cross-discipline or subject-integrated lesson. A **cross-discipline lesson** includes a combination of curriculum-specific areas, such as math or science, that are integrated with language arts. A **subject-integrated lesson** is a lesson that integrates multiple skills such as speaking, reading, thinking, and writing with multiple subject areas such as math, science, and language arts to create a more holistic learning experience. An interdisciplinary curriculum can combine various skills or disciplines to make a lesson more fully integrated for authentic and inquiry-based learning. Figure 7-37 shows a curriculum-integration activity, called *Natural Disasters Occur Everywhere*, that integrates technology in the subject areas of writing, research, science, social studies, health, and art.

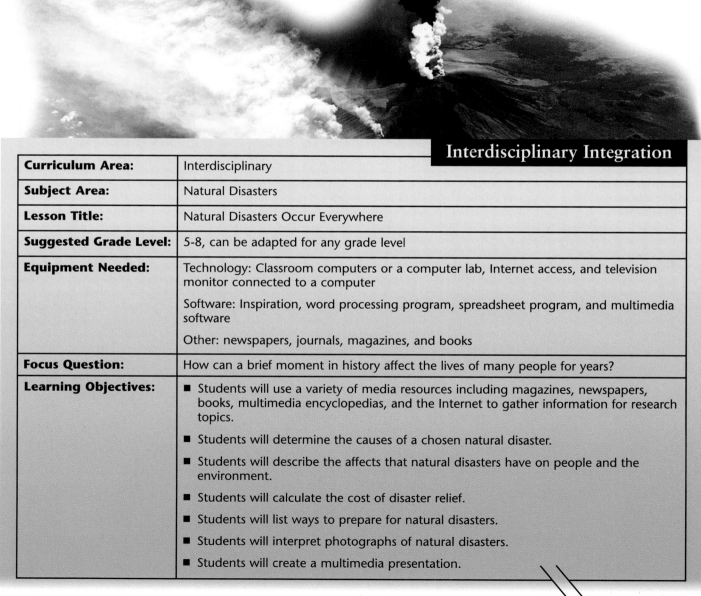

Interdisciplinary Integration

Curriculum Area:	Interdisciplinary
Subject Area:	Natural Disasters
Lesson Title:	Natural Disasters Occur Everywhere
Suggested Grade Level:	5-8, can be adapted for any grade level
Equipment Needed:	Technology: Classroom computers or a computer lab, Internet access, and television monitor connected to a computer Software: Inspiration, word processing program, spreadsheet program, and multimedia software Other: newspapers, journals, magazines, and books
Focus Question:	How can a brief moment in history affect the lives of many people for years?
Learning Objectives:	■ Students will use a variety of media resources including magazines, newspapers, books, multimedia encyclopedias, and the Internet to gather information for research topics. ■ Students will determine the causes of a chosen natural disaster. ■ Students will describe the affects that natural disasters have on people and the environment. ■ Students will calculate the cost of disaster relief. ■ Students will list ways to prepare for natural disasters. ■ Students will interpret photographs of natural disasters. ■ Students will create a multimedia presentation.

Figure 7-37 An interdisciplinary lesson plan for *Natural Disasters Occur Everywhere*.   *(continued)*

Instructions:	Introduce the task by asking the focus question. Allow several students to respond. Introduce the term natural disaster. Create a KWL chart to determine what students know about natural disasters and what they want to learn. Divide students into groups of three or four and have each group go to ndrd.gsfc.nasa.gov to select a natural disaster that they would like to research. Distribute a predetermined assessment rubric and cover the evaluation procedures for the final project.
	Students will use the Internet and other resources to collect data on their chosen natural disaster. Students will use Inspiration to organize their data into a web; students should include information such as the type and cause of the natural disaster, where the disaster occurred, the effect on people and environment, and the type of aid currently being sent.
	Students will find and save photographs that depict the affect the natural disaster had on people and the environment.
	Using the knowledge that they gained from their research, students will determine what type of aid they could put into a relief-care package for a family of four with a $100 budget. Students should also use the food pyramid as a guide to help choose healthy food items to include in their care package. Students will gather the prices of each item using newspaper ads, the Internet, and other available resources. They will use a spreadsheet program to calculate the cost of the care package with appropriate sales tax.
	Using the computer lab or classroom computers, students will create a culminating multimedia presentation to present their research findings and their plans for aiding the victims.
Evaluation of Content:	Teacher observation along with the project rubric will be used to evaluate this activity. Students will be evaluated on usage of the Web and other technology tools. The quality of research and information utilized and the extent to which the focus question was answered also will be assessed.
Evaluation of Curriculum Integration:	Students' ability to access, analyze, and apply information from different resources will be observed. Students' motivation and enthusiasm when creating the multimedia presentation also will assist with evaluating the technology.

Figure 7-37 *(continued)*

Finding Funds to Support Classroom Technology Integration

One of the more difficult aspects of implementing technology in schools is finding and obtaining the funds for new technologies and the associated ongoing expenses. At present, many school districts do not have sufficient funding to incorporate technology at all levels throughout the district. For this reason, a classroom may not contain all the hardware and software to fully integrate technology into the curriculum.

While the continued drop in computer and educational software prices lessens the problem, obtaining funding for classroom technology is challenging. Many teachers, however, find that persistence often produces dramatic results. To increase the quantity and quality of technology in a classroom, a teacher first should ask the principal and other district administrators for additional classroom equipment and software. If you still need to obtain additional technology funding, you can turn to numerous other sources, including local school districts, public and private businesses, and government agencies.

FUND-RAISING DRIVES AND ACADEMIC CONTESTS

Class car washes, bake sales, and other activities can help raise money to purchase additional computers, hardware components, and software for classrooms. Local businesses such as banks, car dealerships, grocery stores, and department stores often respond to solicitations to improve the educational quality of the schools in their areas with donations. Corporations frequently are eager to become involved in active school technology programs — whether it is to contribute equipment, funds, or expertise. Teachers regularly write letters to local school business partners stating the school's needs in order to enlist their support. Even relatively small amounts of acquired funding can make a difference in the availability of technology in your classroom. Raising $100 will fund a new ink-jet printer, numerous educational CDs/DVDs, or a color scanner; $1,000 will allow the purchase of a high-end multimedia computer with software, or several PDAs with software and accessories. [Figure 7-38].

Figure 7-38
Teachers organize all kinds of class events, such as car washes and bake sales, to raise funds to purchase computers, printers, scanners, digital cameras, educational software, and other items for use in integrated classrooms.

WEB INFO

For more information about how to obtain equipment for your classroom, visit the Teachers Discovering Computers Web site, click Chapter 7, click Web Info, and then click Free Equipment.

Another way to obtain hardware and software for the classroom is to enter academic contests. Teachers may locate information about hundreds of academic contests on the Web and in educational journals and magazines.

Teachers should involve the community, especially parents, in fund-raising. The local school community holds its schools accountable for everything that goes on in the classroom, so enlisting the help of parents and business partners will broaden the base of support for the school's educational technology efforts. In addition, parents may have contacts or affiliations with local businesses or be able to provide further information on how to obtain funding. Another avenue for locating potential sources for technology funding is to showcase your classroom's use of technology for parents, business leaders, and school board members at your school's Parent Teacher Association (PTA), Parent Teacher Organization (PTO), or Parent Teacher Student Organization (PTSO) meetings.

Schools also should consider asking for volunteer services from the community in addition to or instead of asking for funds to pay for services. If funding for equipment maintenance is not available, for example, a local consultant may be willing to donate services. Many schools find that a combination of financial and volunteer support demonstrates the community's commitment to technology integration and strengthens the long-term community-school partnerships.

GRANTS

The majority of outside funding sources for technology fall under a general category called grants. **Grants** are funds provided by a funding source that transfers money, equipment, or services to the grantee. The **grantee** is the teacher, school, or organization to which the grant funds or equipment are transferred. Grants can be obtained from school districts, state Departments of Education, federal sources, foundations, and corporations. Grants range from a few hundred to millions of dollars. Many corporations maintain or support foundations that provide grants, both large and small, for creative projects.

To obtain a grant, a school district, school, or teacher must submit a grant proposal in response to a request for proposal (RFP). A **request for proposal (RFP)** is a document provided by the grant source that details the information teachers and schools need to provide to write a successful grant proposal. A **grant proposal** is the document the potential grantee sends to the funding source. Grant proposals can vary from a simple one-page application to an extensive multipage document.

When writing a grant, schools can take one of several approaches. A single person may write the grant proposal; teachers may write grant proposals with other teachers, media specialists, technology coordinators, and school district personnel; or if the proposal is extensive, the school districts may even employ a grant-writing specialist or consultant to write the proposal to increase the availability of technology in their classrooms.

The principal and curriculum coordinator usually receive notification of grant opportunities. In addition, teachers can locate many grant opportunities on the Web [Figure 7-39].

Figure 7-39 Many Web sites provide teachers and administrators with current, extensive information on grants for education.

Creating a Curriculum Page

As you learned earlier in this chapter, curriculum pages are wonderful tools for enhancing your students' learning experience. The special feature at the end of Chapter 3 provided you with step-by-step instructions for creating a basic teacher's home page using Microsoft Word. The special feature that follows this chapter builds on your knowledge and enhances your Web page development skills by providing you with step-by-step instructions for creating a curriculum page using Microsoft Word. You also can download a similar step-by-step project that provides you with instructions on how to create a curriculum page in the latest version of Netscape Composer.

Summary of Evaluating Educational Technology and Integration Strategies

Technology will not make a difference in the quality of students graduating from K-12 schools unless teachers learn how to use it as an integration tool to enhance learning. This chapter first introduced the various tools and resources teachers use to evaluate the appropriateness of educational technology and the effectiveness of technology integration. Next, a number of strategies were presented for integrating technology into one-computer classrooms and other K-12 instructional settings along with seven subject-specific curriculum integration activities. Finally, the chapter provided information on how to obtain funding to increase the availability of technology in your classroom.

WEB INFO

For more information about grant opportunities for educators, visit the Teachers Discovering Computers Web site, click Chapter 7, click Web Info, and then click Grants.

In Brief

WEB INFO

IN BRIEF

KEY TERMS

CHECKPOINT

TEACHING TODAY

EDUCATION ISSUES

INTEGRATION CORNER

SOFTWARE CORNER

IN THE LAB

LEARN IT ONLINE

✴ FEATURES...

Timeline 2004

Guide to WWW Sites

Buyer's Guide 2004

Professional Sites

State/Federal Sites

Interactive Labs

Search Tools

HOME

Web Instructions: To display this page from the Web, start your browser and enter the URL, www.course.com/tdc3. Click Chapter 7 at the top of the Web page and then click In Brief on the left sidebar. Click the links for current and additional information. To listen to an audio version of this In Brief, click the Audio button to the top left of these instructions.

1. Evaluating Educational Technology

Evaluation of educational technology is important before instruction begins, during the instructional period, and after the instruction takes place. Educators can rely on a variety of resources to help them identify and evaluate the appropriateness of educational technologies, including resources available from school districts, state Departments of Education, professional educational organizations, catalogs, and Web sites.

2. Evaluating Software Applications

Teachers should evaluate software for appropriateness and accuracy of content and consider its relevance to curriculum learning objectives. Software evaluation rubrics help teachers evaluate educational software. A **rubric** is a detailed assessment tool that allows individuals to assess the quality of software or other items. A software evaluation rubric should list a number of important evaluation criteria, including content, documentation and technical support, ability and academic levels, technical quality, and ease of use.

3. Evaluating Web Resources

When evaluating a Web site as an instructional resource, teachers should consider characteristics such as authority, affiliation, audience, currency, and Web site design. **Authority** refers to the credibility of the author of the Web page or Web site. **Affiliation** refers to the professional organization, school, school district, university, company, or government office with which a particular Web site is connected. **Content** is the information provided on a Web page. The **audience** is the individual or group intended to view the Web page. **Currency** is a measure of how up-to-date, or timely, the Web page content is and how often it is updated.

4. Evaluating the Effectiveness of Technology Integration

When integrating technology, some teachers and schools are moving towards a nontraditional approach of student assessment, known as alternative assessment. **Alternative assessment** is using nontraditional methods to determine if students have mastered content and skill level. **Authentic assessment**, **project-based assessment**, and **portfolio assessment** refer to alternative ways to evaluate student performance to determine how well and in what way students are able to accomplish learning objectives and standards.

5. Evaluation Tools

When using authentic assessment, many teachers use checklists, rating scales, rubrics, and teacher observation. A **checklist** is a predetermined list of performance criteria. A **rating scale** is a more complex form of a checklist that lists a numerical value, or rating, for each criterion. A **rubric** is a detailed assessment tool that makes it easier for teachers to assess the quality of an item, such as a learning project. **Teacher observation** is when teachers actively observe their students during the learning process.

In Brief

WEB INFO

IN BRIEF

KEY TERMS

CHECKPOINT

TEACHING TODAY

EDUCATION ISSUES

INTEGRATION CORNER

SOFTWARE CORNER

IN THE LAB

LEARN IT ONLINE

✱ FEATURES...

Timeline 2004

Guide to WWW Sites

Buyer's Guide 2004

Professional Sites

State/Federal Sites

Interactive Labs

Search Tools

HOME

6. Evaluating Technology-Based Student Projects

Checklists, rating scales, and teacher observation are valid assessment tools for technology-based student projects. Curriculum goals and objectives should define and guide the selection and creation of the assessment tool. Student projects should be evaluated for content, planning, and creativity. Planning tools include flowcharts and concept maps. **Flowcharts** are diagrams that show the step-by-step actions that must take place through a sequence of events. A **concept map** or **story web** helps students use flowcharting to understand the attributes and relationships of the main subject and provides a visual tool for brainstorming and planning.

7. Integration Strategies

To help meet the constant challenge of motivating students to learn, teachers must change their traditional roles to become facilitators of learning. Instructional strategies help teachers integrate technology into a one-computer classroom, a multicomputer classroom, and a computer lab. Most teachers will teach in a classroom with one multimedia computer, often referred to as the **one-computer classroom**. The most common usage of one computer is for classroom presentations and demonstrations. The most important advantage of using a computer lab is that all students are provided hands-on experience with using computer technology.

8. Curriculum Pages

Teachers who integrate the Internet successfully are utilizing it in ways to engage students in problem solving, finding research information, and developing high-order thinking skills. Crucial to the successful use of the Internet in the classroom is supervising students and controlling Web activities by using curriculum pages. A **curriculum page** is a teacher-created document that contains hyperlinks to teacher-selected sites that have been evaluated for content and age appropriateness.

9. Creating Lesson Plans

To be successful when integrating technology, teachers must rethink and redesign activities and create new teaching and learning strategies. New technology tools require new instructional lessons. Teachers do not have to originate and create technology-enriched lesson plans and activities. They may find a multitude of lesson plans and activities at thousands of educational Web sites. Many educational Web sites provide search engines that allow teachers to locate curriculum-specific lesson plans and activities for almost any K-12 curriculum area.

10. Finding Funds to Support Integration

Teachers can obtain funding for classroom technology from a number of sources, including people within their school district, businesses, private organizations, foundations, and the government. Class car washes, bake sales, and other activities raise money to purchase additional computers, other hardware components, and software for classrooms. Other ways to obtain these tools are to solicit corporate donations and enter academic contests.

11. Grants

The majority of outside funding sources for technology fall under a general category called grants. **Grants** are funds provided by a funding source that transfers money, equipment, or services to the grantee. The **grantee** is the teacher, school, or organization to which the grant funds or equipment are transferred. To obtain a grant, a school district, school, or teacher must submit a grant proposal in response to a request for proposal. A **request for proposal** (RFP) is a document provided by the grant source that details the information teachers and schools need to provide to write a successful grant proposal. A **grant proposal** is the document sent to the funding source.

Key Terms

WEB INFO

IN BRIEF

KEY TERMS

CHECKPOINT

TEACHING TODAY

EDUCATION ISSUES

INTEGRATION CORNER

SOFTWARE CORNER

IN THE LAB

LEARN IT ONLINE

*FEATURES...

Timeline 2004

Guide to WWW Sites

Buyer's Guide 2004

Professional Sites

State/Federal Sites

Interactive Labs

Search Tools

HOME

Web Instructions: To display this page from the Web, start your browser and enter the URL, www.course.com/tdc3. Click Chapter 7 at the top of the Web page and then click Key Terms on the left sidebar. Scroll through the list of terms. Click a term to display its definition and a picture. Click Key Terms on the left to redisplay the Key Terms page. Click the TO WEB button for current and additional information about the term from the Web.

ability level [7.09]
academic level [7.09]
affiliation [7.10]
alternative assessment [7.12]
appropriate [7.02]
arts curriculum [7.37]
AskERIC [7.29]
assessment [7.12]
audience [7.11]
authentic assessment [7.14]
authentic learning [7.14]
authority [7.10]

block schedule [7.20]

checklist [7.15]
concept map [7.19]
content [7.11]
creativity [7.19]
cross-discipline lesson [7.41]
currency [7.11]
curriculum page [7.28]

design [7.11]
documentation [7.09]

e-folio [7.15]
ease of use [7.09]
EDTECH [7.05]
electronic portfolio [7.15]

embedded assessment [7.15]
evaluate [7.02]
exceptional education
    curriculum [7.39]

flowcharts [7.19]

grant proposal [7.44]
grantee [7.44]
grants [7.44]

Inspiration [7.19]
interdisciplinary curriculum
    [7.41]

KWLQS chart [7.25]

language arts curriculum [7.30]
learning process [7.11]

mathematics curriculum [7.33]

objectivity [7.11]
one-computer classroom [7.22]

physical education and health
    curriculum [7.36]
portfolio assessment [7.15]
project-based assessment [7.15]
project-based learning [7.15]
purpose [7.11]

rating scale [7.15]
reliable assessment [7.12]
request for proposal (RFP)
    [7.44]
rubric [7.06, 7.15]

science curriculum [7.35]
social studies curriculum [7.31]
software evaluation rubric
    [7.06]
special education curriculum
    [7.39]
storyboard [7.19]
story web [7.19]
student performance [7.12]
subject-integrated lesson [7.41]

teacher observation [7.17]
technical quality [7.09]
technical support [7.09]
technology conference [7.04]
traditional assessment [7.12]

valid [7.06]
visual learning techniques
    [7.19]

Web evaluation rubric [7.12]
Web scavenger hunt [7.26]

Checkpoint

Web Instructions: To display this page from the Web, start your browser and enter the URL, www.course.com/tdc3. Click Chapter 7 at the top of the Web page and then click Checkpoint on the left sidebar. Click a blank line for the answer. Click the links for current and additional information.

WEB INFO

IN BRIEF

KEY TERMS

CHECKPOINT

TEACHING TODAY

EDUCATION ISSUES

INTEGRATION CORNER

SOFTWARE CORNER

IN THE LAB

LEARN IT ONLINE

✱ FEATURES...

Timeline 2004

Guide to WWW Sites

Buyer's Guide 2004

Professional Sites

State/Federal Sites

Interactive Labs

Search Tools

HOME

1. Label the Figure

Instructions: Identify the various categories used to evaluate Web sites.

2. Matching

Instructions: Match each term from the column on the left with the best description from the column on the right.

_____ 1. curriculum page

_____ 2. request for proposal

_____ 3. checklist

_____ 4. evaluate

_____ 5. concept map

a. to determine the value or to judge the worth

b. provides a visual tool for brainstorming and planning

c. teacher-created document that contains hyperlinks to teacher-selected Web sites

d. predetermined list of performance criteria

e. a document provided by a grant source that details the information needed to write a grant

3. Short Answer

Instructions: Write a brief answer to each of the following questions.

1. Describe four resources where teachers can find information about how to evaluate educational software. Why is it important for teachers to evaluate software before using it in the classroom? _____

2. Should teachers evaluate Web resources for instructional value in the same way they evaluate print resources? Why or why not? _____

3. Describe three techniques for evaluating students' technology projects. _____

4. Briefly describe three uses of technology in a one-computer classroom. Why does having more than one computer in a classroom allow for more flexibility and greater integration of technology? _____

5. Briefly describe grant funding for K-12 schools. Why are grants so important for many K-12 schools? Describe three ways in which teachers can obtain funding for classroom technology. _____

Level 1
1. _____ No author is listed and no e-mail contact is provided.
2. _____ It is unclear what institution supports this information.
3. _____ The purpose is unclear or cannot be determined.
4. _____ The Web page is a virtual soapbox.
5. _____ The information on the Web site does not relate to my objectives.
6. _____ The information will not challenge learners to think, reflect, discuss, compare, or classify.
7. _____ The Web pages are not appropriate for my audience.
8. _____ Information on the site has not been revised since 2002, or no date can be located.
9. _____ The Web site is not appropriate for my audience.

Teaching Today

WEB INFO

IN BRIEF

KEY TERMS

CHECKPOINT

TEACHING TODAY

EDUCATION ISSUES

INTEGRATION CORNER

SOFTWARE CORNER

IN THE LAB

LEARN IT ONLINE

* FEATURES...

Timeline 2004

Guide to WWW Sites

Buyer's Guide 2004

Professional Sites

State/Federal Sites

Interactive Labs

Search Tools

HOME

Web Instructions: To display this page from the Web, start your browser and enter the URL, www.course.com/tdc3. Click Chapter 7 at the top of the Web page and then click Teaching Today on the left sidebar. Click the links for current and additional information.

1. The Parent Teachers Organization (PTO) at your school has raised money to purchase software for all classes in your grade level. Your principal asks you to work with other teachers in your grade to make recommendations for software purchases to enhance the curriculum. Your principal asks you and the teachers to supply a wish list with seven to ten different titles, a detailed evaluation of each title, and pricing for each. Based on what you have learned in this chapter, what would be your next step in identifying appropriate software packages and then evaluating each? Where can you find software reviews? To what extent are these reviews helpful? What type of information can you gather about the software from these reviews? What kind of site-licensing and pricing are available for each package?

2. In your classroom, you may have one, two, or more computers. You may even have access to a wireless mobile lab. While this is exciting, it presents new challenges for you as a teacher and for your students. No matter how many computers or technologies are available to you, effective class management is crucial and you have to plan and be well-organized. One of the more difficult issues to manage is scheduling student use of various technologies. How would you set up your classroom to maximize the use of one, two, or more computers and how would you manage your class to ensure that all students get time on the computers? In what ways could you create learning communities in your classroom? Where could you locate ideas and suggestions to help you?

3. You teach students with special needs in a middle school. You want to integrate multimedia software applications into your curriculum to enhance your students' learning. You are looking for software applications that can be used in more

than one curriculum area. You are familiar with multimedia authoring programs such as PowerPoint and HyperStudio and already are using them in different curriculum areas. Describe the ways in which the other applications described in this chapter may be used in more than one curriculum area. Explore subject-specific software such as Where in the U.S.A. is Carmen Sandiego? (social studies software). Can this type of software be used in other curriculum areas as well? Why or why not?

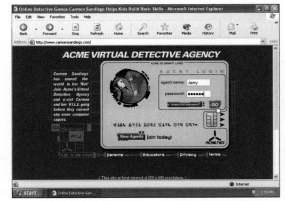

4. As you begin to integrate technology into your curriculum, you need alternative ways to assess student performance. In this chapter, you read about the rubrics that teachers use to assess performance. Itemize the key points to remember when evaluating student work. What alternative assessment tools can you use in your classroom? When is using alternative assessment tools most appropriate? When are other types of assessment tools most appropriate?

Education Issues

7

Web Instructions: To display this page from the Web, start your browser and enter the URL, www.course.com/tdc3. Click Chapter 7 at the top of the Web page and then click Education Issues on the left sidebar. Click the links for current and additional information to help you respond to the Education Issues questions.

WEB INFO

IN BRIEF

KEY TERMS

CHECKPOINT

TEACHING TODAY

EDUCATION ISSUES

INTEGRATION CORNER

SOFTWARE CORNER

IN THE LAB

LEARN IT ONLINE

✱ FEATURES...

Timeline 2004

Guide to WWW Sites

Buyer's Guide 2004

Professional Sites

State/Federal Sites

Interactive Labs

Search Tools

HOME

1. Simulation Software

Increasingly sophisticated software applications not only have impacted business, entertainment, and recreation, but education as well. Simulation software gives students experience with designing a city, constructing buildings, flying airplanes, or saving a forest. Many educators feel simulation software assists students in developing high-order thinking skills and problem-solving skills. Opponents argue, however, that using these types of software merely leads students and does not help develop problem-solving skills. Opponents stress that simulation software programs are no more than fancy games. Do you agree with either side? Why or why not? Support your position with documentation. What advantages, if any, do simulation software applications offer? Do you think disadvantages may become evident when using the simulation software in the classroom? How might another application described in this chapter be used to teach high-order thinking skills or problem solving?

2. Graduation Concerns

You are a high school counselor. Two years ago your state initiated a state-mandated exit exam that all seniors must pass before they can receive a high school diploma. You have three students who earned As and Bs throughout high school. They are all well-rounded, good students with high aptitudes for learning. One has taken several Advanced Placement (AP) classes. This year, none of these three passed the exit exam. This means they have the credits to graduate but will not receive a high school diploma; instead they will receive only a certification of completion. What do you think about this situation? What could be the underlying and contributing issues that resulted in their failure to pass? How will you counsel the students, teachers, and parents?

Education Issues

WEB INFO

IN BRIEF

KEY TERMS

CHECKPOINT

TEACHING TODAY

EDUCATION ISSUES

INTEGRATION CORNER

SOFTWARE CORNER

IN THE LAB

LEARN IT ONLINE

✱ FEATURES...

Timeline 2004

Guide to WWW Sites

Buyer's Guide 2004

Professional Sites

State/Federal Sites

Interactive Labs

Search Tools

HOME

3. Evaluating Web Sites

A great deal of <u>information exists on the Internet</u> that is not what it appears to be. Sometimes material seems authoritative and well-written, but upon closer inspection, the material is biased, inaccurate, or out of date. Your school board feels it is a teacher's responsibility to teach students to recognize the quality and authority of information they find on the Internet. Do you agree or disagree? Why? How will you teach your students to do this? What criteria should students use when evaluating Web sites? Do students need to evaluate all Web sites? Support your answer with illustrations from exiting Web sites.

4. Grants for Training

You locate a request for proposal (RFP) to fund a grant for notebook computers for all the teachers in your school. The grant will provide the notebook computers, but the school has to provide the teacher training. You want to develop the proposal with the help of the technology committee. You recognize this is a great opportunity to get technology into the hands of all teachers through the use of their own notebook computers. You think your school has an extremely good chance of being funded. The principal immediately says, "NO!" She feels the teachers should write grants only to obtain student computers. She also states that no funds are available for teacher training. Do you see a solution to this dilemma? What should you do? Where can you go to obtain more information and creative ideas for <u>writing the grant</u> and solving the <u>training issues</u>? How will you convince the principal that putting a notebook computer in each teacher's hands is an important initial step toward technology integration?

5. Alternative Assessment

Your first teaching job is at a very progressive new school that has technology in every classroom. During your college education, you learned a great deal about assessing student achievement through testing. You learned how to create appropriate traditional tests for subjects. This new school, however, has no traditional testing program. It has implemented an innovative approach to learning that uses only alternative assessment. No grades are assigned and all assessment is based on mastery learning. Do you think this is a good strategy? Support your position with reasons based on educational research. What <u>alternative assessment tools</u> can you use to meet the school's standards? Describe the advantages and disadvantages of this type of assessment.

Integration Corner

WEB INFO

IN BRIEF

KEY TERMS

CHECKPOINT

TEACHING TODAY

EDUCATION ISSUES

INTEGRATION CORNER

SOFTWARE CORNER

IN THE LAB

LEARN IT ONLINE

✱ FEATURES...

Timeline 2004

Guide to WWW Sites

Buyer's Guide 2004

Professional Sites

State/Federal Sites

Interactive Labs

Search Tools

HOME

Web Instructions: To display this page from the Web, start your browser and enter the URL, www.course.com/tdc3. Click Chapter 7 at the top of the Web page and then click Integration Corner on the left sidebar. Click any Corner and then click the various links for extensive and curriculum-specific information.

Integration Corner is designed for teachers and other educators who are looking for innovative ways to integrate technology into their content-specific curriculum. Integration Corner not only provides great Web sites with current information but also shows what other educators are doing in the field of educational technology. These Corners are designed for all educators regardless of their area of interest. Review information and Web sites outside of your teaching area because many great integration ideas in one area can be modified easily for use in other curricular areas.

Teachers and administrators will find other colleagues in their areas with whom to connect and share the successes and hurdles of integrating technology in a classroom or an entire school system. Consider this your one stop for integration ideas and resources. Links to educational Web sites are organized in the following 12 Corners, and different Web resources are available for each chapter. Figure 7-40 shows examples of the Web resources provided in the Chapter 7 Administrator Corner.

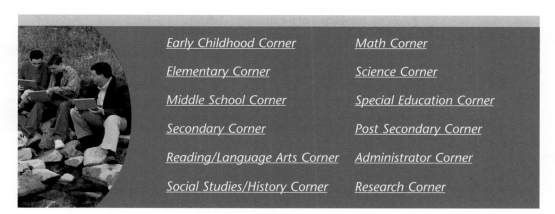

Early Childhood Corner *Math Corner*

Elementary Corner *Science Corner*

Middle School Corner *Special Education Corner*

Secondary Corner *Post Secondary Corner*

Reading/Language Arts Corner *Administrator Corner*

Social Studies/History Corner *Research Corner*

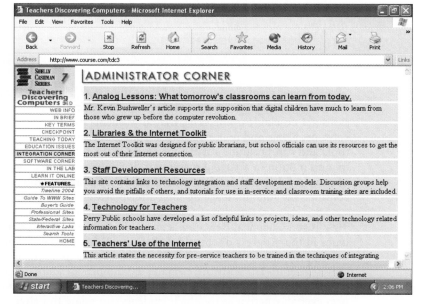

Figure 7-40 Examples of the Web resources provided in the Chapter 7 Administrator Corner.

Software Corner

WEB INFO

IN BRIEF

KEY TERMS

CHECKPOINT

TEACHING TODAY

EDUCATION ISSUES

INTEGRATION CORNER

SOFTWARE CORNER

IN THE LAB

LEARN IT ONLINE

✱ FEATURES...

Timeline 2004

Guide to WWW Sites

Buyer's Guide 2004

Professional Sites

State/Federal Sites

Interactive Labs

Search Tools

HOME

Web Instructions: To display this page from the Web, start your browser and enter the URL, www.course.com/tdc3. Click Chapter 7 at the top of the Web page and then click Software Corner on the left sidebar. Click the links for additional information and instructions on how to download or receive an evaluation copy.

1. Inspiration is a powerful software product that allows students to think visually through webbing, concept mapping, and more. Inspiration provides students in grades 4-12 and beyond with the ability to organize and develop their thoughts before creating essays, reports, presentations, and more. Language arts teachers will find Inspiration an awesome writing and literature tool. History and science teachers can use Inspiration to create timelines and plan research reports and projects. Inspiration can be integrated into all areas of the curriculum and will inspire your students to new heights!

2. Are you looking for a way to create a more professional looking Web site that integrates products such as Adobe Photoshop to help give your Web site a distinctive look? Adobe GoLive is the perfect solution. Web creation, Web design, and Web site management tools are all at your disposal. If you are a novice just beginning to design Web pages or a skilled Web site developer, Adobe GoLive offers an intuitive environment for creating everything from simple, elegant Web pages to complete online courses.

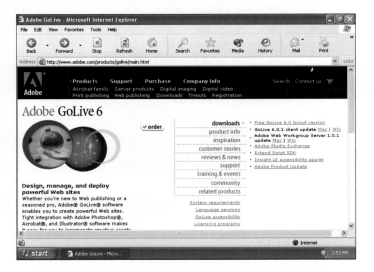

3. Do you want to get your students thinking? Thinkin' Things: Galactic Brain Benders is an enhanced multimedia version of the award-winning Thinkin' Things collection 3. Critical-thinking skills are crucial learning skills that all students must possess. Using high-order thinking skills to solve problems and make decisions, your students organize and experiment with special-effects tools and can program a half-time show at the Intergalactic Rocket Bowl. Plus, they can alter gravity and motion in a virtual metal world! Students are challenged to imagine, test hypotheses, observe results, and develop conclusions. Additional Web-based challenges are provided to continue the fun and learning long after blast-off into the Galactic Brain Benders has started!

4. Just a Chemical Reaction is an awesome piece of software that lets you teach key facts and dates in the progress of chemistry. Because of its video game graphics, Just a Chemical Reaction will appeal to middle and high school students, helping them begin to understand chemistry before they realize it! The software contains 20 minutes of animated narration and 93 scientific concepts. It also includes 14 interactive activities and an illustrated periodic table. Just a Chemical Reaction uses everyday activities to which students can relate to better understand and explain chemistry's influence in their daily lives.

In the Lab

WEB INFO

IN BRIEF

KEY TERMS

CHECKPOINT

TEACHING TODAY

EDUCATION ISSUES

INTEGRATION CORNER

SOFTWARE CORNER

IN THE LAB

LEARN IT ONLINE

* FEATURES...

Timeline 2004

Guide to WWW Sites

Buyer's Guide 2004

Professional Sites

State/Federal Sites

Interactive Labs

Search Tools

HOME

Web Instructions: To display this page from the Web, start your browser and enter the URL, www.course.com/tdc3. Click Chapter 7 at the top of the Web page and then click In The Lab on the left sidebar. Click the links for tutorials, productivity ideas, integration examples and ideas, and more.

PRODUCTIVITY IN THE CLASSROOM

Introduction: As you have learned, many kinds of curriculum pages exist. For example, a curriculum page can serve as a guide, assisting students in locating quality information on the Internet. Teachers easily can create curriculum pages using a variety of software programs and Web editors. You already are familiar with using Microsoft Word to create Web pages, and Word is available on many home and school computers. In addition, Netscape, which includes the Web editor, Composer, can be downloaded free from the Web. Microsoft Publisher also can be used to create Web and curriculum pages. Some popular stand-alone Web editors used by educators include Adobe GoLive, Macromedia Dreamweaver, and Microsoft FrontPage.

Teachers can use curriculum pages in a variety of ways. One type of curriculum page is a list of annotated links focusing on one area of the curriculum or supporting one particular project. A curriculum page also can present students with a learning task, guidelines for how the task will be evaluated, and provide preselected Web sites that support the task.

Utilizing curriculum pages in the classroom provides many benefits. Students develop independent thinking and working skills, as well as high-order thinking and problem-solving skills. Furthermore, teachers preselecting Web sites maximizes the time students spend on the Internet and helps teachers to better supervise their students. Students also can create curriculum pages to provide evidence of their learning. This can be a powerful and exciting way for students to demonstrate their newly acquired knowledge and skills.

1 Creating and Formatting a Dental Health Curriculum Page

Problem: You are beginning a unit on dental health in your first grade classroom. You want to create a curriculum page to use with the class to enhance the students' learning experience. Also, by using a curriculum page, the students will be able to go back and review Web sites after the unit is finished. The curriculum page is shown in Figure 7-41 on the next page. Open Microsoft Word, Netscape Composer, or any Web editing software and create the curriculum page as described below. Using the skills you learned by completing the special feature following Chapter 3, download the background and clip art image located on this chapter's special feature Web page (see page 7.61 for the Web page URL) or use any appropriate background and clip art image to personalize the page. (*Hint:* Use Help to understand the steps better.)

Instructions: Perform the following tasks.

1. Insert the background image.
2. Display the first heading line, Let's Learn About Teeth, in 24-point Times or Times New Roman dark blue font.
3. Display the second heading line in 18-point Times or Times New Roman dark blue, bold font. Personalize the curriculum page by inserting your name instead of Ms. Yoshimura's name.
4. Insert a table with one row and two columns. Format the table to display as shown in Figure 7-41.
5. Insert an appropriate picture, image, or clip art graphic in the left column.
6. The two paragraphs and the bulleted list in the right column display in 14-point Times New Roman dark blue, bold font.
7. The line following the table and the bulleted list display in 14-point Times New Roman dark blue, bold font.

In the Lab

WEB INFO

IN BRIEF

KEY TERMS

CHECKPOINT

TEACHING TODAY

EDUCATION ISSUES

INTEGRATION CORNER

SOFTWARE CORNER

IN THE LAB

LEARN IT ONLINE

✱ FEATURES...

Timeline 2004

Guide to WWW Sites

Buyer's Guide 2004

Professional Sites

State/Federal Sites

Interactive Labs

Search Tools

HOME

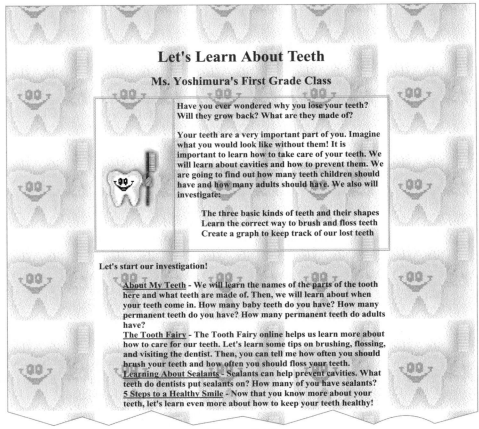

Figure 7-41

8. Link the words, About My Teeth, to http://www.ms-flossy.com/myteeth.html. Link the words, The Tooth Fairy, to http://www.toothfairy.org/index.html. Link the words, Learning About Sealants, to http://www.ms-flossy.com/sealants.html. Link the words, 5 Steps to a Healthy Smile, to http://www.healthyteeth.org/prevention/5steps.html.

9. Save the curriculum page on a floppy disk with a file name of your choice. Print the curriculum page and then follow your instructor's directions for handing in the assignment.

2 Creating and Formatting a Science Curriculum Page

Problem: Your eighth grade science class has been studying the weather. As a final project, students must gather research and create a multimedia presentation. You create a curriculum page to facilitate their research. The curriculum page is shown in Figure 7-42. Using the skills you learned by completing the special feature following Chapter 3, download the background and clip art image located on this chapter's special feature Web page (see page 7.61 for the Web page URL) or use any appropriate background and clip art image to personalize the page. (*Hint:* Use Help to understand the steps better.)

Instructions: Insert the background image. Display the first heading line in 24-point Times or Times New Roman font. Insert your name in place of Mr. Pawlinger's in 18-point Times or Times New Roman font. Insert a table with one row and two columns and format the table as shown in Figure 7-42. Insert a graphic in the left column of the table. The text and bulleted list in the right

In the Lab

WEB INFO

IN BRIEF

KEY TERMS

CHECKPOINT

TEACHING TODAY

EDUCATION ISSUES

INTEGRATION CORNER

SOFTWARE CORNER

IN THE LAB

LEARN IT ONLINE

✳ FEATURES...

Timeline 2004

Guide to WWW Sites

Buyer's Guide 2004

Professional Sites

State/Federal Sites

Interactive Labs

Search Tools

HOME

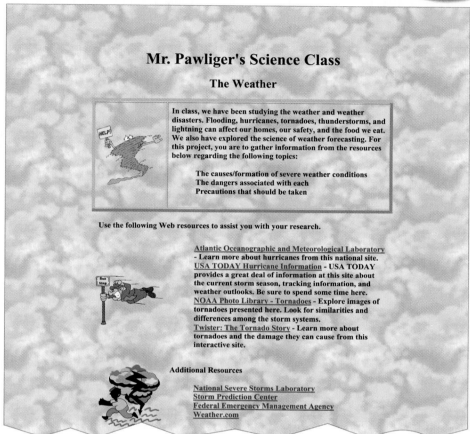

Figure 7-42

column display in 12-point Times New Roman bold font. The line below the table displays in 12-point Times New Roman bold font.

Insert a table with two rows and two columns to help organize the links. Format the table to display as shown in Figure 7-42. (*Hint:* Format the table to display without borders.) The text and bulleted lists display in 12-point Times New Roman bold font. Insert graphics and create the hypertext links using the Web site addresses (URLs) listed in the table below.

Internet Resources

Linked Text	Web Site
Atlantic Oceanographic and Meteorological Laboratory	www.aoml.noaa.gov
USA TODAY Hurricane Information	www.usatoday.com/weather/hurricane/whur0.htm
NOAA Photo Library - Tornadoes	www.photolib.noaa.gov/nssl/tornado1.html
Twister: The Tornado Story	whyfiles.org/013tornado/index.html
National Severe Storms Laboratory	www.nssl.noaa.gov
Storm Prediction Center	www.spc.noaa.gov
Federal Emergency Management Agency	www.fema.gov
The Weather Channel	www.weather.com

In the Lab

WEB INFO

IN BRIEF

KEY TERMS

CHECKPOINT

TEACHING TODAY

EDUCATION ISSUES

INTEGRATION CORNER

SOFTWARE CORNER

IN THE LAB

LEARN IT ONLINE

✱ FEATURES...

Timeline 2004

Guide to WWW Sites

Buyer's Guide 2004

Professional Sites

State/Federal Sites

Interactive Labs

Search Tools

HOME

After you have typed and formatted the curriculum page, save the curriculum page on a floppy disk with a file name of your choice. Print the curriculum page and then follow your instructor's directions for handing in the assignment.

3 Creating and Formatting a Subject-Specific Curriculum Page

Problem: You want to create a curriculum page to support a concept you are teaching in your classroom and to provide students with preselected Internet resources.

Instructions: Create a curriculum page similar to the curriculum page illustrated in Figure 7-42 on the previous page. Use appropriate layouts, font types, font styles, font sizes, and clip art images. Include your name and the subject area you teach. After you have created the curriculum page, save the curriculum page on a floppy disk using an appropriate file name. Print the curriculum page, and then follow your instructor's directions for handing in the assignment.

INTEGRATION IN THE CLASSROOM

1 While studying the fifty states, you have your elementary students work in pairs to design and create a curriculum page about the state of their choice. They are to include their names and the name of the state at the top of the curriculum page. They also will include a graphic of either the state or the state flag, a brief paragraph about the state, and a bulleted list that includes the state capital, state bird, and state flower. The students then will include three links to Internet resources that provide additional information about their state. Create a sample curriculum page for your students using the state of your birth or the state in which you currently live. Include your name on the curriculum page.

2 To help your middle school language arts students develop reading, vocabulary, and writing skills and increase their awareness of community and global issues, you begin a unit using newspapers in your classroom. You arrange for local newspapers to be donated to your classroom so each student has a copy. You also have students explore local newspapers and news sources online. You direct students to select an article from either a local newspaper or an online news source and create a curriculum page that summarizes the news item and contains at least three links to Internet resources that support or give further information on their selected topic. Students will present their curriculum pages to the class and you will have them posted on your school's server so all students can access the information. Create a sample curriculum page for your students. Include your name and school at the top of the curriculum page. Include your e-mail address and the current date at the bottom of the curriculum page.

3 Your music class has been studying famous composers. To prepare for the end-of-unit exam, you divide the students into five groups and have each group research one composer. The groups then will create a curriculum page for other students to use to study. On their curriculum pages, students are required to include a graphic image, a brief paragraph about the composer, a bulleted list of the titles of at least five famous pieces, and at least four annotated links to Web resources. The curriculum pages will be placed on the computers in the classroom, media center, and computer lab. In addition, you will post the curriculum pages on the Web to assist the students in studying at home. Select a famous composer and create a sample curriculum page for your students. Include your name on your curriculum page. Include your e-mail address and the current date at the bottom of the curriculum page.

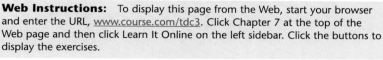

Learn It Online

WEB INFO

IN BRIEF

KEY TERMS

CHECKPOINT

TEACHING TODAY

EDUCATION ISSUES

INTEGRATION CORNER

SOFTWARE CORNER

IN THE LAB

LEARN IT ONLINE

*FEATURES...

Timeline 2004

Guide to WWW Sites

Buyer's Guide 2004

Professional Sites

State/Federal Sites

Interactive Labs

Search Tools

HOME

Web Instructions: To display this page from the Web, start your browser and enter the URL, www.course.com/tdc3. Click Chapter 7 at the top of the Web page and then click Learn It Online on the left sidebar. Click the buttons to display the exercises.

1. Evaluating Internet Resources

Evaluating information found on the World Wide Web is a critical skill that teachers and students must possess. Click the button to the left to complete an exercise and learn how to evaluate the quality of Internet resources.

2. Evaluating Student Projects

Designing effective evaluation tools to assess student learning requires thought and preparation. One popular assessment tool is an assessment rubric. Click the button to the left to complete an exercise on how to create effective rubrics.

3. Integration Strategies

When integrating technology into the curriculum, teachers use different strategies depending on the number of computers in their classrooms. Many teachers have only one or two modern computers in their classrooms. Click the button to the left to complete an exercise and learn more about integration strategies in the one-computer classroom.

4. Graphic Organizers

Concept maps, flowcharts, story webs, storyboards, visual learning techniques, and other graphic organizers assist students with visualizing concepts and organizing information. Click the button to the left to complete an exercise to learn more about these concepts.

5. Web Scavenger Hunt

A Web scavenger hunt is an excellent method of allowing students to explore the resources on the Web using discovery learning. Click the button to the left to complete an exercise to learn more about Web scavenger hunts.

6. Who Wants To Be a Computer Genius?

Click the button to the left to find out if you are a computer genius. Directions on how to play the game will display. When you are ready to play, click the PLAY button. Submit your score to your instructor.

7. Crossword Puzzle Challenge

Click the button to the left to complete the puzzle to reinforce skills you learned in this chapter. Directions on how to play the game will be displayed. When you are ready to play, click the SUBMIT button. Submit the completed puzzle to your instructor.

8. Practice Test

Click the button to the left and answer each question. When completed, enter your name and click the Grade Test button to submit the quiz for grading. Make a note of any missed questions. If required, print a copy to submit to your instructor.

Creating a Curriculum Page Using Microsoft Word

As you have learned, many different kinds of curriculum pages exist, and you can use them many different ways. Curriculum pages should provide students with quality Internet resources that will enhance their learning of a particular concept. In addition, students should be able to gather information, learn more about a concept, and use Web resources to help prepare for a task. Instead of listing all information on one page, making it very long and intimidating, many teachers elect to create separate pages and link them to their home page. You link two pages together by creating a hyperlink between the two pages, also called a **relative link**. The result is that you create a **Web site**, which is a group of related HTML documents linked together.

This special feature provides you with step-by-step instructions on how to create a curriculum page that provides students with assignment information and Web links for a five-day period. The Web page, Mr. Handley's Home Page, which you created in the special feature that followed Chapter 3, will be used as the home page in this project. If you have not done so, you need to create the Web page detailed in the special feature following Chapter 3 before starting this project.

In this project, you will use many features of Microsoft Word to create a curriculum page, called Mr. Handley's American History Class, which is linked to Mr. Handley's Home Page that you created earlier (Figure 1). Recall that Mr. Handley is a history teacher at Ridgedale High School. You will find it helpful to refer back to Figure 1 to see the completed Web page as you work through this project. Included in this special feature are step-by-step instructions for using Word 2002 (part of Office XP) installed on a PC. You also can create this project using Word 2000 installed on a PC or Word installed on a Macintosh computer; however, you may encounter slight variations from the step-by-step instructions in this project.

As you learned, another popular and very easy to use program for creating Web and curriculum pages is Netscape Composer, which is included with Netscape Communicator. If you do not have Netscape Communicator installed on your home or school computer, you can download a free copy from the Web. Detailed step-by-step instructions for completing this project in the latest version of Netscape Composer are available to download and print from the World Wide Web at www.course.com/tdc3/sf7 (the same Web site that you will use later in this project to download graphics).

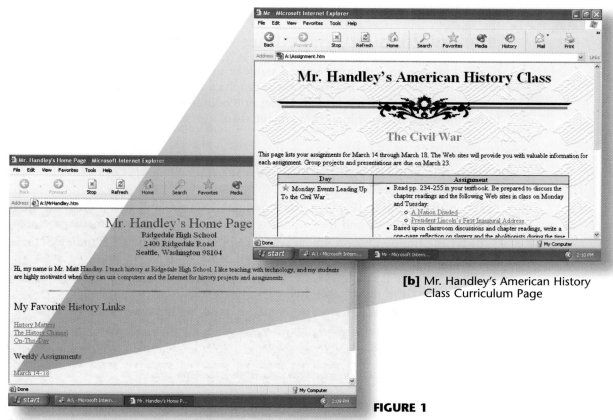

[b] Mr. Handley's American History
    Class Curriculum Page

[a] Mr. Handley's Home Page

FIGURE 1

In this project, you will learn how to download graphics from the World Wide Web, open a new Web page to create your curriculum page, select a background image, create a title, insert and format text and headings, insert a horizontal line graphic and other graphics, use tables to organize assignment information, create numerous links to teacher-selected and evaluated history Web sites, and save your curriculum page. Next, you will open your previously created Web page, Mr. Handley's Home Page, and link the home page to your curriculum page. You will need the floppy disk on which you saved the Web page, Mr. Handley's Home Page. This project assumes that you possess basic word processing skills and have completed the Mr. Handley's Home Page project. You might find it useful to review the step-by-step instructions that you used to create Mr. Handley's Home Page.

Downloading Image Files

Clip art images are graphical images you can use on Web and curriculum pages. This project requires you to download three graphics from the Web, including one used for the curriculum page background. Using procedures learned earlier, perform the following steps to download three image files.

TO DOWNLOAD IMAGE FILES

1. Start your browser, type the URL www.course.com/tdc3/sf7 in the Address text box, and then press the ENTER key.
2. When the textbook Web page for this special feature appears, right-click the flags background image, and then point to Save Picture As on the shortcut menu.
3. Insert the floppy disk on which you saved the Web page, Mr. Handley's Home Page, in drive A and then click Save Picture As.
4. When the Save As dialog box displays, click the Save in box arrow, click 3½ Floppy (A:) in the Look in list, and then click the Save button.
5. Repeat Steps 2 through 4 to download two additional images: the yellow star and the horizontal line images.
6. Close your browser.

Three additional image files are saved on your floppy disk.

Starting Microsoft Word and Opening a New Web Page

Perform the following steps to start Word and open a new Web page, so you can begin developing Mr. Handley's American History Class curriculum page.

TO START WORD AND OPEN A NEW WEB PAGE

1. Click the Start button on the Windows taskbar, point to All Programs on the Start menu, and then click New Office Document on the All Programs submenu.
2. When the New Office Document dialog box appears, if necessary, click the General tab, click the Web Page icon, and then click the OK button.
3. If necessary, click the Font Size box arrow on the Formatting toolbar and then click 12 in the Font Size list to change the font size to 12.

Word is opened and displays a new blank Web page (Figure 2). Depending on the computer you are working on, the default font size may display 10 or 12. Font size 12 is required for this Web page.

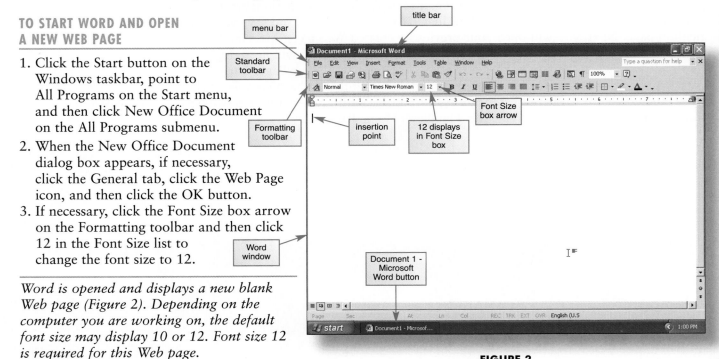

FIGURE 2

Inserting a Background Image and Entering and Formatting a Title

Recall that the background of a Web page is created by tiling a small graphic image many times across the page. For this project, you will use the flags background image that you downloaded as the background for this Web page. Perform the following steps to insert a background image.

Steps to Insert a Background Image

1 **Click Format on the menu bar, point to Background, and then click Fill Effects on the Background submenu. When Word displays the Fill Effects dialog box, click the Picture tab, and then point to the Select Picture button.**

Word displays the Picture sheet in the Fill Effects dialog box (Figure 3).

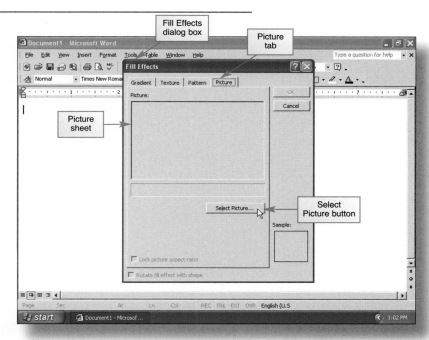

FIGURE 3

2 **Click the Select Picture button. When Word displays the Select Picture dialog box , if necessary, click the Look in box arrow and then click 3½ Floppy (A:). Double-click the background image, flags, and then click the OK button in the Fill Effects dialog box.**

Word tiles the flags image across the Web page (Figure 4).

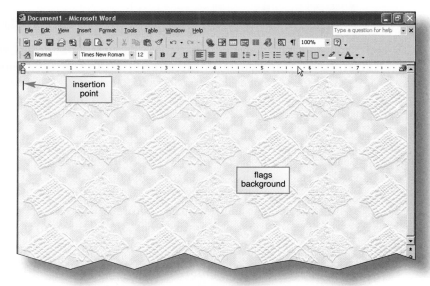

FIGURE 4

Entering and Formatting a Title

Perform the following steps to enter and format a title for the curriculum page.

TO ENTER AND FORMAT A TITLE

1. Type Mr. Handley's American History Class and then press the ENTER key.
2. Select the text just entered, click the Font Size box arrow on the Formatting toolbar, and then click 26 in the Font Size list. With the text still selected, click the Bold button and then click the Center button on the Formatting toolbar.
3. Click below and to the left of the text to position the insertion point at the beginning of the next line.

The formatted title text appears as shown in Figure 5.

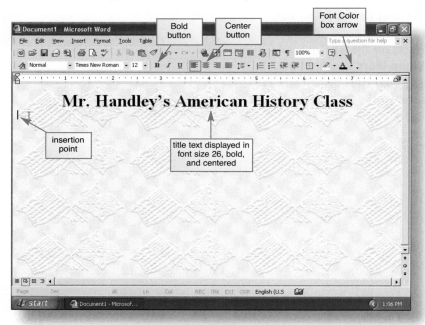

FIGURE 5

Inserting a Horizontal Line, a Heading, and Text

Next, you will enter a curriculum-appropriate and colorful horizontal line that you downloaded from the Web. You then will enter a curriculum-descriptive heading and text. Recall that horizontal lines are used to set apart different sections of a Web page. Perform the following steps to insert a horizontal line.

TO INSERT A HORIZONTAL LINE

1. Press the ENTER key and then click the Center button on the Formatting toolbar.
2. Click Insert on the menu bar, point to Picture, and then click From File on the Picture submenu.
3. When the Insert Picture dialog box appears, if necessary, click the Look in box arrow and then click 3½ Floppy (A:). Double-click the horizontal line image.

Word inserts the horizontal line graphic centered at the insertion point (Figure 6). The horizontal line may display differently than shown depending on the computer you are working on and the version of Word you are using.

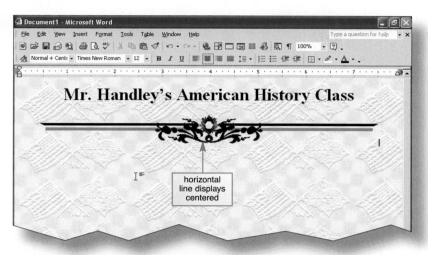

FIGURE 6

Entering a Heading

Next, you will enter a heading that describes the week's history topic.

TO ENTER A HEADING

1. Press the ENTER key twice and make sure the insertion point still is centered.
2. Type The Civil War and then press the ENTER key.
3. Select the text just entered, click the Font Size box arrow on the Formatting toolbar, and then click 22 in the Font Size list. Click the Bold button on the Formatting toolbar.
4. With the text still selected, click the Font Color box arrow on the Formatting toolbar, and then click the color Red (row 3, column 1) on the Font color palette.
5. Click below the text you just entered to position the insertion point centered on the next line.

Word displays the heading centered, bold, in red, and in font size 22 (see Figure 7 on the next page). The insertion point appears centered on the next line.

Entering Text

Perform the following steps to enter the text that provides students with information concerning the dates of the assignments, group projects, and more.

TO ENTER TEXT

1. Press the ENTER key and then click the Align Left button on the Formatting toolbar.
2. Type This page lists your assignments for March 14 through March 18. The Web sites will provide you with valuable information for each assignment. Group projects and presentations are due on March 23. and then press the ENTER key.

The text is entered and left-aligned. Word displays the insertion point at the beginning of the next line (Figure 7 on the next page).

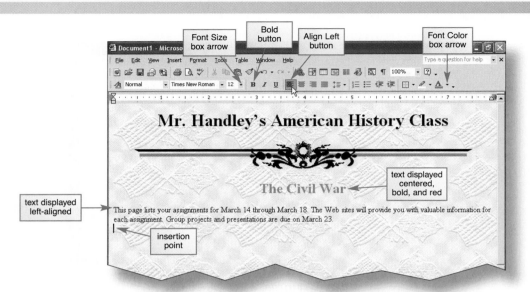

FIGURE 7

Inserting a Table

A Word **table** is a collection of rows and columns. The intersection of a row and column is called a **cell**. Using tables is a great way to organize and align information on a Web page. Word allows you to manipulate tables in many ways, including arranging rows and columns, changing column widths, typing text and inserting graphics in individual cells, and formating individual cells or the entire table with different colors and shadings. Sometimes, teachers completely remove the borders so all you see is the organized text and graphics. To learn more about using Word tables, use the Word Help system. Perform the following steps to insert a table.

Steps to Insert a Table

1 **Press the ENTER key. Click Table on the menu bar, point to Insert, and then click Table on the Insert submenu. When Word displays the Insert Table dialog box, type 2 in the Number of columns text box. Press the TAB key and then type 4 in the Number of rows text box. Point to the OK button.**

Word displays the Insert Table dialog box, 2 displays in the Number of columns text box, and 4 displays in the Number of rows text box (Figure 8).

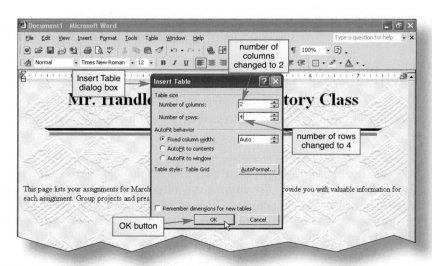

FIGURE 8

2 **Click the OK button.**

Word inserts an empty table with 2 columns and 4 rows into the Web page. The insertion point displays in the first cell (row 1, column 1) of the table (Figure 9).

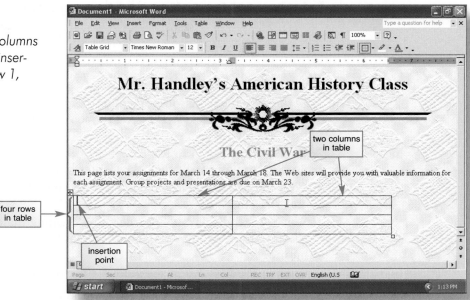

FIGURE 9

Formatting a Table

Word allows users to do many things with tables, including centering a table on a page, changing column widths, entering and formatting text and graphics, creating bulleted lists, inserting hyperlinks, formatting cells, and much, much more. The easiest way to move from cell to cell in a table is to use the TAB key.

Centering a Table and Changing Column Widths

Perform the following steps to center the table on the page and change the width of the columns.

TO CENTER A TABLE AND CHANGE COLUMN WIDTHS

1. Position the mouse pointer in the left margin at the top of the table and drag to select the entire table. Once the entire table is selected, click the Center button on the Formatting toolbar.

2. Click in the first cell of the first row to remove the selection.

3. Position the mouse pointer on the border between the two columns and then drag the border until it is positioned as shown in Figure 10 (at the 2" mark on the ruler).

Word centers the table and changes the width of both columns (Figure 10). To center a table on the page, the entire table must be selected.

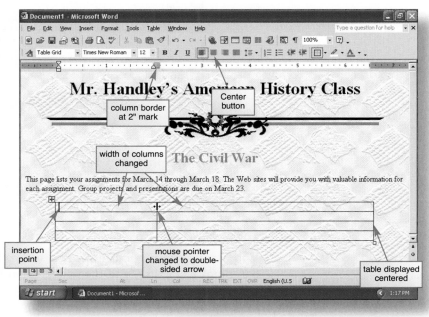

FIGURE 10

Entering and Formatting the Column Headings

Next, you will enter the column headings, center the column headings, and shade the cells containing the column headings.

TO ENTER AND FORMAT THE COLUMN HEADINGS

1. Make sure the insertion point is in the first cell (row 1, column 1), type Day and then press the TAB key. Type Assignment in the second cell in the heading row (row 1, column 2).
2. Click in the margin to the left of the first row to select only row 1. Click the Bold button and then click the Center button on the Formatting toolbar.
3. With the row still selected, click Format on the menu bar, and then click Borders and Shading.
4. When Word displays the Borders and Shading dialog box, click the Shading tab, click Gray-15% on the Fill color palette (row 1, column 5), and then click the OK button.
5. Click in the first cell in the second row to remove the selection.

The column headings appear bold, centered, and shaded gray (Figure 11).

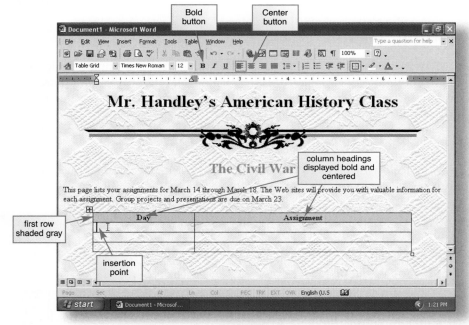

FIGURE 11

Inserting a Graphic and Text

Next, you will enter a star graphic and a short description for Monday's assignment.

TO INSERT A GRAPHIC AND TEXT

1. With the insertion point in the first cell of the second row, click Insert on the menu bar, point to Picture, and then click From File on the Picture submenu.

2. When Word displays the Insert Picture dialog box, if necessary, click the Look in box arrow and then click 3½ Floppy (A:). Double-click the yellow star image.

3. Press the SPACEBAR, and then type Monday: Events Leading Up To the Civil War as the assignment text.

Word inserts the star graphic, and the text is entered (Figure 12).

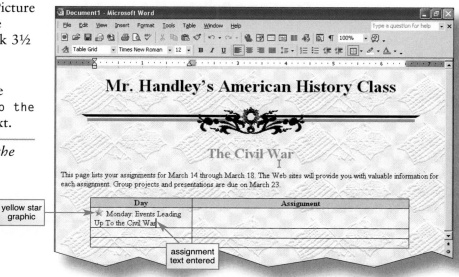

FIGURE 12

Entering Assignment Information

Next, you will enter the assignment information for Monday's assignment. You will create a bulleted list, indent bullets, and create hyperlinks to teacher-selected Web sites. Perform the following steps to enter the text.

Steps to Enter Assignment Information

1 **Press the TAB key to position the insertion point in the second cell in row 2. Type** Read pp. 234-255 in your textbook. Be prepared to discuss the chapter readings and the following Web sites in class on Monday and Tuesday: **and then press the ENTER key.**

2 **Type** A Nation Divided **and then press the ENTER key. Type** President Lincoln's First Inaugural Address **and then press the ENTER key.**

3 **Type** Based upon classroom discussions and chapter readings, write a one-page reflection on slavery and the abolitionists during the time leading up to the Civil War. The reflection is due on Wednesday. **as the final text entry.**
Do not press the ENTER key; doing so would insert a blank line.

The text appears in the second cell of the second row (Figure 13).

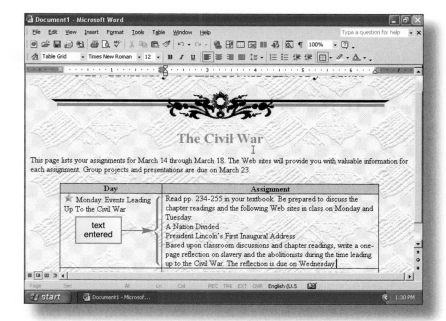

FIGURE 13

Creating a Bulleted List in a Table

Perform the following steps to format the text you just entered as a bulleted list and then indent two of the text entries.

Steps to Create a Bulleted List in a Table

1 **Select all of the text just entered in the right column of the second row and then click the Bullets button on the Formatting toolbar. Click within the cell to remove the selection.**

Word formats the text as a bulleted list (Figure 14). The bullet style may be different depending on the computer you are working on and the version of Word you are using.

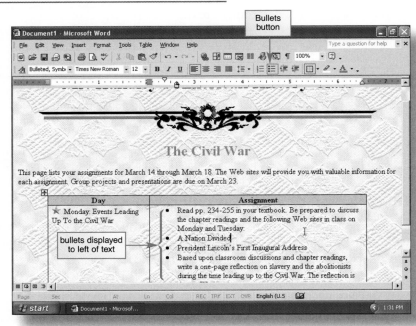

FIGURE 14

2 **Select the second and third bullets. Click the Increase Indent button on the Formatting toolbar. Click within the cell to remove the selection.**

Word increases the indent of the two lines of text and changes the bullet style (Figure 15). The bullet style may be different depending on the computer you are working on and the version of Word you are using.

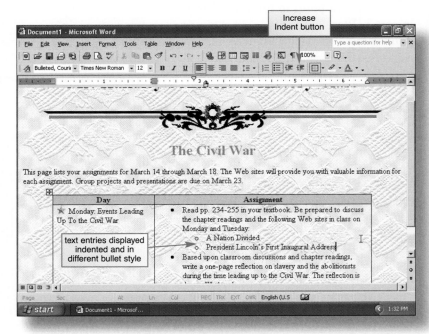

FIGURE 15

If you would like to change the bullet style, select the entire bulleted list, right-click the list, and then click Bullets and Numbering on the shortcut menu. When Word displays the Bullets and Numbering dialog box, if necessary, click the Bulleted tab. Click the desired bullet style and then click the OK button in the Bullets and Numbering dialog box.

Creating Links to Web Sites

Recall that using text and graphic links, you can create links for your students to Web sites on the World Wide Web. Recall that curriculum pages contain links to Web sites that have been evaluated by the teacher to ensure they are appropriate and meet curriculum objectives. Perform the following steps to link text entries to Web sites by entering the Web site's Uniform Resource Locator (URL).

TO CREATE LINKS TO WEB SITES

1. Select the first text entry to be linked, A Nation Divided, and then click the Insert Hyperlink button on the Standard toolbar.
2. When Word displays the Insert Hyperlink dialog box, if necessary, click the Existing File or Web Page button on the Link to bar, type `http://www.historyplace.com/civilwar` in the Address text box, and then click the OK button. In Word 2000, type the URL in the Type the file or Web page name text box that is located below the Text to display text box.
3. Repeat the procedures in Steps 1 and 2 to link the text entry, President Lincoln's First Inaugural Address, using the following URL: http://showcase.netins.net/web/creative/lincoln/speeches/1inaug.htm

Word links the text to the entered Web sites and displays the linked text underlined in the default color blue (Figure 16).

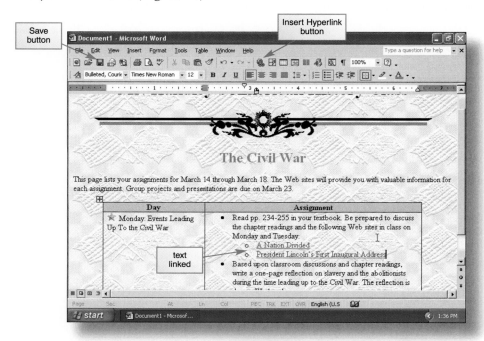

FIGURE 16

Saving a Web Page and Completing the Table

As you know, it is a good practice to save your documents regularly to eliminate retyping information in the event of a power or computer failure. To save the curriculum page on your floppy disk in drive A using the file name, Assignment, perform the following steps.

TO SAVE A WEB PAGE

1. Click the Save button on the Standard toolbar.
2. When Word displays the Save As dialog box, type Assignment in the File Name text box. If necessary, click the Save in box arrow, click 3½ Floppy (A:) in the Look in list, and then click the Save button in the Save As dialog box.

Completing the Table

Using the procedures presented on pages 7.68 through 7.71, enter the yellow star graphic and the text for Wednesday's short description. Enter and format the text for Wednesday's assignment information.

TO COMPLETE WEDNESDAY'S ASSIGNMENT INFORMATION

1. If necessary, click the scroll bar to see row 3 of the table and then add Wednesday's assignment information in both cells of the third row as shown in Figure 17.
2. Create links using the following URLs:
   Battle of Gettysburg: http://www.americancivilwar.com/getty.html
   Battle of Fort Sumter: http://www.civilwarhome.com/ftsumter.htm

Wednesday's assignment information is entered and formatted (Figure 17).

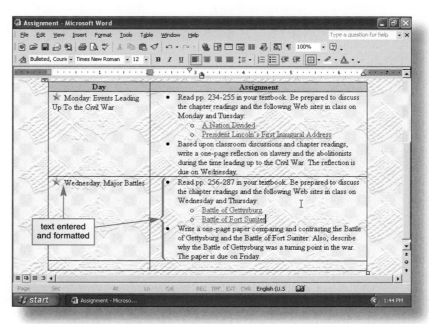

FIGURE 17

Using the procedures presented on pages 7.68 through 7.71, enter the yellow star graphic and text for Friday's short description and then enter and format the text for Friday's assignment information.

TO COMPLETE FRIDAY'S ASSIGNMENT INFORMATION

1. If necessary, click the scroll bar to see the final row of the table. Complete the table as shown in Figure 18.
2. Create links using the following URLs:
   Gettysburg Address: http://lcweb.loc.gov/exhibits/gadd/
   Gettysburg National Military Park: http://www.nps.gov/gett/index.htm
   The American Civil War Homepage: http://www.sunsite.utk.edu/civil-war
   The Valley of the Shadow: http://jefferson.village.virginia.edu/vshadow2
   Civil War Medicine: http://www.civilwarhome.com/civilwarmedicineintro.htm
   Rose O'Neal Greenhow Papers: http://scriptorium.lib.duke.edu/greenhow

Friday's assignment information is entered and formatted (Figure 18).

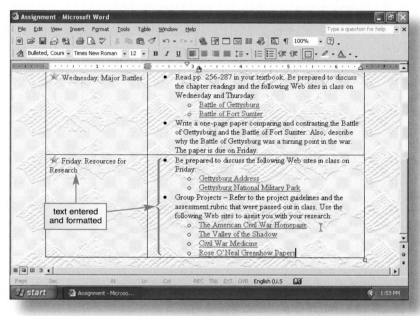

FIGURE 18

Checking Spelling and Saving the Web Page

Before you hyperlink the curriculum page you have created, you should check it for spelling and grammar errors and then save it. Perform the following steps to check spelling and correct any errors and then save your curriculum page.

TO CHECK SPELLING AND SAVE THE WEB PAGE

1. Press CTRL+HOME to display the top of the curriculum page and then click the Spelling and Grammar button on the Standard toolbar. Correct any errors.
2. Click the Save button on the Standard toolbar.

Opening a Previously Created Web Page

After you have created and saved a Web page, you can open the Web page and revise it at any time, just like any other Word document. The following steps show how to open a previously created Web page so you can hyperlink Mr. Handley's Home Page to Mr. Handley's American History Class curriculum page.

TO OPEN A PREVIOUSLY CREATED WEB PAGE

1. With your floppy disk in drive A, click File on the menu bar and then click Open.
2. When Word displays the Open dialog box, if necessary, click the Look in box arrow, click 3½ Floppy (A:), and then double-click the file, MrHandley.

Word displays the MrHandley Web page that you created previously in a Word window (Figure 19).

Editing a Web Page and Creating a Relative Link

The curriculum page that you created in this project will be linked to Mr. Handley's Home Page. First, you will edit Mr. Handley's Home Page and then you will link Mr. Handley's Home Page to the Mr. Handley's American History Class curriculum page using the Insert Hyperlink button. Recall that the hyperlink between two pages of a Web site is called a **relative link**. To edit a Web page and create a relative link, perform the following steps.

Steps to Edit a Web Page and Create a Relative Link

1 **Click to the right of the On-This-Day link and then press the ENTER key twice to position the insertion point.**

2 **Type** Weekly Assignments **and then press the ENTER key. Select the text just entered and then click the Font Size box arrow on the Formatting toolbar. Click 14 in the Font Size list. Click below the text entry to position the insertion point.**

The text is inserted and formatted. The insertion point appears below the Weekly Assignments text (Figure 19).

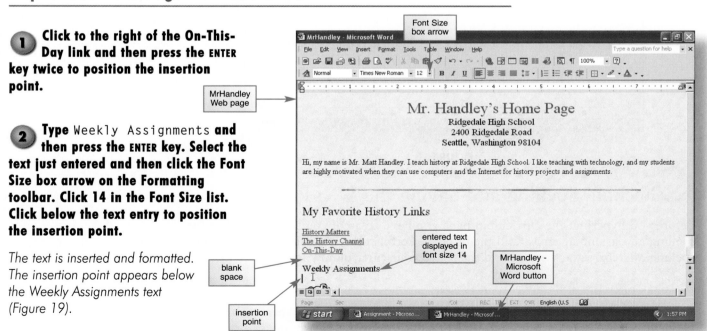

FIGURE 19

3 **Press the ENTER key twice and then press the UP ARROW key once. Type** March 14-18 **and then select the text just entered. Click the Insert Hyperlink button on the Standard toolbar.**

Word displays the Insert Hyperlink dialog box.

4 **If necessary, click the Existing File or Web Page button on the Link to bar. If necessary, click the Look in box arrow, click 3½ Floppy (A:), click Assignment, and then point to the OK button. In Word 2000, click the File button in the Browse for area. When Word displays the Link to File dialog box, if necessary, click the Look in box arrow, click 3½ Floppy (A:), and then double-click Assignment.**

Word displays the files stored on the floppy disk in drive A and the Assignment Web page is selected (Figure 20).

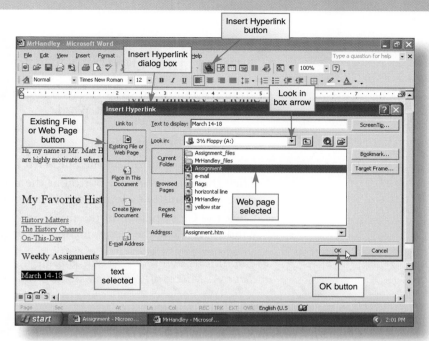

FIGURE 20

5 **Click the OK button.**

Word inserts a hyperlink for the selected text to the Assignment Web page and the selected text displays underlined in the default color blue (Figure 21).

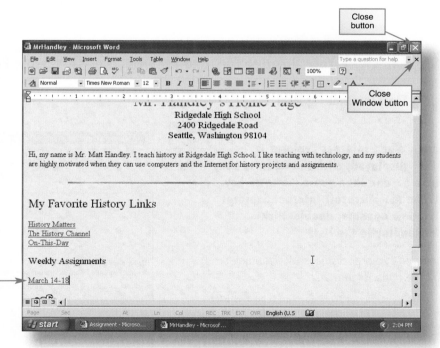

FIGURE 21

Saving and Quitting Word

Perform the following steps to save the changes you made to Mr. Handley's Home Page and then quit Microsoft Word.

TO SAVE AND QUIT WORD

1. Click the Save button on the Standard toolbar.
2. Click the Close Window button at the upper-right corner of the Word window to close Mr. Handley's Home Page (see Figure 21 on the previous page).
3. Click the Close button in the upper-right corner of the title bar of the Word window to close the Assignment Web page and Microsoft Word.

The additions you made to Mr. Handley's Home Page are saved on your floppy disk in drive A. Microsoft Word closes and the Windows desktop appears.

Checking Your Relative Link and Previewing Your Curriculum Page

Congratulations, you now have created a Web site using Microsoft Word. You have linked Mr. Handley's Home Page to your newly created Assignment Web page using a relative link. Perform the following steps to preview the curriculum page you just created in your browser by using the link on Mr. Handley's Home Page.

Steps to Check Your Relative Link and Preview Your Curriculum Page

1 **Start Internet Explorer.**

2 **When Internet Explorer is displayed, click the Address box,** type a: **and then press the ENTER key. When A:\-Microsoft Internet Explorer Window appears, double-click MrHandley in the list.**

Internet Explorer displays Mr. Handley's Home Page (Figure 22).

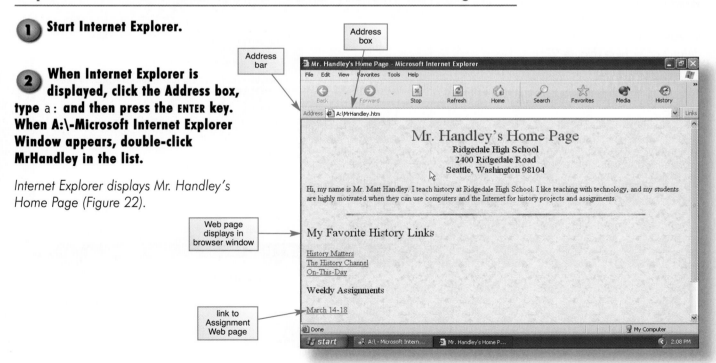

FIGURE 22

③ **Click the relative hyperlink March 14-18.**

Internet Explorer displays Mr. Handley's American History Class Web page (Figure 23).

curriculum page displays in browser window

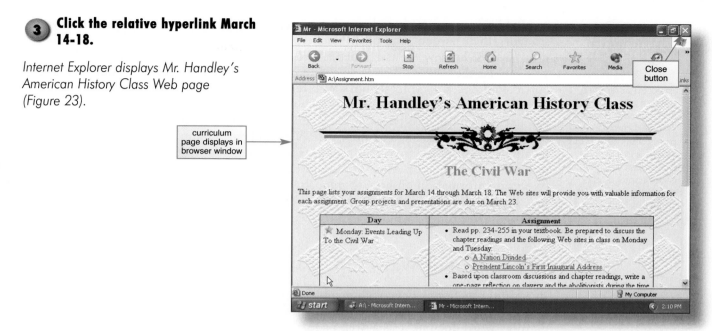

FIGURE 23

Quitting Internet Explorer

With your Web site created and previewed, your project is complete. To quit Internet Explorer, perform the following steps.

TO QUIT INTERNET EXPLORER

1. Click the Close button on the upper-right corner of the Internet Explorer title bar (see Figure 23).
2. If necessary, click the Close button on the upper-right corner of the 3½ Floppy (A:) – Microsoft Internet Explorer title bar.

Both windows close and the Windows desktop is displayed.

As you have learned, you do not have to be a programmer to create Web and curriculum pages and link them together. Microsoft Word provides a wealth of Web page creation tools. In addition, you will find that applying basic formatting options and using numerous other design techniques can help you easily create a variety of curriculum and Web pages. The following sections will describe a few of the techniques and tools that you may find useful as you increase your Web development skills using Microsoft Word.

Publishing Web Pages to a Web Server

You do not have to publish your Web and curriculum pages to a Web server to integrate effectively the multitude of resources available on the Internet in your classroom curriculum. You can have your students access your curriculum pages stored on either floppy disks or the hard disks on the computers in your classroom. You also can create shortcuts to your Web and curriculum pages directly on the desktop of your PC or Macintosh classroom computers.

WEB INFO

To access a free Web site that allows teachers to publish their Web and curriculum pages, visit the Teachers Discovering Computers Web site, click Chapter 7, click Web Info, and then click Web Publishing.

Publishing your Web and curriculum pages to a Web server, however, allows your students, their parents, and other teachers to access your curriculum materials, schedules, lessons, homework assignments, and more at anytime and any place. In Word, you can use the Save as Web Page command on the File menu to save your Web and curriculum pages on your school's Web server or on your Internet service provider's (ISP) Web server. Many schools and ISPs also provide tools and/or techniques that you can use to publish Web pages on their servers. Many free education Web sites also provide space for teachers to store their Web and curriculum pages. You can get help to publish your pages from many sources, including your instructor and your school's technology coordinator. Most universities and ISPs have Help desks that you can call to obtain information on how to publish your Web pages. In addition, most universities, ISPs, and free education Web sites provide tutorials at their Web sites that you can use to learn how to publish your Web and curriculum pages on their servers.

Additional Ways to Create Web Pages Using Word

In addition to creating curriculum and other Web pages starting with a blank Web page, Word provides three other techniques for creating Web pages. You can save any existing Word document as a Web page, use a Web page template, or utilize Word's Web Page Wizard.

Saving a Word Document as a Web Page

Perform the following steps to save a Word document as a Web page.

TO SAVE A WORD DOCUMENT AS A WEB PAGE

1. Start Word and open any Word document.
2. Click File on the menu bar and the click Save as Web Page.
3. When Word displays the Save As dialog box, type the Web page name in the File name text box and then select the location to save the Web page.
4. Click the Save button in the Save As dialog box.
5. Close Word.

Word saves the Word document as a Web page and displays it in Web Layout view after you perform step 4.

Using Word Templates or the Word Web Page Wizard

You can create a Web page from scratch using a Word Web page template or you can use the Word Web Page Wizard.

TO USE A WORD TEMPLATE OR THE WORD WEB PAGE WIZARD

1. Start Word, click File on the menu bar and then click New.
2. When Word displays the New Document task pane, click the General Templates link in the New from template area. When Word displays the Templates dialog box, if necessary, click the Web Pages tab.

Word displays several Web page template icons and the Web Page Wizard icon in the Web Pages sheet of the Templates dialog box (Figure 24).

Double-click any template icon to open a Web page template or double-click the Web Page Wizard icon to use the wizard. You also can download hundreds of education-related templates from the Web.

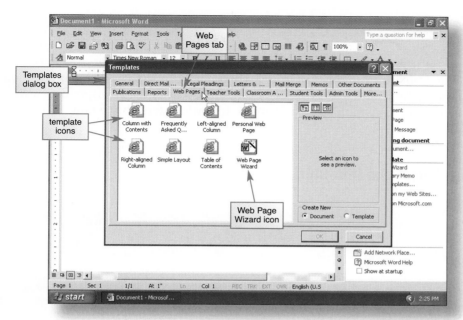

FIGURE 24

Creating a Curriculum Page without Typing URLs

Many URLs can be long and it is very easy to make mistakes when typing them into a Web browser. In Word, you can create a curriculum page without having to type URLs. Recall that curriculum pages can be simple or detailed. Often, teachers want to create a quick curriculum page such as the one shown in Figure 7-27a on page 7.28. A basic curriculum page with teacher-evaluated links is valuable to both teachers and students. It allows students to access those pages in class without having to type lengthy URLs. Creating hyperlinks without having to type URLs is quick and easy to do; they can be created in a matter of minutes from your list of favorites or bookmarked sites. You and your students can use two techniques that will eliminate the need to type URLs: copying and pasting using the keyboard or having Word insert links automatically through the Insert Hyperlink dialog box.

Copy and Paste Using Keyboard Shortcut Keys

The easiest way to prevent errors when entering URLs or e-mail addresses on curriculum or other Web pages is to copy and paste the Web or e-mail address using keyboard shortcut keys. Perform the following steps to copy and paste using keyboard shortcut keys.

TO COPY AND PASTE USING KEYBOARD SHORTCUT KEYS

1. Start your browser and then display the desired Web site.
2. Select the URL in the Address box and then press CTRL+C to copy the address to the Windows Clipboard.
3. Switch to a curriculum page, the Insert Hyperlink dialog box, or any Office document, and then press CTRL+V to paste or insert the address at the insertion point.
4. Close Word and close your browser.

Having Word Enter Web Site Names and URLs Automatically

Word also allows you to add the name of a Web site and the corresponding URL without typing either. Word will enter this information automatically in the Insert Hyperlink dialog box, utilizing the information in your browser. The following section details how to add the name of a Web site and link the text to its corresponding URL on a curriculum page automatically. Perform the following steps to see how easy it is to do.

Steps to Have Word Enter Web Site Names and URLs Automatically

① Start Internet Explorer.

② Start Microsoft Word and open a new blank Web page or any other previously created curriculum page.

③ Position the insertion point where you would like to create a hyperlink. Click the Insert Hyperlink button on the Standard toolbar to display the Insert Hyperlink dialog box.

④ Click the Internet Explorer button on the Windows taskbar to switch to Internet Explorer and then access the desired Web site.

⑤ Click the Word button on the Windows taskbar to switch back to the Word Web page.

Word automatically enters the name and URL of the Web page in the Text to display and Address text boxes in the Insert Hyperlink dialog box (Figure 25).

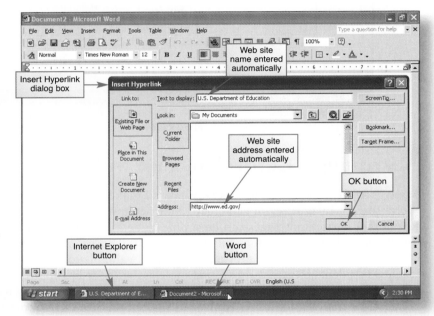

FIGURE 25

⑥ If desired, edit the Web site name in the Text to display text box and then click the OK button in the Insert Hyperlink dialog box.

Word enters the Web site name at the insertion point and hyperlinks the Web site name to its corresponding URL (Figure 26).

⑦ Close Word and close your browser.

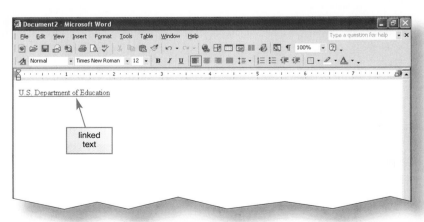

FIGURE 26

Editing a Web Page in Your Browser

One of the powerful features Office XP offers is the ability to edit a Web page directly in Internet Explorer. The following steps illustrate how to open and edit your Assignment Web page in Internet Explorer.

Steps to Edit a Web Page in Internet Explorer

1 If necessary, insert the floppy disk that contains the Assignment Web page file in your computer's floppy disk drive.

2 Start Internet Explorer. When Internet Explorer appears, click the Address box. Type a: and then press the ENTER key. Double-click the Assignment Web page. When the Web page appears, click File on the menu bar and then point to Edit with Microsoft Word.

Internet Explorer displays the Assignment Web page (Figure 27). Internet Explorer determines which Office program you used to create the Web page and associates that program with the Edit button, Microsoft Word in this case.

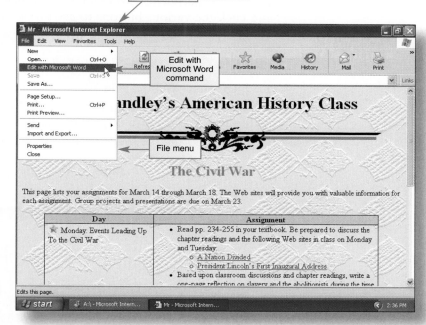

FIGURE 27

3 Click Edit with Microsoft Word.

Internet Explorer starts Microsoft Word and displays the Assignment Web page in the Word window in Web Layout view. You now can edit the Web page in Word as needed and then preview your changes in Internet Explorer (Figure 28).

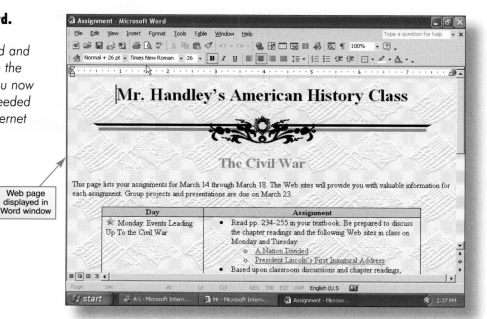

FIGURE 28

Using the Web Tools Toolbar

Word has many other Web page authoring features. For example, you and your students can include sounds, videos, pictures, scrolling text, bullets, check boxes, option buttons, list boxes, text boxes, and much more on your Web pages. A floating Web Tools toolbar contains icons that provide access to a number of these authoring features (Figure 29). The Web Tools toolbar is **floating** because you can drag it anywhere on your desktop. The easiest way to see which of these tools can benefit you is to experiment with them. Open a blank Web page and the Web Tools toolbar and click the various buttons to use the Web authoring tools. To display the Web Tools toolbar, perform the following steps.

TO DISPLAY THE WEB TOOLS TOOLBAR

1. Open a new Web page in Word using the steps on page 7.62.
2. Click View on the menu bar, point to Toolbars, and then click Web Tools on the Toolbars submenu to display the Web Tools toolbar.
3. After exploring the Web tools, close Word.

Word displays the Web Tools toolbar after you perform step 2 (Figure 29).

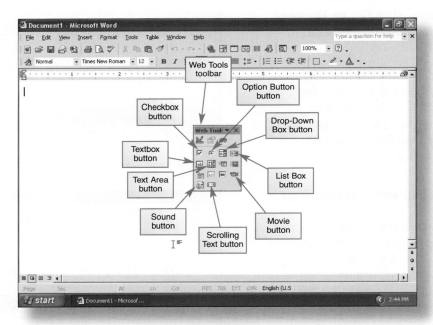

FIGURE 29

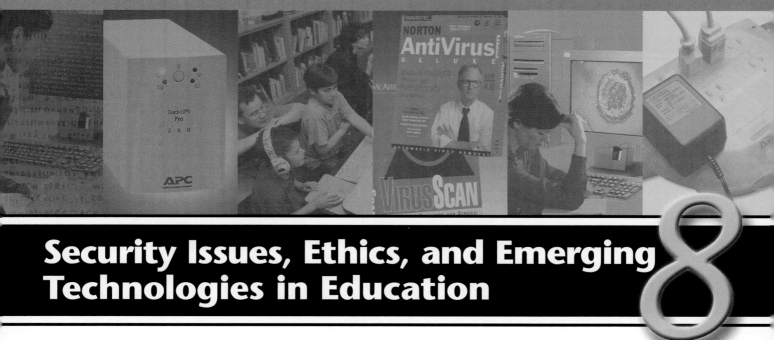

Security Issues, Ethics, and Emerging Technologies in Education

8

Objectives

After completing this chapter, you will be able to:

- Identify security risks that threaten home and school computers

- Describe how computer viruses and malicious software programs work and the steps you can take to prevent viruses

- Describe different ways schools safeguard computers and networks

- Explain why computer backup is important and how it is accomplished

- Define what is meant by information privacy and its impact on schools

- Identify the components of copyright that impact education

- Describe the ethical issues related to Internet usage and steps schools are taking to address them

- Identify safe and healthy uses of technology resources

- Describe the emerging technologies that will transform traditional classrooms

Every day, businesses, schools, and individuals depend on computers to perform a variety of significant tasks, such as tracking sales, recording student grades, creating reports, searching the Web, and sending e-mail. People increasingly rely on computers to create, store, and manage critical information, so it is important to ensure that computers and software are protected from loss, damage, and misuse. School districts, for example, must take precautions to guarantee that student information, such as grades, attendance rates, personal and family data, and learning problems, is protected from loss and kept confidential.

This chapter identifies some potential risks to computers and software, and describes a number of safeguards that schools, businesses, and individuals can implement to minimize these risks. The chapter also discusses information privacy, including the current laws that keep certain data confidential. The chapter then reviews concerns about the ethical use of computers and which activities are right, wrong, or even criminal. Next, the chapter covers security, privacy, and the ethical issues that relate to how teachers and students use the information they find on the Internet. Finally, the chapter concludes with a discussion about health issues and emerging technologies in education.

Computer Security: Risks and Safeguards

Any event or action that has the potential of causing a loss of computer equipment, software, data and information, or processing capability is a **computer security risk**. Some of these risks, such as viruses, unauthorized access and use, and information theft, are a result of deliberate acts that are against the law. Any illegal act involving a computer generally is referred to as a **computer crime**. The following sections describe some of the more common computer security risks and the measures that you and your school can take to minimize or prevent their consequences.

COMPUTER VIRUSES

At 4:30 in the afternoon, Mrs. Vicki Reamy of Ridgedale High School is in her classroom making last-minute adjustments to the Excel spreadsheet she plans to use in tomorrow's third-period Business Education class. As she opens the spreadsheet file to make one last change, the top of the spreadsheet displays the message, "Something wonderful has happened, your PC is alive." Dismayed, she realizes that a computer virus has corrupted her spreadsheet and she has lost all her work.

A **virus** is a potentially damaging computer program designed to affect your computer negatively without your knowledge or permission by altering the way it works. More specifically, a virus is a segment of program code that implants itself in a computer file and spreads systematically from one file to another. Figure 8-1 shows one way that a virus can spread from one computer to another.

Computer viruses, however, do not generate by chance. Creators of virus programs write them for a specific purpose — usually either to spread from one file to another, to trigger a symptom, or cause damage. Many viruses, for example, are designed to destroy or corrupt data stored on the infected computer. The symptom or damage caused by a virus, called the **virus payload**, can be harmless or cause

Figure 8-1 A virus spreads from one computer to another as illustrated in this figure.

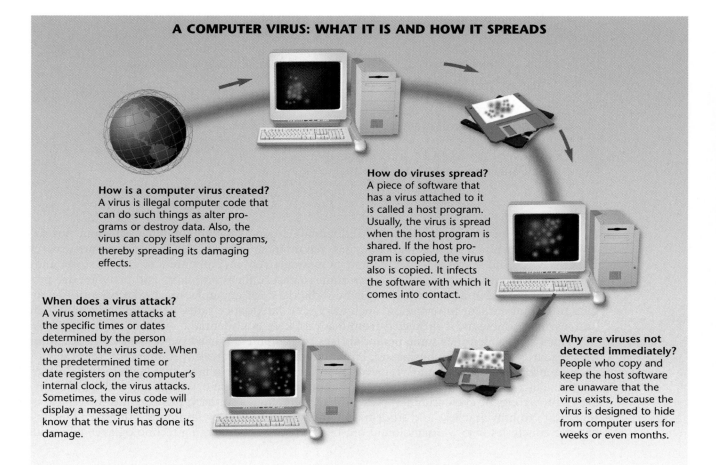

A COMPUTER VIRUS: WHAT IT IS AND HOW IT SPREADS

How is a computer virus created?
A virus is illegal computer code that can do such things as alter programs or destroy data. Also, the virus can copy itself onto programs, thereby spreading its damaging effects.

When does a virus attack?
A virus sometimes attacks at the specific times or dates determined by the person who wrote the virus code. When the predetermined time or date registers on the computer's internal clock, the virus attacks. Sometimes, the virus code will display a message letting you know that the virus has done its damage.

How do viruses spread?
A piece of software that has a virus attached to it is called a host program. Usually, the virus is spread when the host program is shared. If the host program is copied, the virus also is copied. It infects the software with which it comes into contact.

Why are viruses not detected immediately?
People who copy and keep the host software are unaware that the virus exists, because the virus is designed to hide from computer users for weeks or even months.

significant damage, as planned by the creator. Figure 8-2 outlines some common symptoms of virus infections.

Unfortunately, Vicki Reamy's experience is not unusual. Although viruses are a serious problem for both PC and Macintosh computer users, the majority of virus programs are intended to infect PCs. Currently, more than 62,000 known viruses or variants exist, and hundreds of new viruses or variants are identified every month. The increased use of networks and the Internet makes the spread of viruses easier than ever. Viruses commonly infect computers through e-mail attachments. Figure 8-3 on the next page shows how a virus can spread from one computer to another through an infected e-mail attachment. Before you open or execute any e-mail attachment, you should ensure that the e-mail message is from a trusted source and scan the attachment using antivirus software.

Although numerous variations are known, three main types of viruses exist: boot sector viruses, file viruses, and macro viruses. A **boot sector virus** replaces the boot program used to start the computer with a modified, infected version of the boot program. When the computer runs the infected boot program, it loads the virus into the computer's memory. Once a virus is in memory, it spreads to any disk inserted into the computer. A **file virus** inserts virus code into program files; the virus then spreads to any program that accesses the infected file. A **macro virus** uses the macro language of an application, such as word processing or spreadsheet, to hide virus codes. When you open a document with an infected macro, the macro virus loads into memory. Certain actions, such as saving the document, activate the virus. Macro viruses often are part of templates, so they will infect any document created using one of the templates.

Two common variations of computer viruses, often called **malicious software programs**, are worms and Trojan horses. A **worm** is a program that copies itself repeatedly in a computer's memory or on a network, using up resources and possibly shutting down the computer or network. Creators of worms often play on user psychology to entice people to download and run them. As a result, a number of well-known worms have hijacked e-mail systems and sent copies of themselves around the world in a matter of hours. The notorious Melissa worm quickly spread around the world causing serious harm to millions of computers. A **Trojan horse** (named after the Greek myth) is a malicious software program that hides within or is designed to look like a legitimate program.

Some viruses are relatively harmless pranks that temporarily freeze a computer or cause it to display sounds or messages. The computer plays a few chords of music when the Music Bug virus is triggered, for example. Other viruses cause extensive damage to computer files and spread quickly throughout a network. For example, if a state administrator sends an e-mail message with an attached Excel spreadsheet infected with a macro virus to every school district in the state, the virus could quickly infect hundreds of computers.

For more information about computer viruses, visit the Teachers Discovering Computers Web site, click Chapter 8, click Web Info, and then click Viruses.

Signs of Virus Infection

- An unusual message or graphical image appears on the computer screen
- An unusual sound or music plays randomly
- The available memory is less than what should be available
- A program or file suddenly is missing
- An unknown program or file mysteriously appears
- The size of a file changes without explanation
- A file becomes corrupted
- A program or file does not work properly

Figure 8-2 Viruses attack computers in a variety of ways. Listed here are some of the more common signs of virus infections.

Step 1:
Unscrupulous programmers create a virus program. They hide the virus in a Word document and attach the Word document to an e-mail message.

Step 2:
They use the Internet to send the e-mail message to thousands of users around the world.

Step 3b:
Other users do not recognize the name of the sender of the e-mail message. These users do not open the attachment — instead they immediately delete the e-mail message. These users' computers are not infected with the virus.

Step 3a:
Some users open the attachment and their computers become infected with the virus.

Figure 8-3 How a virus can spread through an e-mail attachment.

Some viruses are considered logic bombs or time bombs. A **logic bomb** is a program that activates when it detects a certain condition. One disgruntled worker, for example, planted a logic bomb that began destroying files when his name was added to a list of terminated employees. A **time bomb** is a type of logic bomb that activates on a particular date. A well-known time bomb is the **Michelangelo virus,** which destroys data on your hard disk on March 6, the date of Michelangelo's birthday. The World Wide Web is a great source for finding information about viruses and malicious software programs.

VIRUS DETECTION AND REMOVAL

Completely effective ways to keep a computer or network safe from computer viruses simply do not exist. You can, however, take precautions to protect your home and classroom computers from virus infections. Viruses normally are spread between computers by inserting an infected floppy disk in a computer or downloading an infected file from the Internet or via an e-mail attachment. **Figure 8-4** lists a number of safe computing tips that may help you minimize the risk of viruses.

FAQ

Should I inform others if my computer gets a virus?

If you share data with other users, such as via e-mail attachments, instant messages, floppy disks or Zip disks, you should inform these users of your virus infection. This courteous gesture allows fellow users to check their computers for viruses. In addition, you should inform your school's network specialists if you shared files or data with your school's computers.

Safe Computing Tips

A number of simple steps teachers can take will protect their home and classroom computers from viruses.

- **Purchase reliable antivirus software.** Most programs offer free virus updates. Upgrade antivirus software every week.

- **Scan all disks.** Floppy disks are common culprits for carrying viruses from one computer to another and spreading viruses throughout networks. If someone hands you a disk that has been used in another system — scan it.

- **Scan all files downloaded from the Internet.** The number-one source for viruses is downloaded files. To be safe, download all files into a special folder on your hard drive and scan them for viruses immediately after downloading.

- **Scan all attached files before reading them.** It is possible to transfer a virus to your system by opening an attachment. While it is not likely that you will get a virus from reading your e-mail, many e-mail programs allow users to preview an e-mail message before or without opening it. Some sophisticated viruses and worms can deliver their payload when a user simply previews the message. Thus, users should turn off message preview in their e-mail programs.

- **Scan all software before using even if it is shrink-wrapped.** Viruses have been found in manufacturer-supplied software. Scan before installing software.

- **Avoid pirated, illegal copies of copyrighted software.** Not only is using them illegal, but they are a favorite source of viruses.

- **Never start your computer with a floppy disk in drive A,** unless the floppy disk is an uninfected rescue disk.

- **Install antivirus programs on all of your school and home computers.** The cost of antivirus software is much less than the cost of rebuilding damaged files.

- **Have a bootable system disk.** Always have a clean, bootable system disk available.

- **Back up your files often.** Even with the best antivirus software, realize that your computer's files can be infected. Be prepared to deal with the problem.

- **Set your antivirus program to scan automatically.** Most antivirus programs can be set up to scan the system automatically when booted and check it whenever floppy drives are accessed or files are opened.

Figure 8-4 Teachers can use a number of safe computing tips to minimize the risk of viruses.

WEB INFO

For details about antivirus programs, visit the Teachers Discovering Computers Web site, click Chapter 8, click Web Info, and then click Vaccines.

Using an antivirus program is one of the more effective ways to protect against computer viruses. An **antivirus program** is designed to detect, disinfect, and protect computers and networks from viruses. Antivirus programs, also called **vaccines**, work by looking for programs that attempt to modify the boot program, the operating system, or other programs that normally are read from but not written to [Figure 8-5].

In addition to providing protection from viruses, most antivirus programs also have utilities to remove or repair infected programs and files. If the virus has infected the boot program, however, the antivirus program may require you to restart the computer with a rescue disk. A **rescue disk** is a floppy disk that contains an uninfected copy of key operating system commands and startup information that enables the computer to restart correctly. After you have restarted the computer using a rescue disk, you can run repair and removal programs to remove infected files and repair damaged files. If the program cannot repair the damaged files, you may have to replace or restore them with uninfected backup copies of the files. Later sections in the chapter explain backup and restore procedures.

To help protect against viruses, most schools install antivirus programs on their networks and on individual computers throughout the school. Two popular antivirus programs used in schools and homes, shown in Figure 8-6, are Symantec Norton AntiVirus and McAfee VirusScan.

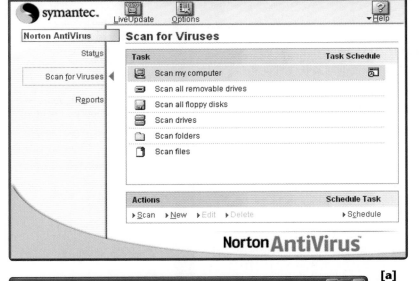

[a]

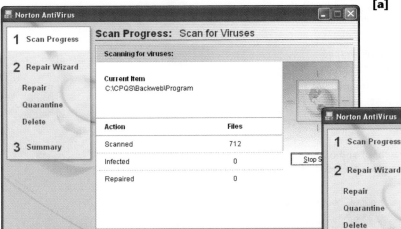

[b]

[c]

Figure 8-6 Symantec Norton AntiVirus and McAfee VirusScan are two popular antivirus programs used in schools, businesses, and homes.

Figure 8-5 Antivirus programs check disk drives and memory for computer viruses. Figure 8-5a displays the Scan for Viruses screen that allows you to select the disk drives or files to be scanned. Figure 8-5b displays the status during the scan, and Figure 8-5c shows the results.

When you install an antivirus program, you should set up the program to monitor a computer continuously for possible viruses, including continual scans of all floppy disks and files downloaded from the Internet [Figure 8-7]. You also should set your antivirus program so it updates automatically every week.

False warnings about viruses often spread via e-mail and over the Internet. Known as **virus hoaxes**, these warnings describe viruses that are not actually known to exist. Given the damage viruses cause, however, you should take the time to research the validity of any virus warnings you receive, in the event they are real. The Symantec Security Response – Hoax Web page regularly releases new virus hoax names. If you think you have received a message about a false new virus, you can verify it at the Hoax Web page.

UNAUTHORIZED ACCESS AND USE

Unauthorized access is the use of a computer or network without permission. An individual who tries to access a computer or network illegally is called a **cracker** or hacker. The term, **hacker**, although originally a complimentary word for a computer enthusiast, now has a derogatory connotation because it refers to people who try to break into a computer, often intending to steal or corrupt its data. Crackers and hackers typically break into computers by connecting to the system via a modem and logging in as a user. Some intruders have no intent of causing damage to computer files; they merely want to access data, information, or programs on the accessed computer before logging off. Other intruders leave some evidence of their presence with a message or by deliberately altering data.

Unauthorized use is the use of a computer or data for unapproved or possibly illegal activities. Unauthorized use ranges from an employee using a company computer to send personal e-mail or track his or her child's soccer league scores to someone gaining access to a bank system and completing an unauthorized transfer.

One way to prevent unauthorized access to and use of computers is to implement **access controls**, which are security measures that define who can access a computer, when they can access it, and what actions they can take while using the computer. To prevent unauthorized use and access to sensitive information, schools install different levels and types of access controls. Schools set up their networks so that users have access only to those programs, data, and information for which they are approved. Most schools and businesses provide authorized users with unique user identification, or **user ID**, and a **password** that allows them to log on to the network to use e-mail, transfer files, and access other shared resources [Figure 8-8]. When a user logs on to a computer or network by entering a

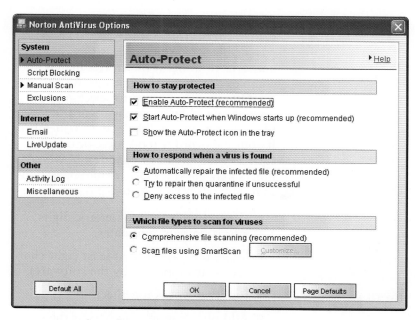

Figure 8-7 Using Norton AntiVirus Auto-Protect, users can opt for several different virus protection options.

Figure 8-8 Many schools require administrators, teachers, staff, and students to log onto the school's network with a unique user ID and password.

user ID and a password, the operating system checks to see if the user ID and password match the entries stored in an authorization file. If the entries match, the computer or network grants access.

Often you are asked to select your own password by choosing a word or series of characters that will be easy to remember. If your password is too simple or obvious, such as your initials or birthday, however, others may guess it easily. Some suggestions to follow when you create a password are:

- Use a combination of letters, digits, words, initials, and dates.

- Make the password at least eight characters (if supported by the software).

- Join two words together.

- Add one or more numbers at the beginning, middle, or end of a word.

- Choose words from other languages.

- Choose family names far back in your family tree.

- Choose a password you can type easily without looking at the keyboard.

Generally, the more creative your password, the harder it is for someone else to figure out. Even long and creative passwords, however, do not provide complete protection against unauthorized access. Some basic precautions to take include:

- Do not post passwords near your computer.

- Use a password that is easy to remember, so that you do not have to write it down.

- Change your password frequently.

- Do not share your password with anyone.

Following these guidelines helps to ensure that others will not use your password to access data, programs, or sensitive information stored on your computer or a school network.

At many schools, each user ID and password is associated with a specific level of computer and network access. The following is a brief description of some basic

access levels schools use to prevent unauthorized access and use of sensitive information.

- Students usually can access only instructional materials and software. Many schools also provide student access to the Internet and Web — although many schools install filtering software on the networks to prevent students from viewing inappropriate Web sites. Students do not have network access to grades, attendance rates, and other sensitive and personal information.

- Teachers typically have access to all the programs, data, and information to which students have access; they usually have access to selected information about their students, such as grades and attendance. Teachers normally do not have access to information about other teachers, students, or any administrative files.

- Principals and assistant principals normally have access to all information that pertains to students enrolled at their schools; they may not, however, access information about students attending other schools in the district.

- School district administrators and superintendents usually have access to all information stored on their districts' network servers.

FIREWALLS

Despite efforts to protect the data on your computer's hard disk, it still is vulnerable to attacks from hackers. A **firewall** is a security system consisting of hardware and/or software that prevents unauthorized access to data and information on a network. Schools use firewalls to deny network access to outsiders and to restrict both student and teacher access to sensitive data [Figure 8-9]. Many schools route all communications through a proxy server. A **proxy server** screens all incoming and outgoing messages.

Home and home office computer users should install a personal firewall. A **personal firewall** is a software program that detects and protects your personal

WEB INFO

For more information about unauthorized access, visit the Teachers Discovering Computers Web site, click Chapter 8, click Web Info, and then click Unauthorized Access.

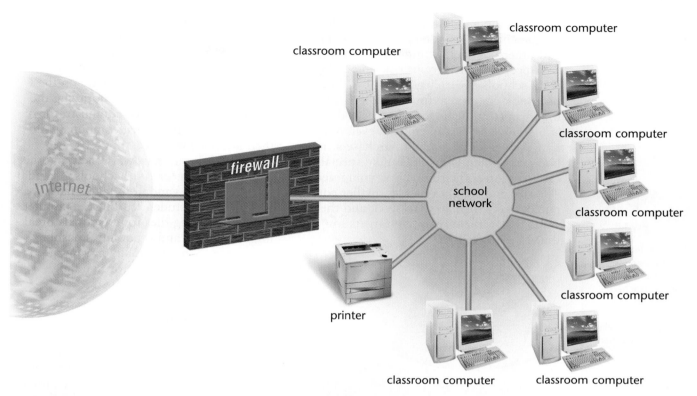

Figure 8-9 A firewall restricts unauthorized intruders from accessing data, information, and programs on networks and individual computers.

computer and its data from unauthorized intrusions. These products constantly monitor all transmissions to and from your computer and inform you of any attempted intrusions. These easy-to-use products are definitely worth their expense, which usually is less than $40. Figure 8-10 lists popular personal firewall products. If you are using Mac OS X, you already have a personal firewall that protects your computer from unauthorized access by monitoring all incoming network traffic.

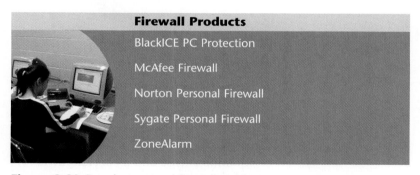

Firewall Products

BlackICE PC Protection

McAfee Firewall

Norton Personal Firewall

Sygate Personal Firewall

ZoneAlarm

Figure 8-10 Popular personal firewall products.

HARDWARE THEFT AND VANDALISM

For schools, hardware theft and vandalism present a difficult security challenge. To help minimize the theft of computers and associated equipment, schools can implement a variety of security precautions. In addition to installing security systems, many schools also install additional physical security devices such as cables that lock the equipment to a desk, cabinet, or floor [Figure 8-11]. Schools also normally install deadbolt locks and alarm systems to protect the equipment in their computer labs.

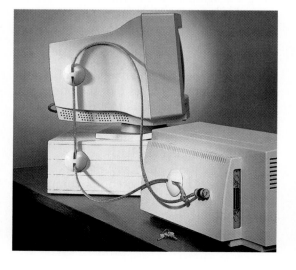

Figure 8-11
Using cables to lock computers can help prevent the theft of desktop and mobile computer equipment.

With the increasing use of portable equipment such as notebook computers and other handheld computers, hardware theft poses a more serious risk. Increasingly, K-12 schools and colleges are providing notebook computers for teachers and loaning them to students for short periods. Some universities and colleges even require that each entering student purchase a notebook computer. Users must take special care to protect their notebook computers. The size and weight of these smaller computers make them easy to steal, and their value makes them tempting targets for thieves [Figure 8-12].

WEB INFO

For more information about notebook computer security, visit the Teachers Discovering Computers Web site, click Chapter 8, click Web Info, and then click Security.

Figure 8-12 The size and weight of notebook computers make them easy to steal, and their value makes them tempting targets for thieves. Schools and teachers need to take special precautions to prevent the theft of their notebook computers.

Common sense and a constant awareness of the risks are the best preventive measures against theft of notebook computers and other portable equipment. You should never, for example, leave a notebook computer unattended or out in the open in a public place, such as the cafeteria or on the seat of a car. Some schools install physical devices such as cables that temporarily lock notebook computers to a desk or table. As a precaution in case of theft, you also should back up the files stored on your notebook computer regularly.

Many schools purchase insurance policies to cover their notebook computers, desktop computers, and other computer equipment. In addition, schools also can purchase a service that actually can track down a stolen notebook computer.

WEB INFO

For an overview of software and technology law, visit the Teachers Discovering Computers Web site, click Chapter 8, click Web Info, and then click Software.

This unique system often is called by its nickname, *the Lojack of the Computer World*. As soon a person who has stolen a notebook computer uses the computer to access the Internet, the software on the computer sends a message, notifying the school's system network administrator of the location of the stolen computer, who then notifies the police.

In addition to hardware theft, another area of concern for K-12 schools is vandalism. **Computer vandalism** takes many forms, from a student cutting a computer cable or deleting files to individuals breaking in a school and randomly smashing computers. Schools usually have written policies and procedures for handling various types of vandalism.

SOFTWARE THEFT

Like hardware theft and vandalism, software theft takes many forms — from a student physically stealing a CD to intentional piracy of software. **Software piracy** — the unauthorized and illegal duplication of copyrighted software — is by far the most common form of software theft.

When you purchase software, you actually do not *own* the software; instead, you have purchased the right to use the software, as outlined in the software license. A **software license** is an agreement that provides specific conditions for use of the software, which users must accept before using the software. Manufacturers usually print the terms of a software license on the software packaging, or in the case of software downloaded via the Web, a page at the manufacturer's site. The same agreement generally displays on a licensing acceptance screen during the software's setup program [Figure 8-13]. Installation and use of the software constitutes the user's acceptance of the terms.

The most common type of license agreement included with software packages purchased by individual users is a **single-user license agreement**, or **end-user license agreement (EULA)**. An end-user license agreement typically includes numerous conditions, including the following:

- Users may install the software on only one computer.

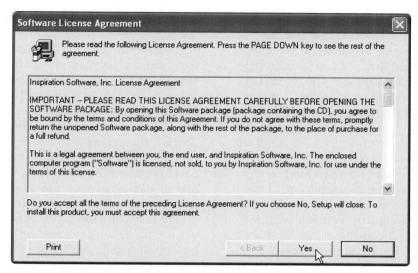

Figure 8-13 Purchasers of single-use software usually have to accept all the terms of the licensing agreement during installation of the software.

- Users may not install the software on a network, such as a school computer lab network.

- Users may make *one* copy for backup purposes.

- Users may not give copies to friends and colleagues.

Unless otherwise specified by a software license, you do not have the right to loan, rent, or in any way distribute software you purchase. This means you cannot install the software on both your home and classroom computer or on more than one classroom or home computer. Doing so not only is a violation of copyright law, it also is a federal crime.

Software piracy introduces a number of risks into the software market: it increases the chance of viruses; reduces your ability to receive technical support; and significantly drives up the price of software for all users. Experts estimate that for every authorized copy of software in use, at least one unauthorized copy is made.

One recent study reported that software piracy results in worldwide losses of more than tens of billions of dollars per year. Software piracy continues for several reasons. Some countries do not provide legal protection for software, while other countries rarely enforce laws. In addition, many buyers believe they have the right to copy the software for which they have paid

hundreds, even thousands of dollars — particularly when it is on an inexpensive floppy disk, CD, or DVD.

Newer Microsoft Office and Windows products contain software-based product activation technology, which means you need to activate your Office and Windows products to use them. **Product activation** is an antipiracy technology designed to verify that software products have been licensed legitimately. Microsoft states that product activation is quick, simple, unobtrusive, and that it protects customer privacy.

Product activation works by verifying that a software program's product key, which you must use to install the product, has not been used on more personal computers than intended by the software's license. Software companies take illegal copying seriously and prosecute some offenders (including school districts, school administrators, and teachers) to the fullest extent of the law. Penalties include fines up to $250,000 and up to five years in jail.

Most schools have strict policies governing the installation and use of software and enforce their rules by periodically checking classroom and lab computers to ensure that all software is properly licensed. Teachers who are not completely familiar with their school's policies governing installation of software always should check with the school's technology coordinator before installing any software on a classroom computer.

WEB INFO

For a list of freeware for the PC or Mac, visit the Teachers Discovering Computers Web site, click Chapter 8, click Web Info, and then click PC Freeware or Mac Freeware.

Two additional types of software, shareware and freeware, also require license agreements and are protected under copyright law. As you learned in Chapter 1, **shareware** is software that is distributed free for a trial period. If you want to use a shareware program beyond the trial period, the developer (person or company) expects you to send a small fee. **Freeware**, by contrast, is software provided at no cost to a user by an individual or company. You should carefully read the license included with any shareware or freeware to familiarize yourself with the usage terms and conditions. Some shareware licenses, for example, allow you to install the software on several computers for the same fee, while others allow you to install the software on an unlimited number of computers in the same school for a minimal additional fee. Always scan shareware and freeware programs for viruses before installation and use.

To reduce software costs for schools and businesses with large numbers of users, software vendors often offer special discount pricing or site licensing. With discount pricing, the more copies of a program a school district purchases, the greater the discount. Purchasing a software

Figure 8-14 A summary of the various types of software licenses used in education.

site license gives the buyer the right to install the software on multiple computers at a single site. Site licenses usually cost significantly less than purchasing an individual copy of the software for each computer; many school districts, in fact, purchase software site licenses that allow for use on computers throughout the district, thus gaining substantial savings.

Network site licenses for many software packages also are available. A **network site license** allows network users to share a single copy of the software, which resides on the network server. Network software site license prices are based on a fixed fee for an unlimited number of users, a maximum number of users, or per user.

A **community site license** gives an entire region or state the right to install an unlimited number of educational copies of a particular software program on individual computers or a network. As with other site licenses, a community site license provides substantial savings. Figure 8-14 summarizes the various types of software licenses used in education. A number of major software companies, such as Microsoft, provide site licenses for some of their software to K-12 schools at drastically reduced rates.

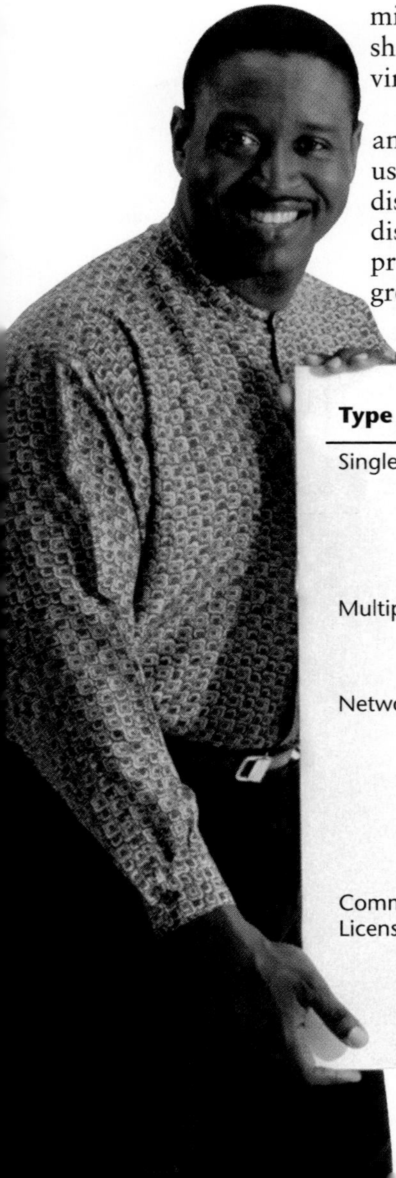

Type of License	Characteristics	Use in Schools
Single-user	Can be installed on only one computer.	Used when a school needs only a few copies of a particular software. Commonly found in small schools and when purchasing specialized software programs.
Multiple-user	Software can be installed on a set number of computers, typically 5, 10, 50, or more.	Cost-effective method to install software on more than one computer. Most commonly used in schools.
Network License	Software is installed on the school's network. The license will specify and the software will control a specific number of simultaneous users, such as 50, 100, 250, or 500.	Cost-effective method of allowing students and teachers throughout the school to have access to an application software program. As schools continue to install networks, network licenses are becoming very common.
Community/State License	Frequently used with software distributed on CDs/DVDs. Any number of programs can be purchased for either Macintosh or PC platforms.	Very cost-effective method for schools to purchase large quantities of software. Savings can be significant over individual CD or DVD pricing.

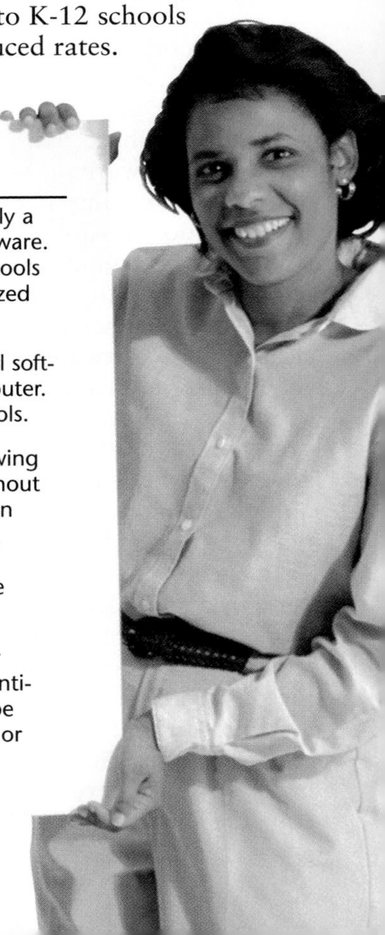

INFORMATION THEFT

As you have learned, information is a valuable asset to an organization, such as a school district. The deliberate theft of information, causes as much or more damage than the theft of hardware. Information theft typically occurs for a variety of reasons — organizations steal or buy stolen information to learn about competitors and individuals steal credit card and telephone charge card numbers to make purchases. Information theft often is linked to other types of computer crime. An individual, for example, first may gain unauthorized access to a computer and then steal credit card numbers stored in a firm's accounting files.

Most organizations prevent information theft by implementing the user ID controls previously mentioned. Another way to protect sensitive data is to use encryption. **Encryption** is the process of converting readable data into unreadable characters by applying a formula that uses a code, called an **encryption key**. The person who receives the message uses the same encryption key to decrypt it (convert it back to readable data). Both the sender and receiver computers use the same encryption software. Any person illegally accessing the information sees only meaningless symbols [Figure 8-15].

School networks do contain a great deal of important and confidential information about students, teachers, and staff. While information theft is not a major problem in schools, the potential is taken seriously. As a result, schools implement many of the security precautions described in this chapter.

SYSTEM FAILURE

Theft is not the only cause of hardware, software, data, or information loss. Any of these also can occur during a **system failure**, which is a malfunction of a computer. System failures occur because of electrical power problems, hardware component failure, or software error.

One of the more common causes of system failures in schools and homes is an abrupt variation in electrical power, which can cause data loss or damage computer components. In a school network, for example, a single power disturbance can damage multiple computers and their associated equipment. Two more

For more information about encryption software, visit the Teachers Discovering Computers Web site, click Chapter 8, click Web Info, and then click Encryption.

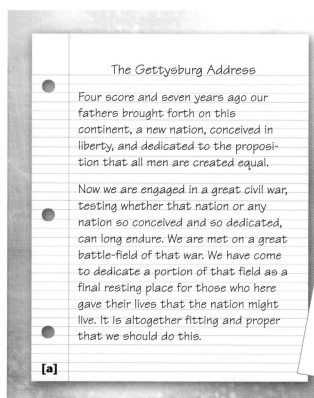

The Gettysburg Address

Four score and seven years ago our fathers brought forth on this continent, a new nation, conceived in liberty, and dedicated to the proposition that all men are created equal.

Now we are engaged in a great civil war, testing whether that nation or any nation so conceived and so dedicated, can long endure. We are met on a great battle-field of that war. We have come to dedicate a portion of that field as a final resting place for those who here gave their lives that the nation might live. It is altogether fitting and proper that we should do this.

[a]

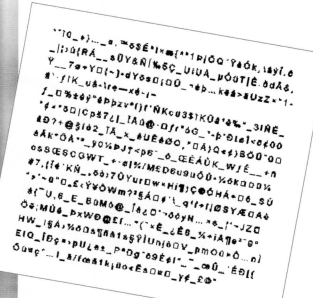

[b]

Figure 8-15 The first two paragraphs of the Gettysburg Address in plain text [a] and after the text is encrypted [b].

common electrical power variations that cause system failures are undervoltages and overvoltages.

An **undervoltage** occurs when the electrical power supply drops. In North America, electricity normally flows from the wall plug at approximately 120 volts. Any significant drop below 120 volts is considered an undervoltage. A **brownout** is a prolonged undervoltage; a **blackout** is a complete power failure. Undervoltages cause data loss and computer crashes but generally do not cause serious equipment damage.

An **overvoltage**, or **power surge**, occurs when the incoming electrical power increases significantly above the normal 120 volts. A momentary overvoltage, called a **spike**, occurs when the power increase lasts for less than one millisecond (one thousandth of a second). Spikes are caused by uncontrollable disturbances, such as lightning, or controllable disturbances, such as turning on a piece of equipment that uses the same electrical circuit. Overvoltages can cause immediate and permanent equipment damage.

To protect your computer equipment from overvoltages, you should use surge protectors. A **surge protector** is a device that uses special electrical components to smooth out minor voltage errors, provide a stable current flow, and keep an overvoltage from damaging computer equipment [Figure 8-16]. Schools should use surge protectors for all classroom and lab computers and printers.

Electrical power surges also can occur over communications lines, such as telephone lines. Home users thus should purchase a surge protector that includes a connection for the telephone line connected to your modem [Figure 8-17]. Overall, surge protectors provide an inexpensive way to protect computers and associated equipment. Basic surge protectors cost less than $15 and surge protectors that include protection from power surges over telephone lines cost less than $20.

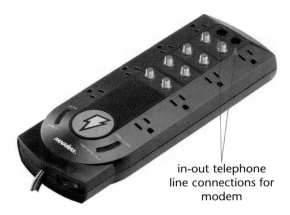

in-out telephone line connections for modem

Figure 8-17 Home users should purchase a surge protector that includes an in-and-out connection for the telephone line to the computer's modem.

While a surge protector absorbs a small overvoltage without damage, a large overvoltage, such as that caused by a lightning strike, will cause the surge protector to fail in order to protect the computer components. Surge protectors also are not completely effective; large power surges may bypass the surge protector and repeated small overvoltages may weaken a surge protector permanently.

For additional electrical protection, many home and school users connect their computers and printers to an uninterruptible power supply, instead of a surge protector. An **uninterruptible power supply** (**UPS**) is a device that contains surge protection circuits and one or more batteries that provide power during a temporary or permanent loss of power [Figure 8-18]. The amount of time a UPS allows you to continue working depends on the electrical requirements of the computer and the size of the batteries in the UPS. A less expensive UPS provides enough time for users to

Figure 8-16 Circuits inside a surge protector safeguard equipment against overvoltages.

save their current work and properly shut down the computer after a power outage (about 10 minutes).

Figure 8-18 If power fails, an uninterruptible power supply (UPS) uses batteries to provide electricity for a limited time. A UPS also contains circuits that safeguard against overvoltages.

To ensure that their networks will continue to operate in the event of a power loss, most schools and businesses install UPSs to protect their network servers. Home users also should consider investing in a UPS, especially if they live in an area prone to power surges, power failures, and lightning strikes. For home users, the $75 to $150 investment in a UPS can prevent user frustration associated with most power-related computer problems, crashes, and loss of data. Some UPS manufacturers pay for any damage your computer sustains from power surges, including lightning strikes.

BACKUP PROCEDURES

To prevent data loss caused by a system failure or a computer virus, many schools, businesses, and home users back up their important files. A **backup** is a duplicate of a file, program, or disk that may be used if the original is lost, damaged, or destroyed. When a file is corrupted or destroyed, the backup copy is used to **restore**, or reload, the file on a computer or network file server. Schools and home users often overlook storing

backup copies at another location, called an **offsite location**, as an additional precaution. This simple precaution prevents a single disaster, such as a fire, from destroying both the primary and backup copies of important files.

Most schools have a **backup procedure** that outlines a regular plan of copying and backing up important data and program files. At many schools, the backup procedures cover only essential school programs, information, and data, such as student grades, attendance, and other personal information. Schools normally do not back up the files individual teachers or students create on their classroom computers. If your school does not provide backups for the files you create in your classroom, you should make backup copies of your school files periodically and store them on Zip disks or CDs. Likewise, you should back up the files you create on your home computer. Whether at school or home, backing up your important files prevents loss of lesson plans, curriculum pages, handouts, tests, and more — files that represent years of work. Teachers also should teach their students how to back up their homework, projects, and other files.

Creating backup copies of your files is not a difficult procedure. The easiest way is to copy your important files from your hard disk to a Zip disk, CD, or USB drive. In addition, most personal computer operating systems include an easy-to-use backup utility program [Figure 8-19]. Such utilities not only allow users to back up their important files, they also compress the backed up files so they require less storage space than the original files.

WEB INFO

To learn more about Microsoft Backup, visit the Teachers Discovering Computers Web site, click Chapter 8, click Web Info, and then click Backup.

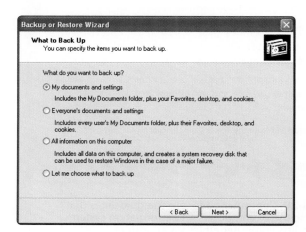

Figure 8-19 Microsoft Backup is a utility program that comes with Microsoft Windows and is an easy way to back up your important computer files.

Ethics and the Information Age

As with any powerful technology, individuals can use computers for both good and bad actions. The standards that determine whether an action is good or bad are called **ethics**. **Computer ethics** are the moral guidelines that govern the use of computers, networks, and information systems [Figure 8-20]. Five areas of computer ethics frequently discussed are (1) unauthorized use of computers, (2) hardware, software, and information theft, (3) information privacy, (4) copyright, and (5) the existence of objectionable materials on the Internet.

Unauthorized use of computers and hardware, copying software, and information theft were discussed earlier in this chapter. The following sections present the issues surrounding information privacy and copyright. The ethical issues related to objectionable materials on the Internet will be discussed later in this chapter.

Computer Ethics for Educators

1. An educator will not use a computer to harm other people.

2. An educator will not interfere with others' computer work.

3. An educator will not look at others' computer files.

4. An educator will not use a computer to steal.

5. An educator will not use a computer to lie.

6. An educator will not copy or use software without paying for it.

7. An educator will not use others' computer resources without permission.

8. An educator will not use others' work.

9. An educator will think about the social impact of the programs he or she creates.

10. An educator always will use a computer in a way that shows respect and consideration for other people.

Modified from the *Ten Commandments for Computer Ethics* by the Computer Ethics Institute.

Figure 8-20 Computer ethics are the guidelines that govern the use of computers and information systems. This table lists computer ethics for educators.

INFORMATION PRIVACY

Information privacy is the right of individuals and organizations to deny or restrict the collection and use of information about them. In the past, information privacy was easier to control because information was kept in separate locations, individual schools in a large school district maintained their own files, individual stores had their own credit files, government agencies had separate records, doctors had separate files, and so on.

Now it is feasible, both technically and economically, for schools, businesses, and other organizations to store large amounts of related data in a database or on one network server because of the widespread use of networks and increased storage capacity. These organizations also use computers to monitor student and employee activities. As a result, many people have concerns about how the unauthorized collection and use of data and monitoring effects their privacy. Figure 8-21 lists actions you can take to make your personal data more private.

UNAUTHORIZED COLLECTION AND USE OF INFORMATION Most individuals are surprised to learn that national marketing organizations often purchase the information individuals provide for magazine subscriptions, product warranty registration cards, contest entry forms, and other documents.

By combining this acquired data with other information obtained from public sources, such as driver's licenses and vehicle registration information, national marketing organizations create an **electronic profile** of an individual. The organizations then sell this electronic profile to organizations that distribute information on a product, service, or cause to a specific group of individuals (for example, all sports car owners over 40 years of age living in the southeastern United States).

Direct marketing supporters say that using information in this way lowers overall selling costs, which in turn, lowers product prices. Critics contend that the information combined in these electronic profiles reveals more about individuals than anyone has a right to know. These same individuals believe that, at a minimum, companies should inform the

How to Safeguard Personal Information

1. Fill in only necessary information on rebate, warranty, and registration forms.

2. Do not preprint your telephone number or Social Security number on personal checks.

3. Have an unlisted or unpublished telephone number.

4. If Caller ID is available in your area, find out how to block your number from displaying on the receiver's system.

5. Do not write your telephone number on charge or credit receipts.

6. Ask merchants not to write credit card numbers, telephone numbers, Social Security numbers, and driver's license numbers on the back of your personal checks.

7. Purchase goods with cash instead of credit or checks.

8. Avoid shopping clubs and buyers' cards.

9. If merchants ask personal questions, find out why they want to know before releasing the information.

10. Inform merchants that you do not want them to distribute your personal information.

11. Ask, in writing, to be removed from mailing lists.

12. Obtain your credit report once a year from each of the three major credit reporting agencies (Equifax, Experian, and TransUnion) and correct any errors.

13. Request a free copy of your medical records once a year from the Medical Information Bureau.

14. Limit the amount of information you provide to Web sites. Just fill in required information.

15. Install a cookie manager to filter cookies.

16. Clear your history file when you are finished browsing.

17. Set up a free e-mail account. Use this e-mail address for merchant forms.

18. Turn off File and Print Sharing on your Internet connection.

19. Install a personal firewall.

20. Sign-up for e-mail filtering through your Internet service provider or use an anti-spam program such as Brightmail.

21. Do not reply to spam for any reason. It may not be a good idea to unsubscribe to unsolicited spam; by sending back a message, you may only confirm that your e-mail account is active.

22. Surf the Web anonymously with programs such as Freedom or through an anonymous Web site such as Anonymizer.

Figure 8-21 Techniques to keep personal data private.

FAQ

Why would a hacker want to access my home computer?

One reason hackers access home computers is to search for personal information, for example, credit cards numbers, bank account numbers, Social Security numbers, wills, resumes, and more.

individuals whose personal information they intend to sell or release and give the individuals the right to deny such use.

SPAM Spam is an unsolicited e-mail message or newsgroup posting sent to many recipients or newsgroups at once. The content of spam ranges from selling a product or service, to promoting a business opportunity, to advertising offensive materials. One study indicates the average user receives more than 1,000 spam e-mail messages each year.

Many organizations have teamed up to stem the flood of unsolicited e-mail that is costing business billions of dollars a year. In the spring of 2003, Microsoft launched a major anti-spam initiative with other industry leaders, including AOL, Yahoo!, and EarthLink. These companies are committed to work with the government to curb spam through technological innovation, industry efforts, and legal action. In the summer of 2003, Microsoft announced that it had filed 13 civil suits in the U.S. against offenders for sending unwanted, deceptive commercial e-mail to Microsoft customers.

Until the spam issue is resolved, you can reduce the amount of spam you receive using several techniques. Some e-mail programs have built-in settings that delete spam automatically. Other e-mail programs, such as Outlook Express, also allow you to set up message rules that block all messages from a particular sender or subject. You also can sign up for e-mail filtering from your Internet service provider. **E-mail filtering** is a service that blocks e-mail messages from designated sources. You can block unwanted e-mail messages by using an **anti-spam program** that attempts to remove spam before it reaches your inbox. The disadvantage of using e-mail filters and anti-spam programs is that sometimes they remove valid e-mail messages.

PRIVACY LAWS The concern about privacy has led to federal and state laws regarding storing and disclosing personal data and other issues [Figure 8-22].

Common points in some of these laws include the following:

- A business or government agency collecting data about individuals should limit the information collected and only store what is necessary to carry out the organization's functions.

- After it has collected data about individuals, an organization must make provisions to restrict data access to only those employees who must use it to perform their job duties.

- An organization should release an individual's personal information outside the organization only after the individual has agreed to its disclosure.

- When an organization collects information about an individual, the organization must inform the individual that it is collecting data and give him or her the opportunity to determine the accuracy of the data.

Schools and school districts have a legal and moral responsibility to protect sensitive information, whether it is in printed form or stored electronically on school computers. Just like any other business, school districts must follow state and federal laws concerning storage and release of personal information about students, teachers, and staff personnel. For these reasons, school districts generally restrict access to sensitive information stored on their networks and in printed materials on a strict need-to-know basis.

Teachers also must follow federal and state laws concerning the storage and release of information about their students. Teachers should carefully read and make sure they understand all school district policies concerning the release of sensitive information as related to their students.

EMPLOYEE AND STUDENT MONITORING
Employee monitoring uses computers to observe, record, and review an individual's use of a computer, including communications such as e-mail, keyboard activity (used to measure productivity), and Internet sites visited. A frequently discussed issue is whether or not an employer has the right to read an employee's e-mail messages. Actual policies vary widely, with some organizations declaring they will review e-mail messages regularly, while others state they consider e-mail private and will protect it just like a letter sent through the postal service.

Most schools usually have very specific rules governing the use of e-mail and school networks by teachers, administrators, staff, and students. Some schools randomly monitor e-mail messages and the Internet sites visited by teachers, administrators, staff, and students, while other schools do not. Some schools also randomly monitor files stored on the school network.

Teachers should familiarize themselves with all school policies concerning e-mail and computer and Internet usage. To ensure that individuals understand these policies, most schools require that teachers, students, staff, and parents sign an Acceptable Use Policy (AUP) that provides specific guidance for using school computers, networks, and the Internet. Teachers also should ensure that students fully understand that school personnel or their future employers may monitor their use of the organization's computer resources.

COPYRIGHT LAWS
As discussed earlier in this chapter, copyright laws cover software programs to protect them from piracy. Copyright law

WEB INFO

For a crash course on copyright basics, visit the Teachers Discovering Computers Web site, click Chapter 8, click Web Info, and then click Crash Course.

DATE	LAW	PURPOSE
2003	Health Insurance Portability and Accountability Act (HIPAA)	HIPAA became effective on April 14, 2003. The act describes how personal medical information may be used and disclosed.
2002	Dot Kids Implementation and Efficiency Act	The Act establishes the Dot Kids domain that will list only Web sites that conform to policies to protect children under the age of 13. It will function similarly to the children's section of a library.
2001	Provide Appropriate Tools Required to Intercept and Obstruct Terrorism (PATRIOT) Act	Gives law enforcement the right to monitor people's activities, including Web and e-mail habits.
2000	Children's Internet Protection Act (CIPA)	Protects children from obscene and pornographic materials by requiring libraries to install filtering software on their computers. Upheld by the Supreme Court in July 2003.
1998	Children's Online Privacy Protection Act (COPPA)	Protects personal information for children under the age of 13.
1997	No Electronic Theft (NET) Act	Closed a narrow loophole in the law that allowed people to give away copyrighted material (such as software) on the Internet without legal repercussions.
1996	National Information Infrastructure Protection Act	Penalizes theft of information across state lines, threats against networks, and computer system trespassing.
1994	Computer Abuse Amendments Act	Amends 1984 act to outlaw transmission of harmful computer code such as viruses.
1992	Cable Act	Extends privacy of Cable Communications Policy Act of 1984 to include cellular and other wireless services.
1991	Telephone Consumer Protection Act	Restricts activities of telemarketers.
1988	Computer Matching and Privacy Protection Act	Regulates the use of government data to determine the eligibility of individuals for federal benefits.
1988	Video Privacy Protection Act	Forbids retailers from releasing or selling video-rental records without customer consent or a court order.
1986	Electronic Communications Privacy Act (ECPA)	Provides the same right of privacy protection for the postal delivery service and telephone companies to the new forms of electronic communications, such as voice mail, e-mail, and cellular telephones.
1984	Cable Communications Policy Act	Regulates disclosure of cable television subscriber records.
1984	Computer Fraud and Abuse Act	Outlaws unauthorized access of federal government computers.
1978	Right to Financial Privacy Act	Strictly outlines procedures federal agencies must follow when looking at customer records in banks.
1974	Privacy Act	Forbids federal agencies from allowing information to be used for a reason other than for which it was collected.
1974	Family Educational Rights and Privacy Act	Gives students and parents access to school records and limits disclosure of records to unauthorized parties.
1970	Fair Credit Reporting Act	Prohibits credit reporting agencies from releasing credit information to unauthorized people and allows consumers to review their own credit records.

Figure 8-22 Summary of the major U.S. government laws concerning privacy.

WEB INFO

To learn more about fair use, visit the Teachers Discovering Computers Web site, click Chapter 8, click Web Info, and then click Fair Use.

includes many other aspects, however, that teachers need to understand. The Copyright Act of 1976 and its numerous amendments apply to all creative works.

A **copyright** means the original author or creator of the work retains ownership of the work and has the exclusive right to reproduce and distribute the creative work. All educators need to understand how copyright laws impact the manner in which they and their students use information created by others. Such an understanding is important because the building blocks of education use the creative works of others: books; videos; newspapers, magazines, and other reference materials; software; and information located on the World Wide Web.

U.S. Copyright Law: Fair Use

(U.S. Code, Title 17, Chapter 1, Section 107)

§ 107. Limitations on exclusive rights: Fair use

Notwithstanding the provisions of sections 106 and 106A, the fair use of a copyrighted work, including such use by reproduction in copies or phonorecords or by any other means specified by that section, for purposes such as criticism, comment, news reporting, teaching (including multiple copies for classroom use), scholarship, or research, is not an infringement of copyright. In determining whether the use made of a work in any particular case is a fair use, the factors to be considered shall include:

(1) the purpose and character of the use, including whether such use is of a commercial nature or is for nonprofit educational purposes;

(2) the nature of the copyrighted work;

(3) the amount and substantiality of the portion used in relation to the copyrighted work as a whole; and

(4) the effect of the use upon the potential market for or value of the copyrighted work.

The fact that a work is unpublished shall not itself bar a finding of fair use if such finding is made upon consideration of all the above factors.

Figure 8-23 The Copyright Act of 1976 provides the structure for copyright law. Section 107 of the U.S. Copyright Law defines Fair Use.

Three areas of copyright directly impact today's classrooms: (1) illegal copying or using copyrighted software programs; (2) fair use laws and their application to the use of both printed copyrighted materials and copyrighted materials accessible on the Internet; and (3) use of copyrighted materials on teacher and student Web pages. The first area (illegal copying or using licensed and copyrighted software) was covered earlier in this chapter; the following sections cover the other two areas of copyright.

FAIR USE The Copyright Act of 1976 established **fair use**, or guidelines that allow educators to use and copy certain copyrighted materials for nonprofit educational purposes. Figure 8-23 shows Section 107 of U.S. Copyright Law, which deals with fair use. Copyright issues are complex and sometimes the laws are vague. School districts thus provide teachers with specific guidelines for using copyrighted materials in their classrooms. Schools can interpret copyright issues differently, so school policies concerning the use of copyrighted materials vary widely. Teachers need to read school policies concerning copyright carefully and understand them.

In addition to providing printed school policies on copyright issues, most schools provide teachers with information and answer questions about copyright issues. For information or answers to questions concerning software copyright issues, teachers should ask their school or district technology coordinator. For all other issues concerning copyright, fair use, and associated school district policies, teachers should speak with their media specialist. Media specialists receive training on copyright issues and deal with them on a daily basis. If in doubt, teachers should contact the creator of the work and ask for written permission to use his or her material.

Fair use guidelines apply to copyrighted materials on the Internet just as they apply to a copyrighted article published in a magazine. Basically, Web sites include two kinds of information: original copyrighted information and information without copyright restriction. Web pages that contain original information generally include a copyright statement on the page; the copyright statement normally contains the copyright symbol, the year, and the creator's name [Figure 8-24].

If a teacher uses copyrighted materials from the Internet, he or she must follow fair use guidelines, school policies, and any restrictions listed on the Web site. If the information located on the Web site does not include copyright restriction, it does not mean the creator is waiving his or her privileges under copyright. To be safe, you should assume everything on the Web is copyrighted, and always follow fair use guidelines and school policies when using Web materials for educational purposes in a classroom. In addition, always give proper credit and use citations if appropriate.

These guidelines do not apply only to text-based materials on the Web. The Web also contains a multitude of graphics, animations, and audio and video files teachers can download and use for educational purposes or classroom presentations. When teachers download and use these materials, they must adhere to fair use guidelines, school policies, and any other restrictions noted on the Web site.

TEACHER AND STUDENT WEB PAGES
Teachers and students in school districts all over the country are creating and publishing their own Web pages [Figure 8-25]. As previously discussed, **Web publishing** is the development and maintenance of Web pages. When developing these pages, teachers and students must take care to respect copyright laws and follow the guidelines outlined in the previous section.

Copyright laws do protect any original materials created by students and teachers and published on the Web. To ensure that this is clear, however, teachers and students may want to include a copyright statement at the bottom of their home page.

The use of copyrighted materials (text, graphics, animations, audio, and video) on teacher or student Web pages requires permission from the creator of the materials. Most Web pages include an

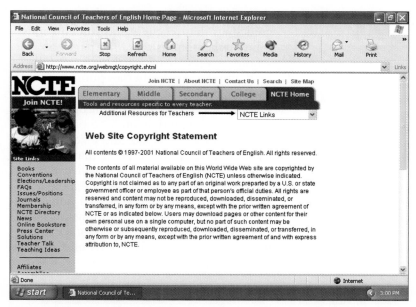

Figure 8-24 This educational Web page has a copyright statement. The copyright statement includes basic copyright information as well as other information.

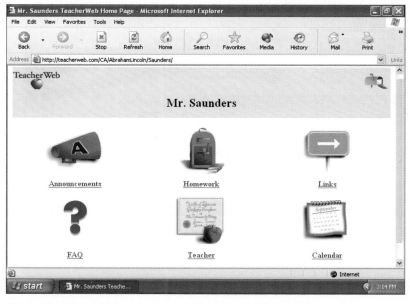

Figure 8-25 Teachers and students in school districts all over the country are creating and publishing their own Web pages.

e-mail link to use when asking for permission to use copyrighted materials. To use the materials on the Web, simply send a short e-mail message to the creator of the work, explaining how you will use his or her work on your Web page. Many authors are more than willing to allow teachers to use their original text or artwork for educational purposes as long as they receive proper credit.

Many school districts have specific guidelines that teachers and students must follow when publishing Web pages on school servers. Teachers should carefully read all school rules before publishing any teacher or student Web pages. Some schools, for example, prohibit using any copyrighted materials on Web pages. In such instances, students and teachers must use only original material or material that is not copyrighted. Teachers generally may use materials from government-sponsored Web sites, which are considered public domain [Figure 8-26]. Anything considered **public domain** — including software or creative works — is free from copyright restrictions.

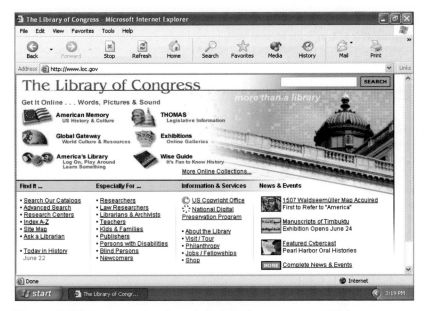

Figure 8-26 An example of a public domain government Web page. Government Web pages usually have a URL that ends in .gov.

Most school districts have access to and purchase copyright-free CDs and DVDs or subscribe to services that contain thousands of clip art images, photos, graphics, and audio and video clips. They make these copyright-free materials available for teachers and students to use on their Web pages and in class presentations and projects [Figure 8-27]. In addition to respecting copyright law, teachers also must consider other issues related to Web page publishing. Teachers, for example, must protect their students from Internet users who might want to harm them.

Figure 8-28 lists some basic guidelines that teachers should consider when creating Web pages.

Figure 8-27 Web Graphics is a popular software package that provides teachers and students with thousands of graphics they can use on their published Web pages.

Finally, a broadly interpreted issue known as intellectual property rights is beginning to play an important role in public education. The major intellectual property rights issue currently being discussed is who owns online content and courses, both in higher and K-12 education. A recent survey found that most institutions of higher education see content as the property of the instructor. More than half also believe that the instructor owns the actual course. Currently, most K-12 districts handle ownership of items such as tests, lesson plans, and other teaching materials as a nonissue. Some districts are beginning to clarify the ownership of online courses.

Internet Ethics and Objectionable Materials

As you already have learned in this chapter, the widespread use of the Internet — especially in today's schools and classrooms — raises many issues regarding security, privacy, and ethics. Of all of these, one issue is of particular concern for teachers and parents: the availability of **objectionable material** on

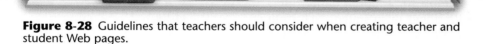

Web Page Guidelines

- Always protect the identity of your students.

- Never list student last names, telephone numbers, home addresses, or e-mail addresses.

- Use only first names of students on a Web site, but never in conjunction with other identifying information, such as a photograph.

- Use caution when including digital pictures of classrooms; avoid pictures that show close-ups of students.

- Never provide links to sites that are not appropriate for K-12 students or educational settings.

- List the function of all linked Web pages. Link only to pages that inform, explain, or teach a concept or curriculum area to students. Beware of linking to Web sites that persuade students.

- Avoid providing links to sites whose primary purpose is selling noneducational products and services, unless relevant to the subject under discussion.

- Avoid linking to Web pages that are not updated on a regular basis.

- Provide links to sites that help you achieve instructional and curriculum goals.

- Avoid discussing controversial issues on your Web site or linking to Web sites that discuss controversial issues, unless these issues are part of your curriculum.

- Carefully read and follow all guidelines and policies that your school district provides.

Figure 8-28 Guidelines that teachers should consider when creating teacher and student Web pages.

WEB INFO

For more information about Web page guidelines, visit the Teachers Discovering Computers Web site, click Chapter 8, click Web Info, and then click Guidelines.

the Internet, including racist literature, obscene pictures and videos, and even gambling.

Teachers and other school personnel must be concerned with three different types of Internet materials that fall under the general term, objectionable material. The first area includes all materials that most people consider pornographic, such as obscene pictures, stories, graphics, articles, cartoons, and videos. The second area includes racist literature, controversial subjects such as gambling, and other similar materials. Teachers and parents usually easily identify Web sites that contain materials in these first two areas.

The third area includes Web sites that contain incorrect material and thus are inappropriate for K-12 students. Identifying this type of Web page is more difficult than identifying the first two. Because anyone may create and publish a Web page or Web site, some people deliberately create and publish materials on Web pages to fool unsuspecting people. Young students are extremely vulnerable to being fooled by these sites. These Web sites appear perfectly appropriate for K-12 students, but contain information that is historically and otherwise inaccurate. An elementary student may not know the difference between a site that is historically

inaccurate about America's founding fathers and an educational site that is accurate.

Before the explosive growth of the Internet, it was difficult for most K-12 students to obtain and view objectionable materials, such as pornographic magazines. Today, anybody with Internet access may view a vast array of obscene and other inappropriate materials on the Web. Many people want to ban such materials from the Internet, while others would only restrict objectionable materials so they are not available to minors. Opponents argue that banning any material violates the constitutional right of free speech. Opponents state that instead of limiting Internet access and materials, schools should teach students right from wrong.

RECENT GOVERNMENT ACTIONS

Two recent government actions will help protect children from being exploited while on the Internet: the Dot Kits Implementation and Efficiency Act and the Children's Internet Protection Act.

DOT KIDS IMPLEMENTATION AND

EFFICIENCY ACT President George W. Bush signed the Dot Kids Implementation and Efficiency Act on December 4, 2002. **Dot Kids** is part of the U.S. domain on the Internet and functions much like the children's section of a public library with content suitable for children under thirteen. As President Bush stated, "This bill is a wise and necessary step to safeguard our children while they use computers and discover the great possibilities of the Internet. Every site designated .kids will be a safe zone for children. The sites will be monitored for content, safety, and all objectionable materials will be removed. Online chat rooms and instant messaging will be prohibited, unless they can be certified as safe. The Web sites under this new domain will not connect a child to other online sites outside the child-friendly zone." The administrators of the domain also will work with the U.S. Department of Justice and other federal agencies to prevent children using Dot Kids from being targeted by predators.

WEB INFO

To access the Dot Kids Web site, visit the Teachers Discovering Computers Web site, click Chapter 8, click Web Info, and then click Dot Kids.

CHILDREN'S INTERNET PROTECTION ACT

Congress passed the **Children's Internet Protection Act (CIPA)** in 2000 to protect children from obscene, pornographic, and other information considered harmful to minors. CIPA requires that public libraries install filtering software to block Web sites that contain obscene images or content. As you learned in Chapter 2, filtering software programs prevent browsers from displaying materials from targeted sites or sites that contain certain keywords or phrases. The act was challenged by opponents who argued that this law would obstruct appropriate, nonobscene material from being viewed. In July 2003, the U.S. Supreme Court upheld CIPA, arguing that it does not violate freedom of speech. As a result, all public libraries must install filters on their computers to block access to online pornography or lose federal funding.

Many K-12 schools and parents have taken proactive steps to protect their students and children from the negative aspects of the Internet. While only a small percentage of the information available on the Internet is unsuitable for children at home or in K-12 schools, educators agree that such materials have no place in our classrooms. Teachers and parents need to ensure that children understand that inappropriate materials exist on the Internet, and some individuals may try to exploit them via e-mail messages or in chat room conversations.

PARENTAL CONTROLS

Parents may take a number of steps to prevent children from accessing pornographic and other objectionable materials on the Internet. First, parents need to ensure that their children understand that some Internet sites contain objectionable materials, and that some people who use the Internet would like to harm them.

One approach to restricting access to certain material uses a rating system similar to those used for videos, movies, and television shows. The rating system is understood by your Web browser, which allows you to set limits on the types of material available for viewing

[Figure 8-29]. If content at the Web site goes beyond the rating limitations you set in the Web browser, the site will not display. You prevent the rating limitations from being changed by using a password.

A more effective approach to blocking objectionable materials is for parents to install filtering software programs on any computer with Internet access. Many filtering software programs allow parents to filter harmful Web sites, restrict Internet access, monitor their children's online activities, and prevent their children from accidentally providing personal information in e-mail messages or in chat rooms [Figure 8-30].

Many Internet service providers also provide software that allows users to control the content their Web browser will display. America Online, for example, allows home users to establish different accounts for adults and children. When a user logs on using the child's account, only appropriate pages will display. Parents also can specify various settings, blocks, and access options for their child's account; for example, parents can control who can send their children instant messages. In addition, many Internet security programs that provide firewall and antivirus protection also include Web filtering capabilities [Figure 8-31].

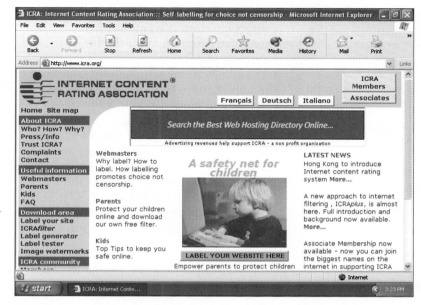

Figure 8-29 Many Web browsers use the ratings of the Internet Content Rating Association (ICRA), which indicate rating levels for material unsuitable for minors.

Figure 8-30 Net Nanny is a popular Internet filtering software program that provides parents with numerous options for protecting their kids as they surf the Web.

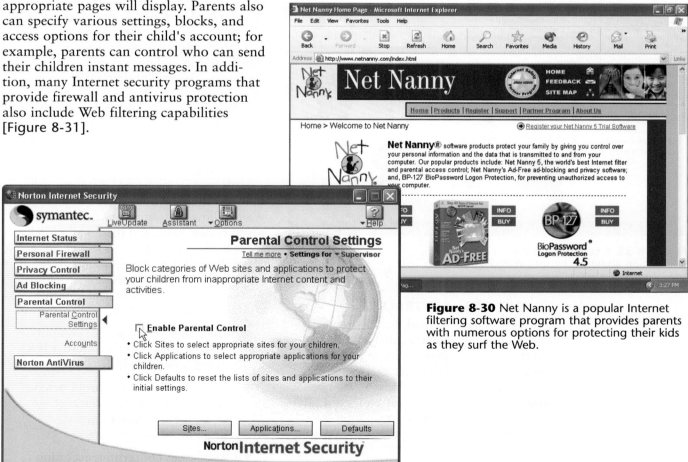

Figure 8-31 Many Internet security programs include content filtering capabilities, by which parents can block Web sites and applications.

Finally, the best way for parents to protect children is to monitor their children's activities while on the Internet both by direct and indirect observations. One technique is to keep the family computer in the family room or in an area where you can observe your children while they are working on the computer.

Because it is difficult always to monitor or observe children's Internet activities directly, you can check which Internet sites children are visiting by viewing the browser's history list [Figure 8-32]. This simple but effective technique is useless, however, if children are allowed to clear the history list.

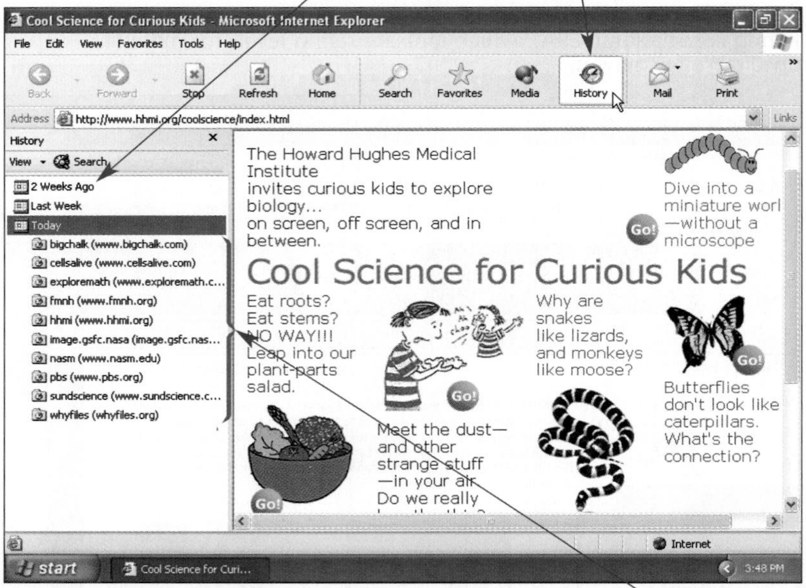

previously accessed Web sites   History button

Figure 8-32 A browser's history list records information about all the sites visited for a predetermined period.

Web sites accessed Today

EDUCATIONAL CONTROLS

As you have learned, businesses and parents have several available options to control access to inappropriate Internet sites. Most school districts also control student access to objectionable materials by implementing these controls and a few additional ones. For schools, attacking this problem requires a four-pronged approach: filtering software, Acceptable Use Policies, use of curriculum pages, and teacher observation. All four prongs of the approach are discussed in the following sections.

FILTERING SOFTWARE As previously discussed, **filtering software programs** prevent the browser from accepting material from targeted sites or material that contains keywords or phrases. Schools install Internet filtering software on their networks and then constantly update the software programs to keep them as current as possible. While very effective, these filtering software programs do not prevent access to all objectionable and inappropriate materials. One drawback to using filtering software is that it also can block access to legitimate materials or research on controversial issues. A filtering software program is the first level of protection that many school districts use.

ACCEPTABLE USE POLICIES Recognizing that teachers, students, administrators, and staff personnel need guidance, most schools develop specific standards for the ethical use of computers, school networks, and the Internet. These standards are called Acceptable Use Policies. As discussed in Chapter 1, an **Acceptable Use Policy (AUP)** is a set of rules that governs the use of school and school district computers, networks, and the Internet by teachers, administrators, staff, and students.

Acceptable Use Policies vary greatly from school district to school district. Many schools have separate AUPs for students, teachers, and staff personnel. Many school districts require both students and their parents to sign student AUPs. Some schools publish student AUPs on their Web sites, which allows new students and parents to print, review, sign, and then mail or deliver them to the school [Figure 8-33]. Schools normally will not allow students or teachers to access the school's network or Internet unless a signed AUP is on file. Many AUPs contain the following guidelines:

- Notice that use of school computers, networks, and the Internet is a privilege, not a right

- Notice that students should behave as guests when on the Internet — that is, they should use good manners and be courteous

- List of rules concerning accessing objectionable Internet sites

- List of rules dealing with copyright issues

- Outline of proper use of all networks and computers

- List of rules covering online safety and release of personal information

- Notice that students who violate AUPs will face disciplinary action and possible permanent cancellation of school network and/or Internet access privileges

CURRICULUM PAGES As you learned in Chapter 7, a **curriculum page** is a teacher-created document or Web page that contains hyperlinks to teacher selected and evaluated Web sites that support learning objectives by providing students with quality Web resources, links to additional information, and opportunities to learn more. Using a curriculum page offers several advantages. Students quickly link to excellent sites, instead of the various locations they may find from searching the Internet for information. Because the teacher evaluates the linked sites for content and appropriateness before posting them, a curriculum page significantly reduces the chance students will view an inappropriate site. Furthermore, by providing links for students to click, a curriculum page eliminates the need for students to type URLs. Students often make mistakes typing URLs, which, in addition to wasting time, sometimes links them to inappropriate or incorrect sites.

TEACHER OBSERVATION Teacher **observation** or supervision permits teachers to monitor their students actively and continuously while they are on the Internet [Figure 8-34]. Teacher observation is extremely important and, in most cases, a final measure to prevent students from accessing objectionable and inappropriate materials on the Internet. For teacher observation to be effective, teachers must constantly and actively watch what their students are doing in the classroom and viewing on the Internet. Teachers should direct students that, if they access an Internet site that contains objectionable material, they should immediately click their browser's Back button to return to

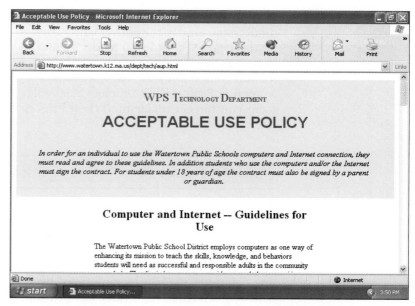

Figure 8-33 Many schools include AUPs on their Web sites so new teachers, students, and parents can print and review, sign, and then mail or deliver them to the school.

the previous page and if this does not work simply close the browser. Either is a quick-and-easy way to prevent objectionable material from displaying in the browser. You also may want students to notify you if such a situation arises, so that you may add that site to the sites restricted by the filtering software. Some schools have installed software programs on their lab computers, such as Apple's Remote Desktop for Macintosh computers, which enables teachers to keep an eye on all the computer screens in a classroom or lab.

Figure 8-34 Teacher observations can prevent students from viewing objectionable or inappropriate material on the Internet.

As a final note, all educators should understand clearly the ethical issues covered in this chapter in order to model these concepts for their students and teach them to be ethical computer users. The questionnaire shown in **Figure 8-38** on page 8.30 will help you further understand these ethical concepts.

Health Issues

Users are a key component in any information system. Thus, protecting teachers and students is just as important as protecting hardware, software, and data. Many health-related issues concerning computer use can be minimized by teaching students at an early age how to use computers properly so they reduce their risk of injury. The following sections discuss health risks and preventions.

COMPUTERS AND HEALTH ISSUES

The Bureau of Labor Statistics reports that work-related musculoskeletal disorders account for one-third of all job-related injuries and illnesses. A **musculoskeletal disorder (MSD)**, also called a **repetitive strain injury (RSI)**, is an injury or disorder of the muscles, nerves, tendons, ligaments, and joints. Computer-related RSIs include tendonitis and carpal tunnel syndrome. The largest job-related injury and illness problems in the United States today are repetitive strain injuries. For this reason, the Occupational Safety and Health Administration (OSHA) has developed industry-specific and task-specific guidelines designed to prevent workplace injuries with respect to computer usage.

Tendonitis is inflammation of a tendon due to some repeated motion or stress on the tendon. **Carpal tunnel syndrome (CTS)** is inflammation of the nerve that connects the forearm to the palm of the wrist. Repeated or forceful bending of the wrist can cause CTS or tendonitis of the wrist. Symptoms of tendonitis of the wrist include extreme pain that extends from the forearm to the hand, along with tingling in the fingers. Symptoms of CTS include burning pain when the nerve is com-

pressed, along with numbness and tingling in the thumb and first two fingers.

Long-term computer use can lead to tendonitis or CTS. Factors that cause these disorders include prolonged typing and mouse usage, or continual shifting between the mouse and the keyboard.

You can take many precautions to prevent these types of injuries both for yourself and your students. Take frequent breaks during computer sessions to exercise your hands and arms [Figure 8-35]. To prevent injury due to typing, place a wrist rest between the keyboard and the edge of your desk. The wrist rest reduces strain on your wrist while typing. To prevent injury while using a mouse, place the mouse at least six inches from the edge of the desk. Finally, minimize the number of times you switch between the mouse and the keyboard, and avoid using the heel of your hand as a pivot point while typing or using the mouse.

HAND EXERCISES

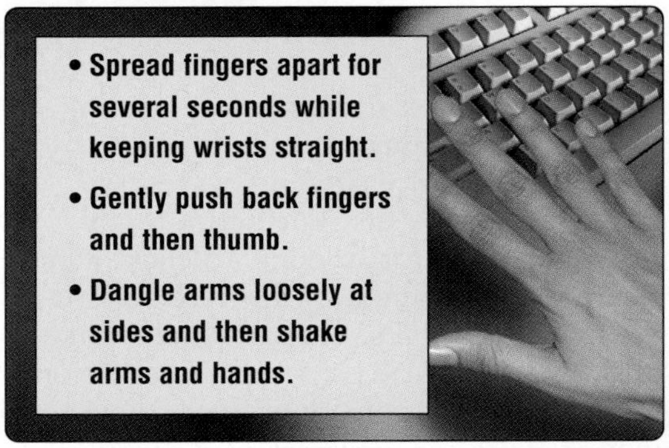

- Spread fingers apart for several seconds while keeping wrists straight.
- Gently push back fingers and then thumb.
- Dangle arms loosely at sides and then shake arms and hands.

FIGURE 8-35 To reduce the chance of developing tendonitis or carpal tunnel syndrome, take frequent breaks during computer sessions to exercise your hands and arms.

Another type of health-related condition due to computer usage is **computer vision syndrome (CVS)**. You may have CVS if you have any of these conditions: sore, tired, burning, itching, or dry eyes; blurred or double vision; distance blurred vision after prolonged staring at a display device; headache or sore neck; difficulty shifting focus between a display device and documents; difficult focusing on the screen image; color fringes or after-images when you look away from the display device; and increasing sensitivity to light. Although eyestrain associated with CVS is not thought to have serious or long-term consequences, it is disruptive and unpleasant. Figure 8-36 outlines some techniques you can follow to ease eyestrain.

TECHNIQUES TO EASE EYESTRAIN

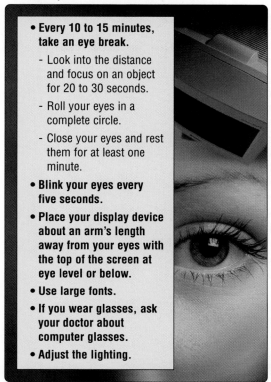

- **Every 10 to 15 minutes, take an eye break.**
  - Look into the distance and focus on an object for 20 to 30 seconds.
  - Roll your eyes in a complete circle.
  - Close your eyes and rest them for at least one minute.
- **Blink your eyes every five seconds.**
- **Place your display device about an arm's length away from your eyes with the top of the screen at eye level or below.**
- **Use large fonts.**
- **If you wear glasses, ask your doctor about computer glasses.**
- **Adjust the lighting.**

FIGURE 8-36 Following these tips may help reduce eyestrain while working on the computer.

People who spend their workday using the computer sometimes complain of lower back pain, muscle fatigue, and emotional fatigue. Lower back pain sometimes is caused by poor posture. Always sit and have your students sit properly in the chair. Take a short break every 30 to 60 minutes — stand up, walk around, or stretch.

ERGONOMICS

Ergonomics is an applied science devoted to incorporating comfort, efficiency, and safety into the design of items in the workplace. Ergonomic studies have shown that using the correct type and configuration of chair, keyboard, display device, and work surface helps users work comfortably and efficiently, and helps protect their health [Figure 8-37].

Many display devices and keyboards have features that help address ergonomic issues. Some keyboards have built-in wrist rests and can be purchased from any computer supply store. Other keyboards have an ergonomic design specifically to prevent RSI. Display devices usually have controls that allow you to adjust the brightness, contrast, positioning, height, and width of images. Most monitors have a tilt-and-swivel base, allowing you to adjust the angle of the screen to minimize neck strain and reduce glare from overhead lighting.

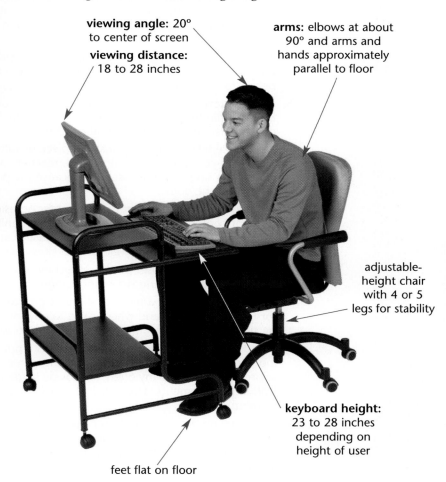

viewing angle: 20° to center of screen

viewing distance: 18 to 28 inches

arms: elbows at about 90° and arms and hands approximately parallel to floor

adjustable-height chair with 4 or 5 legs for stability

keyboard height: 23 to 28 inches depending on height of user

feet flat on floor

FIGURE 8-37 A well-designed work area should be flexible to allow adjustments to the height and build of different individuals. Good lighting and air quality also are important considerations.

COMPUTER ETHICS QUESTIONNAIRE

	Ethical	Unethical	Crime
1. A teacher uses her computer at school to send e-mail to her friends and family.	☐	☐	☐
2. A teacher uses the Web at school to access stock market reports. So that he can periodically check the market, he leaves the Web connection running in the background all day.	☐	☐	☐
3. A principal installs a new version of a word processing program on her office computer. Because no one will be using the old version of the program, she takes it home and installs it on her home computer so her husband and children can use it.	☐	☐	☐
4. While checking teachers' e-mail messages, the principal finds that one of his teachers is using the district's e-mail system to bet on football games.	☐	☐	☐
5. A school technology facilitator has his students develop HyperStudio tutorials. When the projects are completed, he offers to sell the tutorials to another school.	☐	☐	☐
6. A principal tells a teacher to install a piece of software on numerous computers on campus. The teacher knows the software has a single-user license, but because the principal said to install it, he does.	☐	☐	☐
7. Personnel in the district's computer center occasionally monitor computer use in the schools. They monitor how often and for what lengths of time particular teachers are connected to the Internet, as well as what sites have been visited.	☐	☐	☐
8. The media specialist uses photo retouching software to put her school name on another school's logo.	☐	☐	☐
9. A teacher downloads a piece of shareware software. He uses it for the allotted time and when asked to pay for the software, he simply closes the window and continues to use it.	☐	☐	☐
10. An educational learning company contacts a principal requesting information about students, including names and addresses. The company offers to provide students with free learning supplements. The principal sends the company her student database.	☐	☐	☐
11. Your students are creating Web pages of their own. They search the Internet for ideas. One of them finds a very cool home page and decides to copy the page, change the name, and use it.	☐	☐	☐
12. You are doing a unit on famous cartoon characters and go to the Disney Web site to get clip art for your curriculum page.	☐	☐	☐

Figure 8-38 Indicate whether you think each described situation is ethical, unethical, or a crime. Discuss your answers with other teachers as well as your students.

Emerging Technologies

The classrooms and schools you attended throughout your 12 years of K-12 education probably were similar to the classrooms in which your parents sat — for some of you, the schools and furniture were exactly the same. More importantly, your educational experience and the educational experiences of your parents also probably were very similar. Unlike society, which has dramatically changed, many schools and school curriculum have been slow to change during the past few decades.

Fortunately, the infusion of modern multimedia computers, high-speed networks and Internet access, higher-quality educational software, and a realization by administrators that teachers must receive extensive and appropriate technology training is beginning to transform many classrooms. In some cases, the transformation is remarkable.

Due to the infusion of informational technologies and the World Wide Web, teachers no longer are bound by the four walls of traditional classrooms and the two covers of traditional textbooks [Figure 8-39]. Furthermore, technology has helped a number of schools significantly improve the quality of their graduates.

Because of the strong commitment of federal, state, and local governments, thousands of organizations dedicated to improving education, and millions of concerned parents, the infusion of computer technologies into schools will continue — and continue explosively. Technology has only begun to influence the way teachers instruct and students learn. The following sections summarize six emerging areas of educational technology that will continue to influence significantly the public education system: the World Wide Web, the next generation of software on DVDs, assistive technologies, Web-enhanced textbooks, Web-based distance learning, and wireless technologies.

[a]

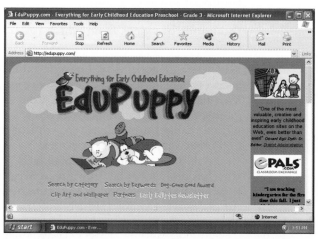

[b]

[c]

Figure 8-39 The Web has enormous potential to change the way teachers instruct and students learn due to the vast amount of current and education-related information available at thousands of Web sites.

THE WORLD WIDE WEB

The federal government is committed to ensuring that every K-12 classroom has high-speed Internet access and is investing billions of dollars to meet the goal. The following specific Internet improvements will directly influence the quality of the K-12 educational experience:

- The speed of the Internet will increase dramatically.

- Students will be able to access full-motion videos on demand. Streaming video technology will allow teachers to bring live video footage of current and historical events into their classrooms, simply by clicking a video link. Teachers and students will have thousands of videos from which to choose.

- Teachers and students will have instant access to tens of thousands of interactive Web-based educational software programs, including tutorials, exercises, virtual-reality tours, science experiments, and other subject-related activities. Many of these online educational software programs will be fully interactive, thus opening up incredible opportunities for discovery learning [Figure 8-40].

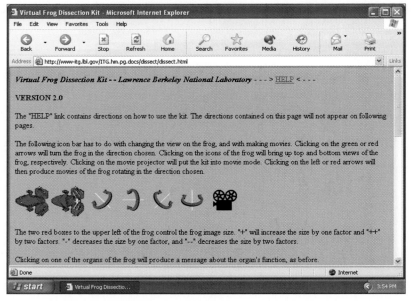

Figure 8-40 Many educational Web sites are offering students and teachers opportunities to explore education topics interactively. This Web site, for example, allows students to dissect a frog, just as if they were in a school biology lab.

EDUCATIONAL SOFTWARE ON DVD

During the last ten years, the influx of multimedia computers with CD-ROM drives and the availability of hundreds of high-quality CD-based educational software programs impacted education significantly.

During the next five years, the availability of DVD-based education software programs will have an even greater impact on education. The huge storage capacity of DVDs will allow educational software developers to build programs that contain vast amounts of information, graphics, animations, video, and interactive links. These next-generation educational software programs on DVDs will include hours of high-quality full-motion video that teachers and students may access instantly.

ASSISTIVE TECHNOLOGIES

Dramatic improvements are being made in hardware, software, and Web-based tools that teachers will use to help instruct students with special needs. As you learned earlier, **assistive technologies** are innovative technologies that modify or adapt the classroom for special learning needs. Assistive technologies aid in teaching students who have physical, sensory, or cognitive disabilities. Emerging assistive technologies will provide teachers with innovative tools to help students with special needs overcome the disability that blocks or impedes their learning process.

Nationwide, funding for assistive technologies is increasing significantly. Teacher education programs and K-12 schools are placing more emphasis on assistive technologies, due to the number of students with disabilities who are mainstreamed into regular classrooms. According to the Individuals with Disabilities Education Act (IDEA) Amendments of 1997, regular classroom teachers must be part of the cross-curriculum and interdisciplinary team that teaches all students. Technology is the bridge that provides new strategies for all students to learn and succeed [Figure 8-41].

In addition, many leaders express concern that current technologies are widening the gap between the economic haves and have-nots. Federal funding, private funding, and emerging technologies will help slow this crisis facing America. Schools will be provided funding and guidance to ensure that at-risk students have equal access to current and emerging technologies.

Figure 8-41 Technology can be the bridge that provides new strategies for all students to learn and succeed, including students with physical and other challenges.

FEDERAL ACCESSIBILITY INITIATIVE

In 1998, Congress amended the Rehabilitation Act to require federal agencies to make their electronic and information technology accessible to people with disabilities. Under **Section 508**, agencies must give employees with disabilities and members of the public access to technology that is comparable to the access available to others. The law applies to all federal agencies when they develop, procure, maintain, or use electronic and information technology.

Education agencies can verify easily that their Web sites and pages meet Section 508 requirements by using Bobby. **Bobby** is a software program that analyzes Web sites and pages to see if they meet the World Wide Web Consortium's (W3C) Web content Accessibilities Guidelines. For example, for a Web site to be Bobby approved, it must (partial list):

- Provide text equivalents for all nontext elements (such as images, animations, video, and audio)

- Provide summaries of graphs and charts

- Ensure that all information displayed in color also is available without color

Bobby is a free software program, created by the Center for Applied Special Technology (CAST) and allows Web authors to identify needed changes to their pages so users with disabilities can more easily use their Web pages. Using Bobby is simple; Web authors enter their URL and Bobby will analyze their Web site for compliance [Figure 8-42].

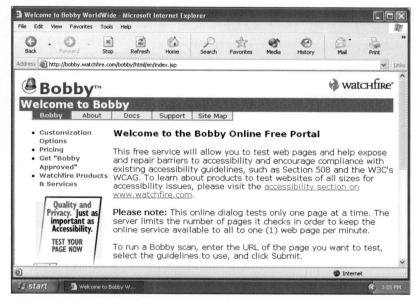

Figure 8-42 Bobby allows Web authors to check their sites to ensure that the sites meet accessibility guidelines.

WEB-ENHANCED TEXTBOOKS

For many years, K-12 textbooks remained basically unchanged. Recently, however, this began to change as the Web became an integral part of K-12 books. Traditional textbooks will fade into history as all areas of education create increasingly interactive and extensive Web-enhanced textbooks. Many of these books will correlate to national and state curriculum standards and benchmarks.

Imagine teaching social studies, biology, or English literature using a Web-enhanced textbook with an extensive Web site that continuously is updated and maintained by a team of experienced educators and provides students with discovery learning avenues and information about thousands of topics from thousands of sources all over the world. These exciting and interactive Web-enhanced textbooks

WEB INFO

To see an example of a Web-enhanced science textbook, visit the Teachers Discovering Computers Web site, click Chapter 8, click Web Info, and then click Textbook.

will crumble the concrete and brick walls of traditional classrooms and remove the covers of traditional textbooks.

WEB-BASED DISTANCE LEARNING

Due to the increasingly diverse population of students, education is changing in an effort to meet the needs of this diverse and changing student body. These changes bring the Web to the forefront of instructional strategies in education — specifically, the use of Web-based distance learning.

Web-based distance learning already has experienced phenomenal growth in institutions of higher education and K-12 schools. The more common approach for schools to take, however, is to use the Web to enhance classes and instruction.

These Web-based teaching strategies are new and will continue to evolve for many years. Web-based strategies offer creative solutions for homebound students, home-schooled students, at-risk students, students who are physically challenged, and shortages of teachers for specialized positions. Because many small or rural schools cannot offer students courses such as Latin and French, or advanced-placement courses in math and science, states and school districts now offer students these specialized courses using the Web. Depending on the situation

and school district policies, students take these Web-based courses at home, at a public library, or in a classroom — Internet access is the common agent for this remote instruction. For example, Florida Virtual School provides online classes and instruction to all public, private, and home-school students in Florida and other states [Figure 8-43].

A WORLD WITHOUT WIRES

The last decade of the twentieth century was dominated by the evolution of the World Wide Web. While it seems certain that the Web will continue to evolve and mature, it is clear that the first decade of the twenty-first century is being dominated by the wireless revolution that is taking place globally. Today's wireless technology represents an evolution in products and services that quickly is transforming the way people live, work, learn, and teach. Wireless technology will continue to impact our K-20 education system dramatically in the following ways:

■ Wireless communications will allow teachers and students to connect their smart phones, PDAs, notebook computers, Tablet PCs, and other wireless devices to a truly global high-speed network.

To learn more about a Web-enhanced high-school class, visit the Teachers Discovering Computers Web site, click Chapter 8, click Web Info, and then click Class.

Figure 8-43 The Florida Virtual School opened in 1997 as a two-county initiative. Today, more than 15,000 high school students from all 67 Florida county school districts, charter and private schools, and other states enroll in more than 75 classes every year.

- Wireless desktop computers, Tablet PCs, mobile labs, and other devices will ensure that educational technology is used seamlessly at the point of instruction.

- Global wireless access will ensure that all children, regardless of their socio-economic status, will have access to educational classroom materials and the world itself from their homes, their schools, and many other locations throughout their communities.

Wireless technologies already have changed the way you communicate with relatives, colleagues, and friends. Indeed, you are taking part in the wireless revolution that is sweeping the world and is just beginning to change and influence the way we teach and learn in our schools.

To learn more about the wireless revolution and how it will impact you, your students, and your family, review the special feature, A World Without Wires, that follows this chapter.

Summary of Security Issues, Ethics, and Emerging Technologies in Education

The livelihood of businesses, schools, and individuals depends on the computers and networks in use every day. This increased reliance on computers and information sent over networks makes it essential to take steps to protect the systems and information from known risks. At the same time, employees, teachers, and students also have an obligation to use computers responsibly and not abuse the power computers provide. This responsibility presents constant challenges, which sometimes weigh the rights of the individual against increased efficiency and productivity. Schools have the added responsibility and challenge of protecting their students from unethical practices and people.

Educational technologies are the tools whose effectiveness is determined by the knowledge, skill, experience, level of training, and ethics of the user. The educational technology knowledge you acquire should help you be better able to participate in decisions on how to use computers and other educational technologies, and using the Internet efficiently and ethically.

Summary of Teachers Discovering Computers

To be effective in using educational technology in their classrooms, teachers must be computer literate, information literate, and most importantly, integration literate. This textbook provided you with knowledge and skills in all three areas. What you have learned is only a beginning.

Teachers must continuously update their technology and technology integration skills. Teachers have an incredible responsibility — a far greater responsibility than any previous generation of teachers. The amount of knowledge that teachers must instill in their students is enormous and continues to expand at a phenomenal rate. To continue to prosper in the 21st century, educational institutions must provide students with a solid foundation of the basic skills and other core subjects. Used as instructional and productivity tools, current and emerging technologies help teachers make a difference in the quality of their students. Teachers can use and integrate technology to influence future generations in immensely positive ways. The possibilities really are limitless [Figure 8-44].

Figure 8-44 Teachers make a difference in the quality of their students' education when they integrate technology effectively.

In Brief

Web Instructions: To display this page from the Web, start your browser and enter the URL, wwwcourse.com/tdc3. Click Chapter 8 at the top of the Web page and then click In Brief on the left sidebar. Click the links for current and additional information. To listen to an audio version of this In Brief, click the Audio button at the top left of these instructions.

WEB INFO

IN BRIEF

KEY TERMS

CHECKPOINT

TEACHING TODAY

EDUCATION ISSUES

INTEGRATION CORNER

SOFTWARE CORNER

IN THE LAB

LEARN IT ONLINE

✱FEATURES...

Timeline 2004

Guide to WWW Sites

Buyer's Guide 2004

Professional Sites

State/Federal Sites

Interactive Labs

Search Tools

HOME

1. Computer Security Risks

A **computer security risk is** any event or action that can cause a loss of or damage to computer equipment, software, data and information, or processing capability. A **computer crime** is any illegal act involving a computer.

2. Computer Viruses

A **virus** is designed to affect computers negatively by altering the way they work. Many viruses are designed to destroy or corrupt data. A **boot sector virus** replaces the boot program used to start the computer with a modified, infected version of the boot program. A **file virus** inserts virus code into program files. A **macro virus** uses the macro language of an application to hide virus codes. Two common variations of computer viruses, often called **malicious software programs,** are worms and Trojan horses.

3. Virus Detection and Removal

Antivirus programs are designed to detect, disinfect, and protect computers and networks from viruses. Antivirus programs work by looking for programs that attempt to modify the boot program, the operating system, and other programs that normally are read from but not written to. Most antivirus programs also have utilities to remove or repair infected programs and files.

4. Unauthorized Access and Use

Unauthorized access is the use of a computer or network without permission. The term, **cracker** or **hacker,** refers to a person who tries to break into a computer often with the intent of stealing or corrupting its data. **Unauthorized use** is the use of a computer or data for unapproved or possibly illegal activities. Unauthorized access is prevented by establishing **access controls**, which are security measures that define who may access a computer or information.

5. Theft

Common sense and a constant awareness of the risks are the best preventive measures against theft of notebook computers and other portable equipment. **Software piracy** is the unauthorized and illegal duplication of copyrighted software. Software piracy is a violation of copyright law and is a federal crime. A **software license** is an agreement that provides specific conditions for use of the software, which users must accept before using the software.

6. System Failure

A **system failure** is a computer malfunction. System failures occur because of electrical power problems, hardware component failure, or a software error. An **undervoltage** occurs when the electrical power supply drops. An **overvoltage**, or **power surge**, occurs when the incoming electrical power increases significantly above the normal 120 volts. A **surge protector** keeps an overvoltage from damaging computer equipment.

7. Copyright Laws

The Copyright Act of 1976 applies to all creative works. A **copyright** means the original author or creator of the work retains exclusive ownership of the work. **Fair use** guidelines allow educators to use and copy certain copyrighted materials for nonprofit educational purposes.

In Brief 8

WEB INFO

IN BRIEF

KEY TERMS

CHECKPOINT

TEACHING TODAY

EDUCATION ISSUES

INTEGRATION CORNER

SOFTWARE CORNER

IN THE LAB

LEARN IT ONLINE

✴ FEATURES...

Timeline 2004

Guide to WWW Sites

Buyer's Guide 2004

Professional Sites

State/Federal Sites

Interactive Labs

Search Tools

HOME

8. Internet Ethics

Objectionable materials on the Internet include racist literature and obscene pictures and videos. <u>Computer ethics</u> are the moral guidelines that govern the use of computers, networks, and information systems. **Filtering software programs** prevent browsers from displaying materials from targeted sites or materials that contain certain keywords or phrases.

9. Educational Controls

<u>Controls</u> to prevent student access to inappropriate Internet sites include filtering software, Acceptable Use Policies, use of curriculum pages, and teacher observation. An **Acceptable Use Policy (AUP)** is a set of rules that governs the use of school and school district computers, networks, and the Internet. A **curriculum page** is a teacher-created document or Web page that contains links to teacher chosen and evaluated Web sites that match curriculum goals. **Teacher observation** involves teachers monitoring their students actively and continuously while they are on the Internet.

10. Health Issues

A **repetitive strain injury (RSI)** is an injury or disorder of the muscles, nerves, tendons, ligaments, and joints. Common RSIs include tendonitis and <u>carpal tunnel syndrome</u>. **Tendonitis** is the inflammation of a tendon due to repeated motion or stress on the tendon. **Carpal tunnel syndrome (CTS)** is the inflammation of the nerve that connects the forearm to the palm of the hand. **Ergonomics** is an applied science devoted to incorporating comfort, efficiency, and safety into the design of items in the workplace.

11. Emerging Technologies

Emerging educational technologies that will influence public education significantly include the World Wide Web, the next generation of software on DVDs, <u>assistive technologies</u>, Web-enhanced textbooks, Web-based training, and wireless technologies.

Key Terms

Web Instructions: To display this page from the Web, start your browser and enter the URL, wwwcourse.com/tdc3. Click Chapter 8 at the top of the Web page and then click Key Terms on the left sidebar. Scroll through the list of terms. Click a term to display its definition and a picture. Click Key Terms on the left to redisplay the Key Terms page. Click the TO WEB button for current and additional information about the term from the Web.

WEB INFO

IN BRIEF

KEY TERMS

CHECKPOINT

TEACHING TODAY

EDUCATION ISSUES

INTEGRATION CORNER

SOFTWARE CORNER

IN THE LAB

LEARN IT ONLINE

＊FEATURES...

Timeline 2004

Guide to WWW Sites

Buyer's Guide 2004

Professional Sites

State/Federal Sites

Interactive Labs

Search Tools

HOME

Acceptable Use Policy (AUP) [8.26]
access controls [8.07]
anti-spam program [8.18]
antivirus program [8.06]
assistive technologies [8.32]

backup [8.15]
backup procedure [8.15]
blackout [8.14]
Bobby [8.33]
boot sector virus [8.03]
brownout [8.14]

carpal tunnel syndrome (CTS) [8.28]
Children's Internet Protection Act (CIPA) [8.24]
community site license [8.12]
computer crime [8.02]
computer ethics [8.16]
computer security risk [8.02]
computer vandalism [8.10]
computer vision syndrome (CVS) [8.28]
copyright [8.20]
cracker [8.07]
curriculum page [8.27]

Dot Kids [8.24]

electronic profile [8.16]
e-mail filtering [8.18]
employee monitoring [8.18]
encryption [8.13]
encryption key [8.13]

end-user license agreement (EULA) [8.10]
ergonomics [8.29]
ethics [8.16]

fair use [8.20]
file virus [8.03]
filtering software programs [8.26]
firewall [8.08]
freeware [8.12]

hacker [8.07]

information privacy [8.16]

logic bomb [8.05]

macro virus [8.03]
malicious software programs [8.03]
Michelangelo virus [8.05]
musculoskeletal disorder (MSD) [8.28]

network site license [8.12]

objectionable material [8.22]
offsite location [8.15]
overvoltage [8.14]

password [8.07]
personal firewall [8.08]
power surge [8.14]
product activation [8.11]
proxy server [8.09]
public domain [8.22]

repetitive strain injury (RSI) [8.28]
rescue disk [8.06]
restore [8.15]

Section 508 [8.33]
shareware [8.12]
single-user license agreement [8.10]
site license [8.12]
software license [8.10]
software piracy [8.10]
spam [8.17]
spike [8.14]
surge protector [8.14]
system failure [8.13]

teacher observation [8.27]
tendonitis [8.28]
time bomb [8.05]
Trojan horse [8.03]

unauthorized access [8.07]
unauthorized use [8.07]
undervoltage [8.14]
uninterruptible power supply (UPS) [8.14]
user ID [8.07]

vaccines [8.06)
virus [8.02]
virus hoaxes [8.07]
virus payload [8.02]

Web publishing [8.21]
worm [8.03]

Checkpoint

Web Instructions: To display this page from the Web, start your browser and enter the URL, www.course.com/tdc3. Click Chapter 8 at the top of the Web page and then click Checkpoint on the left sidebar. Click a blank line for the answer. Click the links for current and additional information.

WEB INFO

IN BRIEF

KEY TERMS

CHECKPOINT

TEACHING TODAY

EDUCATION ISSUES

INTEGRATION CORNER

SOFTWARE CORNER

IN THE LAB

LEARN IT ONLINE

★ FEATURES...

Timeline 2004

Guide to WWW Sites

Buyer's Guide 2004

Professional Sites

State/Federal Sites

Interactive Labs

Search Tools

HOME

1. Label the Figure

Instructions: Identify each type of software license.

Type of License	Characteristics	Use in Schools
1._____	Can be installed on only one computer.	Used when a school needs only a few copies of a particular software. Commonly found in small schools and when purchasing specialized software programs.
2._____	Software can be installed on a set number of computers, typically 5, 10, 50, or more.	Cost-effective method to install software on more than one computer. Most commonly used in schools.
3._____	Software is installed on the school's network. The license will specify and the software will control a specific number of simultaneous users, such as 50, 100, 250, or 500.	Cost-effective method of allowing students and teachers throughout the school to have access to an application software program. As schools continue to install networks, network licenses are becoming very common.
4._____ _____	Frequently used with software distributed on CDs/DVDs. Any number of programs can be purchased for either Macintosh or PC platforms.	Very cost-effective method for schools to purchase large quantities of software. Savings can be significant over individual CD or DVD pricing.

2. Matching

Instructions: Match each term from the column on the left with the best description from the column on the right.

____ 1. filtering software
____ 2. curriculum page
____ 3. Trojan horse
____ 4. Web publishing
____ 5. computer ethics

a. teacher-created Web page that contains links to teacher chosen and evaluated Web sites

b. moral guidelines that govern the use of computers, networks, and information systems

c. prevents browser from displaying materials from certain Web sites

d. a virus designed to look like a legitimate program

e. the development and maintenance of Web pages

3. Short Answer

Instructions: Write a brief answer to each of the following questions.

1. What are computer security risks? What different types of security risks threaten school computers? What are some safeguards that minimize security risks? _____

2. What is a virus? Describe three types of viruses. Why are viruses commonly found in schools? What can teachers do to minimize the impact of viruses both at home and at school? _____

3. What is a single-user software license agreement? How is a single-user software license agreement different from a network site license? What types of software licenses are found typically in schools? _____

4. What is an overvoltage? What precautions should teachers take to protect their computers and other electronic equipment from overvoltages, both at home and at school? _____

5. What is an Acceptable Use Policy (AUP)? Why are AUPs so important for K-12 schools? Describe two other ways to limit student access to inappropriate Internet sites. _____

Teaching Today

Web Instructions: To display this page from the Web, start your browser and enter the URL, www.course.com/tdc3. Click Chapter 8 at the top of the Web page and then click Teaching Today on the left sidebar. Click the links for current and additional information.

WEB INFO

IN BRIEF

KEY TERMS

CHECKPOINT

TEACHING TODAY

EDUCATION ISSUES

INTEGRATION CORNER

SOFTWARE CORNER

IN THE LAB

LEARN IT ONLINE

✱ FEATURES...

Timeline 2004

Guide to WWW Sites

Buyer's Guide 2004

Professional Sites

State/Federal Sites

Interactive Labs

Search Tools

HOME

1. **You are an innovative teacher** with three multimedia computers connected to the Internet in your classroom. You also have access to a wireless mobile lab and many other technologies. Your school has a school-wide Acceptable Use Policy (AUP) for teachers, staff, students, and parents. You have been thinking, however, about having an additional AUP for your students and their parents, not only to protect the students, but also to have your students learn how to use different technologies responsibly and safely. What key components do you think your AUP should include? Do you think you should let your students help you create the AUP? Do you think this might be a good learning experience for the students? Why or why not? What are some consequences you think students should face for violating your classroom AUP? How will you enforce the AUP with students and parents?

2. **Recently, you have been hearing a lot about viruses.** You have two computers in your classroom and they are connected to the Internet. In the past, you have not worried about viruses because your computers have never been infected. Other teachers, however, have been discussing a new virus affecting their computers. Where can you get reliable information about viruses? What kind of support is available on the Internet? Can you get a virus from the Internet? How can you protect your computers from getting a virus?

3. **Based on Section 107** of the Copyright Act of 1976, also known as fair use, teachers are allowed to photocopy and use copyrighted materials in their classrooms for educational purposes. With the advent of multimedia, the Internet, and the World Wide Web, legislators have had to reexamine fair use. How do you think fair use rules apply to multimedia, the Internet, and the Web? Is using materials found on the Web different from using materials found in a copyrighted book? How can you determine if your use of copyrighted materials is governed by fair-use rules? Because it has become so easy to copy materials from so many different sources, how will you teach your students about copyright laws and fair use?

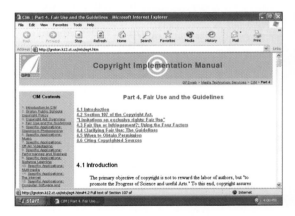

4. **Parents are concerned about objectionable materials** found on the Internet and are looking for some kind of protection. Your district is considering installing filtering software. What are the benefits of filtering software? Is filtering software foolproof? Why or why not? What are the disadvantages of filtering software? What type of report would you make to your school board about installing filtering software? How could an Acceptable Use Policy address the issue of objectionable materials?

Education Issues

8

Web Instructions: To display this page from the Web, start your browser and enter the URL, www.course.com/tdc3. Click Chapter 8 at the top of the Web page and then click Education Issues on the left sidebar. Click the links for current and additional information to help you respond to the Education Issues questions.

WEB INFO

IN BRIEF

KEY TERMS

CHECKPOINT

TEACHING TODAY

EDUCATION ISSUES

INTEGRATION CORNER

SOFTWARE CORNER

IN THE LAB

LEARN IT ONLINE

✱ FEATURES...

Timeline 2004

Guide to WWW Sites

Buyer's Guide 2004

Professional Sites

State/Federal Sites

Interactive Labs

Search Tools

HOME

1. Essays and Term Papers

For years, the only way to write a term paper was to visit the library, walk through shelves of texts and journals to find what you needed — before you even started to write. Today, obtaining a paper is as easy as clicking a mouse button. Several sites on the Web now provide a searchable database of term papers gathered from college and high school students. Students can download a term paper, make any necessary changes, print a copy, and then turn it in as their own. How can instructors keep students from claiming the work of others as their own? Can you explain how using the Web for research differs from using it to copy someone's work? What should be the consequences for plagiarizing from a Web site?

2. Teacher and Student Monitoring

Your school district maintains a policy that states classroom computers and Internet access are to be used for instructional purposes only. The district instructs teachers not to send or receive personal e-mail messages or instant messages (IMs), surf the Internet for fun, or play games on classroom computers. The district observes Internet activities with monitoring software. Some teachers feel they should be allowed to use the Internet, play games, or work on their personal projects during their lunch periods and after school. What limits, if any, should be placed on teachers' use of class-room computers? How closely should the school district be able to monitor teacher and student use? Why? Network specialists and administrators can see anything and everything on your com-puter. Should administrative personnel be allowed to monitor your e-mail messages and files on your school computer? Why or why not? Should you be allowed to monitor your students' e-mail messages? Why or why not?

3. Software Ethics

You recently purchased a DK Multimedia CD using your own funds for use on one computer in your classroom. Another teacher likes the software and borrows your CD so she can evalu-ate it for use in her classroom. A few weeks later, you find out that numerous other teachers in your school have a copy of the DK Multimedia CD. You ask the teacher about this and she says, "Oh, this is so cool. I have a CD-RW on my home computer and it is so easy to copy CDs. I am so proud of myself! I made one for every-one!" You know this breaks copyright laws, could get the school fined, and that it also is

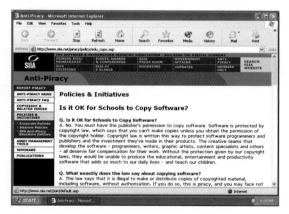

morally and ethically wrong. What to do! Should you tell the teacher, your principal, or technology facilitator? Could you be liable because you loaned her the original CD? How will you solve this dilemma?

4. Software Piracy

Software manufacturers are watching school districts closely for evidence of illegal use of software. Recently, a major school district was fined $300,000 for having multiple copies of non-licensed software installed on classroom computers. Teachers often illegally install multiple copies of single-user programs on their classroom computers. What are some of the ethical issues regarding soft-ware piracy? Why is illegally installing software so prevalent in K-12 schools? How does the software industry deal with violators of software copyright law? Describe several ways in which school districts can prevent illegal software from being installed on school computers.

Integration Corner

WEB INFO

IN BRIEF

KEY TERMS

CHECKPOINT

TEACHING TODAY

EDUCATION ISSUES

INTEGRATION CORNER

SOFTWARE CORNER

IN THE LAB

LEARN IT ONLINE

✱ FEATURES...

Timeline 2004

Guide to WWW Sites

Buyer's Guide 2004

Professional Sites

State/Federal Sites

Interactive Labs

Search Tools

HOME

Web Instructions: To display this page from the Web, start your browser and enter the URL, www.course.com/tdc3. Click Chapter 8 at the top of the Web page and then click Integration Corner on the left sidebar. Click any Corner and then click the various links for extensive and curriculum-specific information.

Integration Corner is designed for teachers and other educators who are looking for innovative ways to integrate technology into their content-specific curriculum. Integration Corner not only provides great Web sites with current information but also shows what other educators are doing in the field of educational technology. These Corners are designed for all educators regardless of their area of interest. Review information and Web sites outside of your teaching area because many great integration ideas in one area can be easily modified for use in other curricular areas.

Teachers and administrators will find other colleagues in their areas with whom to connect and share the successes and hurdles of integrating technology into the classroom or an entire school system. Consider this your one stop for integration ideas and resources. Links to educational Web sites are organized in the following 12 Corners, and different Web resources are available for each chapter. Figure 8-45 shows examples of the Web resources provided in the Chapter 8 Research Corner.

Early Childhood Corner   Math Corner

Elementary Corner   Science Corner

Middle School Corner   Special Education Corner

Secondary Corner   Post Secondary Corner

Reading/Language Arts Corner   Administrator Corner

Social Studies/History Corner   Research Corner

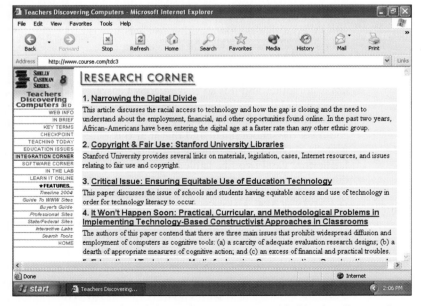

Figure 8-45 Examples of the Web resources provided in the Chapter 8 Research Corner.

Software Corner

Web Instructions: To display this page from the Web, start your browser and enter the URL, www.course.com/tdc3. Click Chapter 8 at the top of the Web page and then click Software Corner on the left sidebar. Click the links for additional information and instructions on how to download or receive an evaluation copy.

WEB INFO

IN BRIEF

KEY TERMS

CHECKPOINT

TEACHING TODAY

EDUCATION ISSUES

INTEGRATION CORNER

SOFTWARE CORNER

IN THE LAB

LEARN IT ONLINE

✱ FEATURES...

Timeline 2004

Guide to WWW Sites

Buyer's Guide 2004

Professional Sites

State/Federal Sites

Interactive Labs

Search Tools

HOME

1. Biomes and Natural Cycles explores the earth using seven different maps that describe everything from ecosystems to precipitation and more! Students will learn about water cycles, the different biomes and climates of the world, as well as the fluctuation of energy. Biomes and Natural Cycles is a wonderful instructional tool with many graphics and video segments when explaining the water, carbon, and nitrogen cycles to students.

2. Computer viruses spread faster than the common cold! When you and your students download files from the Internet, open e-mail attachments, or transport files between computers, you are at risk of getting a virus. Norton AntiVirus or McAfee's VirusScan will detect viruses in e-mail attachments, in files, on floppy disks, and on your computer's system files. Both companies allow users to update their virus protection files online to protect computers from the most current viruses. These antivirus programs can be set up to scan your computer automatically on a regular basis. Their Web sites provide information about the latest viruses as well as news releases and virus tips to help consumers better protect themselves. By visiting these Web sites, students can learn about computer viruses and research what viruses are affecting different regions of the world!

3. Solving problems, working cooperatively, expressing ideas, and understanding concepts are essential for student learning. Create Together uses object-oriented programming to allow students to produce their own multimedia encyclopedias, animated games, randomly generated puzzles, interactive simulations, searchable multimedia databases, hyperlinked presentations, and much more. This software is unique and has built-in collaboration tools so students can work individually or in groups on projects. The possibilities for teaching and learning with Create Together are limitless!

4. Getting middle school students interested in science is easiest when students can connect science with their everyday lives. Riverdeep strives to create this connection through real-life scenarios in its Logal Science series. The science curriculum spans from middle school to college level science concepts. Activities are designed with multimedia, streaming audio, animation, and a complete toolbox for student activities. Activities are packaged with lesson plans and printable screen shots for documentation. Within the safety of the computer environment, students engage in activities and investigate science concepts. You can download science simulation activities and demos from Logal Middle School Science Gateways, Logal High School Science Gateways, or Logal High School Science Explorer at this Web site.

In the Lab

Web Instructions: To display this page from the Web, start your browser and enter the URL, www.course.com/tdc3. Click Chapter 8 at the top of the Web page and then click In The Lab on the left sidebar. Click the links for tutorials, productivity ideas, integration examples and ideas, and more.

WEB INFO

IN BRIEF

KEY TERMS

CHECKPOINT

TEACHING TODAY

EDUCATION ISSUES

INTEGRATION CORNER

SOFTWARE CORNER

IN THE LAB

LEARN IT ONLINE

✱ FEATURES...

Timeline 2004

Guide to WWW Sites

Buyer's Guide 2004

Professional Sites

State/Federal Sites

Interactive Labs

Search Tools

HOME

PRODUCTIVITY IN THE CLASSROOM

Introduction: Effectively integrating technology in the curriculum allows students to demonstrate their learning using creative, motivating, and nontraditional means. Multimedia projects and presentations, as well as other technology-oriented presentations provide students with authentic learning activities and require a different form of assessment. Rubrics can provide teachers with a more authentic assessment tool.

Chapter 7 introduced the use of rubrics as a means of alternative assessment. Rubrics assist students in understanding teacher expectations and provide a clear outline when creating projects. Students also can use rubrics as a self-assessment tool. This encourages students to be more involved and responsible for their learning.

Teachers easily can create rubrics using numerous software applications, such as word processing, spreadsheet, Web editors, or other commercial products. Free online resources also are available that walk teachers through the process of creating a variety of rubrics and performance checklists.

1 Creating and Formatting a Problem-Solving Math Rubric

Problem: To encourage students in your 6th grade math class to use high-order thinking skills, you are beginning a unit on problem solving. Students will be given problems and have to write out how they solve the problem and their reasoning for selecting the approach they use. You design a rubric to guide your students through this process. The rubric is shown in **Figure 8-46**. Open your word processing, spreadsheet, or Web editing software and create the rubric as described below. (*Hint:* Use any appropriate clip art image and font to personalize the rubric. Use Help to understand the steps better.)

Instructions: Perform the following tasks.

1. Insert the clip art image.
2. Format the first heading line, Mrs. Georgiev's, in 20-point Times or Times New Roman bold font. Personalize the rubric by inserting your name instead of Mrs. Georgiev's.
3. Format the second heading line, 6th Grade Math Class, in 20-point Times or Times New Roman bold font.
4. Format the third heading line, Math Problem-Solving Rubric, in 18-point Times or Times New Roman font.
5. Insert a table with six rows and five columns.
6. Center the row headings and format them in 12-point Times New Roman bold font.
7. Format the text in 12-point Times New Roman font.
8. Personalize the school name and insert the current date. Format the school name and date in 12-point Times or Times New Roman bold font. Insert your e-mail address instead of Mrs. Georgiev's. Format the e-mail address in 12-point Times or Times New Roman, blue bold font.
9. Save the rubric on a floppy disk with a name of your choice. Print the rubric and then follow your instructor's directions for handing in the assignment.

In the Lab

WEB INFO

IN BRIEF

KEY TERMS

CHECKPOINT

TEACHING TODAY

EDUCATION ISSUES

INTEGRATION CORNER

SOFTWARE CORNER

IN THE LAB

LEARN IT ONLINE

✱ FEATURES...

Timeline 2004

Guide to WWW Sites

Buyer's Guide 2004

Professional Sites

State/Federal Sites

Interactive Labs

Search Tools

HOME

Mrs. Georgiev's
6th Grade Math Class
Math Problem-Solving Rubric

Task	Beginning 1 - 2	Developing 3 - 4	Advancing 5	Score
Student uses math language to explain the problem.	Used a few math terms in the explanation of the solution and the explanation was brief.	Used some math terms in the explanation of the solution and the explanation was adequate.	Used math terms correctly throughout the explanation of the solution and the explanation was thorough and complete.	
Student's explanation demonstrates understanding of the problem.	Misinterpreted parts of the problem.	Solved the problem with minor interpretation errors.	Answer demonstrates complete understanding of the problem.	
Student articulates plan for solving the problem.	The plan for solving the problem is partially correct.	The plan for solving the problem is correct but may lead to minor errors.	The plan for solving the problem is accurate and will lead to a correct solution.	
Student correctly solves the problem.	The answer is incorrect or not solved.	Part of the problem is solved correctly.	The answer is correct and the work supports the answer.	
TOTAL POINTS				

Woodrow Wilson Middle School
April 12, 2005
b_georgiev@tricounty.k12.ia.us

Figure 8-46

In the Lab

WEB INFO

IN BRIEF

KEY TERMS

CHECKPOINT

TEACHING TODAY

EDUCATION ISSUES

INTEGRATION CORNER

SOFTWARE CORNER

IN THE LAB

LEARN IT ONLINE

✱ FEATURES...

Timeline 2004

Guide to WWW Sites

Buyer's Guide 2004

Professional Sites

State/Federal Sites

Interactive Labs

Search Tools

HOME

2 Creating and Formatting a Multimedia Research Rubric

Problem: You want to introduce your high school students to a systematic approach to research. The students will access, evaluate, and use information from a variety of sources on an assigned topic. They then will write a research paper and create a multimedia presentation to present their findings to the class. At the beginning of the unit, you pass out the rubric shown in Figure 8-47. (*Hint:* Use any appropriate clip art images and fonts to personalize the page. Use Help to understand the steps better.)

Mr. Hernandez
World History Class
Multimedia Research Project Rubric

Student Name: _____   Topic: _____   Date: _____

Research Process:	Level 1	Level 2	Level 3	Level 4	Self–Score	Teacher Score
Gathered information from journals, books, CDs, and the Internet	0 1 2	3 4 5	6 7 8	9 10		
Resources are current and reliable	0 1 2	3 4 5	6 7 8	9 10		
Extracted, synthesized, and applied appropriate information	0 1 2	3 4 5	6 7 8	9 10		
Writing Process:						
Organized information from resources to complete research paper	0 1 2	3 4 5	6 7 8	9 10		
Wrote paper following steps in writing process	0 1 2	3 4 5	6 7 8	9 10		
Documented references using MLA citation style	0 1 2	3 4 5	6 7 8	9 10		
Multimedia Project:						
Presentation includes title slide, a minimum of seven content slides, and bibliography slide	0 1 2	3 4 5	6 7 8	9 10		
Graphic images are used appropriately and gathered from a variety of resources	0 1 2	3 4 5	6 7 8	9 10		
Presentation is well–organized, visually appealing, and flows well	0 1 2	3 4 5	6 7 8	9 10		
Presentation:						
Demonstrates good speaking skills	0 1 2	3 4 5	6 7 8	9 10		
TOTAL POINTS:						

Figure 8-47

In the Lab

WEB INFO

IN BRIEF

KEY TERMS

CHECKPOINT

TEACHING TODAY

EDUCATION ISSUES

INTEGRATION CORNER

SOFTWARE CORNER

IN THE LAB

LEARN IT ONLINE

✱ FEATURES...

Timeline 2004

Guide to WWW Sites

Buyer's Guide 2004

Professional Sites

State/Federal Sites

Interactive Labs

Search Tools

HOME

Instructions: Format the first and second heading lines in 16-point Lucinda Sans Unicode bold font. Insert your name in place of Mr. Hernandez. Format the third heading line in 14-point Lucinda Sans Unicode bold font. Insert a clip art or graphic image. Format the Student Name, Topic, and Date headings in 10-point Lucinda Sans Unicode bold font. Format the section headings in 10-point Lucinda Sans Unicode bold underlined font. Format the the text in 10-point Lucinda Sans Unicode font.

After you have typed and formatted the rubric, save the rubric on a floppy disk with a file name of your choice. Print the rubric and then follow your instructor's directions for handing in the assignment.

3 Creating and Formatting a Subject-Specific Rubric

Problem: You want to create a rubric to evaluate student learning of a concept you are presenting. The rubric also will serve as a guide for students as they create their end-of-unit project that demonstrates their learning.

Instructions: Create a rubric similar to the rubrics illustrated in **Figures 8-46** or **8-47**. Use an appropriate layout; font types, styles, and sizes; and clip art images. Include your name and the subject area you teach. After you have created the rubric, save the rubric on a floppy disk using an appropriate file name. Print the rubric and then follow your instructor's directions for handing in the assignment.

INTEGRATION IN THE CLASSROOM

1 At the beginning of the school year, you want to establish classroom rules and criteria for positive behavior in your 2nd grade special education classroom. You decide to create a behavior rubric together with your students that will be used and sent home weekly to parents. You ask the students for their ideas about positive classroom behavior, and together, you and your students create a rubric on which you all agree. Create a sample behavior rubric for your students. Include your name, school name, and the current date on the rubric.

2 The students in your Earth Science class have been studying the environment and environmental hazards such as acid rain and oil spills. As a final project for the unit, students will work in groups and conduct a research activity. They will present their findings in either a PowerPoint presentation or a video. To encourage the students to take responsibility for their learning, you first assign each group to the task of developing a rubric that outlines the assessment criteria for their final project. You will assist the students as necessary; however, you believe they will have more ownership in their learning and be more motivated if they establish the majority of the criteria themselves. Create a sample rubric for your students to use as a guide. Include your name, subject area, project topic, and current date on the rubric.

3 Ask your students to research Web page evaluation rubrics on the Internet to prepare them to create Web pages. The students will work in groups to locate and print a minimum of five different Web page evaluation rubrics. They then will compare and contrast the different rubrics and determine what is important when creating a Web page. As a class, you will brainstorm, create a rubric, and then use this rubric to create Web pages. Include a column for self-evaluation. Locate at least three different Web page evaluation rubrics. From your research, create a rubric to use as an example for your students. Include your name and class at the top of the rubric. Include your e-mail address and the current date at the bottom of the rubric.

Learn It Online

WEB INFO

IN BRIEF

KEY TERMS

CHECKPOINT

TEACHING TODAY

EDUCATION ISSUES

INTEGRATION CORNER

SOFTWARE CORNER

IN THE LAB

LEARN IT ONLINE

✱ FEATURES...

Timeline 2004

Guide to WWW Sites

Buyer's Guide 2004

Professional Sites

State/Federal Sites

Interactive Labs

Search Tools

HOME

Web Instructions: To display this page from the Web, start your browser and enter the URL, www.course.com/tdc3. Click Chapter 8 at the top of the Web page and then click Learn It Online on the left sidebar. Click the buttons to display the exercise or the Interactive Lab.

1. Shelly Cashman Series Keeping Your Computer Virus Free Lab

Click the button to the left to start and use the Shelly Cashman Series Keeping Your Computer Virus Free Lab.

2. Shelly Cashman Series Exploring the Computers of the Future Lab

Click the button to the left to start and use the Shelly Cashman Series Exploring the Computers of the Future Lab.

3. Internet Filtering Software

Internet filtering software allows parents and teachers to block students from having Internet access to objectionable materials. To learn more about Internet filtering software, click the button to the left and complete this exercise.

4. Software Piracy

Software piracy is a problem in K-12 schools. The Business Software Alliance (BSA) Web site provides the latest information about software piracy. BSA fights against software piracy by conducting educational programs and operating antipiracy hotlines. To learn more, click the button to the left and complete this exercise.

5. State Standards

Click the button to the left to locate and learn more about your state's content standards.

6. Who Wants To Be a Computer Genius?

Click the button to the left to find out if you are a computer genius. Directions on how to play the game will display. When you are ready to play, click the PLAY button. Submit your score to your instructor.

7. Crossword Puzzle Challenge

Click the button to the left to complete the puzzle to reinforce skills you learned in this chapter. Directions on how to play the game will display. When you are ready to play, click the SUBMIT button. Submit the completed puzzle to your instructor.

8. Practice Test

Click the button to the left and answer each question. When completed, enter your name and click the Grade Test button to submit the quiz for grading. Make a note of any missed questions. If required, print a copy to submit to your instructor.

A World Without Wires

Each time you use your smart phone, tune your television to a soccer game being played on another continent, or listen to satellite radio in your car, you are enjoying the benefits of the world of wireless communications. New wireless devices, including smart phones and pagers, PDAs, Tablet PCs, and notebook computers with high-speed Internet access, simplify and expand your communications abilities. Wireless technology also is changing many other hardware devices that traditionally needed cords to transmit data, such as printers and video projectors.

Wireless communications technology is not new. More than 100 years ago, Guglielmo Marconi sent the first wireless message by using radio waves. Today, Marconi's discoveries allow you to connect peripherals to your desktop computers without using wires and build a wireless home network. You also can keep in touch with family and associates from anywhere in the world by telephone or e-mail using a variety of wireless products.

Wireless technology has transformed the way people work, communicate, and learn and has won popular acclaim worldwide in a very short period. Even the casual observer notices dramatic changes in the way computer users in homes, schools, and businesses, send e-mail, communicate, access the Internet, display photos, and create and share files. Today's teachers and students are part of this wireless revolution – a revolution that is fundamentally changing the way students and teachers communicate and collaborate with each other.

Although Marconi laid the foundation for wireless technology more than a century ago, today's wireless products and standards represent an evolution of his original discoveries. Each day, the number of wireless devices increases as the price of connectivity decreases. As the world goes wireless, Asia and Western Europe have emerged as world leaders in wireless device use (Figure 1).

This special feature looks at a wide variety of wireless products and illustrates how various segments of society, including K-20 education, use wireless technology. The following section provides a brief overview of wireless networks and some of the terms often associated with wireless technology.

WIRELESS NETWORKS AND TERMINOLOGY

Several years ago, Nicholas Negroponte, founder and director of MIT's Media Lab, predicted what has come to be known as the Negroponte Flip. Negroponte predicted that communications media that formerly were wireless would become wired, and media that were formerly wired would become wireless. Evidence of the Negroponte Flip can be seen today in the emergence of cable television (wireless to wired) and the explosion in voice and data services over wireless networks (wired to wireless).

Wireless networks can be characterized generally by the area they cover. The following sections briefly describe wireless personal area networks, wireless local area networks, and wireless metropolitan and wide area networks.

Wireless Personal Area Network (WPAN)

A **wireless personal area network (WPAN)** is a short-range wireless network often based on Bluetooth technology. **Bluetooth** technology uses short-range radio waves to transmit data between two Bluetooth devices such as smart phones, headsets, microphones, digital cameras, fax machines, printers, desktop computers, Tablet PCs, notebook computers, and many other wireless devices. Bluetooth-equipped devices *discover* each other and form *paired* connections. Examples of paired connections include a cellular telephone and a headset, a keyboard or printer and PC, a notebook computer, and a PDA (Figure 2). To communicate with each other, Bluetooth devices should be within approximately 10 meters, or 33 feet, of each other.

Many devices that traditionally have required wires, such as printers, keyboards, scanners, and digital cameras are now manufactured with integrated Bluetooth technology. Bluetooth can also be added to existing wire-dependent equipment through the use of PC Cards or USB devices. Both Mac OS X and Windows XP have built-in Bluetooth support that allows users easily to configure Bluetooth communications.

Number of Wireless Devices

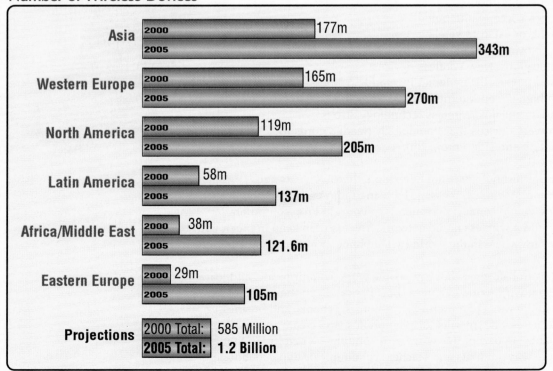

FIGURE 1   By 2005, more than 1.2 billion wireless devices will be in use, millions of which will be capable of accessing the Web. Asia and Western Europe are the biggest users of wireless devices.

FIGURE 2 Bluetooth technology allows users to connect devices wirelessly in a multitude of ways.

Wireless Local Area Networks (WLAN)

A **wireless local area network (WLAN)** is a network that uses wireless media, such as radio waves, to connect computers and devices in a limited space, such as a home, classroom, office building, or school. Wireless LANs are based on the Institute of Electrical and Electronics Engineers (IEEE) 802.11 standard. The term **802.11** refers to a family of specifications developed for wireless local area networks that allows computers and other devices to communicate via radio waves. The nonprofit organization, **Wi-Fi Alliance**, was established in 1999 and certifies the interoperability of 802.11 products (Figure 3). **Wi-Fi**, short for *wireless fidelity*, is a popular term used when referring to any type of 802.11 network.

FIGURE 3 The Wi-Fi Alliance certifies 802.11 products and provides extensive information and resources on wireless networks.

Currently, three implementations of the 802.11 specification exist. The first and most common is 802.11b; 802.11a and 802.11g are more recent. In the summer of 2003, the Wi-Fi Alliance approved the newer and much faster 802.11g standard, which is backward compatible with existing 802.11a/b standards.

Wi-Fi networking hardware is becoming standard equipment on many notebook computers, PDAs, and other wireless devices. In many public locations, people connect their computers or devices to the Internet wirelessly using Wi-Fi standards through a **public Internet access point**. Users can connect to the Internet if their computers or devices have an appropriate network card and as long as they are in a hot spot. A **hot spot** is an area with the capabilities of wireless Internet connectivity. The area of most hot spots ranges from 100 to 300 feet when located inside a building and up to 1,000 feet when located in open or outdoor areas. Today, Wi-Fi public Internet access points are emerging everywhere, including bookstores, malls, airports, city parks, universities, downtown areas of major cities, and many other locations (Figure 4).

Access to the Internet is now available via wireless devices in many places outside of your home, school, or office. A **cybercafé** is a coffeehouse or restaurant that provides computers with Internet access to its customers. Many cybercafés today provide hot spots and Wi-Fi Internet access points for their customers. In addition, you can access the world wirelessly while traveling on airplanes, trains, ferries, cruise ships, and even your car.

FIGURE 4   Users can access the Web from many locations using Wi-Fi technology.

Currently, tens of thousands of Wi-Fi hot spots exist worldwide and this number is expected to increase dramatically over the next few years. You can locate hot spots in your community and around the world by using the ZONE Finder search tool at the Wi-Fi Alliance Web site (Figure 5).

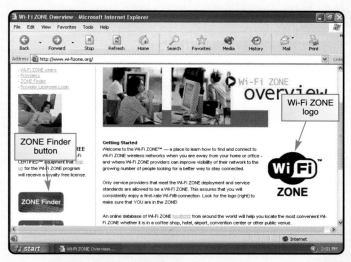

FIGURE 5 The ZONE Finder site lists service providers that meet industry standards.

FIGURE 6 This warchalking symbol indicates an open node, which is an area offering free wireless Internet access.

Although some Wi-Fi distributors provide free Internet access, most charge a per-hour or per-minute fee. Users can easily identify hot spots by looking for the **Wi-Fi ZONE** logo (see Figure 5). In addition, a grass roots movement called warchalking is helping users identify hot spots that provide free Wi-Fi access. **Warchalking** refers to the practice of using chalk to draw a series of symbols on sidewalks to direct people to places that provide wireless access (Figure 6). The term warchalking originated during the Great Depression to describe the practice of hobos who used chalk marks to indicate which homes would provide a meal.

Wireless Metropolitan Area and Wide Area Networks

A **wireless metropolitan area network (WMAN)** is a wireless network designed to cover an urban area. WMANs are being installed in both large and small cities by organizations and for-profit companies dedicated to providing free or for-a-fee wireless access in public spaces.

For example, NYCwireless promotes wireless hot spots in public spaces such as parks, coffee shops, and building lobbies throughout the New York City region (Figure 7). NYCwireless also is working with public and other nonprofit organizations to provide broadband wireless Internet access to under-served communities.

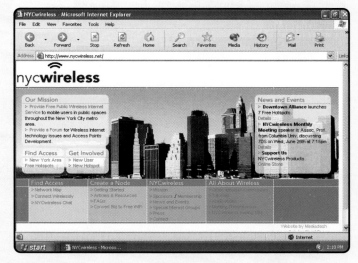

FIGURE 7 The mission of NYCwireless is to provide free wireless Internet service in public spaces throughout the New York City area.

A **wireless wide area network (WWAN)** is a wireless network that covers a wide geographic area and uses a variety of technologies including radio, satellite, and mobile telephone technologies. A number of major corporations such as Verizon, Sprint, AT&T, MCI and others are creating wireless wide area networks to provide their customers access to the Internet from any location at any time.

WIRELESS TECHNOLOGY AND EDUCATION

Wireless networking is becoming commonplace in institutions of higher education. According to the 2002 Campus Computing Survey of The Campus Computing Project, nearly 68 percent of surveyed institutions reported the use of WLANs, and 10 percent reported the use of full-campus wireless access (Figure 8).

For example, the University of Central Florida (UCF) has made wireless networking available over its entire campus; in classroom buildings, the library, administrative offices, the student union, residence halls, and even outdoor locations where students gather (Figure 9). In addition, students who visit the UCF library without their own notebook computers can check out wireless notebook computers for use throughout the library.

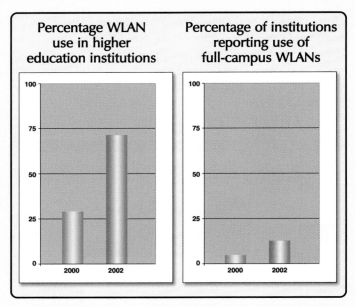

FIGURE 8   The trend is clear; in the very near future, wireless local area networks will be the standard networking choice of colleges and universities.

FIGURE 9   The campus of the University of Central Florida and all new classroom buildings are designed to take advantage of the benefits of wireless networking, allowing students access to information, their classes, and each other from any campus location.

Today, schools and institutions of higher learning use wireless networks to access the same applications used on wired networks: electronic mail, Web access, and instant messaging. The main advantage that wireless brings is flexibility, which allows users to access e-mail and the Web at any time and from any location. Wireless networks also offer other unique benefits, such as the ability to easily set up temporary computing locations, network buildings that would be difficult or impossible to wire, or provide connections to every student in a classroom, auditorium, or outdoor setting.

Wireless networks also are becoming common in many K-12 schools and school districts. Every day, schools all over the world are discovering new benefits and advantages of using wireless networks. For example, teachers now can use interactive wireless computers to determine how well students comprehend class material. They can ask students to respond to a multiple-choice or true-false question using a wireless keypad resembling a remote control. Within seconds, an infrared reader captures the students' responses, and a computer tabulates the results and tracks their scores. Students react exceedingly well to this type of interactivity in the assessment process (Figure 10).

FIGURE 10   Students are actively engaged in taking a *wireless practice quiz*. Similar engagement, excitement, and competitiveness are difficult to create using traditional paper-and-pencil quizzes.

The trend is clear, many K-12 schools and institutions of higher education are replacing their wired networks with high-speed or broadband wireless networks that use a variety of wireless devices, including the Tablet PC.

Wireless Tablet PC

The wireless Tablet PC is the ideal tool for today's classroom for many reasons. About the size of a spiral notebook, the Tablet PC combines all the power and speed of a desktop computer with Windows XP Tablet PC software, which enables pen- and voice-based computing (Figure 11). Just as the Internet is breaking down the traditional four walls of the classroom, the Tablet PC will break down traditional pencil-and-paper learning.

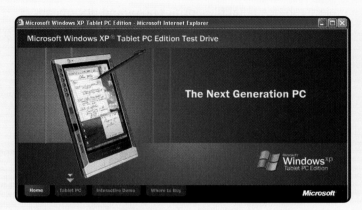

FIGURE 11   The Tablet PC has the potential to change paper-and-pencil learning forever.

WIRELESS TECHNOLOGY AND SOCIETY

Messaging is driving the wireless market explosion. By the end of 2004, experts predict that more than 1 billion people will send 244 billion text messages monthly. Wireless nodes allow individuals to connect their cellular telephones and notebook computers to wireless Web modems and their handheld computers to school and corporate networks. People can access their e-mail, view photographs, run applications, and more (Figure 12).

FIGURE 12   By the end of 2004, industry experts predict that more than 1 billion people will send 244 billion text messages monthly.

The following sections describe just a few of the ways that the Wi-Fi revolution is impacting society.

Wireless Home Networking

A **wireless home network** connects your home computers and peripherals without the use of wires. Family members simultaneously can collaborate on projects, share digital files, print photos and documents, and access the Internet. Notebook computer users can roam around the house and work as far as 500 feet from the wireless access point, which is the central network hub. Many home networking products are based on Wi-Fi standards and are becoming more affordable, plentiful, and easy to use; some manufacturers claim a buyer can link two computers together and to the Internet in less than one hour for less than $100. Figure 13 shows the steps to set up a wireless home network.

Service Industry

Health-care professionals, police officers, package couriers, and retail sales personnel are using handheld computers to help them work more efficiently. Ambulance crews use PDAs to collect and transmit patient data while en route to hospitals. Doctors and nurses access patients' records and then record treatments and prescribe medications.

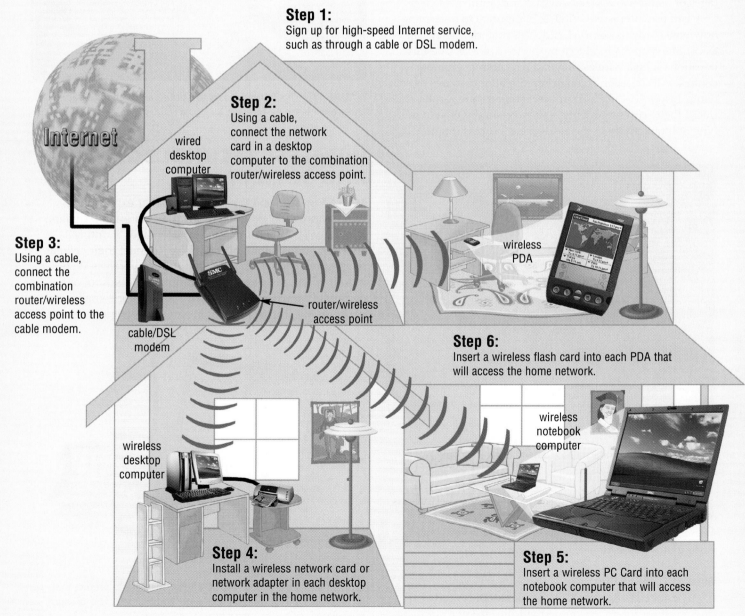

FIGURE 13   This figure shows the steps necessary to set up a wireless home network.

Patrol officers conduct vehicle registration checks (Figure 14) and record crime scene details. Delivery personnel scan package bar codes to track pickup and delivery times and record signatures. Retail managers use PDAs to monitor, transfer, and reorder product inventory.

Global Positioning

Millions of hikers, boaters, pilots, drivers, and other navigators never feel lost with the aid of global positioning system (GPS) devices. These products rely on 24 satellites that circle the Earth twice a day in very precise orbits and transmit data back to Earth. The GPS products then use between 3 to 12 of these satellites to determine the receivers' precise geographic locations (Figure 15). Some GPS devices include color mapping capability that gives detail for any United States city. GPS modules also are available for handheld computers. By the middle of this decade, analysts predict that 25 million vehicles, including all new cars, will be equipped with GPS navigational devices.

FIGURE 14 Instant wireless communications and wireless devices have changed the way police officers and other professionals do their jobs.

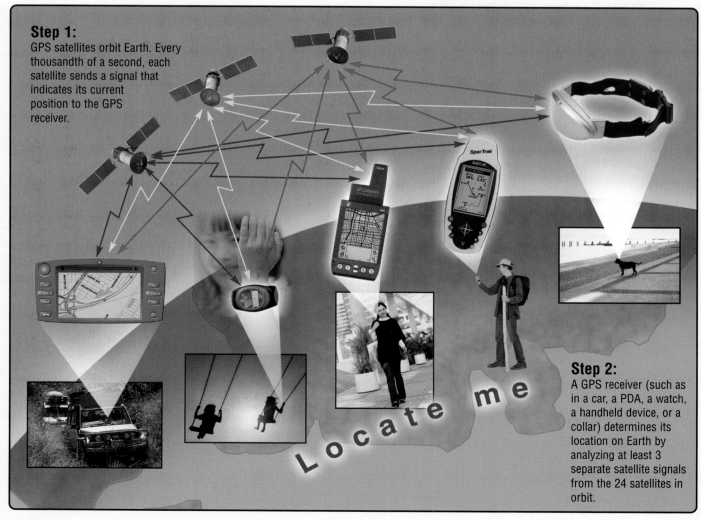

Step 1:
GPS satellites orbit Earth. Every thousandth of a second, each satellite sends a signal that indicates its current position to the GPS receiver.

Step 2:
A GPS receiver (such as in a car, a PDA, a watch, a handheld device, or a collar) determines its location on Earth by analyzing at least 3 separate satellite signals from the 24 satellites in orbit.

Locate me

FIGURE 15 How a GPS works.

Anyplace, Anytime Connectivity

Anyplace, anytime wireless connectivity makes it easy to synchronize files on your handheld computers and notebook computers. When you are on the road, you can connect your wireless devices to a school or office network and automatically transfer databases, appointments, to-do lists, and other files, just as if you were seated in front of your computer. Back at school or your office, you can update your notebook computer and handheld computer the instant you enter the room (Figure 16).

WIRELESS SUMMARY

Your pockets, purses, book bags, and backpacks may be overflowing with small electronic devices, but the wireless revolution is making headway to combine some of these products and simplify your life. Wireless networks are growing throughout the world, driven by convenience, cost, and access and are changing forever the ways people communicate and learn and how they work at home, school, or the office. At one time, computing abilities were limited by the length of wires; now communications and computing have no physical limitations. Wireless communication has removed the wires and opened the doors to anyplace, anytime communications and connectivity – creating a world without boundaries and a world without wires.

FIGURE 16   Wireless technology allows anyplace, anytime computing with the power of instant updating of information between devices.

Appendix A

Guide to Professional Educational Organizations

WEB INSTRUCTIONS: To gain World Wide Web access to additional and up-to-date information regarding this Appendix and links to these organizations, start your browser and enter the URL, www.course.com/tdc3. When the Teachers Discovering Computers home page is displayed, click the Professional Sites link on the lower-left side of the home page.

Many public and private nonprofit professional organizations provide educators with a variety of Web Resources, assistance with important issues that educators deal with on a daily basis, and much more. Professional educational organizations are dedicated to promoting and supporting improvement in student learning and educational practices and provide for professional growth in K-12 education and teacher education. These organizations also provide networking opportunities, information, and leadership in a variety of education areas, including information technology and other technologies integrated into the educational environment. A continually updated Guide to Professional Organizations, which links the most current URLs for a representative cross section of professional organizations, can be found at the Teachers Discovering Computers Web site.

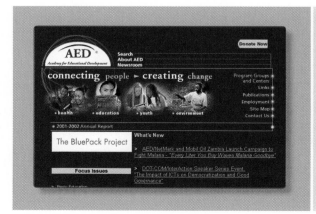

Academy for Educational Development (AED)
www.aed.org

This independent nonprofit organization is committed to solving critical social problems in the U.S. and abroad through education, social marketing, research, training, policy analysis, and innovative program design and management.

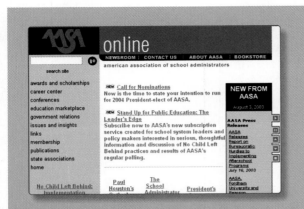

American Association of School Administrators (AASA)

www.aasa.org

The AASA, founded in 1865, is the professional organization for more than 14,000 educational leaders throughout the United States and abroad. The organization's focus is on supporting and developing effective school system leaders who are dedicated to the highest quality public education for all children.

American Federation of Teachers (AFT)

www.aft.org/index.html

Founded in 1916, the American Federation of Teachers is a national organization committed to teachers' professional interests. The AFT has more than 1 million public and professional members nationwide.

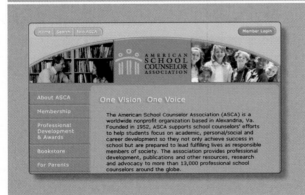

American School Counselor Association (ASCA)

www.schoolcounselor.org

ASCA is a professional organization for licensed school counselors that provides information and resources that support school counselors' efforts to help students focus on academic, personal/social, and career development.

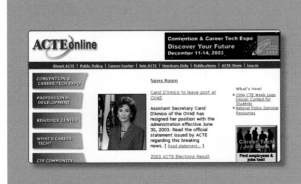

Association for Career and Technical Education (ACTE)

www.acteonline.org

The Association for Career and Technical Education is the largest national education association in the United States that is dedicated to the advancement of career education for both youth and adults. ACTE offers a wide variety of valuable resources for teachers, counselors, and administrators. Start by reading About ACTE where you will find a complete explanation of what it is and what it does. Do not miss the Member Services area with details on the many benefits offered through association membership.

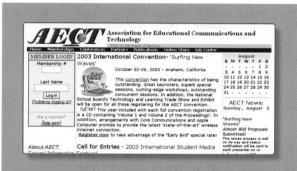

Association for Educational Communications and Technology
aect.org

The mission of the Association for Educational Communications and Technology, founded in 1923, is to provide leadership in educational communications and technology by linking professionals holding a common interest in the use of educational technology and its application to the learning process.

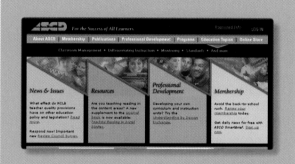

Association for Supervision and Curriculum Development (ASCD)
www.ascd.org

The ASCD, founded in 1943, is a unique international, nonprofit, nonpartisan association of professional educators of all grade levels and subject areas; it provides a forum for education issues and shares research, news, and information.

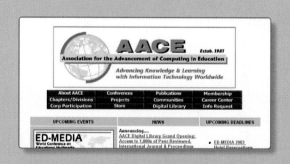

Association for the Advancement of Computing in Education (AACE)
www.aace.org

AACE, founded in 1981, is an international, educational, and professional not-for-profit organization dedicated to the advancement of the knowledge and theory, and the improvement of the quality of learning and teaching at all levels with information technology.

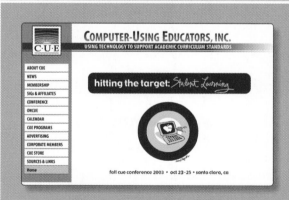

Computer-Using Educators (CUE)
www.cue.org

Computer-Using Educators, Inc. was founded in 1978 with the goal to promote and develop instructional uses of technology in all disciplines and at all educational levels from preschool through college. CUE is the largest organization of this type in California and one of the largest in the country.

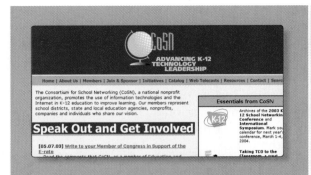

Consortium for School Networking (CoSN)
www.cosn.org

The Consortium for School Networking (CoSN) promotes the use of telecommunications to improve K-12 learning. Members represent state and local education agencies, nonprofits, companies, and individuals. CoSN is dedicated to promoting leadership development, advocacy, coalition building, and emerging technologies.

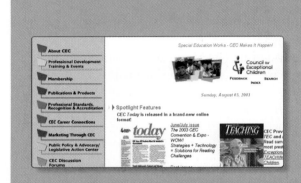

Council for Exceptional Children (CEC)
www.cec.sped.org/index.html

The Council for Exceptional Children (CEC) is the largest international professional organization dedicated to improving educational outcomes for individuals with exceptionalities, students with disabilities, and/or gifted students. Visit this Web site to find out how CEC campaigns for appropriate governmental policies, sets professional standards, provides continual professional development, advocates for newly and historically underserved individuals with exceptionalities, and helps professionals obtain conditions and resources necessary for effective professional practice.

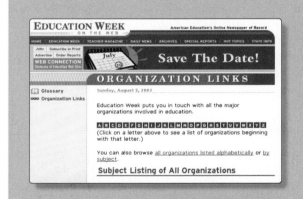

Education Week on the Web
www.edweek.org/context/orgs

Education Week maintains a listing of dozens of education organizations with links to their home pages. You can review or search the list alphabetically or by subject.

International Society for Technology in Education (ISTE)
www.iste.org

ISTE is comprised of international leaders in educational technology. The organization promotes appropriate uses of information technology to support and improve learning, teaching, and administration in K-12 and teacher education.

National Art Education Association (NAEA)
www.naea-reston.org

Founded in 1947, NAEA comprises more than 22,000 art educators from every level of instruction, from early childhood to university education. The NAEA is dedicated to quality art education in schools.

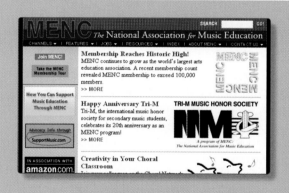

National Association for Multicultural Education (NAME)
www.nameorg.org

NAME is an active, growing organization that is working to bring together individuals and groups with an interest in multicultural education at all levels of education, different academic disciplines, and from diverse educational institutions and occupations. Membership includes educators from preschool through higher education and representatives from businesses and communities in 22 states.

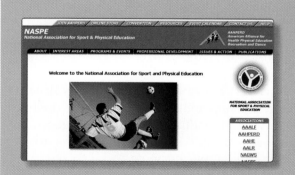

National Association for Music Education (MENC)
www.menc.org

MENC's mission is to advance music education as a profession, and to ensure that every child in America has access to a balanced, sequential, high-quality education that includes music as a core subject of study.

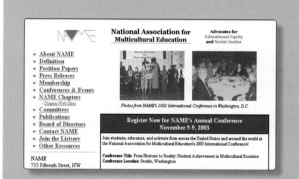

National Association for Sport and Physical Education (NASPE)
www.aahperd.org/naspe

The National Association for Sport and Physical Education enhances knowledge and professional practice in sport and physical activity through scientific study and dissemination of research-based and experiential knowledge to members and the public.

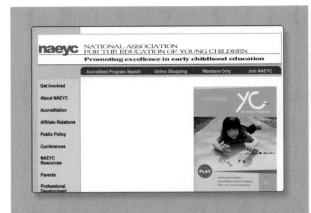

National Association for the Education of Young Children (NAEYC)
www.naeyc.org

Founded in 1926, NAEYC, the nation's largest and most influential organization of early childhood educators, constantly is striving to improve professional practice and working conditions in early childhood education and to build public support for high-quality early childhood programs for children from birth through third grade.

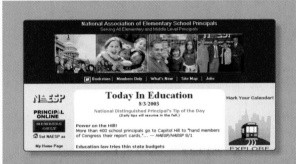

National Association of Elementary School Principals (NAESP)
www.naesp.org/index.html

The mission of NAESP is to lead in the advocacy and support of elementary school principals, middle school principals, and other education leaders in their commitment to all children.

National Association of Secondary School Principals (NASSP)
www.principals.org

This professional organization, founded in 1916, includes tens of thousands of middle level and high school principals, assistant principals, and aspiring principals from the United States and other countries around the world. Its mission is to promote excellence in school leadership by offering a wide variety of programs and services to assist members in administration, supervision, curriculum planning, and staff development.

National Business Education Association (NBEA)
www.nbea.org

The National Business Education Association (NBEA) is the nation's largest professional organization devoted exclusively to serving individuals and groups engaged in instruction, administration, research, and dissemination of information for and about business.

National Council for the Social Studies (NCSS)
www.ncss.org

NCSS engages and supports elementary, secondary, and college teachers of history, geography, economics, political science, sociology, psychology, anthropology, and law-related education. Check out this Web site and find out how to become an NCSS member and join the ranks of thousands of K-12 classroom teachers, college and university faculty members, curriculum designers and specialists, social studies supervisors, and leaders in the various disciplines.

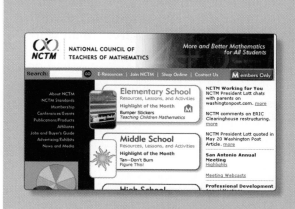

National Council of Teachers of English (NCTE)
www.ncte.org

NCTE's mission is to improve the teaching and learning of English and the language arts at all levels of education. Since 1911, NCTE has provided opportunities for teachers to continue growing professionally. In addition, they founded a forum to deal with issues that affect the teaching of English.

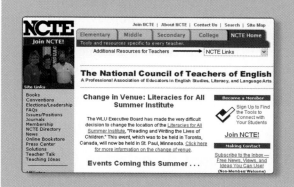

National Council of Teachers of Mathematics (NCTM)
www.nctm.org/

For more than 75 years, NCTM has been a recognized leader in efforts to ensure excellent mathematics education for all students, and an opportunity for every mathematics teacher to grow professionally. With about 100,000 members, NCTM is the largest association of mathematics educators in the world, providing professional development opportunities by holding annual regional leadership conferences, and publishing journals, books, videos, and software.

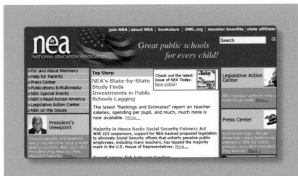

National Education Association (NEA)

www.nea.org

Founded in 1857, NEA is America's oldest and largest organization committed to advancing the cause of public education with more than 2.7 million members who work at every level of education, from preschool to university graduate programs. NEA has affiliates in every state and in more than 13,000 local communities across the United States dedicated to helping students.

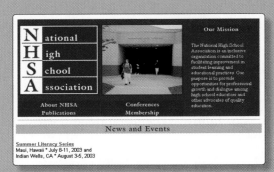

National High School Association (NHSA)

www.nhsa.net

The National High School Association is a nonprofit membership association dedicated to improving the professional knowledge of high school educators so that all high school students may experience academic success. Members include administrators, teachers, parents, policymakers, and others interested in student achievement.

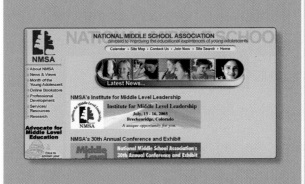

National Middle School Association (NMSA)

www.nmsa.org

The National Middle School Association is dedicated to improving the educational experiences of adolescents by providing vision, knowledge, and resources to all who serve them in order to develop healthy, productive, and ethical citizens. Learn how to become one of the 30,000 members that include principals, teachers, central office personnel, professors, college students, parents, community leaders, and educational consultants across the United States, Canada, and 46 other countries.

National PTA

www.pta.org

PTA is the largest volunteer child advocacy organization in the United States. It is an association of 6 million parents, educators, students, and other citizens who are active leaders in their schools and communities in facilitating parent education and involvement in schools.

National School Boards Association (NSBA)
www.nsba.org

The mission of the NSBA is to foster excellence and equity in public education through school board leadership. The NSBA believes local school boards are the nation's preeminent expression of grass roots democracy and that this form of governance of the public schools is fundamental to the continued success of public education.

National Science Teachers Association (NSTA)
www.nsta.org

Founded in 1944, NSTA is the largest organization in the world committed to promoting excellence and innovation in science teaching and learning. NSTA's current membership of more than 55,000 includes science teachers, science supervisors, administrators, scientists, business and industry representatives, and others involved in science education.

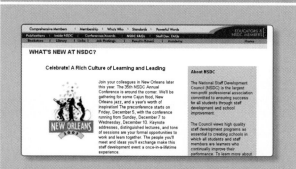

National Staff Development Council (NSDC)
www.nsdc.org

NSDC is the largest nonprofit professional association committed to ensuring success for all students through staff development and school improvement.

Phi Delta Kappa (PDK)
www.pdkintl.org

Phi Delta Kappa (PDK) is an international association of professional educators. PDK's mission is to promote quality education, with particular emphasis on publicly supported education.

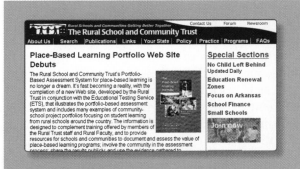

Rural School and Community Trust
www.ruraledu.org

Visit this Web site and you will learn more about this nonprofit educational organization dedicated to enlarging student learning and improving community life by strengthening relationships between rural schools and communities and engaging students in community-based public work.

Teachers of English to Speakers of Other Languages, Inc. (TESOL)
www.tesol.org/index.html

TESOL's mission is to develop the expertise of its members and others involved in teaching English to speakers of other languages to help them foster effective communication in diverse settings while respecting individuals' language rights.

Guide to State and Federal Government Educational Web Sites

WEB INSTRUCTIONS: To gain World Wide Web access to additional and up-to-date information regarding this appendix and links to these sites, start your browser and enter the URL, www.course.com/tdc3. When the Teachers Discovering Computers home page appears, click the State/Federal Sites link on the lower-left side of the home page.

The federal government, state governments, and state institutions and organizations provide a multitude of Web resources for K-12 teachers and students. Every day, hundreds of new and exciting education Web resources are added to these sites. A continually updated Guide to State and Federal Government Educational Web sites, which links to the most current URLs, can be found at the Teachers Discovering Computers Web site.

State Departments of Education

Site Name	Location (site locations begin with http://)
Alabama	www.alsde.edu/html
Alaska	www.educ.state.ak.us
Arizona	ade.state.az.us
Arkansas	arkedu.state.ar.us
California	www.cde.ca.gov
Colorado	www.cde.state.co.us
Connecticut	www.state.ct.us/sde
Delaware	www.doe.state.de.us
District of Columbia	www.k12.dc.us
Florida	www.fldoe.org
Georgia	www.doe.k12.ga.us
Hawaii	doe.k12.hi.us
Idaho	www.sde.state.id.us/Dept
Illinois	www.isbe.state.il.us
Indiana	www.doe.state.in.us
Iowa	www.state.ia.us/educate
Kansas	www.ksbe.state.ks.us
Kentucky	www.kde.state.ky.us
Louisiana	www.doe.state.la.us
Maine	www.state.me.us/education
Maryland	www.msde.state.md.us
Massachusetts	www.doe.mass.edu
Michigan	www.michigan.gov/mde
Minnesota	www.education.state.mn.us
Mississippi	www.mde.k12.ms.us
Missouri	services.dese.state.mo.us
Montana	www.opi.state.mt.us
Nebraska	www.nde.state.ne.us

State Departments of Education

Site Name	Location (site locations begin with http://)
Nevada	www.nde.state.nv.us
New Hampshire	www.ed.state.nh.us
New Jersey	www.state.nj.us/education
New Mexico	sde.state.nm.us
New York	www.nysed.gov
North Carolina	www.dpi.state.nc.us
North Dakota	www.dpi.state.nd.us
Ohio	www.ode.state.oh.us
Oklahoma	sde.state.ok.us
Oregon	www.ode.state.or.us
Pennsylvania	www.pde.state.pa.us
Rhode Island	www.ridoe.net
South Carolina	www.sde.state.sc.us
South Dakota	www.state.sd.us/deca
Tennessee	www.state.tn.us/education
Texas	www.tea.state.tx.us
Utah	www.usoe.k12.ut.us
Vermont	www.state.vt.us/educ
Virginia	www.pen.k12.va.us/go/VDOE
Washington	www.k12.wa.us
West Virginia	wvde.state.wv.us
Wisconsin	www.dpi.state.wi.us
Wyoming	www.k12.wy.us

Federal Government

Site Name	Location (site locations begin with http://)	Comment
AskERIC	www.askeric.org	AskERIC is a personalized Internet-based service providing education information to teachers, librarians, counselors, administrators, parents, and anyone interested in education throughout the United States and the world. Simply AskERIC.
Ben's Guide to U.S. Government for Kids	bensguide.gpo.gov/subject.html	Ben's Guide provides a comprehensive listing of government Web sites for kids.
Bureau of Land Management	www.blm.gov/education	This site, created by the U.S. Department of the Interior, presents learning opportunities associated with the 262 million acres of public lands that the Bureau of Land Management manages for all Americans. Included is extensive information for students, teachers, and adult learners to use in the classroom, informal outdoor settings, or virtual classrooms.
Comprehensive Regional Assistance Centers	www.ed.gov/EdRes/EdFed/EdTech Ctrs.html	The Department of Education funds these fifteen K-12 regional assistance centers to provide services to states, local education agencies, and schools.
Department of Defense (DoD)	web.lmi.org/edugate/	This Web site provides general information about educational programs sponsored in whole or in part by the Department of Defense. This gateway to education effort is sponsored by the DoD.
Department of Energy's KidZone	www.energy.gov/engine/content.do ?BT_CODE=KIDS	This site, maintained by the Department of Energy Education, provides educational resources in science, technology, energy, math, and more. The site includes an Energy Glossary with more than 4,000 energy definitions, as well as other energy-related terms for middle and secondary students.

Federal Government

Site Name	Location (site locations begin with http://)	Comment
Department of Justice Kids and Youth	www.usdoj.gov/kidspage/ index.html	This informative Web site is designed for all students, teachers, and parents and provides great resources on Internet crimes, drug prevention, cyberethics for kids, justice for kids, and more.
EDSITEment	edsitement.neh.gov	This subject-based catalog from the National Endowment for the Humanities provides access to the top humanities sites on the Web. It includes online humanities resources from some of the world's great museums, libraries, cultural institutions, and universities for use directly in your classroom.
Educational Resources Information Center (ERIC)	www.eric.ed.gov	A nationwide information network funded by the U.S. Department of Education that acquires, catalogs, summarizes, and provides access to education information from many sources.
EPA — Kids, Students, and Teachers	www.epa.gov/epahome/ students.htm	This U. S. Environmental Protection Agency (EPA) Web site provides fact-sheets, interactive games, and more for kids, students, and teachers who want to learn about the environment or share what they know with others. The Web site can help you with all sorts of information about the EPA and the environment.
ERIC Clearinghouse for Science, Mathematics, and Environmental Education	www.ericse.org	This Web site, provided by ERIC, offers a variety of resources for teaching and learning about science, mathematics, and the environment.
Federal Communications Commission (FCC)	www.fcc.gov/learnnet	The FCC LearnNet Web site provides information about FCC programs that are working to bring every school in America into the information age.
Federal Resources for Educational Excellence (FREE)	www.ed.gov/free	FREE provides hundreds of Internet-based education resources supported by federal agencies available at one great Web site.
FedWorld	www.fedworld.gov	FedWorld is a comprehensive central access point for searching, locating, ordering, and acquiring government information.
FirstGov.gov	www.firstgov.gov	Visit the U.S. government's official Web portal that makes all of America's government services available worldwide.
FirstGov for Kids	www.kids.gov	This U.S. government interagency Kids' Portal provides links to federal kids' sites along with some of the best kids' sites from other organizations all grouped by subject.
Food and Drug Administration (FDA)	www.fda.gov	Learn about the latest FDA developments that will help keep you and your students informed about important health issues.
healthfinder®	www.healthfinder.gov	This Web site is an important source for educators to find reliable consumer, health and human services information.
Institute of Education Sciences	www.ed.gov/offices/IES	The U. S. Department of Education provides educational research resources funded by congress at this Web site.
Kidz Privacy	www.ftc.gov/bcp/conline/edcams/ kidzprivacy/index.html	This site from the Federal Trade commission covers the very important issue of children's privacy and how it affects kids, their parents, and teachers.
Library of Congress	www.loc.gov	The Library of Congress is an incredible library resource for students and teachers.
National Aeronautics and Space Administration (NASA)	www.nasa.gov	This awesome Web site covers NASA's extensive education program.
National Archives and Records Administration (NARA)	www.archives.gov/ digital_classroom/index.html	The NARA site presents the Digital Classroom, which encourages teachers of students at all levels to use archival documents in the classroom.
National Endowment for the Humanities	www.neh.fed.us	Online projects at this Web site support learning in history, literature, philosophy, and other areas of the humanities.
National Gallery of Art	www.nga.gov	The National Gallery of Art (NGA) is home to the world's finest paintings and sculptures. This site offers a wealth of culture. It includes a link to NGA Kids for exciting animation and interactivity.
National Oceanic and Atmospheric Administration (NOAA)	www.noaa.gov	NOAA provides information about the weather, oceans, satellites, fisheries, climates, and more.

Federal Government

Site Name	Location (site locations begin with http://)	Comment
National Park Service (NPS)	www.nps.gov/learn	LearningNSP is your one stop for finding education materials about America's national parks; includes TeacherZONE and GoZONE for kids.
National Register of Historic Places: Teaching with Historic Places (TwHP)	www.cr.nps.gov/nr/twhp	TwHP offers great lesson plans and guidance on using historic places in teaching and learning.
National Science Foundation (NSF)	www.nsf.gov	The NSF Web site promotes the progress of science and health; it is a must stop for science teachers.
Peace Corps	www.peacecorps.gov/wws/index.html	The Peace Corps World Wise Schools education program is designed to help students gain a greater understanding of other cultures and countries.
Recreation.gov	www.recreation.gov/index.cfm	This is a fantastic Web site for anyone searching for information about recreational opportunities on federal lands.
Regional Education Laboratories	www.ed.gov/EdRes/EdFed/RegLab.html	This Web site offers details about the K-12 educational laboratories that are funded by the U. S. Department of Education and work to help schools solve problems.
Regional Technology Consortia Program	bcol02.ed.gov/Programs/EROD/org_list.cfm?category_ID=RTC	This Web site gives information about the programs that are funded by the U. S. Department of Education to help K-12 schools integrate technology.
Smithsonian Center for Education and Museum Studies	educate.si.edu	This essential source includes lesson plans, resource guides, field trips, and more for all educators.
students.gov	www.students.gov/STUGOVWebApp/index.jsp	This Web site contains great links to federal Web site resources for post-secondary students.
The Kennedy Center ARTSEDGE	artsedge.kennedy-center.org	The National Arts and Education Network links the arts and education through technology.
United States Department of Agriculture (USDA)	www.reeusda.gov	The USDA provides extensive sources of research and education information about many important subjects for all ages.
United States Geological Survey (USGS)	www.usgs.gov/education	The USGS Learning Web site is dedicated to K-12 education, exploration, and life-long learning.
U.S. Census Bureau	www.census.gov	Through this Web site, expose your students to timely, relevant, and quality data about the people and economy of the United States.
U.S. Department of Health and Human Services (HHS)	www.os.dhhs.gov	The HHS offers a wealth of information related to public health, privacy issues, grant programs, and more at this Web site.
U.S. Department of Education	www.ed.gov	All teachers should make this Web site a first stop as they embark on their teaching careers. The site provides information about student readiness, gives lesson ideas and materials, includes training and development sources, offers guidelines for applying for grants, and much more.
U.S. Department of Energy: Office of Science	www.science.doe.gov/index.htm	This Web site is dedicated to helping educate America's next generation of scientists.
U.S. Depart of the Interior (DOI)	www.doi.gov	The DOI is dedicated to the internal development of the United States and the welfare of its people.
U.S. Fish and Wildlife Service	www.fws.gov	Learn how to protect the homes and lives of fish and wildlife at this interesting Web site.
USDA Forest Service	www.fs.fed.us	This Web site is a great resource for information about public lands in the United States; it includes a special section just for kids.
USDA for Kids	www.usda.gov/news/usdakids	This extraordinary Web site contains a treasure-trove of resources for children; adults will be intrigued too.
Welcome to the White House	www.whitehouse.gov	Welcome to the White House provides links to many collections, programs, and products of significant educational benefit; offers a wealth of information and news about the president, government, and history; it includes virtual tours and interactivity of value to all ages.

References

This Third Edition of *Teachers Discovering Computers* was created using information that was gathered, reviewed, and researched from various Web sites and other resources. You can review many of these resources by accessing the Teachers Discovering Computers, Third Edition Web site at www.course.com/tdc3. The textbook Web site contains links to hundreds of resources, including many research articles and Web sites dedicated to educational theory, education practice, instructional models, and research-based integration solutions. The following are additional references that were used in the preparation of this textbook.

Anderson, R., & Speck, B. (2001). *Using technology in k-8 literacy classrooms*. Columbus, OH: Prentice Hall.

Bitter, G., & Pierson, M. (2002). *Using technology in the classroom* (5th ed.). Boston: Allyn & Bacon.

Branigan, C. (2003). Schools urged to teach '21st-century' skills. Retrieved March 24, 2003, from http://www.eschoolnews.com/news/showStoryalert.cfm?ArticleID=4506

Dean, K. (2002). PDAs good for education. Retrieved April 23, 2003, from http://www.wired.com/news/school/0,1383,56297,00.html

Dexter, S., & Anderson, R. (1999). Teachers' views of computers as catalysts for changes in their teaching practice. *Journal of Research on Computing in Education*, 31(3), 221-239.

eSchool News Staff Report. (2003). Quick! Tell me how to buy classroom & curriculum planning software. Retrieved Feb 23, 2003, from http://www.eschoolnews.com/resources/reports/classroom.cfm

Flores, A. (2002). Learning and teaching mathematics with technology. Retrieved April 2, 2003, from http://my.nctm.org/eresources/article_summary.asp?URI=TCM2002-02-308a&from=B]

Forcier, R., & Descy, D. (2002). *The computer as an educational tool: productivity and problem solving* (3rd ed.). Columbus, OH: Prentice Hall.

Grable, M., & Grable, C. (2000). *Integrating the Internet for meaningful learning*. Boston: Houghton Mifflin Company.

Gredler, M. (2001). *Learning and instruction* (4th ed.). Columbus, OH, Upper Saddle River: Prentice Hall.

Gunter, G. (2001). Making a difference — using emerging technologies and teaching strategies to restructure an undergraduate technology course for preservice teachers. *Education Media International, 38*(1), 13-20.

Gunter, G., & Murphy, D. (1997). Technology integration: The importance of administrative support. *Education Media International, 34*(3), 136-139.

Heinich, M., Molenda, M., Russell, J., & Smaldino, S. (2002). *Instructional media and technologies for learning* (7th ed.). Columbus, OH: Prentice Hall.

Intel Teach to the Future. (2003). Retrieved March 3, 2003, from http://www97.intel.com/education/teach/index.htm

International Society for Technology in Education. (2003). National educational technology standards (NETS) project. Retrieved April 3, 2003, from http://cnets.iste.org

Kellough, R., & Kellough, N. (2003). *Teaching young adolescents: A guide to methods and resources* (4th ed.). Columbus, OH: Prentice Hall.

Lever-Duffy, J., McDonald, J., & Mizell, A. (2003). *Teaching and learning with technology*. Boston: Allyn & Bacon.

Matematica Policy Research, Inc. (2001). *Analysis of the 1999-2000 annual performance reports for preparing tomorrow's teachers to use technology final report*. Retrieved July 5, 2003, from http://www.ed.gov/offices/OUS/PES/higher.html#pt3

Meyer, K. (2003). The Web's impact on student learning. *T.H.E. Journal, 30*(10), 14-24.

Microsoft. (2002). *Microsoft computer dictionary* (5th ed.). Redmond, WA: Microsoft Press.

Morrison, G., Lowther, D., & DeMeulle, L. (1999). *Integrating computer technology into the classroom*. Columbus, OH: Merrill Education/Prentice Hall.

National Council for Accreditation of Teacher Education. (2001). Technology and the new professional teacher: Preparing for the 21st century classroom. Retrieved February 22, 2003, from http://www.ncate.org/accred/projects/tech/m-technology.htm

National Center for Educational Statistics. (1999). Teachers' tools for the 21st century: A report on teachers' use of technology. Publication # NCES 2000102. Retrieved June 23, 2002, from http://nces.ed.gov/pubsearch/pubsinfo.asp?pubid=2000102

New Measure. (2003). Helping you design rubrics. Retrieved May 17, 2003, from http://www.rubrics.com

Newby, T., Stepich, D., Lehman, J., & Russell, J. (2000). *Instructional technology for teaching and learning: Designing instruction, integrating computers, and using media* (2nd ed.). Columbus, OH: Prentice Hall.

Ornstein, A., & Hunkins, F. (1998). *Curriculum foundations, principles, and theory* (3rd ed.). Seattle, WA: Allyn & Bacon.

Policy Information Center. (2000, October). *How teaching matters*. Princeton, NJ: Education Testing Service.

Preparing Tomorrow's Teachers to Use Technology. (2002). Retrieved March 3, 2003, from http://www.pt3.org

President's Committee of Advisors on Science and Technology. (1997). Report to the president on the use of technology to strengthen k-12 education in the United States. Retrieved June 19, 2001, from http://www.agiweb.org/hearings/pcastedu.html

Robyler, M. (2003). *Integrating educational technology into teaching* (3rd ed.). Columbus, OH: Prentice Hall.

Schunk, D. (2004). *Learning theories: An educational perspective* (4th ed.). Columbus, OH: Merrill Education/Prentice Hall.

Shelly, G., Cashman, T., Gunter, R., & Gunter, G. (2002). *Teachers discovering computers: Integrating technology in the classroom* (2nd ed.). Boston: Course Technology.

Shelly, G., Cashman, T., Gunter, R., & Gunter, G. (2003). *Teachers discovering and integrating Microsoft Office: Essential concepts and techniques*. Boston: Course Technology.

Shelly, G., Cashman, T., & Vermaat, M. (2002). *Microsoft Office xp: Introductory concepts and techniques*. Boston: Course Technology.

Shelly, G., Cashman, T., & Vermaat, M. (2003). *Discovering computers 2004: A gateway to information*. Boston: Course Technology.

Thompson, A., Simonson, M.R., & Hargrave, C. (1996). *Educational technology: A review of the research* (2nd ed.). Ames, IO: Association for Educational Communications and Technology.

United States Department of Education. (2002). No child left behind. Retrieved January 18, 2003, from http://www.nclb.gov

Universal Service Administrative Company. (2003). *E-rate.* Retrieved March 18, 2003, from http://www.sl.universalservice.org

Web-Based Education Commission (2000). The power of the Internet for learning. The president and the congress of the United States. Retrieved May 17, 2002, from http://interact.hpcnet.org/webcommission/index.htm

Welliver, P. (1990). *Instructional transformation: a module for change.* A report of the Pennsylvania regional computer resource center. University Park, PA: Pennsylvania State University.

Willis, J., Thompson, A., & Sadera, W. (1999). Research on technology and teacher education: Current status and future directions. *Educational Technology Research and Development, 47*(4), 29-45.

Wise, A. (1997). Technology and the new professional teacher - preparing for the 21st century. Retrieved June 14, 2000, from http://www.ncate.org/projects/tech/TECH.HTM

Index

802.11: Family of specifications developed for wireless local area networks by the Institute of Electrical and Electronics Engineers (IEEE). **8.51**

Ability level: Student's current competency level or the skill level they can achieve for a specific learning objective. **7.09**

Absolute hyperlinks: Hyperlinks to another document on a different Internet computer that could be across the country or across the world. **2.22**

Academic level: Evaluation based on grade level with increments to determine if a student is performing at the appropriate level. **7.09**

Acceptable Use Policy (AUP): Set of rules that governs the use of school and school district computers, networks, and the Internet by teachers, administrators, staff, and students. **2.36, 8.26**

Access controls: Security measures that define who can access a computer, when they can access it, and what actions they can take while using the computer. **8.07**

Accommodation: Process of a child learning by fitting information or experiences to his or her knowledge base, defined by Piaget. **6.50**

Accuracy of computer, 1.11

Active learning: Type of learning that provides students with the opportunity to be involved and interested in their own learning and gives them a sense of ownership of the information with which they are presented because they are actively involved in the learning process. **6.12, 6.14, 6.24**

Adapter card, *see* **Expansion card**

Address: Unique number identifying the location of a byte in memory. **4.07**

Address
  e-mail, 2.31
  Internet, 2.19-20
  Web page, 2.21-22

Address book: Feature of personal information manager used to organize names, addresses, and telephone numbers. **3.22**

Adobe GoLive: Web page authoring program. **3.28**

Advanced learning system, *see* **Open learning system**

Advanced Research Projects Agency (ARPA): Department of Defense agency that developed a networking project that the Internet has roots in, called ARPANET. **2.13**

Affective domain: A student's emotions, interests, attitude, attention, and awareness, identified by Bloom. **6.62**

Affiliation: Professional organization, school, school district, university, company, or government office with which a particular Web site is associated. **7.10**

Alternative assessment: Assessment that uses nontraditional methods to determine whether students have mastered appropriate content and skill level; approaches include authentic, performance-based, or project-based assessment. **7.12-17**

America Online, 1.18

American Standard Code for Information Interchange (ASCII): Most widely-used coding scheme to represent data on many personal computers. **4.03**

Analog: Representation of data using continuous signals. **4.02**

Analog formats: Video camera formats including 8mm, Hi8, VHS-C, and Super VHS-C. **5.52**

Analog signal: A continuous electrical wave. **2.04**

Anchor: Concepts and information that form a basis for other information upon which to connect and build. **6.52**

Anchored instruction: Provision of a knowledge base on which students can build; learning and teaching activities are designed around an anchor (or situation) that provides a scenario or problem enhanced with curriculum materials that allow exploration by the learner. **6.12, 6.52**

Animated GIF: Popular type of animation where a group of several images are combined into a single GIF file. **2.28**

Animation: Multimedia element that creates the appearance of motion by displaying a series of still images in rapid sequence. **2.27, 5.06**
Web and, 2.27

Anonymous FTP: Ability for anyone accessing an FTP site to transfer some, if not all, available files. **2.32**

Anti-spam program: Program used to block unwanted e-mail messages that works by attempting to remove spam before it reaches an e-mail inbox. Sometimes anti-spam programs remove valid e-mail messages. **8.18**

Antivirus program: Program designed to detect, disinfect, and protect computers and networks from viruses; they work by looking for programs that attempt to modify the boot program, the operating system, or other programs that normally are read from but not written to. In addition to providing protection from viruses, most antivirus programs also have utilities to remove or repair infected programs and files. Also called vaccines. **8.06**

Apple Computer, *see* **Macintosh computer**

AppleWorks: Popular integrated software package for Macintosh computers. **3.25**

Application, *see* **Application software**

Application software: Programs designed to perform specific tasks for users; examples include educational, business, and scientific computer programs. Also called application, or software application. **1.14-16, 3.04-37**
buying computer and, 4.54
database, 3.15-17
evaluating, 7.06-09
home and personal use, 3.32-34
learning aids, 3.34-35
multimedia, 3.25-28
PDA, 3.23-24
personal information manager (PIM), 3.22-23
presentation graphics, 3.17-21
productivity, 3.10-25
school, 3.29-32
spreadsheet, 3.13-15
starting, 3.05-06
suites, 3.24-25
upgrades, 3.35
versions, 3.35-36
word processing, 3.10-13
working with, 3.06-08

Appointment calendar: Feature of personal information manager used to schedule activities. **3.22**

Appropriate: Describes educational technology that is suitable for the educational situation and promotes learning at the correct levels of ability and academic achievement. **7.02**

Arithmetic operations: Performed by the arithmetic/logic unit, include addition, subtraction, multiplication, and division operations. **4.07**

Arithmetic/logic unit (ALU): CPU component that performs the execution part of the machine cycle; includes performing arithmetic, comparison, and logical operations. **4.07**

ARPANET: Networking project that the Internet has roots in, developed by the Department of Defense, which effectively linked together scientific and academic researchers in the United States. **2.14**

Article: Message on a newsgroup. **2.33**

Arts curriculum: Curriculum that usually incorporates instruction in the visual and performing arts of drawing, painting, dance, music, and theater. **7.37**

AskERIC: Federally funded Internet-based service that provides educational information to teachers, media specialists, administrators, parents, and other interested persons throughout the world; provides a question-and-answer service, virtual library, lesson plans, and searchable database that contains more than one million abstracts of documents and journal articles on educational research. **7.29**

Assessment: Any method used to understand the current knowledge a student possesses; it can range from a teacher's subjective judgment based on a single observation of a student's performance to a state-mandated standardized test. **7.12**

Assimilation: New knowledge absorbed as a child experiences new things and learns new information, defined by Piaget. **6.50**

Assistant, *see* **Wizard**

Assistive technologies: Innovative technologies that modify or adapt the classroom for special learning needs. **8.32**

ASSURE Model: Instructional model that is a procedural guide for planning and delivering instruction that integrates technologies and media into the teaching process. **6.22**

Audience: Individual or group intended to view a Web page. **7.11**

Audio: Digitized music, speech, or any other sound that is stored and produced by a computer. **2.28, 4.22, 5.06**
downloading, 2.12
streaming, 2.29
Web and, 2.28-29

Audio input: Process of recording music, speech, or sound effects. **4.19**

Audio output: Any music, speech, or other sound produced by a computer; widely available on the Internet. **4.28**

AUP, *see* **Acceptable Use Policy**

Authentic assessment: Alternative assessment method that measures learning by evaluating a student's ability to master practical learning standards. Also called performance-based assessment. **7.14**

Authentic learning: Learning experiences that demonstrate real-life connections between students' lessons and the world in which they live. **6.12, 6.14, 7.14**

Authoring tool, *see* **Multimedia authoring software**

Authority: When evaluating Web sites, the credibility of the person or persons who author and create the site. 7.10

Authorware: Multimedia authoring software program. 5.29

AutoSave: Feature that automatically saves open documents as specified time periods. 3.08

Auxiliary storage, *see* **Storage**

Backbone: High-speed network that connects regional and local networks to the Internet. 2.14, 2.18-19

Background (Web page): Backdrop against which other elements of a Web page are shown. 3.50, 3.54-55

Backup: Duplicate of a file, program, or disk that can be used if the original is lost, damaged, or destroyed. 4.31, 8.15

Backup procedure: Procedure that outlines a regular plan of copying and backing up important data and program files. 8.15

Banking, technology used in, 1.03

Bar code: Identification code that consists of a set of vertical lines and spaces of different widths. 4.18

Beaming: Transfer of data from one PDA to another through an infrared port. 3.23

Behaviorism: Theory that centers on learning as it relates to behavior. 6.54

Benchmark: Specific, measurable learning objective or indicator that usually is tied to a curriculum standard. Also called learning objective. 6.04

Binary: Numbering system that uses just two unique digits: 0 and 1. 4.03

Bit: Short for binary digit, representation of the smallest unit of data a computer can handle. 4.03

Blackout: Complete power failure. 8.14

Block schedule: Alternative way of scheduling classes in which classes meet every other day instead of every day. 7.20

Bloom, Benjamin, 6.62-63

Bloom's Taxonomy: Levels used to acquire knowledge about a topic, identified by Bloom. 6.63

Bluetooth: Technology that uses short-range radio waves to transmit data between two Bluetooth devices. 8.50

Bobby: Software program that analyzes Web sites and pages to see if they meet the World Wide Web Consortium's (W3W) Web content Accessibilities Guidelines. 8.33

Body Works: Multimedia educational software application for teaching all related concepts about the human body. 6.13

Bookmark: Method of keeping track of Web pages that have been viewed; records the Web page title and URL, on a computer for use in future Web sessions. Also called favorites. 2.25

Books, electronic, 4.24, 5.10

Boot sector virus: Virus that replaces the boot program used to start a computer with a modified, infected version of the boot program. When the computer runs the infected boot program, it loads the virus into the computer's memory. Once a virus is in memory, it spreads to any disk inserted into the computer. 8.03

Border: Decorative line or pattern along one or more edges of a page or graphic. 3.11

Branching: Nonlinear approach used by tutorials that offers alternative paths through a lesson based on students' responses. 5.22

Broadband: Technologies that transmit signals at much faster speeds than traditional network configurations. 2.06, 2.10

Brownout: Prolonged undervoltage. 8.14

Browser, *see* **Web browser**

Bruner, Jerome, 6.47-49

Button: Graphical element (usually a rectangular or circular shape) that, when selected, causes a specific action to take place. 3.06

Buying guide, for personal computers, 4.52-67

Byte: Eight bits grouped together as a unit. 4.03

Cable modem: High-speed modem that uses broadband technology to send and receive data over the cable television network. 2.05-06, 2.17

Cafeteria manager, computer use by, 1.23

Carpal tunnel syndrome (CTS): Inflammation of the nerve that connects the forearm to the palm of the wrist, which can be caused by repeated or forceful bending of the wrist, such as occurs during computer use. 8.28

Cars, computers in, 1.03

Catalogs, technology evaluation and, 7.04

Cathode ray tube (CRT): Large glass tube that is the core of most monitors. 4.22

CD, *see* **Compact disc**

CD-ROM, 1.08

CD-ROM drive: Drive that can read CDs. 1.07, 1.08, 4.33

CD-RW, 1.08

CD-RW drive, 1.07

Cell (spreadsheet): The intersection of a column and a row in a spreadsheet. 3.14

Cell (table): The intersection of a column and a row in a table. 7.66

Centers: Breaking a classroom into many different types of learning environments without ever leaving the room, allowing students to rotate around the classroom to complete projects or activities. Also called learning centers. 6.28

Central processing unit (CPU): Electronic device on the motherboard that interprets and carries out the instructions that operate a computer. Also called a processor. 1.06, 4.05

Chart: Graphical illustration of numeric data. 3.15

Chat: Real-time typed conversation that takes place on a computer. 2.34

Chat client: Program on computer that allows connection to a chat server. 2.34

Chat room: Communications medium, or channel, that permits users to chat with each other. 2.12, 2.34

Checklist: Predetermined list of performance criteria. 7.15

Checkpoint section, 1.26

Children's Internet Protection Act (CIPA): Act passed by Congress in 2000 to protect children from obscene, pornographic, and other information on the Internet considered harmful to minors. 8.24

Chip: Small piece of semiconducting material usually no bigger than one-half-inch square and is made up of many layers of circuits and microscopic components that carry electronic signals. 1.06, 4.05. *See also* **Central processing unit (CPU); Memory**

Citizenship, preparing students for, 1.02, 1.18

Classic conditioning: Behavioral process defined by Pavlov, which refers to the natural reflex that occurs in response to a stimulus. 6.55

Classroom
mobile lab, 6.19-20
networking, 2.07-11
technology integration, *see* **Technology integration**
wireless, 2.07, 6.19

ClearType: Technology developed by Microsoft to improve the quality of reading materials on LCD screens, such as e-books. 5.10

Clicking: Mouse operation that involves pressing buttons on the mouse. 4.15

Clip: Segment of video. 5.07

Clip art: Type of graphic that may include drawings, diagrams, and photographs and can be inserted in other documents. 3.11

Clip art collections: Sets of previously created digital images that can be inserted into a document. 3.11, 5.04

Clip art/image gallery: Collection of clip art images, pictures, video clips, and audio clips. 3.18

Clipboard: Temporary storage location for text or other information during cut or copy operations. 3.07

Clock speed: Speed at which a processor executes instructions. 4.07

Coaxial cable, 2.04

Codec: Specification of how audio and video is compressed and stored within a file. 5.54

Cognitive domain: A student's intellectual level, defined by Bloom. 6.62

Cognitive scaffold: Mental bridge to build an understanding of complicated concepts. 6.13

Collaborative learning: Learning that takes place when a child is challenged by some form of expertise, such as an advanced peer or teacher, defined by Vygotsky. 6.52

Colleges
distance learning and, 5.18
Web use, 2.01

Color scanner: Scanner that converts images into a digitized format for use in multimedia applications. 5.28

Commands: Instructions that cause a computer program to perform specific actions. 3.06, 4.12

Communications: Process in which two or more computers or devices transfer data, instructions, and information; sometimes called telecommunications. 1.12, 2.03
learning effects, 2.02

Communications channel: Path that data follows as the data is transmitted from the sending equipment to the receiving equipment in a communications system. 2.04

Communications device: Hardware that enables a computer to exchange data, information, and instructions with another computer. 1.08

Communications networks, *see* **Networks**

Communications protocol: Rules that define how devices connect to each other and transmit data over a network. 2.16

Communications software: Programs that manage the transmission of data between computers. 2.04

Community, computer use by, 1.25

Community site license: Software license that gives an entire region or state the right to install an unlimited number of educational copies of a particular software program on individual computers or a network. 8.12

Compact disc (CD): Flat, round, portable, metal-coated plastic storage medium that is usually 4.75 inches in diameter and less than one-twentieth of an inch thick; stores data, instructions, and information in microscopic pits that are on the top surface. 1.08, 4.33-34

Compact disc read-only memory (CD-ROM): Type of optical disc that uses the same laser technology as audio CDs for recording and can contain text, graphics, animation, video, and sound. A CD-ROM can hold 650 MB of data. 4.34

Compact disc-recordable (CD-R): Compact disc that information can be recorded onto; part of the disc can be written on at one time and another part at a later time. Each part can be written on only one time and the disc's content cannot be erased. 4.36

Compact disc-rewriteable (CD-RW): Erasable disc that can be written on multiple times. **4.36**

Comparison operations: Operations performed by the arithmetic/logic unit that involve comparing one data item to another to determine if the first item is greater than, equal to, or less than the other. 4.07

Compression
audio, 2.28
video, 5.08, 5.54

Compression (picture): Reduction of a digital camera's image file size. 5.48

Computer: Electronic machine, operating under the control of instructions stored in its own memory, that can accept data (input), manipulate the data according to specified rules (process), produce results (output), and store the results for future use. 1.04
buying guide, 4.52-67
categories of, 1.09-11
data representation in, 4.02-04
example of school use, 1.21-25
functions of, 1.04-05
hardware, *see* **Hardware**
maintaining, 4.71-72
power of, 1.11-12
use of, 1.01-02, 1.03

Computer crime: Any illegal act involving a computer. 8.02

Computer ethics: Moral guidelines that govern the use of computers, networks, and information systems. 8.16

Computer games: Games that use a combination of graphics, sound, and video to create a realistic and entertaining game situation. 5.14

Computer history, timelines in, 1.27

Computer lab: Designated classroom filled with computers and technology for groups of students to use. Also called technology lab. 6.06

Computer lab on wheels, *see* **Wireless mobile lab**
traditional, 6.05-06, 6.19
wireless mobile, 6.19-20

Computer literacy: Knowledge and understanding of computers and their uses. 1.04, 6.01

Computer program: Series of instructions that tells the computer how to perform the tasks necessary to process data into information. Also called software, or program. **1.12**
application, *see* **Application software**

Computer programmers: People who write the instructions necessary to direct the computer to process data into information, called software programs. Also called programmers. **1.16**

Computer security risk: Any event or action that has the potential of causing loss of computer equipment, software, data and information, or processing capability. 8.02

Computer vandalism: Vandalism that takes many forms, from a student cutting a computer cable or deleting files to individuals breaking in a school and randomly smashing computers. 8.10

Computer virus, *see* **Virus**

Computer vision syndrome:

Computer-assisted instruction (CAI): Software designed to help teach facts, information, and/or skills associated with subject-related materials. 5.21

Computer-based training (CBT): Tool in which individuals learn by using and completing exercises using instructional software on computers. 5.09

Concept map: Planning tool that helps students use flowcharting to understand the attributes and relationships of the main subject and provides a visual tool for brainstorming and planning. Also called a story web. 7.19

Connectors: Device on a port that allows connection to the system unit. 4.10

Constructivism, *see* **Constructivist**

Constructivist: Theory based on a type of learning in which the learner forms, or constructs, much of what he or she learns or comprehends. Also called constructivism. 6.46

Content: Refers to information a Web page provides. 7.11

Context-sensitive: Feature that means Help information is related to the current instruction being attempted. 3.35

Control unit: Component of the CPU that directs and coordinates most of the operations in a computer. 4.06

Cooperative learning: Method of instruction where students work collaboratively in groups to achieve learning objectives and goals. 1.18, 6.15

Copy: Process of duplicating a portion of a document and electronically storing it in a temporary storage location called the Clipboard. 3.07

Copyright: Retention of ownership of a work by the original author or creator of the work and giving the creator exclusive rights to reproduce and distribute the creative work. 8.20

Cordless keyboard: Input device that is a battery-operated keyboard that transmits data using wireless technology. 4.14

Cordless mouse: Mouse that is battery powered and transmits data using wireless technology. Also called wireless mouse. 4.15

Courseware: Interactive CBT software usually available on CD-ROM, DVD-ROM, or the Web. 5.09

CPU, *see* **Central processing unit**

Cracker: Individual who tries to access a computer or network illegally. 8.07

Creating: Process of developing a document by entering text or numbers, designing graphics, and performing other tasks using an input device such as a keyboard or mouse. 3.07

Creativity: Elements of originality, imaginative and innovative approaches, and artistic abilities in student projects. 7.19

Creativity applications: Educational software that often allows students to start with a blank canvas, allowing them to use imagination and ingenuity. 5.25

Critical-thinking applications: Educational software that stimulates students to use critical-thinking skills in a variety of ways. 5.25

Cross-discipline lesson: Lesson that includes a combination of curriculum-specific areas, such as math or science, that are integrated with language arts. 7.41

CTS, *see* **Carpal tunnel syndrome**

Currency: Measure of how up to date, or timely, Web page content is and how often it is updated. 7.11

Curriculum: All of the experiences a learner has under the supervision and guidance of teachers, consisting of a plan or written document that includes a series of required goals and learning outcomes. 6.02-04
benchmarks, 6.04
spiral, 6.49
standards, 6.03-04
technology integration and, 6.08-09, 7.01-45

Curriculum frameworks: Documents that describe curriculum goals and objectives for learning, and often include direction for specific content areas, benchmarks, activities, and forms of evaluation. Also called curriculum guides. 6.02

Curriculum goal, *see* **Curriculum standard**

Curriculum guides, *see* **Curriculum frameworks**

Curriculum integration, *see* **Technology integration**

Curriculum page: Teacher-created document or Web page that contains hyperlinks to teacher-selected and evaluated sites that assist in teaching content-specific curriculum objectives. 3.28, 7.28, 8.27
creating using Microsoft Word, 7.60-82

Curriculum standard: Standard that defines what a student is expected to know at certain stages of education. Also called a curriculum goal. 6.03

Curriculum-specific learning: Learning how to apply teaching principles, knowledge, and ideas to authentic and practical classroom lessons and projects that can benefit students. Also called discipline-specific learning. 1.02-03

Custom software: Program developed at a user's request to perform specific functions. 1.16

Cut: Process of removing a portion of a document and electronically storing it in a temporary storage location called the Clipboard. 3.07

Cybercafé: Coffeehouse or restaurant that provides computers with Internet access to its customers. 8.52

Data: A collection of unorganized facts that can include words, numbers, images, and sounds. Data is manipulated and processed by computers to create information that is useful. 1.04, 4.12
accuracy of, 1.11
communications system and, 2.04
representation in computer, 4.02-04

Data projector: Output device that projects an image that displays on a computer screen onto a large screen, so that an audience, such as a classroom or school assembly, can see the image clearly. 4.26, 5.31

Database: Collection of data organized in a manner that allows access, retrieval, and use of that data. 1.15, 3.16

Database file: Collection of related data organized in records. 3.16

Database software: Software used to create a computerized database; add, change, and delete data; sort and retrieve data from the database; and create forms and reports using the data in the database. 3.15-17

Decoding: Control unit process of translating an instruction into commands the computer understands. 4.06

Delete: Process of removing text or other information from a document's existing content. 3.07

Design: Arrangement of a Web site — that is, the way it uses instructional design principles to deliver content to the user. 7.11

Desktop: Onscreen work area that uses common graphical elements such as icons, buttons, windows, menus, and dialog boxes, all of which can display on the desktop. 3.06

Desktop computer: Name given to personal computers because they are designed so the system unit, input devices, output devices, and any other devices fit entirely on a desk. 1.10
purchasing, 4.52-57

Desktop publishing (DTP) software: Software used to design, produce, and deliver sophisticated documents that contain text, graphics, and brilliant colors. 3.25

Dewey, John, 6.53-54

Dialog box: Special window displayed by a program to provide information, present available options, or request a response using command buttons, option buttons, text boxes, and check boxes. 3.08

Dial-up access: Connection to the Internet using a computer and a modem to dial into an ISP or online service over regular telephone lines. 2.17

Digital: Representation of data using two discrete states: on and off. 4.02

Digital cameras: Type of cameras that allow a user to take pictures and store the photographed images digitally (electronically) instead of on traditional film. 1.05, 4.19, 5.28, 5.48
image files, 5.49
selecting, 5.48
storage media, 4.38
using, 5.48-49

Digital formats: Video camera formats that include Mini-DV, MICROMV, Digital8, and DVD. 5.52

Digital images, 5.46-57

Digital imaging technology: Process of capturing and manipulating still photographic images in an electronic format. 5.48

Digital modems, 2.05

Digital signals: Individual electrical pulses that a computer uses to represent data. 2.04

Digital subscriber line (DSL): High-speed alternative to a modem that uses broadband technology to transmit data on existing standard telephone lines. 2.18

Digital-to-analog converter: Hardware used to save digital video on a standard video tape. 5.56

Digital video disc read-only memory, see **DVD-ROM**

Digital video technology: Technology used to input, edit, manage, publish, and share videos using a personal computer. 5.52-58

Director: Multimedia authoring software program. 5.29

Disabled students, see **Students with exceptionalities**

Discipline-specific learning, see **Curriculum-specific learning**

Discovery learning: Inquiry-based, nonlinear method of learning and teaching that involves branching off and investigating related topics as they are encountered. 1.18, **2.22**, 6.13

Discussion board, 2.32

Discussion groups, 2.12

Disk: Commonly-used storage medium, which is a round, flat piece of plastic or metal on which data, instructions, and information can be encoded. 4.29

Disk drive, 1.07

Diskette, see **Floppy disk**

Display device: Output device that displays text, graphics, and video information. 4.22

Distance education, see **Distance learning**

Distance learning: Delivery of education from one location to another; the learning takes place at this other location. Also called distance education or Web-based education. 5.17, 8.31

Document: Piece of work created with an application program and saved on a disk with a unique file name. 3.06
hypermedia, 2.22
hypertext, 2.22
Web page, see **Web page**

Documentation: Any printed or online information that provides assistance in installing, using, maintaining, and updating the software. 7.09

Domain name: Text version of a computer address. 2.20

Dot Kids: Part of the U.S. domain on the Internet that functions much like the children's section of a public library with content suitable for children under thirteen, implemented in 2002 when the Dot Kids Implementation and Efficiency Act was signed by the President. Dot Kids Web sites will be a safe zone for children when using the Internet. 8.24

Dot pitch: Factor in monitor quality, the distance between each pixel on a monitor. 4.25

Dot-matrix printer: Printer that produces printed images when tiny pins on a print head mechanism strike an inked ribbon. 4.25

Double-clicking: Mouse operation that involves pressing and releasing a mouse button twice without moving the mouse. 4.15

Download: Process of copying a file using a network. 2.32
audio files, 2.12, 2.29
FTP, 2.32
image files, 3.52
video files, 2.12, 2.30

Dragging: Mouse operation that involves moving data from one location to another. 4.15

Drill-and-practice software: Software that first supplies factual information and then through repetitive exercises allows students to continue to work on the specific materials to remember or memorize the information. Also called skills-reinforcement software. 5.21

DSL, see **Digital subscriber line**

DSL modem, 2.05

Dual inline memory module (DIMM): Small circuit board that contains multiple RAM chips. 4.08

DVD and CD mastering software: Software used to create slide show presentations on a recordable DVD or CD. 5.51

DVD-ROM (digital video disc read-only memory): Extremely high capacity CD capable of storing from 4.7 GB to 17 GB of data of a quality that far surpasses that of a CD. 1.08, **4.37**
educational software on, 8.31

DVD-ROM drive: Drive used to read a DVD-ROM. 1.07, **4.37**

Early learning applications: Educational software designed to provide students in grades K-3 with a developmental head start in reading, language arts, math, science, and other curricular areas. 5.26

Ease of use: Refers to anything that makes software easy to use. Also called user-friendliness. 7.09

E-book: Type of electronic book that uses a small, book-sized computer that can hold thousands of pages of text and small graphics. 5.10. *See also* **Electronic book**

Editing: Process of making changes to a document's existing content. 3.07

Editing video, 5.54-56

EDTECH: Large, well-known mailing list that allows educators from many different areas — teachers, administrators, technology coordinators, media specialists, and university faculty — to exchange information, comments, and ideas on educational issues. 7.05

Education
electronic references and, 5.10
impact of Internet and World Wide Web on, 2.36-37
networks and, 2.07-11
software for, 3.26-27
technology integration and, 6.01-31
wireless technology and, 8.54-55

Education Issues section, 1.27

Education Rate: Federal Communications Commission government initiative designed to provide discounts to schools and libraries on all communications services. Also called E-Rate. 1.21

Education search tools, 2.60-68

Education software, 1.15

Educational computer simulation: Computerized model of real life that represents a physical or simulated process. 5.23

Educational equalizer: Name given to the Internet and the World Wide Web because they give students of all backgrounds, socioeconomic levels, learning styles, and learning abilities access to the same information. 6.14

Educational games: Games used to teach information through repetition and practice. 5.22

Educational research, 6.45-66

Educational software: Software designed for the learning environment. 3.34
curriculum-specific, 5.25-28
integrating with multimedia, 5.01-33

Educational software application: Computer software products used to support teaching and learning of subject-related content. 5.20

Edutainment: Experience meant to be both educational and entertaining. 5.14

E-folio, see **Electronic portfolio**

Electronic book (e-book): Small, book-sized computer that allows users to read, save, highlight, bookmark, and add notes to online text. 4.24, 5.10

Electronic magazine: Digital publication available on the Web. Also called e-zine. **5.12**

Electronic mail (e-mail): Electronic exchange of messages and files to and from other computer users via a computer network. **1.12, 2.31**

Electronic portfolio: Electronically-stored portfolio that contains student assignments or projects. Also called an e-folio. **7.15**

Electronic profile: Combining acquired data about individuals with other information obtained from public sources. **8.16**

Electronic reference text: Digital version of a reference text, which uses text, graphics, sound, animation, and video to explain a topic or provide additional information. **5.10**

Electronic whiteboard, *see* **Interactive whiteboard**

E-mail, *see* **Electronic mail**

E-mail address: Combination of a user name and a domain name that identifies a user so he or she can receive messages. **2.31**

E-mail link, inserting, 3.62-64

E-mail program: Program used to create, send, receive, forward, store, print, and delete e-mail messages. **2.31**

Embedded assessment, *see* **Portfolio assessment**

Emoticons: Keyboard characters used in combinations to express emotion. **2.36**

Employee monitoring: Use of computers to observe, record, and review an individual's use of a computer, including communications such as e-mail, keyboard activity (used to measure productivity), and Internet sites visited. **8.18**

Encryption: Process of converting readable data into unreadable characters. **8.13**

Encryption key: Code that converts readable data into unreadable characters. **8.13**

End-user license agreement (EULA), *see* **Single-user license**

ENERGY STAR: Label that identifies a monitor as an energy-efficient product as defined by the Environmental Protection Agency (EPA). **4.25**

Entertainment, multimedia and, 5.14

Entertainment software: Software that includes interactive games, videos, and other programs designed to support a hobby or just provide amusement and enjoyment. **3.34**

ePALS: Project designed to enable students to develop an understanding of different cultures through student e-mail exchanges. **2.37**

E-Rate, *see* **Education Rate**

ESL and foreign language applications: Educational software that provides K-12 students with assistance in learning English and other languages. **5.26**

Essential questioning technique: Looking for the most important or fundamental part of a topic. **6.29**

Ethics: Standards that determine whether an action is good or bad. **8.16-27**

Evaluate: Process of determining an item's value or judging its worth. Evaluating educational technology involves determining if the technology is appropriate and enhances the teaching and learning process. **7.02**

Evaluation: Method of appraising or determining the significance or worth of an item, action, or outcome. **6.24**

Evaluation process: Process that includes assessing learner outcomes, reviewing, critiques of the learners' work or works

based on specific standards, and evaluating reviews of the media and materials used. **6.24**

Exceptional education curriculum: Curriculum that usually contains instruction in all curriculum areas with adaptations made for students with unique characteristics or special needs, including students who are gifted, learning disabled, physically disabled, emotionally disabled, or mentally disabled. Also called special education curriculum. **7.39**

Execute: Process of a computer performing a program. **1.12**

Executing: Control unit process of carrying out commands. **4.06**

Expansion board, *see* **Expansion card**

Expansion card: Circuit board inserted into a motherboard that adds new devices or capabilities to a computer. Also called adapter card or expansion board. **4.09**

Expansion slot: Opening, or socket, where a circuit board can be inserted into the motherboard. **4.09**

External hard disk: Separate, portable hard disk that connects to a USB or FireWire port by a cable. **4.32**

E-zine, *see* **Electronic magazine**

Facilitator of learning: Person who motivates students to want to learn, guides the student learning process, and promotes a learning atmosphere and an appreciation for the subject. **6.09**

Facsimile (fax) machine: Output device that transmits and receives documents over telephone lines. **4.27**

Fair use: Guidelines that allow educators to use and copy certain copyrighted materials for non-profit educational purposes. **8.20**

FAQ (Frequently Asked Questions): Answers to frequently asked questions contained in many Web pages and newsgroups. **2.36**

FAQ boxes, 1.25

Favorite, *see* **Bookmark**

Favorites: Bookmark list stored on a computer. **2.25**

Fetching: Control unit process of obtaining a program instruction or data item from memory. **4.06**

Fiber-optic cable, 2.04

Fields: Collection of related facts in a database. **3.16**

File: Named collection of data, instructions, or information, such as a document, a program, or a set of data used by a program. **3.08**
audio compression, 2.28
digital camera, 5.49
downloading, *see* **Download**
exchanging, 2.12
software versions and, 3.36
uploading, *see* **Upload**
video camera, 5.52, 5.54, 5.57
video compression, 5.08

File name: Unique set of letters, numbers, and other characters that identifies a file. **3.08**

File transfer protocol, *see* **FTP**

File virus: Virus that inserts virus code into program files; the virus then spreads to any program that accesses the infected file. **8.03**

Filtering software programs: Programs that allow parents, teachers, and others to block access to certain materials on the Internet. **2.35, 8.24**

Find: Feature that locates all occurrences of a particular character, word, or phrase. Also called search feature. **3.11**

Firewall: General term that refers to both hardware and software used to restrict access to data on a network. **2.35, 8.08**

FireWire: Port that can connect multiple devices that require fast data transmission speeds to a single connector. Also called FireWire. **4.11, 5.47, 5.52**

Flame wars: Exchanges of flames. **2.36**

Flames: Abusive or insulting messages sent on the Internet. **2.36**

Flat panel monitor, *see* **LCD monitor**

Floppy disk: Portable, inexpensive storage medium that consists of a thin, circular, flexible plastic disk with a magnetic coating enclosed in a square-shaped plastic shell. **1.08, 4.30**

Floppy disk drive: Device that can read from and write on a floppy disk. **1.07, 4.30-31**

Flowcharts: Diagrams that show the step-by-step actions that must take place by plotting a sequence of events. **7.19**

Font: Name given to a specific design of characters. **3.07**

Font size: Size of characters in a particular font. **3.07**

Font style: Feature that adds emphasis to a font, such as **bold,** *italic,* and underline. **3.07**

Footer: Text at the bottom of each page. **3.12**

Formatting (disk): Process of preparing a disk (floppy disk or hard disk) for reading and writing by organizing the disk into storage locations called tracks and sectors. **3.36, 4.30**

Formatting (document): Process of changing the appearance of a document. **3.07**
Web page text, 3.55-57

Formula: Calculations performed on numeric data in a spreadsheet; results are displayed in the cell containing the formula. **3.14**

Frame rate correction: Tools included with some video editing programs that help fix the problem of lost video frames during the transfer of video. **5.54**

Freeware: Software provided at no cost to a user by an individual or company. **1.16, 8.12**

Frequently Asked Questions, *see* **FAQ**

FTP (File Transfer Protocol): Internet standard that allows the exchange of files with other computers on the Internet. **2.32**

FTP server: Computer that allows users to upload and download files using FTP. **2.32**

FTP site: Collection of files on an FTP server including text, graphics, audio, video, and program files. **2.32**

Function: Predefined formula that performs common calculations such as adding the values in a group of cells. **3.15**

Funding, 2.02, 2.07, 7.44

Future
of computer use, 1.04
of Internet and World Wide Web, 2.38

Gagne, Robert, 6.58-59

Games
educational, 5.22
input devices for, 4.17

Garbage in, garbage out (GIGO), 1.1

Gardner, Howard, 6.59-61

Gas plasma monitor: Flat-panel display that uses gas plasma technology, which substitutes a layer of gas for the liquid crystal material in an LCD monitor. **4.23**

Gigabyte (GB): Approximately one billion bytes. **4.08**

Gigahertz (GHz): One billion ticks of a system clock. **4.07**

Global positioning system (GPS), 8.57

GPS, *see* **Global positioning system**

Grade book software: Program that allows teachers to track and organize student tests, homework, lab work, and other scores. **3.30**

Grade Level Expectations (GLEs): Content and skills that students are expected to master for each subject area that are incorporated by some states and districts into curricula. **6.03**

Grant proposal: Document a potential grantee sends to a funding source. **7.44**

Grantee: Teacher, school, or organization to which grant funds or equipment are transferred. **7.44**

Grants: Funds provided by a funding source that transfers money, equipment, or services to a grantee. **7.44**

Graphical image, thumbnail of, 2.27

Graphical user interface (GUI): User interface that combines text, graphics, and other visual cues such as icons that allow a user to interact with software. **1.14, 3.04**

Graphics: Digital representations of nontext information, such as images, drawings, charts, pictures, photographs, animations, illustrations, and other images added to enhance Web pages and multimedia applications. Also called a picture or image. **2.27, 4.22, 5.04, 5.28**

multimedia and, 3.25-27, 5.02, 5.04-06

Web and, 2.27

Web page, 2.22, 3.51, 3.62-64

word processing software and, 3.11

Groceries, technology used in buying, 1.03

GUI, *see* **Graphical user interface**

Hacker: Originally a complimentary word for a computer enthusiast, now with a derogatory connotation because it refers to people who try to break into a computer often intending to steal or corrupt its data. **8.07**

Handheld computer: Computer small enough to fit in one hand while being operated with the other hand. **1.11**

input devices for, 4.19

service industry and, 8.56

storage media, 4.38

Hard copy: Name given to printed information because it is a more permanent form of output than that presented on a monitor. **4.25**

Hard disk: Storage device that usually consists of several inflexible, circular disks, called platters, on which items such as data, instructions, and information are stored electronically. 1.08, **4.32**

Hard disk drive, 1.07

Hardware: Electric, electronic, and mechanical equipment that makes up a computer. **1.04, 1.05-08, 4.01-38**

communications, 2.04-06

determining needs, 6.26

input, 1.05, 4.12-21

output, 1.06, 4.21-29

storage devices, 1.07-08, 4.29-38

system unit, *see* **System unit**

Header: Text at the top of each page in a document. **3.12**

Headings: Text used to set off different paragraphs of text or different sections of a page. **3.51, 3.58-60**

Health, electronic references and, 5.10

Help: Feature integrated into an application software package that is the electronic equivalent of a user manual; provides assistance in learning how to use an application software package. **3.34**

High schools, distance learning and, 5.18

High-definition television (HDTV): Type of television set that works with digital broadcasting signals, supports a wider screen, and displays at a higher resolution than a standard television set. **4.23**

High-order thinking skills: Abilities to solve problems, engage in critical thinking, and interpret and solve complex issues. **1.18, 6.15**

History list: Method of keeping track of Web pages that have been viewed during time online. **2.25**

Home

Internet connections, 2.17

software for, 3.32-34

Home network: Network that connects computers in a home or home office. **2.06**

wireless, 8.56

Home page: Starting point for a Web site which is similar to a book cover or table of contents for the site and provides information about the site's purpose and content. **2.21**

Horizontal lines: Lines that display across a page and are used to separate different sections of the page. Also called horizontal rules. **3.51**

Horizontal rules, *see* **Horizontal lines**

Host: Main computer in a network of computers connected by communications links. **2.14**

Hot spot: An area with the capabilities of wireless Internet connectivity, ranging from 100 to 300 feet when located inside a building and up to 1,000 feet when located in open or outdoor areas. **8.52**

How-to guides: Multimedia applications that include step-by-step instructions and interactive demonstrations to teach practical new skills. **5.12**

HTML, *see* **Hypertext markup language (HTML)**

HTML editors: Software programs specifically designed for creating Web pages. **3.50**

http:// (hypertext transfer protocol): Communication protocol used to transfer pages on the Web; beginning of most Web page URLs. **2.21**

Hyperlinks: Areas of a Web page, text or graphics, that when selected cause a browser to display another file or Web page, or play sounds or videos. Also called links. **2.21, 3.51**

absolute, 2.22

creating, 3.60-62

e-mail, 3.62-64

relative, 2.22

subject directories and, 2.25

target, 2.22

text, 3.51

Hypermedia: Web page document that contains text, graphics, video, or sound hyperlinks to other documents. **2.22**

HyperStudio: Easy-to-use multimedia authoring software program that allows the author to combine multimedia elements into a series of interactive cards. **3.27, 5.30**

Hypertext: Web page document that contains text hyperlinks to other documents. **2.22**

Hypertext markup language (HTML): Set of special codes, called tags, used to create and format Web pages. **2.23, 3.50**

Hypertext transfer protocol, *see* **http://**

IBM PC, 1.09

IBM-compatible computers, 1.09

Icon: Small image that represents a program, instruction, or some other object. **1.14, 3.06**

Ideas, applying, 1.02

ILS, *see* **Integrated learning system**

IM, *see* **Instant messaging**

Image editing software: Software used to draw pictures, shapes, and other graphics using various tools on the screen such as a pen, brush, eye dropper, and paint bucket and is used to modify existing graphics. **3.26**

Image files, downloading, 3.52

Images: Graphics and pictures contained on a Web page. **3.51**

background, 3.54-55

digital, 5.46-57

inserting for Web page, 3.62-63

Impact printer: Printer that forms marks on a piece of paper by striking a mechanism against an ink ribbon that physically contacts the paper. **4.25**

Import: Process of bringing objects into a document. **3.11**

In Brief sections, 1.26

In the Lab sections, 1.27

Information: Data that is organized, has meaning, and is useful. **1.04**

Information age, ethics and, 8.16-27

Information kiosk: Computerized information or reference center that allows a user to select various options to browse through or find specific information. **4.17, 5.16**

Information literacy: Knowing how to find, analyze, and use information; the ability to gather information from multiple sources, select relevant material, and organize it into a form that will allow the user to make decisions or take specific actions. **1.04, 6.01**

Information privacy: Right of individuals and organizations to deny or restrict the collection and use of information about them. **8.16**

Information processing cycle: Cycle of input, process, output, and storage. **1.04, 1.11**

Ink-jet printer: Type of nonimpact printer that forms marks by spraying tiny drops of liquid ink onto a piece of paper. **4.26**

Input: Any item entered into the memory of a computer, including data, programs, commands, and user responses. **1.04, 1.11, 4.12**

Input device: Any hardware component that allows a user to enter data, programs, commands, and user responses into the memory of a computer; includes a keyboard, a mouse, and a microphone. **1.05, 4.13-21**

Insert: Process of adding text or other information to a document's existing content. **3.07**

Insertion point: Symbol that indicates where on the screen the next character typed will appear. **4.14**

Inservice: Training teachers after they have entered the profession of teaching. **6.26**

Inspiration: Software planning tool used to help students and teachers quickly develop and communicate ideas using flowcharts, concept maps, and story webs. **7.19**

Install: Process of loading software on a computer's hard disk. **1.12**

Instant messaging (IM): Real-time Internet communications service that notifies a user when one or more people are online and then allows the user to exchange messages or files, or join a private chat room with them. **2.35**, 8.55

Instructional model: Systematic guide for planning instruction or a lesson. **6.22-25**

Instructional resources, 1.18

Instructional strategies, changing, 6.09-10

Instructor-led training: Online professional development training that involves continuous interaction with an instructor courses are structured, often including schedules and assignment due dates. **5.20**

Integrated learning system (ILS): Sophisticated software package usually developed by an established educational software corporation as a complete educational software solution in one package. **5.23-24**

Integrated software: Software that combines applications such as word processing, spreadsheet, and database into a single, easy-to-use package. **3.24**

Integration: Process of bringing different parts together to combine into a whole. **6.05**

Integration Corner, 1.27

Integration literacy: Ability to use computers and other technologies combined with a variety of teaching and learning strategies to enhance student learning; matching appropriate technology to learning objectives, goals, and outcomes. **1.04**, **6.01**

Intelligence: Ability to gain knowledge, apply knowledge, manipulate one's environment, and think abstractly. **6.59**

Interactive learning, 1.18

Interactive multimedia: Multimedia application that accepts input from a user by means of a keyboard, voice, or a pointing device such as a mouse; and performs an action in response. **5.02**

Interactive whiteboard: Electronic whiteboard that turns a computer and data projector into a powerful tool for teaching and learning. **5.31**

Interactivity: One of the essential features of multimedia applications that allows for individualized instruction and exploration. **5.01**

Interdisciplinary curriculum: Curriculum that includes two or more academic disciplines or curriculum areas to form a cross-discipline or subject-integrated lesson. **7.41**

Internal modem: Modem built on a circuit board that is installed inside a computer and attaches to a telephone socket using a standard telephone cord. **2.05**

International Society for Technology in Education (ISTE): Leading organization that supports education and educators in the use of technology; a non-profit group that promotes the use of technology to support and improve teaching and learning. **1.19**

Internet: World's largest network, a worldwide collection of networks that link together millions of businesses, governments, educational institutions, and individuals using modems, telephone lines, and other communications devices and media. Also called the Net. 1.04, **1.17**, 2.01-02, **2.11-38**
access to, 2.10, 2.15-16, 2.36

addresses, 2.19-20
connecting to, 1.18, 2.16, 2.17-18
functions of, 1.17-18
future of, 2.38
history of, 2.13-15
how it works, 2.15-20
impact on education, 2.01, 2.36-37
netiquette and, 2.35-36
popularity of, 2.01
public access point, 2.18, 8.52
security, 2.35-36
smart phone accessing, 1.11
uses of, 1.11, 2.11-12
World Wide Web and, *see* **World Wide Web**

Internet backbone: Main communication lines that have the heaviest amount of traffic (data packets) on the Internet. **2.18**

Internet etiquette, *see* Netiquette

Internet Explorer, *see* **Microsoft Internet Explorer**

Internet service provider (ISP): Organization that has a permanent connection to the Internet and provides temporary connections to individuals and companies for a fee. 1.18, **2.16**, 2.24
selecting, 4.57

Internet2 (I2): New Internet being developed, an extremely high-speed network that will develop and test advanced Internet technologies for research, teaching, and learning. **2.15**

ISP, *see* **Internet service provider**

ISTE, *see* **International Society for Technology in Education**

Joystick: Pointing device that is a vertical lever mounted on a base. **4.17**

JPEG file, 5.49

K-12 curriculum: Any and all subject areas offered or taught in a K-12 school environment. **6.02**

Key Terms sections, 1.26

Keyboard: Primary input device used with a computer that is a group of switches resembling the keys on a typewriter. 1.05, **4.13-14**

Keyword: Special word, phrase, or code that a program understands as an instruction. **4.12**

Keywords, searching World Wide Web using, 2.25, 2.64

Kilobyte (K, or KB): 1,024 bytes. **4.08**

Kiosk: Freestanding computer that provides information for a user. **4.17**, 5.16

Knowledge, applying, 1.02

KWHL chart: Alternative version of a KWL chart, an instructional planning tool, that adds an additional component — How they will learn. **6.20**

KWL chart: Instructional planning chart used to assist a teacher in identifying curriculum objectives by stating what students already Know, what they Want to know, and what they will Learn. **6.20**

KWLQS chart: Instructional planning chart used to identify curriculum objectives by stating what students already Know, what they Want to know, what they will Learn, further Questioning, and Sharing projects with fellow students. **7.25**

Label: Text entered in a spreadsheet cell used to identify data and help organize a spreadsheet. **3.14**

LAN, *see* **Local area network**

Landscape orientation: Printed page that is wider than it is tall, with information printed across the widest part of the paper. **4.25**

Language arts applications: Educational software that supports student learning throughout the reading and writing process. **5.26**

Language arts curriculum: Curriculum that usually includes instruction in reading, writing, listening, viewing, speaking, and literature. **7.30**

Laptop computer, *see* **Notebook computer**

Large display monitors: Large monitors that allow an audience or a group of students in a classroom to view images and multimedia displayed on a computer easily. **4.23**

Laser printer: High-speed, high-quality nonimpact printer. Operating similarly to a copy machine, a laser printer uses powdered ink, called toner, which is packaged in a cartridge. When electrically charged, the toner sticks to a special drum inside the printer and then is transferred to the paper through a combination of pressure and heat. **4.26**

LCD monitor: Monitor that uses liquid crystal, instead of a cathode-ray tube (CRT), to present information on a screen. Also called flat panel monitor. **4.24**
ClearType and, 5.10

Learn It Online sections, 1.27

Learning: Process of gaining knowledge or skills acquired through instruction or study, or to modify behavior through exposure to a type of conditioning or form of gaining experience. **6.45**
active, 6.12, 6.14, 6.24
authentic, 6.12, 6.14, 7.15
collaborative, 6.52
cooperative, 1.18, 6.15
curriculum-specific, *see* **Curriculum-specific learning**
discovery, 1.18, 2.22, 6.13
distance, 5.17-18, 8.31
facilitator of, 6.09
impact of networks on, 2.02
interactive, 1.18
linear, 2.22
mastery, 6.63
multimedia and, 5.03
new environments, 1.02
nonlinear, 2.22, 6.13
objectives, 1.04, 1.18
online, 2.12
technology integration and, 6.11-16
visual, 5.04

Learning aids, for software, 3.34-35

Learning centers, *see* **Centers**

Learning disabilities, 3.32

Learning objective, *see* **Benchmark**

Learning process: Process of content engaging students to use high-order thinking skills to go beyond the simple acquisition of knowledge. **7.11**
technology and, 6.11-16

Learning style: How individuals learn, including how they prefer to receive information, process information, and retain information. Learning styles vary among individuals. **6.09**

Learning theories: Theories that provide frameworks for interpreting the conditions and observations of teaching and learning and provide the bridge between education and research. **6.45-66**

Legal software: Software that assists in the preparation of legal documents and provides legal advice to individuals, families, and small businesses. **3.34**

Lesson plans, 1.03, 6.20-22, 7.28-42

Linear learning, 2.22

Link: Any clickable object such as text, graphics, animation, or videos that allows users to access information quickly and navigate from one topic to another in a nonlinear fashion. **5.03.** *See also* **Hyperlinks**

Linux: Popular, multitasking UNIX-type operating system that is one of the faster growing operating systems in use today. Linux is open source software, which means its code is available free to the public. **3.04**

LISTSERV: Popular software program used to manage mailing lists. **2.34**

Local area network (LAN): Communications network that covers a limited geographical area such as a school, an office, a building, or a group of buildings. A LAN consists of a number of computers connected to a central computer, or server. 1.16, **2.06**

schools and, 2.07-08

Local ISP: Internet service provider that provides one or more telephone numbers limited to a small geographic area. **2.16**

Logic bomb: Virus that is a program that activates when it detects a certain condition. **8.05**

Logical operations: Performed by the arithmetic/logic unit, operations that work with conditions and logical operators. **4.07**

Mac OS version 9.1: Version of MAC OS operating system used by most users of Apple and Macintosh school computers. 1.09, **1.13, 3.03**

Mac OS X: Version of Macintosh operating system, released in 2001 that is a significant upgrade to the previous Macintosh operating systems. **3.03**

Machine cycle: Control unit operation that includes repeating a set of four basic operations: (1) fetching an instruction, (2) decoding the instruction, (3) executing the instruction, and, if necessary, (4) storing the result. **4.06**

Macintosh computer: Personal computer introduced by Apple Computer Company in 1984. **1.09,** 1.10

purchasing, 4.53

working with, 3.03

Macro virus: Virus that uses the macro language of an application, such as word processing or spreadsheet, to hide virus codes. When a document is opened that contains an infected macro, the macro virus loads into memory. Certain actions, such as saving the document, activate the virus. Macro viruses often are part of templates, so they will infect any document created using one of the templates. **8.03**

Macromedia Dreamweaver: Web page authoring program. **3.28**

Magazines, multimedia, 5.12

Mail server: Internet service provider server that contains user's mailboxes and e-mail messages. **2.31**

Mailbox: Storage location for e-mail that usually resides on the computer that connects a user to the Internet. **2.31**

Mailing list: Group of e-mail names and addresses given a single name. **2.34**

Malicious software programs: Viruses that include worms and Trojan horses. **8.03**

Margins: Portion of a page outside the main body of text, on the top, bottom, and sides of paper. **3.11**

Marquee: Text animated to scroll across the screen. **2.28**

Mastery learning: A model for learning in which students continue to gain information and knowledge, working through modules or teacher instruction until they have mastery of content. **6.63**

Math applications: Educational software that helps students master basic and complex mathematics. **5.27**

Mathematics curriculum: Curriculum that usually includes instruction in basic number concepts, measurements, geometry, algebra, calculus, and data analysis. **7.33**

Media literacy, 1.04

Media specialist, 1.23, 6.27

Medicine, electronic references and, 5.10

Megabyte (MB): Approximately one million bytes. **4.08**

Megahertz (MHz): One million ticks of a system clock. **4.07**

Megapixels (MP): A measurement of digital camera image resolution, megapixels are millions of pixels. **5.48**

Memory: A series of electronic elements on the motherboard that temporarily hold data and instructions while they are being processed by the CPU. **1.06, 4.07**

document in, 3.08

input device and, 1.05

operating system and, 1.13, 3.02

RAM, *see* RAM

ROM, *see* ROM

software and, 1.12

Mentorship program: Program that teams new teachers with experienced teachers to encourage new teachers to learn to integrate technology resources. **6.16-17**

Menu: List of commands from which a user can select. **3.06**

Message boards: Popular Web-based type of discussion groups that do not require newsreaders. Also called discussion boards. **2.33**

Michelangelo virus: Time bomb that destroys data on a hard disk on March 6, the date of Michelangelo's birthday. **8.05**

Microbrowser: Special type of browser used by Web-enabled mobile devices that is designed for small screens and limited computing power. **2.24**

Microphone, 1.05, 3.08

Microprocessor: Single chip in a personal computer that contains the CPU. **4.06**

Microsoft Encarta: Interactive multimedia encyclopedia. **6.13**

Microsoft FrontPage: Web page authoring program. **3.28**

Microsoft Internet Explorer, 1.18

printing and opening Web page in, 3.66

Microsoft Network, The (MSN), 1.18

Microsoft PowerPoint: Presentation graphics program that allows teachers and students to create multimedia presentations that can incorporate text, graphics, animation, audio, video, links, and most importantly interactivity. 3.21, **5.30**

Microsoft Windows: Most used personal computer operating system and graphical user interface in the world. Also called Windows. 1.09, **1.13, 3.02**

Microsoft Windows 98: Operating system upgrade to Windows 95 that still is a commonly-used version of Windows. 3.02-03

Microsoft Windows 2000: Operating system upgrade to Windows 98 marketed in two versions: Windows Millennium Edition, or Windows ME, for home users; and Windows 2000 Professional, which is a network version for businesses and schools. 3.03

Microsoft Windows XP: Significant upgrade to the Windows operating system that is available in two main versions: Windows XP Home edition and Windows XP Professional for businesses and schools. A version also is specifically tailored for Media Center PCs. 3.03

Microsoft Windows XP Tablet PC Edition: Windows operating system that includes all the features of Windows XP Professional with additional features unique to using a Tablet PC. 3.03

Microsoft Word

creating curriculum page using, 7.60-82

creating teacher's Web page using, 3.50-66

Microsoft Works: Popular integrated software package for PCs. **3.25**

Microwave transmission, 2.04

Mobile computer, 1.10-11

purchasing, 4.52-53

Modem: Communications device that converts digital signals into analog signals, enabling computers to communicate via telephone lines. 1.08, **1.12, 2.06**

Monitor: Output display device that conveys text, graphics, and video information visually and is housed in a plastic or metal case. 1.06, **4.22**

Morphing: Special effect in which one video image is transformed into another image over the course of several frames of video, creating the illusion of metamorphosis. **5.55**

Mosaic: Graphical Web browser developed in 1993. **2.24**

Motherboard: Circuit board in the computer that contains many of the electronic components in the system unit. **4.04**

Mouse: Most widely used pointing device; input device used to control the movement of a pointer on the screen and make selections from the screen. 1.05, 1.09, **4.15,** 5.03

Mouse pad: Rectangular rubber or foam pad that provides traction for a mouse. **4.15**

Moving Pictures Experts Group (MPEG): Group that has defined a popular standard for video compression and decompression. **5.08**

Mozilla, 1.18

MPEG, *see* **Moving Pictures Experts Group**

MSN, *see* **Microsoft Network, The**

Multifunction device (MFD): Single piece of equipment that provides the functionality of a printer, fax machine, copier, and scanner. **4.28**

Multimedia: Combination of text, color, graphics, animation, audio, video, and virtual reality. **2.25, 5.02**

applications, 5.08-28

creating applications, 5.28-31

educational software applications, 5.20-28

elements of, 5.02-08

integrating applications, 5.01-33

interactive, 5.02
on Web, 2.25
presenting, 5.30-31
Multimedia application: The use of multimedia technology in education, business, and entertainment. 5.08-20
Multimedia authoring software: Software used to create interactive multimedia presentations that can include text, graphics, video, audio, and animation. Also called an authoring tool. **3.27, 5.29**
Multimedia magazine: Digital version of a magazine distributed on CD-ROM, DVD-ROM, or via the World Wide Web. **5.12**
Multimedia newspaper: Digital version of a newspaper distributed on CD-ROM, DVD-ROM, or via the World Wide Web. **5.12**
Multimedia software: Any computer-based presentation or application software that uses multimedia elements. **3.25-27, 5.02**
Musical Instrument Digital Interface (MIDI): Port; and the electronic music industry's standard that defines how digital musical devices electronically represent sounds. **5.07**

National Council for Accreditation for Teacher Education (NCATE): Official body for accrediting teacher education programs. **1.19-20**
National Educational Technology Standards for Teachers (NETS-T): Fundamental concepts, knowledge, skills, and attitudes for applying technology in K–12 educational settings, developed by the International Society for Technology in Education (ISTE). **1.20**
National ISP: Internet service provider that provides local telephone numbers in most major cities and towns nationwide. **2.16**
National Science Foundation (NSF): Organization that connected its huge network of five supercomputer centers, called NSFnet, to ARPANET. **2.14**
NCATE, *see* **National Council for Accreditation for Teacher Education**
Net, *see* **Internet**
Netiquette: Short for Internet etiquette, the code of acceptable behaviors users should follow while on the Internet. **2.35**, 2.36
Netscape, 1.18
Netscape Composer: Web page authoring feature that is part of the Netscape Communicator software package. **3.28, 7.60**
Network: Collection of computers and other equipment organized to share data, information, hardware, and software. Also called communications network. **1.12, 1.16,** 2.01, **2.04-39**
educational applications, 2.07-11
future of, 2.38
hardware, 2.04-06
home, 2.06
Internet, *see* **Internet**
learning effects, 2.02
local area, *see* **Local area network**
software, 2.04
wide area, *see* **Wide area network**
wireless, 2.04, 2.06, 2.10, 8.49-58
World Wide Web and, *see* **World Wide Web**
Network interface cards (NICs): Communications devices that connect computers directly to a school or business network without using a modem. **2.06**
Network site license: Software license that allows network users to share a single copy of software, which resides on a network server. **8.12**
News server: Computer that stores and distributes newsgroup messages. **2.33**
Newsgroup: Online area in which users conduct written discussions about a particular subject. **2.33**
Newspapers, multimedia, 5.12-13
Newsreader: Program that enables access to a newsgroup to read previously entered messages, add articles, and keep tracks of which articles a user has and has not read. **2.33**
NICs, *see* **Network interface cards**
Nine events of instruction: Events identified by Gagne to maximize the potential for the internal process of learning to occur. **6.59**
Nonimpact printer: Printer that forms marks on a piece of paper without actually striking the paper. **4.26**
Nonlinear learning, 2.22, 6.13
Nonvolatile memory: Type of memory in which contents are not lost when power is removed from a computer; example is ROM. **4.08**
Normal text: Text that makes up the main information content of a Web page. **3.51**
Notebook computer: Portable, personal computer small enough to fit on a user's lap. Also called a laptop computer. **1.10**
purchasing, 4.60-62
storage media, 4.38
Notepad: Feature of personal information manager used to record ideas, reminders, and other important information. **3.22**
NSFnet: National Science Foundation network of five supercomputer centers, connected to ARPANET, serving as the major backbone network of the Internet until 1995. **2.14**
Numeric keypad: Calculator-style arrangement of keys on a keyboard representing numbers, a decimal point, and some basic mathematical operators; used to facilitate entering numbers. **4.14**

Objectionable material: Material that includes racist literature, obscene pictures and videos, and even gambling. Internet materials classified as objectionable material include (1) all materials that most people consider pornographic, such as obscene pictures, stories, graphics, articles, cartoons, and videos; (2) racist literature, controversial subjects such as gambling, and other similar materials; and (3) Web sites that contain incorrect material and thus are inappropriate for K–12 students. **8.22-23**
Objectivity: Process of determining or interpreting the intent or purpose of a Web page and if it is free of bias, such as advertising. **7.11**
Offsite location: Location for storing backup copies. **8.15**
One-computer classroom: Classroom that is equipped with one multimedia computer. **6.19, 7.22**
Online course, *see* **Web-based course**
Online learning, 2.12
Online service provider: Organization that provides access to the Internet, as well as members-only features that offer a variety of special content and services. 1.18, **2.16,** 2.24
selecting, 4.57
Online shopping, 2.01
Open learning system: Integrated learning system that includes software titles from leading publishers. Also called an advanced learning system. **5.24**
Open source software: Software that has code available free to the public. **3.04**
Operant conditioning: Learning that is controlled and results in shaping behavior through the reinforcement of stimulus response patterns, described by Skinner. **6.56**
Operating system: System software containing instructions that coordinate all of the activities of hardware devices and instructions that allow a user to run application software. **1.13, 3.02**
role of, 3.02
types of, 3.02-04
Optical character recognition (OCR): Type of optical reader technology that involves reading typewritten, computer-printed, and in some cases handwritten characters on documents and converting the images into a form the computer can understand. **4.18**
Optical mark recognition (OMR): Type of optical reader technology that reads hand-drawn marks such as small circles or rectangles. **4.18**
Optical mouse: Mouse that has no moving mechanical parts, instead it emits and senses light to detect the mouse's movement. **4.15**
Optical reader: Input device that reads characters, marks, and codes and then converts them into digital data. **4.18**
OSP, *see* **Online service provider**
Output: Data that has been processed into a useful form called information. Four common types of output are text, graphics, audio, and video. **1.04, 1.11, 4.21**
Output device: Hardware used to convey the information generated by a computer to a user; includes a printer, a monitor, and speakers. **1.06, 4.22**
Overvoltage: Situation that occurs when incoming electrical power increases significantly above the normal 120 volts. Also called power surge. **8.14**

Packaged software: Application software designed to meet the needs of a variety of users. **1.15**
Packet switching: Technique of breaking a message into individual packets, sending the packets along the best route available, and reassembling the data. **2.16**
Packets: Small pieces of data sent over the Internet. **2.15**
Page layout: Process of arranging text and graphics in a document. **3.25**
Paint software: Software used to draw pictures, shapes, and other graphics using various tools on the screen such as a pen, brush, eye dropper, and paint bucket. **3.26**
Parents, computer use by, 1.24-25
Paste: Process of placing items stored on the Clipboard into a document. **3.07**
Pavlov, Ivan, 6.55
PC, *see* **Personal computer**
PC Card: Special type of expansion card for notebook and other mobile computers. **4.10**
PDA, *see* **Personal digital assistant**
Performance-based assessment, *see* **Authentic assessment**
Peripheral device: Any external device that attaches to the system unit. **1.07**

Personal computer (PC): Computer designed for use by one person at a time. 1.09-10
buying guide for, 4.51-67
installing, 4.68-70
maintaining, 4.71-72
working with, 3.36-37
Personal digital assistant (PDA): Mobile device that provides personal organizer functions such as a calendar, appointment book, address book, calculator, and notepad, often is Web-enabled allowing a user to check e-mail and access the Internet. 1.11
purchasing, 4.53, 4.66-67
service industry and, 8.56
Personal finance software: Simplified accounting program used to pay bills, balance a checkbook, track personal income and expenses, track investments, and evaluate financial plans. 3.32
Personal firewall: Software program that detects and protects a personal computer and its data from unauthorized intrusions. 8.08
Personal information manager (PIM): Software that includes an appointment calendar, address book, and notepad used to organize personal information such as appointments and task lists. 3.22
Personal use, software for, 3.32
Photo-editing software: Software used to edit digital photographs. 3.26
Physical education and health curriculum: Curriculum that usually includes instruction in basic health and physical education literacy. 7.36
Piaget, Jean, 6.49-50
Picture CD: Type of compact disc from Kodak that stores digital versions of a single roll of film using a .jpg file format. 1.08, **4.35**
Pictures
on Web page, 3.51
See also **Digital cameras**
Pixel (short for picture element): Single point in an electronic image. 4.23
ClearType and, 5.10
Pixilated: Image that is blurry. 5.50
Planning
lessons, *see* **Lesson plans**
for technology integration, 6.17
Platter: Inflexible, circular disk in a hard disk that is made of aluminum, glass, or ceramic and is coated with a material that allows data to be magnetically recorded on its surface. **4.32**
Player: Program that can play the audio in an MP3 file on a computer. 2.28
Plug and Play: Computer's capability to configure automatically expansion cards and other devices as they are installed. 4.10
Plug-in: Program which extends the capability of a browser. 2.26
Pocket PC: A type of PDA that uses the Pocket PC operating system software developed by Microsoft. 3.22
Point of instruction: Having technology in the teachers' classrooms at the teachers' and students' fingertips. 6.06
Pointing device: Input device that allows a user to control a pointer on the screen. 4.15, 5.02
Pointing stick: Pressure-sensitive pointing device shaped like a pencil eraser that is positioned between keys on a keyboard. 4.16
Points: Measurement system for font size; a single point is approximately 1/72 of one inch in height. **3.07**

Port: Point of attachment to a system unit. 4.10
Portfolio assessment: Evaluation of student assignments or projects over a period of time. Sometimes called embedded assessment. 7.15
Portrait orientation: Printed page that is taller than it is wide, with information printed across the shorter width of the paper. 4.25
Posting: Adding a message to a newsgroup. 2.33
PowerPoint, *see* **Microsoft PowerPoint**
Pragmatism: Early education movement that stated that the truth of a theory could be determined only if a theory worked. 6.54
Preoperational: Second stage in cognitive development, defined by Piaget, which occurs when children begin to use symbols and images. 6.49
Presentation graphics software: Software used to create presentations, which are used to communicate ideas, messages, and other information to a group. 1.15, **3.17-21**
Presentations: Documents created with presentation graphics software, used to communicate ideas, messages, and other information to a group. 3.17
commercially produced, 3.27
multimedia, 5.30-31
Principal, computer use by, 1.22
Printer: Output device that produces text and graphical information on a physical medium such as paper or transparency film. 1.06, **4.25**
impact, 4.25
nonimpact, 4.26
Printing: Process of sending a file to a printer to generate output on a medium such as paper. **3.08**
digital pictures, 5.47, 5.50
Problem solving, teaching, 1.18
Problem-based instruction: Component of anchored instruction in which students use the background (anchor) information to begin to solve and understand complex problems or concepts. 6.12-13
Process, 1.04, 1.11
Processor, *see* **Central processing unit (CPU)**
Product activation: Anti-piracy technology designed to verify that software products have been legitimately licensed. 8.11
Productivity software: Software designed to make people more effective and efficient while performing daily activities; includes applications such as word processing, spreadsheet, database, presentation graphics, personal information management, and software suites. 1.15, **3.10-25**
Productivity tool, 1.02
Professional development, 1.02, 5.19
Professional organizations, 7.04, A.47-56
Program, *see* **Computer program; Software**
Programmers, *see* **Computer programmers**
Progressive education: Movement in the early 1900s that focused on educating the whole child. 6.54
Project Gutenberg: E-book project that makes thousands of literary and reference books and materials available free to everyone. 5.10
Project-based assessment: Alternative assessment method that focuses on assessing student projects. 7.15
Project-based learning: Model for teaching and learning that focuses on creating learning opportunities for students by engaging them in real-world projects where they have an active role in completing meaningful tasks,

constructing their own knowledge, solving problems, or creating realistic projects. 7.15
Proxy server: Server that functions as a firewall by screening all incoming and outgoing messages. 8.09
Pruning: Process of cutting out unwanted scenes or portions of scenes during video editing. 5.55
Psychomotor domain: A student's motor skills and physical abilities, categorized by Bloom. 6.62
Public Internet access point: Wireless connection to the Internet in a public location, such as an airport, hotel, or coffee shop. 2.18, 8.52
Public-domain software: Free software or creative works that have been donated for public use and have no copyright restrictions. 1.16, 8.22
Purchasing computers, 4.52-67
Purpose: Reason a Web site was created or the intent of the Web site. 7.11

RAM (random access memory): Volatile memory in which its contents are lost (erased) when a computer's power is turned off. 4.08
Random access memory, *see* **RAM**
Rating scale: Complex checklist that lists a numerical value, or rating, for each criterion that is assessed. 7.15
Read-only memory, *see* **ROM**
Real time: Something that occurs immediately. 2.34
Record: Collection of fields (related facts) in a database. 3.16
Recorded: Process of writing data, instructions, and information to a storage medium. 4.34
Reference, electronic, 5.10
Reference software: Software that provides valuable and thorough information for everyone in an educational setting and in the family. 3.31, 6.13
Reflective evaluation: Evaluation by teachers using thoughtful reflection on the components of the teaching and learning process and determination of the effectiveness of the learner outcomes and the use of technology during the process. 6.24
Refresh rate: Speed at which monitor redraws images on the screen. 4.25
Registrar: Organization used to register for a domain name that maintains a master list of names for a particular top-level domain. 2.21
Relative hyperlinks: Hyperlinks to another document on the same Internet computer. **2.22, 7.60**
Reliability of computers, 1.11
Reliable assessment: Information that provides accurate estimates of student performance, permits appropriate generalizations about the students' skills and abilities, and enables teachers or other decision-makers to make appropriate decisions. 7.12
Remediation: Review of content many times until a student grasps the concepts being taught. 5.22
Replace: Feature that substitutes existing characters or words with new ones. 3.11
Request for proposal (RFP): Document provided by a grant source that details information teachers and schools need to provide to write a successful grant proposal. 7.44

Rescue disk: Floppy disk that contains an uninfected copy of key operating system commands and startup information that enables a computer to restart correctly. **8.06**

Research, educational, 6.45-66

Resolution (digital camera), 5.48

Resolution (monitor): Describes sharpness and clarity of a monitor and is related directly to the number of pixels it can display, expressed as two separate numbers: the number of columns of pixels and the number of rows of pixels a monitor can display. **4.25**

Resources: Hardware devices, software programs, data, and information shared by users connected to a network. **1.16**

Restore: Process of reloading files on a computer or network file server. **8.15**

ROM (read-only memory): Nonvolatile memory that stores information or instructions that do not change; retains its contents even when power to a computer is turned off. Instructions and data are permanently recorded on ROM chips by manufacturers. **4.09**

Routers: Hardware devices that packets travel along to a recipient's computer. **2.15**

Rubric: Detailed assessment tool that provides a number of important evaluation criteria, including content, documentation and technical support, ability and academic levels, technical quality, and ease of use to help assess the quality of software or other items. **7.06, 7.15-16**

Saving: Process of copying a document from memory to a storage medium. **3.08**

Scaffolding: Building or constructing a child's learning experiences based on the child's level of cognitive/social development, defined by Vygotsky. **6.52**

Scanner: Input device that electronically can capture an entire page of text or images such as photographs or artwork and converts the data into digital data that can be stored on a disk and processed by the computer. **1.05, 4.18**

color, 5.28

Scenes: Smaller pieces that video is split into during the editing process. **5.54**

Schema: Cognitive understanding or development at any given time while learning, defined by Piaget. **6.50**

Schemata: Organized way of creating or providing a cognitive mental framework for understanding and remembering information. **6.52**

School district

networking, 2.07-11

technology evaluation and, 7.02

technology integration and, 6.16-17

School management software: Centralized program that allows district and school personnel to manage school district operations. **3.29**

School secretary, computer use by, 1.22

Schools

funding for, 2.02, 2.07, 7.44

networking, 2.07-11

Science applications: Educational software that assists students in learning a wide variety of science concepts. **5.27**

Science curriculum: Curriculum that usually contains instruction in physical sciences, earth and space sciences, and life sciences. **7.35**

Scrolling: Process of moving different portions of a document onto the screen into view. **3.11**

Search, *see* **Find**

Search engine: Search tool that finds Web sites, Web pages, and Internet files that match one or more keywords entered by a user. **2.25, 2.60, 2.63-68**

Search tools: Tools that enable users to locate specific information found at Web sites; include search engines and subject directories. **2.25**

Searching techniques, guide to, 2.52-68

Secondary storage, *see* **Storage**

Section 508: Federal accessibility initiative that requires federal agencies to give employees with disabilities and members of the public access to technology that is comparable to the access available to others. **8.31**

Sector: Pie-shaped section of a disk, which breaks tracks on the disk into small arcs. **4.30**

Security, 2.35-36, 8.01-15

Self-paced training: Online professional development training in which teachers typically sign up for a specific course or module, and after completing all the requirements they receive credit for the training. **5.19-20**

Sensorimotor: First stage in cognitive development, defined by Piaget, which occurs when learning takes place primarily through a child's senses and motor actions. **6.49**

Server: Computer that manages the resources on a network and provides a centralized storage area for software programs and data. **2.06**

chat, 2.34

FTP, 2.32

mail, 2.31

school network, 2.07

Web, *see* **Web server**

Shareware: Software that is distributed free for a trial use period. If a user wishes to use a shareware program beyond the trial period, the developer (individual or company) expects a small fee. **1.16, 8.12**

Shopping online, 2.01

Short message service (SMS): Internet service used by smart phone, cellular telephone, or PDA users to send and receive brief text messages on their Web-enabled devices. **2.35**

SimCity: Very popular simulation program for education in which students design cities, communities, neighborhoods, and businesses. **5.23**

Simulations: Computer-based models of real-life situations. **5.09**

educational, 5.23

Single-user license agreement: Software license included with software packages purchased by individual users, which contain conditions about installation and distribution of the software. Also called end-user license agreement (EULA). **8.10-11**

Site license: Software license that gives a buyer the right to install software on multiple computers at a single site. **8.12**

Skill assessment survey: Planning tool designed to identify individual students' academic and technology skill levels and then create a starting point for developing instructional strategies. **6.20**

Skill building, 1.18

Skills-reinforcement software, *see* **Drill-and-practice software**

Skinner, B.F., 6.56-57

Slide sorter: Feature of presentation graphics software that allows viewing of small versions of all slides, used to organize a presentation. **3.19**

Slides: Document produced for a presentation that is displayed on a computer's monitor or a large-screen television, or projected on a screen; can be made into traditional overhead transparencies, or printed and given as handouts. **3.17**

SMART Board: Interactive whiteboard produced by Smart Technologies that can be used to access and control any computer application. **5.31**

Smart phone: A web-enabled device that has basic telephone capabilities as well as allowing a user to send and receive e-mail and access the Internet. **1.11**

SMS, *see* **Short message service**

Social constructivist theory: Learning theory that states learning is influenced significantly by social development. **6.51**

Social studies curriculum: Curriculum that usually encompasses instruction in history, geography, civics, and economics. **7.31**

Social studies software applications: Educational software that encourages high-order thinking skills, provides reinforcement of facts, and allows students to define their own path. **5.28**

Society

technology-rich, 1.18

wireless technology and, 8.55-58

Soft copy: Describes information shown on a display device because the information exists electronically and is displayed for a temporary period of time. **4.22**

Software: Series of instructions that tells hardware how to perform tasks. Also called a computer program, or program. **1.04**

application, *see* **Application software**

custom, 1.16

determining needs, 6.26

development, 1.16

educational applications, 5.20-28

evaluating, 7.06-09

installing, 1.12-13

multimedia, *see* **Multimedia software**

network access, 2.07

system, *see* **System software**

types of, 1.14-16

Web browser, *see* **Web browser**

Software application, *see* **Application software**

Software Corner, 1.27

Software evaluation rubric: Rubric used to evaluate educational software. **7.06**

Software license: Agreement that provides specific conditions for use of software, which users must accept before using the software. **8.10**

Software package: Name given to a particular software product, such as Microsoft Word. **3.05**

Software piracy: Unauthorized and illegal duplication of copyrighted software. **8.10-11**

Software suite: Collection of individual application software packages sold as a single package. **1.15, 3.24**

Sound, *see* **Audio**

Spam: Unsolicited e-mail message or newsgroup posting sent to many recipients or newsgroups at once. **2.36**

Speakers: Audio output devices that either can be separate devices that can be placed on either side of the monitor or built into the monitor or system's unit case. Stereo speakers are connected to ports on the sound card. **1.06, 4.28**

Special education curriculum, *see* **Exceptional education curriculum**

Special needs software: Software designed specifically for students with physical impairments or learning disabilities, to assist them in completing school assignments and everyday tasks. **3.32**

Speech recognition, *see* **Voice recognition**

Speech synthesis software: Software used by students with speech and vocal muscle disorders to participate in classroom discussions. **3.32**

Speed of computer, **1.11**

Spell checker, *see* **Spelling checker**

Spelling checker: Spelling review feature that compares words in a document to an electronic dictionary that is part of the software. Also called spell checker. **3.12**

Spike: Momentary overvoltage that occurs when a power increase lasts for less than one millisecond (one thousandth of a second); caused by uncontrollable disturbances, such as lightning, or controllable disturbances, such as turning on a piece of equipment that uses the same electrical circuit. **8.14**

Spiral curriculum: Curriculum organized so that students continually build upon what they already have learned. **6.49**

Splitting: Process of reducing video into smaller pieces during editing. **5.54**

Spoiler: Message that reveals a solution to a game or ending to a movie or program. **2.36**

Spreadsheet: Rows and columns of numeric data. Also called a worksheet. **1.15, 3.13**

Spreadsheet software: Software used to organize numeric data in rows and columns. **3.13-15**

State bid list: List of companies that states contracts with to purchase specific software applications at reduced prices. **6.26**

State departments of education, technology evaluation and, **7.02**

Storage: The media on which data, instructions, and information are kept when they are not being processed, as well as the devices that record and retrieve these items. Also called secondary storage. **1.04, 1.11-12, 4.29**

CD-ROM, **4.34**

compact discs, **4.32-34**

digital camera images, **5.49**

digital video, **5.47, 5.53**

DVD-ROM, **4.37**

floppy disks, **4.30-31**

hard disks, **4.32**

high-capacity removable disks, **4.31**

Storage device: Hardware used to record and retrieve data, information, and instructions to and from a storage medium; often functions as a source of input because it transfers items from storage into memory. **1.07-08, 4.29**

Storage medium: The physical material on which data, instructions, and information are kept. **1.07, 4.29**

Storing: Control unit process of writing results to memory. **4.06**

Story web, *see* **Concept map**

Storyboard: Planning tool, which is a drawing that allows students to design and lay out a

project or assignment before creating it on a computer. **7.19**

Streaming: Process of transferring data in a continuous and even flow. **2.29**

Streaming audio: Process of transferring audio data in a continuous and even flow, allowing user to listen to a sound file as it downloads to the computer. **2.29**

Streaming video: Process of transferring video data in a continuous and even flow, allowing user to view longer or live video images as they are downloaded to the computer. **2.30**

Student management software: Program that allows administrators, teachers, and other staff to manage and track information on students. **3.29**

Student objectives: Statement of the type of performance a teacher expects students to be able to demonstrate at the end of instruction. **6.22**

Student performance: Assessment of technology integration to ensure that students meet the learning objectives. **7.12**

Student projects, evaluating, **7.17-19**

Students

decision making by, **1.04**

preparing for citizenship, **1.02, 1.18**

Students with exceptionalities

curriculum for, **7.39**

input devices for, **4.20-21**

multimedia applications, **5.24-25**

output devices for, **4.28-29**

Subject directory: Search tool that allows users to navigate to areas of interest without having to enter keywords; instead links are followed to specific topics. **2.25, 2.60-63, 2.65**

Subject-integrated lesson: Lesson that integrates multiple skills such as speaking, reading, thinking, and writing with multiple subject areas such as math, science, and language arts to create a more holistic learning experience. **7.41**

Submenu: List of commands that displays when a command is selected on a previous menu. **3.06**

Subscribe: Process of saving a newsgroup location so it can be accessed easily in the future. **2.33**

Superintendent, computer use by, **1.21-22**

Surge protector: Device that uses special electrical components to smooth out minor voltage errors, provide a stable current flow, and keep an overvoltage from damaging computer equipment. **8.14**

S-video: Cables used to transfer video. **5.52**

Synchronize: A feature of PDAs that allows users to transfer information and programs from a PDA to a personal computer and vice versa. **3.22-23**

Synchronous dynamic RAM (SDRAM): Most common form of RAM used in personal computers. **4.08**

System clock: Small chip that synchronizes, or controls the timing of, all computer operations. **4.07**

System failure: Malfunction of a computer that occurs because of electrical power problems, hardware component failure, or software error. **8.13**

System software: Programs that control the operations of a computer and its devices; includes the operating system and utility programs. System software serves as the

liaison between a user and the computer's hardware. **1.13-14, 3.02**

System unit: Box-like case made from metal or plastic that houses the computer electronic circuitry. **1.06, 1.11, 4.02**

components of, **4.04-11**

Systems analyst: Person who manages the development of a program, working with both the user and the programmer to determine and design the program. **1.16**

Table: Collection of rows and columns in a Word document. **7.66**

Tablet PC: Special type of notebook computer that allows a user to input data by writing on the screen using a digital pen or by using the attached keyboard. **1.10-11**

purchasing, **4.52, 4.63-65**

wireless, **8.55**

Tags: Set of special codes used in hypertext markup language that define the placement and format of text, graphics, video, and sound on a Web page. **2.23, 3.50**

Target hyperlinks: Hyperlinks to another location in the same document. **2.22**

Tax preparation software: Software that guides individuals, families, or small businesses through the process of filing federal taxes. **3.33**

TCP/IP, *see* **Transmission control protocol/Internet protocol)**

Teachable moment: Open window of opportunity for information to be comprehended in greater detail by students; the time when students are interested and ready to learn more about a topic. **6.06**

Teacher observation (Internet use): Teachers monitoring their students actively and continuously while they are on the Internet. **8.27**

Teacher observation (learning process): Active observation by teachers of their students during the learning process. **7.12, 7.17**

Teacher's manual: Booklet that contains information, rules and regulations, rights and responsibilities, and policies and procedures. **6.25**

Teacher's Web page, creating, **3.50-66**

Teachers

example of computer use by, **1.23-24**

professional development, **5.19**

professional organizations, **1.19-20, 5.47-52**

Teaching principles, applying, **1.02**

Teaching Today sections, **1.27**

Technical quality: Refers to how well software presents itself and how well it works. **7.09**

Technical support: Service that hardware and software manufacturers and third-party service companies offer to customers to provide answers to questions, repairs, and other assistance. **7.09**

Technology

evaluating, **7.02-21**

reasons for using, **1.18-20**

Technology committee: Committee that consists of teachers, administrators, and staff who consider, investigate, advise, and make recommendations to the principal and technology coordinator on technology-related issues. **6.25**

Technology conference: Meeting dedicated to provide a vast array of information and resources for teachers. **7.04**

Technology coordinator, **1.22-23**

Technology integration: Combination of all technology parts, such as hardware and software, together with each subject-related area of curriculum to enhance learning. Also called curriculum integration. 6.01, 6.05-31
barriers to, 6.10-11
curriculum and, 7.01-45
introduction to, 1.01-27
learning environment and, 6.28-29
learning process and, 6.11-16
planning for, 6.17-20
Technology lab, *see* **Computer lab**
Technology plan: Outline that specifies a school district's procedures for purchasing equipment and software and training teachers to use and then integrate technology into their classroom curriculum. 6.16
Telecommunications, *see* **Communications**
Text: Output that consists of characters that are used to create words, sentences, and paragraphs. 4.22, 5.04
hyperlinks, 3.51
multimedia and, 5.02, 5.04
normal, 3.51
Web page, 3.51, 3.55-58
word processing software and, 3.10-11
The Microsoft Network (MSN), *see* **Microsoft Network, The**
Theory: Scientific set of principles presented to clarify or explain a phenomenon. 6.45
Thread: Original newsgroup article and all subsequent related replies. Also called threaded discussion. 2.33
Threaded discussion, *see* **Thread**
Thumbnail: Small version of a larger graphical image that can be clicked to display the full-sized image. 2.27
TIFF file, 5.49
Time bomb: Type of logic bomb that activates on a particular date. 8.05
Timelines in computer history, 1.27
Title (Web page): Text that appears on the title bar of the browser window when the page is being displayed; also can refer to the first line or main heading of a Web page. 3.50
Title bar: Located at the top of a window, a horizontal space that contains the window's name. 3.06
ToolBook: Multimedia authoring software program. 5.29
Touch screen: Monitor that has a touch-sensitive panel on the screen, used for input. 4.17
Touchpad: Small, flat, rectangular pointing device sensitive to pressure and motion. 4.16
Track: Narrow storage ring around a disk. 4.30
Trackball: Stationary pointing device with a ball mechanism on its top. 4.16
Trade books: Books available to help a user learn to use the features of software application packages. 3.35
Traditional assessment: Assessment that uses tests in the form of multiple choice, fill-in-the-blank, true/false, short answer, and essay questions. Traditional forms of assessment also can be used to evaluate the effectiveness of technology. 7.12
Traffic: Communications activity on the Internet. 2.14
Training
computer-based, 5.09
professional development, 5.19
technology integration and, 6.10-11
Web-based, 5.17

Transmission control protocol/Internet protocol (TCP/IP): Protocol used to define packet switching on the Internet. 2.16
Transmission media: Physical materials or other means used to establish a communications channel. 2.04
Trojan horse: (named after the Greek myth) Malicious software program that hides within or is designed to look like a legitimate program. 8.03
Tutorials: Step-by-step instructions using real examples that show a user how to use an application. 3.35, 5.22
Twisted-pair cable: The most widely used transmission medium consisting of pairs of plastic-coated copper wires twisted together; used in standard home telephone lines. 2.04

Unauthorized access: Use of a computer or network without permission. 8.07
Unauthorized use: Use of a computer or data for unapproved or possibly illegal activities. 8.07
Undervoltage: Situation that occurs when electrical power supply drops. 8.14
Uniform Resource Locator (URL): Unique address for each Web page on a Web site; consists of a protocol, domain name, and sometimes the path to a specific Web page. 2.21, 2.24
Uninterruptible power supply (UPS): Device that contains surge protection circuits and one or more batteries that provide power during a temporary or permanent loss of power. 8.14
Universal serial bus (USB) port: Port that connects up to 127 different peripheral devices with a single connector type. 4.11, 5.47, 5.52
Universities, distance learning and, 5.18
UNIX: Multitasking operating system originally developed for mainframe computers but used today for computers of all sizes. 3.03-04
Unsubscribe: Process of removing name from mailing list. 2.34
Upgrade: New version of software product designed to replace an older version of the same product. 3.35
Upload: Process of copying a file to an FTP site. 2.32
UPS, *see* **Uninterruptible power supply**
URL, *see* **Uniform Resource Locator (URL)**
USB drives: Portable mini-external hard drives that may be carried on a key chain and plug into a USB or FireWire port. 4.32
USB port, *see* **Universal serial bus (USB) port**
USB 2.0 port: The latest version of a universal serial bus (USB) port that is more advanced and with speeds 40 times faster than the original USB port. 4.11
Usenet: Entire collection of Internet newsgroups, containing thousands of newsgroups on a multitude of topics. 2.33
User: Person who communicates with a computer or uses the information it generates. 1.04
User interface: Part of all software with which a user interacts that controls how data and instructions are entered (input) and how the computer presents information on the screen (output). 1.14, 3.04
User name: Unique combination of characters that identifies a user. 2.31
User response: Answer to a question asked by a program. 4.12

Utility program: System software that performs a specific task, usually related to managing a computer, its devices, or its programs. 1.14

Vaccines, *see* **Antivirus program**
Valid: Software that has well-grounded instructional properties, provides appropriate content, and teaches what is intended. 7.06
Value: Number in a spreadsheet cell. 3.14
Version: Number designation for software. 3.35
Video: Photographic images that are played back at speeds that provide the appearance of full motion in real time. 2.29, 3.27, 4.22, 5.07
digital technology, 5.52-57
downloading, 2.12
multimedia and, 5.02, 5.07-08
streaming, 2.29
Video cameras, 5.52-57
Video compression: Process of decreasing the size of video files. 5.07-08
Video input: Process of entering a full-motion recording into a computer. Also called video capture. 4.19
Virtual reality (VR): Use of a computer to create an artificial environment that appears and feels like a real environment and allows a user to explore space and manipulate the setting; appears as a three-dimensional (3-D) space. 2.30, 5.15-16
Virtual tours: Tours that allow a user to walk through doorways, down halls, and see everything in a three-dimensional world via a computer, as if being there. 6.08
Virus: Potentially damaging computer program designed to effect a computer negatively without a user's knowledge or permission by altering the way it works. More specifically, a virus is a segment of program code that implants itself in a computer file and spreads systematically from one file to another. 8.02-07
Virus hoaxes: False warnings about viruses often spread via e-mail and over the Internet. 8.07
Virus payload: Symptom or damage caused by a virus. 8.02
Visual learners: Individuals who learn concepts faster or retain a higher percentage of material if they see the information presented graphically. 5.04
Visual learning techniques: Methods that present ideas and information through graphical webs, used in planning projects. 7.19
Voice recognition: Computer's capability of distinguishing spoken words. Also called speech recognition. 3.08, 4.19
Volatile memory: Type of memory in which contents are lost (erased) when a computer's power is turned off; example is RAM. 4.08
VR world: 3-D Web site that contains infinite space and depth. 2.30
Vygotsky, Lev, 6.51-52

WAN, *see* **Wide area network**
Warchalking: The practice of using chalk to draw a series of symbols on sidewalks to direct people to places that provide wireless access. 8.53
WBT, *see* **Web-based training**
Web, *see* **World Wide Web (WWW)**
Web browser: Program that interprets HTML and displays Web pages and enables user to link to other Web pages and Web sites. Also called a browser. 1.18, 2.23
plug-in, 2.26

Web evaluation rubric: Detailed scoring guide for assessing the value of Web sites. **7.12**

Web Info boxes, 1.25

Web page: Electronic document viewed on the Web. 1.18, **2.21**
  address, 2.21
  bookmark, 2.25
  development of, 2.23
  history list, 2.25
  how it works, 2.22-23
  hyperlinks, *see* **Hyperlinks**
  images on, 3.51, 3.62-64
  teacher's, 3.50-66

Web page authoring software: Software used to create Web pages, in addition to organizing, managing, and maintaining Web sites. **3.28**

Web publishing: Development and maintenance of Web pages. **2.23**, **3.28**, **8.21**

Web resources, evaluating, 7.09-12

Web scavenger hunt: Inquiry-oriented activity in which students explore the resources of the Web using discovery learning to find the answers to teacher-created questions; encourages high-order thinking skills. **7.26**

Web server: Computer that delivers (serves) requested Web pages. **2.21-23**

Web site: Collection of related Web pages. **2.21**, **7.60**
  creating links to, 3.60-62
  textbook, 1.25-27

Web surfing: Process of exploring the Web by displaying pages from one Web site after another, similar to using a remote control to jump from one TV channel to another. **2.23**

Web-based course: A course that is taught mostly or completely on the Web, rather than in a traditional classroom. Often called an online course. **5.18**

Web-based education, *see* **Distance learning**

Web-based training (WBT): Approach to computer-based training that uses the technologies of the Internet and the World Wide Web and typically consists of self-directed, self-paced instruction on a topic. **5.17**

Web-enabled: Devices that can connect to the Internet wirelessly; include handheld computers, PDAs, and smart phones. **1.11**

Web-enhanced course: Course that uses the Web to enhance the content of the course. **5.18**

Web-enhancing: Classes enhanced by providing students with Web resources to enrich their learning experiences. **5.18**

Webmaster: Individual responsible for developing Web pages and maintaining a Web site. **2.23**

Wellivers Instructional Transformation Model: Model that describes five hierarchical stages of technology integration through which all teachers must progress to integrate technology effectively; stages are: familiarization, utilization, integration, reorientation, and revolution. **6.10**

Wheel: Steering-wheel type input device, used with games software. **4.17**

Wide area network (WAN): Network that covers a large geographical region (such as a city or school district) and uses regular telephone cables, digital lines, microwaves, wireless systems, satellites, or other combinations of communications channels. A WAN can consist of numerous local area networks organized into one larger network. 1.16, **2.06**

Wi-Fi: Short for wireless fidelity, a popular term used when referring to any type of 802.11 network. **2.38**, **8.51**

Wi-Fi Alliance: Nonprofit organization that certifies the interoperability of 802.11 products. **8.51**

Wi-Fi ZONE: Logo that identifies hot spots. **8.53**

Window: Rectangular area of the screen used to display a program, data, and/or information. **3.06**

Windows, *see* **Microsoft Windows**

Wireless home network: Network that connects computers and peripherals inside a home without the use of wires. **2.38**

Wireless keyboard, *see* **Cordless keyboard**

Wireless LAN (WLAN): Local area network that uses no wires; instead, uses wireless media such as radio waves to connect computers and devices in a limited space. 2.04, **2.06**, 2.10, **8.51**

Wireless metropolitan area network (WMAN): Wireless network designed to cover an urban area. **8.53**

Wireless mobile lab: Portable cart with wireless notebook computers that can be transported from one classroom to another. Also called a computer lab on wheels. **6.19**

Wireless mouse, *see* **Cordless mouse**

Wireless network, 2.04, 2.06, 2.10, 8.49-58

Wireless personal area network (WPAN): Short-range wireless network often based on Bluetooth technology, connecting devices that are within 33 feet of each other. **8.50**

Wireless service provider (WSP): Company that provides wireless Internet access to users with wireless modems or Web-enabled handheld computers or devices. **2.16**

Wireless wide area network (WWAN): Wireless network that covers a wide geographic area and uses a variety of technologies including radio, satellite, and mobile telephone technologies. **8.53**

Wizard: Automated tool that helps a user complete a task by asking questions and automatically performing actions based on the answers. Also called assistant. **3.12**

WMAN, *see* **Wireless metropolitan area network**

Word processing software: Most widely-used application software, used to create, edit, and format documents that consist primarily of text. 1.15, **3.10-13**

Word processor
  creating curriculum page using, 7.60-82
  creating teacher's Web page using, 3.50-66

Wordwrap: Positioning of text that extends beyond a page margin or window margin at the beginning of the next line, performed automatically by a word processor. **3.11**

Worksheet, *see* **Spreadsheet**

World Wide Web (WWW): Worldwide collection of electronic documents on the Internet that have built-in hyperlinks to other related documents (Web pages). Also called the Web. **1.18, 2.21**
  animation and, 2.27-28
  audio and, 2.28-29
  evaluating resources, 7.09-12
  future of, 2.38
  graphics and, 2.27
  impact on education, 2.36-37
  learning process and, 6.14
  multimedia and, 2.25-30, 5.16-17
  popularity of, 2.01
  searching for information on, 2.25
  video and, 2.29
  virtual reality and, 2.30

Worm: Malicious software program that does not reproduce itself; instead worms spread by indirect means. **8.03**

WPAN, *see* **Wireless personal area network**

WWAN, *see* **Wireless wide area network**

WWW, *see* **World Wide Web**

Zip disk, 1.08

Zip drive: Special high-capacity disk drive developed by Iomega Corporation, which uses a special 3.5-inch Zip disk, which can store 100-250 MB of data. 1.07, **4.31**

Zone of proximal development: The difference between the problem-solving ability a child has learned and the potential the child can achieve from collaboration with a more advanced peer or expert, defined by Vygotsky. **6.51**

Photo Credits